NAVAL ENGINEERING
A N D
AMERICAN SEAPOWER

With Fifteen Contributors

Editor: Rear Admiral Randolph W. King, USN (Ret)
Associate Editor: Lt. Commander Prescott Palmer, USN (Ret)
Graphics Editor: Commander Bruce I. Meader, USN (Ret)

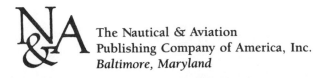
The Nautical & Aviation
Publishing Company of America, Inc.
Baltimore, Maryland

ISBN: 0-933852-73-8

Library of Congress Catalog Card Number: 89-60473

Printed in the United States of America

All photos are official U.S. Navy

Library of Congress Cataloging in Publication Data

Naval Engineering and American Seapower
Bibliography: p.
Includes index.
1. Sea-power—United States—History. 2. Naval architecture—History. 3. Marine
engineering—United States—History. 4. Munitions—United States—History.
5. Shipbuilding industry—United States—Military aspects.
I. King, Randolph W. II. Palmer, Prescott.
VA55-N24 1989   359'.03'0973   89-060473
ISBN 0-933852-73-8

TABLE OF CONTENTS

P R E F A C E

The latter half of the nineteenth century was a period of great technical ferment in many areas, including maritime endeavors. The National Academy of Sciences was established in the United States in 1863 by Congressional Act of Incorporation, with a broad scope in scientific matters but notable specific involvement in important naval developments from its beginning. In 1860, the Royal Institution of Naval Architects was founded, followed in 1883 by the Royal Corps of Naval Constructors. In the United States, a major start was made to provide associations for individuals of similar technical interests by the founding of six professional societies. Interest in scientific and technical matters was amply demonstrated, further, with the founding, in 1886, of the Society of Sigma Xi and, in 1888, of the National Geographic Society. The Society of Naval Architects and Marine Engineers (SNAME) was formed in 1893.

In 1888, a small group of about twenty forward-looking officers of the Engineering Corps of the United States Navy met informally to develop means for disseminating technical information within the Navy relative to the field of naval engineering. One of the officers present, Assistant Engineer A. M. Mattice, proposed an organization to be known as the American Society of Naval Engineers (ASNE) for the purpose of promoting naval engineering and professionalism. The Society was born.

The early context of naval engineering was mechanical, most particularly energy conversion devices to provide propulsion for the Navy's ships. Over the years, the scope of naval engineering has broadened to include most aspects of military ships and craft and their support systems, and engineering development and operation in maritime commerce, whether ocean-going, coastal, or on the Great Lakes and inland waterways. In short, naval engineering now encompasses many disciplines, with the aim of improving our government, civil, and commercial endeavors at sea. This is reflected in today's definition of naval engineering by ASNE:

> NAVAL ENGINEERING includes all arts and sciences as applied in the research, development, design, construction, operation, maintenance, and logistic support of surface and subsurface ships and marine craft, naval maritime auxiliaries, ship related aviation and space systems, combat systems, command control, electronic and ordnance systems, ocean structures and fixed and mobile shoe facilities which are used by the naval and other military forces and civilian maritime organizations for the defense and well-being of the nation.

Sea power is the aggregate of a nation's capabilities to use the seas for national purposes. Naval engineering provides its technical foundation.

It is our goal in this volume to provide a chronicle of development of naval engineering over a century of monumental change. The authors have accepted this challenge, aided by many personal observations and documents responding to a broad request for input. The centennial of ASNE provided impetus to undertake the book and timing for its publishing. We go back several years in chapter 1 to highlight events of great importance to naval engineering and portray the environment leading to the significant first ASNE meeting in 1888.

There was general consensus among those who reviewed portions of the manuscript that this work fills a significant maritime history void by addressing naval engineering. Criticism has focused on consistency of approach. In this multiple-author work, each contributor addressed the era for which he was asked to write, within general guidelines but in his own style. Exchange of material and ideas continued throughout the project, but non-uniform treatment of the material is acknowledged. An apology might be offered that the enormity of the task and its volunteer nature mandated multiple authors. The more important and positive aspect, however, is that fifteen authors with mixed backgrounds and perceptions bring to the table more detail and richness than a single author. Faults resulting from abridging and organizing the submitted material lie solely with the Editor.

This is not a technical document, but, rather, selected narratives aimed at wide civil and uniformed readership—those who are interested in the history of maritime engineering and its implications. We cover, primarily, developments and individuals in the United States, not from chauvinism, but to keep the project manageable. In many cases, however, there was such strong influence or interaction that we must refer to events and naval engineers in other countries. No work of similar purpose or scope has been found, although there are many fine sources for various specific aspects of the field; and certainly there are first rate volumes and articles on maritime history. With few exceptions, such as John Adolphus Dahlgren, John Ericsson, Benjamin Franklin Insherwood, Hyman George Rickover, and David Watson Taylor, it has been particularly difficult to associate developments with specific people.

We hope that this book will suggest and trigger further efforts to fill the gaps, supplement scanty coverage, or correct the record of naval engineering, particularly concerning the vital matters of how decisions were made, who made them, and their basis. Individuals are encouraged to make their papers and reminiscences available to the several organizations providing archival and reference services. Naval engineering is a continuing process and there is every reason to be confident that future decades will always provide important new information meriting careful elucidation and publication.

ACKNOWLEDGMENTS

There are special pitfalls in acknowledging assistance provided from myriad widely scattered and diverse sources. There are too many to attempt a complete list and serious problems of omission in citing examples. Nonetheless, we shall wander into the minefield of the latter approach.

Many discussions resulted in useful leads and specific input as well as much needed encouragement to move ahead. Of great assistance were the nearly one hundred commenters, including multiple responders in several cases, who provided many more than one hundred letters, along with photographs, drawings, and memorabilia. We hope that no one was missed as we acknowledged with great appreciation their input during the four years of this work. Their contributions were invaluable.

Enthusiasm and encouragement, in addition to specific suggestions on sources, approaches to the task, vignettes, recollections, and anecdotes to provide personal flavor to the narrative came to us on a continuing basis from many sources. To cite a few:

Captain Henry A. Arnold, USN (Ret)
Mr. John Arrison
Mr. Arthur Davidson Baker
Rear Admiral Edgar H. Batcheller, USN (Ret)
Captain Edward L. Beach, USN (Ret)
Mr. Joseph Breickner
Mr. Robert C. Browning
Dr. Bernard H. Carson
Vice Admiral Kenneth K. Cowart, USCG (Ret)
Rear Admiral Cabell S. Davis, USN (Ret)
Captain F. A. Edwards, Sr., USN (Ret)
Captain Dennett K. Ela, USN (Ret)
Rear Admiral Frank Jones, USN (Ret)
Dr. William P. Jones

Captain Hal A. Kauffman, USN (Ret)
Professor Emeritus Neville T. Kirk
Rear Admiral Lauren S. McCready, USMS (Ret)
Rear Admiral John H. McQuilkin, USN (Ret)
Captain Richards T. Miller, USN (Ret)
Rear Admiral John B. Oren, USCG (Ret)
Captain Henry P. Rumble, USN (Ret)
Mr. Philip Sims
Mr. Frank Smollon
Mr. Don L. Stevens, Jr.
Mr. A. Steven Toby
Vice Admiral Thomas R. Weschler, USN (Ret)
Rear Admiral Kenneth E. Wilson, Jr., USN (Ret)

Information needed on several organizations, schools, and various technical areas such as ship design, shipbuilding, radar, combat systems, the Naval Tactical Data System, and propulsion came from many individuals, including:

Dr. George J. Billy
Mr. W. J. Coops
Mr. Joseph L. Duffy, Jr.

Rear Admiral Wayne E. Meyer, USN (Ret)
Mr. Tim B. Nichols
Dr. William R. Porter [Captain, USN (Ret)]

Rear Admiral James M. Farrin, USN (Ret)
Rear Admiral Robert B. Fulton, USN (Ret)
Mr. Mark Jacobsen
Captain Bryce D. Inman, USN (Ret)
Rear Admiral P. L. Krinsky, USMS

Rear Admiral M. H. Rindskopf, USN (Ret)
Vice Admiral Benedict L. Stabile, USCG (Ret)
Captain Edward C. Svendsen, USN (Ret)
Captain Erick N. Swenson, USN (Ret)

Contact points within their organizations were provided by the Commanders of the Naval Sea Systems Command and Military Sealift Command, the Maritime Administrator, and the Commandant of the Coast Guard, significant indication of support and interest from these major organizations. The resources of the Director of Naval History and the Naval Historical Center were made available and were vital to the effort. The Navy's Chief of Information expressed enthusiasm in a most supportive letter.

The most superficial review of references in this book reveals the dependence on information from Norman Friedman's encyclopedic *Illustrated Design History* series on U.S. naval ships, published by the Naval Institute Press. The authors and editors gratefully acknowledge this debt to Dr. Friedman and his colleagues, and further cite the degree to which the accuracy and detail of their information complements that of other sources.

The small but industrious staff of the American Society of Naval Engineers, headed by Captain James L. McVoy, USN (Ret), provided administrative support for this project, including correspondence, filing, arrangements for meetings, tens of thousands of copies, myriad mailings, drafts and smooth copy for at least two chapters, and on and on. Heather Dell Aversano provided initial staff focus for this effort until personal plans led to her departure. Diane Quinn served as the histories project staff assistant, carrying a heavy load during a busy middle phase with energy, talent, and good humor. Captain William A. Ellis, USN (Ret), who spent many creative years as principal ASNE staff person for the *Naval Engineers Journal*, assisted in editing portions of the manuscript and contributed in other helpful ways.

SPECIAL ACKNOWLEDGMENT

For a substantial part of the lengthy period in which this volume was being prepared, a group of volunteers, appointed by the President of the American Society of Naval Engineers, devoted considerable time in service as an Editorial Board. This Board was broadly representative of the field of naval engineering, and included notable expertise in history. Its mission was to help structure an approach to this work, assess overall progress on the project, determine possible pitfalls during the process, suggest preventive or remedial action, and review drafts of chapters and sections of the manuscript. The work of these dedicated individuals is deeply appreciated:

Rear Admiral James K. Nunneley, USN (Ret), Chairman
Rear Admiral John D. Beecher, USN (Ret)
Dr. Warren C. Dietz [Commander, USN (Ret)]
Captain Jerome J. Fee, USN (Ret)
Captain James E. Grabb, USCG (Ret)

Mr. Norman O. Hammer
Rear Admiral Frank C. Jones, USN (Ret)
Commander Kathleen K. Paige, USN
Dr. Robert L. Scheina
Dr. Michael E. Vlahos

CHAPTER
ONE
1797–1887

The Making of an American Style

by Michael E. Vlahos

There is an oil portrait of a ship hanging in the old Washington Navy Yard. It shows a sleek cruiser under full steam, making off from its kill. In the distance, just a smudge of black smoke, is the horizon tell-tale of its pursuers. The cruiser is American, but it is not a modern warship made of powered steel: it has a black hull of white oak and four tall funnels, three masts, and a bark-rig. It is the USS *Wampanoag*, the wonder ship, the fastest thing afloat, shown in its element, raiding British commerce in a war that never was.

Before Captain Alfred Mahan, before the battlefleet, before America's rise to world power, this was the image of Yankee technology at war. This was the Navy mission: to be the Shield of the Republic. American national security tradition said that this nation could only be threatened by sea, that only Britain had a navy that could threaten our shores (after all, they had burned Washington), and that the United States could never equal the might of British seapower. The job of the smaller U.S. Navy was

to break the stranglehold of blockade and raid British shipping. American cruisers had done this twice. In 1868, when the *Wampanoag* was built, it seemed they might need to do so again.

The American naval tradition was predicated on two apparent historical truths that would continue to dominate: an advanced British industrial economy and the Royal Navy. As the United States industrialized in Britain's wake, the press to experiment and to apply marine technology was driven by the weight of British competition. The United States was a developing nation. It sought "high technology" to counterbalance British naval strength, while lacking a comparative advantage to apply these technologies as efficiently as the British. This frustration extended equally to the American merchant marine. The United States spent the nineteenth century competing with Britain at sea, and looked to new marine technologies as an equalizer.

The American Society of Naval Engineers [ASNE] called its first meeting in September

1888. It was already the eve of America's transformation from nativism to world power. Pacing the internal recognitions of changing national identity by historical visionaries Alfred Thayer Mahan and Frederick Jackson Turner, professional societies like ASNE were part of a metamorphosis of the American world view. The world of steam engineering, after all, was merely the physical, the visible cutting edge of change: the naval architects and engineers now were shaping the ships that placed America on a world stage. A new Navy and a new concept for Americans—the battlefleet—would become the glorified example of change. Not only were the ships and new steam technologies debated at ASNE different from the ships of the old America, but the mission they embodied had forever changed.

The story of American steam engineering and ship design before 1888 is the story of an America detached, linked to the world only through its commerce. There was for young America, however, a distinct sense of an American style of ship design and of an American approach to applied marine technology. U.S. ships of war and of trade reflected an American ethos that exalted its own uniqueness: Americans were exceptional; so were their ships. As much as our national spirit was advertised in crafts as in literature, so it was with ships and the new industrial technology of the sea.

To understand the ways in which the work of American designers and engineers subtly, but innocently, shaped national mission into steel in the modern era, it is important to search out continuities from a time of white oak and forged iron. American ships and their designers emerged from a society that saw itself as something newly hewn from the wilderness of the New World. The United States was at once superior to Europe and in comparison unsophisticated: a state both less corrupted and less advanced. American shipwrights sought to make of their vessels fitting representatives of the new republic. This was easy in the eighteenth century, when British and American industrial infrastructures mirrored each other. In the nineteenth century, however, as Britain mastered the new technologies of iron and steam, the United States labored increasingly to compete at sea.

MARINE TECHNOLOGY AND THE AMERICAN ETHOS

The world of American shipbuilding, design, and technology can be understood only in relation to the larger transatlantic maritime world of the United States, Canada, and Great Britain. American oceanic enterprise was intimately intertwined within the British imperial weave, both as colleague and competitor. The ability of American ship designers, builders, and engineers to hold their own against a larger and more efficient British marine industrial base, however, remained tenuous throughout the nineteenth century. Before the vulcanian age of steam and iron, the great timber stands of North America gave the United States a choice comparative advantage in shipbuilding. The industry lacked only economy of scale, which the shipyards of New York and New England soon would develop, to equal Britain by the 1850s.

Iron and coal, however, remade Britain at sea. Britain, the first industrial nation, pushed its pig-iron production from 442,000 to 3,876,700 tons between 1823 and 1860. The annual rate of growth averaged 5.9 percent, the highest in British history. This meant cheap iron. The more that was smelted each year, the cheaper it got. Prices dropped from £6.30 per ton in 1810 to £2.60 in 1840.[1] Not only was finished iron cheaper, it could be provided in any shape or form, as an established fabrication plant developed.[2] When iron became a preferred material for shipbuilding, this meant cheaper ships, ton for ton. When the demand rose for ships driven by steam, the capacity to produce high-quality forgings and large pieces of close-tolerance rolled iron meant better, stronger engines and boilers, and faster ships.

In comparison, the United States lagged. Between 1800 and 1860, America grew from five to thirty-one million people, while Britain merely doubled its population to thirty million.[3] But at the height of the Civil War, annual American pig iron production stood at just over one million tons, only a quarter of England's output.[4] The United States was, industrially, still a developing nation at mid-century. In shipbuilding, this was disguised by a continuing comparative advantage in wooden sailing ships. The American merchant marine jumped from 1.2 million tons in 1830 to 5.4 million in 1860, while the British merchant marine grew from 2.5 to 5.7 million tons. But nearly all America's oceangoing tonnage was in wood and sail.[5]

Throughout the nineteenth century, the United States would continue to compete against a society that had 1) a larger, more mature industrial base; 2) maritime industries pursuing a deliberate policy of capital investment in advanced technology design, fabrication, and material; and 3) state support for maritime industries with an imperial preference system and longterm subsidies. These factors added up to a powerful, persistent, British advantage in the maritime world. To offset this, Americans looked to their native genius, "Yankee ingenuity," as embodied in their ship designers and engineers.

In young America, the ships of the U.S. Navy and the merchant marine were the Republic's representatives abroad. Given America's geographic isolation, they were to a large extent its physical and social links to the wider world as well. Before the dominance of the new marine technologies of steam and iron, the United States managed to wrest, if only for a time, the image of first place at sea. It did so with a great shipbuilding plant working in wood alone, and through the speed and grace of its sailing hulls and rigs.

And, all of this happened while the British were quietly pushing ahead with steam and iron. Popular mythology decries Confederate raiders as the cause of decline. But the American merchant marine did not fall to swashbuckling Confederate naval commander Raphael Semmes. It was hoist by its own old-tech petard: it clung to a fleeting advantage in wooden, sailing ship technology while oblivious to the technological change that would alter that advantage. Americans designed the best in sail and wood—and sail and wood would live forever!

TECHNOLOGY AND THE AMERICAN SAILING NAVY

The new republic certainly saw itself as advanced—the prototype for the future, the seat of human progress. The triumphs of American shipwrights and designers only perpetuated the myth of a natural American supremacy, ship for ship, at sea. Americans saw their navy and merchant marine as physical symbols of a national mission, demonstrating to the world the superiority of American values.

In a sense, the tour de force of maritime America—the world's best, and fastest ships—to mid-century was built on design innovation within a dying technology. The technological ferment in British maritime industries was not understood in the United States. It was a parochial world view held by a shallow and backward design community: there were no academic institutions applying developments in the physical sciences to naval architecture, and there were no professional societies to impose membership standards or to promote an intellectual "critical mass."

For example, the earliest American naval architects were British emigres. Josiah Fox, designer of the big frigates, the *Constitution*, *United States*, and *President*, exerted a dominant influence on American sailing warship design. He was trained in England, apprenticed to the master shipwright at Plymouth Dockyard.[6]

The success achieved by American shipbuilders before 1860 was a function of relative demand, dependent on the genius of a few gifted native naval architects: J.W. Griffiths (who designed the *Rainbow*), George Steers (designer of the renowned yacht *America*), Samuel Pook, William H. Webb, Donald McKay, and Samuel Hall. The Yankee hull forms' fame of being the fastest rested on the superior models these men made in Boston and New York.[7]

There was, as yet, no science of naval architecture in the United States; ships were built by eye from models. There were few good draftsmen and far fewer shipwrights skilled in mathematics, physics, hydraulics, and applied mechanics. Until mid-century there were only two major treatises on naval architecture written by Americans, those of Lauchlan McKay and J.W. Griffiths.[8]

In spite of these design limitations, however, a distinctly American approach to marine technology and the design process emerged between 1780 and 1850. The original attitudes and values that drove how America approached ship design and the uses of marine technology should be spelled out, for two reasons. First, self-consciously, American influences aimed at celebrating the "American-ness" of the ship. Second, the belief that innately American designs should represent us has persisted long after the end of sail and wood. It is still with us.

There are three areas in which this native approach to design and technology is highlighted:

• in distinct patterns of native design,
• in America's sensitivity and insensitivity to European trends, and
• in the limits of the U.S. marine industrial base.

Patterns of Native Design

Patterns of native design during the sailing era can be seen most clearly in the U.S. Navy. A distinct American warship "type" was common parlance by 1815, and almost a caricature by 1856, the year the great steam frigate *Merrimac* began its European tour. Quite simply, the American Navy built big ships. And these big ships carried big guns. And they were fast.

Before the Civil War, the U.S. Navy promoted no really new nor unusual marine technology. Two memorable private entrepreneurs—Robert Fulton and Robert Stevens—pursued their own pathfinding naval visions. They were ignored by naval society. Innovation was consciously limited to traditional technology and purely a function of design integration. The goal was to produce individually superior ships. This goal was met, and exceeded, to the point that this flamboyant excess came to symbolize to Europeans the image of America itself: brash, rough-hewn, bigger-than-life.

The U.S. Navy between 1797 and 1860 actually created a tradition of progressive warship design while reinforcing desired continuities in American naval culture. The very first Navy ship program inspired a trio of frigates that codified a characteristic ship type. The big 44s, the *Constitution*, *United States*, and *President*, became archetypes, both for future American capital ships and for a Navy tradition. Their heroic performance in the War of 1812 established a Navy mission. American commerce-raiding would be led by cruising ships more powerful than standard British ships-of-the-line.

British fleets historically were preoccupied

with the containment of continental European battle squadrons. War with the United States would force the Royal Navy to detach a disproportionate slice of their main order of battle to deal with a clutch of American battlecruisers. Given their preoccupation with European navies, this would be politically impossible; the U.S. would be safe from British coercion. So, our big frigates of 1797, the line-of-battle ships of 1816, and the steam frigates of 1853 were the substance of an American naval deterrent.

The big 44s set the trend. They were superficially a melange of British hull forms and French proportions, but they took matters a step further than European frigates. Their tonnage equaled the standard British Third-Rate, 74-gun battleship. Their great innovation was their raw size, which, combined with a hull sharpness comparable to the post-Civil War downeasters, made them fast sailers. A full length spar deck and heavy gundeck enabled them to carry over fifty heavy guns. Their war armament gave a broadside of 654 pounds against almost 680 pounds for a standard British turn-of-the-century 74.[9] In other words, they were the strength and gun equal of the standard British battleship, with the speed and sailing qualities to catch and kill any other frigate. In the parlance of Jackie Fisher, they were true battlecruisers. Their utility in the War of 1812 literally stunned the Royal Navy. The heroic tradition they inspired bonded the young U.S. Navy to the giant frigate image as its badge of identity and national uniqueness.

But, war with Britain showed that frigates were not enough. The United States needed powerful, line-of-battle ships capable of breaking a British blockade. The first three were experiments with the type, and unexceptional. They were followed, however, by a series of magnificent sailing battleships. The *Delaware*-class battleship and the *Ohio* extended the American design vision of the big frigate to battleships. The result was ships of their type faster and more powerful than any single warship in the Royal Navy.[10]

Political objectives were more than achieved. Again, a few individually superior American ships forced the British to sit up and take notice. In fact, they did more than that. The British called a special Cabinet Council on Naval Armament in July 1826 to deal with the threat of the big American battleships. It was stressed with some alarm that the broadside of the *Ohio* at 1,792 pounds, outgunned the biggest British First Rate, the *Caledonia*, a nominal 120-gun ship that could discharge only 1,568 pounds. The American ship also carried heavier single guns: 42-pounders. An alarmed Admiralty was forced to lay down seven improved First Rates just to compete.[11]

In the 1820s, the French also were paying homage to American warship design. The French Marine's program of 1824 focused on giant frigates of sixty guns "in the American manner."[12] British fears of new, ever more monstrous ships were heightened by the giant framing of the *Pennsylvania*, thought by European naval opinion to mount 140 guns.[13] The very presence of such ships in the American naval order of battle undermined British contingency planning. Even though few in number, U.S. battleships would overload the Royal Navy in a crisis. It would be impossible for the Admiralty to face both the U.S. Navy and a local European naval rival simultaneously. Since the French and Russian fleets were far more threatening to British security, the American approach paid off: given a larger global balance of power, a small, but powerful, American battle line would deter any British diplomatic or military threat.

The now-famous American blend of heavy, long-range gunpower and fast sailing continued with big corvettes/sloops of the 1840s. Now, contemporary mercantile hull design innovations were folded in. They were cut like fast packet ships—the kind that had captured the transatlantic passenger trade for the United States. With straight-rising floors and little deadrise, they were considered the finest examples of their class in the world. An authentic, native approach to warship design had paid off for a fledgling republic unable to buy and man a big fleet; it built big ships instead. American naval architects had taken the symbolic value of warships to their limit. The U.S. Navy defended the nation with the emotional force of visible symbols, not through the reality of ready force.[14]

Sensitivity and Insensitivity to European Trends

The United States was relatively insensitive to European trends in ship design and marine technology before the Civil War. Several examples show both American design independence and stubbornness.

American shipping interests were not responsive to the emergence of the iron-hulled, steam-driven passenger liner until it was too late to compete. The dominance of sailing packets (in which the United States excelled) fell from 96 percent in 1856 to 68 percent by 1862. The trend toward steam and iron was made irreversible by the low-priced, immigrant steamships of the Collins Line (U.S. government subsidized, but soon to fail), Cunard Line, and especially the Inman Line. Only 1 percent of all passengers departing New York City by 1869 chose sailing craft.[15] This crucial example highlights the incapacity of maritime America to respond to the subsidized iron and steam passenger lines of Great Britain.

In contrast, American designers rejected the fashion among late sailing warships set by the Royal Navy's surveyor, William Symonds. His emphasis on high-rise-of-floor, deep-draught ships (which were neither suited to steam conversion nor effective as gun platforms) had been tried years before in the United States. Here, sharp deadrise had already been discarded for large warships. An earlier American experience with the "Symondite" hull midsection—Humphreys' pilot-boat schooner *Nimble* of 1806—rightly lead to a rejection of this European "innovation."[16]

In fact, through the first half of the nineteenth century, it was British naval architects that were sensitive to American design innovation. This began with three 74s razed down to frigates in 1814, in an attempt to deal with the big American 44s.[17] In the 1820s, Britain's first two-decker 90s were designed as an explicit response to the *Ohio*, the finest of the American sailing battleships.[18] Finally, reports of the "monster" *Pennsylvania* helped spur the design of huge line-of-battle ships like the *Royal Albert*, laid down in 1844.

Before the 1850s, the Royal Navy was haunted by fears of technological and design backwardness.[19] These fears lead to the establishment of the School of Naval Architecture at Portsmouth in 1811, responding to a long-standing sense of inferiority to French and Spanish designs and their sailing qualities. The notion, however, of

training formal "superior shipwright appren-
tices" was resisted by the older generation, and
the School's graduates were neglected. The
School itself was closed a decade later. British
design was as dependent on individuals like
Robert Seppings and Symonds, and on trial and
error initiatives like "experimental squadrons,"
as was the U.S. Navy.[20] In 1844, the Construction
Board of the Admiralty would declare in exasperation: "There is not at present any fixed principle by which the construction of our ships is
regulated."[21]

The single example of American design-
borrowing in this period was the *Pennsylvania*.
Its draught was actually based on plans obtained
by Samuel Humphreys for the giant Havana-
built, Spanish turn-of-the-century three-decker
Santissima Trinidad, captured at Trafalgar.[22]

The Limits of the Marine Industrial Base

The American marine industrial base was
severely limited in crucial areas before 1860. The
integration of related industries, moreover,
tended to reinforce the dominance of wood in
shipbuilding. There were several reasons for this
built-in resistance to materials innovation.

First, comparative costs in labor, raw materials,
and materials-working heavily favored wood
over iron before 1880.

Second, general industrialization in America
created an environment of partial mechanization
of shipbuilding operations. Rising labor costs
were offset with the appearance of steam-driven
sawing machinery, tilting saws for frames and
planking, and lathes for treenails,[23] all preserving the competitiveness of wood as opposed to
iron.[24]

Finally, the decade 1847-57 was a boom-time
for large ship construction. The average annual
output of ships (including bark-rigs) launched
by American yards was 259. The peak year, 1855,
saw 381 ships go down the ways, a total of
308,000 tons. In contrast, the years 1831-46 held
an average of only 93 ships per year, and 99,700
tons. During the generation of the Civil War,
from 1858-78, the annual average was only 83,
although the increasing size of merchant sailing
ships is reflected in an average annual tonnage
of 196,000.

But this boom was deceptive, and fostered a
false sense of perpetual American competitiveness in wooden square-riggers. In reality, this
wood and canvas industrial plant was completely
handcraft-intensive. Throughout this era, the
production line introduced few economies of
scale, and the entire industry was minced: a
highly-competitive and vulnerable multiplicity
of small shipbuilding yards. When the industry
expanded in the 1850s, growth took the form of
more local yards in a shipbuilding center, not
bigger and more efficient yards. For example,
there were 31 shipbuilding plants in New York
City alone in 1855.[25]

America's shipbuilding strength must have
seemed unshakeable—a force of nature—to any
contemporary observer. Had not the United
States outbuilt Great Britain in sailing ships
between 1847 and 1857 by two to one (3.4 to 1.7
million tons), and Canada by more than two to
one (3.4 to 1.2 million tons)? But what proud
Yankees casually ignored were pernicious
technological and industrial trends. In this same
decade, British yards built 550,000 tons of ocean-
going steam ships, and fully 30 percent of all
British ships built in 1860 were of iron.[26] In
contrast, American builders managed only a
handful of iron ships, and the bulk of steamers
were built for coastal and river traffic.

The American warship building plant, in effect, was limited equally by the lack of civilian
innovation in marine technologies. American
sailing warship design might even be superior to
British, but the capacity of American designers
to translate their designs into efficient ships was
constrained by the shipbuilding base. The gap,
moreover, would grow as steam and, later, iron
(and armored) warships became the norm.

High labor costs at Navy yards also limited the
ability of the U.S. Navy to build ships quickly. In
the wood and sailing world, it was possible to
evade the full impact of labor costs by stretching
the time of construction. For example, the
Pennsylvania took fifteen years [1822-37] to
complete, while of the six 74s appropriated in
1818, four were kept on the stocks until the
1860s. Of the nine frigates of 1821, the last, the
Sabine, was completed in 1854. Unburdened by
high-maintenance machinery, a wooden hull
could be kept on the ways, unfitted but structurally complete, for decades. Expensive capital

ships could be held in a nineteenth century equivalent of "mothballs," to be launched and outfitted quickly in case of national emergency.[27]

The U.S. Navy world view operated within an assumption that war mobilization equated to the readying of uncompleted but already existing ships. This attitude spilled over into an age of more complex marine technology, and may help explain the U.S. Navy's slide into decrepitude after 1865. It certainly did not encourage capital investment in war-mobilization capability.

THE TRANSITION, 1845-60

By 1845, the Navy was aware of the necessity of steam propulsion. After a period of experimentation, steam technology seemed mature enough for a long-term fleet shipbuilding program. Approved in April 1854, during the Pierce administration, its core was twelve big screw-ships: six frigates (the "rebuilding" of the *Franklin* was approved in 1853), five sloops, and one giant corvette (classed as a frigate). Although they mounted big shell guns, engines, and coal-fired boilers, they were the lineal descendants of the big sailing 44s and 74s, of the *Constitution* and the *Ohio*. And, they were big, powerful ships.

Boynton, historian of the Navy in the Civil War, wrote that when they first appeared, they had no equal:

> . . . the result was, a class of frigates more formidable than any other ships afloat. . . . The *Minnesota* would so far have overmatched an English line-of-battle ship as to have made the contest a useless waste of life.[28]

Alfred Thayer Mahan also provides a powerful recollection of them:

> . . . they could, acting together, have presented a line of battle extorting very serious consideration from any probable foreign enemy. It was for such purpose they were built. . . .[29]

And of course, they achieved their objective, at least in terms of British perception. Their equipment was essentially equivalent to the latest in the Royal Navy ships, while certain aspects of American design were more innovative than any of Her Majesty's ships. The big American frigates, especially the *Niagara*, introduced heavy shell guns that had no counterpart in the Royal Navy.

The American merchant marine fared less well with steam.

In 1836, the British government promoted a leap-ahead in marine technology, by introducing long-term, fast steamship subsidies. Subsidies were promoted on the basis of: 1) support for infant industries, 2) improved imperial communications, and 3) national defense. The result was revolution in the transatlantic passenger trade, going from sail to steam in a generation. The United States attempted to respond with an Act of Congress, 3 March 1847, which authorized the Secretary of the Navy to offer a subsidy to E.K. Collins for five steamships. These were to exceed 2,000 gross tons and to generate at least 1,000 horsepower.

What followed was a shocking snapshot of what was slowly going wrong with American shipbuilding. Their building hewed to areas of American comparative advantage in marine technology: they were framed in wood and were paddle-driven. They were the largest wooden ships built to that time except for McKay's *Great Republic*. But a comparative advantage in wooden square-rig building turned into a 25 to 33 percent disadvantage with British wooden steamships. Collins first four liners cost $735,000 each, as compared to $575,000 apiece for the Cunard Line's *Asia* and *Africa*, or $600,000 for the U.S. Navy's paddle-driven frigates *Missouri* and *Mississippi*.

After the *Arctic* was lost at sea in 1855, President Franklin Pierce vetoed an extra subsidy. The *Pacific* was lost in 1856. Throughout this period the Collins Line operated at a deficit, while British lines such as the Cunard made money. Collin's last ship, the huge *Adriatic* of 4,144 gross tons when compared to the latest British iron screw-ships, was obsolete when launched.[30] A deliberate American effort to stay competitive in a vital area of ocean trade had collapsed by 1860, due in large part to U.S. technological backwardness in maritime industries, steam engineering, and naval architecture.

Let's look at how this decline permeated through maritime America, and show, as well, remaining areas of a healthy marine technology. Three areas in the American approach to maritime technology in the sailing era will be looked at:

• Native design patterns—the persistent and customary patterns in design evolution by marine improvisation and innovation, in contrast to areas neglected or considered taboo. Exploring this area will help explain why some marine technologies were highlighted while others were ignored.

• Sensitivity and insensitivity to European trends, both in ship design and applied marine technology—includes changes in American dependence on European design and marine technology, in terms of perceived importance to American maritime competitiveness.

• The limits of the marine industrial base, in terms of: 1) the ability of naval architects (and later, engineers) to prepare advanced designs, 2) the capacity of industry to realize these designs, and 3) the potential of the larger, national industrial base to support the competitive development of maritime industries.

These areas reveal broad national trends in marine technology. Next, by showing how specific technologies were applied, we can better assess the impact of the American ethos (our own patterns of behavior) on the use of marine technology in a period of ferment and flux. There are six key areas to examine in applied marine technology from the 1840s to the 1880s:

• Steam propulsion
• Hull design
• Materials
• Ordnance
• Traditional motifs and symbols
• Ship design integration

Steam Propulsion

Great Britain seemed to be the first to apply crucial innovations in marine technology. The British were the first to adopt the screw propeller, even though it was first tested in the United States. Samuel Hall developed the surface steam condenser for the recycling of steam in marine boilers, allowing higher pressures. Charles Rudolph and John Elder perfected the compound engine, which utilized higher boiler pressures more efficiently. This increased the range and reliability of steamships, which, in turn, helped to encourage the gradual abandonment of auxil-

iary sails. These innovations were in general use in British shipping by the end of the 1860s.[31]

The United States, in contrast, lagged behind in the centrally important area of steam engineering. The U.S. Navy, for example, was generally accused of technological backwardness by the 1860s for keeping paddle-driven war steamers. Hans Busk was scathing in 1859:

America, moreover, is now perhaps the only country where paddle steamers for war purposes have not virtually been abolished. . . .[32]

This was perhaps a bit unfair, coming from a British commentator, for the last U.S. paddle frigate, the *Powhatan*, was launched in 1850, while the last British paddle frigate, the *Valorous*, was launched in 1851.

Part of the problem was a hardening to change and innovation in U.S. Navy world view just as the Royal Navy was opening to the revolution in marine technology and institutionalizing design evolution. The big steam frigates of 1854 were in fact lineal descendants of the *Constitution*, in reality as well as in spirit. They were sailers first, with steam intended as a pure auxiliary. The Navy ethos clung to sail, unwilling to give up its pride of place. In Admiral Samuel Dupont's diary we read of the passage of the new steam frigate *Minnesota* to the East India Station in 1857, and feel his glee when the big ship topped 17 knots with straining sheets!

Innovation in American ship design was limited, and not just within the Navy, to areas of marine technology that reinforced national maritime traditions. Innovation that abridged the fundamental core of that tradition was rejected, diminished, or delayed to hold off its inevitable impact.

So British criticisms of the steam plants installed in the big American screw frigates really hit home. The Royal Navy's Surveyor, Baldwin Walker, built six big frigates—*Doris*, *Diadem*, *Ariadne*, *Galatea*, *Mersey*, and *Orlando*—with outputs of over 3,000 horsepower. They all could make 13 knots in smooth water. The *Merrimac* and her sisters, in contrast, could generate at best 1,200 horsepower, and less than 9 knots under steam. The *Niagara* did better with 11 knots.[33]

American steamers generally were noted for extremely inefficient power plants. Boilers were meant for firewood. There were no condensers, so the water supply had to be continuously replenished. The whole steam shipbuilding industry, moreover, was dominated by river side- and stern-wheelers, powered craft with no requirement for continuous operation. "Marine engineers" were really no more than marine blacksmiths. There was also an industry-wide lack of proper metal working drills, planers, and milling machines. Parts tended to be made by hand, with boilers of copper, hand-punched and riveted. Even though tariffs on importation of foreign machinery averaged 28 percent between 1833 and 1865, a competitive native industry did not develop.[34]

In spite of their more advanced industrial plant, the British also were plagued by steamship breakdowns. The Lisbon trials of 1850 showed that all powerplants in the experimental squadron were breaking down after five days of continuous steaming. This recognition led to a formal conclusion that ship design for screw-ships should in no way detract from sailing qualities.[35]

Finally, American steamship building, ocean vessels intended for foreign trade—the competitive cutting edge of the merchant service—grew glacially compared with the progress of the British steamship industry. Fully 25 percent of Britain's shipbuilding output from 1847 to 1857 was steam-propelled (550,000 tons steam versus 1.7 million tons sail).[36] The same proportion held for the U.S. (841,000 tons steam versus 3.3 million tons sail) during the same decade.[37] The share of American steam ocean-going ships designed for foreign trade, however, was miniscule. We were reinforcing an insular world view with insular marine technology: the riverine paddle-steamer.

Hull Design

The United States Navy had a reputation building "monster" warships, or in the words of a contemporary British writer:

> The United States has not yet abandoned the principle of building gigantic vessels, in order to carry a few heavy guns.[38]

In fact the *Niagara*, which carried only twelve great guns, was as big as the biggest British three-decker!

But the British, ultimately, had the same problem. In an attempt to make the paddle-frigate type equivalent in gunpower to sailing frigates, the model was enlarged to the point where the HMS *Terrible* was larger than the last of the 74-gun battleships, and even then it only mounted 19 guns.[39] The *Mersey* and *Orlando*, the biggest of steam frigates, like the *Niagara*, equalled the largest 101- and 120-gun screw-battleships.[40] The British mutated the U.S. model of the "monster" steam frigate, outdoing the Americans in sheer size. They also eventually followed, though with less abandon, the American style of mounting a few very heavy shell guns.

Materials

The big American frigates and passenger steamships built by Collins suffered from hogging problems stemming from the excessive elasticity of their wooden hulls. But the British suffered similar problems with their countervailing frigates. The HMS *Mersey* and *Orlando*, in fact, suffered from far more severe hogging, with seams opening up in the hull nine inches wide, a weakness that curtailed their active service life.[41] In contrast, American naval designers during the Civil War applied iron hull-strapping so robust that many a wooden cruiser postwar, though rotting within, could trust its iron to let it keep the sea.

This problem of premature rot in U.S. naval vessels was often attributed to the use of improperly seasoned yellow pine. British commentators were especially severe in their criticism of American timber seasoning practices.[42]

The continued reliance on wood, however, created a synergy of design problems for American naval architects. The problems encountered by the big steamships of the Collins Line are a useful illustration. Hull strain was just one issue; weight of materials was another. The heavier weight of wood over iron for equal strength meant a significant loss of carrying capacity. Wood also had a shorter structural life than iron, in spite of the most creative counterefforts through more and more iron strapping,[43] which, after all, also added more weight. Then, the vibration of engines, boiler heat, and the constant straining of paddle wheels on a continuously flexing wooden hull shortened service life. Finally, wooden hulls had less cubic and dead-weight capacity than comparably sized iron hulls.[44]

The U.S. Navy's reliance on wood can be understood within the contemporary context of what was seen as a failed British experiment in iron warship construction in the 1840s. The British experimental program was large, culminating in four iron screw-frigates ordered in 1845. The size of the program and the exhaustive series of firing trials at Woolwich Arsenal in 1846 made the abandonment of iron warships look authoritative.[45] The British civilian iron shipbuilding scene was far more assertive. Moreover, American builders continued to ignore the 30-percent share of iron in British shipbuilding in 1860. Finally, iron returned to Royal Navy warships in 1860 with the great iron frigate, the *Warrior*.

These were more than just portents of change in materials technology; they were the very substance of change itself. The entrenched, if subconscious, resistance of maritime America to iron could be summed in its meager shipbuilding effort: only 1,500 gross tons of iron ships per year in the 1850s.[46]

Ordnance

The warship design innovations of the first half of the nineteenth century were huge, sharp hulls and big guns. Ironically, this was a characteristic feature in American battleship design in the first half of the twentieth century as well. Although the French were the first to introduce the shell gun, the U.S. Navy was the first to positively celebrate large-caliber shell pivot guns. European reaction was to see this American practice through a traditional cultural lens: the United States consisted of people of excess whose lack of balance and moderation constantly diminished their efforts.

For example, European commentators said that big guns at upper deck heights would roll more than those on the traditional gundeck and so would be inaccurate. They conveniently ignored the advantages of freedom from spray and wave interference and the capacity of a few pivot guns to cover the same arcs of fire of several dozen broadside truck guns. Actual experiments

afloat were conducted by Dahlgren in the 1850s with a 15,000 pound, 11-inch pivot gun high-mounted on a relatively small sloop, the *Plymouth*. The results showed that big guns could be mounted effectively on relatively small ship platforms—that such guns mounted high were actually *more* efficient than smaller, broadside guns in heavy seas, and suffered less from ship motion.[47]

Combat in the Crimean turned European opinion around. The utility of large pivot guns was demonstrated during the bombardment of Sevastopol by the Anglo-French fleet on the night of 17 October 1854. The only effective fire delivered against the granite Russian bastions came from the big pivot guns of the *Terrible*, which knocked out barbette guns at Fort Constantine, and caused a tremendous explosion— and this from a ship with only nineteen guns![48]

But, even with increasing private and public criticism of the obsolescent armaments on British battleships after 1857, the Admiralty was reluctant to put large-caliber shell guns on their capital ships, and no more than a token bow and stern pair of 68-pounder pivots. Real political arm-twisting was needed to push Walker to try mounting an all-heavy shell-gun armament on the *Diadem*, *Doris*, *Ariadne*, and *Galatea*, the first steam frigates built in response to the *Merrimack*-class. Conservative opinion still held that line-of-battle ships needed rapid, close-range fire volume to "smother" the enemy line. But others were writing:

> As compared with the *Niagara*, our *Duke of Wellington* and *Marlborough* seem unfit to be our First Rates . . . could they not come within fair range, I should fear for our three-deckers.[49]

Here the USS *Niagara* caused the greatest stir of all. Its visit to the United Kingdom in April of 1857 created a sensation. No checkered bands of gunports along its broadside, just twelve seven-and-one-half ton pivot guns, throwing 130-pound shells that could smash the towering sides of Britain's three-deck "wooden walls."

Traditional Motifs and Symbols

In armaments and gun arrangement, especially, the British were entrenched in the social and mythic implications of "broadside" numerology. There was, after all, an explicit social linkage between the number of guns a ship carried and the rank of her captain, an association hallowed in the seventeenth century tradition of "rates." The Royal Navy was an extension of a larger social hierarchy where the badges and symbols of rank were important in reassuring the permanence of station and its capacity to resist change. In mythic terms, moreover, the British were wedded to a lineage of ship-image. The sea victories that made Britain were the stuff of heavy cannonade from the tall tumble-home of multidecked battleships, stuffed with scores of iron guns. In contrast, Americans always underrated the number of guns they carried, and celebrated victories over British ships that on paper carried more cannon. American sailors cherished, perhaps as a sea-expression of frontier rifle tradition, the long-range, well-placed shot, the nautical equivalent of backwoods marksmanship. So, there was a kind of cultural value to a concentrated armament of few heavy guns.[50]

Ship Design Integration

In summary, for reasons of advantage misconstrued, maritime America remained backward in materials. A limited industrial base and a cultural aversion to steam meant that the United States was also lagging behind in steam engineering. Competitive efforts in hull design and in armaments continued to produce warships equal to the best of Britain's. In the balancing of tradition and innovation, American ships succeeded in armament and failed in propulsion.

What of the overall design goals of American ships before 1860? How well integrated were the components of ship technologies in terms of a balanced ship system? American warships were the prime examples of our maritime "state-of-the-art," and we have seen how they served self-consciously as symbols of American national stature. They were held up to Europe, and especially to Great Britain, as totems of American naval competitiveness and national maturity. How well did they fulfill this role?

Britain's chief naval constructor during this era, Edward Reed, also claimed that building costs in U.S. naval yards were significantly higher than in Britain, and that a standard British steam frigate like the HMS *Shannon* could be maintained at 45 percent of the operating costs of,

say, the USS *Merrimac*. This typical British claim for greater design efficiency, however, is contradicted by their program of big frigates in "the American manner."[51]

But the success of the big steam frigates is self-evident. It emerges from contemporary British commentaries like a back-handed compliment that cannot be denied.

First, the big frigates were prototypical. They prefigured the capital ship of the future: big as was possible to build, carrying a few heavy guns that could be brought to bear at long-range and with concentrated fire effect. The British not only slavishly imitated the American model almost immediately, though not gladly, but they also followed it up with the first armored battleship, which in arrangement and in form was nothing more than an iron-slabbed, iron-framed steam frigate.

Second, the big steam frigates of the 1850s demonstrated a general American technological equivalence with the United Kingdom.[52] They were not as fast, but this was a conscious choice. Their equipment was not inferior to the best produced in mid-century industrial Britain.

Then, there was the truest test, the operational response of the adversary. The *Trent* Affair of 1861-62 was almost a paean to the strategic success of American naval technology in the 1850s. It happened before any significant deployment of new British ironclads, so it is a picture of the American steam frigate mission in action. During the crisis, which brushed the possibility of Anglo-American war, the Royal Navy ranged almost half of all its available capital ships against the United States Navy. The Admiralty deployed eleven of twenty-three active capital ships manned and ready for sea to North America. What better tribute to those seven American frigates![53]

American maritime success in the 1850s, however, was fleeting. The great clipper boom busted after 1857, and the steam frigates were relegated from "capital" to cruiser status by iron and armor and rifled guns. The steamship subsidy failed, and the ships built to compete with British passenger liners failed, as though all of the deeper American resistances to new maritime technologies welled up at once. While the United States had the industrial potential to compete in an era of rapid change in marine industry, it did not have the intellectual capacity to recognize the urgent need for change or to adapt older habits of doing maritime business that could implement such change.

Things were different in Britain. Their shipbuilders had adapted to the loss of native timber, and the process was eased by a mature coal-and-iron industrial plant. For the Royal Navy, adaptation could also "piggy-back" off of a dynamic industrial infrastructure. They needed only to take advantage of national resources. Symonds had resisted both the introduction of steam and iron to the Royal Navy. His fall in 1846 became the signal that this recognition had been made by the Admiralty, not merely for naval architecture, but for the application of new marine technologies to ship design. After Symond's departure, ship design at last was transferred from the Royal Navy's "seaman officer" to a chief constructor and a chief engineer.[54]

Finally, in January 1860, the Institution of Naval Architects (INA) held its inaugural meeting. This professional society quickly and successfully lobbied for a permanent school of naval architecture, which opened in November 1864. The development in tandem of both a learned society and a professional school created a foundation for the continued dominance of British marine technology, pioneering advanced ship engineering and design concepts, which would last into the 1920s.[55]

The United States would have no professional counterpart to the INA until 1888.

WAR AND UNREALIZED METAMORPHOSIS, 1861–65

The Civil War should have forever changed the Navy. With change, traditional Navy notions, no matter how romantically entrenched, should have been discarded, as well. For the first time, the Navy had been used as a strategic tool. In a protracted, mobilization war, the Navy became the binding agent of ultimate victory. The battles themselves were just episodic bloodletting; they needed to be cemented into a passage to victory. This the Navy did both from within and from without the continental theater of war. From within, the stern-wheel ironclads and river steamers pushed and sustained the armies of the

republic, up and downriver, penetrating the heart of the Confederate nation. From without, the monitors and steam frigates of the blockading squadrons starved the South of all succor, as though it had been stripped of the harbors and coves of all ten thousand coastal miles.

The Navy contribution to the War of Rebellion should have asserted to the Navy that it had been central to the fulfillment of America's first exercise in grand strategy and total war. Moreover, American society should have recognized that the sailors, engineers, and builders of maritime America showed a stunning capacity for improvisation under stress.

As an institution, the Navy showed that it could cast off its romantic mission expectations from the War of 1812 and fight a war on a scale and in a theater undreamed of in peace. American naval architects and steam engineers showed that they could come up with radical native designs neatly suited to a coastal and river war. The maritime industries, finally, showed that they could expand their shipbuilding plants; convert from mercantile to war construction; and provide both the raw hulls and the guns, engines, and armor of a new fleet. It was a fleet that British intelligence reports in 1864 warned would come to rival the Royal Navy itself.

Simply, maritime America had proved that it could produce the men, ships, and industrial base to create a navy that could, in time, achieve any national goals in the wider world. It remained only for American society to voice what those goals should be.

The fleet ordered up during the Civil War was not tailored simply to the immediate needs of strangling and penetrating the Confederacy. War building programs deliberately envisaged a big postwar navy, with the leverage to exert American influence in the world, with a suasion unavailable to an earlier, fledgling republic. Britain and France had been hostile neutrals. While the Union struggled to survive, Britain permitted private builders to sell commerce raiders to the South, which crippled Yankee commerce, and France had cynically invaded Mexico. By war's end, unresolved diplomatic wrangles implied an expanded American postwar naval mission.

How did this new fleet respond to areas that had earlier stifled technological innovation: native design patterns, sensitivity and insensitivity to European trends, and the limits of the marine industrial base? Did this fleet reveal the capacity for a wider mission in how it applied its technology in key areas?

Steam Propulsion

War's strategic demands finally seemed to displace the symbolic sway of sail. Steam was exalted; it was literally and symbolically the enginery of victory. The revolution in marine technology had at last caught the American navy in its embrace.

Part of this was a pure function of necessity. Naval operations upriver and blockading offshore could not have been executed without steam propulsion.

Steam shipbuilding shot upwards in Union yards during the war, helping to develop the industrial infrastructure of steam engineering. During the four years of peak war deliveries, from 1863 to 1866, steam vessel production increased 75 percent [100 percent over prewar if Southern shipbuilding is discounted]. Also, for these four years, steamship tonnage built passed the 50-percent mark compared to pure sailing ships (54 percent).[56]

The culmination of the cult of steam came just after the war. The *Wampanoag* was one of seven ships ordered in the late spring of 1863 as part of a fast cruiser competition. The legends among American steam engineers, John Ericsson and Benjamin Isherwood, vied along with the great George Steers and Cramp & Sons, Philadelphia, to build the fastest commerce raider of all time— but for the first time in the American experience *not under sail*. Monster machinery was now, if only a brief precursor of things to come, the *deus ex machina* of a new Navy ethos.

Hull Design

Basic design backwardness persisted in American naval architecture. Drafting, as an essential construction technique, was poorly developed. There was, as a consequence, much waste in labor and materials during building. For iron ships, no specifications were sent to the mills, and hull frames were cut at the building yard. Inefficiencies mounted during construction. Over one-third of all shell plating was wasted,

owing to mistakes in cutting and punching. As a legacy from the era of wood and shipwrights, builders were comfortable working up a design as they went along, so full plans were rarely made. A glaring example can be seen in the tenders for the *Monitor* bid in 1860. Even though submitted in the rush of war, there was only one set of detailed plans offered among thirty submissions.[57]

The *Monitor*, however, was the triumphal hull design of the war. Its design reverberations hit European navies like a great wave. The Admiralty wrestled with its uncomfortable innovations for decades, before finally giving in and building turret battleships. The United States built them first, thanks to an emigre naval architect, John Ericsson. The monitors led the advance on Western rivers and up mid-Atlantic tidewater, and so caught the American national imagination. Their very insularity of employment mirrored a native resistance to the capital ship concept, the embodiment of oceanic imperialism. Here was a native design that captured the spirit of American national security, a true "Shield of the Republic."

Materials

Although the Admiralty had ten ironclads with iron hulls under construction before the end of 1861, they had also authorized the conversion to armored ships of eight wooden, screw, two-deckers. The results were no more satisfactory than American wooden-hulled war steamers. The long hulls of the nineteen fast cruisers, laid down in 1863 and 1864, stretched 300 feet and more. The squat British wooden ships were weighed down by iron appliques and huge new engines for their ironclad role. Heavy iron strapping could not prevent sagging from the moment of completion, nor hogging in a seaway. The problem of hull distortion in the *Prince Consort* class was so severe that the shafting had to be realigned constantly.[58]

American war-built cruisers and monitors were strong enough, though built of wood. They were cursed by their wood, white oak and yellow pine with no time to season. It was green and it decayed fast.

Britain's capacity to build iron ships cheaper than wood was beginning to put the United States out of the naval running in applied materials technology. Wooden cruisers like the USS *Wampanoag* could be given native steam plants competitive with the best from Britain, but their long hulls could not be iron-built. Worse yet, the age of iron had become an age of iron armor. The monitors' thick turret armor might be able to shrug off British shot (from Armstrong and Blakeley and Whitworth rifled cannon sold to the South), but their layers of 1-inch laminated plate were only a fraction as efficient as the fine, thick, rolled wrought-iron of English ironclads. America's armor-making backwardness would increase with each advance in metallurgy and even twenty years after the Civil War, the United States was slavishly dependent on British plate.

Ordnance

The United States continued to awe the British with its big guns. The American 15-inch smoothbore directly penetrated the British naval imagination. With eighteen new ironclads building, the Royal Navy had a complete new fleet of capital ships to replace the now-fragile wooden walls. But, they were sheathed by only 4½ inch plate, which the 15-inchers of the American monitor fleet could pierce with ease at 500 yards. Invulnerable to French shot, the great iron frigates were as thin-skinned as if they were wood to America's big Rodman smoothbores.[59] Nor was there consolation in heavier iron plate, for the Americans had a 20-incher coming! The standard British naval gun, the 68-pounder, could not penetrate the 10- to 15-inch turrets of the monitors. It was clear by 1864 that the British battlefleet could not pretend to have the potential to blockade Union ports.

The smoothbore cannon might have seemed obsolete by 1865, but the Royal Navy gave up on breechloaders in 1866 (save for boat guns) and was still experimenting with big smoothbores, two of which—a 6.5-ton, 9.2-inch tube called the "Somerset" and a 12-ton, 10.5-inch model— were mounted on Her Majesty's Ships in 1863-64.[60] The British were still looking over their shoulder at American innovation.

Traditional Motifs and Symbols

The emergence of the monitor as the first native American capital ship design showed the capacity of our national world view to adapt

fully to new marine technologies. It would be a decade before the Royal Navy could bring itself to build a turret battleship without full masts and sailing rig. So intent was its corporate orthodoxy to force the turret into a fully rigged hull that a great iron ship, the *Captain*, and its crew of 472 were sacrificed in the pursuit of a cherished symbol.

America's embrace of the monitor should not be seen as fully flattering to the Navy world view. The monitor concept fit nicely within an American naval mission whose evolution had bifurcated into two basic ship types. The *Monitor* could trace her lineage to the block ship, the harbor defender, the blockade-buster. Her other bloodline was a romantic path of descent: the great frigate-battlecruiser. This other icon of American naval tradition implied speed and graceful line *under sail*. The new cruisers, especially the fast five—the *Ammonoosuc*, *Pompanoosuc*, *Madawaska*, *Neshaminy*, and *Wampanoag*—clearly subordinated sail to steam. With their four towering funnels, they anticipated the ship shapes of the 1900s. How would these figures play with a postwar navy?

Ship Design Integration

In scrambling for specialized ships of war, the Navy Department paid good greenbacks for some pretty green vessels. Mutations like the *Keokuk*, or the *Galena*, or the entire slew of nineteen *Casco* shallow-draft monitors leap to mind. Even the monitors, for all of their fighting record, were unbalanced designs. The *Patapsco* sank in 15 seconds from a mine, a mere 60-pound charge exploded 35 feet from the hull. The *Tecumseh* took 25 seconds to capsize from a mine at Mobile Bay. But the big two-turret monitors—the *Miantonomoah* and *Monadnock*—each made long ocean voyages under their own power, weathering gales (as did the *Lehigh* off Hatteras) like big transatlantic packets.[61]

With thirty-two seagoing Yankee armored ships built or building in 1864, the British Admiralty had cause for alarm. That year, they received a secret report from their main U.S. agent, Captain James Goodenough. He wrote of the Union ironclad fleet:

> Of these classes a&b are fit for coast and harbor defense, and, in the event of a port being block-

THE MAKING OF AN AMERICAN STYLE 17

aded, class a [*Kalamazoo, Puritan,* and *Mian-tonomoah* classes] are able to make destructive excursions against the blockading squadrons and probably, as they are more heavily armored than any ships yet built to cross the ocean, to relieve the blockade during moderate weather.[62]

This was news indeed. And there was worse to come. There were also twenty-eight big cruisers under construction, as fast or faster than any British steam frigate. Goodenough called them, plainly:

> . . . the most formidable class of steamers ever built for the purpose of injuring an enemy's commerce.[63]

His unvarnished assessment: if war came between the United States and Great Britain, the merchant marine of the British empire would die, and there was nothing that the "black battle-fleet" could do to stop them. If a clutch of Confederate raiders built in British yards and named by British crews could effectively eviscerate Yankee commerce, what might be the prospect of a score of fast Federal cruisers with heavy guns let loose on British sea lanes? This was a bleak vision to an Admiralty preoccupied with French ironclad competition.

Any superficial glance would have placed American marine technology at the world's forefront in 1865. France and Italy both showed their homage to Union "high-tech" by buying American ironclads. The French marine picked up the uncommissioned *Dunderberg*—a giant, Confederate-stylized Union casemate ship—and the double-turrent *Onandaga,* while Count Cavour of Savoy commissioned William Webb of New York to build two armored frigates, the *Re d'Italia* and the *Re di Portogallo.* The British never bought a Federal war steamer, but they did buy several of their own abortive exports to the South, designed specifically to tackle the monitors of the North Atlantic Blockading Squadron. Beyond recognizing the threat of the U.S. Navy's monitor concept, they kowtowed to its promise. They built a quartet of "breastwork monitors" of their own, the *Cerberus* class, and modeled the *Glatton* on Ericsson's single turret and twin guns, the *Dictator.*[64]

Adaptation to revolution in applied marine technologies was in fact roughly parallel in both the Navy Department and the Admiralty. This can be seen in the similarity and course of engineering debates: rifle versus smoothbore, turret versus broadside, the balance between steam and sail, wood and iron. Even the experimental ships produced to settle some of these debates looked the same. For example, both the U.S. and Royal Navies each tried cutting down one of their biggest wooden steam capital ships for conversion to turret battleship: the Americans the big frigate *Roanoke,* the British the three-decker *Royal Sovereign.* Each was cut down to the same deck, each had three turrets, and they were converted within a year of each other.[65] Although lagging in industrial fabrication, the United States in war had proven its capacity to shape an integrated design, and equip it with an advanced propulsion plant and modern armament. In 1865, briefly, the United States at sea was the functional equal of the first industrial nation: Great Britain.

POSTWAR PAROCHIALISM, 1865–85

And what of the recognitions that should have come out of the war? Not one of them took hold. The ability of the Navy to discard its own embedded parochialism, the capacity of marine designers to imagine, and the readiness of maritime industry to forge new ships could have catapulted the United States into world power standing in the late 1860s.

But basic American values denied the legitimacy of great power status. We did not seek it. Power was the pursuit of European kings, it was the road to empire and so, for America, to national corruption. The Civil War had been fought for reform and expiation, not for material reward and expansion.

The South had been beaten in battle, but the war was not over. Now the arena shifted to a struggle for national purification and renewal, a battle over "hearts and minds" called "reconstruction." In the space of an instant, as American world view shifted from war to postwar reform, the Navy was relegated to its traditions. This was the first blow to the evolution of a naval mission now America's by right (if not by inclination).

The second blow was a willing reassertion of Navy romantic tradition within the service itself, an embrace forced in the face of immediate, pulsing war experience. It was almost as though the Navy denied what it had just done, as if it had been an interesting episode or aberrant combat excursion, irrelevant to past and future, and to the true sources of identity. If the national spirit of the postwar age rejected American engagement in the world, then so too would the Navy. The chronicle of decline encompassed more than just the naval service. In the process, an American maritime world that had become dependent on government grants and guidance was boosted into decline.

The decline of maritime America ensured as well the atrophy of its naval architecture and engineering. Congress authorized few new ships, which helped to render naval and civilian shipbuilding competitively obsolescent. It was during this generation, from Appomatox to the late 1880s, that the consequences of maritime parochialism, congratulating itself for the wrong innovations and the wrong technology path, became horribly visible.

But it did not happen all at once. The immediate postwar picture was one of open-ended maritime potential. A sense of U.S. freedom of action at sea was braced by the host of new ships just launched or on the stocks. This fleet, however, was a wasting capital asset. Its rapid erosion as a diplomatic tool just about paced the actual rot of unseasoned yellow pine of the fleet's timbers.

The American fast cruiser program of 1863 impressed British observers. When the *Wampanoag* reached 17.75 knots on its speed trials, 11 February 1868, Americans knew they had image-dominance over Britain. Here was a ship that no British war steamer could catch. At the very moment of the *Wampanoag* trials, U.S. senators were demanding huge indemnities from Her Majesty's Government for damages suffered by American commerce under the guns of Confederate raiders. The British indignantly refused to pay.

The House of Representatives had already passed a bill in 1866 permitting private shipbuilders to sell warships to foreign states at war. William Webb had recently built (in addition to two ironclad frigate for Savoy) a "monster" 68-gun screw-frigate, the *General Admiral*, for Imperial Russia.[66] Now the British Admiralty could savor the bitter prospect of America return-

ing the *Alabama* favor if war with Russia re-erupted. Although at peace with Petersburg since 1856, Russia's 1870 repudiation of the Black Sea clauses of the Treaty of Paris renewed the prospect of war, and Russian "war scares" were serious political issues in 1878 and 1885. The image of a series of *Wampanoag*s with names like *Dmitri Donskoi* or *Alexander Nevski* ravaging the sea lanes helped bring the Court of St. James to the arbitration table.

At least jingoistic Americans, flush with postwar complacency, saw things that way.

But jingoism did not equate to expansionism. Baron Edouard de Stoeckel, Russian minister to the United States, spent the enormous sum of $200,000 (perhaps $20 million in 1988 dollars) on propaganda, parties, and bribes before the Senate would agree to buy Alaska. Similar tactics by Raasloff, the Danish minister, failed to sell the Virgin Islands, and no exertions by President U.S. Grant would move the Senate to pick up Samana Bay for a song (the Dominican Republic had actually offered itself to the U.S. if it would cover its public debt of $1,500,000). Hawaii was out, though Seward managed Midway. Americans just wanted nothing of foreign affairs, let alone foreign "entanglements."

The naval image cashed in by the State Department during the *Alabama* claims was in full, literal rot by 1873, when a real crisis hit the United States. Forty U.S. citizens were summarily executed by Spanish authorities in Cuba that October, in what is remembered as the *Virginius* Incident. Grant mobilized the U.S. Fleet at Key West.

What a motley assemblage it was! Monitors with rusting armor and rotting or rusting hulls, wooden cruisers limited to 7 or 8 knots under steam. . . . Spain, in contrast, had seven new black battleships, iron-sheathed broadside frigates that could have shattered the American navy.[67] The great, crusty David Dixon Porter was even more emphatic: " . . . one ship like the British iron-clad *Invincible* ought to go through a fleet like ours and put the vessels *hors de combat* in a short time. . . ."[68] And Spain had seven such ships!

Responding to the shame of the *Virginius* Affair, Congress authorized the Secretary of the Navy to use about $900,000 for the "reconstruction" of the armored fleet. Five monitors were selected: the still-incomplete *Puritan* and the four *Miantonomoahs*, which would in effect become new ships, for their wooden hulls were almost completely rotted. Work was suspended in 1876, however, when Navy Secretary Robeson failed to get the $2.3 million needed to complete the ships. His 1875 report to Congress listed twenty-one monitors, five reconstructing, the harbor-bound *Roanoke*, and fifteen surviving single-turret ships. The big *Kalamazoos* were too deteriorated even to list, though their armor and machinery plants were still held in the Navy yards. Work on new monitors would not be authorized again until 1883.[69]

In effect, from the 1870s to the 1890s, the U.S. had no working armored ships, while domestic political authorities would point to a mighty fleet of twenty-one, pacifying all electoral opinion.

The American electorate, after all, saw what it wished to see. After Appomattox, officials could point to a boundless reservoir of ships and naval weaponry. In 1865, the Federal fleet listed 471 ships and 2,455 modern guns. The guns were stockpiled; like a great coastal fort, they were viewed by the people as the nation's "permanent" arsenal for national defense. They were battle-tested and proven. A misguided American tradition of national defense dominated any recognition that technological change demanded constant military modernization. For Congress and the electorate, the false but soothing perception that military goods once appropriated were durable and good for generations persisted. Like the sailing battleships held in readiness for launching, decade after decade, in case of national emergency, Americans assumed that the ships and guns built for war would serve as an enduring insurance of peace for an entire era.

America's merchant marine was also in full decline. Confederate raiders had crippled the American merchant marine. The collapse of the whaling industry in the 1860s added momentum to the slide. The descent can be measured in terms of its share of our foreign trade: 67 percent in 1855-59, 46 percent in 1864, 44 percent in 1866, 38 percent in 1870; and in the size of the fleet engaged in foreign trade: 2,379,396 tons in 1855; 1,448,846 tons in 1870.[70]

There were other factors contributing to the decline of the American merchant marine. A major pre-Civil War demand for sailing ships had largely disappeared by 1870. The slowly reviving cotton trade to Great Britain was now picked up by steam tramps. Sail passenger packets had given way to the new iron transatlantic liners, and the great symbol of American internalization, the transcontinental railroad, could now replace the Cape Horners. Denied any hope of a commercial niche in trades that demanded high technology—fast, iron ships—American shipbuilders and fleet owners naturally shifted their focus to transport markets where wooden, square-rigged ships still had a comparative advantage. So developed a postwar American dominance in the grain trade from Pacific Coast to Europe. Here sail still offered strengths in carrying capacity and economy of operation. At 2,000 gross tons, American grain ships averaged two times or more the size of the typical freighter of the 1850s.[71]

Within this last American square-rigged niche, there were even good times. During the boom of 1870-74, 224,000 gross tons of square-rigged ships and barks were built, 80 percent in Maine yards. In 1875-79, output reached 401,000 gross tons. But then the final decline set in. From 1880-84, production fell to 165,000 gross tons, and from 1885-89, it fell to only 35,000 gross tons.[72]

The final consequence, in professional and industrial terms, of entrenched postwar parochialism was the collapse of an American sense of marine technology and the design process. An embracing set of national beliefs had denied the consequences of technological change to American naval power. This innocent but fixed attitude had an extended impact on the Navy and maritime America as a whole. Research and development in maritime technologies and new maritime industries tended to be withheld.

Shipbuilding had become dependent on government intervention during the Civil War. Postwar evaporation of federal support had handed the North Atlantic carrying trade to the British. For the Navy, government neglect had direct results: its capacity to compete with evolving European design would be dependent on Congressional authorization. Years of atrophy resulted not merely in a neglected naval order of battle; it ensured a backward, neglected industrial infrastructure and an impoverished design base. In contrast, European marine technology was surging ahead, propelled by massive state support, in all component areas of ship design.

Steam Propulsion

Sail continued to control American oceangoing shipping in foreign trade. In 1869, the gross tonnage of the U.S. merchant sailing fleet was 1,353,170, compared to a mere 213,252 tons for steamships. This relationship held until 1902, when steamships finally won out.[73] But actual tonnage employed tells only part of the story. In terms of gross-ton miles covered per year, sailing ships as late as 1901 racked up 3473 billion, while steamships pulled only 981 billion.

In contrast, in Great Britain, steamship building had passed the output of pure sailing rigs in the 1860s.[74] In the United States, steam first surpassed sail in 1879-82, declined for three years, and then after 1885 outdistanced sailing ships for good. Unhappily, shipbuilding statistics continued to show steam dominant in domestic trade on the rivers of America, not in foreign trade.[75]

British steamship building, moreover, continued to demonstrate a high annual growth over a thirty-year period. From an average of 46,300 tons in the 1850s, it swelled to 107,900 tons in the 1860s, and to 258,600 tons in the 1870s.[76] By comparison, an American annual steam vessel output of 75,000 tons during the 1850s grew to an annual average of 89,000 tons in the 1860s, much of this due to Federal war orders, and then sank back to an average of 75,000 tons in the 1870s.[77]

Hull Design

American hulls were still predominantly wooden, and so hull design in the United States still focused on the characteristic problems of wooden structural integrity. The shapes themselves were excellent. The big grain ships of the 1870s had full, yet easy lines, embodying many of the advances of the clipper era, while avoiding the clippers' disadvantages of low capacity and heavy crew costs. These were achieved by employing long and level keels, flat floors, semi-clipper bows, and broad square sterns with fair runs. To handle large bulk cargoes, builders

became obsessed with hull stiffening; very deep keelsons with heavy iron plating, iron cross-strapping on frames amidships, and heavy floors and futtocks became hallmarks of American hull design.[78]

Materials

Creative but cumbersome iron hardware was a necessity in American shipbuilding, where in 1884 wood still surpassed iron in the merchant fleet by a factor of ten to one (3,885 to 387,000 gross tons). Iron and steel did not surpass wood until 1908.[79]

So, the focus on improving wooden ship integrity and durability continued. A major innovation in wooden shipbuilding technology was introduced by J.W. Griffiths' frame-curving machinery. It offered all wood-framed ships the strength of iron framing. It was successfully demonstrated in the New Era in 1870, to enthusiastic reviews. The machinery, however, was complex and costly. The innovation was not adopted, and for decades American shipbuilders continued to rely on a material that was inferior to iron in strength, was heavier, and demanded more hull volume.[80]

By the 1870s, the comparative cost advantages of wood were evaporating. The available timber supply was in full-scale decline, the result of using up forests along the entire eastern seaboard. The big grain ships required from 200 to 300 full-grown oaks each. New supplies could be had from the Great Lakes and Ohio Valley, or cheap Canadian hackmatack and Oregon pine could be hauled from the Pacific Northwest by railroad. But these could be had only with higher costs.

In Britain, however, the cost per ton of iron ships continued to fall: from £17-18 in 1860 to £13-14 in 1870. This rate equalled the lowest price for New England wooden sailing ships. By the 1880s, British yards were building steel sailing ships better than iron and lighter at $50-65 per gross ton. The predictable result: British steel sailing-ship building reached an all-time peak in 1892 at 287,000 net tons, mostly at the expense of the United States. In comparison, American yards at that time built only three big, iron, square-rigged ships, in 1882-83, and one steel sailing ship, in 1894. Even France and

Germany were forging ahead of American square-rig shipbuilding.[81]

American shipbuilding, by clinging to wood, had doomed itself. In 1884, Henry Hall, in an official report attached to the U.S. Census, declared:

> . . . it is almost impossible to entertain the slightest hope of ever replacing the timber [supplies] when it has finally been cut off . . . the United States cannot depend upon the oak supply of the country for many years longer. . . . ship-building timber on the Atlantic coast is diminishing now so fast that wooden ships are likely to rise materially in price in the next twenty years.

Even with substantial stocks on the Pacific coast, the handwriting was on the wall.[82] The passion for wood is all the more remarkable given the expansion in American iron production. In 1884, when Hall submitted his report, pig iron smelting in the United States was four times higher than in 1864, at the height of the Civil War.[83] The irony is that American shipbuilding lost its competitiveness in sailing-ship building, in which it had always excelled, and for which a strong market still existed.

Of thirty-six passenger liners flying the United States flag in 1870, only three were built of iron, and of these, only the Brazilian liner *Merrimac* was a real oceanliner. At that time, all 102 British, French, and German liners were iron-built.[84] Part of the problem for native builders was that the price of American iron did not fall until the 1880s. In the 1870s, wood ships could still be framed for $65-80 per ton, while an iron ship cost $110-135 per ton.[85]

Unfortunately, wide-scale steel shipbuilding overtook Europe while the United States was just beginning to enter an economical iron age![86] Iron remained the preferred construction material of the U.S. Navy. The "reconstructed" monitors authorized in 1874 were still building in iron at the end of the 1880s. Professional opinion within the Navy actually opposed the use of steel, in stubborn resistance to European trends. Chief Engineer Benjamin Isherwood, and naval constructors John Lenthal, T. D. Wilson, and Philip Hichborn managed to reject the use of steel several times before their prejudice could be overridden.[87]

The British were already using steel for warship construction with the battleship *Bellerophon* in 1868. Their first all-steel warship was the *Iris* of 1876.[88] In fairness, the British still held an apparently unassailable lead in industrial infrastructure through the 1870s. The United States shared roughly the same limitations in marine technology as most European states. The French, for example, were still building ironclads of wood to the end of the 1870s. Suddenly, however, they were ready and able to skip a materials' generation and switch to steel.[89] The United States did much the same with its "New Navy" in the 1880s.

American marine industry was peculiarly backward in specific, applied marine technology. One major limitation was an incapacity to roll armor plate. The Civil War monitors had wrapped themselves in layers of thin laminated wrought iron plates, a crude expedient. Of the sixteen new warships actually built for the U.S. Navy in the 1870s, all were cruising ships, for which armor was impracticable.

But, there were five big monitors rebuilding, and still there was no state or private capacity to roll thick plate. Halfway through the "reconstruction" of the *Miantonomoah*, the Navy was forced to contract with the British firms of John Brown and Charles Cammell for 2,240 tons of steel plates for $118,000 in 1883.[90] America's naval industries were beginning to resemble the contemporary, nineteenth century version of a Third World regional power: the Ottoman, Spanish, or Chinese empires. Each represented a majestic economy unharnessed. In spite of major resources and human capital, industrial development was passing them by, a function in part of pervasive cultural disinterest. Was American society so different in its attention to maritime industry?

Ordnance

In military technology, the United States could build hulls of inferior materials (wood), equip them with serviceable steam plants, but had to go abroad for their essential martial fittings: armor and guns.

The atrophy of gun-founding was especially galling. The Union had cast numbers of great guns during the Civil War, guns without peer. The 15-inch Rodman was 42,000 pounds, and at the end of the war, several monstrous pieces of 20-inch caliber and 117,000 pounds were cast. Between 1865 and 1880, no attempts were made by the United States Government to create a modern weapons-forging industrial plant. When foreign style decreed rifled artillery at sea, old Civil War smoothbores were converted to rifled cannon by the simple expedient of lining an 11-inch Dahlgren with rifled tube. Huzzah—an 8-incher! Inaction persisted until 1880, when the Navy forged its first built-up, steel, breechloading gun.[91]

Going late to breechloaders was not necessarily a sign of backwardness; the Royal Navy also clung to muzzle-loaders until 1884. After a premature initiative, the Admiralty actually had declared *against* breechloaders in 1868. It took a terrible accident aboard the battleship *Thunderer* in January 1879 to show the backwardness of muzzleloaders and to bring back the future. Bureaucratic inertia decreed that this would be a future still eight years away; Britain's first battleship breechloaders did not enter sea service until 1886, on the *Colossus*.[92]

Traditional Motifs and Symbols

Most elegant of all the traditional symbols of a navy consecrating mummified traditions at the expense of a vital mission is the conversion of the fast cruiser *Madawaska* to the steam frigate *Tennessee*. The metamorphosis (it would be improper and misleading to call it a "refit") itself was representative of the Navy's postwar rejection of its future in an attempt to reassert its past. The *Madawaska* was one of the five *Wampanoags*, ships built for steam engines and boilers and little else: in its original form she was the incarnation of the revolution in marine technology, and of a wartime navy's understanding of its implications.

In the early 1870s the *Madawaska* was transformed from a badge of modernism to a totem of romantic tradition. Not just its white oak hull, but all of the traditional ship fittings of the old sailing navy were there. The pieces that transformed the original *Madawaska* recalled a prewar world where "Young America" was supreme at sea: knee-bows, stern galleries, spar decks. A loss of fighting power, with no bow-heavy pivot gun, was regrettable but subordinate to the ship's

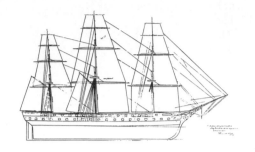

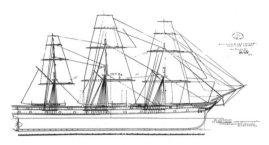

FIGURE 1-1—The USS Franklin (top) represented the apogee of the pre-Civil War frigate: a true capital ship of the 1850's. She was robust and loaded with heavy shell guns (notice the number of gun ports). The USS Tennessee (lower), in contrast, shows its cruiser lines. In spite of the addition of a spar deck, she retained a long, sleek hull, with only a single gun deck. With her graceful knee bow, the Tennessee exemplified the post-Civil War abandonment of the concept of an oceangoing American battleship embodied in the Franklin, built just a few years before.

major role, which was primarily symbolic in an age of American withdrawal. The *Tennessee* did not need to tackle British or French steel cruisers; it was enough to "show the flag" in impressive fashion, where visual delight at the sheer line of wooden hull and high sparring seemed to identify the Navy mission.

After all, American designers could insist that the British were still building ironclads with square rigs, right up to the armored cruiser *Imperieuse* in 1887.[93] But what was only a badge of identity for the British, French, and Russians, a mere motif, had become a sacred hereditary emblem for the American navy. As with all such totems, the original meaning had been lost. In the nineteenth century, the big frigates, sailing battleships, and "monster" steam-frigates, too, had sought to exploit marine technology to create an individual ship deterrent. This deterrent had been the core of the Navy mission. And it had been lost.

The U.S. Navy of the 1870s, in its exaltation of symbol over the thing represented, had come to resemble the Royal Navy of the 1840s, clinging to checker-painted wooden walls.

Ship Design Integration

However magnificent a vision at the frontiers of technology she seems now to us, the *Wampanoag* was excoriated by a bigoted Navy Department review board as an example of poor design integration: " . . . scarcely more than naval trash. . . ." They could point to internal arrangements that were unbearably cramped, of crew spaces and armament that should not be those of a proper fighting ship. They could also protest that its giant engines were too inefficient for its intended oceanic cruiser-raider role. The same would be said of the torrentially fast Italian cruisers of the 1920s, but they caused a sensation anyway, and did no harm to Italy's reputation in naval architecture.[94]

If the *Wampanoag* lacked design balance, this was a consequence of the pressures to experiment during a period of rapid technological change. During these times, the presentation of balanced ships should not be the test of design judgement. The fruits of research and development, especially the willingness to build complete ship prototypes to test applications and potential system-synthesis, form a better test. In this sense, the *Wampanoag* and its designer, Isherwood, should not be judged for offering an immature prototype. The *Wampanoag* was the essense of an experimental ship, which could have been a real "technology test bed" (in today's jargon), leading a research and development program that would have extended the design edge of the U.S. Navy after 1865. In contrast, the Navy judgements on the *Wampanoag* express a kind of mental atavism, a clutch of attitudes and assumptions that constitute a throwback in maritime world view. For the cruiser tradition, this meant spar-decks and clipper knees, telescoping funnels, retractable screws, and a genteel curbing of armament.

For the indigenous American capital ship concept, the monitor, resistance to experiment meant an end to evolution. We had the perfect design, the perfect ship to defend America's coast and harbors. The monitor was a design whose exact lines had become equated to the symbol of its function. To change or to enlarge it might mean a corollary expansion of the mission itself. And it was, moreover, a design that seemed forever "modern."

American technology looked unassailable in 1866. That year the monitors went overseas. The biggest hit was the grand tour of the *Miantonomoah* through Europe in 1866. Everywhere it was feted as a wonder ship. In the Russian capital, its crew was the toast of the town, "receiving such a reception that it is an event still told of in St. Petersburg. . . ."[95] The Russians did the U.S. Navy a further and greater honor by building ten monitors, essentially copies of the *Passaic*-class.[96]

The French and British also built monitors and turret ships, and through their experiments, the monitor concept evolved to the prototype of the modern battleship: Reed's *Devastation* of 1873. His criticisms of Ericsson's uninflected American monitor concept—low freeboard and a single, unobstructed turret—highlights contemporary European opinion of U.S. design atrophy.[97]

The revised monitor designs of the 1870s and 1880s, although incorporating iron construction and breechloading cannon (both armor and guns forged in British furnaces), were, in spirit, no more than extrapolated replicas of Civil War ships.[98] Nothing had been learned; but, then, nothing needed to be learned. The fate of the monitor concept from 1865 to 1895, when the first ocean-going battleship, the *Indiana*, hoisted colors was a fate decreed by its success in physically embodying inward-looking national values. As symbol, the *Monitor* was the naval guarantor, as well as the physical protector, of parochial America.

In contrast, the Royal Navy profited from American war lessons. After 1865, research and development ruled procurement. The Admiralty spent £10.5 million on new ships, many of them experimental, in the eight years after 1865.[99] A commitment to test-bed research in the Royal Navy was exemplified by the *Thunderer* trials, which attempted to define the "state-of-the-art" limits of ship-system performance.[100]

This commitment extended to the design and construction of actual capital ships to test new concepts. Perhaps the best example of this was the battleship *Inflexible*. Like many British capital ships from this era, it was never intended as a standard ship type. The *Inflexible* was an attempt to push certain concepts about what a capital ship should be, and what military and marine technologies should be incorporated for the future. Among the innovations built into the *Inflexible* were such firsts as electric lighting and antiroll tanks.[101]

The British Admiralty approach to naval experimentation did lead to a menagerie of capital ship types and a heterogeneous fleet. Many ironclads were militarily obsolete the day they were commissioned. During the 1870s, the Royal Navy added to the fleet: 1) breastwork monitors, 2) a masted turret-ship, 3) a two-storied central-battery ship, 4) a central-battery ship with barbettes, 5) a one-deck broadside battery ship, 6) citadel turret ships, 7) small redoubt single turret ships, and 8) partially belted broadside ships.[102]

In this context, technological hypertrophy, exemplified by the HMS *Inflexible* became a design dead-end. A critic might admit that by testing the state-of-the-art so rigorously, certain design verities were demonstrated, but at great cost, with little return. Another view, however, might contest this notion. Certainly, the British could hardly lay claim to a battle-ready force during the "dark ages of the Victorian Navy."[103] But did it really matter? The decade of the 1870s, the apogee of English scientific-technical dominance, was used to advantage by White, and then Fisher, to prepare the way for the fine standard battleships of the next century. In fact, the capacity of the Royal Navy to compete technically with the new industrial superpowers of Germany, the United States, and Russia might be seen as a result of developing a technical design establishment a generation before it was needed.

The Royal Navy gave up little for its Gilded Age experimentations. The French were hardly a strategic threat after their defeat in 1871, and the Russians and Germans would not begin to constitute effective naval orders-of-battle until the early part of the twentieth century. Much was gained at little risk.

Also, it must be remembered that in the 1870s,

only the French and the Russians were really building their own native designs. The Germans were still buying British-built ironclads until the mid-70s, while Japan would not complete its first home-built battleship, the *Tsukuba*, until 1907.[104]

In contrast, when the U.S. Navy finally attempted to "go it alone" in the early 1880s, it had to clear several hurdles, several of them self-imposed.

First, by this time, native American design concepts no longer existed. And "modern" warship designs were dependent on European models. Hat-in-hand, American officers made technical pilgrimages to the Old World to purchase foreign designs. The U.S. Navy paid $2,500 in 1886 for the latest British notions of the perfect warship for their navy and Japan's. Secretary of the Navy William C. Whitney, like a bureaucrat from the Third World today, confessed that " . . . our true policy is to borrow the ideas of our neighbors *so far as they are thought to be in advance of our own* (italics mine)."[105] This attitude held for all the combatants of our new steel navy that were built through to the small battleship *Texas*, designed by Barrow Shipbuilding in 1887.[106]

Second, industrial limitations in fabrication and material production forced the United States to buy from European industry. The Rodgers Board, charged by President Garfield to think about a new navy, underscored the failings of the domestic steel industry, and its incapacity to forge heavy ordnance above 6-inch caliber.[107] When the first steel ships were authorized, the builder, John Roach, labored under massive cost overruns building the first of warships of their kind in America.[108]

Third, there was the persistence of sailing navy traditions, which forced naval architects and engineers to consider the most backward of European models, simply because these embodied needed emotional motifs. The first steel cruisers of the "New Navy" were shaped to preserve sail-rigs. This practice was barely acceptable for cruising ships during the 1880s; it was inexcusable for an ironclad. The *Maine*, taken from a British design for Brazil, worked in a full bark-rig at the expense of its fighting power.[109]

Fourth, there was an erosion of clear Navy

mission concepts, either from the time of "Young America" or from the Civil War, accelerated by the physical decay of the U.S. fleet itself. In an official statement by the Navy Department in 1884, its civil powers declared that, "It is not now, and never has been, a part of (our navy) policy to maintain a fleet able at any time to cope on equal terms with the foremost European armament." A nation enthralled with its internal development wished nothing more from the Navy than defense of its coasts.

The monitors under "reconstruction" would cost $1.6 million, but the same report bent to popular will by assuring Americans that "It has never been claimed for the monitors that they would be a match for the enormous ironclad battleships of Europe, costing $4,000,000 each."[110] This popular aversion to "monster weapons" (a term from today's political lexicon used every time a new carrier is requested) was contrary to pre-Civil War national security norms. Then, the United States deliberately maintained a squadron of frigates individually superior to the latest European battleships, even if each was an uncharacteristic combination of line-of-battle ship and cruiser.

In effect, the functional division of ship types as a result of Civil War experience reinforced very old popular traditions, emerging from the myths of the War of 1812, where fleet composition was seen by the Congress and electorate as a mix of blockade-busters and commerce-raiders. America of the 1870s and 1880s merely updated this schema of national defense to coast defense armored ships and steel cruisers. The mature pre-Civil War Navy concept—centered around a small, but powerful squadron of first-class capital ships—was dead.

When fleet obsolescence became so pronounced that a renewal was required, the Rodgers Board (First Advisory Board)—simply restated postwar and traditional American notions of a normal fleet makeup: seventy unarmored cruisers (there were sixty-one cruising ships on the current list) and twenty-one monitor-like ironclads (there were twenty-one armored hulls listed). The Board called for steel in construction, so displaying "modernity," and yet averred that "in time of peace ironclads were not necessary for carrying on the work of the United States

Navy." Their 1881 report led to a 1882 naval appropriations bill which authorized completion of five monitors and construction of two steel cruisers.[111] A Second Advisory Board under Commodore Robert W. Shufeldt merely reinforced the former, lingering parochialism, but it led to real money for real ships: $1.3 million for four cruisers and a dispatch boat.[112]

But through the internalized American age, between the Civil War's end and the first ship of the "New Navy," some forty new war steamers had been added to the Fleet. Although not yet finished, five big iron monitors had been launched between 1876 and 1883. Certainly, the "Old Navy" between 1865 and 1885 was backward, slow to adpot evolving marine technology, slower still to adopt to European naval trends, and bereft of innovative native designs. The vision of the "New Navy" spun by the Rodgers Board, moreover, was no more than the old fleet in new packaging.

But the United States Navy reflected a wider American way. National values shaped its mission, and its institutional behavior. The real "New Navy" began only in June of 1890, when the first ocean battleships since the big steam frigates of 1854 were authorized by Congress. Navy metamorphosis could not precede a transformation of American world view. A re-emergence of Navy vitality, where the mission of the Service lay at the oceanic horizon of national mission was dependent on a national recognition of an American mission.

And that recognition came with a rush at the very end of the 1880s.

THE FERMENT BEFORE TRANSFORMATION, 1885–1888

Several things seemed to happen at once. America had been turning outward for years in ways it did not see: a world of immigrants were coming to our shores, wrenching our world view; trade with Europe and Asia and Latin America was booming; and the fast steamships of the 1880s were pulling the world to us.

American industrial production was accelerating, like a dynamo rushing to threshold speed, and Americans began to believe that they must compete with the other industrial superpowers, especially Britain and Germany, for foreign markets if American prosperity was to survive. At the center of this portrait, a fierce canvas of struggle, was technology. American industry was still backward in many areas. To win in the new world economic competition, the United States must seize the forefront of technology.

Steel came to be seen as the ultimate arbiter of national progress, and by 1890 output of American steel surged past British output. In 1870, the United States smelted 77,000 short tons, while in 1890 the tonnage stacked up to 4,779,000.[113] In comparison, from 1871 to 1874, British furnaces produced 468,000 short tons to 176,000 in American fires; from 1890 to 1894, however, Britain produced only 3,143,000 compared with 4,796,000 by the United States.[114]

This was not enough for the Navy. It needed specialized steel fabrication plants, especially armor forging and rolling, and heavy gun foundries. The cost of developing a domestic armor and artillery plant for the Navy was estimated at $17,000,000 by the Simpson Gun Foundry Board in 1884.[115] To pull in private industry, Congress would need to create a naval program large enough to interest the big steel and shipbuilding firms in capitalization. Rear Admiral Edward Simpson declared that even if a deliberate, well-funded program were begun in 1885, the lead time for heavy guns was five years minimum.[116]

Congress responded to the need. The Whitney Naval Bill of 1886 incorporated a clause demanding that all warship-system components (except shafting) be manufactured domestically, and included capitalization for ordnance plants. The 1888 bill included $5 million "towards armor and armament of domestic manufacture."[117] Final foreign armor contracts were let in March 1885, for $327,000 of British plate and gun steel.[118] By the end of the 1880s, however, American industry had created a foundation strong enough to quickly capitalize the fabrication of new naval technologies.

If, for a generation, from 1865-85, maritime America acted as though the United States was no more than a Third World power, this was decreed by an inward-facing national ethos. America rejected world involvement for twenty years while celebrating its own uniqueness. When our world view shifted at the end of the

1880s, maritime America "came in from the cold."

This displacement of world view came with a suddenness of national recognition. In 1890, Frederick Jackson Turner spoke in symbolic terms of what many had begun to feel years earlier: that the American frontier was gone. The myth of the American western frontier was itself a binding image reinforcing national insularity after the Civil War. Now its presence, and its calling, had ended.

That same year, Alfred Thayer Mahan's *Influence of Sea Power Upon History* thrust a substitute vision on the national imagination. Having lost our old myth of historical progress as a nation, we were offered another. Mahan reshaped familiar American expectations of national progress and historical passage within the course of European intellectual currents. He fit American world view into a larger spirit of the age without stripping it of older mythic content. The United States had a new calling, or historical mission, within a global context.

In recasting the national mission, Mahan skillfully positioned navies as the central instrument of world power. This necessitated scuttling traditional U.S. Navy notions, which put the service at the margins of national life. No longer mere protector of American rights and American sovereignty, the U.S. Navy was to be the actual and the symbolic agency of America's destiny. Mahan was able to weave changing American cultural attitudes and economic needs into a tapestry bordered by the Navy.

And the Navy's success would depend on the most advanced technology, applied by American industry in the form of a fleet of battleships. A modern battlefleet would emblemize American competitiveness and would also insure it, protecting the wider, global economic interests of the United States. What the Soviets today call the "scientific-technical revolution" was identified by Mahan as the centerpiece of his agenda. If the battleship was key to the Navy mission, as the Navy to a larger national mission, then realization of battleship technology would unlock all. Gone were parochial ship concepts, limited to the commerce-raiding cruiser and the coastal blockade-breaker.

With the recognition of America in a great

world competition, however, came the pressing awareness that the United States was still weak in human capital. An age of industrial technology required an educational network of technical training and professionalism to sustain us in the race. This sense of intellectual urgency helps to explain the welling-up of professional societies, the upsurge in engineering graduates, and the clamorous expansion of higher degree programs among American universities.

Figures here are indicative. The number of institutions of higher learning grew from 563 in 1870 to 998 in 1890.[119] The number of degrees conferred rose from 9,372 in 1870 to 16,703 in 1890. Numbers of a new degree, the Ph.D., grew from the very first in 1870 to 149 in 1890.[120] Also, between 1879 and 1894 nearly fifty U.S. Navy steam engineers were sent out to American universities to help create and shape a nation-wide engineering program. The effort was similar to the way in which Third World states today have tried to use their precious human capital as a foundation for national scientific-technical development.

America was "taking off" technologically. Alexander Graham Bell was in full operation, while Edison and the Wright brothers were just around the corner. There was a fertility of native invention. As only a hint of impending change, of all patents issued, the number granted to new inventions grew from 4,357 in 1860 to 25,313 in 1890.[121]

In purely naval terms, it was recognized how much the competitiveness of the U.S. Navy had suffered from its dependence on self-made, isolated individual naval architects and engineers. While a few brilliant men might come forth— Ericsson, Steers, Isherwood—their own prejudices might eventually do as much to hold back the cause as their farsightedness had once advanced it. Isherwood's tenacious crusade against steel in ship construction, Ericsson's insistance on a spindle-mounted, single-turret monitor as a pure and eternal naval form, and Steer's perfect sailing hull vision all show the down side of the dominance of the individual in American naval architecture and steam engineering. A professional society that would instill a sense of corporate mission, blending its institutional calling with a larger sense of national mission, was needed. The linkage was more than casual; it was explicit.

Naval engineering can be seen, within the bounds of a competitive and exuberant age, as self-consciously symbolizing America as world competitor *and* as world power. For the Navy, steam engineers were like midwives at the rebirth of a Phoenix. For maritime America had once before been dominant, once before tested the standard of the world. Now it was doing so again, and now as part of a larger, embracing national movement. Where shipwrights had once been sorcerers of draught line and model, their naval engineer-architect successors were part of a national vision, the prefiguring of America's future and of those who would realize it through technology.

Notes

1   Headrick, Daniel R., *The Tools of Empire: Technology and European Imperialism in the Nineteenth Century.* Oxford: Oxford University Press, 1981, p. 46.

2   Hutchins, John G. B., *The American Maritime Industries and Public Policy, 1789-1914.* Cambridge, Mass.: Harvard University Press, 1941, p. 258.

3   *Ibid.,* p. 259.

4   U.S. Department of Commerce, Bureau of the Census, *Historical Statistics of the United States: Colonial Times to 1970.* Washington, D.C.: U.S. Government Printing Office, 1975, p. 600.

5   Hutchins, *Maritime Industries and Public Policy,* p. 259.

6   Chapelle, Howard I., *The History of the American Sailing Navy.* New York, N.Y.: W. W. Norton, 1949, p. 121, 126.

7   Hutchins, *Maritime Industries and Public Policy,* p. 288.

8   *Ibid.*

9   Lavery, Brian, *The Ship of the Line.* London, England: Conway Maritime Press, 1983, p. 188, 210. Also Chapelle, *Sailing Navy,* p. 132.

10   Chapelle, *Sailing Navy,* pp. 316-318.

11   Hamilton, Sir Richard Vesey, ed., *Letters and Papers of Admiral of the Fleet Sir Thomas Byam Martin.* Lon-

don, England: The Navy Records Society, 1900, pp. 97-98.

12 Tupinier, Jean, *Rapport sur le Materiel de la Marine.* Paris, France (1837), p. 19.

13 Hamilton, *Letters*, p. 154.

14 Chapelle, *Sailing Navy*, pp. 438-440.

15 Hutchins, *Maritime Industries and Public Policy*, pp. 319-320.

16 Chapelle, *Sailing Navy*, p. 450. Also Brown, D. K., *A Century of Naval Construction: The History of the Royal Corps of Naval Constructors.* London, England: Conway Maritime Press, 1983, p. 29.

17 Archibald, E. H. H., *The Wooden Fighting Ship in the Royal Navy.* New York, N.Y.: Arco Publishing, 1970, p. 83.

18 Lavery, *Ship of the Line*, p. 146.

19 Busk, Hans, *The Navies of the World: Their Present State and Future Capabilities.* London, England: Routledge, Warnes, and Routledge, 1859, p. 119.

20 Chapelle, *Sailing Navy*, pp. 368-369.

21 Lambert, Andrew, *Battleships in Transition: The Creation of the Steam Battlefleet, 1815-1860.* Annapolis, Md.: Naval Institute Press, 1984, p. 16.

22 Chapelle, *Sailing Navy*, pp. 338-339.

23 Sims, A. J., "Warships, 1860-1960," *Transactions of the Royal Institution of Naval Architects*, Vol. 102 (1960) p. 54.

24 Hutchins, *Maritime Industries and Public Policy*, p. 299.

25 *Ibid.*, pp. 275-277.

26 *Ibid.*, p. 303.

27 Chapelle, *Sailing Navy*, pp. 372-374.

28 Boynton, Charles B., *The History of the Navy During the Rebellion.* New York, N.Y. (1867) p. 125.

29 Mahan, Alfred Thayer, *From Sail to Steam: Recollections of Naval Life.* New York, N.Y. (1907) p. 36.

30 Hutchins, *Maritime Industries and Public Policy*, pp. 355-358.

31 Headrick, *Tools of Empire*, p. 147.

32 Busk, *Navies of the World*, p. 105.

33 Parkes, Oscar, *British Battleships.* London, England: Seeley Service, 1956, p. 8. Also Bennett, Frank M., *The Steam Navy of the United States.* Pittsburgh, Penn., 1896, pp. 145-151.

34 Hutchins, *Maritime Industries and Public Policy*, pp. 330-331.

35 Lambert, *Battleships in Transition*, pp. 31-32.

36 Hutchins, *Maritime Industries and Public Policy*, p. 303.

37 Bureau of the Census, *Historical Statistics*, GPO (1975), p. 751.

38 Busk, *Navies of the World*, p. 105.

39 Lambert, *Battleships in Transition*, p. 19.

40 *Ibid.*, p. 53, 140.

41 *Ibid.*, p. 140.

42 Busk, *Navies of the World*, p. 118.

43 Hutchins, *Maritime Industry and Public Policy*, p. 355.

44 Fassett, F. G., ed., *The Shipbuilding Business in the United States of America.* New York, N.Y.: The Society of Naval Architects and Marine Engineers (SNAME), 1948, p. 33.

45 Brown, D. K., "Attack and Defense," *Warship*, Vol. V, pp. 138-142. Also Brown, D. K., *Century of Naval Construction*, p. 31.

46 Hutchins, *Maritime Industry and Public Policy*, p. 449.

47 Busk, *Navies of the World*, p. 105, 109-110.

48 Brown, D. K., "Shells at Sevastopol," *Warship*, Vol. III, p. 76.

49 Lambert, *Battleships in Transition*, pp. 59-60, 149.

50 Chapelle, *Sailing Navy*, pp. 421-422.

51 Busk, *Navies of the World*, p. 107.

52 *Ibid.*, pp. 113-115.

53 Vlahos, Michael, "Historical Continuities in Naval Power Projection," *The Projection of Power*, Uri Ra'anan, ed. New York, N.Y.: Lexington Books, 1982.

54 Brown, *Century of Naval Construction*, p. 32, 37.

55 *Ibid.*, p. 39.

56 Bureau of the Census, *Historical Statistics*, GPO (1975) p. 751.

57 Hutchins, *Maritime Industry and Public Policy*, p. 450.

58 Parkes, *British Battleships*, p. 55-56.

59 Basow, Richard, William Grehegan, Frank Merli, ed., "A British View of the Union Navy, 1864," *American Neptune*, Vol. XXVII (January 1967). Also Parkes, *British Battleships*, p. 34.

60 Parkes, *British Battleships*, pp. 35-37.

61 *Conway's All the World's Fighting Ships, 1860-1905.* Greenwich: Conway Maritime Press, 1979, pp. 121-122.

62 Basow, Grehegan, and Merli, *American Neptune*, (1967), p. 38.

63 *Ibid.*, p. 39.

64 Parkes, *British Battleships*, p. 172.

65 *Ibid.*, pp. 44-48.

66 *Conway's Ships*, p. 172.

67 *Ibid.*, pp. 380-381.

68 Cooling, Benjamin Franklin, *Gray Steel and Blue Water Navy: The Formative Years of America's Military-Industrial Complex, 1881-1917.* Hamden, Conn.: Archon Books, 1981, p. 18.

69 Friedman, Norman, *U.S. Battleships: An Illustrated Design History.* Annapolis, Md.: Naval Institute Press, 1985, pp. 406-407.

70 Hutchins, *Maritime Industries and Public Policy*, p. 324.

71 Fassett, *Shipbuilding Business*, p. 34.

72 *Ibid.*, p. 36.

73 Hutchins, *Maritime Industries and Public Policy*, p. 398.

74 Mathias, Peter, *The First Industrial Nation: An Economic History of Britain, 1700-1914.* New York, N.Y.: Charles Scribner's Sons, 1969, p. 311.

75 Bureau of the Census, *Historical Statistics*, GPO (1975) p. 751.

76 Mathias, *First Industrial Nation*, p. 489.

77 Bureau of the Census, *Historical Statistics*, GPO (1975) p. 751.

78 Fassett, *Shipbuilding Business*, p. 34.

79 Bureau of the Census, *Historical Statistics*, GPO (1975) pp. 749-750.

80 Hall, Henry, *Report on the Ship-Building Industry of the U.S.*, Library Editions, 1970, p. 95. (Reprint of 1884 edition.)

81 Fassett, *Shipbuilding Business*, pp. 35-36.

82 Hall, *Report on Ship-Building Industry*, pp. 245-248.

83 Bureau of the Census, *Historical Statistics*, GPO (1975) p. 532.

84 Hutchins, *Maritime Industries and Public Policy*, p. 454.

85 *Ibid.*, p. 416.

86 Brown, *Naval Construction*, p. 48.

87 Sloan, Edward W., "Progress and Paradox: Benjamin Isherwood and the Debate over Iron vs. Steel in American Warship Design," *Naval Engineers Journal* (August 1982) p. 42.

88 Cooling, *Gray Steel*, p. 20.

89 *Conway's Ships*, p. 289.

90 Cooling, *Gray Steel*, p. 40.

91 *Ibid.*, p. 23.

92 Parkes, *British Battleships*, pp. 287-288.

93 *Ibid.*, p. 311.

94 Cooling, *Gray Steel*, p. 22.

95 Bennett, *Steam Navy*, p. 592.

96 Tupinier, "Rapport," 1837, p. 175.

97 Brown, *Naval Construction*, p. 43.

98 Friedman, *Battleships*, pp. 406-407.

99 Cooling, *Gray Steel*, p. 19.

100 Brown, *Naval Construction*, p. 46.

101 *Ibid.*, p. 47.

102 Parkes, *British Battleships*, p. 231.

103 *Ibid.*, p. 230.

104 *Conway's Ships*, p. 244.

105 Cooling, *Gray Steel*, p. 63.

106 *Ibid.*, p. 81.

107 *Ibid.*, p. 30.

108 *Ibid.*, p. 39.

109 Friedman, *Battleships*, p. 21.

110 Cooling, *Gray Steel*, p. 40, 52.

111 *Ibid.*, pp. 29-31.

112 *Ibid.*, p. 35.

113 Bureau of the Census, *Historical Statistics*, GPO (1975) p. 694.

114 *Ibid.*, p. 692. Also Mathias, *First Industrial Nation*, p. 484.

115 Cooling, *Gray Steel*, p. 53.

116 *Ibid.*, p. 63.

117 *Ibid.*, p. 65, 79.

118 *Ibid.*, p. 80.

119 Bureau of the Census, *Historical Statistics*, GPO (1975) p. 383.

120 *Ibid.*, p. 386.

121 *Ibid.*, p. 958.

CHAPTER
TWO
1888–1898

Growth of the New American Navy

by John D. Alden

INTRODUCTION

The decade between 1888 and 1898 marked such momentous changes—strategic, tactical, and technological—in the United States Navy that its characterization as the "New Navy" era is no exaggeration. Although its conception is properly dated to 1883, the gestation of the New Navy was long and rather desultory. The shipbuilding programs of 1883 to 1887 initiated under Secretaries of the Navy William E. Chandler and William C. Whitney had resulted in the authorization of eighteen steel warships, including the armored ships *Maine* and *Texas*, a monitor, eight protected cruisers, four gunboats, a despatch vessel, the "dynamite cruiser" *Vesuvius*, and a single torpedo boat. Also, the impetus provided during President Grover Cleveland's first administration produced a final large increment in the authorization of eleven more ships in 1888.[1]

However, the active fleet of 1888 still consisted of little more than wooden, and a few iron, cruising ships and gunboats carrying full sail-rigs with auxiliary steam power. Their strategic role was merely to "show the flag" and protect American commercial interests in undeveloped parts of the world. With the merchant marine in a state of continuing decline except for coastwise trade, there was little high-seas commerce to be protected. The mission of defending the coasts of the United States was entrusted to Army forts and the isolation provided by the wide ocean expanses; the Navy had only a few leftover Civil War monitors rusting "in ordinary." Naval vessels mostly operated singly and independently, far removed from central control.

Yet, only ten years later, the United States would become a world power with far-flung territorial possessions, while its Navy would be on the way to becoming second only to Great Britain's. In commission or on the drawing boards would be first-class armored battleships, fast cruisers, torpedo-boat destroyers, submarines, and fleet auxiliaries of many kinds. Sails would be a nautical anachronism; technology in the form of steam and mechanical power, hydraulics, electricity, chemistry, and metallurgy would have taken over. The need for technical skills and training would have superseded past reliance on brawn and raw bravery.

The end of the 1880s marked a turning point whose importance has been largely overlooked in the development of the new steel Navy. The ships authorized in 1888 differed markedly from those of preceding construction programs. They differed because of the drive of a few key men who led not only in strategic vision but also in technological professionalism. The revolutionary changes of the decade that followed continued to be strongly influenced by individual leaders and innovators. Alfred T. Mahan, Stephen B. Luce, and others preached the strategy of sea power. Benjamin F. Tracy, Hilary Herbert, and Theodore Roosevelt led in providing the political impetus. Their vision was turned to reality by the technical genius of a small cadre of key naval constructors and engineers.

Because of the controlling influence of these powerful personalities, and the short time frame within which radical changes were made, the era is best understood in terms of year-by-year developments. Shipbuilding programs authorized by Congress provided the driving force for technological progress—each new ship incorporated something new in configuration, machinery, ordnance, equipment, even metallurgy. Yet such is the slow pace of shipbuilding that the ships completed in 1898 reflected technologies and concepts that were already obsolete in comparison to those then being designed.

THE STATUS OF THE
STEEL NAVY IN 1888-1889

As of 1888 only three of the ships authorized in 1883 had been completed and few of the later ones had even been laid down. The Bethlehem Iron Company had barely begun to tool-up to fulfill the consolidated contract for heavy gun forgings and armor plate awarded by Secretary Whitney only the year before as a means of "rendering us independent" of foreign industry.[2] Guns of larger bore than 6 inches still had to be procured abroad. With no domestic shipyards

capable of building the two armored ships authorized in 1886, their construction had been assigned to the New York and Norfolk Navy Yards; but these government facilities were even less well equipped. In fact, the Navy Yards were still being described in 1889 as in "tumble-down condition."[3]

To add to the Navy's problems, the four original ships of the ABCD group, already under severe attack as being technologically and militarily inferior to their European contemporaries,[4] if not actually obsolete, had been tarred with the political scandal associated with their builder, John Roach, of Chester, Pennsylvania. One of Secretary Whitney's first acts on taking office had been to declare Roach's contract invalid and refuse to accept the dispatch vessel *Dolphin*, thus forcing Roach's shipyard into receivership.[5] In an effort to vindicate the quality of the new ships, the Navy ordered the little *Dolphin* off on a cruise around the world. Starting from New York on 21 January 1888, the ship steamed a total of 50,350 miles before returning to the United States in September 1889. During that time, her engine was inoperative for adjustments for less than 2 hours, a fine tribute to her builders and her engineers.[6]

The ships of the 1888 program—one armored cruiser, one large protected cruiser, five smaller cruisers, and a practice vessel for the Naval Academy—were envisioned at that time as slightly improved versions of earlier designs. Since only the *Dolphin* had been completed, the Navy had practically no experience with its steel warships to serve as a guide. In the end, all of the 1888 ships were held up by the new administration, and many of them came out as entirely different types, much superior to those originally contemplated; consequently, they will be described later.

In March 1889, a "lame duck" Congress authorized an additional two gunboats and a harbor-defense ram. The addition of the gunboats closely followed the losses of the *Trenton* and *Vandalia* and the grounding of the *Nipsic* in a typhoon at Apia, Samoa, all of which glaringly revealed the weakness of the engineering plants of these wooden steamships of 1872-1874 vintage.[7] The *Vandalia*, after struggling against the wind and sea at full engine power for 12 hours, finally dragged onto a reef and sank with the loss of many lives. The *Trenton* lost steam when water washed in through the hawsepipes on the berth deck and gradually flooded the engine room; it soon fetched up alongside the *Vandalia*. The *Nipsic* lost her stack when a German ship drifted into her, and soon went aground. But she was salvaged after the storm. Her commanding officer reported that she would have become a total loss if her engines had not functioned as well as they did. Her engineering officer, Chief Engineer George W. Hall, who was then over 50 years of age, died a few weeks later from the effects of the exposure suffered during the typhoon.[8] The hawsepipes of the *Chicago* were raised after being damaged in 1891, possibly in reaction to the disaster in Apia.[9]

MELVILLE AND THE GROWTH OF ENGINEERING PROFESSIONALISM

George W. Melville, who was appointed Engineer-in-Chief in 1887, played a major role in the design of the machinery for most of the ships authorized from then until 1903. He was selected by Secretary of the Navy Whitney, primarily on the strength of the energy and heroic leadership he had demonstrated in the Arctic under Lieutenant Commander George W. DeLong on the ill-fated *Jeannette* expedition of 1879-1882.[10] Melville had spent most of his Navy career at sea, had no reputation as a machinery designer, and was well down on the seniority list; consequently, his appointment over forty-four more senior officers came as quite a surprise to himself and a shock to the Engineer Corps.[11] However, he quickly mastered both the technical and political requirements of the job, and began immediately to introduce innovations in the machinery of the new ships that came under his cognizance. As a result, naval engineering made great advances during Melville's tenure, which spanned the metamorphosis of the U.S. Navy from obsolescent stagnation to world-power status.

One of Melville's first acts "was to outlaw the venerable notion that the engines of a war vessel should be horizontal [so] that they might be stowed in the bottom of a ship, below the water-line, and in any space that might be left after

other departments had made choice of all they wanted."[12] To this end, he introduced vertical triple-expansion engines in the armored cruiser (later second-class battleship) *Maine*, which had been authorized in 1886 but was not started until 1888. This type of engine had received its first operational test only the year before, in a British cruiser, and its adoption led to the rapid increase in steam pressures and greatly-improved engine efficiency that took place during the next few years. For example, the cruiser *Charleston*, commissioned in 1889, had compound engines operating at 90 pounds per square inch (psi). These engines weighed 113 pounds per indicated horsepower (IHP). The boilers weighed an additional 133 pounds and required 3.0 pounds of coal per IHP. Six years later the comparable figures for the *Olympia* were 66, 95, and 2.3 pounds, respectively.[13]

For the monitor *Monterey*, Melville specified four Ward coil boilers in addition to two traditional Scotch boilers. The Ward was an early version of the water-tube boiler, which was then being developed to provide steam at higher pressures than could be generated by fire-tube, or Scotch, boilers. The triple-expansion engine commonly used steam at 140-170 psi and was not efficient over 200 psi. The next most advanced type, quadruple expansion, needed steam at 225 psi and higher. Such engines were already being built for the torpedo boat *Cushing*, which also had coil boilers rated at 250 psi. The great increase in engine efficiency achieved thereby is apparent in her engine weight of 31.2 pounds, boiler weight of 38.2 pounds, and coal requirement of 2.0 pounds per horsepower.[14]

The Navy was taking another look at oil fuel at this time, after having rejected it outright in 1867. A board of engineers in 1888 recommended that it be tried in torpedo boats and coast defense vessels, but nothing was done at that time.[15]

It was also noted regarding Melville that "after his accession to the office of engineer-in-chief bidders for new vessels ceased supplying machinery designs of their own and gladly accepted those furnished by the Bureau of Steam Engineering."[16] However, Melville's most prominent trademark was the extremely high stacks, ultimately as tall as 100 feet over the boiler grates, that he introduced into later ships as a means of providing a strong draft without the use of forced-draft blowers.[17]

Hull design came under the cognizance of the Bureau of Construction and Repair, which was headed by Chief Constructor Theodore D. Wilson from 1882 to 1893 and included several talented younger naval architects, largely educated in Europe. The team of Melville with Wilson, and later with Philip Hichborn, thus deserves major credit for the technological progress in ship construction and engineering made by the Navy during its crucial period of transition into the modern era. The achievements of these leaders in developing the Navy's in-house design and construction capability are all the more remarkable when it is recalled that most of the ships of the New Navy prior to 1888 were built in private yards to foreign or commercial plans due to the paucity of experienced naval personnel and the lack of modern facilities.

The rapid growth in shipbuilding activity after 1885 had one unfortunate side effect on the relationship between the Engineer Corps and the civilian engineering educational establishment. The officers formerly available for detail as instructors to many of the nation's engineering schools under the legislation of 1879 were increasingly needed in the Navy's own billets. Although seven officers were newly assigned as college instructors in 1888, the number dwindled rapidly thereafter. Only two details were made after 1891, and these only as the result of "political influence too powerful for the Navy Department to withstand."[18] These two cases were the assignment of Passed Assistant Engineer[19] Thomas W. Kincaid to Pennsylvania State College (now Pennsylvania State University) and Chief Engineer John D. Ford to Maryland Agricultural and Mechanical College (now the University of Maryland). Both had served earlier at other colleges and were apparently highly regarded as teachers. Ford went on to become George Dewey's fleet engineer and to be commended and advanced because of his performance on the *Baltimore* during the Battle of Manila Bay. Promoted to the rank of rear admiral on retirement, he stayed on active duty as the Inspector of Machinery and Ordnance at Sparrow's Point, Maryland.[20] The flush-deck destroyer DD-228 was named after him and,

appropriately, received battle stars for service with the Asiatic Fleet in World War II.

The Engineer Corps' official involvement with civilian engineering education ended in 1896. The program had given major impetus to the development of mechanical and marine engineering programs on some of the most prestigious campuses in the United States, thereby greatly enhancing the reputation of the Engineer Corps, as well as the professional advancement of the officers involved. With its termination, naval engineering became much more isolated from the mainstream of engineering education and its contributions gradually faded from memory and were almost forgotten. (Many more recent naval engineers today have regretted that their official duties made it difficult for them to have much involvement with their civilian academic counterparts.)

In the midst of the ferment and change of 1888, a small group of naval engineers gathered in the Bureau of Steam Engineering after working hours on 30 September to exchange technical information and ideas.[21] Passed Assistant Engineer George W. Baird, who had been in the Corps since 1863 and was apparently the senior officer present, presided over the meeting. As he recorded the occasion in his diary, those present besides himself were Passed Assistant Engineers Asa M. Mattice, William S. Moore, and William H. Naumann; Assistant Engineers Frederick C. Bieg, William H. Chambers, Robert S. Griffin, G. Kaemmerling, Harold P. Norton; "and some others." Baird had earlier proposed starting a journal, which suggestion had been discussed among his fellow engineers without conclusion.[22] However, the idea was picked up at the meeting and Mattice offered a motion to form a society, to be called ASNE (The American Society of Naval Engineers), as the appropriate body to publish a professional journal. The motion was enthusiastically adopted, and ASNE became the seventh engineering society to be established in the United States. Griffin was chosen as secretary and assigned to correspond with the younger members of the Corps, while Baird undertook to solicit members from the "old engineers and to invite that prince of engineers, Mr. Isherwood (Benjamin F. Isherwood, Engineer-in-Chief of the Navy during the Civil War), to edit the journal."[23]

If there were actually others present at the founding meeting, their names are not definitely known. ASNE identifies at least eight other officers as being members of the society since 30 September 1888: Ira N. Hollis, Isherwood, Charles E. Manning, Walter M. McFarland, Frederick G. McKean, George Melville, James H. Perry, and Nathan P. Towne. Indeed, Towne was elected as the Society's first president. However, the context of Baird's notes makes it improbable that most, if any, of these officers were present. Isherwood had been retired since 1884. Melville, the current Engineer-in-Chief, would surely have presided at the meeting if he were there, as would have Towne or McKean, who were Chief Engineers, or Perry, who, although still a Passed Assistant Engineer, had been in the service longer than Baird. It, therefore, appears likely that these senior officers were enrolled within a day or two of the meeting and accorded the honorary status of founding members. Hollis, Manning, and McFarland were in the younger group and may well have been among those present but not identified specifically by Baird.

What manner of men were these founders of ASNE? Melville, in addition to being respected as a mechanical engineer, was a founding member of the National Geographic Society.[24] Isherwood, although recognized primarily because of his work during the Civil War, was still very active in experimental steam engineering. Baird had served in the Civil War and later was associated with Isherwood at Mare Island. In 1882 he was posted to the Fish Commission, where he supervised the construction of the steamer *Albatross* and the installation therein of the first electric light plant on any government vessel.[25] In 1888 he was on special duty as assistant superintendent of the State, War and Navy Department Building, in the course of which he installed the electric lighting system in the White House. After serving as chief engineer of the *Dolphin* from 1892 to 1895, when that ship was being used as the presidential yacht, he returned to the State, War and Navy Building as superintendent until his retirement in 1905. Baird continued his unusual career in civilian life as president of the District of Columbia Board of Education.

Towne, the first president of ASNE, had entered the Navy in 1862 directly from civilian life

with a classical education and a natural aptitude for engineering. In the early 1890s he was in charge of the machinery design for the cruisers *Oregon, Brooklyn, Columbia,* and *Minneapolis.* In 1892 he was granted leave to accept a temporary appointment with the Cramp Shipbuilding Company as supervising marine engineer, and left the service shortly thereafter when offered the position on a permanent basis.

McFarland was instrumental in supporting the reorganization that amalgamated the Engineer Corps into the General Line of the Navy, but resigned after the Spanish-American War to become a vice-president of the Westinghouse Electric and Manufacturing Companies. From 1910 until 1931 he was the manager of the Marine Department of The Babcock & Wilcox Company. He also served as chairman of the Committee to Coordinate Marine Boiler Rules in 1929, and at various times as president of the Society of Naval Architects and Marine Engineers, vice president of the American Society of Mechanical Engineers, and president of Webb Institute of Naval Architecture.

Probably the most notable of the younger founders of ASNE was Robert S. Griffin, who served as the Society's secretary for much of the period up to 1908. Since the Society initially had no paid staff, its headquarters consisted of the secretary's desk in the old State, War and Navy Department Building (now the Executive Office Building at Pennsylvania Avenue and 17th Street in Washington) and its records were kept in a pocket notebook and ledger. After a series of increasingly responsible assignments at sea and ashore, Griffin became Chief of the Bureau of Steam Engineering in 1913, ostensibly for a term of four years. However, he was retained in that office through World War I and served through the major expansion of the Navy until 1921. He was particularly active in making the transition from coal to oil fuel and fought strongly, and successfully until his retirement, to preserve the Naval Oil Reserve from private exploitation. In addition to being responsible for many other machinery developments during his tenure, he played an important role in the adoption of electric drive for major naval warships. During the Second World War, the submarine tender AS-13 was appropiately named the *Griffin* in his honor.

Several of the founders left the Navy and made major contributions in civilian life. Mattice and Manning resigned their commissions before the end of 1891. As a consulting engineer, Mattice was responsible for designing the machinery for the Calumet and Hecla copper mines. He also worked for the Remington Arms Company and became chief engineer for the Westinghouse Electric Company and the Allis-Chalmers Company. Manning played a key role in developing the Amoskeag Cotton Mills. Oddly enough, neither Manning, Moore, nor Perry ever published a paper in the *ASNE Journal* (*Naval Engineers Journal* since May 1982). Most of the others added their contribution to professional knowledge in the form of articles to the *Journal* and other engineering publications. Baird, Isherwood, and McFarland were especially prolific authors of technical papers in the early years of the Society. McFarland became essentially the historian of the Society and its main link with the past, contributing many obituaries and biographical articles on notable naval engineers. Hollis resigned in 1893 and went on to achieve great recognition as a professor of engineering at Harvard University, president of the American Society of Mechanical Engineers, and president of Worcester Polytechnic Institute.

During its early years, the Society relied solely on its journal, the first issue of which was published in 1889, as a means of disseminating technical and professional information. By 1898 it had broadened its activities to sponsor a prize essay; the initial award was made that year to Passed Assistant Engineer William W. White for his paper on the machinery of the cruiser *Minneapolis*.

As might have been expected, the *ASNE Journal*, throughout its first decade, was dominated by detailed technical papers. Reports of various tests and trials of new ships and machinery installations were most prominent, followed closely by articles on the various types of boilers and associated equipment that were being developed during the period. Other articles covered the entire range of naval engineering: steam engines, auxiliary machinery, coal and later oil fuel, propellers, metallurgy, electrical machinery and equipment, construction techniques, and studies of operational experiences and casualties.

Within a few years, articles with a more theoretical basis began to appear, dealing with such subjects as mathematical techniques, vibration, metal fatigue, and even quality assurance. Foreign and commercial developments were covered more or less regularly, and later in the decade a few writers offered their thoughts on the education and role of the naval engineer. In general, however, the Society continued to focus primarily on technical topics.

Possibly because ASNE in its early years limited its membership to officers of the Navy's Engineer Corps, and probably desiring to appeal to the broader civilian shipbuilding community, a group of naval architects founded another professional organization, the Society of Naval Architects and Marine Engineers (SNAME), in 1893 with Clement A. Griscom as president and Naval Constructor Theodore D. Wilson as first vice-president. This society also included several influential line officers and forward-looking naval engineers in its membership. Engineer-in-Chief George Melville was among the nine original vice-presidents, and engineers Walter McFarland and Charles H. Haswell were among the initial members.[26] Leading members of the Construction Corps filling SNAME offices included Philip Hichborn, Washington L. Capps, Francis T. Bowles, Charles H. Loring, Frank L. Fernald, and John C. Kafer. Melville's approach to naval issues was reflected in the important papers he presented before SNAME almost every year. The papers dealt with engineering-related subjects in a way that encompassed operational and policy matters as well as technical details. (Not until 1909 did Melville publish a paper in the *ASNE Journal*.)

PROGRESS UNDER BENJAMIN F. TRACY

The election of 1888 brought a change in administration and a shift of political control to the Republican party under Benjamin Harrison, who named as his Secretary of the Navy Benjamin F. Tracy, a lawyer, party loyalist, and former Civil War general.[27] However, Tracy was an expansionist and advocate of a strong Navy. His strategic ideas were already similar to those of Captain Alfred T. Mahan, ideas that were expressed most fully in the latter's seminal work,

The Influence of Sea Power Upon History, 1660-1783, published in 1890. Unfortunately, Mahan's opponents had become influential under Secretary Whitney, and Tracy allowed Mahan's Naval War College to be shut down during 1890 and 1891. Thereafter, he became a strong supporter of the college, and in 1892 he reappointed Mahan as its president and brought in James R. Soley, Mahan's close associate, as Assistant Secretary of the Navy. ASNE stalwarts Hollis and McFarland were chosen to lecture on engineering to the War College students in 1892 and 1893.

Declaring, "We must have armored battleships" and disdaining the further construction of gunboats, Tracy immediately launched a sweeping series of reforms.[28] Stopping work on the designs of the ships authorized in 1888, he organized a Board of Construction consisting of the heads of the Bureaus of Construction and Repair, Steam Engineering, Equipment and Recruiting, Ordnance, and Yards and Docks to review the characteristics of those ships. He then appointed a Policy Board under Commodore W. P. McCann to study and recommend the long-term structure of the fleet, a Drydock Commission to determine the Navy's needs for such facilities, and a board to investigate the causes of stagnation in the officer corps. He established new rules for naming the ships of the fleet and reshuffled the responsibilities of the material bureaus, moving recruiting to the Bureau of Navigation and shifting the responsibility for electric lighting from that bureau to the renamed Bureau of Equipment. Reorganization of the Bureau of Provisions and Clothing into the Bureau of Supplies and Accounts took a bit longer but was completed in 1892. Ashore, he initiated the acquisition of ordnance proving grounds at Indianhead, Maryland; coaling facilities at Tutuila, Samoa; and land for a new navy yard at Puget Sound.

In response to reports of the *Dolphin's* success in mitigating the heat of the tropics during that ship's world-girdling cruise,[29] Tracy issued General Order 371 in June 1889 directing that the hulls of all iron and steel ships be painted white instead of black, with masts and stacks a light straw color. He thus initiated the peacetime color scheme that would remain in effect, with minor variations, until 1909. Then, he ordered the formation of the famous Squadron of Evolution under Rear Admiral John G. Walker to evaluate operations and tactics with the new steel warships *Chicago, Boston, Atlanta*, and *Yorktown*, to which were added the *Newark, Concord, Bennington*, and *Cushing* when these ships were commissioned in the next two years.[30] The squadron really provided the first experience most U.S. naval officers were to have in operating a group of modern warships under steam, revealing the need for improvements in command, control, and communications and stimulating developments of all kinds. However, it would take years of experimentation before electrical equipment and more effective procedures for ship control and communications would become the norm.

The Navy Department also took early action to exploit the advantages of self-propelled torpedoes and establish a domestic manufacturing source to replace European suppliers.[31] At first, interest was focused on one invented by Commander John A. Howell, 14.2 inches in diameter and powered by a heavy flywheel that had to be spun at 10,000 revolutions per minute by a small steam turbine before it could be fired.[32] The torpedo left no wake and appeared to be effective in early tests, so in 1888 the Navy placed an order for them from the Hotchkiss Ordnance Company, while the purchased wooden torpedo boat *Stiletto* was outfitted to test them. Because of delayed deliveries of the Howell weapon, one hundred 17.7-inch (nominally 18-inch) Whitehead torpedoes were ordered from England in 1890 for use with the *Cushing*, but in 1891 the E. W. Bliss Company was given a contract to produce them in the United States on license. The Navy also experimented with the wire-controlled, electric-powered Edison torpedo, the Cunningham "rocket" torpedo, and one proposed by inventors named Patrick and Sims. Ultimately, the Whitehead type proved to be superior, but as late as 1893 antiquated spar torpedo outfits were still being delivered to several new cruisers![33]

While Tracy was preoccupied with shaking up the naval establishment, no new ships were authorized in 1889, except a second dynamite cruiser. This was apparently strictly a congressional initiative, since the *Vesuvius* was still incomplete. The authorization included the proviso that no funds be spent until the Secretary of the Navy was satisfied with the first ship; as a result, the second was never built.

In the meantime, the bureaus, the Board on Construction, and the Policy Board were all hard at work on designs for the delayed ships of 1888, all of which Congress had mandated to be entirely of domestic manufacture. (Previous authorizations had allowed exceptions for components that were then unavailable in the United States.) Since different naval architects and engineers were involved in all three agencies, where they were accustomed to operate rather freely in implementing their own ideas as to appropriate designs for the ships under consideration, it is not always easy to relate a particular ship to the characteristics that were recommended by one or another group. The Secretary of the Navy had the last word within the Navy Department, but Congress was by no means reticent in specifying exactly how its appropriations should be spent.

Many influences are apparent in the ships that ultimately resulted from the 1888 program. The extent to which this program marked a new departure in the Navy's development was reflected in that year's report of the venerable Admiral of the Navy, David D. Porter. "The days of old fashioned ships have passed away," he wrote. "New kinds of ships, new kinds of guns, including machine and rapid-firing guns and torpedoes, will take the place of old means of offense and defense."[34] Porter, who had played a major role in the Navy's affairs since 1869, although a persistent and outspoken advocate of naval strength, was also described as "often impatient, biased and impracticable."[35] Unfortunately, one of his biases was against steam propulsion and engineers. When he died in 1891, the positive heritage that he left to the New Navy was marred by a legacy of discrimination and long-festering antagonism between the General Line and the Engineer Corps.

The largest of the 1888 ships, a 7,500-ton armored cruiser, had originally been conceived as a ship similar to the *Maine*, which was still designated as an armored cruiser at that time. Ships of her type had been generally looked upon as potential opponents of similar ships

then possessed or being acquired by several South American navies.[36] Tracy, however, wanted a Navy that could stand up to any of the European powers except England, and deter aggression from the latter country by posing a genuine threat to its commerce. The armored cruiser design that emerged in 1890 was for a fast and powerful ship of 8,200 tons, the *New York*, protected by a belt of 4-inch armor and armed with four 8in/35 breech-loading rifles (BLR) in armored turrets, sixteen 4in/40 rapid-fire (RF) guns in casemates, and three above-water torpedo tubes.[37] (There is considerable confusion as to the actual torpedo armament of the ships designed and built in the early 1890s, some of which were designed for 18-inch Whitehead torpedoes and some for the 14.2-inch Howell type. Consequently, many changes in the torpedo armament of the ships of this period were made in the design stage, during construction, or soon after completion.) Apparently, Tracy himself was responsible for having four of the 4-inchers replaced by two additional 8-inch weapons, placed singly in lightly shielded mounts on either beam and operated entirely by manual power.

In this ship, Melville provided, by far, the most powerful propulsion plant yet seen in the U.S. Navy; in fact, he declared that the engines of the *New York* increased the horsepower of the fleet by 17 percent when the ship was commissioned.[38] To produce the 16,000 IHP needed to make the contract speed of 20 knots (21 knots on trials), Melville used four vertical triple-expansion engines on two shafts, so arranged that the after engines were normally used for cruising, while the forward units were coupled manually to their shafts for full power. Each engine had cylinders of 32, 47, and 72 inches diameter with a piston stroke of 42 inches. The engines were fed by steam at 160 psi from six double-ended Fox fire-tube boilers, each with eight fireboxes, with smokepipes rising 80 feet from the grates. The fireroom arrangement originally designed by the Bureau of Steam Engineering would have placed boilers three abreast in two firerooms such that the outboard boilers would have been close to the sides of the ship, but was changed at the instigation of the builder, Charles Cramp, to a less vulnerable layout of three firerooms separated by bulkheads. Two single-ended auxiliary boilers were placed higher in the ship, above the armored deck—an obviously dangerous location. The cruiser's endurance was established as 4,800 miles at 10 knots, which necessitated a maximum coal capacity of 1,279 tons (750 tons normal). The auxiliary machinery was all powered by steam—in fact, there were ninety-two separate engines with 170 steam cylinders on board, including those that drove the hydraulic pumps used for turning the turrets.[39] In addition to the usual pumps and fans, there were two evaporators and two distillers for 10,000 gallons of fresh water per day, an Allen "dense air" ice machine of the model first used on the *Chicago* in 1890, an improved air compressor, and three dynamos providing a total of 46 kilowatts of electricity.

When completed, the *New York* was regarded as one of the finest armored cruisers in the world, and was said to be one of the steadiest ships ever built for the U.S. Navy. As the flagship of the North Atlantic Squadron, she led a landing force to Port of Spain, Trinidad, to put down an outbreak of arson and looting. The following year, she attracted much attention, including the admiration of Kaiser Wilhelm II, as the Navy's chief representative at the opening of the Kiel Canal. Oddly enough, the *New York* as well as the slightly later *Columbia* and *Minneapolis* were fitted with British-style stern walks, apparently the only time these ever appeared in American warships.

The large protected cruiser became the famous *Olympia*. Instead of being an improved version of the *Baltimore* or *San Francisco* "second-generation" designs, she had a unique arrangement of four 8in/35 BLRs in two turrets, ten 5in/40 RF guns, and six 18-inch torpedo tubes. Her equipment was generally similar to that of the *New York*, but her designed endurance—13,000 miles—was even greater and she clocked 21.69 knots on trials. Her main machinery consisted of two vertical triple-expansion engines rated at 6,750 IHP each and four double-ended fire-tube boilers. Her builders, the Union Iron Works of San Francisco, lengthened her by 10 feet to provide more space in the boiler rooms, at their own expense. The *Olympia* has usually been considered to have been intended to serve as a typical commerce raider, as claimed by Sec-

retary Tracy, for which she would have been reasonably well suited. (However, one is tempted to speculate that her heavy main battery in its unusual turret arrangement and her extraordinary endurance were also intended to fit her for particular service on the Asiatic Station as a "colonial battleship" of sorts. The fact that the only bidder for her construction was the Union Iron Works hints at some prearrangement.) In any case, the *Olympia* was there when needed at Manila Bay in 1898.

Congress had imposed a cost limit on the two 3,000-ton protected cruisers that became the *Cincinnati* and *Raleigh*, as well as mandating a speed of 19 knots. This required shoehorning a 10,000 IHP power plant into a very small hull, such that the twin triple-expansion engines were designed with two low-pressure cylinders instead of the usual one. The engine spaces were terribly overcrowded and inadequately ventilated. Additionally, the designers provided the very heavy armament of one 6in/40 and ten 5in/40 guns, plus four torpedo tubes, and a 2.5-inch protective armored deck in the effort to make these gunboat-sized ships the equivalent of contemporary cruisers. Because of the cost and speed restrictions, no commercial shipyard would bid for these contracts, and they were assigned to the New York and Norfolk Navy Yards, which built both the engines and the hulls. These yards had been struggling with the armored ships assigned to them earlier, and the Navy Department may well have been glad to have an excuse to give them additional work as part of the effort to develop effective government-owned facilities. It is not surprising that both the armament and propulsion plants of these ships ultimately had to be reduced in size. Indeed, they were used as gunboats later in their careers, and the Navy's experience with them proved useful in designing the "peace cruisers" of 1899.

The three 2,000-ton ships of the 1888 program were authorized as either cruisers or gunboats, and Congress left it up to the Navy Department to specify their speed. Characteristically, Tracy and his assistants opted for a cruiser-type speed of 18 knots and an armament of two 6in/40 and eight 5in/40 guns (raised from the 4-inch battery originally chosen by the designers) and three torpedo tubes. Again the private yards refused to bid within the appropriated limit, and the Navy had to reduce the speed requirement to 17 knots. When completed, their bureau-designed engines produced 19 knots and a bonus for the builders of the *Montgomery, Detroit*, and *Marblehead*. However, the ships were unstable and the excessive armament had to be reduced to ten 5-inchers, which was still a pretty formidable battery for such small ships. They were later downgraded to gunboats or noncombatant types.

The training ship *Bancroft* was essentially a gunboat of about 840 tons displacement, armed with four 4-inch guns and two torpedo tubes for the instruction of naval cadets, as the midshipmen were then called. Although of little fighting strength or technical interest, the *Bancroft* did provide tangible evidence of the Navy's commitment to the training of its officer corps. The *Bancroft* was used as a gunboat after 1896 until transferred to the Revenue Service in 1906 as the cutter *Itasca*.

The two gunboats added by Congress just before President Harrison took office, the *Machias* and *Castine*, were ordered from the Bath Iron Works in Maine. Like the other ships of the period, they were overgunned for their size with eight 4in/40 RF guns; when first put into service they proved to be dangerously unstable and had to be lengthened by 14 feet at the New York Navy Yard.

The final vessel of the group, also ordered from Bath, was the harbor defense ram *Katahdin*, the brainchild of Rear Admiral Daniel Ammen, who had been pestering the Navy Department for years to build such ships. (In 1885, Congress had established the joint Army-Navy Endicott Board on harbor fortifications and floating batteries, for which special funds were earmarked each year. Such funds had previously been used for the torpedo boat *Cushing* in 1886 and the monitor *Monterey* in 1887, which explains how these anomalous vessels got into the respective shipbuilding programs.)[40] Although obsolete in concept, the *Katahdin* included a number of unusual structural and engineering features. The hull was essentially a single longitudinal girder converging to a massive cast-steel ram and covered with turtleback armor. Horizontal triple-expansion engines had to be used because of the limited overhead, and all below-deck arrange-

ments were more like those of a submarine or a Civil War monitor than a conventional warship. Even her paint scheme—a dull sea green—was unorthodox.[41] Living and working conditions within her were atrocious, and the Navy was happy to decommission her after a year's shakedown.

Even the old monitors, although well along in construction, were revamped in 1889.[42] The *Puritan*'s main battery was increased to 12-inch guns in barbettes in place of 10-inch weapons in turrets and her boilers were upgraded. The *Monterey* was given two 12-inch and two 10-inch guns, instead of the impractical armament of a single 110-ton 16-incher and a dynamite gun as initially proposed, in addition to the new boilers mentioned previously. Less extensive changes were made in the machinery of the other monitors, in several cases as a means of testing competing installations as well as updating the obsolete original equipment.[43]

Although the revamped ships of the 1888 program reflected many new ideas, the input of the Policy Board was directly felt in 1890 after the hiatus of 1889. The board, carried away by its visions of the distant future, had conceived of a fleet of no fewer than ten first-class seagoing battleships, twenty-five slower coast-defense battleships, twenty-four large cruisers, fifteen torpedo cruisers, five special cruisers for the China station, ten rams, one hundred first-class and numerous lesser torpedo boats, and three torpedo-boat depot and repair ships. When word of this extravagant program leaked out prematurely (as was common then as well as in more recent times), opponents of expansion raised a great outcry and Secretary Tracy, whose own plans were more realistic, was greatly embarrassed. After the uproar died down, Congress approved the 1890 shipbuilding program of three battleships, a large protected cruiser, a torpedo cruiser, and a torpedo boat. The torpedo boat *Ericsson*, a follow-on to the newly completed *Cushing*, was awarded to the Iowa Iron Works in Dubuque, suffered an inordinate number of delays and casualties, and was not completed until 1897. The torpedo cruiser—with size, speed, and cost all specified by Congress—could not be built for the funds authorized. In the other ships, Tracy and his supporters got what they really wanted—"real bone and sinew" for the New Navy.[44]

There was no delaying with these ships. The cruiser, which became the *Columbia*, was a logical development from the *Olympia*. In this case, there was no doubt as to the cruiser's role as a commerce raider; in fact, Chief Engineer Nathan P. Towne, who was then in charge of the drafting room at the Bureau of Steam Engineering, jokingly tagged her "the Pirate," a name that was picked up in the press.[45] Designed to track down shipping in the North Atlantic, including the fastest passenger liners, she mounted two 6in/40 caliber guns on the forecastle, eight 4in/40s in side sponsons, four torpedo tubes, and a single 8in/35 stern-chaser to hold off more powerful enemy warships. This was actually a very light armament for a ship of 7,375 tons; she was far longer than any other ship in the Navy, and her overall length of 412 feet was not exceeded until after the turn of the century. In fact, most of her space was devoted to a massive power plant and voluminous coal bunkers. To make the prescribed speed of 22 knots, Engineer-in-Chief Melville designed the first three-shaft arrangement in the modern Navy, driven by vertical inverted triple-expansion engines totaling 20,500 IHP.[46] (The low pressure cylinders in the *Columbia*, as in the *Olympia*, were a full 8 feet in diameter.) Steam was provided by ten fire-tube boilers, which vented into four impressive stacks. Her coal was estimated to be sufficient to steam for 103 days or 25,520 miles at 10 knots, which would take her around the world without refueling. The *Columbia* made 22.8 knots on her sea trials, but gave an even more impressive demonstration when ordered in 1895 to cross the Atlantic Ocean from Southampton, England to New York at full speed without forced draft. The run was made at an average speed of 18.4 knots, a performance that could be beaten by only a few of the fastest liners.[47]

Tracy completed his commerce raider program with the *Minneapolis*, a duplicate of the *Columbia* except for having two stacks instead of four. The only new ship authorized in 1891, she was rushed to completion by the Cramp shipyard within a few months of her older sister.

The three battleships of 1890—the *Indiana*, *Massachusetts*, and *Oregon*—really ushered the United States into the era of naval power. In concept, they represented the Policy Board's coast-defense battleships "of limited coal endurance," since the nation was not yet prepared to take the full leap to an ocean-going fleet. The coast-defense role was also evident in their low freeboard and slow speed, but in other respects, especially armament, they outmatched their contemporaries abroad. On a displacement of 10,288 tons was mounted a battery of four 13in/35 guns in armored turrets at bow and stern, plus eight 8 in/35 guns in four wing turrets and four 6 in/40s in casemates. All of these guns were slow-firing breech-loading rifles. The designers had originally planned to have a uniform secondary battery of 5-inch RF guns, but at that time, the United States did not yet have the capability of manufacturing such guns.[48] The substitute intermediate battery of 8-inch guns gave the impression of great power and was not unreasonable in view of the short firing ranges and rudimentary methods of fire control then in use. (In retrospect, it seems to have been a major factor in delaying the introduction of the "all big gun" or dreadnought-type battleship for 15 years.) The Bureau of Ordnance wanted to adopt turrets with conical sloping sides, but these would have required a major redesign of the gun mounts and loading arrangements, so the familiar pillbox shape dating from the Civil War was retained.

The battleships were protected by an armor belt of 18-inch Harveyized (face-hardened) nickel steel and a 2.75-inch deck. Since the Bethlehem Iron Company, the only domestic manufacturer of armor, was having difficulty starting production, Secretary Tracy contracted with Carnegie, Phipps and Company to provide a second source. The Midvale Steel Company was similarly established as the second source for heavy gun forgings. Carried out simultaneously, were major ordnance and armor test programs, which naturally led to rapid advances in both guns and armor during the 1890s. The propulsion plants consisted of vertical inverted triple-expansion engines driving twin shafts, with four double-ended Scotch (fire-tube) main boilers and two single-ended auxiliary boilers. As in the armored cruiser *New York*, most of the auxiliary machinery was steam powered. However, the rammers and elevating gear for the 13-inch guns were hydraulically operated, as were the turret training motors in the earlier *Oregon*.[49] The 8-inch guns were loaded and elevated by hand power alone. Electric power was adopted for the 8-inch and smaller ammunition hoists and for portable ventilating fans, in addition to the usual illuminating system and searchlights.[50]

As coastline battleships, these three were designed for only 15 knots and a normal coal capacity of only 400 tons. They could actually carry four times that amount, but the armor belt was not spaced accordingly and was often nearly submerged during operations. The various calibers of guns were located so close together that their blasts interfered with each other. They also suffered from unbalanced turrets, which caused the ships to heel when the main guns were trained, and from the absence of bilge keels, which were included in the design but could not be installed because of the limited drydock facilities then available. (During a voyage in 1896, the *Indiana* had both main turrets come adrift and swing out of control until they were finally lashed down by heavy hawsers.) They were far more impressive in appearance than effective in operation, but still represented a major achievement and a positive source of pride for the emerging American Navy.

A now long-forgotten feature of the ships built during the early 1890s was the use of various formulations of "woodite" or cellulose packed into cofferdams as a supplement to regular armor, on the theory that if the hull were punctured, water would cause the material to swell and plug the hole. Initially, the cellulose was extracted from coconut husks as granules having a density of 8 pounds per cubic foot, about a quarter of that of cork.[51] This was mixed with a small proportion of coconut fiber and pressed into briquettes. These were further compressed into the cofferdam spaces under a pressure of 200 psi. Later, American corn pith was found to provide a cheaper, as well as lighter, cellulose.[52] Unfortunately, minor leakage or condensation in the cofferdams caused the cellulose to deteriorate, leaving a rotten mess that was more of a hazard than a help. No one was sorry to see it eliminated.

Developments were also taking place on other fronts during these years, not the least significant of which was the initiation of the Army-Navy football contest in 1890! On the international scene, the Navy continued to be called on to intervene and protect U.S. nationals and economic interests in a variety of distant countries. Marines had been landed in Haiti and Korea in 1888 and in Hawaii in 1889, but these were minor compared to the so-called "Baltimore incident" of 1891.[53]

With civil war raging in Chile, the new cruisers *San Francisco* and *Baltimore* were ordered to Valparaiso, where both factions took umbrage at their presence. When the captain of the *Baltimore*, Winfield Scott Schley, injudiciously permitted a liberty party to go ashore, insults led to injuries and the death of two bluejackets at the hands of an enraged mob. For a while, war between the United States and Chile seemed imminent, and Tracy quietly had the Navy make preparations to fight, actually going so far as to charter the steamship *Ohio* to be fitted out as a floating machine shop to support the ships away from any American port. In the end, diplomacy prevailed, Chile apologized and made reparations, and the crisis blew over.

On the technological front, the Navy installed its first internal communication telephone system in the cruiser *Philadelphia* in 1891. Naval constructors took initial steps to apply scientific principles to the problem of launching ships; the *Raleigh* and *Texas* launchings in 1892 were the first in which mathematical calculations of stresses played a part.[54] In the same year, Secretary Tracy, acting in response to an earlier recommendation by a board of naval engineers, asked Congress for funds to equip a torpedo boat with an oil-fueled propulsion plant. Such radical ideas, however, were not to be implemented without due deliberation.

During 1891, an effort was made to revive the merchant marine, the United States having practically abandoned ocean traffic after 1871.[55] (Figures compiled later put the decline from 2,500,000 tons in 1861 to 800,000 in 1897. Coastwise shipping, on the other hand, had increased from 2,800,000 to nearly 4,000,000 tons during the same period.)[56] The Dingley Shipping Bill, in typical congressional fashion, approached the problem indirectly by authorizing mail contracts to subsidize ships that could be used as armed merchant cruisers in wartime. When the International Navigation Line sought to reregister the British-built *City of New York* and *City of Paris*, which it had purchased, Congress allowed the transaction with the proviso that the line order U.S.-built ships of similar size. These two ships, the *St. Louis* and *St. Paul*, designed and built by Charles H. Cramp, were the equal of leading foreign liners in state-of-the-art technology as well as passenger comfort: 554 feet long, measuring 10,700 gross tons, and carrying 1,420 passengers.

Cramp had a low opinion of the British practice of designing passenger ships with low metacentric height to give an easy roll, then using water ballast to ensure stability. He also objected to the use of large propellers whose blades extended well below the keel, both on grounds of efficiency and in recognition that a 28-foot draft was the maximum that was commercially feasible in American ports at that time. Since he considered that 12,000 IHP was the mechanical limit that could be produced by a marine reciprocating engine without running at an unacceptable speed, he gave his new ships twin screws, each driven by a quadruple-expansion engine using 200 psi steam. No other American oceanliners were built, as Congress refused to provide further operating subsidies.

Coastwise shipping, which included United States-to-Hawaii and United States-to-Central America routes, was a different matter because American operators were protected by law from foreign competition. Although the years 1894-95 were described as "the dullest in the history of American steel [commercial] shipbuilding,"[57] some excellent ocean-going cargo and passenger-cargo ships were built throughout the 1880s and 1890s by such yards as the newly-formed Newport News Shipbuilding and Dry Dock Company, the Union Iron Works, and the reorganized John Roach Delaware River works. Representative of such ships were the *Standard* of 1888, the first American bulk tanker, built by the Roach yard;[58] the *Pomona*, a 1,264-ton passenger-cargo ship built by Union in 1888 and believed to have the first triple-expansion engine in an American-built merchant ship;[59] and the 4,600-ton *El*

Norte, Newport News' first steel-hulled ship, started in 1891.[60] By 1897 there were twenty subsidized steamers available as naval auxiliaries, but the bulk of commercial work was the building of coastal and river craft, wooden and iron sailing vessels, and ferry boats. The revival of the shipbuilding industry in the 1890s really depended on construction for the Navy.

In 1892, Tracy got his first ocean-going capital ship, although it was still described as a "sea-going coast-line battle ship" in the authorizing legislation. (In fact, this terminology continued to be used through 1899, apparently in an effort to imply the absence of imperialistic intent.) Also authorized was another armored cruiser similar to the *New York*. Many improvements were made in the designs of both ships.[61] The battleship *Iowa* was increased moderately in size and displacement, but her major improvement was the addition of a long forecastle deck that not only made her much more seaworthy but also gave the forward turret a better elevation and provided desirable berthing space for the crew. Although the armament layout was similar to that of the earlier battleships, the main guns were reduced to 12in/35 BLRs, which were considered as effective as the earlier 13-inchers by virtue of a higher muzzle velocity and slightly greater rate of fire. The 8-inch intermediate battery was retained, but the ship's sides were given an extreme tumble-home that reflected the French influence on her design and provided a much clearer field of fire without interfering with other guns. The secondary battery was changed to six 4in/40 RF guns in recognition of the devastating effect explosive shells could have on the upper works of enemy ships. Four above-water beam torpedo tubes were installed for 14.2-inch Howell torpedoes, apparently the only ones of this type ever actually fitted in a battleship. Her engine horsepower was increased to 11,000, which gave an additional knot in speed, while the number of main boilers was reduced to three. These were fitted with the Navy's first feedwater heaters, of a primitive design that was rapidly improved in later plants. The most distinguishing feature of her engineering plant was the towering, straight 100-foot stacks (favored by Melville), which reached their extreme height at this time. All told, the *Iowa* was quite successful for her time, but was soon outdated by the steady advancement in all areas of technology.

The armored cruiser *Brooklyn* bore much the same relationship to the *New York* that the *Iowa* did to the *Indiana* class, even to her high stacks, raised forecastle, and extreme tumble-home. Many features of her external appearance also reflected the contemporary French influences. A longer hull enabled her to make a slightly higher speed with the same engines as those installed in her near-sister and only five double-ended Fox boilers; the auxiliary boilers were relocated to a less vulnerable position below the armored deck. Her builder, Charles Cramp, proposed using two quadruple-expansion engines in lieu of the Bureau design, but was turned down. (Her contract was the last in which a bonus or penalty was provided for each quarter-knot deviation from the specified speed.) The reduction in topside weight achieved by the narrower upper works, and the reduction of her armor belt to 3-inch Harvey steel, permitted the addition of two 8-inch guns, the enclosure of all of them in powered twin turrets, and the increase of the secondary battery to much more effective 5in/40 RF guns with telescopic sights devised by Lieutenant Bradley Fiske.[62] These, plus five 18-inch torpedo tubes, made her the most heavily armed armored cruiser in the world—for a few years at least. Her 8-inch guns were equipped with newly designed breeches for electrical firing, but their barrels, as forged by the inexperienced Midvale firm, were weakened by inclusions of slag and clay and were initially rejected, only to be accepted at reduced cost 2 years later because the company could not provide better ones. Not surprisingly, three of these guns had their muzzles blown off during target practice in 1904.

Problems with earlier models of steam, hydraulic, and pneumatic turret-turning machinery had led the Bureau of Ordnance to conduct experiments with an electrical system. The Chief of the Bureau, Captain William T. Sampson, turned the problem over to the inventive Lieutenant Fiske, who worked with the General Electric Company to develop a suitable installation. Both the Chief Constructor and the Engineer-in-Chief preferred to stay with the familiar steam-hy-

draulic system, but the Secretary of the Navy (by then Hilary Herbert) agreed to let General Electric put its system into the forward and starboard turrets, at the company's risk, for competitive trials. Conducted in 1896, these demonstrated the superiority of the electrical system and led to its adoption as the Navy's standard.

The priorities of the Navy Department during the Tracy administration are clearly indicated in the progress of work on the various ships under construction or authorized while he was in office. The first to be completed was the armored cruiser *New York* in 1893, followed by the *Cincinnati* and *Montgomery* class cruisers, then the *Columbia* and *Minneapolis* in 1894, the *Olympia* and *Indiana* in 1895, the *Massachusetts*, *Oregon*, and *Brooklyn* in 1896, and the *Iowa* in 1897. By contrast, the obsolescent *Maine*, *Texas*, and monitors, the useless *Katahdin*, and the experimental torpedo boats (which would have been ineffective in numbers even if completed sooner) took much longer to complete. The influence of Melville and the naval constructors has already been mentioned, and would continue with the next administration. The work of George Dewey as chief of the Bureau of Equipment, and Montgomery Sicard (until 1890) and William M. Folger as heads of the Bureau of Ordnance also contributed greatly to the advances made in those areas. Although Tracy did not stay in office long enough to see his ideas come to fruition, his programs were well along by the time the Democrats came to power again in the elections of November 1892.

CONTINUED DEVELOPMENT UNDER HILARY HERBERT

When Grover Cleveland took office for his second term in 1893, he named Hilary P. Herbert as his Secretary of the Navy. Herbert was then a congressman from Alabama, having served some 15 years, for 6 of which he chaired the Committee on Naval Affairs. During the Civil War, he had fought on the Confederate side and was wounded at the Battle of the Wilderness; oddly enough, his predecessor, Benjamin Tracy, had been wounded in the same battle on the Union side.[63] While in Congress, Herbert had originally opposed the construction of battleships, but by

1893 he had become a convert to the cause of a strong Navy. Even so, one of the first actions taken after his accession to office was the forced transfer of Captain Alfred T. Mahan from the Naval War College to command of the new cruiser *Chicago*. The chief of the Bureau of Navigation, Francis M. Ramsay, thought naval officers belonged at sea and had no business writing books, and he had long sought to pry Mahan away from his scholarly activities. Actually, the command of the *Chicago* was a desirable post at that time, and Herbert made up for Mahan's temporary loss by giving the War College a permanent staff starting in 1894.

Herbert made a rather clean sweep of the top positions in the Navy Department, bringing in William G. McAdoo, a New Jersey congressman who had also been a member of the Committee on Naval Affairs, as Assistant Secretary. William T. Sampson became the chief of the Bureau of Ordnance, French E. Chadwick took over the Bureau of Equipment, and Philip Hichborn replaced Theodore Wilson as Chief Constructor. However, Herbert wisely kept George Melville in the job of Engineer-in-Chief. Despite the change in personnel, the new team followed the policy of the previous administration with little change, although Herbert relaxed Tracy's policy on navy yard hirings to the extent of equalizing the balance of patronage between the two major political parties.

The country had drifted into a depression by 1893 and government spending was being drastically reduced. This, plus the normal hiatus in ship construction associated with a change in administration, caused naval appropriations to be cut to about half of their former level. The "lame-duck" Congress in March 1893 produced a shipbuilding program of only three gunboats. (It also authorized the New Navy's first submarine, but no action was taken on this craft for another 2 years.) The insignificant contribution of these gunboats to the ocean-going fleet did not detract from the careful attention given to their designs by the constructors and engineers. Although all three were comparable in size and armament, they fell into two distinct classes that were intended, and optimized, for different kinds of service. The *Nashville* was designed as a general-purpose gunboat for foreign service, with

seagoing capabilities but a shallow draft to suit undeveloped ports and rivers. Her berthing arrangements were unusually spacious and well-ventilated to not only provide more comfortable living conditions for the crew but also to leave space available to house refugees or carry troops when needed. The main propulsion plant was quite innovative, consisting of two four-cylinder quadruple-expansion engines fed by a combination of Scotch and Yarrow water-tube boilers. For ordinary cruising, the low-pressure cylinder could be cut off, leaving the engine to run as a normal triple-expansion plant. At full power, the Yarrow boilers delivered steam at 250 psi directly to the high-pressure cylinder, while the single-ended fire-tube boilers provided theirs at 160 psi to the exhaust receiver of the first stage. This unusual design was the work of two Passed Assistant Engineers, Frank H. Bailey and Ira N. Hollis, both of whom were active in the affairs of ASNE.[64] Like most gunboats of the period, the *Nashville* was provided with auxiliary sail power. In practice, her unusual power plant was difficult to operate and was ultimately converted to triple-expansion operation alone.

The other two ships, the *Wilmington* and *Helena*, were designed specifically as river gunboats for China service and, as such, represented the application of what are today called systems concepts.[65] With a draft of only 9 feet and twin screws, they had oversized double rudders to provide maneuverability and inner bottoms under the engineering spaces to provide protection against damage during inevitable groundings. The combination armored conning tower and military mast, enclosing a spiral staircase, was made high enough to give the officers a view over 50-foot river banks and dikes as well as to protect them from rifle fire. Like the *Nashville*, they had commodious berthing spaces and tall, straight "Melville" stacks, but no sails. The *Wilmington* (renamed *Dover*) actually remained in service through World War II, a tribute to the quality put into her by her designers and builders. All three gunboats were built by the Newport News Shipbuilding and Dry Dock Company, the first of many warships the Navy would receive from that shipyard.

Other significant events were taking place in 1893, as the first of Tracy's new generation of ships, the armored cruiser *New York*, was placed in commission. Settlers in Hawaii overthrew the native monarchy and established a provisional government. Marines were landed during the disturbances and it was apparent that the question of sovereignty over the islands would soon have to be resolved. In June, the sinking of the British battleship HMS *Victoria* after a collision with the *Camperdown* during maneuvers in the Mediterranean had several important consequences: it reinforced belief in the effectiveness of the ram as an instrument of war at a time when weapons developments had rendered it useless, and it stimulated interest in improving the watertight integrity of ships.[66] This led rather quickly to better compartmentation, the elimination of all but truly necessary bulkhead doors, and closer attention to penetrations of all kinds. The tragedy also highlighted problems in controlling ships at sea and further stimulated improvements in that area.

An interesting experiment in coaling at sea was carried out during the year between the cruiser *San Francisco* and the old steam sloop *Kearsarge*, the latter simulating a collier.[67] The rig consisted of a 235-foot cable strung from shear poles erected on the stern of the cruiser to a block on the foremast of the *Kearsarge* and tensioned by a 1,600-pound counterweight. Bags containing 200 pounds of coal were slid down the cable, each taking 14 seconds for the trip. The system was evaluated as having little value, especially in rough weather, and no follow-up action was taken until the war with Spain showed the essentiality of refueling at sea.

The greatest excitement during 1893 was occasioned by the Columbian Exposition and the international naval review that preceded it. The theme of the entire affair was such as to ensure that the Navy would have a major role in it, and indeed, naval engineers were intimately involved in every phase. Replicas of Columbus' caravels *Pinta* and *Nina* were constructed in Spain at the expense of the United States and towed to Havana by the cruiser *Newark* and gunboat *Bennington*. From there, they were sailed by Spanish crews to New York for the naval review, and thence to Chicago. Most of the warships—twelve American, four British, three French, three Brazilian, two Russian, two Italian, two German, and one Dutch—assembled at Hampton Roads on 24

April and sailed in formation to New York. There, they were joined by another Russian, an Argentinian, and three Spanish warships, plus the monitor *Miantonomoh*; all were reviewed by President Cleveland in the *Dolphin* on the 27th.

The Exposition itself had been set up in Chicago. The machinery exhibit, consisting of 30 acres of equipment on display, was under the supervision of Chief Engineer Lewis W. Robinson, who had been detailed to this special duty.[68] Possibly the most spectacular feature of the fair was a full-scale model of an *Indiana*-class battleship suggested by Rear Admiral Richard W. Meade, built of brick, wood, and steel on pilings in Lake Michigan, and dubbed "USS Illinois."[69] Over three million visitors were reported to have inspected the "ship" and the naval exhibits displayed on its decks. The whole affair was a real publicity coup for the Navy. Perhaps in hopes of reaping similar advantages from the Midwinter Fair in San Francisco the following year, the Bureau of Steam Engineering allowed Passed Assistant Engineer Andrew M. Hunt to take leave as head of the mechanical arts exhibit, where he made such a hit that he was persuaded to resign from the service for a civilian job that was too good to turn down.[70]

With the economic slump continuing in 1894, Congress turned down the Navy Department's request for a new battleship and authorized a new construction program of only three torpedo boats, utilizing funds appropriated in 1889 for the unbuilt second dynamite cruiser. It will be recalled that the New Navy's first torpedo boat, the *Cushing*, had been completed in 1890. Although the second, the *Ericsson*, was encountering all sorts of construction problems at its Iowa building yard, the Navy now had some experience with the type, which would have to be available in quantity to be employed effectively. The new boats—the *Foote, Rodgers*, and *Winslow*—were slightly improved versions of the previous Bureau designs, 160 feet long by 16 feet in the beam, displacing 142 tons, and armed with three 18-inch torpedo tubes and three 1-pounder guns. Fitted with twin triple-expansion (some sources say quadruple-expansion) engines and either Thornycroft or Mosher water-tube boilers, they had a designed speed of 25 knots on 2,000 horsepower.[71]

On the international scene, the outbreak of

the Sino-Japanese War led to growing concern over the expansionist intentions of Japan. The Battle of the Yalu, in which the Chinese fleet was decisively defeated, demonstrated the destructive effect of wood and steel splinters produced by the explosion of medium-caliber shells in unarmored superstructures. Warship designers turned their attention to better methods of protection as well as stronger secondary batteries of rapid-fire guns. Hurried changes were made to eliminate much of the wooden structure being incorporated in the *Iowa* and existing in older ships. The battle also revealed the problem of maintaining internal communication with the primitive means then available to ship commanders. Lieutenant Albert P. Niblack emphasized the need to incorporate such considerations in the design of new warships.[72] He lamented the inadequacy of voice pipes, noting that "the voice gets confused and drowned amongst the several pipes, especially if the wind is blowing." As for the confusion of battle, he reported that "Captain McGiffin, late of the Chinese Navy, says that, in a modern action, a commanding officer, after a few moments, is half blind and totally deaf." Relays of word-passers had to be used to transmit orders from the bridge to other stations throughout the ships. Chief Constructor Hichborn felt that torpedoes were no longer appropriate weapons for battleships, pointing out that the Japanese had jettisoned theirs during the battle to avoid having them detonated by enemy fire.[73] All of these ideas would have their effect on future ship characteristics.

The concepts advanced by the line officer faction represented by Lieutenant Niblack and Rear Admiral Meade, while progressive in many ways, also reflected a continuing antagonism toward the engineers and constructors. Niblack attacked the "craze for speed," which he tended to blame for the shortcomings in other areas,[74] and indeed, the Navy Department ceased offering shipbuilders a premium for exceeding the contractual requirements. Meade strongly recommended building slow 14- or 15-knot cruisers with full sail-rigs and composite (wood planking on steel frames) hulls, and even slower sailing gunboats, useful only for showing the flag in backward countries during peacetime.[75]

More disruptive was an attack on the Marine Corps pursued relentlessly by Lieutenant William F. Fullam.[76] As commanding officer of the *Raleigh* in 1894, he launched a major effort to have the Marine detail removed from his ship. The drive was supported by petitions drawn up by enlisted personnel throughout the fleet; Captain Robley D. Evans requested that no Marines be assigned to his ship, the nearly completed *Indiana*; and a bill was introduced in the Senate to transfer the Marine Corps to the Army. Saner heads prevailed. Secretary Herbert, who knew a political hot potato when he saw one, not only disapproved Fullam's and Evans's requests, but emphasized the integral role of the Marines in ships' companies, prescribed the exact number to be assigned, and spelled out their duties in detail. Even this failed to squelch Fullam, who continued to agitate against the Corps, with results that led to serious personnel and morale problems in the decades to come.

Secretary Herbert made an important advance in improving the coordination of ship construction by assigning the Bureau of Construction and Repair lead responsibility for all phases of the ultimate design and modifications thereto. (This one change may have been sufficient to delay the consolidation of the material bureaus, especially Construction and Repair and Engineering, by at least 45 years. Although reformers had long been calling for such action, the separate bureaus managed to preserve their independence until 1940.) Another advance this year was the congressional authorization for the Secretary of the Navy to loan ships to the growing state naval militias. Also in 1894, the Naval War Records Office, which had been organized by Professor James R. Soley, finally published the voluminous official records of the Union and Confederate Navies during the Civil War, thus making that material available for general study.

Naval engineers and constructors continued to seek improvements in equipment, materials, and techniques. In an effort to understand the remote effects of underwater explosions, tests were made on a boat filled with animals (this being before the days of recognition of animal rights), from which it was concluded that no harm would be expected as long as the hull itself was not breached. Several papers in the ASNE and SNAME journals discussed continuing European experiments with liquid fuel. These involved the use of petroleum residuals, the well known thick black oil used in Navy boilers until well after World War II, that were, however, disparaged as "refuse" from inferior Russian petroleum. United States oils were considered too pure to leave useful amounts of these residues, and the author of one paper concluded that "Unless unexpected supplies of petroleum should be discovered it hardly seems likely that it will become a fuel for general purposes on war vessels."[77]

By 1895 the economy had strengthened and the country was ready to support further naval expansion. Secretary Herbert asked for three battleships, with the further request that the legislation specifically authorize one to be named after the famous Civil War steam sloop *Kearsarge*, which had been lost on a reef the preceding February. The program as approved included the two battleships *Kearsarge* and *Kentucky*, three more torpedo boats, and six composite gunboats of the type favored by Rear Admiral Meade.

With the current emphasis on heavy armament in preference to speed, the Bureau of Construction and Repair designed a battleship enlarged somewhat from the *Indiana*, with a low forecastle and less coal capacity than the *Iowa*.[78] Displacement was increased to 11,540 tons and designed speed was kept at 16 knots. The proposed armament consisted of four 12-inch and four 8-inch guns, with the latter's turrets spaced as far apart as possible to leave clear space for a heavy secondary battery of fourteen 5-inch RF guns in a casemate protected by 6 inches of armor.[79] The Bureau of Ordnance preferred the heavier 13-inch guns, noting that proving-ground tests on the *Iowa*'s armor had shown that it could withstand 12-inch but not 13-inch projectiles, and insisted that the supply of ammunition for all calibers of gun be increased.

At this point, Ensign Joseph Strauss came up with the idea of mounting the 8-inch turrets directly on top of the 13-inch housings. (This two-story arrangement was termed "superposed," while turrets arranged with one behind and higher than the other were described as "superimposed.") The concept offered the advantages of a full arc of fire for both calibers, no blast interference, less total weight of armor around the guns and ammunition tubes, and control of the two turrets by a single officer. The

disadvantages appeared to be the inability to train the turrets separately, a very high concentration of weight, and increased trunnion pressure. The hull structure had to be strengthened to support these added loads, and the main gun mounts had to be moved farther back in the turrets to accommodate the larger 13-inch rifles without unbalancing them. This necessitated enlarging the gun ports to allow full elevation of the guns, a weakness for which these ships would be roundly criticized. The recoil cylinders of the 13-inch guns were improved and strengthened by incorporating a combination of springs and hydraulic loading. The armor belt of 16.5-inch Harvey steel was raised 6 inches on the sides of the hull so that it would not be submerged at full load, and a thinner 4-inch belt was carried all the way to the bow. The array of smaller guns included eight 6-pounder Hotchkiss cannon in hull embrasures and twelve more on the upper deck along with four Hotchkiss 1-pounders. Maxim-Nordenfeldt automatic 1-pounders and Colt 6-millimeter machine guns were mounted in the fighting tops, and there were four above-water torpedo tubes.

The 10,000 horsepower main propulsion plant consisted of two three-cylinder triple-expansion engines, with forged steel support columns designed by Passed Assistant Engineer Frank H. Bailey in place of the heavy castings used up to that time. There were three double-ended and two single-ended Scotch boilers generating steam at 180 psi, and no special auxiliary boilers. Seven General Electric dynamos provided 350 kilowatts of electricity at 160 volts to power the turret training, gun elevating and ramming, and ammunition hoisting motors. This was a remarkable increase in both voltage and capacity over previous installations and was perhaps a bit too radical for the time, as it was not repeated in later classes.

The three torpedo boats represented a departure from the previous Bureau type. The *Porter* and *DuPont* were ordered from the Herreshoff Manufacturing Company to its own plans, the company having guaranteed to raise speed to 27.5 knots. Dimensions were increased to 175 by 18 feet and displacement to 165 tons. Armament consisted of three 18-inch torpedo tubes and four 1-pounders. The propulsion plant provided by Herreshoff consisted of two quad-ruple-expansion engines producing 3,200 horse-power with three Normand water-tube boilers. (Lieutenant Niblack later characterized the Her-reshoff torpedo boats as the best in the world and the previous Bureau design as the worst, but this judgment does not appear to have been borne out by the service records of the ships concerned.[80] Melville thought that the *Ericsson*, "the only torpedo boat fully to Bureau plans," had the best record in the Spanish-American War.)[81]

The third boat, the *Rowan*, was built to a new Bureau design. Slightly smaller than the Her-reshoff craft, it had a high forecastle, a displace-ment of 182 tons, a designed speed of 26 knots, and Mosher boilers. The high forecastle, in-tended to improve seakeeping ability over the turtleback design that was then typical of most torpedo boats, was a feature that would ulti-mately become standard for destroyers. However, the contract was awarded to the Moran Brothers Company of Seattle and the *Rowan* was not com-missioned until 1899.

This year marked the end of an earlier experi-ment in torpedo boat applications when two portable boats intended to be carried on the *Maine* and *Texas* failed to pass their trials.[82] These were 15-ton craft, 62 feet long, with a single 18-inch bow tube and a 1-pounder gun. They had miniature quadruple-expansion en-gines and Mosher water-tube boilers operating at 220 psi with closed firerooms under forced draft. The reason given for their failure was ina-bility to make designed speed, but the bow tor-pedo tube had already been abandoned in larger torpedo boats because of a tendency for the boat to overrun the torpedo. Also, the concept of having battleships slow down in order to lower a torpedo boat, which may have appeared practi-cal in 1886, was entirely out of keeping with thinking a decade later. The little boats were stored away at Newport where they faded into obscurity.

The new gunboats were of two types. The larger group consisted of the *Annapolis, Vicks-burg, Newport*, and *Princeton*. These were 13-knot cruising vessels of 1,010 tons with composite hulls (copper-sheathed wooden planking on steel frames) and full bark-rigs, yacht-like in

appearance and quite anachronistic in the New Navy. The second group, the *Wheeling* and *Marietta*, also had composite hulls, and were similar to the others in size, speed, and arma-ment of 4-inch guns, but did not have sails. The first four were parceled out to three builders, but the last two went to the Union Iron Works on the West Coast. Most were completed in time to serve in the war with Spain despite their obvious limitations, and the *Wheeling* actually survived as a training hulk until 1946.

The Navy maintained a close interest in ships operated by other government agencies, espe-cially the Revenue Marine (a predecessor of the Coast Guard), the Lighthouse Service, and the U.S. Fish Commission, whose ships would be-come available to the Navy in time of war. Secre-tary Tracy had suggested back in 1889 that the Revenue Marine be merged fully with the Navy, but nothing came of it. However, in 1897-98 Navy influence was obvious in five new revenue cutters that were built with 4-inch guns and a bow torpedo tube, very similar to the Navy's small gunboats of the period.

In reaction to the agitation against high speed, the Navy Department ordered the *Columbia* to demonstrate the reliability of her engines by crossing the Atlantic at full speed in what was publicized as a race with the German liner *Augusta-Victoria*.[83] Even so, there was already starting to be a feeling that the Navy was too large and expensive to maintain, and Secretary Herbert proposed that ships be laid up with skeleton crews to reduce costs.

During 1895, the Krupp process, in which armor plates of chrome-nickel steel were face-hardened in a gas atmosphere, was perfected in Europe.[84] This was a major advance over the Harvey process, as it enabled the thickness and weight of armor to be significantly reduced with-out loss of protection, but it would not be avail-able in the United States for 3 more years. The United States did make some experiments in using aluminum for shipboard applications and immediately ran into corrosion problems that would take many years to resolve.[85]

After a long series of false starts, the Navy finally ordered the submarine that Congress had authorized in 1893. Actually, Montgomery Sicard, who was then chief of the Bureau of

Ordnance, had persuaded Secretary Whitney to advertise a competition in 1888 for the design of a submarine torpedo boat according to a rather ambitious set of specifications. Whitney apparently had been assured that Congress would appropriate two million dollars to build the boat that was chosen. John P. Holland, who had already built two successful boats, the so-called "Fenian Ram" and the "Zalinski Boat," had the devoted support of Navy Lieutenant William W. Kimball, who persuaded him to enter the competition in partnership with shipbuilder Charles Cramp.[86] Holland won the competition, but the Navy backed out when Cramp would not guarantee to meet the difficult performance requirements. Whitney reopened the competition in 1889 and again Holland was the winner, but with the change in administrations the project was sidetracked until the second Cleveland administration. On 3 March 1893, Congress appropriated the initial funds for a new design competition, which was entered by Holland, Simon Lake, and George Baker. The latter had already completed an experimental submarine and offered to demonstrate it to the Navy on Lake Michigan; also, he had strong political support. The Navy's Board on Submarine Torpedo Boats again recommended in favor of Holland, but Secretary Herbert stalled and ordered the test of the effects of underwater explosions that has been described earlier. Matters then stagnated amid political controversy until a contract was let with the John P. Holland Torpedo Boat Company in March 1896.

This submarine was the *Plunger*, a boat 85 feet in length with a hull 11.5 feet in diameter displacing 168 tons submerged and armed with two 18-inch torpedo tubes. To make the speeds of 15 knots surfaced and 8 knots submerged specified by the contract, the power plant consisted of two triple-expansion steam engines fed by a large Mosher boiler for surface cruising, a 70-horsepower electric motor and storage batteries for underwater operation, and a third steam engine running a dynamo to charge the batteries. There were three propeller shafts, two for surface and one for submerged propulsion. The boiler furnace exhausted through a collapsible stack amidships, and the entire after two-thirds of the boat was devoted to the machinery plant. The *Plunger*

was a major departure from Holland's earlier boats and its construction was subcontracted to the Columbian Iron Works of Baltimore. Holland's heart was not in the project: he felt that the Navy's requirements were not only unreasonable and unworkable, but were wrong for submarines. The steam plant would make the boat unbearably hot when submerged, as there was no way the residual heat could be dissipated. Other features insisted on by the cautious Navy merely added encumbrances to Holland's streamlined hull and simple diving system. Holland's interest turned to a new boat that would be built as a private speculation without government interference, the way Holland wanted to build it.

Enthusiasm for submarines was still running high in 1896 when Congress appropriated funds for two more, contingent on acceptance of the first Holland boat. Of greater interest to the Navy, however, was the authorization of three new battleships and up to thirteen torpedo boats. President Cleveland had asked for two battleships and was supported by the Senate, but the House of Representatives voted for four. As usual, the conference committee split the difference. To avoid the controversy that had surrounded the design of the *Kearsarge* class, Secretary Herbert appointed a special battleship design board under Rear Admiral John G. Walker. The board rode the *Indiana*, the only battleship then in service, inspected the incomplete *Iowa*, and listened to the opinions and prejudices of all parties. Taking note of the conflicting desires of commanding officers, but aware of the interdependence of size, armament, endurance, protection, speed, habitability, and seagoing qualities, the board sagely declared: "The necessity of these adjustments is a matter of common knowledge, and is condensed into the axiomatic saying that 'every ship is a compromise.'" The board then recommended that "no feature of their design should be permitted to seriously impair good seagoing and sea-enduring qualities."[87] Their compromise was to retain the hull and armor arrangement of the *Kearsarge* but add the high forecastle of the *Iowa*, leave speed at 16 knots, and eliminate the intermediate 8-inch battery as an unnecessary complication. Battleship drafts were still being limited to 23 feet as recommended by the Naval War College so they could take refuge in harbors on the southern Atlantic and Gulf coasts if necessary. A coal capacity of 1,200 tons (the same as the *Iowa* but less than the *Indiana*) was accepted, but the board insisted that the fighting draft be calculated more realistically at two-thirds of full load to avoid submerging the armor belt as in the *Indiana* class.

The main battery of four 13in/35 caliber guns was mounted in newly designed balanced turrets with flat, sloping faces. This eliminated the oversized gun ports of the *Kearsarge* but necessitated redesigning the recoil cylinders. The secondary battery of 6in/40 caliber RF rifles was arranged with ten in the hull and four on the upper deck. Smaller guns included sixteen 6-pounders, four Maxim-Nordenfeldt and two Hotchkiss 1-pounders, and four .30-caliber machine guns. The usual four underwater torpedo tubes were also provided. The engines were essentially the same as in the *Kearsarge*, but the boiler layout was changed to eight single-ended 180 psi Scotch units arranged athwartships with the furnaces outboard where they were adjacent to the coal bunkers in four separate watertight compartments. This necessitated locating the stacks two abreast, a feature also found in contemporary British battleships but unique in the U.S. Navy. The turrets, guns, and ammunition hoists were electrically operated, as well as the ventilation fans and lights, but all other auxiliary machinery was steam-driven. The electric plant was reduced to 256 kilowatts at 80 volts. These three ships became the *Illinois, Alabama,* and *Wisconsin.*

Although thirteen torpedo boats were authorized, only ten could be ordered within the appropriated funds. With this group, the Navy Department went all-out in experimenting with a variety of designs, mostly smaller than previous models.[88] This reflected earlier distinctions between oceangoing and harbor or coastal types and presaged the divergence of the torpedo-boat destroyer from the standard torpedo boat. One boat, the *Farragut,* was much larger than the rest—214 by 21 feet, displacing 279 tons, armed with four 6-pounder guns and two torpedo tubes, and designed to make 30 knots on 5,800 horsepower. Awarded to the Union Iron Works, the *Farragut* was frequently referred to as a

destroyer because of her size and heavy guns, but had little influence on ultimate destroyer development.

Smaller, but still classed as oceangoing, were the *Dahlgren* and *Craven.* These were ordered from Bath Iron Works to French plans procured from Normand and converted to English dimensions. Supposedly capable of 31 knots, they had 4,200-horsepower power plants and rudders at both bow and stern. When completed, they were judged to be unhandy and unreliable.

The seven others were all still smaller and much slower, with speeds of only 20-23 knots. All had triple-expansion engines and either Thornycroft or Normand boilers, two or three torpedo tubes, and from one to three 1-pounder guns. The *Davis* and *Fox* were ordered from Wolff & Zwicker of Portland, Oregon to a design submitted by the builder. Herreshoff offered two designs, the 105-ton *Morris,* which was distinguished by a sharp cutaway bow, and the much smaller *Talbot* and *Gwin,* 100 feet in length and displacing only 46 tons. These had high, straight bows and single stacks. Almost as small were the *MacKenzie,* built by the Charles Hillman Co. of Philadelphia, and the *McKee,* by the Columbian Iron Works. Although the two are usually listed as sister ships, they differed slightly in size and other characteristics. Since the Columbian Iron Works is reported to have prepared its own design, the *MacKenzie* may have been built to a similar plan provided by the Bureau of Construction and Repair. The Navy Department considered the Herreshoff designs the best of this group, but none of these boats saw much active service, nor can they be viewed as contributing much to the development of the Navy.

A number of the older cruisers, including the *Atlanta, Chicago, Charleston, Baltimore,* and *Philadelphia* were taken in hand between 1895 and 1898 to be re-engined, reboilered, rearmed, or otherwise modernized, having rapidly become outdated with advances in naval technology. In 1896, the model basin requested by the naval architects since 1888 was finally authorized by Congress to be built at the Washington Navy Yard.[89] The million-gallon facility was put into operation shortly after the turn of the century. Congress also provided funds to buy armament for the subsidized merchant ships designated as auxiliary cruisers, of which twenty-nine were now on hand. During the year, the Navy acquired the ammunition magazine at St. Julien's Creek, Virginia, to serve its growing fleet, and President Cleveland put most of the Navy Department's white collar employees under Civil Service. Marines were landed in Nicaragua, and Lieutenant Robert E. Peary embarked on his first Arctic expedition, followed by the second a year later. Of greater immediate interest to the Navy's bluejackets were the opening of the first ship's store in the battleship *Indiana*[90] and the issuance of General Order 466, which prohibited the use of holystones on ships' decks except "when absolutely necessary." Brushes or other means were to be used so as not to wear down the wooden decks. Earlier, Naval Constructor Francis T. Bowles had declared: "The most offensive weapon that the Navy now possesses is what 'Jackie' calls a file scraper. Whenever he hasn't anything else to do, he scrapes off the paint somewhere."[91] Apparently, neither the complaints of naval architects nor general orders of the Secretary of the Navy would prove effective in altering the traditional employment of sailors.

An event of particular interest to naval engineers was the publication in 1896 of Frank M. Bennett's monumental history, *The Steam Navy of the United States*. Reflecting the growing animosity between line and staff, Bennett closed his book on a somber note. Citing the long struggle to overcome the "iron-bound . . . rules of past practice" in achieving technological progress, he complained that the corps of naval engineers had "not yet succeeded in gaining similar recognition for its own members." The grievances of the engineers were focused in the issues of command authority and relative rank. "By custom and the requirements of service," Bennett wrote, "the engineer officer exercises all the functions of subordinate command over what is usually the largest division of men in the ship," yet statute law held that engineers could not legitimately exercise such authority.[92] Similarly, engineers were denied military rank equivalent to line officers; their various grades were assigned only "relative rank," which had been downgraded since the Civil War to make the engineers clearly inferior to their line counterparts in pay and prestige, although having com-

parable or greater responsibility. The antagonism of line officers against the various staffs, reflected in 30 years of discriminatory actions (and in 1896 directed especially at the Marine Corps) would soon reach proportions that would stress the Navy's personnel effectiveness beyond tolerable limits.

THEODORE ROOSEVELT AND WAR WITH SPAIN

The elections of 1896 brought another political reversal with the return to power of the Republican Party under William McKinley. When the new administration took office in March 1897, John D. Long, a Harvard-educated lawyer, former governor of Massachusetts, and one-time member of Congress, became Secretary of the Navy and Theodore Roosevelt became Assistant Secretary. Long made a practice of delegating much responsibility to his subordinates, and the energetic Roosevelt was eager to accept it. The Cuban struggle for independence was approaching a crisis, sympathies in the United States were overwhelmingly on the side of the revolutionaries, and the nation was in a self-confident, expansionist mood.

As had been characteristic of earlier changes in political control of the government, the administration called a virtual halt on naval appropriations while it took stock of affairs; thus, only three torpedo boats were authorized in 1897. These, like the *Farragut* of the previous year, were considerably larger than the typical torpedo boat, and were also often referred to as destroyers, although that was not the intent of their design.[93] The largest of the three, the 340-ton, 228-foot long *Stringham*, was ordered from the Harlan & Hollingsworth Co. Although completed in 1899, the ship suffered four machinery accidents, failed to pass her acceptance trials, had to be re-engined, and was not commissioned until 1905. The slightly smaller *Goldsborough* was even less successful. Designed by her builder, Wolff & Zwicker, she failed to make the designed speed of 30 knots. When the Navy refused to accept her, the company forfeited the contract and went bankrupt. The Navy then had Puget Sound Navy Yard install new engines, but the port unit was wrecked during trials and the torpedo boat's completion was delayed until 1909. The 235-ton *Bailey*, built by the Gas Engine & Power Co. and Charles L. Seabury & Co. and completed in 1901, was distinguished as the first U.S. Navy ship to have four stacks and Seabury water-tube boilers.

In most respects, 1897 was a rather uneventful year. The old torpedo boat *Stiletto* finally received the Navy's first oil-fueled propulsion plant,[94] but the sailors of the fleet would have to coal ship for many years before such installations would become standard. Ordnance continued to be improved, particularly with the introduction of the Johnson soft-steel cap for armor-piercing projectiles. Probably the most significant technical development to affect the world's fleets took place in England. The British had assembled a massive naval review at Spithead for Queen Victoria's Diamond Jubilee, at which the United States was represented by the proud armored cruiser *Brooklyn*. Inventor Charles Parsons had been experimenting with steam turbines since 1884, and a decade later had built the yacht *Turbinia* as a test vehicle.[95] The results were dramatically revealed to the world when the little craft, without advance warning, sped through the long ranks of warships and signaled the coming obsolescence of their massive reciprocating engines.

However, trouble was brewing over Cuba and the Navy Department quietly started making long-range plans and improving the fleet's readiness for a war that appeared almost inevitable. To guard Spain's colonies in the Pacific, of which the Philippines was the richest, Roosevelt strengthened the Asiatic Squadron as much as possible, given the few ships available for that purpose, and arranged for a strong leader, Commodore George Dewey, to take over its command. On the East Coast, the armored ships of the North Atlantic Squadron were shifted south and concentrated at Key West and other ports.

As 1898 opened, tension mounted, marked by rioting in Havana and brutal repressive measures by an intransigent and inept Spanish colonial government. War sentiment was inflamed by politicians, propagandists, and newspaper publishers eager to exploit the latest atrocity story. A news reporter's coded dispatch from Havana was misread, leading the administration to believe that American citizens were in danger, and McKinley peremptorily ordered the second-class battleship *Maine* to proceed to Havana on a "friendly" visit.[96] The Spanish reciprocated by having their cruiser *Vizcaya* visit New York. While the *Maine* swung quietly at anchor, the situation appeared to stabilize until 15 March, when the forward magazines of the battleship erupted in a volcanic blast of flame. Within a few minutes 251 American sailors were dead and the twisted wreckage of their ship lay awash in the muck of Havana harbor. In the investigation that followed, keel plating was found to have been forced upward, leading to the conclusion that the explosion was caused by a mine outside the ship. (No corroborating evidence of Spanish sabotage has ever come to light, and many naval authorities suspected an internal explosion right from the start. A recent study placed the probable blame on overheated powder in a magazine adjacent to a smoldering coal bunker.)[97]

Whatever the cause, the powder train that detonated the *Maine*'s magazines burned on to ignite the inevitable war. Congress appropriated $50 million for national defense and the Navy rushed to mobilize. Cruisers and gunboats were recalled from widely scattered stations, the battleship *Oregon* was ordered to steam from the West Coast to the Atlantic, and ships laid-up in ordinary were hastily recommissioned. The Navy hastened to requisition the steamers subsidized under the legislation of 1891. The big Cramp-built liners *St. Louis* and *St. Paul* became auxiliary cruisers, as did seven of the larger and faster freighters. The former Inman liners *New York* and *Paris* were similarly armed but diverted to duty as military transports under the new names of *Harvard* and *Yale*. Naval agents sought out surplus warships that might be purchased from other navies or shipbuilders; commercial vessels of all types, including pleasure yachts, were purchased or chartered to serve as auxiliaries;[98] and the fleet's white and buff ships were hastily painted war gray. The United States demanded that Spain negotiate an armistice with the Cuban rebels; Spain refused. Congress passed a resolution authorizing the President to take whatever steps were necessary to bring about Cuban independence; the Navy was ordered to blockade Cuban ports. Spain considered this an act of war; Congress made it official as of 21 April.

Although the U.S. Navy was actually considerably stronger than that of Spain, this was not immediately recognized, especially by the public. The main battle force consisted of only five battleships—the *Texas, Indiana, Massachusetts, Oregon*, and *Iowa*—none having been in commission more than 3 years, and the armored cruisers *New York* and *Brooklyn*. These were backed by little more than the few protected cruisers and gunboats of the New Navy, old wooden ships, and the obsolete coast defense monitors. The fleet was particularly deficient in torpedo boats and had no destroyers at all. Organizationally, the Navy Department was better prepared. A Coaling Facilities Board had determined the location of depots along the Atlantic and Gulf coasts, and the Naval War Board was hastily established to oversee the conduct of the war.[99] Spain, on the other hand, was very poorly prepared. Her one battleship, the elderly *Pelayo*, was under refit and her newest armored cruiser, the *Cristobal Colon*, was still without heavy guns. Governmental neglect had reduced the navy to a hollow, but still flashy, shell.

The outcome, in retrospect, was inevitable, but first the United States had to overcome a bad case of nerves as residents of coastal cities demanded to be protected from what they thought would be imminent invasion. National confidence revived in a hurry when Dewey drew first blood at Manila Bay on 1 May 1898. Led by the protected cruiser *Olympia*, his makeshift squadron totally destroyed the assembled Spanish ships without losing a single American life. On 21 June a landing party from the cruiser *Charleston* accepted the surrender of Guam, whose small Spanish garrison did not even realize it was at war. As an indirect consequence of the war, the United States annexed Hawaii on 7 July.

In the Atlantic, Spanish Admiral Pascual Cervera led a force of four armored cruisers and three torpedo-boat destroyers past the American blockade and soon holed-up with most of his force in the harbor of Santiago. Assistant Naval Constructor Richmond P. Hobson of Admiral William T. Sampson's staff came up with a bold plan to seal the harbor by scuttling the collier *Merrimac* in the narrow entrance.[100] Ten torpedoes were strapped to the collier's port side below the waterline to ensure that she would sink quickly, and Hobson with seven other volunteers slipped the darkened ship into the harbor entrance late one night. Detected and fired upon by the Spaniards, the *Merrimac* was sunk slightly out of place and Hobson and his crew were taken prisoner. Admiral Cervera was so impressed with their gallantry that he sent his chief of staff out under a flag of truce to let the Americans know that the prisoners were safe. Hobson, of course, became a popular hero as a result of his exploit. After being bottled up for over a month by a greatly superior U.S. force, Cervera led his ships on a futile sortie to destruction on 3 July. Again, the victory was completely one-sided; only one U.S. sailor was killed in the battle. With Spanish power effectively wiped out, hostilities ceased in August and a peace treaty was signed on 10 December.

The war was marked by several notable engineering achievements. The long dash of the *Oregon* around South America and her superb handling during the battle off Santiago were hailed as operational successes, but behind them lay some remarkable engineering performance.[101] Chief Engineer Robert W. Milligan, backed by Captain Charles E. Clark, insisted that the limited supply of fresh water be rationed to avoid introducing any salt water into the boilers, and the engineering gang stoically put up with boiler room temperatures that at times reached or exceeded 140 degrees. For most of the trip around South America, three of the four main boilers were used in rotation for steaming, while recurring steam leaks were repaired in the idle one. The engines themselves operated perfectly for the entire trip of some 14,700 miles at an average speed of 11.6 knots. Four coaling stops were carried out in accordance with advance arrangements, with much labor on the part of the crew, during the 71 days between leaving San Francisco and arriving at Jupiter Inlet, Florida. Among the junior officers in the Engineering Department were Assistant Engineer Joseph M. Reeves, who shifted to the General Line when the Engineering Corps was disbanded and went on to become Commander-in-Chief of the U.S. Fleet from 1934 to 1936, and Naval Cadet

William D. Leahy, who ended his career as President Franklin D. Roosevelt's Chief of Staff during World War II.

The *Oregon*'s superb engineering performance continued at Santiago, where the battleship outraced every other ship except the cruiser *Brooklyn*, which was rated at least 5 knots faster, and was instrumental in cutting off and destroying the Spanish cruisers. Milligan achieved this by keeping banked fires under all boilers at all times, while the engineers of other ships shut down boilers or disconnected engines to save coal. Also, during one of the South American coaling stops, he had taken aboard high-grade Welsh coal, some of which he set aside in a padlocked bunker for use in battle, to excellent purpose. For his performance, Milligan was recommended by Engineer-in-Chief Melville for special commendation.

Other noteworthy performances were given by the crews of the monitors *Monterey* and *Monadnock*. The only ships with heavy guns left on the West Coast after the *Oregon* was detached, the two clumsy monitors were urgently prepared for the long trip to Manila, where they arrived in due course to reinforce Dewey's squadron in anticipation of a Spanish attack. The engineering performance of many other ships was far from commendable, although perhaps excusable under the exigencies of war. Most of the purchased ships had to be manned by naval militiamen or inexperienced volunteers and operated without benefit of thorough overhauls or careful maintenance. There was no standardization of equipment and no time for training. The use of salt water in many of the boilers, which was still a common practice with low-pressure fire-tube boilers, contributed to machinery casualties and breakdowns; the finely-tuned torpedo boat engines were especially vulnerable to abuse or neglect. According to Melville, "the machinery of some was in a condition which can only be described as horrible, where boilers were burnt, cylinder covers broken, pistons and valves stuck, and everything in bad shape." There were simply too few experienced engineers to meet the Navy's needs. "A man without previous training does not become at once a skilled engineer by assuming charge of machinery," he declared.[102]

While individual exploits received the head-lines, the major contribution of the naval engineers and constructors was in the field of what would later be called logistics. Despite the Navy's relative unpreparedness, it successfully activated and manned decommissioned ships, from the commerce-raiding cruisers *Columbia* and *Minneapolis*, to the useless ram *Katahdin*,[103] and several antiquated Civil War monitors; purchased two cruisers, a gunboat, and two torpedo boats abroad; acquired and converted four passenger liners, eighteen colliers, nineteen other cargo ships, twenty-seven tugs, twenty-eight yachts, and several miscellaneous types; and took over twenty-four vessels from other government agencies. In the course of hostilities, it captured or salvaged about thirty-five Spanish warships and took a large number of merchant prizes. A number of the captured gunboats were refitted and commissioned as U.S. ships, while the old cruiser *Reina Mercedes*, which had been scuttled by the Spanish at Santiago, was raised and towed to the United States, where she served for many years as a floating barracks and brig at the Naval Academy.

Several of the conversions provide evidence of long-range planning for fleet needs, clearly presaging the great mobile logistics force of World War II. The humble colliers, of course, provided the fuel constantly required to keep warships on station. Such refueling was conducted alongside at sea but not underway, and frequently resulted in damage to one ship or another. Captain Robley D. Evans of the *Iowa* recorded that his ship gave the *Justin* "some pretty hard knocks" without punching holes in her plating, but was disgusted with the *Sterling* for "having sides like paper."[104] The *Texas*, with great overhanging sponsons for her turrets, could not coal alongside at all. Coaling problems and experience during the war provided direct impetus to new experiments with rigs for coaling at sea that led to the development of the Navy's capability for underway replenishment and refueling. Although oil was still practically unknown in the fleet as a fuel, it was needed in large quantities as a lubricant, and the *Arethusa* was acquired as the Navy's first oiler. The refrigerator ships *Celtic, Glacier,* and *Culgoa* were used to supply the fleet with fresh meat, provisions, and ice from the United States and Australia.

Other auxiliaries received more extensive conversions. The *Iris* and *Rainbow* were fitted with distilling plants capable of producing 60,000 gallons of fresh water a day, but were not completed in time to play a part in the war. The coastal steamer *Creole* became the "ambulance ship" *Solace* to carry wounded and sick personnel back to the States. The *Chatham* was taken in hand and hastily equipped with machine shops and tools to become the repair ship *Vulcan*. Stationed at captured Guantanamo Bay, her artisans were instrumental in keeping the blockading ships operating.[105] Engineer-in-Chief Melville later wrote that "with the exception of the battleship *Oregon*, there was not a vessel on the south side of Cuba that contributed indirectly more to the destruction of Admiral Cervera's squadron." In the words of Captain French Chadwick, "No one can understand the value of such an adjunct who has not had to look around for ships to go on duty, the long list of waiters for repairs or overhauling was sometimes heartbreaking; a full third of such a fleet as ours had at all times been counted off as unavailable for such reasons and others."[106] Experience with the emergency conversions was put to use after the war when a number of the purchased auxiliaries were retained and converted into regular repair ships and tenders.

Post-War Developments

The war taught the Navy a number of important lessons. Oddly enough, the experience was obtained almost entirely with ships and equipment that in no way represented the technology that was even then going into ships under construction. As a result, much criticism was voiced against material and practices that had already been changed but had not yet worked their way into the fleet. Gunfire control with the old weapons was so poor that the intermediate 8-inch guns appeared more impressive than the larger main battery rifles. Thus, although they had been abandoned in the *Illinois* and *Maine* classes on theoretical grounds, they gained new favor in the post-war predreadnoughts.[107] The operators learned, as the engineers already knew, that steam could not be raised in Scotch boilers as fast as it was needed in an emergency, and that

high-capacity distilling plants were essential to preclude having to feed seawater into boilers. The experiment of having two engines in line on a shaft was proved to be a serious mistake when the *New York* could not take the time to slow down and engage the forward engines without having the Spanish cruisers escape. The need for refrigeration and cold storage facilities was made clear to all after extended operations in the tropics. Deficiencies in command, control, communications, and organization called for immediate attention, as did inadequacies in personnel and training; state militias were shown to be no substitute for an adequate reserve force. There was no end of problems for the Navy to chew on in the post-war years.

Although the Navy's efforts during 1898 were focused largely on the short-term needs of the war, a new construction program was authorized that continued the steady expansion of the fleet. The core of the program was three more battleships (although only one had originally been recommended by Secretary Long), the first of which was appropriately named the *Maine*. Equally significant for the future was the authorization of sixteen torpedo-boat destroyers, the Navy's first of the type.[108] Continued emphasis on coast defense was reflected in twelve torpedo boats and—the ultimate anachronism—four monitors. The program was developed in the absence of any real war experience, although some wartime lessons would, of course, be incorporated in design changes during the construction of individual ships.

The battleships *Maine, Missouri,* and *Ohio* were initially envisioned as near-repeats of the previous *Illinois* class, but the Navy Department, strongly urged by Engineer-in-Chief Melville, agreed to see if their speed and endurance could be increased by allowing bidders to submit alternative designs. They ended up 20 feet longer and some 700 tons heavier than their predecessors, with a designed top speed of over 18 knots.[109] This necessitated raising their engine horsepower to 16,000 with a corresponding increase in the number of boilers, a return to the fore-and-aft arrangement of boiler rooms, and the addition of a third stack. The main engines were of the triple-expansion type, although Melville wanted to go to a five-cylinder quadruple-expansion design, but differed in each ship. Those in the *Maine* had the usual three cylinders, while the others each had four, with two low-pressure cylinders. The *Ohio* ships had these together at the end of the engine, an arrangement that was found to be poorly balanced. Chief Engineer C. F. Bailey of the Newport News Shipbuilding and Dry Dock Company devised a better arrangement for the *Missouri*, with one low-pressure cylinder at each end of the engine. These battleships were the first to receive water-tube boilers: twelve Thornycroft in the *Missouri* and *Ohio*, but twenty-four Niclausse small-tube units in the Cramp-built *Maine*.[110] (These were responsible for the *Maine*'s later notoriety as a coal eater.)

The caliber of the main battery guns was once again reduced to 12 inches, but these were for the first time designed to use smokeless powder; consequently, they produced double the muzzle energy of the *Iowa*'s guns and greater destructive power than the 13-inch in spite of the reduced weight of the projectiles. The secondary battery increased to sixteen 6in/50 caliber RF guns with new quick-acting breech mechanisms. Although two torpedo tubes were provided, they were of the Elswick design, fitted with hollow ball joints at the hull and relocated below the waterline, as would be the case in later classes of battleships. The torpedoes were charged with compressed air at 2,225 psi and ejected by air. The development of Krupp cemented face-hardened armor enabled the main belt to be reduced to 11 inches without a nominal sacrifice in protection. The electrical system was kept at 80 volts as in the previous class. The *Ohio* was given a hydraulic steering engine; the others, steam. Habitability improvements on the *Missouri* included the Navy's first dishwashing machine, potato peeler and masher, ice cream and dough mixers, meat slicer, and cafeteria-style steam tables.[111] An important damage control feature was the "long arm" system for closing watertight doors by remote control.[112] Overall, this class was about equivalent to contemporary foreign battleships and was generally typical of the later U.S. predreadnoughts.

The four latter-day monitors of the *Arkansas* class were given the names of states to imply that they were substitutes for battleships in the coast defense role, and they carried two modern 12-inch guns in a single forward turret. Although they had conventional triple-expansion engines, different types of boilers—Thornycroft, Niclausse, Mosher, and Babcock & Wilcox—were used in each ship. In this respect, as well as with later modifications, they were given some experimental value to compensate for their worthlessness as modern warships.

In view of the lack of progress on the three experimental large torpedo boats authorized in 1897, nine of the twelve new torpedo boats were simply ordered as updated versions of the previous Bureau (*Winslow* class) design with the rounded sides eliminated to provide more deck room. The three *Bagley*-class boats were built to the French Normand plans used by Bath Iron Works. The destroyers, on the other hand, were a new departure. In the absence of prototypes, the Bureau of Construction and Repair produced a wholly new design but gave bidders the option of proposing their own versions. In the event, nine were ordered to the Bureau design and the rest to three different private designs. The general characteristics called for ships of about 250 feet in overall length, displacing a nominal 420 tons, and capable of 26 knots. They were armed with two 3-inch guns, four 6-pounders, and two 18-inch torpedo tubes. The story of the development of the destroyer type from these primitive beginnings to its present form will be the subject of later chapters.[113]

Several other events took place and decisions were made just prior to or during the Spanish-American War that now stand out as harbingers of the future. At Lewis Nixon's Crescent Shipyard in Elizabethport, New Jersey, on 17 May 1897, John P. Holland launched, as a private speculation, the hull (Holland VI) that was to become the Navy's first submarine and a model for the future development of most undersea warships.[114] Shortly thereafter, Simon Lake, on 15 December 1897, demonstrated his submarine *Argonaut* in the Patapsco River near Baltimore.

The Navy has been blamed for the fiasco of the original *Plunger* and for dragging its heels in accepting the *Holland*. Holland himself constantly complained about the Navy's actions and inactions. However, the record shows that Holland's progress had been followed quite keenly by various naval personnel since the early 1880s. Lewis Nixon, the owner of the shipyard where the submarine was built, was a retired Naval Constructor who had designed several ships of the New Navy, including the *Indiana*-class battleships, and Assistant Naval Constructor George H. Rock represented the Navy at its launching. One of Holland's close associates, William F. C. Nindemann, had been with Melville on the *Jeannette* expedition, and presumably the two men remained in touch with each other. When the first sea trials were held on 27 March 1898, Lieutenant Nathan Sargent from the Board of Auxiliary Vessels was there and reported favorably on the results. On 10 April, Theodore Roosevelt wrote to Secretary of the Navy Long urgently recommending purchase of the boat.

Very shortly thereafter, a Board of Inspection headed by Captain C. S. Sperry observed further sea trials and noted a number of defects, which was not particularly surprising since the boat had sunk accidentally at her dock the previous October and grounded all of the electrical equipment. (A young electrician, Frank T. Cable, had succeeded in restoring it without disassembling the submarine.) On 12 November 1898, formal trials were held under a Board of Inspection and Survey headed by Captain Frederick Rodgers, with the boat actually under the command of a naval officer, Commander W. H. Emory. Chief Engineer John Lowe operated the propulsion plant and Lieutenant W. J. Sears successfully fired a Whitehead torpedo from the single forward tube. Considerable difficulty was experienced in steering the boat while submerged, and although some of the problem was attributed to inexperience on the part of the operators, Holland completely redesigned and rebuilt the stern section and rudder of the submarine before it was finally accepted by the Navy in 1899. This was accomplished by allowing Holland to take back the unfinished *Plunger* and repay the funds advanced by the government for that boat, with the Navy taking the *Holland* in its place under the original authorization of 1893.

An action that was to have a direct effect on the Engineer Corps and its members was the appointment of the Naval Personnel Board of 1898.[115] One of the objectives of this board was to resolve the long-simmering controversy regarding the status of staff officers, especially the engineers. The board's recommendation to amalgamate the Engineering Corps into the General Line, strongly supported by Theodore Roosevelt on the principle of making "every officer a fighting engineer," was not implemented until after the war.[116]

The indefatigable Roosevelt, ever on the lookout for new developments, noted the experiments of Samuel P. Langley with a flying machine, foresaw the possibility of military applications, and instigated the appointment of a board of officers to look into the matter. Although little came of either Langley's experiments or the board's report (after all, there was a shooting war going on!) this marked the beginning of the Navy's continuing interest in aviation.

Conclusion

The end of 1898 found the Navy victorious in war, basking in public adulation, and clearly on the way to becoming a first-class sea power. Its supporters occupied high political office in both the executive and legislative branches of the government. Public sentiment was in full support of a new role for the United States as a world power, with the Navy providing the nerves and sinews to connect the country to its new overseas territories and possessions. The nation now had the industrial plant and engineering know-how to free it from critical dependence on foreign sources. Scientific and technological development was advancing at a breathless pace, and already showed promise of extending the Navy's operations below the surface of the water, into air, and into the realm of long-distance radio communications. With unmitigated confidence and optimism, the Navy looked forward to the wonders of the twentieth century.

Notes

1 Students of this period are fortunate in having historical resources of probably unequalled richness in the form of detailed annual reports by the Secretary of the Navy and his principal aides, especially the chiefs of the Bureau of Construction and Repair and the Bureau of Steam Engineering. The technical information in these reports is amplified by excellent papers, many written by top naval officers, published by the newly organized professional societies, the American Society of Naval Engineers and the Society of Naval Architects and Marine Engineers. The SNAME papers in particular were usually followed by extensive discussion and comment, adding further to their value. Together with the Navy Department reports, the society journals constitute the primary sources for this chapter. The most significant documents are referenced in the text, but it should be recognized that this chapter is an amalgam of information and data from many published sources in which the same topics were covered from a variety of viewpoints and in various degrees of detail. The following general references were used extensively throughout the chapter.

A. Alden, John D., *American Steel Navy*. Annapolis, Md.: Naval Institute Press, 1972.

B. Bauer, K. Jack, *Ships of the Navy 1775-1969*. Troy, N.Y.: Rensselaer Polytechnic Institute, 1969.

C. Bennett, Frank M., *The Steam Navy of the United States*. Pittsburgh, Penn.: Warren & Co., 1896.

D. Friedman, Norman, *U.S. Battleships: An Illustrated Design History*. Annapolis, Md.: Naval Institute Press, 1985.

E. Friedman, Norman, *U.S. Cruisers: An Illustrated Design History*. Annapolis, Md.: Naval Institute Press, 1984.

F. Gardiner, Robert (Editorial Director), *Conway's All the World's Fighting Ships 1860-1905*. Greenwich: Conway Maritime Press, Ltd., 1979. (Naval Institute Press Edition, New York, N.Y.: Mayflower Books.)

G. Herrick, Walter R., Jr., *The American Naval Revolution*. Baton Rouge, La.: Louisiana State University Press, 1966.

H. Hovgaard, William, *Modern History of Warships*. London, England: Conway Maritime Press, Ltd., 1920. (New Impression, United States Naval Institute, 1971.)

I. *Journal of The American Society of Naval Engineers* (Naval Engineers Journal). Washington, D.C.: Vol. I, 1889-. Also *Cumulative Index 1889-1979*. (Hereafter referred to as ASNE.)

J. Musicant, Ivan, *U.S. Armored Cruisers—A Design and Operational History*. Annapolis, Md.: United States Naval Institute, 1985.

K. *Naval War College Review—Centennial Issue 1884-1984*.

L. Paullin, Charles O., *Paullin's History of Naval Administration 1775-1911*. Annapolis, Md.: United States Naval Institute, 1968.

M. Reilly, John C., Jr. and Robert L. Scheina, *American Battleships 1886-1923*. Annapolis, Md.: Naval Institute Press, 1980.

N. *Transactions of the Society of Naval Architects and Marine Engineers*. New York, N.Y.: Vol. I, 1893-; also *Historical Transactions 1893-1943*. (Hereafter referred to as SNAME.)

O. U.S. Navy, *Dictionary of American Navy Fighting Ships*. Vols. I-VIII. Washington, D.C.: Government Printing Office, 1959-1981.

P. U.S. Navy Department, *Annual Report of the Secretary of the Navy*. Washington, D.C.: Government Printing Office, 1886-1902. (Hereinafter referred to as Annual Report.)

Q. U.S. Naval Institute *Proceedings*. Annapolis, Md.: Vol. I, 1888-. (Hereafter referred to as USNIP.)

2 Annual Report 1886.

3 Annual Report 1889.

4 Actually, the early ships of the U.S. steel navy were quite similar to comparable types of foreign ships of contemporary design. Excellent illustrations of typical ships of the period may be found in *World Warships in Review, 1860-1906* by John Leather. Annapolis, Md.: Naval Institute Press, 1976.

5 Swann, Leonard A., Jr., *John Roach, Maritime Entrepreneur*. Annapolis, Md.: U.S. Naval Institute, 1965.

6 Annual Report 1889. Also Hart, E. H., *The New Navy of the United States*. (No date—U.S. Naval Academy Library.)

7 Gray, J. A. C., "The Apia Hurricane of 1889." USNIP, June 1960, pp. 34-39. Also, McKean, F.G.,"Some Lessons from Samoa (Typhoon Disaster)." ASNE I (1889) pp. 209-222.

8 Bennett, *Steam Navy*, p. 762.

9 Annual Report 1891.

10 Bennett, *Steam Navy*, p. 686 et. seq.

11 Bennett, *Steam Navy*, p. 805.

12 Bennett, *Steam Navy*, p. 806.

13 Busley, Carl, "Development of the Marine Engine." ASNE I (1889) pp. 151-162. Also Melville, George W., "Notes on the Machinery of the New Vessels of the United States Navy." SNAME I (1893) pp. 140-175.

14 Potts, Stacy, "Machinery of the Torpedo Boat *Cushing*." ASNE II (1890) pp. 215-222.

15 Annual Report 1888.

16 Bennett, *Steam Navy*, p. 806.

17 "High Smoke Pipes." Note Memorandum, submitted by the Engineer-in-Chief of the Navy to the Navy Department. Reprinted from *Iron Age*. ASNE V (1893) pp. 175-181.

18 Bennett, *Steam Navy*, pp. 732-743. Also Hayes, John D., "The Naval Academy and Engineering Education." Reprinted from *Shipmate*. ASNE, February 1969, pp. 33-35.

19 The ranks of naval engineers after 1874 and the comparable line ranks were Assistant Engineer (equivalent to Ensign or Master), Passed Assistant Engineer (equivalent to Master or Lieutenant), and Chief Engineer, whose equivalency ranged from Lieutenant through Captain. The overlapping rank structures effectively subdivided the engineer ranks according to the line rank with which each individual was equivalent.

20 Various issues of the ASNE *Journal* include obituaries giving much biographical information on prominent naval engineers, several of which have been used in this chapter. Unfortunately, the ASNE cumulative index does not include these sketches.

21 Madden, R. B., "The American Society of Naval Engineers." ASNE, August 1954, pp. 553-558. Also "The American Society of Naval Engineers Pre-Diamond Anniversary Bulletin." ASNE, 4 May 1962.

22 The *Proceedings* of the United States Naval Institute had, since 1874, provided a forum for discussing topics of naval interest. However, its papers reflected the interests of the line officers and included few on engineering subjects during the nineteenth century.

23 Sloan, Edward W., III., *Benjamin Franklin Isherwood, Naval Engineer*. Annapolis, Md.: United States Naval Institute, 1962.

24 *National Geographic*, Vol. 173, No. 1 (January 1988) p. 4.

25 McFarland, Walter M., "Rear Admiral George Washington Baird, U.S. Navy." Associates Notes, ASNE, November 1930, p. 720. The first installation of electric lights on a U.S. naval ship was on the *Trenton* in 1883 (Annual Report 1887), and the first installation on any ship was on the SS *Columbia* in 1880 (SNAME Hist. Trans. 85).

26 SNAME I (1893) prefatory pages.

27 Herrick, *Naval Revolution*, pp. 39-53.

28 Annual Report 1889.

29 "The USS Dolphin." USNIP, July 1954, p. 837.

30 Annual Reports 1889-1891.

31 Annual Report 1892.

32 McCandless, Bruce, "The Howell Automobile Torpedo." USNIP, October 1966, pp. 174-176.

33 Annual Report 1893.

34 Annual Report 1888.

35 Paullin, *Naval Administration*, p. 324.

36 Reilly and Scheina, *American Battleships*, p. 22. Also Friedman, *Battleships*, p. 23.

37 Wilson, Theodore D., "The Steel Ships of the United States Navy." SNAME I (1893) pp. 116-139. Wilson describes most of the ships designed up to 1893.

38 Annual Report 1894. Also Melville, SNAME I (1893) "Machinery." Also McFarland, Walter M., "The Modern Marine Engine, Boilers, Etc." ASNE VI (1894) pp. 647-703.

39 Bennett, *Steam Navy*, p. 810.

40 Herrick, *Naval Revolution*, p. 35.

41 *Jane's Fighting Ships*. London: 1898.

42 Bennett, Frank M., "Reconstructed American Monitors (Ironclad Vessels)." ASNE IX (1897) pp. 525-548.

43 Kinkaid, T. W., "The U.S.S. *Terror* and the Pneumatic System as Applied to the Guns, Turrets and Rudder." ASNE IX (1897) pp. 14-39.

44 Hichborn, Philip. "Recent Designs of Vessels for the United States Navy." SNAME III (1895) pp. 159-183. Hichborn describes many ships of the period.

45 Bennett, *Steam Navy*, p. 821.

46 Melville, George W., "The United States Triple-screw Cruisers *Columbia* and *Minneapolis*." SNAME II (1894) pp. 95-148.

47 Bennett, *Steam Navy*, pp. 826-834.

48 Davenport, Russell W., "Production in the United States of Heavy Steel Engine, Gun and Armor Forgings." SNAME I (1893) pp. 70-90.

49 Ståhl, Albert W., "Hydraulic Power for Warships." SNAME II (1894) pp. 203-240.

50 Greene, S. Dana, "Electricity on Shipboard—Its Present Position and Future Development." SNAME II (1894) pp. 51-68.

51 Cheneau, Emmanuel, "Cellulose and its Application to Warships." SNAME II (1894) pp. 73-94.

52 Cramp, Henry W., "American Corn-pith Cellulose." SNAME IV (1896) pp. 65-72.

53 Herrick, *Naval Revolution*, pp. 125-130.

54 Baxter, William J., "Notes on Launching." SNAME II (1894) pp. 241-260.

55 Cramp, Charles H., "Evolution of the Ocean Greyhound." SNAME I (1893) pp. 1-27.

56 Nevitt, Cedric R., "American Merchant Steamships." SNAME Hist. Trans., pp. 54-73. Also Perrott, William, "The Cramp Shipyard." SNAME Hist. Trans., pp. 213-217. Also Rigg, E. H. and A. J. Dickie, "History of the United States Coastwise Steamers." SNAME Hist. Trans., pp. 74-96.

57 Newell, W. S., "History of Bath Iron Works Corporation." SNAME Hist. Trans., p. 199.

58 Frear, Hugo P., "History of Tankers." SNAME Hist. Trans., pp. 135-144.

59 Rigg and Dickie, "Coastwise Steamers," p. 85.

60 Furgason, Homer L., "The Newport News Shipbuilding and Dry Dock Company." SNAME Hist. Trans., pp. 218-221.

61 Wilson, SNAME I (1893) "Steel Ships." Also Melville, SNAME I (1893) "Machinery."

62 Fiske, Bradley A., *From Midshipman to Rear Admiral.* New York, N.Y.: Century, 1919.

63 Paullin, *Naval Administration*, p. 367.

64 Bennett, *Steam Navy*, p. 841.

65 Woodward, Joseph D., "Recent Light-Draught Gunboats for the U.S. Navy." SNAME II (1894) pp. 285-295. Also "Special Navy Supplement." *Scientific American Supplement* XLV (30 April 1898) pp. 1-40. This publication contains excellent descriptions of many ships that served in the Spanish-American War.

66 "The Sinking of HMS *Victoria*." ASNE V (1893) pp. 693-703. Also "Loss of HMS *Victoria*." ASNE VI (1894) pp. 47-149.

67 Miller, Spencer, "Coaling Vessels at Sea." SNAME VII (1899) pp. 155-166. Also Miller, Spencer, "Coaling of the USS *Massachusetts* at Sea." SNAME VIII (1900) pp. 155-166.

68 Bennett, *Steam Navy*, p. 764.

69 Annual Report 1893.

70 Bennett, *Steam Navy*, pp. 767-768.

71 Gillmor, Horatio G., "Torpedo-boat Design." SNAME VI (1898) pp. 51-80. Gillmor describes all U.S. torpedo boats designed up to 1898.

72 Niblack, Albert P., "Tactical Considerations Involved in Warship Design." SNAME III (1895) pp. 149-158.

73 Hichborn, SNAME III (1895), "Recent Designs."

74 Niblack, "Tactical Considerations."

75 Meade, Richard W., "Some Suggestions of Professional Experience in Connection with the Naval Construction of the Last Ten Years." SNAME II (1894) pp. 1-26.

76 For a full discussion, see Heinl, Robert Debs, Jr., *Soldiers of the Sea.* Annapolis, Md.: United States Naval Institute, 1962.

77 Annual Report 1893. Also McFarland. ASNE VI (1894), "Engine, Boilers, Etc." p. 680.

78 Hichborn, SNAME, Vol. III.

79 O'Neil, Charles, "Development of Modern Ordnance and Armor in the United States." SNAME X (1902) pp. 235-271.

80 Niblack comment, discussion on torpedo-boats. SNAME VI (1898) pp. 53-55.

81 Hichborn, Philip, "Experience Gained With Our New Steel Ships' Care and Preservation," Comment on. SNAME, Vol. II, (1894) pp. 159-182.

82 Reilly and Scheina, *Battleships*, p. 30. Also Special Navy Supplement." *Scientific American.*

83 Bennett, *Steam Navy*, pp. 826-833.

84 Sampson, William T., "The Present Status of Face-Hardened Armor." SNAME II (1894) pp. 183-202.

85 McGuire, James C., "Aluminum—Its Alloys and Their Use in Ship Construction." SNAME III (1895) pp. 69-98.

86 Morris, Richard K., *John P. Holland 1841-1914, Inventor of the Modern Submarine.* Annapolis, Md.: United States Naval Institute, 1966.

87 Reilly and Scheina, *Battleships*, pp. 98-99. Also Hichborn, Philip. "The New Battleships." SNAME IV (1896) pp. 73-92.

88 Gillmor, "Torpedo-boat Design."

89 Taylor, David W., "The United States Experimental Model Basin." SNAME VIII (1900) pp. 37-62.

90 *All Hands*, March 1970, p. 40.

91 Comment on Hichborn, SNAME II (1894).

92 Bennett, *Steam Navy*, pp. 846-852. Also Paullin, *Naval Administration*, pp. 458-459.

93 Gillmor, "Torpedo-boat Design."

94 Annual Report 1898.

95 "Parsons' Steam Turbine" Abridged from *Engineering*. ASNE V (1893) pp. 899-922. Also Parsons, Charles, "The Application of the Compound Steam Turbine to the Purpose of Marine Propulsion." ASNE IX (1897) pp. 374-384.

96 Meriwether, Walter S., "Remembering the Maine." USNIP, May 1948, pp. 549-555.

97 Rickover, H. G., *How the Maine Was Destroyed.* Washington, D.C.: Naval History Division, Department of the Navy, 1976.

98 Stephens, W. P., "The Steam Yacht as a Naval Auxiliary." SNAME VI (1898) pp. 89-112.

99 Annual Report 1898. Also U.S. Navy, *Naval Operations of the War with Spain: Appendix to the Report of the Chief of the Bureau of Navigation.* Washington, D.C.: GPO, 1898. Also Chadwick, French E., *The Relations of the United States and Spain: The Spanish-American War.* New York, N.Y.: Scribners, 1911.

100 Annual Report 1898. Also Hobson, Richmond P., *The Sinking of the Merrimac.* New York, N.Y.: Century, 1899.

101 Offley, C. N., "The Work of the *Oregon* During the Spanish-American War." ASNE, November 1903, pp. 1144-1162. This subject is also discussed in Annual Report 1898 and in "Topical Discussion," SNAME VI (1898) pp. 210-211.

102 Annual Report 1900.

103 For an entertaining description of service on the *Katahdin*, see Potter, David, "'Old Half-Seas Under,' Experiences in the United States Ram *Katahdin*

During the War with Spain." USNIP, January 1942, pp. 57-69.

104 Miller, SNAME VII (1899), "Coaling Vessels."

105 Annual Report 1898; also in "Topical Discussion," SNAME VI (1898) pp. 212-214.

106 Annual Report 1902.

107 O'Neil, SNAME X (1902), "Ordnance and Armor."

108 Dickie, George W., "Torpedo-boat Destroyers." SNAME VI (1898) pp. 43-74.

109 Hichborn, Philip, "Designs of the New Vessels for the United States Navy." SNAME VI (1898) pp. 115-138.

110 Melville, George W., "Causes for the Adoption of Water-tube Boilers in the U.S. Navy." SNAME VI (1898) pp. 1-18. The 1906-07 issue of *Jane's Fighting Ships* contains excellent descriptions and diagrams of the principal types of boilers then in use.

111 *All Hands*, March 1970, p. 40.

112 Cowles, William B., "Watertight Bulkhead Doors and the 'Long-arm' System on the USS *Chicago*." SNAME V (1897) pp. 1-32.

113 Friedman, Norman, *U.S. Destroyers*. Annapolis, Md.: Naval Institute Press, 1982.

114 Morris, *John Holland*.

115 Annual Report 1898. Also Paullin, *Naval Administration*, pp. 459-463.

116 Annual Report 1902.

CHAPTER THREE
1899–1913

The Rise of American Naval Power

by John J. Fee

INTRODUCTION AND HISTORICAL BACKGROUND

The period from 1899 to 1913 was not an especially active historic period for the United States, but it was an extremely important chapter in the development of naval engineering. New ship types emerged; naval aviation was born; and incredible advances were made in ship propulsion, ordnance, electrical plants, and communications. Yet, the history and political climate of the period cannot be ignored, because they had a profound influence on the naval development.

The Roosevelt Administration

Assessment of American naval policy at the turn of the twentieth century focuses on the administration of Theodore Roosevelt. Roosevelt took office in 1901 as the young, reform-minded chief executive who had been Assistant Secretary of the Navy for the four previous years. During his administration, Roosevelt nearly doubled naval spending, and, although he had his own well-founded ideas, he depended heavily on well-qualified naval officers, such as Admirals William D. Sims and Bradley A. Fiske.

The General Board

It was also about this time that the Navy General Board was created. This top-level group, together with the Army's General Staff, "conferred upon, discussed and reached common conclusions regarding all matters calling for cooperation of the two services." Independently, the Board discussed matters of ship design, designation of bases, and the updating and preparation of war "color" plans. The members of the Board were essentially of the Mahan school: they recognized the pivotal role of sea power in American defense policy. With this philosophy, they helped shape American foreign affairs by advocating overseas bases; construction of an isthmian canal to permit selective, rapid reinforcement of the Atlantic and Pacific fleets; and a strong battle force with which to protect overseas holdings.[1]

The Spanish-American War

The United States was beginning to see itself as a giant island between the Atlantic and Pacific oceans. The Spanish-American War had just shown the American public the importance of a strong navy. As Mahan had observed, and Americans came to believe, "It is not likely that the United States will ever again be confronted with an enemy as inept as Spain proved to be." This observation furthered the argument to have the American coasts better protected from a fleet superior to the Spanish.[2]

The Spanish-American War had also shown that two fleets were needed, for fighting against even one enemy could require operations in two oceans. The United States had had to govern events taking place in both the Caribbean and the far western Pacific in the war with the Spanish.

American Industrial Growth

It has been shown in the previous chapter how the surge of post-Civil War industrial growth provided the foundation for the American naval build-up. Worldwide naval policy during the Roosevelt and Taft administrations placed great emphasis on capital ships. Roosevelt used the Navy in the Chilean crisis, Nicaragua, Haiti and Dominican Republic campaigns, Cuban uprisings in 1906 and 1912, the Boxer Rebellion, and the Vera Cruz action. Significant as they may have appeared at the time, they cannot be viewed in history as a time of great national testing. And the dreadnoughts had little effect on later actions in World War I, where the United States' involvement was limited primarily to smaller ships and craft.

The Ivory Fleet and Foreign Policy

Roosevelt sent the Great White Fleet on a world cruise in 1907 as a thinly veiled show of strength to the world, especially to the Japanese. Additionally, Roosevelt wanted to promote domestic support for his naval program, as well as to test the Navy's ability to operate the fleet in extended deployment. Roosevelt succeeded splendidly in all these goals with the 14-month circumnavigation. Yet, as further chapters will show, this moment of glory was short-lived and the Great White Fleet soon would become ob-

solete dinosaurs in naval warfare. This chapter will focus on the advances in engineering that made the Great White Fleet possible.

Naval Friction with Germany

After the Battle of Manila Bay, there was a certain uneasiness in the Philippines as the German Pacific Squadron arrived in Manila Bay. Dewey maintained a blockade awaiting American troops. The German Squadron, superior to the American, made hostile motions of occupation. The British, who were also present in numbers, stood with the Americans and perhaps saved the day. From this point on, an atmosphere of suspicion toward Germany developed, and the United States set out to surpass Germany's navy. It was apparent that the U.S. Navy had come to an era where they would be expected to exercise worldwide responsibility.

Major Ship Improvements

It may have been in response to this challenge that U.S. ship design advanced so dramatically. The result was that during the early 1900s ships became obsolete only 1 or 2 years after they were built. The size and capability of these ships, including their guns, armor, engines, and boilers, all advanced tremendously. By 1913 ships could engage the enemy at great ranges, rather than having to follow the Nelsonian dictate of drawing alongside the enemy, as was still the case in the 1890s. The more efficient, powerful, and convenient fuel oil replaced coal; electrical lights replaced kerosene lamps; and steam turbines burst onto the scene. The new wireless radio extended ship-to-ship and ship-to-shore communications from visual range to several thousand miles. Ships had to take into account the new threat of an underwater attack by torpedo. Consideration was already being given to protective measures against aerial bombs.[3] The designs of ships, large and small, changed significantly, and new craft emerged, such as the submarine, destroyer, and dreadnought.

But, the cost of ships was also rising rapidly. The cost of a battleship in 1903 was $5,382,000. By 1907, the cost of a battleship had risen to $8,225,000 and by 1914, the cost had gone up to $15,000,000-$20,000,000. This rise in cost was due in part to an increase in size. In 1900, a typical battleship was 400 feet long and displaced about 15,000 tons. As an example, the USS *Mississippi* and USS *Idaho* were each about 13,000 tons. By 1914, United States' battleships, such as the 32,000-ton USS *Pennsylvania*, were being built with 14-inch guns and 12 inches of armor. The crew complements, the size of the armaments, the thickness of the armor, and the speed of these ships all increased in general proportion with the increase in tonnage. Even though the ships built in the early 1900s were obsolete by 1913, ships built in 1913 were still in use some 30 years later.[4]

The battleship was not the only ship that was changing. At the turn of the century, the U.S. Navy had no destroyers, but, by 1914, there were thirty-four in commission, along with numerous torpedo boats. (The development of torpedo boats was partly due to the improvement of the torpedo. At the turn of the century, a torpedo was just as likely to strike the launching vessel as the target; by 1914, it had become a much more reliable weapon.)

BATTLESHIPS

Change in American Requirements

The increase in battleship size was, in part, due to its changing role in the United States Navy. Prior to 1898, battleships had been needed only for coastal continental defense. The government now realized that it needed battleships with greater range to protect its newly acquired territories and foreign interests. This posed new problems for American naval engineers. Ships with higher speeds and greater cruising radius were needed in sufficient numbers for two fleets, one in the Pacific and one in the Atlantic. Because of this demand, construction of coastal defense battleships was discontinued. The USS *Mississippi* and USS *Arizona* were the last two ships of this type authorized.[5] Since monitors were discontinued also because of their ineffectiveness against the ever-increasing gun ranges, shell power, and armor of the new battleships and dreadnoughts, the monitor money was then diverted into building the new battleships. Roosevelt sought to make the United States Navy second only to the British. When Roosevelt took office, the U.S. Navy was ranked fifth among the world's sea powers based on tonnage, but when

he left office in 1909, it had risen to second, even surpassing Germany's expanding armada.[6]

Competition with the Germans

However, by 1912 the United States was again outmatched by Germany in naval power. Even though the United States still led Germany in pre-dreadnought displacement by almost 100,000 tons, Germany's more rapid build-up in dreadnought battleships overtook the Americans in this more effective class by 130,000 tons. This change reflected the slowdown of American naval building during the Taft administration following Roosevelt's departure from office.[7]

Other Developments

It was not just the transition to the battleship and then to the dreadnought concept that was important to this period. Rapid development was occurring in many areas of naval engineering, from the seemingly mundane, like the successful use of fuel oil tank gages in the USS *New York*,[8] to more visible items, such as developments in gun turrets.

American Turret Development

Before 1905, basic battleship design provided for a forward turret, an after turret, and a pair of turrets amidships to allow simultaneous firing in a broadside. Stacked turrets were tried and, in time, rejected. This was in part due to experiments with the *Kearsarge*'s turrets in 1895, which proved highly ineffective. The lower turret was virtually uninhabitable during firing, due to noise and percussion. In 1905, experiments were begun in the monitor *Florida*, with one turret superimposed above and abaft the other. Animals were placed in the lower turret and the upper turret guns were fired, with no apparent injury to the animals. After repeating the experiment using people, with the same results, the United States adopted this concept for future battleship designs. As a further development, the USS *Texas* was laid down in 1911 with forward and after pairs of superimposed turrets of 14-inch guns. This would set the stage for basic battleship turret arrangements for the next 35 years.[9]

Propulsion Improvement

From the earliest days of sail, ship speed was a sought-after performance characteristic. But, the importance of speed lessened somewhat as gun ranges increased. In 1905, the design speed of battleships was 19 knots. By 1910, design speed had only increased to 20 knots with the design of the *Arkansas* class. And a year later, the *New York* class achieved only 21 knots. This was not to say that progress was not being made in propulsion engineering. As turbine speeds increased, the imbalance between engine speed and propeller speed also increased. Reduction gearing would eventually solve the basic problem of high-turbine versus low-propellor speed. In the meantime, naval engineers experimented with turbo-electrical drive and reciprocating engines for ships with constant cruising speeds to achieve improved fuel economy.[10] These experiments met with some success, but the steam turbine was emerging as the principal form of propulsion for warships.

Damage Control

The Russo-Japanese War of 1904 had been closely followed by naval engineers who were always eager to feed back actual battle experience into their designs. During the Battle of Tsushima, several Russian ships had been lost from hits on the boiler uptakes, which ultimately led to disastrous damage in the boiler spaces. This lesson was assimilated by United States constructors, and in time, the new three-gun-turret battleships, the *Nevada* and *Oklahoma*, were designed with armored uptakes.[11]

Recognition of the need to protect the integrity of a ship's buoyancy, despite battle damage, came to the fore about 1900. Watertight compartmentation of hull space was developed to confine flooding and preserve ship buoyancy after damage below the waterline. Refinements of related closures, ducts, steam lines, and fittings followed appropriately. But, the basic protection was seen to be provided by armor. United States battleship side armor thickness had reached 12 inches, as it had on comparable ships of other countries.[12]

Improvements in Fire Control

During this period, there were rapid improvements in fire control as reformers Fiske and Sims pushed for more reliable and accurate gunnery equipment and more effective performance. This emphasis was a consequence of the recognition of the relatively poor American gunnery performance in the Spanish-American War. Fewer than 5 percent hits were achieved, however adequate this may have been against the inept Spanish.[13]

DESTROYERS AND TORPEDO BOATS

Bainbridge Class

The era of the American destroyer began with the authorization of the *Bainbridge* class on 4 May 1895. Sixteen such destroyers were authorized, all commissioned by 1904. The largest of the *Bainbridge* class displaced a modest 400 tons and was 250 feet long. The class was lightly armed, with just two 3-inch, 50-caliber guns, and equipped with two 18-inch torpedo tubes. The main attribute of these ships, which were thought of as just extra-large torpedo boats, was their top speed of 29 knots, 11 knots greater than the speed of most battleships.[14]

Destroyer Evolutions

Destroyer design evolved through a combination of experimentation, accident, and necessity. Torpedo boats were the forerunners of destroyers. In 1898, twenty-eight torpedo boats were authorized, and the first was launched shortly after.[15] By 1900, there were thirty-four torpedo boats, but there were still no true destroyers.

A need for a new ship class became apparent during the Spanish-American War. The United States had seen a significant threat from Admiral Cerveras' small, fast coastal vessels during the Santiago campaign.[16] It seems to have been the intention of the General Board to provide for a nimble ship that could launch torpedos, evade guns, and then retire. President Roosevelt was a strong advocate of what was originally called torpedo boat-destroyers and was instrumental in twenty-six ships of this type being constructed by the time he left office in 1909.

The design of these ships launched during his administration rapidly evolved from that of earlier torpedo boat-destroyers. Displacement nearly doubled, from 400 tons to 750 tons, but with a slight decrease in length. The number of torpedo tubes and guns were doubled.[17] The mission of this new class evolved over time, but, initially, as indicated by their original name of "torpedo-boat destroyer," they were to protect the fleet from enemy torpedo boats. By 1910 their numbers were large enough and they had become sufficiently important that the era of the true destroyer is considered to have begun.

Destroyers as Test Beds

Oddly enough, because of a lack of clarification of their role and lack of an opportunity to prove their utility in battle, destroyers were not fully appreciated at first. Yet, they were inexpensive and this permitted development of incrementally successful prototypes. They also provided test beds for new engineering systems prior to installing them on the larger, more expensive battleships and cruisers. For example, in the early 1900s, effects of strain and distortion on destroyer hulls were measured and analyzed, and served to improve the hull designs of later destroyer classes.[18] Boiler comparison tests also were conducted during the early 1900s in various destroyer classes. Normand, Thornycroft, and Yarrow boilers were installed on different destroyers of the same class and their performance was compared and analyzed. Similar experiments were conducted with turbines. Curtis, Perkins, Streth, and Parsons turbines all were tested. As we will see later, the turbine-drive destroyer USS *Smith* (DD-17), commissioned in 1909, made an important contribution to steam-turbine propulsion. Also, oil-fuel experiments conducted on these early destroyers lead to the USS *Roe*, the first fully oil-burning destroyer launched about the same time as the *Smith* was launched.[19]

SUBMARINES

Introduction of Submarines

The submarine was probably the most significant innovation in naval craft to evolve in the early 1900s. Initially, the submarine was seen as a novelty, but there were farsighted individuals, including Admiral Dewey, who saw its potential. At first, submarines were discounted as too hazardous and unreliable to be effective. In fact, the early designs were so primitive and inefficient that it is surprising that the submarine was ever further developed. Two men dominated early submarine development in the United States, John Holland and Simon Lake. John Holland received the first Navy contract in November of 1899 for the submarine bearing his name.[20] But, Simon Lake was just as instrumental in the early designs of submarines. Lake was in competition with John Holland for the first Navy contract and, even though he was not awarded a contract, his design contained some innovative ideas. Lake's *Arganaut Jr.* had two large wheels that allowed it to be propelled along the bottom and a diving hatch that permitted a diver to leave or enter the craft while submerged. Simon Lake also designed a submarine called the *Protector*. The *Protector* had a primitive snorkel, double-hull construction with fuel tanks outside the pressure hull, an escape hatch in the conning tower, and an early, crude periscope. The *Protector* was never developed further because diving had to be delayed at least 10 minutes to secure the steam plant.[21]

Simon Lake eventually built the *Plunger*, which was 85 feet in length, 11.5 feet in diameter, displaced 186 tons, had five torpedos, two forward and three aft, and one 300-horsepower and two 600-horsepower engines. The *Plunger* was significantly different from the USS *Holland*, which was only 53 feet in length and 10 feet in diameter.

The *Holland*, however, had a number of advantages over the *Plunger*. The *Holland* contained significant reserve buoyancy; 12 tons of main ballast water plus ½ ton of water in each trim tank and some removable 50-pound weights on deck. A ⅝-inch thick hull gave the *Holland* an operating depth of 60 feet; however, due to an open battery, diving or climbing at angles of more than 15 degrees could not be attempted. A 150-horsepower electric motor provided a submerged speed of 9 knots, while a 120-horsepower, 2-cycle, 400-rpm gasoline engine provided an 8-knot surface speed.

There were also problems with ventilation in the *Holland*.[22] But, they were not as great as the ventilation problems in the *Plunger*. Excessive heat from the *Plunger*'s engines became too great to remain below for any period of time. This was the main reason that the *Plunger* was not accepted by the Navy. Ventilation problems continued to plague the *Holland* also, and, on one occasion, leaky exhaust pipes nearly asphyxiated the seven-man crew. Later, white mice were carried to indicate poisonous gas leakage. In spite of all this, the Navy accepted the *Holland* on 18 April 1900 for $100,000. Lt. H. H. Caldwell took command and the Navy's submarine service was born.[23]

Tactical Use

The submarine was first designated to be a harbor defense weapon. Before 1905 it seemed too unstable, unreliable, unseaworthy, and slow for an open-sea vehicle. It was debated whether the U.S. Navy was to invest time and money in submersibles or in submarines. Submarines could submerge, dive, climb, and operate under water. Submersibles, in contrast, could only submerge and then re-emerge from the water. The considerable interest in submersibles was because submarines were considered too dangerous, since a number of submarine accidents had occurred in diving and in attempting to surface.[24]

Design Refinements

Submersibles were laid out in a surface-ship-like design, with a somewhat conventional hull form and a flat deck. The ship-like shape of the early submersibles allowed a gun to be mounted forward and provided for greater crew living and operating space.[25] Most early submarine shapes were of a spindle or cylindrical type design. Their cylinder or spindle shape was modeled after a fish, but this shape gave the submarine a tendency to plunge unexpectedly. The only real advantage of the spindle shape was lesser underwater resistance. A compromise submarine hull form gradually evolved. Its underwater resistance was increased, but handling and arrangements were improved. This basic submarine hull design would prevail for the next 40 years, except pressure hulls gradually tended toward a more circular cross-section since it provided the greatest hull strength for a given structural weight of material. When operating on the surface, this circular cross-section also left the submarine with a large part of the hull submerged.[26]

D. W. Taylor contributed to submarine improvement with his investigation of stemmed bows and sterns to improve longitudinal equilibrium. He also experimented with reserve

buoyancy, which eventually resulted in the increase of reserve buoyancy in submarines from 5 to 30 percent of displacement.[27]

The Navy's first A-class *Holland*-design prototype was the A-1. This submarine was a poor diver, never really seaworthy, and inadequately armed. Later A-class designs (A2, A3, and A4) had more torpedo tubes and were better divers. The modified stemmed bow increased speed and seaworthiness. The early A-boats, tested in 1902, had gasoline engines because the early diesels were too heavy to be accommodated within the A-class design and they could only cruise at 8 knots on the surface for 400 miles, which limited their role until their cruising radius was increased.[28]

Operational Concepts

In 1905, the strategic and tactical roles of the submarine were still ambiguous. Even though development had made it seem possible to expand the operating radius to permit offensive employment, some admirals still saw the submarine as limited to its original coastal defense role. Some even wanted to eliminate it totally, considering it a "dishonorable weapon" of sneak attack.[29] In the early 1900s, the U.S Navy designed submarines in three categories: those for defense of ports and other key naval areas, those for attack at extended ranges, and small submersibles transported by a ship and released close to targets. The second category came to be the dominant submarine design during World War I, and the other two designs remained only secondary concepts, never actively being developed.

Submarines Come of Age

Submarine design progressed from the A-class through an H-class design by 1913, with enough marked improvements to establish the submarine as a legitimate part of the naval force. But the United States had fallen somewhat behind in relative submarine production. In 1904, the U.S. Navy had the world's second largest submarine fleet with seventeen submarines, but soon fell to fifth place by 1906, behind England, France, Russia, and Spain. The policy behind this decline was that submarine design was changing so fast that design improvement and quality were more important than a force strength that would be obsolete within a few years.[30]

From 1902 to 1906, submarines increased in displacement from 120 to 300 tons; propulsion power increased from 150 to 850 horsepower, operational radius doubled, and surface speed increased from 7½ to 13 knots. By 1904, articles in the *American Society of Naval Engineers Journal* (*ASNE Journal*) discussed the threat to shipping of these increasingly effective former novelties. By 1908, the Navy Department's seagoing submarine program demanded a trial surface speed of 20 knots with radius of attack equivalent to that of torpedo boats and destroyers. The submarine's speed and the radius of attack remained its weakest tactical link. But, as these two performance factors improved, aided by the introduction of the diesel engine, so did the submarine's lethal power.

The invention of the periscope by Sir Howard Grubb gave the submarine substantially increased tactical submerged visibility, enabling submerged attack, but only at speeds less than 8 knots, above which periscope vibration produced a wake that could readily be detected.[31] This problem was eventually solved, as well as the problem of submerged trim and immersion, by the invention of larger horizontal control planes.

Submarine Engines

Submarine engines could be classified in the following categories: Otto-cycle engines using a mixture of air and volatile fuels such as gasoline or benzine, engines using less volatile hydrocarbons such as kerosene, and diesel engines burning heavy oils. Gasoline engines were more easily installed, lighter, easier to start, and thus preferred over kerosene engines. Benzine engines had problems with noise and highly visible underwater exhaust.[32] Kerosene engines also required water injection, and more constant attention to the fuel.

By 1910, both 2- and 4-cycle diesel engines proved more effective than gasoline and kerosene engines and were increasingly adopted. Diesels, however, remained undesirably heavy. Diesels by this time could burn heavy oils to a specific density of 0.9. These fuels provided safety against fires and explosions and required no preheating.[33]

Although submarine surface propulsion was a debate not completely resolved until adoption of nuclear power, submerged propulsion by electric power became standard with the development of adequate storage batteries. Electric power offered uniform weight during an operating period, low noise, minimum heat, no deteriorization of crew air, and flexibility of motor operation.[34]

Torpedoes

Refinement of submarine design was accompanied by many modifications to torpedoes, resulting in increased reliability over the period from 1894 to 1909. By 1902, submarines firing at targets in motion succeeded in hitting their target as much as 80 percent of the time.[35]

The largest torpedo in 1899 carried charges of 1,350 pounds, while in 1909, torpedoes carried explosive charges weighing up to 2,250 pounds. Torpedoes grew in length from 14 feet to 20 feet and also increased in speed. In 1909 the propulsive power of torpedoes was increased by shifting from compressed air to a compressed air and alcohol-fueled steam engine. The speed of a 21-inch diameter torpedo was increased by 50 percent, but the cost of the new torpedoes was $7,100 compared to the $2,500 that they had been in 1903.[36] What made the torpedo so successful by 1913 was its newly designed propulsion and guidance controls.

The reciprocating steam engine torpedo was replaced by types powered with miniature turbines, which gave the torpedo better balance and allowed space for more fuel, increasing its speed and range. At first, torpedoes were guided by a small gyroscope called the "obry device." This increased torpedo ranges from to 2,000 to 3,000 yards. Unfortunately, the obry gear steered badly if there were any dents at all in the torpedo, and if the torpedo launching ship was moving, it had a tendency to tumble, deflecting the torpedo from the target.[37]

During this period, the U.S. Navy experimented with the Whitehead torpedo, which had a speed of 30 knots. Instead of running on compressed air, it used propulsive energy from a flywheel operating at 10,000 rpm. However, the Whitehead was not a great success because of difficulties in bringing the flywheel up to speed before launching and because of a lack of ruggedness.

The obry was replaced by the turbine gyroscope that was kept in continuous motion by constant-impulse air, increasing smoothness and allowing the torpedo to travel in a straight track, instead of a sinuous one. The new turbine gyro made it possible to launch torpedoes at angles of up to 120 degrees from the target. Above-water launching in torpedo boats was now also much safer, and safety innovations made a torpedo explosion in the tube no more likely than a shell exploding in a gun.[38]

ENGINES

On the Verge of Change

Returning to the issue of propulsion, in 1899, reciprocating steam engines were still standard, and the latest model of the reciprocating engine was designed and installed in the USS *Kentucky* and the USS *Kearsarge*. Yet, in England, Charles Parsons was busy perfecting the turbine engine that, within 10 years, would render the reciprocating engines obsolete for many classes of vessels. In 1906, the SS *Governor Cobb* was the first American ship fitted with Parsons turbines.[39] Just prior to that, in 1904, the Curtis turbine, the American competitor to the British Parsons turbine, was installed in the SS *Revolution* and SS *Creole*. Congress authorized a comparison of these two turbines with the reciprocating engine. To do this, a three-ship class was built, each containing a different engine. The *Birmingham* had reciprocating engines, the *Chester* had Parsons turbines, and the *Salem* had Curtis turbines. The Parsons turbines performed best, but turbines still seemed too inefficient and unreliable to let a 1- or 2-knot speed advantage promote adoption over the old reliable reciprocating engines.[40]

The following year, in spite of some opposition, the battleships *Florida* and *Utah* were fitted with Parsons turbines. Evaluation of their operations led Admiral Dyson to declare that for cruising under 20 knots, reciprocating engines were more efficient. In 1910, this led to the reversion to reciprocating engines for the battleships *New York* and *Texas*.[41]

Turbine Speed Problem

It quickly became evident that propellers were not driven at efficient speed when directly coupled to the high-speed turbine. This problem was not solved until a reduction gear was developed. In the meantime, improved economy was sought in the USS *Henly* with both a Curtis turbine and reciprocating engines coupled to the same shaft to capture the advantages of each. But, this proved to be unsatisfactory due to the complexity of the installation. Then, in 1910, the collier USS *Neptune* was built with a turbine installation, using a Melville-MacAlpine reduction gear, built by Westinghouse. This was the first, large geared-turbine installed in any United States vessel. Concurrently with these geared-turbine drive developments, electric drive was being tried in the United States as a way to reduce shaft speed from the turbine to the propeller.[42]

Turbines Take Over

The USS *Oklahoma*, laid down in 1912, was the last battleship with reciprocating engines. Her sister-ship, the *Nevada* had turbines.[43] In 1913, the *Pennsylvania* received an all-geared turbine installation, with Curtis turbines coupled to the propeller shafts by single-reduction gears. By 1910, thirty-five ships with 444,200 horsepower were afloat in the United States Navy, second only to the British fleet of 224 ships with 3,128,300 horsepower. In all the warships afloat in the world, the majority of engine installations comprised Parsons turbines. However, reciprocating engines were more efficient for ships traveling at less than 20 knots. Consequently, reciprocating engines continued to be used in cargo ships long after 1910. In addition to high speed, turbines had many advantages over the reciprocating engine. The turbine weighed less for the same amount of power. This was partly due to the elimination of the flywheel, which is not needed in turbines because the steam impulse against rotor blades is continuous. The continuous impulse produces very little vibration in operation, providing another advantage of the turbine over the reciprocating engine. Additionally, the turbine engine takes up much less space than the reciprocating engine, especially vertically, a crucial factor in smaller ships such as destroyers. Finally, the turbine engine is much more adaptable to efficiencies of superheated steam and high exhaust vacuums. The exhaust steam from a turbine is virtually uncontaminated from lubricating oil, a major problem with return steam from the lubricated cylinders of reciprocating engines. With fewer moving parts, the turbine also requires less maintenance.[44]

With the development of efficient reduction gears, steam turbines became the primary method of propulsion. The reduction gear solved the problem of the propeller rotating too fast. Reciprocating engines were relegated to only very specialized use in naval ships.

BOILERS

Boiler selection was a significant problem of the early 1900s. There were several basic boiler designs used by the Navy from 1849 to 1909. But, out of the dozens of boiler manufacturers, a few principal producers began to emerge.

Babcock and Wilcox Boilers

Babcock and Wilcox (B&W) produced the most widely accepted, and probably superior boilers, up to 1910. However, they had more corrosion problems than the other boilers. They were also more difficult to clean because two small doors had to be removed to clean each tube. The first B&W boiler was installed in the USS *Marietta* in 1899. The B&W boiler was improved in the early 1900s, and modified versions were installed in the cruiser USS *Cincinnati*, and proved to be eminently satisfactory.[45] A Royal Navy Boiler Committee report was issued in 1904. The committee evaluated all the current boiler systems, and determined the B&W to be the best, despite its problems.

Niclausse Boilers

Niclausse boilers were preferred by the General Board and they were installed in the USS *Maine* in 1899. Not everybody shared the General Board's preference, especially Admiral Melville, who protested the installation. Admiral Melville's judgement was evidently correct since the *Maine*'s boilers had continual breakdowns and were subsequently determined to be a danger to engineering personnel and were eventually replaced. Shortly after, the Niclausses were replaced on two cruisers and the *Nevada*. In spite of the failures, Niclausse boilers underwent continual modification on other ships, until finally, in 1908, it was clear that little had been done to

overcome defects in the Niclausses, and their use by the Navy was discontinued.[46]

Mosher, Thornycroft, and Yarrow

Mosher, Thornycroft, and Yarrow boilers all were intermittently used through the early 1900s as alternatives to the Babcock and Wilcox boiler. Mosher boilers were first installed in the USS *Florida* in 1899, and the Thornycroft boilers were installed in the *Arkansas, Missouri*, and *Ohio*. Yarrow boilers appeared on the scene a little later and were good enough to impress the Boiler Committee of 1904. The tubes in the Yarrow were vertical, in contrast to the slightly inclined tubes of the Babcock and Wilcox. The tubes in the Yarrow also were smaller in diameter than those in the B&W. The Yarrow boiler could be cleaned more easily, as there was less labor involved in removing the three manhole doors needed to clean the interior tubes.[47]

Evolution of the Modern Boiler

It was not until 1909, with the introduction of the Normand boiler with tube baffling and a steam drum, that a significantly new boiler came into being.[48] This proved to be the design that eventually evolved into the modern boiler.

Up until 1910, a combination of water-tube and fire-tube boilers had been used. But, with a modernization program in 1910, the fleet was finally completely outfitted with water-tube boilers. The old Scotch fire-tube boilers sometimes collapsed after as little as 6 months, and by 1903 Scotch boilers were being seriously questioned. Water-tube boilers had many advantages over the Scotch boilers, and their only drawback was that they required more upkeep. They could raise steam much more rapidly, and their normal heat and pressure limits could be pushed in an emergency without undue hazard. If a tube ruptured, the boiler could be swiftly repaired. In addition, the lighter weight of water-tube boilers contributed to added speed or payload for the ship.

Boiler Water Treatment

Boiler water treatment to control corrosion was now recognized as crucial to the maintenance of boilers and tubes. Before 1900, boiler water treatment was like medieval medicine. Each engineering officer had his own special recipe. There are accounts of everything from potato skins to other assorted garbage being tried to control corrosion. Corrosion was caused by a number of factors, including the fatty acids in oils coating new tubes, and the hydrochloric acid created at high temperature by residual traces of magnesium chloride in the seawater distillate. At the turn of the century, lime was thought to protect boilers from corrosion and scaling. About this time, Frank Lyons, a young officer and member of ASNE, began his own boiler tests. He conducted electrolytic studies of metals and their corrosive properties. He found that while new zinc cathodes provided electrolytic protection, delay in the timely replacement of zincs could actually cause corrosion. Corrosion tests also revealed that dissolved oxygen combines with corrosion products, rather than directly with steel. Further tests determined corrosion rates of residual chemicals on boiler steel. Lyons alertly observed that in a hospital the protection of surgical instruments against corrosion was achieved by setting them in soda water. Testing this principle, Lyons concluded, in 1911, that boilers also could be protected from corrosion with boiler water maintained at or above 3 percent alkaline strength. Subsequently, foaming problems in boilers caused Lyons, by 1913, to reduce the maximum alkalinity to 0.5 percent.[49]

Superheating

Superheating was first discussed as early as the 1870s, and superheated steam was first used on the *Great Lakes* to increase the firemain pressure of steam-driven fire pumps. In 1900, Admiral Isherwood published an article dealing with protecting superheating tubes. Protection was a major consideration because steam pressures were thought to be at the upper limits of the boilers being used. Boiler explosions would take place if pressure limits were exceeded. Superheating, in general, saves fuel by capturing more heat from the fuel; that is, each pound of superheated steam contains more energy than an equal amount of saturated steam at a given pressure. Superheated steam was used for several primary reasons. First, superheating improved turbine operation and turbine life by producing steam free of moisture. This decreased corrosion and eliminated carry-over water, which erodes turbine blades. Superheating also reduced con-

densation in reciprocating engines. In many cases, the use of superheat improved steam pump efficiency up to 40 percent. In 1910, Yarrow introduced a U-shaped superheater array and Foster Wheeler Co. developed a superheater with radial fin tubes. These boilers proved that superheating was safe and practical, and, subsequently, the battleships *Michigan* and *Indiana* were refitted with boilers with superheaters.[50]

NAVAL AVIATION

Naval aviation began with a naval officer observing the Wright brothers' flight in 1908 at Fort Meyer. A Lieutenant Sweet, present at this demonstration, remarked, "The Navy must have that; it will be most important." Earlier, in 1904, a naval officer had made a flight in a Wright aircraft, and in 1910 Eugene Ely flew off the USS *Birmingham*, performing the world's first take-off from a naval vessel. In 1911 Glenn Curtiss carried a naval officer passenger in his seaplane, another first. By 1911, radio experiments had begun, with naval aircraft communicating with ships and shore installations at Annapolis.[51]

A further significant step in naval aviation took place in 1911 with Ely making a landing, on a platform constructed for the purpose, on the deck of the cruiser *Pennsylvania*. Ely then joined the *Pennsylvania*'s captain for lunch and 2 hours later flew back ashore. Ely's aircraft was trapped with a simple arresting gear, weighted cross lines, strung across the platform deck on the *Pennsylvania*.

In 1912, the Navy decided to build its own "flying boat," having been sufficiently impressed by a Curtiss design. This aircraft was designed, tested, and flown in San Diego, California. Across the continent, at the Naval Gun Factory, testing was underway with a catapult to launch aircraft.

Also in 1912, the Navy's first wind tunnel was designed and built by Naval Constructor D. W. Taylor at the Washington Navy Yard in Washington, D.C. The 8- by 8-foot cross-section structure was a very forward step and aided in the research and development of many early naval aircraft.[52]

The first naval operations in which American aircraft were used were in 1914 at Vera Cruz, where seaplanes from the USS *Mississippi* conducted reconnaissance patrols for 43 days and were able to search the channel for mines.[53] This heightened the Navy's interest in aviation and spurred further development. Since there was no established group of aeronautical engineers in the Navy, much of the pioneering in design, construction, and testing of naval aircraft was done by ship naval constructors and engineers.

WIRELESS RADIO COMMUNICATION

Another technological area in which the U.S. Navy took a leading role was in the development of radio communication. Wireless, as it was first called, revolutionized communication at sea. Prior to 1900, communication at sea was limited to semaphore, signal flags, or signal lights. With the development of Marconi's wireless radio, communication between ships, shore installations, and aircraft became possible. Although radio communication of all types was still limited and relatively primitive, by 1913, it had made a brilliant start, and the U.S. Navy led the world with its use and development in many respects.[54]

Introduction Into Naval Use

The first official United States Navy message was sent in 1899. This was a Marconi operation, sending a congratulatory message pertaining to Admiral Dewey's victory at Manila Bay. This message was sent from the steamship SS *Ponce* to Washington, D.C., via the Highland Light shore station in New Jersey. Later in 1899, Rear Admiral Farquhart, in charge of radio tests for the Navy, had Marconi install facilities in the USS *New York* and USS *Massachusetts* for radio transmission. The first official radio message from a U.S. Naval vessel was sent by RADM Farquhart from his flagship the *New York*, via the Navesink Light shore station over 20 miles away, to the Commandant of the Brooklyn Navy Yard. Marconi's specified antenna height necessitated that a spar be added to the *Massachusetts*' top mast.[55]

In other early communications firsts, the *Massachusetts* was able to transmit messages up to 36 miles; in December of 1902, the Navy's coastal radio station at Cape Cod was completed, and on 19 January 1903, President Roosevelt sent a message to King Edward VII, spanning the Atlantic Ocean. By 1904, thirty-three ships and twenty-two shore stations had been provided with radio transmitting equipment. Later that year, federal control regulations were put into effect. It was decided that the Navy should control all coastal and overseas stations, while the Army should control all interior stations.[56]

Operational Naval Use

Later in 1904, war games in Long Island Sound were conducted. Some of the ships participating were equipped with wireless radios, and their value was evident in the results of the games and the praise by participants. This spurred the Navy into establishing more shore stations. Four 25-kilowatt transmitters were established at Key West, Florida; San Juan, Puerto Rico; Guantanamo Bay, Cuba; and Colon, Canal Zone, the most powerful stations up to that time. Additional ships were equipped for experimental wireless transmissions. In 1907, the Navy made its first permanent wireless installations on the battleships *Connecticut* and *Virginia*. They were tested to a range of 20 miles. Following this success, the Navy developed its own wireless in 1908, which the Bureau of Equipment installed in the USS *West Virginia*. It was used during a cruise by President Roosevelt from New Orleans to Washington, D.C. The cruise received national attention, as did the wireless, with Roosevelt being in contact with shore stations around the United States. Many American maritime companies raced to equip their ships with wireless. The North Atlantic Fleet was also equipped in preparation for a global cruise under RADM "Fighting Bob" Evans. It was Evans's intention to have all ships equipped and in contact with each other throughout the voyage.[57]

Radio Arlington

In October of 1908, the National Electric Signaling Company was formed to develop a radio utilizing the Fessendin patents. The contract was signed on 7 May 1909 to erect a 600-foot tower with a 100-kilowatt set in Arlington, Virginia. The Arlington station consisted of three steel masts and the Fessendin transmitter with a Poulsen Arc powered by 100 kilowatts. Construction was finished on 30 December 1912. During tests, messages were exchanged with Mare

Island, Key West, Colon, Guantanamo, San Juan, the Eiffel Tower, and various ships at sea. Development of this station meant that direct communication with the Navy at sea and most coastal stations in the United States became possible.[58]

Radio Distress Communication

Radio also aided in many rescue operations. In 1909, the SS *Republic* sank off the East Coast. A rescue message was sent and a number of radio-equipped ships were able to come to the rescue, saving a number of lives. The famous *Titanic* sank 14 April 1912, but she had been equipped with a wireless that brought other ships within contact who were able to rescue some of her victims. Following this incident, the U.S. Congress passed a law that required all ships of a certain displacement be equipped with some type of wireless radio.[59]

ELECTRICITY

Lighting Leads the Way

Electrical lighting on ships had been experimented with since 1880. In 1902, oil lighting was finally determined to be too dangerous for continued use afloat. There had been too many accidents with oil spills and fires, and a new system using electrical lighting was recommended. Electricity was less expensive than oil and much safer. Electrical lighting, even at this time, provided much more illumination. However, an electrical system to supply power for shipboard functions other than lighting had yet to be developed.[60]

The *Kearsarge* Installation

An electrical generating plant having a 655-kilowatt capacity was first installed in the battleship *Kearsarge*. This capacity was enough to light a small town and was used to power hundreds of internal incandescent lights, as well as searchlights and running lights. It also provided power to dozens of electric motors varying in size from 0.5 to 50 horsepower to power fans, ventilators, ammunition hoists, rammers for turret guns, electric call-bells, annunciators, a telephone system, electric fire alarms, and steering gear.[61]

Safety and Comfort Improved by Electricity

Electricity had other advantages, too. For power systems it was easier to install than steam piping. Electrical cable runs through living quarters did not raise ambient temperatures; steam pipes running through living quarters often raised the inside temperature by as much as 8 degrees. Electrical wiring was also less likely to be damaged by shelling or to cause injury. Steam from a broken pipe could scald people in its vicinity. Electrical wiring was more efficient, reliable, and easier to repair. To protect the crew, lead-covered wiring was braided and run through insulating wood moldings. In crew spaces, wires were supported on porcelain insulators and protected by thin iron guard plates.[62]

The Navy also began using Ardois lanterns for signaling and open motor Sturtevart fans for ventilating. Two- to five-horsepower ammunition hoists also went into general use around 1905.[63]

The Navy began experiments using electrical drive for controlling gun turrets and in 1907 adopted a method developed by Dr. Ward Leonard. The Navy had become dissatisfied with various hydraulic systems because in extreme cold hydraulics had a tendency to freeze. The British, on the other hand, became somewhat dissatisfied with the electric drive for their guns in the early 1900s and went back to using hydraulics. Their rationale was that hydraulic troubleshooting was easier than troubleshooting electrical systems.[64]

Mercantile Application of Electricity

By 1904, electricity was widely used by commercial shipping for many purposes. The White Star liner, HMS *Baltic*, was equipped with electrical equipment, running lights, and masthead lights, as well as indicators to show if the lights were burning properly. An electrical log indicating ship's speed and an electric lead recording depth were among the revolutionary items that the line had. The inventions of electrical cooking and refrigeration equipment were even more attractive because electricity could be wired just about anywhere on a ship.[65]

Electrical Propulsion

As mentioned earlier, electrical drive for propulsion was considered from time to time. In

1910, W. G. R. Emmet, a Naval Academy graduate and trained civilian engineer, submitted an electrical drive design to the Navy. The design used a General Electric high-speed turbogenerator to power a drive shaft motor designed to operate at efficient propeller speeds. Emmet calculated a transmission efficiency of 94 percent for a system designed for installation in a battleship using two turbogenerators driving four motors on two propeller shafts. Shortly thereafter, the Mavor and Carkon electrical drive system also was developed. They used a "squirrel-cage" rotor on a main shaft, a system that provided three speeds in either direction. The Navy decided to test Emmet's electrical drive concept on the new collier *Jupiter*. These trials proved successful and electrical drive was authorized for the new battleship *New Mexico*. Operational experience with the *New Mexico* proved equally successful, and Congress subsequently authorized additional battleships and battlecruisers with turbo-electric drive.[66] In spite of the rise of turbine-reduction gear drive, electric drive would not disappear.

Shipyard Electrification

By the early 1900s, the large public requirement for electric power also stimulated shipyard electrification for lighting and power. Electricity helped reduce production time and cost. A prime example was that old wooden derricks were replaced by electrically driven cranes capable of lifting 5 or more tons.[67]

FUEL OIL

Origins and Requirements

The feasibility of using fuel oil for powering United States naval ships became real with the discovery of the Spindletop oil fields in Texas in 1901. These were the first major oil fields discovered in the continental United States that were adequate to supply the Navy's needs. Up to that point, most large sources of fuel oil were outside of the United States. This discovery ensured a domestic supply, guaranteeing strategic availability.[68]

In 1902, early tests of fuel oil and its heating quality were performed by the Bureau of Steam Engineering. These tests proved inconclusive, and a convincing rationale for the use of oil as a fuel remained lacking. It was to take 15 years before oil became accepted as the optimum naval fuel.[69]

Fuel Oil Advantages

The relative advantages of oil over coal was proved in trials aboard the USS *Venus*. In a 24-hour period, 13.7 tons of fuel oil were used, in comparison with earlier trials where 30 tons of coal were needed. Moreover, the 8-knot speed of the *Venus* using coal was increased to 11.75 knots using oil.[70]

Oil freed a significant amount of shipboard space that previously had been used for coal. Bottom spaces previously used only for water or ballast could be used for fuel oil storage and conveniently reballasted with seawater as oil was consumed.[71]

Fewer men and equipment were necessary when fuel oil was used for heating boilers. Oil was pumped to the boilers, unlike coal that had to be moved by hand from coal bunkers by stokers. A one-third reduction in boiler tenders, one of the most undesirable and dangerous jobs on a ship, was achieved.[72]

Besides reducing a lot of personnel drudgery, fuel oil was much cleaner and the time to load liquid fuel oil aboard a ship was about one-third the time required to load coal.

Cruising radius was also increased and ship speeds were increased 20 percent with the use of oil. In addition, three to three and a half barrels of fuel oil weighing 0.5 ton could do the work of 1 ton of coal.[73]

In 1909, it cost 25 cents more per ton to fire coal than oil. Eliminating coal bunkers, fire bed grates, and ash ejectors; replacing coaling guns with fuel pumps and settling tanks; and then installing an oil-burning apparatus in a battleship saved $5,000 to $10,000 and reduced equipment weight by at least 40 tons. Oil tanks themselves saved upkeep money, since once fitted, they needed less repair than coal bunkers.[74]

Fuel Oil Vignettes

In 1904, the U.S. Navy, along with France and England, developed a gasoline-powered lifeboat. Then, in 1906, the Navy converted the monitor *Wyoming* from coal to oil and the *Wyoming* became the Navy's first oil-fired capital ship. These successes prompted Congress to authorize two oil-burning battleships in 1909, the *North Dakota* and *Delaware*. The *North Dakota*, however, was designed to use both oil and coal. Another early oil burner, the hydraulic dredge *General C. B. Comstock*, was already in use by 1908, which was also the year the first oil-burning destroyer, USS *Roe*, was launched.[75]

In 1913, the U.S. Navy hierarchy maintained considerable pressure to make certain that ships designed for oil use would still be able to operate with coal. According to Admiral Dinger, a respected naval engineer, oil was not readily enough available to be relied upon solely; however, designs that accommodated both the use of coal and oil lost many of the advantages of each.[76]

Underway Replenishment

Fueling at sea became practical with the advent of oil-fired ships and spelled the beginning of the end for the collier. Fueling at sea had been possible with coal, but coal was cumbersome and hard to transport from ship to ship. However, oil could be pumped from one ship to another with a minimum use of manpower. In 1910, the USS *Petroleum*, the Navy's first small tanker, appeared and many others soon followed.[77]

Fuel Oil Disadvantages

Certain disadvantages delayed the use of oil in ships. Oil had to be stored below the waterline where it could be protected from shell attack. Of course, these tanks had to be protected from puncture or torpedo attack.

Oil also had to be stowed where it would not flow into fire rooms in case of damage. The lower deck areas had to be redesigned to hold oil. To prevent leakage, rivets were more closely spaced and more caulking was required. Special ventilation also was required in these storage areas to draw off flammable vapors released by the oil. These ventilation shafts led directly to the weather deck, but to prevent water from pouring down into the tanks, goosenecked cowling tubes were installed.[78]

American Petroleum Sources

By 1910, with automotive development in America, there was such a demand for oil that exploration increased all over the United States.

Oil was discovered in eighteen of the forty-eight states. Along with these discoveries, old refining processes were modified and new tankers were built. These provided for an ever-increasing amount of oil. American naval power was made more secure with the domestic oil discoveries.[79]

Naval Ordnance

Guns and Projectiles vs Armor

Armor and gun armament changed drastically between 1899 and 1910. With both harder and tougher alloys being developed for thicker armor, better projectiles had to be developed to penetrate the armor. Greater kinetic penetration and more powerful explosive charges were needed, and bigger and more powerful guns had to be designed to deliver these projectiles.[80]

Economic Aspects of Armor

With the advent of steel armor in the late 1800s, armor designers and manufacturers raced to outdo each other. Steel manufacturers, and their prices, greatly influenced naval ships under construction. In 1899, for example, construction of the *Georgia*, *Pennsylvania*, and *New Jersey* was delayed 6 months until armor prices came down.[81]

Projectiles

The armor-piercing projectile of 1900 was equipped with a small explosive charge with a detonater at its base. The last solid shot shell passed out of existence about 1905 when large naval defense mortars were discontinued on the East Coast. The projectile was superior because the small explosion that the projectile produced was much more effective than merely punching holes in a target, the end effect of the solid shot.

Projectile Explosive Charges

The explosive filler in the projectiles was changed from gunpowder to high explosives about 1900. The British began using liddite, while the U.S. Navy used the more stable, non-corrosive ammonium-picrate. These new explosives markedly increased the fire power and effectiveness of projectiles.[82]

Projectile Design

The face-hardened armor being used at the turn of the century deflected many projectiles and decreased general penetration. To counter this new protection, a steel nosecap was installed on the end of projectiles that increased penetration, reduced the shock to the shell on impact, and minimized the chance of deflection. Another problem arose because a long, ogival pointed projectile nose was needed over long ranges to reduce wind resistance, while a blunt nose was necessary to ensure penetration of the armor. The solution was to attach a hollow, pointed wind screen of thin steel over the projectile's penetrating cap for streamlining purposes. This out cap collapsed on impact, and further reduced the chances of the armor deflecting the shell.[83]

Armor Piercing Fuses

The last innovation in projectile design during the early 1900s involved the detonator or fuse. It was inside the projectile and provided a built-in delay. Delays varied, but most were set to ignite the charge about 0.03 second after impact. This allowed a shell to penetrate to the inside of a ship before exploding. It was especially effective inside magazines or other ammunition storage spaces.[84]

Advances in Armor

To counteract the new developments in projectiles, new types of armor were developed. In 1899, nickel steel was used as deck armor and in other areas where light armor under 4 inches thick was required. In a short time, nickel steel replaced all previous types of armor and became the first modern, high-alloy steel material used for armor. Harveyized nickel steel replaced regular nickel steel as vertical armor. Harveyized steel, named after its inventor, consisted of nickel steel, with a superhigh carbon, cemented, 1.5-inch face. Harveyized steel was somewhat brittle and tended to crack and break over time. A new material, homogenous chrome-nickel steel, began to be used in the early 1900s. Chrome-nickel steel replaced all-nickel steel armor by 1910.[85]

Smokeless Powders

Smokeless powder was first used in the early 1900s by the U.S. Navy. During the Spanish-American War, visibility had been severely reduced by the amount of smoke produced by gunfire. By proper design of grain shape and size, smokeless powder decreased the smoke and could be tailored to optimize muzzle velocity for penetration and first accuracy. The adoption of smokeless powders was an important part of Sims's plans to increase gunnery effectiveness. Smokeless powder was slow to develop, at first, because many considered it to be dangerous, and a controversy raged over the use of double-base over single-base powders. These new powders were blamed for a number of spontaneous explosions that occurred in magazines and turrets. The British joined the French in restricting the use of smokeless powders while France was investigating the explosion of the *Jena* in 1908. This did not deter the Americans from further use and development of smokeless powders.[86]

REPAIR FACILITIES

The rapid developments of this period were not only confined to improvements in ship design and ordnance. Rapid changes were also occurring in the capability to repair and maintain ships. Important lessons had been learned during the Spanish-American War. One was that if the United States was to have a navy, it also had to have overseas bases with repair facilities.

The Navy not only established overseas bases, it developed mobile facilities that could be deployed to stations at suitable harbors and anchorages. These included both repair ships and floating drydocks capable of being towed long distances in the open ocean.

Meanwhile, in the continental United States, dramatic improvements were being made in graving docks, repair shops, and tools used for ship repair.[87]

VESTIGES OF THE PAST

As the Navy established a foothold in the twentieth century there were still signs of the nineteenth century all around, and they were slow to die. On 8 October 1904 the U.S. Navy decommissioned the USS *Intrepid*, its last sail-rigged ship, an anachronism, recognized to be of little utility to the Navy. Dynamite cruisers and harbor defense rams, now also of little use, were finally phased out.[88] These dinosaurs slowly gave way to a new navy capable of 20 knots by the time of the Great White Fleet. This fleet left Hampton Roads on 16 December 1907 and went 45,000 miles around the world, taking 432 days. During the voyage, engineering competition was introduced. Each ship kept records of speed and fuel consumption. The engineering chief petty officer saving the most coal got a bonus of fifteen dollars and his coal stokers received five-dollar bonuses. This practice, suggested by a Lieutenant Commander Gillis, saved the Navy several thousand tons of coal, and introduced a tradition of competitive efficiency that continues to this day.[89] This was an indication that real engineering had arrived in the Navy right down to the operator level.

SUMMARY

The engineering changes that took place in the U.S. Navy during the brief span of a few years at the turn of the twentieth century were as dramatic as any that had occurred up to that time. Several new ship types emerged, including the dreadnought, submarine, and destroyer. Electrification of ships occurred, and this paved the way for the introduction of shipboard radio communications. The arrival of high-speed steam turbines with reduction gears and oil-fueled boilers revolutionized ship design. Ship size grew dramatically, and ship speeds approached

those of today's ships. Aeronautical engineering was born, and the education of engineers in the Navy took on more importance. The Experimental Model Basin was established by David Taylor in the Washington Navy Yard in 1899, and, in 1903, the Navy began sending officers to the Massachusetts Institute of Technology to obtain graduate degrees in engineering. A postgraduate school in engineering was established at the Naval Academy in Annapolis in 1908, and, in the same year, the Naval Engineering Experimental Station was established across the Severn River from Annapolis.

The engineers in the Navy, who sometimes had been regarded with disdain by their line counterparts were gaining new respect. There would be other decades when engineering accomplishment would approach or exceed that of the first years of the twentieth century, but in most of those cases, the development was sparked by a war-time need. What is remarkable about this period is that it occurred in a time of relative peace and tranquility. Much of the credit can be given to Theodore Roosevelt who, as Assistant Secretary of the Navy, set the stage and, as President, provided the leadership; but, much of the accomplishment was due to the rising new breed of naval engineers who simply had a desire to design and build ships better.

Notes

1 Pratt, Fletcher, *Compact History of the United States Navy*. New York, N.Y.: Hawthorne Press, 1962.

2 *Ibid.*

3 Taylor, D. W., "Recent Advances in the Art of Battleship Design." *ASNE Journal*, August 1912.

4 Pratt, *Compact History.*

5 Taylor, "Advances in Design." *ASNE*, August 1912.

6 Pratt, *Compact History.*

7 *Ibid.*

8 Greene, S. D., "Electricity Onboard Ships." *ASNE Journal*, May 1899.

9 Note, "Design of Battleships." *ASNE Journal*, November 1912.

10 Anderson, E. H. B., "Propelling Machinery of a Battleship." *ASNE Journal*, February 1913.

11 Neuhaus, H. M., "Fifty Years of Naval Engineering in Retrospect." *ASNE Journal*, February 1938.

12 Okum, Nathan, "Armor and Its Applications." *Warship International*, Vol. 2, 1976.

13 Pratt, *Compact History.*

14 Hollis, I. N., "Engineering in the Navy." *ASNE Journal*, August 1903.

15 Durand, W. F., "Electrical Propulsion for Torpedo Boats." *ASNE Journal*, February 1899.

16 Yates, Brock, *Destroyers and Destroyermen*. New York, N.Y.: Harper Bros., 1959.

17 *Ibid.*

18 *Ibid.*

19 *Ibid.*

20 Baird, G. W., "Submarine Torpedo Boats." *ASNE Journal*, August 1902.

21 Note, "Submarine Vessels." *ASNE Journal*, November 1902.

22 Note, "Submarine Boat." *ASNE Journal*, November 1901.

23 Burgoyne, A. H., "Progress of Submarines in 1903." *ASNE Journal*, May 1904.

24 Note, "Stability of Submarines." *ASNE Journal*, August 1906.

25 Lake, Simon, "Submarines Versus Submersibles." *ASNE Journal*, May 1906.

26 *Ibid.*

27 Note, "Submarines." *ASNE Journal*, May 1905.

28 Burgoyne, "Progress of Submarines." *ASNE*, May 1904.

29 Laurenti, G., "Submarine Naval Warfare." *ASNE Journal*, November 1908.

30 Bernay, H., "Improvements in Submarines." *ASNE Journal*, February 1912.

31 Note, "Resistance and Speed of Submarines." *ASNE Journal*, May 1913.

32 Baird, G. W., "A Page in the History of American Torpedo Progress." *ASNE Journal*, August 1911.

33 Note, "Resistance and Speed of Submarines." *ASNE*, May 1913.

34 *Ibid.*

35 Baird, "Torpedo Progress." *ASNE*, August 1911.

36 Hoffmann, A. M., "The Automobile Torpedo of Today." *ASNE Journal*, May 1909.

37 Laurenti, "Submarine Warfare." *ASNE*, November 1908.

38 Baird, "Torpedo Progress." *ASNE*, August 1911.

39 Note, "Turbine Troubles." *ASNE Journal*, February 1911.

40 Note, "Recent Advances." *ASNE Journal*, November 1908.

41 Note, "Future Turbines." *ASNE Journal*, May 1910.

42 Note, "Steam Turbine Governers." *ASNE Journal*, November 1909.

43 Neuhaus, "Fifty Years of Naval Engineering." *ASNE*, February 1938.

44 Parsons, C. A., "Development of the Marine Steam Turbine." *ASNE Journal*, November 1906.

45 Cathcart, W. L., "Water-Tube vs. Cylindrical Boilers." *ASNE Journal*, November 1903.

46 Danville, C., "Report of the Committee on Naval Boilers." *ASNE Journal*, August 1904.

47 *Ibid.*

48 Yates, A. F. H., "The Normand Boilers of the Scout Cruiser *Chester*." *ASNE Journal*, November 1909.

49 Clarke, F. E., "Half a Century of Progress in Naval Boiler Water Treatment." *ASNE Journal*, February 1955.

50 Goddard, F. F. T., "A Note on the Use of Superheated Steam." *ASNE Journal*, February 1955.

51 Bilsten, Roger, *Flight in America*. Baltimore, MD: Johns Hopkins University Press, 1984.

52 Hollis, "Engineering." *ASNE*, August 1903.

53 Bilsten, *Flight*.

54 Robison, S. S., "Developments in Wireless Telegraphy." *ASNE Journal*, February 1911.

55 Schroeder, Peter, *Contact at Sea*. New Jersey: Gregg Press, 1967.

56 *Ibid.*

57 *Ibid.*

58 Howeth, L. S., Captain, U.S. Navy (Ret), *History of Communications—Electronics in the U.S. Navy*. Washington, D.C.: Government Printing Office, 1963.

59 Schroeder, *Contact at Sea*.

60 Greene, "Electricity Onboard Ships." *ASNE*, May 1899.

61 *Ibid.*

62 Note, "Electrical Equipment on the *Harshyer*." *ASNE Journal*, May 1910.

63 Baird, G. W., "Electrically Driven Fans." *ASNE Journal*, August 1909.

64 Emmet, W. L. R., "Electrical Propulsion of Naval Vessels." *ASNE Journal*, February 1911.

65 Note, "Electrical Equipment on the *Harshyer*." *ASNE*, May 1910.

66 Emmet, "Electrical Propulsion." *ASNE*, February 1911.

67 McFarland, W. M., "Electrical Plants for Shipyards." *ASNE Journal*, February 1904.

68 Note, "Oil Fuel Burning on the Pacific." *ASNE Journal*, February 1902.

69 Note, "Oil Consumption." *ASNE Journal*, May 1923.

70 Note, "Oil Fuel Results." *ASNE Journal*, May 1909.

71 *Ibid.*

72 Peabody, E. H., "Oil Fuel." *ASNE Journal*, May 1911.

73 Note, "Oil Fuel Results." *ASNE*, May 1909.

74 Blackinston, G. P., "Oil Versus Coal." *ASNE Journal*, February 1909.

75 Note, "Oil Consumption." *ASNE*, May 1923.

76 Dinger, H. C., "Oil Fuel for Navy Use." *ASNE Journal*, November 1912.

77 Sommer, A., "Petroleum as a Source of Power for Ships." *ASNE Journal*, November 1912.

78 Blackinston, "Oil Versus Coal." *ASNE*, February 1909.

79 Note, "Oil Consumption." *ASNE*, May 1923.

80 Okum, "Armor."

81 *Ibid.*

82 *Ibid.*

83 *Ibid.*

84 *Ibid.*

85 *Ibid.*

86 Note, "Smokeless Powders." *ASNE Journal*, May 1908.

87 Kollock, F. N., Jr., "Electricity at the New York Navy Yard." *ASNE Journal*, November 1901. Also Foley, Paul, Lt. USN, "Thermit for Ships Repairs." *ASNE Journal*, August 1910.

88 Neuhaus, "Fifty Years of Naval Engineering." *ASNE*, February 1938.

89 *Ibid.*

Portsmouth Naval Shipyard Waterfront, about 1890.

The brig *Enterprise* undergoing repairs in Portsmouth Naval Shipyard. *Enterprise* was a wooden sail-and-steam ship.

Wooden ships under construction. Throughout much of the nineteenth century, ships were built without benefit of plans. For guidance, the builder was given a model of the desired ship.

Eight-inch gun aboard *Chicago*, about 1890. In the background is the receiving ship *Vermont*.

Sailors aboard the *Enterprise* gather on deck for a smoke. Seven sailors, seven pipes! In the absence of printed materials, technical information was passed on primarily by word of mouth.

Crew members of iron-clad *Monitor* relax on deck. Photo was taken about five months after *Monitor*'s engagement with *Merrimac* in 1862.

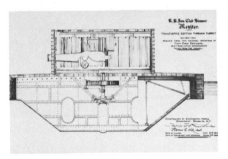

Transverse section through the turret of the *Monitor*; from the original drawing of John Ericsson.

The battleship *Maine* at anchor, 1898.

The Naval Gun Factory, now the Washington Navy yard, built most of the Navy's big breech-loading guns.

Assistant Secretary of the Navy, Theodore Roosevelt poses with officers of the Naval War College in 1897. Roosevelt was an ardent supporter of a strong Navy, both as Assistant Secretary and later as President.

The protected cruiser *Olympia*.
Engineering students as well as sight-
seers visiting Philadelphia can still
board the 5,870-ton *Olympia* and
roam the decks of this fine old veteran
of the Spanish-American War. She is
fitted out just as she was almost 100
years ago. Those without claustro-
phobia can even descend into her
engine room and see her big vertical
triple-expansion engines. At the right
is the *Olympia* as she looked at the
turn of the century.

Members of the "black gang" feed coal to the ravenous
boilers in a ship's fireroom. Temperatures often reached
130°F and more.

Routine shipboard maintenance included removal and
scaling of the boiler tubes.

USS *Langley* (CV-1) was the Navy's first aircraft carrier. She was converted from the collier *Jupiter* and commissioned in 1922. Note horizontal stacks amidships.

On April 11, 1900, the Navy accepted its first submarine, the *Holland*. Lieutenant H. H. Caldwell, *Holland*'s first commanding officer, welcomes midshipmen aboard in photo at left. In right photo, Caldwell poses with his crew.

USS *Ellis* (DD-154) was typical of Navy's "four pipers" of World War I era. This picture was taken in 1920.

The gunboat *Nashville*, commissioned in 1897, fired the first shot of the Spanish-American War. Her quadruple-expansion steam plant was highly advanced for her time. *Nashville* was sold in 1921 to become a lumber ship. She was scrapped in 1957.

CHAPTER
FOUR
1914–1921

World War I Expansion

by Prescott Palmer

BACKGROUND OF THE EPOCH

Major developments, events, and activities of American naval engineering are assessed in this chapter against the background of the years 1914 to 1921. August 1914 marked the outbreak of World War I and the beginning of worldwide naval operations on the part of Great Britain, Germany, France, Italy, Austria, Japan, and later, in 1917, the United States. The year 1921 will always have considerable naval significance, since it marked the end of the pre-Washington Naval Treaty period. Thereafter, as set forth in the next chapter, this treaty had profound impact on the numbers and characteristics of the capital ships of the great powers, with no fleet feeling the impact more than the U.S. Navy.

Maturing American Naval Professionalism

The year 1914, inexorably bringing Europe to "the guns of August," found the U.S. Navy growing and developing in reflection of America's emergent status as a world power. Our navy reflected this emerging status in its growing fleet size, in the gun and armor power of its capital ships, in its advanced and improving technology, and in its broad-based support establishment. But, most of all, the Navy's growth was exemplified in its new professional intellectual stature. It proceeded from the writings and teachings of Luce, Mahan, and other scholar-reformers at the Naval War College at Newport.[1] It proceeded, also, from the brilliance and awareness of dedicated commanders, reformers such as Admirals William S. Sims and Bradley Fiske.[2] Such officers were proving capable of interrelating naval technology, doctrine, and men to meet the sea power requirements of twentieth century national policy. And equally importantly, a maturing generation of American naval engineers and scientists were beginning to match those of Europe in exploiting technology at sea, on land, and (for the first time in man's history) in the air.

Flawed Political Leadership

After the outbreak of European hostilities, the Navy had two and a half years to prepare for naval operations and to deal unsuccessfully with a vexing problem at its very top. It was saddled with a Secretary of the Navy whom many of its senior officers found unsympathetic and difficult. The trouble with Josephus Daniels was that he was a man who knew his own mind, but—prior to his appointment—he knew very little about naval affairs. Confident in his self-made success as a newspaperman, he was not one to be dazzled by the dignity of admirals. As a representative of the populist wing of President Wilson's Cabinet, Daniels's judgement as Secretary of the Navy was colored by distrust of what he thought of as the "militarist" point of view.

His defense ideology affected the material status of the Navy, since he more than shared the commendable intentions of President Wilson and most Americans, to keep America out of the European war. His Assistant Secretary, Franklin D. Roosevelt, was somewhat impatient with his "idealist nonsense."[3] Unfortunately, Daniels also was not of the persuasion that a prepared defense discourages aggression. This thinking, combined with his distrust of "militarist" thinking, obstructed accepting the advice of his naval leaders.[4] He long and stubbornly opposed establishing a Chief of Naval Operations with adequate authority and staff to efficiently direct the affairs of a two-ocean Navy.[5] Even more crucially, he misguidedly refused to undertake many policies that were needed to ready America's Navy for wartime operations,[6] despite the fact that America's involvement in the European struggle was becoming increasingly unavoidable. Not only were material programs procrastinated, but also officer and enlisted recruitment, personnel and fleet training, Naval Reserve mobilization, and support of shipping had to remain at quite inadequate levels, in keeping with Secretary Daniels's avoidance of 'bellicose' preparedness.[7]

The Scope of Naval Engineering

In this period, naval engineering became a continually expanding technological area, defined by the growing technological interests and increasing professional responsibilities and concerns of the members of the American Society of Naval Engineers (ASNE). In the preceding chapters, against the background of maritime America and technology, the Society was shown as coming into existence in response to 'seen need.' That is, in 1888, engineer officers of the Navy Department's Bureau of Steam Engineering were seeking a vehicle for exchange of immediate professional data and information on trials and tests of new ships and engineering plants. Accordingly, the enterprising founders established a professional society and journal for just this purpose. Their, at first somewhat narrowly focused interests on steam power, propulsion, and related machinery and material are well-reflected in the earlier issues of the *ASNE Journal*. The purview, however, can be seen to expand in *Journal*s of succeeding years[8] with the expanding technological interests of the naval engineers, the Navy, and members of the shipbuilding and shipping industries professionally associated with the Society. Later in this chapter, attention will be given to the Society's (and the *Journal*'s) widening interest in hydrodynamics, structural engineering, chemistry, metallurgy, ordnance, optics, electricity, radio, aeronautics, etc. This interest has continued to broaden the purview and definition of "naval engineering," the technological scope of the Society.[9]

NAVAL CONSTRUCTION PROGRAMS

Program Determination

Major U.S. Navy building programs continued to highlight some of the more significant engineering accomplishments during the period of 1914 through 1921. The various ship types, as well as their specifications and performance requirements, were determined by the interaction of a variety of viewpoints. The viewpoints concerned naval policy, strategy, and tactics; they proceeded from the President, the Secretary of the Navy, the Congress, the General Board, the Naval War College at Newport, Rhode Island, and the Fleet.[10]

Fleet Requirements

Naval policy and strategy continued to focus heavily on a battle fleet capable of dealing with any naval challenge to the security of the Western Hemisphere, and to the more recently acquired commitments on the Asian periphery. The battle fleet meant battleships, and possibly battle cruisers, to deal with the equivalent heavies of any challenging power. A battle fleet, of course, required destroyers to assist the battle line in defending itself against torpedo attack by fast surface craft. A battle fleet also meant scout cruisers to locate enemy forces deploying toward friendly waters. Although submarines had been developed to be safe and reliable enough to be accepted for use with the fleet, as well as useful for coastal defense in the absence of the fleet itself, no one, not even the submarine's supporters, foresaw the submarine as a great threat to the capital ships or ocean commerce, which shortly would require heavy investment in escort types. Nor was mine warfare, despite clear evidence from the Russo-Japanese War, seen as much of a threat or opportunity. Lastly, there also was a small group who seemed to think there might be some naval potential for that recent invention of the Wright brothers, the airplane. Most naval strategists, however, were not conceding it much beyond a limited usefulness for reconnaissance, and possibly some nuisance value with dropped explosives.[11]

Capital Ships

Heavily gunned and armored battleships had come to represent the essence of sea power to all world powers. Both the Congress and the influential public had supported a succession of capital ship programs. (The Great White Fleet, in its day, was typical.) By 1914, the new progression that had been initiated 8 years earlier by the Royal Navy's revolutionary battleship *Dreadnought* had been succeeded by a generation of post-dreadnoughts in the fleets of the major powers.[12]

In the U.S. Navy, programs initiated before the period covered in this chapter resulted in delivery of two *New York* (BB-34)-class ships in 1914, and two *Nevada* (BB-36)-class and two *Pennsylvania* (BB-38)-class ships in 1916. The *New Yorks* marked a move for American battleships to 14-inch guns, heavier armor, and an internal gunnery plotting room with splinter protection.[13] The *Nevadas* represented a radical development in battleship design. The *Nevada* armor was concentrated to protect only the most important elements of the battleship system: the big gun turrets, barbettes, and magazines; the boilers, main engines, and uptakes; and the command center conning tower. For the first time in a U.S. battleship, boilers were fired with fuel oil, for the advantages cited in the next section of this chapter, MARINE ENGINEERING. Fuel-oil-fired boilers eliminated the protective coal bunkers;

however, erroneous fear of oil fires caused the fuel oil to be stored in the double-bottoms.[14] (Later, explosive tests evolved protective tanks and voids first used in the *Tennessee*.)[15] The *Nevada* design philosophy was influenced by the Naval War College and the General Board thinking, which saw battleships primarily engaged with their adversary counterparts at extreme ranges (20,000 yards). The long ranges minimized the need for armor against anything other than main battery fire. The essential elements of American battleship design had now evolved and were in place. The jealous Bureaus of Engineering, Construction and Repair, and Ordnance had evolved something of an engineering, tactical, and administrative miracle. Under the pressures of budget constraints, Congressional ideas of reasonable ship size, tactical concepts of big-gun and armor requirements, the realities of engineering and structural design, and deadlines, the basic battleship design concept had been coordinated.[16] Further improvement would be incremental, with the *Pennsylvanias'* displacements increased from 27,000 to 31,000 tons, and the main battery increased from ten to twelve 14-inch guns.[17]

In 1913, although the General Board had called for an entirely new 35,500-ton battleship design, with 16-inch guns, Secretary of the Navy Daniels refused the increase. Five ships, as a result, came in more or less on a par in displacement, protection, and main battery with the previous *Pennsylvanias*: the three *New Mexico*-class in 1919 and the two *Tennessees*.[18]

With the *Tennessees*, however, a type of underwater protection was introduced, designed on the basis of extensive explosive testing with caisson models of battleship partial cross-sections.* The protection consisted of five outboard compartments, with the middle three filled with

---

*It is still not widely recognized that it was just this sort of useful analysis that Brigadier General William Mitchell squandered when, for publicity purposes, he pre-empted the 1921 destructive testing of the old German battleship *Ostfriesland* (contemporary to the *Utah* class). Invited to participate in the Navy program of planned bombing and damage analysis, Mitchell became impatient in the middle of the second day and directed his bombers to conduct a barrage of 2,000-pound bombs that quickly sank the venerable old warship. It, of course, precluded completion of the schedule of inspections and damage measurement, and the Navy had no more war prizes for tests.[19]

fuel oil (found protective rather than a fire hazard when so employed).[20] Moreover, with the *Tennessee*-class, the *Colorado*-class, and the two *Lexington*-class carriers, the use of turbo-electric drive permitted further protective sub-division. Inboard of the protective oil and void sandwiches, four boiler rooms formed inner protective belts on both sides of two tandem centerline turbogenerator rooms. Separate motor rooms for each of the four shafts gave further compartmentalization.[21]

Further Developments

Since 1904, the General Board had pleaded in vain for cruisers that would provide scouting support for fleet operations. Fiscally prudent Congress apparently found it easy to see only an uncomplicated need for Mr. Roosevelt's big stick: battleships. The Navy was unable to convince congressmen that it was unrealistic to have a battle line without a scouting force, and unable to seek out and locate the adversary of that battle force. Finally, however, the Navy was able to get its cruisers authorized in 1916, when a very large naval bill was passed shortly after the Battle of Jutland. Thirteen *Omaha* (CL-4)-class cruisers were then authorized, and built in the 20s. These 7,050-ton, flush-deck cruisers reflected design concepts similar to the World War I destroyers, suitably enlarged to accommodate eight boilers and turbines on four shafts generating 90,000 shaft horsepower. Such a power plant was needed to provide 34-knot speed to operate with fleet destroyers, along with a 10,000-nautical-mile cruising range for scouting.[22] This authorization also included four 32,600-ton *Colorado* (BB-45)-class battleships with eight 16-inch guns, six 43,200-ton *South Dakota* (BB-49)-class battle-ships with twelve 16-inch guns, and six 43,500-ton *Lexington*-class battlecruisers. As a result of the Washington Naval Treaty, however, only three *Colorado*-class were ever built, plus the *Lexington* and *Saratoga*, later completed as the U.S. Navy's first full-size aircraft carriers.[23]

Requirements Not Foreseen

Leading up to this era, it was in regard to destroyers that foresight failed. Naval officers, political leaders, and legislators alike, all failed to anticipate the requirement for escorts, which would prove to be in such short supply once the United States became involved in the war. This was because no one in this country, or in Europe either, fully anticipated the deadly effectiveness of submarines against both naval and merchant shipping.[24]

Destroyers

Like those of other nations, U.S. destroyers had evolved from fast torpedo-boats designed only for attack with torpedoes. The design had grown into a dual-role vessel. It could attack with torpedoes, as well as use its substantially enhanced gun battery to defend the battle line against enemy ships with a torpedo capability. In time, with fine tuning for the defensive role, American destroyer design acquired range and seakeeping capabilities that enabled the ships to stay with the fleet. Then, as World War I and submarine warfare burst on the navies of the world, destroyers were found, gratuitously, to be the only naval vessels possessing a number (but by no means all) of the suitable characteristics needed to engage in anti-submarine warfare.[25] In March 1917, as Norman Friedman records in his wonderfully comprehensive *U.S. Destroyers*: "The General Board urgently recommended massive increases in destroyer production . . . , stating, 'The Destroyer is, so far as now can be seen, the best form of Submarine Chaser.'" There were less than fifty destroyers in the U.S. fleet (various old high-foc's'l ships). The six-ship *Caldwell* (DD-69) class (flush-deckers, some with only three stacks), conveniently in produc-tion, essentially were prototypes for two new basic designs, one by Bath Iron Works and one by Bethlehem Steel. These turbine-powered, oil-fueled, 1,200-ton ships could do 35 knots on four boilers. Commencing then, and continuing until early 1920, orders were placed for 272 flush-deck "four-pipers." This tremendous pro-duction was, perhaps, the largest class of war-ships ever built in this country. For the most part it was accomplished in five private East Coast yards (Bath Iron Works, Cramps, Fore River, Newport News, and New York Shipbuilding Cor-poration), plus the Union Iron Works and Mare Island Navy Yard in California. Mare Island, by dint of pre-fabrication, achieved a possibly all-time record in construction of the USS

Ward (DD-139) in 17 days from keel-laying to launching.[26]

Emergency Program Escorts

To cope with the menace to wartime naval operations and shipping posed by German U-boats, besides the destroyer program, two classes of small escorts were designed and put into production: the 500 ton, 200-foot, turbine-powered PE-class steel "Eagle Boat," and the wooden, 110-foot SC-class subchaser. Although the Ford Motor Company planned production for up to 112 of the rather ugly, slab-sided Eagles at the special production facility built in Highland Park, Michigan, near Detroit, all but PE-1 through PE-60 were canceled in November 1918. Four hundred and forty-eight wooden subchasers were built. After their completions started in July of 1917, they served in their designed anti-submarine warfare role, and in other roles, in domestic and European waters.[27]

Submarines

As indicated in the previous chapter, by 1914, the General Board was moving to provide seagoing submarines for the American fleet distinct from coastal boats for coast defense and cooperation with the fleet in home waters. Need was seen for a "fleet" boat, capable of accompanying battlefleet deployments. The combat experience of both British and German submarines increasingly indicated the necessity for emphasis on high-seas and surface operations. Both found high-seas operations necessary to deploy their boats against the adversary. Both found surface operations to be a tactical necessity, except during the attack phase. Nevertheless, deliveries of scheduled H-, K-, L-, and M-class boats (all under 500 tons displacement) continued, with the three unsuccessful T- or AA-class boats of 1918-1919 (too slow and good only down to 150 feet) being the first U.S. fleet submarines.[28]

In 1914, the Bureau of Construction and Repair commenced preparation of its own submarine designs. Portsmouth Navy Yard was designated as a design agency, and, to start familiarization, an order was placed with Portsmouth to build an L-boat to commercial (Lake Boat Company) designs. In 1916, the Bureau placed a second order with Portsmouth for a Holland-type

O-boat to Electric Boat Company designs. Late that year, the Bureau directed Portsmouth to undertake working plans for a third boat, based on preliminary plans developed by the Bureau, which led to the discontinuance of Lake-type boats. In July 1917, four S-boats built from Portsmouth plans were ordered from Lake, and, in August 1918, four more government-type boats were ordered from Lake to their own plans. Subsequently, no more submarines were ordered from Lake, and the company ceased business as a submarine design agency. Additional boats were not ordered from Electric Boat Company either, but they remained in business as a design agency for various foreign governments. Six K-boats were completed in 1914, followed by a substantial number of L-, H-, N-, O-, R-, and S-boats in the years 1915 through 1921. In particular, S-boats in production (like the flush-deck destroyers) when industrial mobilization got underway for World War I, were built in large numbers (at least fifty-one). During this period, U.S. submarines increased in size and capability, but operating experience during World War I indicated a lack of reliability and capability.[29]

The success of the German U-boat campaign, initially against British warships, but more especially the success against Allied shipping, caused the U.S. Navy to assess German submarines as closely as wartime conditions would permit. A variety of factors were seen as contributing to the efficiency of the German designs, and the German diesels were seen as contributing significantly to successful operation. Assessment of the German U-111 at the end of the war confirmed the superior reliability of the German diesel engines, as well as the operational advantage of its dry bridge. U.S. wartime submarine experience led to new emphasis on surfaced operation, with bridges and decks enlarged and secured with lifelines.[30]

MARINE ENGINEERING

Fuel and Power

Continued steam power domination of propulsion at sea during this period, with improvements in turbines, finally enabled U.S. Navy ship designs to replace reciprocating engines with turbine engines. Diesels were proving to be the optimum system for submarines, and their use for propulsion of large auxiliaries was being tested. With the Spindletop strike in Texas proving a strategic petroleum source was available, fuel oil was replacing coal systems when United States' naval vessels were built or overhauled. The advantages of fuel oil over coal, mentioned in the previous chapter, include:

- greater heat by volume and weight
- convenience and flexibility (in fueling, storage, and use)
- absence of ash removal
- more compact fire rooms
- reduction in personnel
- convenience and flexibility in storage
- elimination of smoke (a tactical advantage)

Testing continued, nevertheless, and boilers and fuel-oil burning were in a constant state of flux. Atomization with compressed air, however, had provided the basic technique for burning heavy fuel oils, and this was further improved with the new Navy fuel oil specifications and the invention of film oil heaters.[31]

Boilers

Scotch boilers were the exception (now used in only a few colliers). By 1915, the so-called 'watertube' boiler that converted boiler water to steam, in arrays of steel tubes directly exposed to boiler furnace flame, had been almost wholly adopted for American naval vessels. Typically, Babcock and Wilcox and Yarrow watertube boilers were used for large ships, the same types— plus Normand, Thornycroft, and White Forster— were used for intermediate-sized vessels and destroyers. Watertube boilers also were used in the mass-produced "Hog Island" freighters (See WAR SHIPPING.) All this wartime use amply established the efficiency, durability, reliability, safety, and ease of maintenance of the watertube boiler.

Boiler-water anti-salinity procedures seem to have remained uniquely static during this era of otherwise increasing engineering efficiency. Navy boiler-water technologists were content to rest with the semi-empirical advances in Frank Lyon's new test kits and the 1913 boiler-water compound (neither yet really well-understood in the Navy engineering community.)[32]

Main Engines

Success in using steam turbines in all navies posed the problem of efficiently coupling the necessarily high speed of turbines with the low-speed regimes needed by propellers. With this problem not yet satisfactorily solved, and despite the earlier use of turbines in the *Utah* and *Wyoming* classes, the need for cruising efficiency (especially in the reaches of the Pacific) caused the return of reciprocating engines in the *Texas*-class battleships and the *Oklahoma* in 1914 and 1916. One Navy solution was to introduce its first all-geared turbine installation in *Oklahoma*'s sister-ship, the *Pennsylvania*, (BB-38) with single-reduction-gear-coupled Curtis turbines.

Some commercial systems found efficiency in turbine installations combining reciprocating engines clutched to a shaft, for cruising or maneuvering at low speed. This was tried on four of the *Cassin*- and *O'Brien*-class destroyers, but not repeated. The destroyer solution was found with single-reduction-gear main turbines tested in the USS *Wadsworth* (DD-60) in 1915.

A parallel improvement in propulsion systems, introduced about this time, was segmentally-pivoted thrust-block bearings (simultaneously conceived by Kingsbury in America and Michel in England), still used in current systems to transmit the thrust of the propeller shaft to the ship.

Several variations of clutched and fixed-geared turbines were tried out in the six flush-deck *Caldwell*-class (forerunners to the wartime mass-produced "four-pipers"). Most of the latter 260 twin-screw ships got cross-compounded Parsons or Westinghouse geared turbines. A number of ships got Curtis high- and intermediate-pressure turbines, in tandem, coupled to one gear pinion, with the low-pressure turbine coupled to the other pinion. A large number of the ships had General Electric tandem high- and low-pressure installations, with a cruising turbine clutched to the main pinion of one shaft.

Initially, under the pressure of wartime production, a number of serious problems and many breakdowns were experienced. Inspection and survey systems gradually diagnosed various problems, including excessive tooth pressure, bad tooth shape, too-narrow gear faces, pinion and gear case deflection, and lack of axial and torsional flexibility. Although major difficulties were largely overcome by 1918, mechanical reduction gears continued to cause problems, due to the state of the art of gear design, metallurgy, and gear cutting.[33]

Turbo-electric Drive

Another solution proposed for achieving optimum simultaneous turbine and propeller speed was the use of turbo-electric drive. Turbo-electric drive was now strongly promoted by proponents such as W.L.R. Emmet, a Naval Academy-educated engineer with General Electric. Turbine-driven generators were proposed, delivering three-phase power to electric motors on the propeller shafts. The concept was carefully and very successfully tested in the collier *Jupiter* and the battleship *New Mexico* (BB-40). The system proved reliable, efficient, and flexible, but quite heavy (even though eliminating the need for astern turbines). Using General Electric turbines, the system was then installed in the five new *Tennessee*- and *Colorado*-class battleships, and the converted battle-cruiser carriers *Lexington* and *Saratoga*. (Eleven more planned turbo-electric capital ships were scrapped by the Washington Naval Treaty of 1922.)[34]

Auxiliary Machinery

The enhancement of propulsion systems was matched with a continuing stream of improvements to auxiliary systems, such as: seawater evaporators; boiler water-saving, exhaust-steam condensers; vacuum pumps; feedwater heaters; air compressors; and forced draft systems; all seeking to extract as much fuel heat as possible in the search for efficiency. Refrigeration, mandated by gunnery requirements for stable magazine temperatures (as well as American food standards), posed a considerable energy expenditure on U.S. Navy ships. Improved efficiency was sought with numerous changes. Damage control considerations ruled out ammonia refrigeration used ashore, and the choice oscillated between CO_2 and so-called "heavy-air" systems.[35]

Diesel Engines

United States submarine diesels, up to and including those of the single-boat M-1 class, launched in 1915, were unreliable and difficult to keep in operation for more than a few hours without casualty. Seeking tactically required surface speeds of about 14 knots, engines were installed that were rather too large for the engine spaces. Air systems for starting and reversing, lube-oil systems, and cooling systems were unnecessarily complicated. Engine accessibility was too difficult to allow proper maintenance. The high horsepower policy was changed with the N-boats of 1916 and 1917, with a reduction to about 600 horsepower. As a result, the engines in this class were satisfactorily reliable, which well compensated for the loss of about a knot in speed. Generally similar engines also were installed in the O-, R-, and S-boats of 1918-1919.

The war situation had tended to freeze in place the developing diesel propulsion technology. State-of-the-art systems were employed for the engines, but numerous minor improvements in equipment, practice, and efficiency resulted from the greatly increased wartime use.[36]

Heavy German Navy investment in diesel development (after Tirpitz's late but sufficiently timely inclusion of U-boats in the Kaiser's fleet) had paid off. It was widely recognized that the resulting efficiency and effectiveness of these engines gave the World War I German submarines the high-seas effectiveness possessed by no other Navy. (This undoubtedly led to the article on the effectiveness of German diesels in the *ASNE Journal* by a perceptive young submarine lieutenant named Chester W. Nimitz.) After the Armistice in 1918, some of the submarines seized by the Allies were operated by American submarine personnel and carefully studied and tested to evaluate their capabilities. It was ascertained that their engines delivered greater power than comparable American diesels and, despite more complicated auxiliary systems, provided adequate reliability. Accordingly, this type of engine was adopted and installed in several S-boats, as well as later classes.[37]

Aircraft Engines

Until the end of this period and the establishment of the Bureau of Aeronautics in July 1921, aircraft engines were a specific responsibility of the Bureau of Steam Engineering. They are discussed later in the NAVAL AVIATION section of this chapter.

New Bureau Name

With all the above general engineering developments in mind, it can be understood why the Navy Department saw fit to seek from Congress (always jealous of its legislative prerogatives in relation to the Bureaus') the authorization to change the name of the Bureau of Steam Engineering to the Bureau of Engineering. The simpler and more appropriate name was authorized on 4 June 1920.[38]

WAR SHIPPING

Background

Over the years, in peace and war, the predominant purchaser of ship tonnage in America has been the government (usually the Navy). American capital has not preferably been invested in ships, shipping, and shipyards—and the years leading up to 1914 were no exception. Foreign bottoms were used extensively to ship American cargoes. In 1915, typically, less than 10 percent of American foreign commerce was being moved in American-flag vessels. Except for the Navy, whose ships were being built in both navy and commercial shipyards, shipbuilding was a lesser industry. It is not surprising, therefore, that in 1915 the American shipbuilding industry produced only twenty-four new merchant ships of 105,000 displacement tons.[39]

The Shipping Emergency

American shippers first felt the effects of the European war as belligerents moved their bottoms out of normal peacetime routes, and into wartime service. Additionally, in 1915, the German U-boat campaign began to take its toll of available tonnage. By 1916, one out of four ships enroute to or from the United Kingdom or Continent was being sunk.[40] This was followed by increases in freight rates by factors of up to ten or twenty. As examples, the shipping rate of coal enroute to Argentina from the United States increased by a factor of 25 times per ton. Cotton enroute to England from the United States had its shipping rate increased from $0.25 per hundred pounds to $5.00 per hundred pounds. In the absence of American-flag bottoms to take up the trade, supply and demand inevitably ran up the price.[41]

American Shipbuilding Starts To Increase

With the increase in shipping needed, American shipbuilding began to perk up. British lines had to look beyond their own overloaded yards, and American firms ordered ships for a share of the increased trade. Deliveries, however, did not become substantial until 1916. Nevertheless, by July 1917, when President Wilson took over the industry and seized all steel merchant ships, there were 431 steel merchant ships under construction, totaling 3,068,431 deadweight tons.[42]

The Emergency Fleet Corporation

In 1916, with the increasing likelihood of the United States participating in the war, Congress passed the War Shipping Act of 1916, a program for the Federal government to acquire, construct, and operate sufficient shipping to ensure protection of national interests. The Emergency Fleet Corporation, an agency authorized by the Act, was given this authority. The task was the world's largest shipbuilding effort in history (only exceeded in World War II). It required building new shipyards, enlarging and renovating old yards, building housing areas, acquiring a wide range of materials, developing new labor resources, and coordinating the administration and financing of the largest industrial operation in the United States.[43]

Yards

In 1913, before the war, there were a total of forty-nine American yards with a total of 184 shipbuilding ways. By 1917, but prior to entry into war, the American shipbuilding industry had already grown to sixty-five yards, with 154 ways for steel ships and 102 ways for wooden ships (over 3,000 deadweight tons). The total peaked in 1919 with seventy-two shipyards with 461 ways for steel ships, plus eighty-seven for wooden seagoing vessels, and seven for concrete ships.[44]

Hog Island

A major project of the Emergency Shipbuilding Corporation was the building and operation of a mammoth ship assembly yard on a tract of land, with deep water on the Delaware River, south of Philadelphia. Its bold scheme called for building a shipyard many times larger than the largest in the country to assemble and mass-produce a simple, pre-fabricated, standardized freighter.[45] The 846-acre tract was chosen for its availability, price, and location as the nearest point to the steel mills and fabricating shops of Pennsylvania and the Middle West, and for its deepwater tidal channel. Its location near, but not in, a large industrial city gave access to a labor pool, some housing, an electrical power net, and three major railroads.[46]

The Hog Island project proceeded with commendable speed. The first keel was laid 5 months after the contract was signed for the fifty-way yard, and the first ship was launched less than 6 months after that; eventually a building rate of a ship every 5 days was achieved. The basic "Hog Islander," designed by Theodore Ferris, was a 7,500-ton cargo-ship, 450 feet long with a 58-foot beam. Her 2,500-horsepower steam turbine plant provided for 11.5 knots.[47] The war ended before any of the 122 "Hog Islanders" were completed (the last ship being completed January 1921), but many remained active in the merchant marine through World War II.[48]

Deliveries

After America's entry into the war in 1917, production of bottoms ultimately reached unprecedented heights. As many as 150 shipyards, employing some 300,000 laborers, succeeded in producing 391,000 tons of shipping in the peak month of October 1918, substantially more than in an entire year before the war. This was a truly astounding achievement, especially considering the slow start-up and given the almost nonexistent shipbuilding industry on which the country had to build.[49] Total American ship production during the war years was as follows:[50]

Fiscal Year	Ships	Gross Tons
1917	49	301,800
1918	410	2,570,000
1919	682	4,291,000
TOTALS	1,141	7,162,800

The U.S. Coast Guard

Establishment During World War I

The Coast Guard was established by an Act of Congress signed into law by President Wilson on 28 January 1915. The Act merged two services, already parts of the Treasury Department: the U.S. Life Saving Service and the U.S. Revenue Cutter Service. The new organization, the U.S. Coast Guard, enjoyed but the briefest breathing spell as a peacetime element of the Treasury Department. As provided under the establishing legislation, entry of the United States into hostilities, in April 1917, transferred the Coast Guard to the Navy Department.[51]

Ships of the Former Revenue Cutter Service

Not long before the amalgamation, the captain commandant of the Revenue Cutter Service, Ellsworth P. Bertholf (soon to be the first captain commandant of the Coast Guard), reported thirty-six cutters on hand, ranging from an ancient dating to 1863 to the newly completed sisters *Tahoma* and *Yamacraw*. They were iron or steel, mostly single-screw, vessels (some also rigged for sail). Exceptions were the wooden ships *Androscoggin*, the later famed (already venerable) *Bear*,[52] and the *Thetis*. The requirement to train cadets in engineering also led to the acquisition of a U.S. Naval Academy training gunboat, the *Bancroft*. Recommissioned as the *Itasca*, she provided training under sail and steam for all Coast Guard cadets and cadet engineers from 1907 until 1922.[53]

Small Craft

Lifesaving stations operated two kinds of craft, lifeboats and surfboats. Lifeboats were used at stations where they could be launched from specially constructed ways on sheltered inlets, bays, and rivers. Surfboats were employed where direct launching into a surf (and recovery, thereafter, back through the surf) was required—evolutions demanding both sound design and the nicest of seamanship. Lifeboats, mostly, were self-bailing, self-righting 34- and 36-footers with gasoline engines, although some pulling lifeboats were used. Surfboats were lighter weight, and included 25-foot, self-bailing, pulling boats; 26-foot, self-bailing powered boats; and a variety of "open" pulling boats that were not self-bailing. All were wooden construction and built at the Curtis Bay 'repair depot,' just south of Baltimore, Maryland. The Coast Guard undertook periodic design review by a Board on Life-Saving Appliances. In 1920, while expressing confidence in current designs, the board recommended more powerful engines and, when available, installation of radio-telephones.[54]

Wartime Tasks

Now, in addition to its regular peacetime responsibilities (only slightly reduced in wartime), the Coast Guard had to undertake new, widespread, additional activities. Its cutters were pressed into service immediately to bolster the Navy's inadequate anti-submarine escort strength, the cutter force required substantial enlargement, a supporting aviation service was to be provided for, Coast Guard crews were required for manning of Navy-operated troop transports, and appropriate communication resources were needed. The engineering implications of this expansion involved significant expansion of the scope and size of Coast Guard engineering activities, and posed a challenging administrative and technical program for the still-nascent Coast Guard. It involved the large-scale acquisition of ships, craft, parts, and equipment. It meant the recruitment and training of engineering personnel. It required the expansion of all maintenance and repair facilities.[55]

Engineer-in-Chief

The engineering activities of the Coast Guard were directed by the Engineer-in-Chief from his office in Coast Guard Headquarters in Washington, D.C., in conformance with the general instructions of the Coast Guard Commandant. The Engineer-in-Chief, Quincy B. Newman, had cognizance over acquisition of new construction, and supervised the construction of new machinery and boilers for the new cutters built during the war. Drawings and prints necessary to show designs for this machinery were prepared in the office of the Engineer-in-Chief.[56]

Superintendent of Construction and Repair

The Superintendent of Construction and Repair, on the staff of the Coast Guard Commandant, was charged with the design and construction of new vessels, as well as all repairs to "floating units and stations." Senior Captains H. M. Broadbent, Howard Emery, J. M. Moore, and William E. Reynolds (the second and next commandant) served in this post between 1917 and 1921. Among the more important work directed

by the superintendents was the repair and fitting out for overseas service of six cutters: the *Algonquin*, *Manning*, *Ossipee*, *Seneca*, *Tampa*, and *Yamacra*; repairs to many Coast Guard cutters (and naval ships) at the Coast Guard's Curtis Bay repair depot; the construction of the new cutters, *Manhattan*, *Kankakee*, and *Yocoha*; and the design and construction of five late-model cutters (the fifth, actually a large seagoing tug) whose construction after the war, on the West Coast, will be discussed later.[57]

The Coast Guard Depot

Formerly the Revenue Cutter Service repair depot, and at one time the site of its School of Instruction, the Coast Guard Depot, South Baltimore, at Arundel Cove on Curtis Bay, was busily engaged throughout the war in "repairing vessels and boats," under the direction of commandant, Captain of Engineers James M. Moore, and engineer officer Captain of Engineers C. G. Porcher. While thus in support of U.S. Navy repair activity, this effort (which extended 9 months past the Armistice) provided for the repair and furnishing of supplies (mostly repairs) to ninety-two Coast Guard, forty Navy, and four other ships, as well as the furnishing of supplies and boat repairs to 276 Coast Guard stations. To a limited extent the depot was used as a recruiting station and as a receiving station for the transfer and discharge of enlisted personnel.[58]

Coast Guard Aviation

The Coast Guard can, of course, claim to have been a part of earliest aviation history. Surfmen from the Kill Devil Lifeboat Station of the Lifesaving Service were part of the Wright Brothers' ground crew at Kitty Hawk.

In 1915, Lieutenants Elmer F. Stone and Norman B. Hall of the Norfolk-based cutter *Onandaga* persuaded Captain Benjamin M. Chiswell to grant permission to undertake what proved to be useful reconnaissance flights. They demonstrated the value of aircraft in locating distressed vessels and derelicts.[59] Reports of their success caused Captain Commandant Bertholf, surely a man of vision himself, to assign Stone and three others to the Navy flight school at Pensacola. Hall was assigned to study aeronautical engineering at the Curtiss Aeroplane and Motor Company. Hall, both technically gifted and energetic, went on to become an important pioneer aeronautical engineer as well as a pilot. Working with Curtiss H-10 flying boats, he developed early aeronavigational systems, assisted the Sperry Gyroscope Company with experimental radio and compass work, and, in the 1930s, designed and built a series of special rescue flying boats for Coast Guard use.[60]

During the war, the six Coast Guard aviators served competently as part of the naval air service, largely at anti-submarine patrols in the Curtiss H-1, 1L, and -2L single-engine flying boats. Several were assigned commands of air stations at Chatham, Massachusetts; Rockaway, New York; and even overseas at Ile Tudy, France.[61] Elmer Stone was chosen to be one of the pilots of the Navy's big NC-4 flying boats on the first transatlantic flight in 1919.

The return of the Coast Guard to the Treasury Department terminated aviation activity for several years. Only in March of 1920 was the first Coast Guard Air Station established at the abandoned naval air station at Morehead City, North Carolina, with six Curtiss HS-2Ls borrowed from the Navy. This lasted scarcely 2 years, when lack of appropriations closed down this activity, too.[62]

Post-War Cutter Construction

At war's end, the Coast Guard suffered from a serious shortage of cutters. Already short four in 1917, the service had lost three more vessels during the war. As noted earlier, designs had been prepared by Construction and Repair, and early in 1920, no longer pre-empted by wartime programs, a contract for four 240-footers and a 158-foot seagoing tug was awarded to the Union Construction Company of Oakland, California. The hull design, by Constructor Frederick A. Hunnewell was traditional—essentially, an enlarged version of the successful *Seneca*, with a plumb bow, counter stern, displacing 1,640 tons. Her compact superstructure provided good working space, amidships, on the main deck. The mast provided adequate antenna space for the extensive radio communications made available by wartime development, and a tall stately stack (old-fashioned looking today) provided increased natural draft. The propulsion plant was not traditional, and reflected the turbo-electric battleship systems pioneered by the Navy before and during the war. This approach gave the more efficient turbines the responsiveness and backing power that previously had made reciprocating engines mandatory for Coast Guard cutters for maneuvering at close quarters in bad sea conditions. The Navy's induction motors, although of sufficient power, unfortunately, were too large for cutters. Engineer-in-Chief Quincy B. Newman cannily found some compact General Electric synchronous motors of adequate power ashore, powering rolling mills. In trials, the power plant fell a little short of the designed 16 knots, and there was early trouble with steering engines, but this was a successful cutter class, with a reputation as "wonderful sea boats."[63]

ORDNANCE

Introduction

In 1914, as the epoch of this chapter began, the Bureau of Ordnance was enjoying what might be called its "golden years" of prestige and influence within the Naval establishment. The reasons were several but mostly stemmed from its role in relationship to battleship material. BuOrd, as it was called, was first of all concerned with the development and supply of all guns, but most especially the big guns, 12-, 14-, and soon 16-inch turret guns with which the battle line was expected to determine the outcome of any naval engagement. Secondly, BuOrd also had cognizance over the determination and acquisition of the heavy armor vital to our battleships' ability to withstand any adversary's big guns. Thirdly, the advanced technology of these and other aspects of ordnance had drawn a professionally committed group of specialist officers and civil servants, highly qualified in the various aspects of the science and engineering involved. They were the technological high priests of the Navy, and they presided over material whose size and performance was awe-inspiring to the Navy and citizens, alike. That this material involved "big-budget" items further contributed to the status of BuOrd, within the Navy, within the influential and contract-hungry American steel industry (also in its hey-day), as well as within the Congress, (ever-sensitive to association of military and financial power).[64]

The Big Guns

The battleship big guns were designed by the officer and civilian ordnance engineers of BuOrd, in continuous consultation and coordination with the admirals of the General Board, the Secretary of the Navy, the fleet, and appropriate bureaus. The guns were fabricated at the Naval Gun Factory on the Annacostia River in Washington, D.C. Starting with rough forgings from the steel industry for gun tubes, breech blocks, and other components, the Gun Factory's immense lathes, planers, and other special machine tools were used to meticulously shape the raw stock to the finest of fractional tolerances. Most especially this giant-scale Swiss-watch machining was needed in shrink-fitting the carefully rifled barrel liners into their built-up reinforcing tubes (after the tubes had been suitably expanded with hours of heat-soaking in monster furnaces).[65]

In 1914, the *Texas*-class battleships introduced the 14in/45 gun into the U.S. fleet, using the twin-gun turret concept employed since 1900. These guns fired a 1,400-pound armor-piercing projectile to a maximum range of 21,000 yards.[66] (It is to be noted that, with a maximum elevation of 15 degrees, these guns sought to penetrate heavy, vertical, side armor with flat trajectory and high velocity, as did their predecessor 12-inchers. The shift to heavier caliber was prompted by the need to increase kinetic penetration without increasing muzzle velocity, which had reached a limit for maximum acceptable bore erosion.)[67] An improved, three-gun turret was introduced early in 1916, for the two lower turrets in the *Nevada* class, and was used subsequently for all four turrets in the *Pennsylvania* class of late 1917.[68] Another gun improvement was introduced next in the *New Mexico* class of 1918, by an increase in length of the 14-inch gun to 50 calibers. This length, together with an appropriately enlarged propellant combustion chamber, increased the maximum range to 25,000 yards.[69] This gun was used again for the *Tennessee* class in 1920.[70] This period's ultimate increase in U.S. naval gun caliber was introduced with the *Maryland* class of 1921, which was equipped with eight 16in/45 guns in four twin turrets. Improved turret design providing 30-degree gun elevation enabled this gun to fire its 2,240-pound armor-piercing projectile to 35,000 yards, an extreme range made useful only with the advent of aircraft spotting and improved fire control.[71] A 16in/50 was designed during this period for the *South Dakota* class that was canceled as a consequence of the Washington Naval Treaty of 1922. Accordingly, this gun never went to sea, but twenty were transferred to the Army Coast Artillery and were installed in batteries in Panama, Hawaii, and California.[72] An 18in/48 gun design started in 1916, halted by the Washington Naval Treaty, and subsequently completed as a 16in/56 ballistics-test weapon, was the Navy's largest gun of this period.[73]

Another big gun development of BuOrd was the design and development of railway gun mounts for the 14in/50 naval gun for use in France against German Army targets. Working in conjunction with the Baldwin Locomotive Works, the project provided twelve single-gun batteries, eight of which reached France before war's end. Five naval gun teams provided useful, previously unavailable, long-range interdiction of rail centers vital to German logistics during final months of the war. The project was marked by remarkably fast design and coordination of fabrication (under 10 months from design initiation to first shot in action).[74]

It is of passing interest that the only big American naval guns to be fired in earnest, at sea, in World War I, were some 14in/45s being built by Bethlehem Steel Corporation for a Turkish battleship under construction in Germany when the war broke out. It was a package deal, complete with twin-gun turrets, armored barbettes, and ammunition. But England's blockade of Germany made delivery impossible, and Bethlehem was not getting paid. Its president, steel magnate (and ace marketeer) Charles Schwab soon went to England to see First Lord of the Admiralty Winston Churchill and First Sea Lord Jackie Fisher. The rest is history. Churchill and Fisher had a scheme for shallow-draft, heavy-gun vessels for possible operations in Belgian and Baltic coastal shallows, a deal was closed, and each of the 14-inch gun turrets became the main battery of a bombardment monitor. Pleased, the Admiralty gave the ships the fine American names of *Admiral Farragut, General Grant, Robert E. Lee,* and *Stonewall*

Jackson. The American ambassador in London, however, representing a sternly nonbelligerent administration, was apparently horrified and hastily requested changes. Accordingly, before the monitors deployed to bombard at Gallipoli, the names of properly venerable British generals were substituted.[75]

Lesser Guns

BuOrd also was heavily occupied in supplying a variety of smaller caliber guns for merchant ships, escorts, destroyers, and fleet auxiliaries. Initially, merchant ships were armed from the Navy's small inventory of some 376 weapons not in use, and this source was quickly used up. Like any gun installation, the work required coordination with the Bureau of Construction and Repair, which undertook deck and bulkhead reinforcement, and Steam Engineering, which provided necessary electrical and command telephone wiring. In relation to the demand for merchant ship arming, the output of smaller caliber guns by the Naval Gun Factory in Washington, D.C. was quite inadequate and, although pushed to the limit, produced only a little over 300 guns and mounts during the war. (Its primary task was the painstaking and slow building of the big battleship guns described above, and it produced thirty of the giants during this period.) The next source tapped for merchant guns was the fleet, where, during the first year of the war, almost 450 secondary battery guns were stripped from "less advantageous locations" on battleships and cruisers. Meanwhile, industrial contracts had been let by BuOrd for the needed weapons. American industry responded effectively and, between 6 April 1917 and war's end, it delivered 2,500 smaller caliber naval guns (37mm to 6-inch).[76]

'Radial expansion' was an important gun barrel fabrication method contributed to BuOrd during the war by A. H. Emory, a Connecticut engineer, and Professor P. L. Bridgeman of Harvard University. It used the interesting technique of sealing a gun tube and expanding it slightly, hydraulically. This was done so the smaller radius inner layers were stressed slightly beyond their elastic limit, to remain slightly enlarged. The outer layers were designed to be precisely large enough to remain within elastic limits during the expansion. With release of hydraulic pressure, the outer layers contracted to grip the now-enlarged inner layers like shrunk-on reinforcing bands, but without any separate fabrication, heating, forcing, and fitting—for great cost-saving.[77]

Fire Control

Fire control, as understood in the U.S. Navy, concerns controlling firing weapons (such as guns and torpedoes) so as to hit the desired target. During the era of this chapter, the important gunnery advance of centralized gunfire control came of age. The world's navies ascertained the great improvement in accuracy, rates of fire, range, and the ultimate pay-off, hits, which were to be gained from salvo main battery gunfire directed from a single control station located advantageously aloft. The U.S. Navy had been moving in the direction of centralized fire control for a number of years. Before the war, BuOrd understood the concept of director fire, but did not fully recognize its advantages.[78] It seems to have entered the U.S. Navy via interaction with Elmer Sperry and his gyrocompass, which provided a reference bearing (true North) in relation to which gun train could be directed. In addition, Sperry's drive system, which synchronized his 'gyro repeaters' to their master gyro, suggested similar elecrical means of transmitting any target or gun train angle required. In the gunnery climate generated by such progressives as Bradley Fiske and William Sims, Sperry coordinated with technically oriented officers, and by 1914 had contrived a system for observing and transmitting target bearing.[79] By 1916, Sperry's system included a telescopic target-bearing transmitter for the fore-top, repeater indicators for the plotting room, as well as train transmitters and indicators for the plot and the turrets. Electrical and automatic, it permitted target bearings selected by a director well above the smoke and spray of naval battle to be sent to the plotting room for addition of deflection and other corrections so as to generate correct turret train. This done, it further provided for transmission of turret train to follow-the-pointer dials at the turret pointers station, and automatic transmission of turret train back to plot so that a gunnery officer in plot could order fire. By 1920 such Sperry fire control systems had been instal-led on thirty American capital ships.[80]

The system also provided for a "battle tracer" in plot that combined electrical inputs of own ship's course and speed, with target bearing and rangefinder range, in an analog computer. It plotted the output on a chart so as to provide a simulation of the relative tracks and positions of both own ship and the target. From this, pre-diction of advanced target range and bearing at the moment of fall of shot could be made. But, although BuOrd took delivery of over twenty battle tracers, the system does not appear to have fulfilled the Navy's needs.[81] BuOrd states that "early in 1916 reports from abroad indicated the necessity of maintaining sight-bar range by means other than spotting" (the battle of Jutland occurred in May 1916). The problem was dis-cussed with Mr. Hannibal C. Ford, a young col-league of Sperry's who had started his own firm, the Ford Instrument Company, in 1914. The result was the delivery of the Ford range keeper Mark I a year later. (This was the first of a line of fire control systems, culminating in the MK 37 system that served the fleet so effectively in World War II.)[82]

BuOrd also called on Ford, in 1918, to man-ufacture a follow-the-pointer system for main battery gun elevation similar to Sperry's target train follow-the-pointer system. Its synchronous "master" and "slave" motors were an improve-ment over the earlier stepping motors, which could be knocked out of phase on occasion by gunfire shock. The new system was installed first in the New Mexico and, subsequently, in all major ships.[83]

British fire control information became avail-able when America entered the war. It was quickly concluded that our capital ships needed follow-the-pointer train and elevation control for their secondary battery guns. The British Vickers system was adopted and built in the United States. Directors and gun attachments were fabri-cated at the New York Navy Yard; synchronous elevation and train data transmission motors were made by the Burke Electric Company of Erie, Pennsylvania; and synchronous receiver and repeater motors (for plotting room and conning tower) were manufactured by Recording & Computing Machine Company of Dayton, Ohio.[84]

A substantially increased amount of this mate-rial had to be acquired by BuOrd as a result of the new developments and because of the war-time naval expansion. It was substantial in vari-eties as well as total numbers. The material in-cluded directorscopes for installation in spotting stations high in ships' structures; a variety of range finders (an area of wartime contribution by Nobel laureate Albert Michelson); periscopes; range receivers, plotting boards, and range keepers for use in gunfire plotting rooms; and numerous types of electrical range and bearing transmitters used to convey information to the elements of a ship's gunnery system.[85]

Torpedoes

In April 1917, the Navy had an inventory of 2,096 torpedoes, of which a little over 1,000 were assigned to ships. The Naval Torpedo Sta-tion at Newport, Rhode Island, was responsible for overhaul, repair, and test. Reserve torpedoes were stored ashore on the East and West Coasts, in the Canal Zone, and in the Philippines. BuOrd's main source of torpedoes had long been the E. W. Bliss Company in south Brooklyn, New York, producing what was known as the Bliss-Leavitt alcohol-fuel steam torpedo. In what can be seen as a "sweetheart contract," Bliss, with over 2,000 torpedoes on order in April 1917, agreed to boost production from some 20 to 300 torpedoes a month. For this, Bliss got a $2,000,000 loan at 4 percent interest to cover a needed 40 percent expansion of their plant. By the summer of 1918, Bliss was falling far behind on torpedo deliveries (and achieved only a maximum of 150 a month in December 1918). This led the Navy to establish its own plant on the Potomac River at Alexandria, Virginia. Al-though conceived as a war measure, the plant was not completed until after the war, and well served the Navy's needs through World War II.[86]

Mines

A major achievement of BuOrd during the war was conceiving the plan for the so-called North-ern Barrage, and developing the necessary min-ing material. This was a large-scale, deep-sea mine blockade to deny U-boats the northern exit of the North Sea. BuOrd designed the 1,400-pound Mark VI mine with 300 pounds of TNT for the task, incorporating it with the British automatic sinker anchor.[87] The Mark VI was actuated by the bimetallic coupling of the mine's copper antenna with the steel hull of a ship (the suggestion of a Massachusetts electrician, see RESEARCH AND DEVELOPMENT). The antenna system very much widened the danger zone of the mine, compared with contact-horn actuation. This made the Barrage project feasible, within the resources available. The Barrage, nevertheless, required the planting of 70,263 mines between the Orkney Islands and Norway. Production amounted to 125,000 mines, of which 85,000 were shipped and assembled overseas.[88]

Depth Charges

BuOrd undertook development of depth charges prior to actual hostilities, shortly after the opening of unrestricted submarine warfare by Germany. The Mark I depth charge, with an inadequate 50-pound explosive charge and a primitive line and buoy actuator, was soon replaced by a Mark II, an improvement of a 300-pound explosive-charge British model. It featured a safer, more reliable hydrostatic firing element designed at the Newport torpedo station by BuOrd's mines and explosives engineer, C. T. Minkler. The Bureau contracted for 10,000 of the Mark II, and subsequently contracted for 20,000 of a Mark III with maximum depth setting improved from 200 to 300 feet. The final development was a Mark IV with a 600-pound TNT explosive charge. In all, 72,000 depth charges were contracted for during the war, from six principal contractors.[89]

Besides discharge from anti-submarine warfare vessels by roll-off release from stern-mounted racks, depth charges also were projected athwartship from deck-mounted mortars. BuOrd engineers developed a very successful "Y-gun," a double-barreled version of the standard British depth charge mortar, whose diverging barrels gave the weapon its name.[90]

NAVAL AVIATION

Promise Unfulfilled

As the new Secretary of the Navy, Josephus Daniels spoke the right words about naval aviation. Hardly in office, he announced early in January 1914 that, "the science of aerial naviga-

tion has reached that point where aircraft must form a large part of our naval force for offensive and defensive operations."[91] But alas, the Secretary lacked the executive insight and organizational drive to match his journalistic gift for phrase. To be sure, in contrast to the dedication and drive of the aviation pioneers, inaction was also due substantially to senior echelon apathy to the potential of naval aircraft. Accordingly, in 1917, the Navy entered the war with only 55 aircraft and under 300 air personnel. In comparison, air operations on the Western Front were by then large-scale. Heavy bombers crossed the Channel, and advanced model Fokker, Sopwith, and SPAD fighters were in use.[92]

Early State of the Art

In 1914, naval aeronautics consisted of less than a dozen "pushers"—several primitive, single-seat, open-frame Curtiss A-type pontoon hydroplanes (later designated AH), and a few two-place Curtiss Model F flying-boats. These aircraft were operated at the training command at Pensacola, Florida. There, the pioneer pilots taught themselves and each other to master the new machines and techniques of flight and tactics.[93]

Administrative Apathy

Early in 1914, the foresighted and gifted Admiral Bradley Fiske took "naval aeronautics" out from under an indifferent Bureau of Navigation. He sought to provide for its growth as the Office of Aeronautics under the aegis of his Division of Operations. However, already locked in a losing battle to get pacifist Secretary Daniels to prepare the Navy for entry into World War I, Fiske had inadequate influence and time to effectively boost naval aviation. After Fiske's exile to the Naval War College, Admiral William S. Benson, the new Chief of Naval Operations established the outlook for aviation by replacing Fiske's hand-picked Director, the able Captain Mark L. Bristol, with a lieutenant (j.g.), and downgraded the position to Officer in Charge.[94]

There appeared to be no guiding policy issuing from Washington directing the pursuance and development of naval aviation doctrine or the acquisition of aircraft and material to fulfill some proposed doctrine. This promising new area of warfare, so filled with potential to be exploited by a well-directed, overall Navy program, was more to be noted for what might have been. Once the U-boat war forced the mossbacks to see a need for aeronautics, the Navy's engineering Bureaus responded with feats of expansion and organization needed for the coordination and acquisition of aviation material.[95] The start, however, was too late, and logistics pipelines started to flow only shortly before the Armistice. It was to be in marked contrast with, say, the Navy's production and planting of the North Sea mine barrage, the "four-piper" destroyer program, or the large scale shipping and convoy of troops and supplies to Europe. It was an object lesson in lack of timely response to a need, with clear-cut centralized authority and proper allocation of appropriate resources. It was not lost on the bright young aristocratic assistant secretary of the Navy, Franklin D. Roosevelt, who did what he could (and learned well for the future).[96]

Technical Arrangements

Technical circumstances were made somewhat more propitious for naval aviation when, in 1914, the gifted naval architect and engineer, David W. Taylor, a strong supporter of naval aviation, was promoted to rear admiral and became Chief of the Bureau of Construction and Repair.[97] Taylor had long provided important technical support in promoting aerodynamic research in the Navy, and in March 1914, a wind tunnel and aeronautical laboratory that Admiral Taylor had helped bring into existence, commenced operation at the Washington Navy Yard.[98] He recalled Naval Constructor Jerome C. Hunsaker (on loan establishing aerodynamics studies at M.I.T.) to be head of his new "Aircraft Division." Subsequently, Naval Constructors Holden C. Richardson, and G. C. Westervelt were added to his team, and later Dr. A. F. Zahm, the distinguished lead scientist at Curtiss was recruited.[99] The Secretary of the Navy's General Order Number No. 41 had assigned material responsibilities for aviation in keeping with Bureau responsibility for ships. The Bureau of Construction and Repair supervised the design and building of aircraft, while the Bureau of Steam Engineering had power plants, electricity, and radios.[100] All Navy weapons, including the few being experimented with by the aviators, continued to come from the Bureau of Ordnance.

The Bureau of Steam Engineering's responsibility for acquisition of aircraft power plants included control of design and development, inspection, expediting of production, and supervision of service operation and maintenance. As early as 1914, Captain Bristol had suggested that the Bureau designate an aircraft engine specialist. In April 1915, Lieutenant Warren G. Child was so detailed and became the Bureau's expert. He set up shop in the Washington Navy Yard, with an aircraft power plant laboratory whose test facilities were technically comparable to the wind tunnel. It was ready and available for the engine tests and competitions to come.[101] Subsequently, in 1916, the Bureau of Construction and Repair, in effect, was made the lead bureau for overall aircraft development and procurement.[102] In that same year, Hunsaker's team completed the design, construction, and preliminary tests of a 6,000-pound gross weight aircraft. It provided experience and information particularly of value for acquisition of aircraft and related material.[103] All these bureau arrangements were an important foundation on which to expand the contracting of aircraft material once America entered the war. These bureaus already had the procedures, experience, and trained personnel familiar with the acquisition of ships and ship material. All this was generally applicable to aircraft, notwithstanding the need to develop knowledge and expertise to deal with aircraft material, per se.

Closer Approach To War

The increasing importance of air operations in the European war could not go unnoticed. Despite Navy inertia, certain Congressional actions proved to have useful long-term results for naval aviation. Recognizing the compelling need for better coordination, not only within the Navy, but also to meet common needs with Army aviation, the Naval Appropriations Act of 1915 provided for a National Advisory Committee for Aeronautics (NACA, the predecessor of the NASA of today) to coordinate military, naval, and other aeronautics. In 1916, Congress virtually forced an aviation budget of $3,500,000 on Secretary Daniels and CNO Benson who wanted only $2,000,000. The budget resulted in a contract for sixty training aircraft.[104] (The trainer was the Navy N-9 floatplane version of the Curtiss JN "Jenny" trainer, designed by B. Douglas Thomas, a Sopwith designer who had been acquired in a hurry by Curtiss to meet U.S. Army and British requirements for a tractor-type trainer.)[105]

Operational Aircraft

When, in April 1917, the United States felt compelled to enter the war against Germany, British and French missions to Washington quickly made clear that the German U-boat campaign threatened to strangle the sea lanes of the theater of war. Having failed to expand its escort fleet, the Navy saw flying boats patrolling key areas as an important part of the solution, and set about acquiring the necessary aircraft, personnel, bases, and other material.[106]

The new aircraft requirements included additional contracts for the Curtiss trainers mentioned earlier. Curtiss built N-9s for the Navy, and the N-9 remained in service as late as 1926. Another model acquired early by the Navy was the Curtiss R series, whose basic design was a more powerful enlargement of the J and N models.[107] It was also used by the U.S. Army and the Royal Naval Air Service, as well as by the U.S. Marines, who used it for anti-submarine warfare patrols in the Azores. After the war, it was used for early experiments with aircraft-launched torpedoes.[108]

Operational requirements for both a long-range, twin-engine, flying boat, and a smaller, short-range, coastal, single-engine boat were determined. Both needs were fulfilled by biplane boats with wood laminate hulls, based on a prewar Curtiss "America" design being sold to and used successfully by the British as the Model H. Production was ordered for an improved "America" designated the H-12, and for the single-engine Curtiss (essentially the Model H scaled down) called the HS-1 (for "H, single-engine"). In October 1917, the HS-1 was used to successfully test America's newly and rapidly developed Liberty engine. The 12-cylinder Liberty's 400 horsepower doubled that delivered by the Curtiss V-X-X engines originally selected for both boats. As a result, the single-engine model was reconfigured for the Liberty as the HS-1L (later, the HS-2L, when 12 feet of wing were added to carry heavier depth bombs). Requirements exceeded Curtiss's production capacity and additional contracts were spread amongst Standard Aircraft of Elizabeth, New Jersey; LWF of College Point, New York; Gallaudet of Greenwich, Connecticut; Boeing of Seattle, Washington; and Loughead (now Lockheed) of Santa Barbara, California. Over 1,100 were built, including 25 at the Naval Aircraft Factory, Philadelphia, Pennsylvania. To accommodate their twin-engine design for Liberty engines, the Navy chose the H-16, an improved H-12 being shipped by Curtiss to the British, as well as a British-improved-hull model designated the F-5L.[109]

Also in 1917, Rear Admiral D. W. Taylor posed the requirement for an even larger flying boat, capable of transatlantic self-delivery, to help defeat the U-boat campaign.[110] This led to the Navy-Curtiss jointly developed NC boats. The multi-engined biplane was a monster for its time (28,000 pounds, 126-foot wingspan). It was too late for the war, but achieved a place in the historical record book by making the first transatlantic flight in 1919.[111]

One last aircraft acquired by the Navy in quantity was the American-built version of the British DH-4 single-engined, two-man bomber. This plane was needed for French-based Marine and Navy squadrons of the Northern Bombing Group to attack the U-boat menace at its source, by bombing submarine pens in Belgium. Some fifty-one DH-4s were transferred from the Army Air Service, but less than half actually arrived in France in time to be used, although with traditional "requisitioning skill" the Marines managed to augment their share. They arranged trade-off of surplus Liberty engines to local British squadrons for a substantial number of Liberty-equipped DH-9As.[112]

Engine Production

In conjunction with the Army Air Service, the Navy participated in engine policy decisions of the Aircraft Production Board (subsequently, Aircraft Board). The Navy's major program for operational aircraft power plants was based on the well-known war-emergency-developed Liberty engine (the name suggested by Admiral D. W. Taylor pursuant to his responsibilities as a

U.S. Navy member of the Aircraft Construction Board).[113]. This engine was designed and produced as a result of the Board's determination, a month after America's war entry, that there was no American aircraft engine of sufficient power and proven reliability for war service. The Liberty was conceived and designed to embody the best features of known engines, and be applicable to American mass production. Its conception and design are a tribute to the genius of E. J. Hall and J. G. Vincent, Aircraft Production Board volunteers from the auto industry. Working around the clock in a suite in Washington, D.C.'s historic Willard Hotel, Hall and Vincent produced the design that led to the delivery of an eight-cylinder prototype in little more than a month (29 May to 3 July 1917). Then, twelve-cylinder prototypes were built and tested. Once the twelve-cylinder engine prototype was approved, contracts were let with Packard, Lincoln, Ford, General Motors, Nordyke, and Marmon; by war's end, production totaled 20,478 engines. The Navy ordered approximately 4,370 Liberty engines to be produced by the Packard Auto Company, almost all of which were delivered.[114] The Liberty engine was widely used in Navy aircraft, during the wartime period and well into the 20s, thereafter. Its reliability and efficiency contributed significantly to the development of naval aircraft engineering and operations, as the aviation pioneers continued to demonstrate the usefulness and importance of this new element of sea power.[115]

Foreign Aircraft

The Navy used French and Italian flying boats primarily for flying patrols from bases in the respective countries, before domestic production made American aircraft available. French coastal patrols were initiated using thirty-four French Tellier boats, augmented subsequently by fifty-six Donnet-Denhauts, a dozen Levy-Lepen HB-2s, and a few Franco-British Aviation FBA Type H boats. In Italy, Macchi M.5 flying boat fighters and French Hanriot HD-1 float fighters were used as bomber escorts, along with Macchi M.8 light bomber flying boats, and a few Italian-manufactured FBA Type H boats. The British furnished fifty-four of the previously mentioned D.H.9As to the Northern Bombing Group, which also acquired nineteen of the large (77-foot wing-span) Italian Caproni Ca-44 twin-fuselage night bombers. At the war's end, the Navy acquired a variety of the more renowned foreign fighters, both for operational use and technical exploitation. These included British S.E.5As and Sopwith Camels, and the French Nieuport 28, used for operations from launch platforms on battleship forward turrets. And mention should be made of six Fokker D.VIIs (considered by many to be the best fighter of either side) transferred to the Navy for Marine Corps use at Quantico, Virginia.[116]

Lighter-Than-Air Aviation

The Navy's acquisition of its first airship, in early 1917, was not auspicious. The nonrigid, twin-engined DN-1 succumbed to the low-bidder weaknesses of its inexperienced builder, Connecticut Aircraft Company. It was underpowered, overweight, and, requiring removal of an engine even to become airborne, made but three flights.[117]

The Navy's next airship was the nonrigid B-series acquired in 1917 and 1918, and designed on the basis of limited pre-alliance information from England. Ten were built by Goodyear, five by Goodrich, and two by Connecticut Aircraft. Its control car was a slightly modified two-place airplane fuselage, suspended beneath an 80,000-cubic-foot envelope, 160 feet long and 35 feet in diameter. Its 100-horsepower Curtiss OXX-2 engine and tractor-mounted propeller achieved a speed of 39 knots.

The following C-series, which first flew in September 1918, was highly successful in coastal and convoy patrols, and strongly influenced design of subsequent Navy nonrigids. It had an 181,000-cubic-foot envelope, 192 feet long and 42 feet in diameter. Two 200-horsepower Hall-Scott engines, mounted on opposite sides of the boatlike four-man control car, achieved a speed of almost 41 knots, with 10 hours endurance. In 1921, the C-7 became the world's first airship to use inert helium gas in place of highly flammable (if more buoyant) hydrogen. Six C-series were built by Goodyear, four by Goodrich. The D-series was a slight larger refinement of the C-series, with external fuel tanks. Two 120-horsepower Union engines drove the Ds at 48 knots, with 12 hours endurance.

In 1919, the Navy also acquired the two-place

E-1 and the three-place F-1, both built as commercial airships. They both had 95,000-cubic-foot envelopes, 162 feet long and 33 feet in diameter. Their 150-horsepower pusher engines gave a speed of 48 knots.

In addition to domestic manufactures, about a dozen British and French nonrigid airships were acquired during the war for overseas anti-submarine patrols in European waters. Arrangements to purchase the new British dirigible R-38 in 1921 terminated when she exploded over the River Humber, killing her British crew and a number of U.S. Navy personnel who were in training.[118]

Early Post-War Naval Aircraft

Shortly after the war, the Navy made two rather substantial aircraft purchases of fighters, a type of aircraft little used until then. One contract commenced what was to be a long relationship with the Chance Vought Corporation. The aircraft were the VE-7, of which a total of 129 were purchased, as well as twenty-one VE-9s, a virtually identical model, configured as a float plane for launch from battleships and cruisers. The Navy manufactured twenty-one of the contract aircraft at the Naval Aircraft Factory in Philadelphia, presumably to maintain expertise in manufacture and costs. The Navy also purchased fifty-five models of another fighter, the Loening M-8 series, shortly after the war. The M-8 was a rather unique two-place monoplane design, whose wing was attached at the upper side of the fuselage.[119]

Further major purchases of naval aircraft, thereafter, were made by the new Bureau of Aeronautics, established by Congress on 12 July 1921, as the era set forth by this chapter ended.[120]

RESEARCH AND DEVELOPMENT

Background

Entering this period, the Navy was already well-committed to engineering research and development as a part of the activities of three Bureaus.[121] The Bureau of Steam Engineering directed the Naval Engineering Experiment Station at Annapolis, Maryland; the Naval Boiler Laboratory at the Philadelphia Navy Yard; and the Radio Telegraphic Laboratory at the U.S.

Bureau of Standards in Washington, D.C. The Bureau of Construction and Repair had cognizance over the Model Basin and an aeronautical wind tunnel at the Washington Navy Yard (both a consequence of the engineering genius, organization skill, and farsightedness of David W. Taylor, now rear admiral and Chief of the Bureau). The Bureau of Ordnance was extensively engaged in research in connection with the development of ordnance at the Gun Factory at Washington, D.C. and the proving grounds at Dahlgren, Virginia; explosives at the Naval Propellant Plant at Indian Head, Maryland; and torpedoes at the Naval Torpedo Station at Newport, Rhode Island.[122]

Influence of World War I

It could be stated that research and development as a concept achieved another major plateau during World War I. It seems to have come about for several reasons. Partially, it was a continuation (under pressure of increased wartime demand for defense technology) of the research and development that had sprung up in America's major industries and campuses during the last quarter of the nineteenth century. It also seems to have been a consequence of the newspaperman awareness Secretary Daniels had of the achievements and potential of American technology—in the war's emergency he set about to put it to work. Less purely, Daniels's initiative also seems to have shown earmarks of publicity seized on to help obscure the absence of war-readiness programs that pacifist Daniels had denied his admirals. He astutely chose Thomas Edison, the revered inventor-entrepreneur to head up this program as Chairman of what was at first called the Naval Advisory Board. Edison had already told the press that

> . . . the Government should maintain a great research laboratory jointly under military and naval and civilian control . . . increasing possibilities of . . . all the techniques of military and naval progression[123]

and the fame of the "Wizard of Menlo Park" would ensure favorable response. The members recruited, and their affiliations, constituted a "Who's Who" of American technology; but, in the end, the effort was frittered away with a minimum contribution to the prosecution of the war. Secretary Daniels lacked both the technical insight and the administrative drive to give it success by directing coordination with the staid Bureaus. The Bureaus, in turn, insisted that the Board's name be changed to reflect what they saw as its proper status: Naval Consulting Board. They saw little need for help from well-publicized landlubbers, however expert. Edison, rather soundly, had his eye set on a Navy version of his Menlo Park laboratory, for brute-force application of technology to solution of the Navy's wartime problems. Members of the Board, not entirely above self-interest, agreed with the need for the lab, but felt that it should be for research, not development, and it should not be a rival to those of industry.[124] Thus, the Board's success was contribution to the future—the founding of the Naval Research Laboratory, on which work began at the end of 1920.[125]

Bureau of Steam Engineering

For the most part, the Engineering Experiment Station, across the Severn River from the U.S. Naval Academy in Annapolis, Maryland, before and during the war, continued in its role of testing equipment and products for use by the U.S. Navy. Test work was charged to proper appropriation, or against a "special deposit" by a manufacturer.[126] Basic investigation and innovation tended to be a fortuitous and incidental by-product of the main testing task.[127] Wartime saw the naval staff reduced by the requirements for officers at sea. Commanding officer Captain Thomas W. Kincaid, nevertheless, succeeded in building his staff of 112 to 168 by war's end.[128] The growth included participating in the World War I expansion in job opportunities for women (particularly as laboratory assistants), but the Navy's progress on this issue did not extend to approving Kincaid's request for female chauffeurs.[129]

As early as 1914, the Vera Cruz incident had closed down the Naval Boiler Laboratory at Philadelphia when commanding officer Lieutenant Commander J. J. Hyland and other officer personnel were ordered to sea. Ten months later, in February 1915, it was reopened under LTJG A. M. Penn (who better, in Philadelphia). Under the pressures of wartime, development of fuel oil equipment slowed, and the plant was occupied

with fuel oil testing, work in connection with new ships, and the training of personnel.[130]

At the Navy Radio Research Laboratory, the director of the Bureau of Standards himself, Dr. L. W. Austin, directed vigorous pursuit of a variety of technical improvements in radio equipment and operation in support of the tremendously expanded wartime Navy radio program.[131] In addition, the Radio Test Shop that was set up at the Washington Navy Yard was increasingly engaged in developing radio procedure, acting as a clearinghouse for new ideas and equipment, and inspecting and testing all new Navy receivers and small transmitters. Both the Lab and the Shop were the first Navy activities to take advantage of the opportunity to move to the new Naval Research Laboratory in 1923.[132]

The Bureau of Steam Engineering was also heavily involved in submarine sound detection effort in conjunction with the National Research Council. What was called the Naval Experimental Station was set up at Ft. Trumbull, near New London, Connecticut.[133] Early it was headed by Nobel laureate Albert A. Michelson, who had loyally returned to the Navy that had educated him. He left the University of Chicago where, as head of the Physics department, he was already working on optical rangefinder research for the Bureau of Ordnance.[134] At Ft. Trumbull, he concluded that the nine other physicists on hand were better qualified for this work than he, and returned to Bureau of Ordnance in Washington to rejoin the rangefinder project. Ft. Trumbull continued to grow, and its work force designed and engineered several early, primitive, sound detection devices, working with target submarines from the base at New London.[135]

The Bureau of Construction and Repair

With D. W. Taylor's promotion to rear admiral and Chief of the Bureau,[136] his protege and colleague at the Model Basin at the Washington Navy Yard, William McEntee, strove to continue the programs Taylor had evolved when he took charge of the new basin.[137] In addition, the establishment was kept extremely busy testing the designs for the various classes of ships that were developed for the Navy's expanded wartime program of battleships, cruisers, submarines, destroyers, and other vessels.[138] In addition, there was an unprecedented amount of testing-for-fee of commercial designs. An experimental wave-maker was developed to test rough water qualities, and a dynamometer system was installed to measure forces developed by self-propelled models.[139] Rolling experiments were instituted, which resulted in placing bilge keels on several naval vessels, most notably the aircraft carrier *Langley* (conversion of the ex-collier *Jupiter*.)[140]

With Admiral Taylor now Bureau chief, McEntee was able to continue the interest and support they both had devoted to aeronautical work.[141] For a number of years, Taylor had worked to establish a major role for the Model Basin in the new field. He had worked for, planned, and built the world's first navy wind tunnel at the Washington Navy Yard during the period 1912-14. Taylor also must be credited with being able to recruit men of the caliber he caused to join McEntee.[142] They included such pioneers of aeronautical engineering as Dr. Alfred Zahm, whose aerodynamics Ph.D. from Johns Hopkins predated Kitty Hawk by 5 years, who patented the airplane control "stick" in 1893, and who built the first wind tunnel in the United States in 1893; Holden C. Richardson, Naval Aviator #13, a 1901 Annapolis graduate, who entered the aerodynamics field via the post-graduate naval architecture studies at MIT; and Jerome C. Hunsaker, a 1912 naval officer graduate of the naval architecture and marine engineering program at MIT, chosen to set up that institution's instruction in the theory and design of aeroplanes (in the process, he was assisted in building a wind tunnel there by newly graduated Donald W. Douglas).[143] It was these men and others who laid the technological foundation for naval air power, so essential to America's security ever since.[144]

The Bureau of Ordnance

For many years the Bureau contained a Special Board on Naval Ordnance composed of officers of long ordnance and sea experience to make judgements about ordnance material. This board was useful for investigating matters of ordnance urgency during the war. Its judgements were also useful in developing new material for the new field of anti-submarine warfare, substitute explosives to circumvent wartime shortages, and

evaluating the many ideas for new naval weapons and equipment from the home mechanics of America. Although only one of these latter ideas proved practical, all were evaluated scrupulously, and the payoff was from a Massachusetts electrician. The idea was a copper wire antenna, actuated by the dissimilar steel of a ship's hull. It added substantially to the danger-space (and, hence, substantially to the efficiency) of the basic British impact-horn mine that the Navy had mass-produced for the North Sea blockade barrage. The board also investigated the ballistics of the Paris Gun of the Germans (built and manned by the Imperial Navy, incidently) supposedly to evaluate its utility, but one suspects a Bureau curiosity such as fascinates gunnery buffs to this day. Another important development approved by the board was for mono-bloc gun barrels. Radial-stretch stressing, by hydraulic pressure from within, was inexpensively substituted for built-up retaining bands.[145]

BuOrd's Experimental Section headed by Lieutenant Commander T. S. Wilkinson (Admiral of World War II), was responsible for the development of many new items of material. These included: depth charges, floating mines, smoke apparatus, an improved Y-gun to launch depth-charges, "aero" bombs, anti-aircraft shells (a new requirement), star shells, and flashless propellant powder.[146]

AMERICAN SOCIETY OF NAVAL ENGINEERS AND THE *ASNE JOURNAL*

Institutional Thrust

In 1914, ASNE carried assets of more than $10,000, a substantial indication (in the dollar value of that day) of its institutional vigor. At the annual banquet, a Professor Lueke reflected commendable forward thinking in addressing "Advanced Engineering Education."

Looking at the Society's membership, it is interesting to note that even at the early date of 1914, the Society's technological appeal was far from limited to the engineering community. Listed on the membership pages of the *Journal* as junior officer members are a number of future line flag officers of World War II, including E. C. Kalbfus, J. O. Richardson, John F. Shafroth, and Harry Yarnell.

Scope of the *ASNE Journal*

Evidence of the progressive naval technological and engineering interests of the Navy is provided in the subject matter addressed in the *Journal* from 1914 through 1921. Understandably, from its origins, the Society selected articles for publication that were predominantly concerned with steam propulsion and associated theory, practice, and equipment.

The careful attention to various aspects of the use of coal as a marine fuel tend to appear as rather archaic technology today. On the other hand, it is also interesting to see that, during this early twentieth-century period, naval engineers were still coming to grips with the concepts and the many as-yet-unsolved problems of fuel oil. Since propulsion already involved the diesel and gasoline internal-combustion engines needed by those recent naval arrivals submarines and aircraft, both also were dealt with at length in the *Journal*.

The article on "Submarine Engines of the German Navy" is of historical interest for the assessments by Lieutenant Chester W. Nimitz, writing from the particular expertise of his own submarine command experience.

Lessons from the War

The *Journal* strove to keep abreast of new developments in warships, in general, including foreign building programs and vessel characteristics. As the European war progressed, with everexpanded naval operations, lessons were to be learned by paying close attention to battle damage to ship structures and armor from gunfire, mines, and torpedoes. These observations about the performance of material in the submarine campaigns, and at Coronel, The Falklands, Dogger Bank, and Jutland, were to be reflected in future U.S. Navy equipment and construction practices.

Similar interest also was shown in all aspects of both heavier-than-air and lighter-than-air aviation. Not only is the previously alluded to technology of their engines addressed, but also aerodynamics (an obvious extension of hydrodynamics), weapons, and tactics. Note especially the appreciation of F. W. Lanchester's seminal concepts and algorithms of operations research implicit in an alert extract from his *Aircraft In Warfare*.

Emphasis on Electrical Technology

The Navy had assigned electricity, as well as its various applications, to the engineers some years back, and its coverage in the *Journal* could be expected. Now, electricity was of even greater engineering interest, as electric drive-coupling showed its promise to solve problems of turbine propulsion. Several articles reported on the new collier *Jupiter* (later converted into the Navy's first aircraft carrier), in which such a propulsion system was being tested with favorable results.

Other General *Journal* Coverage

Metallurgy is, of course, an essential aspect of propulsion engineering plants, as well as auxiliary machinery, and ships, themselves. At this time, *Journal* articles were concerned, for the most part, with ferrous metals in furnaces, boilers, pipes and tubes, turbines, reduction-gears, and shafts, as well as nonferrous-bearing elements, aluminum, and various alloys such as stainless steel, monel, and duralumin. There were articles dealing with metallurgical aspects of manufacture, operation, preservation, and repair; and with theoretical aspects of crystalline structure, physical characteristics, heat treatment, and testing. Ship construction metallurgy was, understandably, particularly concerned with armor.

Society of Naval Architects and Marine Engineers

Not without reason, naval architecture and its supporting science of hydrodynamics seem generally to have been left, appropriately, to the *Transactions* of ASNE's brother organization, the Society of Naval Architects and Marine Engineers (SNAME). Yet, before, during, and after the World War, the *ASNE Journal* saw fit to provide its members with occasional articles on propeller performance, the hydrodynamics of hull forms, and model-tank experiments.

SUMMARY

It can be stated that, in most regards, American maritime technology and production came of age during the period 1914-1921. In almost all of the technical areas discussed in this chapter, American science and technology was applied successfully to most of the engineering and logistical problems posed by a world war on the high seas. Some aspects, like ship and machinery production, gun design and explosive ordnance manufacture, fire control development, and aircraft engine development and production, were particularly successful. In other areas, like turbine gear fabrication and aircraft manufacture, there was partial success marred by wartime priorities and pressures.

There were some failures, too. Torpedo production fell far short of the quantities required. Because these weapons were not tested in the harsh school of combat during World War I, we do not know whether qualitative defects, such as those that plagued our World War II submarine torpedoes, also existed. It also must be admitted that the Navy technical bureaus really failed to properly exploit the potential of civilian scientific research and development for a number of

reasons: a lack of experience, lack of appreciation of what could be achieved in such an effort, and, in some measure, professional arrogance. The naval technical leadership of this era was not disposed to let civilian scientists tell it how to go about its work or solve its problems.

The primary failure besetting the mobilization of maritime technology, however, was lack of preparedness. The problem lay at the very top. The officers charged with responsibility for the nation's naval defenses were frustrated by the ideological commitment of Secretary Josephus Daniels to the belief that avoidance of preparedness would avoid war. It was perhaps our nation's blessing that the Undersecretary of the Navy, Franklin D. Roosevelt, was closely exposed to the consequences of the false concepts of pacifism; they prepared him well to seek preparedness against deadlier enemies in World War II.

Notes

1 Hattendorf, John B., Mitchel B. Simpson, John R. Wadleigh, *Sailors and Scholars: Centennial History of the Naval War College.* Newport, R.I.: Naval War College Press, 1984. Also Morison, Elting E., *Admiral Sims and the Modern American Navy.* Boston, Massachusetts: Houghton Miflin Company, 1942.

2 Morison, *Admiral Sims.* Also Coletta, Paolo L., *Admiral Bradley A. Fiske and the American Navy.* Lawrence, Kansas: The Regents Press of Kansas, 1979.

3 Coletta, *Admiral Bradley A. Fiske.*

4 Morison, *Admiral Sims.* Also Coletta, *Admiral Bradley A. Fiske.* Kittredge, Tracey Barrett, *Naval Lessons of the Great War.* Garden City, N.Y.: Doubleday, Page & Co., 1921.

5 Coletta, *Admiral Bradley A. Fiske.*

6 Kittredge, *Lessons.*

7 *Ibid.*

8 *Cumulative Index of the Naval Engineers Journal Covering 91 Years 1889 through 1979.* Washington, D.C.: The American Society of Naval Engineers, 1981.

9 *Ibid.*

10 Potter, E. B., Editor, *Sea Power, A Naval History.* Annapolis, Maryland: Naval Institute Press, 1981. Also Beach, Edward L., CAPT USN, *The United States Navy.* New York, N.Y.: Henry Holt, & Co., 1986. Also Friedman, Norman, *U.S. Battleships, A Design History.* Annapolis, Maryland: Naval Institute Press, 1985.

11 Turnbull, A. D., CAPT USNR, and LCDR C. L. Lord, USNR, *A History of United States Aviation.* New Haven, Connecticut: Yale University Press, 1949. Also Potter, *Sea Power;* Beach, *U.S. Navy;* and Friedman, *Battleships.*

12 Gardiner, Robert, Editor, *Conway's All the World's Fighting Ships 1906-1921.* London: Conway Maritime Press, Ltd., 1985. Also Hovgaard, William, *Modern History of Warships.* Annapolis, Maryland: Naval Institute Press, 1971; Breyer, Siegfried, *Battleships and Battle Cruisers, 1905-1970.* Garden City, N.Y.: Doubleday & Co., 1973.

13 See references cited in note 12.

14 Rossel, H. E., CDR (CC) USN, "Types of Naval Ships," *Historical Transactions 1893-1943.* New York, N.Y.: The Society of Naval Architects and Marine Engineers, 1945. Also Hone, Thomas and Norman Friedman, "Innovation and Administration in the Navy Department: The Case of the *Nevada* Design," *Military Affairs.* Vol. XLV, No. 2 (April 1981); Friedman, *Battleships;* Hovgaard, *History of Warships;* Breyer, *Battleships and Battle Cruisers.*

15 Jurens, William J., "Underwater Protection of Capital Ships—Technical Approach," *Warship International.* Vol. XXII, No. 4 (1985). Also Gardiner, *Fighting Ships.*

16 Hone and Friedman, "*Nevada* Design," *Military Affairs.* (April 1981).

17 Friedman, *Battleships.* Also Gardiner, *Fighting Ships.* Breyer, *Battleships and Battle Cruisers.*

18 See references cited in note 17.

19 Turnbull and Lord, *History of U.S. Aviation.*

20 Jurens, "Underwater Protection of Capital Ships;" *Warship International* (1985). Also Gardiner, *Fighting Ships.*

21 Gardiner, *Fighting Ships.* Also Breyer, *Battleships and Battle Cruisers.*

22 Friedman, Norman, *U.S. Cruisers: An Illustrated Design History.* Annapolis, Maryland: Naval Institute Press, 1984.

23 Friedman, *Battleships.* Also Gardiner, *Fighting Ships*; Breyer, *Battleships and Battle Cruisers.*

24 Kittredge, *Lessons.* Also Potter, *Sea Power*; Beach, *U.S. Navy.*

25 Hattendorf, et al. *Sailors and Scholars.* Also Morison, *Admiral Sims*; Gardiner, *Fighting Ships*; Breyer, *Battleships and Cruisers.*

26 Friedman, Norman, *U.S. Destroyers: An Illustrated Design History.* Annapolis, Maryland: Naval Institute Press, 1985. Also Owen, W. C., LCDR USN, and J. F. Shafroth, LCDR USN, "War-Time Destroyer Program," *ASNE Journal.* Vol. XXXIV (August 1922); Miller, R. T., CAPT USN, "Sixty Years of Destroyers, A Study in Evolution," *U.S. Naval Institute Proceedings.* (November 1962); Naval History Division, *Dictionary of American Naval Fighting Ships.* Vol. VI, Washington, D.C.: Department of the Navy, 1976; Gardiner, *Fighting Ships.*

27 Friedman, Norman, *U.S. Small Combatants, An Illustrated Design History.* Annapolis, Maryland: Naval Institute Press, 1987. Also *Dictionary of Fighting Ships*, Dept. of the Navy (1976); Gardiner, *Fighting Ships.*

28 McKee, A. I., CAPT USN, "Development of Submarines in the United States," *Historical Transactions 1893-1943.* New York, N.Y.: SNAME, 1945. Also Rodgers, W. L., CAPT USN, "The Suitability of Current Design of Submarines To The Needs of the United States Navy," *Transactions.* Vol. XXIV, New York, N.Y.: SNAME, 1916; Gardiner, *Fighting Ships.*

29 Rodgers, "Suitability of Design of Submarines," SNAME, 1916. Also Gardiner, *Fighting Ships.*

30 Rodgers, "Suitability of Design of Submarines." Also Gardiner, *Fighting Ships.*

31 Neuhaus, H. M., "Fifty Years of Naval Engineering in Retrospect," *ASNE Journal.* (August 1938), Part III, 1908-1921. Also Hamilton, J. E., LT USN, "A Short History of the Naval Use of Fuel Oil," *ASNE Journal.* (November 1933 and February 1935), Parts I and III; Hovgaard, *History of Warships.*

32 King, J. H., and R. S. Cox, "The Development of Marine Watertube Boilers," *Historical Transactions 1893-1943.* New York, N.Y.: SNAME, 1945. Also Clarke, Frank E., "Half A Century of Progress in Naval Boiler Water Treatment," *ASNE Journal.* (February 1955), p. 11; Neuhaus, "Fifty Years of Naval Engineering," ASNE (August 1938).

33 Bowen, Harold G., "One Hundred Years of U.S. Naval Engineering History," *ASNE Journal.* (November, 1937). Also Jung, Ingvar, "The Marine Turbine, A Historical Review by a Swedish Engineer," *Maritime Monographs and Reports.* No. 50, London: Trustees of the National Maritime Museum, 1982; Emmet, W. L. R., "Some Comparisons Relating to Electric Propulsion of a Battleship," *Transactions.* Vol. XXIII, New York, N.Y.: SNAME, 1915; MacDougall, W. D., CAPT USN, *History of the Bureau of Engineering, Navy Department, During the World War.* Washington, D.C.: Government Printing Office, 1922; Hovgaard, *History of Warships*; Friedman, *Destroyers*; Neuhaus, "Fifty Years of Naval Engineering," ASNE (August 1938).

34 Jung, "The Marine Turbine." Also Emmet, *"Some Comparisons Relating to Electric Propulsion;"* Friedman, *Battleships*; Turnbull and Lord, *History of U.S. Aviation*; Jurens, "Underwater Protection of Capital Ships," *Warship International* (1985); Gardiner, *Fighting Ships*; and Hovgaard, *History of Warships.*

35 Nichols, John F., "Development of Marine Engineering," *Historical Transactions 1893-1943.* New York, N.Y.: SNAME, 1945. Also Neuhaus, "Fifty Years of Naval Engineering," ASNE (August 1938).

36 Rossel, "Types of Ships," SNAME (1945); Also McKee, "Development of Submarines," SNAME, 1945; Gardiner, *Fighting Ships.*

37 Nimitz, Chester W., LT USN, "Submarine Engines of the German Navy," *ASNE Journal.* Vol. XXVIII, (May, 1916).

38 MacDougall, *History of the Bureau of Engineering.*

39 Hutchins, John G. B., "History and Development of the Shipbuilding Industry in the United States," Chapter II, *The Shipbuilding Business in the United States of America.* Edited by F. G. Fassett, New York, N.Y.: SNAME, 1948.

40 Secretary of the Navy, *Annual Report of the Navy Department for the Fiscal Year 1920.* Washington, D.C.: Government Printing Office, 1920.

41 Whitehurst, Clinton H., *The U.S. Shipbuilding Industry, Past, Present, and Future.* Annapolis, Maryland: Naval Institute Press, 1986. Also Hutchins, "History and Development of Shipbuilding." SNAME, 1948.

42 Hutchins, "History and Development of Shipbuilding." SNAME, 1948.

43 Bakenhus, R. E., CAPT (CEC) USN, "Development of Shipyards in the United States During the Great War," *Transactions.* Vol. XXVII, New York, N.Y.: SNAME, 1919. Also see references cited in note 41.

44 Hutchins, "History and Development of Shipbuilding." SNAME, 1948. Also Bakenhus, "Development of Shipyards." SNAME, 1919.

45 Taggart, Robert, *Evolution of the Vessels Engaged in the Waterborne Commerce of the United States.* National Waterways Study 83-3, Washington, D.C.: U.S. Army Engineer Water Resources Center, 1983.

46 Blood, W. H., "Hog Island, The Greatest Shipyard in the World," *Transactions.* Vol. XXVI, New York, N.Y.: SNAME, 1918.

47 *Ibid.*

48 Engle, Eloise and Arnold S. Lott, *America's Maritime Heritage.* Annapolis, Maryland: Naval Institute Press, 1975. Also Hurley, Edward N., *The Bridge To France.* Philadelphia, Pennsylvania: J. B. Lippincott Co., 1927; Blood, "Hog Island." SNAME, 1918.

49 Hurley, *Bridge to France.*

50 *Ibid.*

51 Crisp, R. O. Commodore USCG (Ret), *History of the U.S. Coast Guard in the World War.* Vol. 2, 1922. (Unpublished manuscript in the USCG archives.)

52 The famous *Bear* was truly a stout ship—structurally and operationally. A sometime sealer acquired by the Revenue Cutter Service in 1884, she served admirably in Alaskan weather and ice for over 40 years. Controversy as to her soundness, a few years before the Coast Guard decommissioned her in 1929, seemed to turn on the difficulty of making judgement about her hull—her timbers were so thick and dense! Later, as a private ship, the *Bear* provided yeoman service for RADM Byrd's Antarctic expeditions. During World War II, when both the Coast Guard and Navy needed ice-worthy vessels for the Greenland Patrol, RADM Byrd seems to have used the Navy's wartime seniority to "horn-swoggle" the Coast Guard out of its venerable cutter.

53 Johnson, Robert E., *Guardians of the Sea.* Annapolis, Maryland: Naval Institute Press, 1987.

54 *Ibid.*

55 Crisp, *Coast Guard in the World War.*

56 *Ibid.*

57 *Ibid.*

58 *Ibid.*

59 Johnson, *Guardians of the Sea.*

60 Scheina, Robert L., "A History of Coast Guard Aviation," *Commandant's Bulletin 21-96.* Washington, D.C.: USCG, 10 October 1986. Also Swanborough, Gordonn and Peter M. Bowers, *United States Navy Aircraft Since 1911.* New York, N.Y.: Funk and Wagnalls, 1968.

61 Crisp, *Coast Guard in the World War.*

62 Johnson, *Guardians of the Sea.*

63 Newman, Q. B., "Coast Guard Cutters *Tampa, Haida, Modoc,* and *Mojave,*" *ASNE Journal,* November 1921, p. 47.

64 Bureau of Ordnance, Navy Department, *Navy Ordnance Activities, World War 1917-1918.* Washington, D.C.: Government Printing Office, 1920.

65 *Ibid.* Also Peck, Taylor, *Round-shot To Rockets, A History of the Washington Navy Yard and U.S. Naval Gun Factory.* Annapolis, Maryland: U.S. Naval Institute, 1949.

66 Hodges, Peter, *The Big Gun.* Annapolis, Maryland: Naval Institute Press, 1981.

67 Friedman, Norman, *U.S. Naval Weapons.* Annapolis, Maryland: Naval Institute Press, 1983.

68 Breyer, *Battleships and Battle Cruisers.*

69 Hodges, *Big Gun.*

70 *Ibid.*

71 Dulin, R. O. and W. H. Garzke, *Battleships, United States Battleships in World War II.* Annapolis, Maryland: Naval Institute Press, 1976. Also Lewis, E. R., "American Battleship Armament: The Final Generation," *Warship International.* No. 4, 1976; Hodges, *Big Gun*; Friedman, *Battleships.*

72 Lewis, "Battleship Armament," *Warship International.* 1976. Also Friedman, *Battleships.*

73 Friedman, *Battleships.*

74 BuOrd, *Navy Ordnance.* GPO, 1920. Also, Naval Historical Center (Reprint), *The United States Naval Railway Batteries in France.* Washington, D.C.: Government Printing Office, 1988.

75 Buxton, Ian, *Big Gun Monitors.* Annapolis, Maryland: Naval Institute Press, 1978.

76 BuOrd, *Navy Ordnance.* GPO, 1920.

77 *Ibid.*

78 *Ibid.*

79 Hughes, T. P., *Elmer Sperry Inventor and Engineer.* Baltimore, Maryland: The Johns Hopkins Press, 1971.

80 *Ibid.*

81 *Ibid.* Also BuOrd, *Navy Ordnance.* GPO, 1920.

82 BuOrd, *Navy Ordnance.* GPO, 1920. Also Friedman, *Naval Weapons.*

83 BuOrd, *Navy Ordnance.* GPO, 1920.

84 *Ibid.* Also Friedman, *Naval Weapons.*

85 BuOrd, *Navy Ordnance.* GPO, 1920.

86 *Ibid.*

87 *Ibid.*

88 *Ibid.*

89 *Ibid.*

90 *Ibid.*

91 Van Wyen, Adrian O., Lee M. Pearson, and Clarke Van Fleet, *United States Naval Aviation 1910-1970.* 2nd Ed., Washington D.C.: Supt. of Documents, 1970.

92 Caras, Roger A., *Wings of Gold, The Story of United States Naval Aviation.* Philadelphia, Pennsylvania: J. B. Lippincott Co., 1965. Also, Lamberton, W. M. and E. F. Cheesman, *Fighter Aircraft of the 1914-1918 War.* Harleyford Publications, Ltd., Letchworth, Herts, 1960.

93   Turnbull and Lord, *History of U.S. Aviation.* Also Swanborough and Bowers, *Navy Aircraft Since 1911.*

94   Turnbull and Lord, *History of U.S. Aviation.*

95   *Ibid.*

96   Caras, *Wings of Gold.* Also Turnbull and Lord, *History of U.S. Aviation.*

97   Turnbull and Lord, *History of U.S. Aviation.*

98   Van Wyen, et al., *Naval Aviation 1910-1970.*

99   Turnbull and Lord, *History of U.S. Aviation.*

100   *Ibid.*

101   *Ibid.*

102   Van Wyen, et al., *Naval Aviation 1910-1970.*

103   Turnbull and Lord, *History of U.S. Aviation.*

104   *Ibid.*

105   Swanborough and Bowers, *Navy Aircraft Since 1911.*

106   Turnbull and Lord, *History of U.S. Aviation.*

107   Kittredge, *Naval Lessons.*

108   Johnson, Edward C., LCOL USMC, *Marine Corps Aviation: The Early Years 1912-1940.* Washington, D.C.: History & Museums Division, Headquarters, U.S. Marine Corps, 1977. Also Mersky, Peter B., *U.S. Marine Corps Aviation 1912 To The Present.* Baltimore, Maryland: The Nautical & Aviation Publishing Co. of America, 1983; Swanborough and Bowers, *Navy Aircraft Since 1911.*

109   Swanborough and Bowers, *Navy Aircraft Since 1911.* Also Turnbull and Lord; *History of U.S. Aviation;* Van Wyen, et al., *Naval Aviation 1910-1970.*

110   See references cited in 109.

111   *Ibid.*

112   Turnbull and Lord, *History of U.S. Aviation.* Also Swanborough and Bowers, *Navy Aircraft Since 1911;* Johnson, *Marine Corps Aviation: Early Years;* Mersky, *Marine Corps Aviation 1912 to Present.*

113   Turnbull and Lord, *History of U.S. Aviation.*

114   MacDougall, *History of the Bureau of Engineering.*

115   Dickey, Philip S., *The Liberty Engine 1918-1942.* Washington, D.C.: Smithsonian Institution Press, 1968. Also Turnbull and Lord, *History of U.S. Aviation.*

116   Turnbull and Lord, *History of U.S. Aviation.* Also Swanborough and Bowers, *Navy Aircraft Since 1911.* Johnson, *Marine Corps Aviation: Early Years.*

117   Turnbull and Lord, *History of U.S. Aviation.*

118   *Ibid.* Also Swanborough and Bowers, *Navy Aircraft Since 1911.*

119   Swanborough and Bowers, *Navy Aircraft Since 1911.*

120   Van Wyen, et al., *Naval Aviation 1910-1970.*

121   Allison, David K., *New Eye for the Navy: The Origin of Radar at the Naval Research Laboratory.* Washington, D.C.: GPO, 1981. Also Lamb, Carl Jr.,

LT USN, "The U.S. Naval Engineering Experiment Station," *ASNE Journal.* February 1932, Ch. III; BuOrd, *Navy Ordnance;* MacDougall, *History of the Bureau of Engineering.*

122   See references cited in 121.

123   Allison, *New Eye for the Navy.*

124   *Ibid.*

125   History Associates Inc., *History of the David Taylor Research Center.* Bethesda, Maryland: David Taylor Research Center, 1987 (Unpublished manuscript). Also Allison, *New Eye for the Navy.*

126   Beach, *U.S. Navy.*

127   Friedman, *Battleships.*

128   Turnbull and Lord, *History of U.S. Aviation.*

129   MacDougall, *History of the Bureau of Engineering.* Also Lamb, "Engineering Experiment Station," ASNE, Feb. 1932; History Associates, *David Taylor Research Center.*

130   Hamilton, "Short History of Naval Use of Fuel Oil," ASNE, November 1933 and February 1935.

131   MacDougall, *History of the Bureau of Engineering.*

132   Allison, *New Eye for the Navy.* Also History Associates, *David Taylor Research Center.*

133   Howeth, L. S., CAPT USN (Ret), *History of Communications—Electronics in the U.S. Navy.* Washington, D.C.: GPO, 1963.

134   BuOrd, *Navy Ordnance.*

135   Howeth, *History of Communications—Electronics in Navy.* Also Christman, Albert B., *Sailors, Scientists, and Rockets, Origins of the Navy Rocket Program and of the Naval Ordnance Test Station, Inyokern.* Washington, D.C.: GPO, 1971.

136   History Associates, *David Taylor Research Center.*

137   *Ibid.*

138   Secretary of the Navy, *Annual Report of the Navy Department for the Fiscal Year 1915.* Washington, D.C.: GPO, 1915.

139   _____, *Annual Report of the Navy Department for the Fiscal Year 1916.* Washington, D.C.: GPO, 1916.

140   _____, *Annual Report of the Navy Department for the Fiscal Year 1920.* Washington, D.C.: GPO, 1920.

141   History Associates, *David Taylor Research Center.*

142   *Ibid.*

143   Baker, William A., *Report No. 69-3 A History of the First 75 Years.* Cambridge, Massachusetts: MIT Department of Naval Architecture and Marine Engineering, 1969.

144   *Ibid.* Also Secretary of the Navy, *Annual Report 1920.*

145   BuOrd, *Navy Ordnance.*

146   *Ibid.*

CHAPTER
FIVE
1922–1932

The Declining Years

by James V. Jolliff
and Keith B. Schumacher

As noted in the previous chapter, the U.S. Navy had phenomenal growth up to and during the First World War and during the postwar period through 1922. Prior to this time, the United States had obtained naval bases in the Pacific Ocean, with its acquisition of the Philippines and Guam following victory in the Spanish-American War. The Great White Fleet world cruise of 1908 was viewed in Europe as a "flexing of American muscles." During World War I, the United States showed its willingness and ability to project its military might to other seas and shores. By 1922, the United States had shown itself to be a rapidly rising naval and world power, with ships being constructed, or planned for construction that might clearly make her the world's leading naval and maritime power.

Foreign Concerns

Because of this significant naval and maritime growth, the already-established world powers of Europe viewed the United States as a disturbing and unbalancing "upstart" that could possibly prevent them from allotting the power balance among the European powers according to which one of them had triumphed in the most recent wars.

In addition, Japan, rapidly emerging as a Pacific power in its own right, was distressed by what it viewed as competition in terms of a U.S. naval presence and strength in the Far East. Japan had triumphed over Russia and her more long-standing enemy China in recent wars. She was interested in consolidating and extending her power in the Pacific rather than facing a new rival in those waters.

America Calls for Naval Reduction

It was in this setting that the United States hosted the Washington Naval Conference, which began in 1921 and concluded in 1922. An understanding of this conference is of great importance because of its profound impact on naval engineering in the decade that followed. Although some of the growth momentum of previous years carried over into the period 1922 through 1932, the resultant Washington Naval Treaty rang the "death knell" for major new shipbuilding for the U.S. Navy for the next 12 years. In fact, it not only created a tone of "research and development only" for all but a few potential naval growth areas, but it also set the stage for the League of Nations Naval Disarmament Conference in 1925 and the Geneva Naval Limitations Conference in 1927.

The Washington Naval Conference and Five Power Naval Treaty

At the outset of the Washington Naval Conference, two principal bargaining groups formed automatically: the first comprised England, Japan, and the United States; the second France and Italy. The major points evolved by the Washington Naval Conference and finally incorporated into the Five Power Naval Treaty were as follows:[1]

(a) Capital ships were defined as "vessels of war" exceeding 10,000 tons standard displacement or carrying a gun of more than 8-inch caliber. Aircraft carriers were not included in this classification. An allowance of 525,000 tons each was granted to the United States and England, with a maximum individual ship displacement of 35,000 tons. Japan was allowed 315,000 tons, while France and Italy were allowed 175,000 tons each. On those ships retained, 3,000 additional tons were allowed for installation of systems for defense against air and submarine attack. No other alterations were authorized and a maximum limitation of 16-inch caliber guns was established. Age limits of 20 years were specified, with no replacements allowed earlier except for accidental losses.

(b) Aircraft carriers were limited to a total of 135,000 tons, the maximum tonnage of one being 27,000 tons, except that two aircraft carriers of 33,000 tons were permitted, provided the total allowance was not exceeded. Guns were limited to 8-inch caliber.

(c) Cruisers were limited to 10,000 tons with a maximum gun caliber of 8 inches. No limitation was placed on total tonnage.

(d) The treaty provided for the names of new

vessels; vessels to be replaced; dates of authorization and keel laying; and general characteristics such as displacement, dimensions, and armament to be exchanged between the signatory powers.

(e) Standard displacement of a ship was defined as that of a ship complete, fully manned, engined, and equipped ready for sea. This displacement included all armament, ammunitions, equipment, outfit, provisions, fresh water for crew, miscellaneous stores, and implements of every description that would be carried in war, but did not include fuel or reserve feed water. A ton was understood to equate to 2,240 pounds.[2]

(f) A ratio of 5:5:3:1.5:1.5 capital ship construction was established for the United States, England, Japan, France, and Italy, respectively.

The Five Power Naval Treaty came into force in August 1923 and remained in force until December 1936. In the event none of the contracting powers gave notice 2 years before its termination, it was to continue in force for 2 years following such notification, and then was to terminate as regards all contracting powers.

Five Power Naval Treaty Results

As stated earlier, signature of this treaty by the United States in 1923 caused an immediate decline in its Naval power. The fate of the battleship *Washington* clearly demonstrated this point. Nearly three-quarters completed and representing the last word in naval architecture, this great 31,500-ton *Maryland*-class ship was taken out beyond the Virginia Capes one November day in 1924 and sunk before she was even commissioned. Her tough hull withstood the impact of two torpedoes and four 1-ton bombs that were exploded close by. Not until fourteen heavy shells were poured into her by naval gunfire did she finally settle beneath the waves. This was a dramatic sacrifice made, as some would suggest, in the hope for world peace. More than 200 other ships were removed from the Navy list by either sinking, scrapping, or, in a few cases, demilitarization. The old battleships *New Jersey* and *Virginia* were given to the Army to be sunk by its bombers. Numerous other American dreadnoughts, which 15 years earlier had proudly sailed around the world as part of the Great White Fleet, were broken up for scrap. They, at least, were obsolete, as compared to the battleship *Washington*, whose sister ships later fought in World War II. In addition, the partly completed hulls of several other capital ships were scrapped as they lay on the building ways. Had these ships been completed, the United States would have had the mightiest navy afloat. Instead, in a sincere international gesture for peace and resolution of pressing Congressional politics, the United States scrapped actual new ships, while the other Treaty nations scrapped only blueprints of ships they had planned to build in the future.

The Cruiser Controversy

The "Cruiser Controversy" came about because of the building programs instituted by the Five Power Naval Treaty signatories during the 3-year period following the Conference. It is basically agreed by most historians that Japan initiated this new warship race in mid-1922 with the announcement of a major new construction program. During the next 4 years, the Japanese Navy laid down or completed twelve heavy cruisers, establishing a 50 percent lead over the United States in this unrestricted warship category. After some delay, Great Britain and the United States also announced new programs in early 1925. The cruisers laid down under these new programs were generally heavy cruisers, all mounting 8-inch guns and nearly all having displacement at or near the 10,000-ton Five Power Naval Treaty limit. This resulted in a new naval armaments race, with the heavy cruiser replacing the capital ship as its focus. Though less expensive than previous arms races, such growth within the Treaty boundaries was clearly an unsatisfactory situation that needed to be ended as quickly as possible.

British Cruiser Position

The British needed cruisers for two purposes: to work with the main fleets as scouting and covering support and to protect imperial and trade communications. The first purpose involved a mission that was generally common to all navies. The British saw a need for both heavy and light cruisers. The early British preference was for light cruisers, partly because they were cheaper to build and to maintain, and also because the location of British naval stations all over the world precluded the need for long cruising range. Unfortunately, because the heavy cruiser was now in existence, it posed a threat to the growth of a large light cruiser fleet.

Therefore, the British position was clear. First, the heavy cruiser should not be abolished, but no more should be built. Second, further cruisers should be limited to 7,000 tons and 6-inch caliber guns. Third, since the British had a greater need for cruisers than did other navies, the 5:5:3 ratio should not be extended to cruisers, and any limitations agreement should allow the Royal Navy to maintain at least thirty-four light cruisers and twenty-five heavy cruisers, a proposed force much larger than any of the requirements set forth by other naval powers.

The American Cruiser Position

American naval requirements for cruisers were dictated by the need to maintain naval communications with the Philippines and the Far East. Because trade protection was not a major consideration, except in the Far East, a large number of cruisers was not required. But, heavy cruisers, as a class, were extremely vital because American refueling facilities and naval bases in the Pacific were few and far between. In addition, it was opined that the heavy cruiser would be useful in a war in the Pacific against Japan or in the Atlantic and Caribbean in any contest with Great Britain, considered to be a potential enemy by the U.S. Navy throughout the 1920s. American Naval officers saw the heavy cruiser as helping to offset the Royal Navy's advantage in numbers of cruisers. Hence, the American preference was exclusively for development of the heavy cruiser. These considerations, plus insistence on parity with the British, shaped the American position. First, the 5:5:3 ratio should be extended to cruisers. Second, no change in qualitative limitations should be allowed. The maximum individual limits should remain 10,000 tons and 8-inch guns. Third, the total tonnage of cruisers the Americans were willing to accept for the U.S. Navy, and hence for the Royal Navy, was no more than 400,000 tons. Even that amount of tonnage would require considerable construction effort in the United States and it was uncertain whether

Congress would support such a major shipbuilding program.

The Japanese Cruiser Position

Japanese cruiser requirements were simpler than those desired by either Great Britain or the United States. Concerned with defending a smaller area, the Japanese had no need for a large number of cruisers and those required were for fleet work rather than trade protection. Hence, they also preferred the heavy cruiser. But, because they already had several light cruisers, they were willing to accept qualitative limits on future construction below those set at the Washington Naval Conference. They also had no objection to the extension of the ratio principle to auxiliary warships. The one major point that the Japanese sought to secure at the Geneva Arms Limitation Conference was a revision of the Five Power Naval Treaty ratio from 5:5:3 to 10:10:7 for such warships. Thus, the Japanese position was the most flexible of the three major powers. Furthermore, they believed they had a good chance to secure their demand for a 10:10:7 ratio because their early construction start had given them a slight lead over the British in heavy cruisers launched or in commission, and they knew their lead over the United States was quite pronounced.

Cruiser Development Issues at Geneva

The aforestated positions and initial proposals of the three delegations were set forth by their respective leaders at the first preliminary sessions of the Geneva conference in June 1927. The battle lines were drawn! The Americans and British did agree on the same ratio in heavy cruisers, but that was about the extent of initial Anglo-American agreement. It was evident that the road to a limitations treaty at Geneva would be difficult. Yet, each delegation quickly realized that agreement on cruisers was necessary if comprehensive limitations were to be achieved. Therefore, most of the conference time was spent trying to solve the cruiser impasse. Although some headway was made, the stumbling block became the British insistence that the United States agree to total cruiser tonnage of 600,000 tons for each of the two navies and a limitation on further cruiser construction to light cruisers

only. Thus, a stalemate developed over the total cruiser tonnage issue. The other major question, the differences among the delegations concerning the size of the individual cruiser, was, of course, closely related to the question of total cruiser tonnage, and failure to agree on one of these issues practically ensured defeat of the other. The British were insisting on a minimum of seventy cruisers and, therefore, wanted smaller cruisers, both for reasons of economy and to keep total tonnage within the limit demanded by the United States. For their part, the United States maintained its desire for larger cruisers up to the 10,000-ton limit. In addition, the Japanese did not want to build as many cruisers as would be required if the British tonnage proposals were accepted.

Failure of the Geneva Conference

The collapse of the negotiations at Geneva in 1927 meant that the size and complexity of auxiliary warships remained unrestricted. This resulted in yet another round in the naval armaments race. In the United States, where little had been done in naval construction beyond the eight cruiser authorization of 1924 because of the Five Power Naval Treaty and the desires of Congress, the effect was more pronounced. In 1927, the U.S. Navy General Board submitted a building program calling for the construction of twenty-five heavy cruisers and several other warships over a period of 5 years. After considerable discussion, a modified proposal was introduced in Congress early in 1928 and was passed quickly by the House. It involved construction of fifteen cruisers to be laid down over a 3-year period. After spirited debate in the Senate, the "Fifteen Cruiser Bill" was passed on 5 February 1929. The Naval Authorization Act of 1929 put the United States squarely in the cruiser race. And while it stimulated Britain and Japan to consider increasing their own programs, it also increased the desire of all nations to reach a naval limitations agreement to head off another naval shipbuilding race.

London Naval Conference

The London Naval Conference began on 21 January 1930. It was involved with limitations covering all classes of warships, and several issues, particularly those concerning battleships, proved only partly amenable to solution. Thanks to the concessions made prior to the conference, the cruiser problem did not prove intractable. New leadership in the form of President Herbert Hoover of the United States and Prime Minister Ramsay MacDonald of Great Britain led to concessions on both sides. First, the British, who had already agreed to parity with the United States in cruiser strength, accepted a maximum of approximately fifty cruisers totaling 339,000 tons. In return, the Americans agreed to accept a smaller number of heavy cruisers than the number they had previously insisted on.

Major Features of the London Treaty

The major features of the London Naval Treaty of 1930 were: the extension of another 5 years on the prohibition of battleship building previously adopted as part of the Five Power Naval Treaty in 1922, the establishment of qualitative limits on the size and gun power of destroyers and submarines, and a limitation on total tonnages of auxiliary warships. As discussed earlier, the "cruiser controversy" loomed large in the negotiations to secure tonnage limits. As provided in the London Naval Treaty, the total cruiser tonnage, as of the end of 1936, was to be no more than 323,500 tons for the United States, 339,000 for Great Britain, and 208,850 for Japan. In addition, the number of heavy cruisers was fixed at eighteen for the United States, fifteen for Great Britain, and twelve for Japan. Although none of the powers were completely satisfied, the London Naval Treaty did give each country a good portion of what they demanded in terms of cruisers. The Japanese achieved what amounted to a 10:10:7 ratio overall, and the British achieved their objectives of putting a satisfactory limit on the total number of heavy cruisers and allowing a total tonnage in cruisers to meet their minimum needs. As for the United States, it had successfully resisted British pressure to fix lower maximum tonnages for individual cruisers and had maintained a 5:5:3 ratio in heavy cruisers, at least in theory. Furthermore, the establishment of fixed total tonnage figures for cruisers for each navy meant that to reach these figures, the United States would have to build an additional 73,000 tons in light cruisers. Thus, for the United

States, the London Naval Treaty of 1930 represented a naval expansion, unlike the naval limitation that had occurred as a result of the Washington Naval Conference in 1922. All in all, the outcome of the London Naval Conference turned out to be a major triumph for American diplomacy. This is especially true in light of the weak U.S. Naval posture at the time of the conference.

American Lack of Response to the London Treaty

Considering the U.S. Navy's strong preference for the largest possible tonnage for ships in each class, as evidenced in the controversy over the heavy cruiser issue, it was generally believed that the new light cruisers would displace the maximum 10,000 tons permissible under the London Naval Treaty. Yet, the U.S. Navy General Board did not immediately reach this decision. In 1930, a bill was introduced in the House to authorize the construction of enough tonnage to build the Navy up to the treaty strength of 73,000 tons. It was not until 1932 that the General Board recommended construction of, and the Secretary of the Navy presented figures to the Senate Naval Affairs Committee that called for, seven 10,000-ton light cruisers to enable the United States to reach treaty strength by 1937. Nothing was done about any of these requests during the rest of President Hoover's Administration because the Depression and economic recovery preempted attention. Thus, the decline in U.S. Naval sea power, originally brought about by the series of conferences and treaties fostered from 1922 to 1930, continued.

NAVAL CONSTRUCTION

As previously stated, the importance of the period 1922-1932 is more in its historical treaties than in its significant advances in naval engineering because of the deleterious effect of the United States' adherence to the Five Power Naval Treaty. There were, however, advances in shipbuilding resulting from the shipbuilding programs of the previous decade, as well as some authorized programs not treaty-related.

Scout Cruisers for the U.S. Fleet

The year 1923 turned out to be rather significant for the U.S. Navy's shipbuilding program. Ships originally authorized by Congress in the World War I era, including the Scout Cruisers, *Richmond,*[3] *Omaha,*[4] and *Milwaukee,*[5] were all delivered and commissioned. Each had some relatively minor variations, but they all had a waterline length of 550 feet, a design displacement slightly over 7,000 tons, carried a total crew complement of 419 personnel, and achieved 35 knots full power.

USS *Richmond*

The scout cruiser *Richmond,* and the others mentioned above, resembled, in general appearance, earlier destroyers; the principal differences in outboard profile being the tubular tripod foremast with attached lookout and fire control structures, a cutaway upper deck, and installation of twin-gun mounts forward and aft.

The main battery consisted of twelve 6in/53 guns. These guns were served by six ammunition hoists of the step-by-step type, operated by constant-speed electric motors, working through Waterbury variable-speed gears. The maximum rate of delivery was ten rounds per minute. The hoist for the broadside guns delivered on both the main and upper decks. The hoists for the twin-mount guns delivered at the base of the mount, where transfer was made to endless chain hoists that served the guns individually. The anti-aircraft battery consisted of four 3in/50 guns, served by hand-operated hoists. Two 3-pounder guns were supplied for saluting. Two triple torpedo tubes were located on the upper deck.

The machinery layout included three boilers in each fireroom, arranged athwartship. The two forward firerooms were forward of the forward engine room containing the engines for the outboard shafts, numbers 1 and 4. The main condensers were located inboard in the forward engine room.

Just abaft the forward engine room were located the two after firerooms, which were similar to the two forward firerooms. Next came the after engine room, which housed the two inboard shafts, numbers 2 and 3, and the main condensers, which were located outboard. Shaft

horsepower at trial was 93,045, which attained a trial speed of 35 knots.

Other interesting features of the machinery plant included the use of scoop injection at speeds above 12 knots, the use of vacuum traps, and the use of a forced lubrication system for each of the four drive systems.[6]

USS *Raleigh*

In 1924, the USS *Raleigh,* another scout cruiser designed similarly to those commissioned in 1923, entered the fleet. The *Raleigh* had twelve boilers operating at 265 psi steam pressure and had characteristics similar to the USS *Richmond,* particularly in its hull design. However, her appearance was slightly different from her predecessors because her masts were slightly lower and she had hawse pipes, rather than billboards, for anchor stowage. The *Raleigh* was also outfitted to burn Bunker "C" fuel oil by the installation of a fuel oil recirculating system. This system included two additional pumps that were of the same type and size as those used for booster pumps and that were interchangeable with the latter. She also had two additional fuel oil recirculating heaters located in firerooms 1 and 3 and appropriate piping and strainers installed between the heaters and the tanks.[7]

Heavy Cruisers

The USS *Salt Lake City* was commissioned in 1929.[8] It was the first of the eight 10,000-ton 1922 Five Power Naval Treaty ships authorized by the Congress for construction in 1924. The contract for construction of the USS *Salt Lake City* was signed on 9 July 1926 with William Cramp & Sons Ship and Engine Building Company of Philadelphia. Preliminary plans had been made and approved and a considerable amount of material and machinery ordered by the contractor when, on 27 April 1927, the Navy was notified that Cramp & Sons could no longer perform the contract. To offset this setback, a contract was awarded to the American Brown-Boveri Electric Corporation of Camden, New Jersey, to complete all work required on both the USS *Salt Lake City* and the USS *Pensacola.*

In general, these two ships resembled each other in several characteristics; both had an overall length of 585 feet 8 inches, an extreme beam of 65 feet 3 inches, and a draft of 19 feet 6½ inches, and both could reach a speed of 32 knots. Their silhouettes were a radical departure from the "overgrown destroyer" appearance of the earlier 7,500-ton cruisers, resembling more nearly that of a lean battleship, an appearance accentuated by a modified clipper bow. The *Salt Lake City* and *Pensacola* were noticeably larger and more formidable in general appearance than the earlier light cruisers. This impression was increased by the larger turret-size enclosed gun-mounts, the two tripod masts, the two stacks, and the flush deck. The teak deck extending unbroken from bow to stern was not taken up as much with boat and other stowage as on the earlier light cruisers, and the resemblance to an overgrown destroyer had disappeared.

The heavy cruiser's main armament consisted of ten 8in/55 guns, housed in four turrets and disposed as follows: a two-gun turret on the forecastle deck, a three-gun turret directly to rear of it and superimposed; and a corresponding arrangement aft. In addition, four 5-inch anti-air-craft guns and six torpedo tubes were installed. Protection was inadequate, however, because no armor thicker than 1½ inches was worked into the ship, either vertically or horizontally. American naval experts acknowledged that the *Salt Lake City* was overweighted with armament; therefore, in the next six ships of the class, only nine 8-inch guns were mounted in three triple turrets, two forward and one aft.

The main propulsion plant included two fire-rooms, each containing four Babcock and Wilcox White-Forster oil-burning boilers arranged two abreast and back to back. Four sets of main engines, connected to as many propellers, fur-nished power for propulsion. Each unit was designed to develop continuously 26,750 shaft horsepower. A high- and low-pressure geared Parson turbine was fitted with a cruising turbine coupled through a Metten hydraulic clutch and a single reduction gear to the high-pressure turbine shaft. The high- and low-pressure tur-bines, in turn, were connected to the main shaft through a single reduction gear. When operating independently, the cruising turbine was governor controlled at a speed corresponding to about 15 knots. Provision was made for bleeding steam from appropriate stages of the high-pressure

turbine to the auxiliary exhaust for use in feed-water heaters and evaporators. A gland steam exhaust system was installed on the main and cruising turbines.

A large proportion of the auxiliary machinery was electrically driven, although there was some-what of a return to previous designs in that the main air pump, lubricating oil pump, turbine drain pump, and the makeup feed pump were directly driven from the main cruising turbine. In addition, electric hydraulic steering, similar to that in the last five battleships, was built into these ships. In effect, the machinery installations of all eight ships of this heavy cruiser class were practically identical, and in a great measure interchangeable, except for fireroom equipment. In the later six ships of the class, the boilers were arranged in four two-boiler firerooms instead of two four-boiler firerooms.

Of the eight cruisers authorized by Congress in 1924, four additional units were commis-sioned in 1930: the *Pensacola, Northampton, Chester,* and *Houston.*[9] These ships also con-formed to the 1922 Five Power Naval Treaty limitations. USS *Salt Lake City* was actually completed at an announced standard displace-ment of 9,100 tons, some 900 tons under the Five Power Naval Treaty limit. This fact, and several design studies later, quickly led to a new design for the follow-on ships. Except for 8-inch guns, which were already at the limit of ten, the intent was to use the available 900 extra tons to produce more desirable ship characteristics. The first of this new design became the USS *North-ampton,* having an overall length of 600 feet, a beam of 64.5 feet, and a draft of 19.8 feet. As in the case of the *Salt Lake City* design, there was much concern about the *Northampton* being over tonnage throughout the design period. Yet, when commissioned, the *Northampton* was 8,997 tons. It would appear that the designers of the day had trouble determining margins; even later designs, such as the *New Orleans* class, went through extreme weight-saving measures that proved to be excessive upon commissioning. Some of the weight-saving measures made possible by im-proved technology, outside of machinery im-provements, were the use of welding rather than riveting, the use of aluminum rather than steel, and the use of high-strength steels, including improved armor plate. The *Northampton* had a special distinctive feature in that she was the first major American warship designed to include the use of crew bunks rather than hammocks.[10]

Battleships

Because of the Five Power Naval Treaty, the USS *Colorado* and USS *West Virginia,* both commissioned in 1923, were the last battleships to be added to the U.S. Navy until 1941. Both ships had hull characteristics generally similar to those of the earlier battleships *Maryland* and *Tennessee:* a length overall of 624 feet and design displacement of 32,550 tons.[11]

This class of ships differed markedly in profile from any other capital class ship in the United States Navy; the outstanding difference being the very large fire control tops on two conventional cage masts. These tops, together with the new large bridge structures, made the two smoke stacks stand out in marked relief and appear diminutive in size. The cage masts were provided with the usual wireless and signal yards. The mainmast alone had a topmast and the crows nest had vanished. The mainmast was also surrounded with platforms for high-power searchlights. Signal searchlights remained on the bridge area. The hulls of the *Colorado* and *West Virginia* were similar, and each was thoroughly subdivided for protection against underwater attack. A clipper bow marked the abandonment of the old "ram" bow (which had persisted for some years for hydrodynamic purposes) and gave the ships much drier casement gundecks when in a seaway. They also had a catapult aft, the predecessor of those on all subsequent battleships and cruisers.

The battleship's main battery consisted of eight 16 in/45 guns mounted in four turrets of two guns each, two turrets forward and two aft, all on the center line. The guns were mounted in individual slides and could be elevated independently.

The secondary battery consisted of twelve 5in/51 rapid-fire guns, two of which were mounted on the superstructure deck, and the other ten—five on each side—in the enclosed portion of the upper deck. The 5-inch battery was served by eighteen 3-horsepower electrically driven chain ammunition hoists, designed to deliver horizontally a maximum of twenty rounds of ammunition per hoist per minute, the minimum rate of delivery being thirteen rounds of ammunition per hoist per minute. In addition to these hoists, there were also installed four horizontal continuous motion reversible conveyors for transfer of powder cases along the splinter deck passages to the port and starboard amidship hoists. Additionally, there were eight 3in/50 anti-aircraft guns and four 6-pounder saluting guns mounted on the superstructure deck; two 1-pounder boat guns, one 3-inch field piece, and two .30-caliber machine guns.

The torpedo equipment consisted of two 21-inch submerged torpedo tubes mounted in the ship's side just above the second platform between Frames 15 and 24.

The *Colorado* was fitted with a Westinghouse electric drive propulsion unit, while the *West Virginia* had General Electric equipment. Both manufacturers supplied similar material, the principal difference being in the method of starting the main motors. The electric drive propulsion system in these ships facilitated their construction to withstand underwater attack from torpedoes, shell fire, bombs and mines, requirements refined from British and German World War I combat experience.

The propulsion system description for this class will be confined to the *West Virginia.* Two main turbines of Curtis design, ten-stage, and rated 11,000 kilowatts at 2,065 rpm and 250 pounds steam pressure each, drove individual alternating current generators rated at 13,400 kilovolt-amperes, 4,325 volts (series generator connection), 1,550 amperes, and 82 percent power factor. The low-voltage connection was used only when one generator was used to drive all four motors. An interlock was used to cut out the high-voltage combination to prevent possible overload of the generator.

Special features of these installations were the use of steam heating coils in the generators to preserve dryness in the windings, and blowers on both motors and generators for air cooling. Temperature coils imbedded in the motor and generator stators and connected to a special board in the control room provided an easy and rapid means for checking on the condition of the equipment. Electrical and mechanical interlocks were installed to prevent mistakes in the operation of the equipment and to further ensure personnel safety.

Main motors, having a rating of 7,000 horsepower each at 170 rpm were connected through Kingsbury thrust bearings to propeller shafting and thus to the propellers. All were induction motors, with an internal high-resistance starting winding on the General Electric ships and external winding on the Westinghouse ships, which shifted to a low-resistance winding at operating speed. The motors were wound for 72 poles, but through terminal connections were capable of being operated at 36 or 24 poles on three-phase current.

Assuming a steady-state condition on one of the pole combinations, small changes in speed were made by varying the speed of the main alternators, and hence, the frequency. Any change in frequency was immediately reflected in the main motor speed. Control of all main drive features was centralized in a single compartment or control room located abaft the after machinery space and forward of the motor rooms. The governors and throttles of each of the main turbines could be adjusted for any demand by means of a hydraulic transmission from the main control board. Excitation of the main generators was furnished by three 300-kilowatt direct current generators in each machinery space, one noncondensing. Switches on the main control board permitted changing the excitation as the load varied. Additional control was furnished by a booster motor generator manipulated from the control board. Major changes in speed were made through three-pole oil-immersed switches for changing motor pole connections. Reversing the propellers required merely reversing two leads of the three-phase motor's supply. Meters indicated the instantaneous electrical circuit conditions. All cables were heavily insulated with varnished cambric and all exposed electrical parts were located in heavily grilled and screened cells. The successful test of electric drive in the collier *Jupiter* and the battleship *New Mexico* led to its approval for use in all World War I designs, the carriers *Lexington* and *Saratoga*, and merchant ships.[12]

Certain other features of the machinery of this class of battleships are worthy of note. The arrangement of the machinery placed main turbogenerators on an upper machinery flat. This enabled the turbines to exhaust directly downward into the main condensers, an entirely new innovation. In addition, some of these ships had condensers of the new "Lovekin" design, while others were designed by the Bureau of Engineering. A larger than usual number of electrically driven pumps and auxiliaries were also fitted. The evaporators installed marked a return to the low-pressure type, which for several years had been abandoned in the Navy. Operating under a vacuum and thoroughly redesigned, these evaporators gave new economies that corrected past deficiencies. The *Colorado* and *West Virginia* were both equipped with Babcock and Wilcox boilers, with superheater safety valves installed, identical to those in the *Tennessee*.

Aircraft Carriers

The arrival of the U.S. Navy carrier was really due to the perseverance of a number of Naval officers, both non-aviators and aviators, who saw the need for such ships from their experience during World War I. They included Rear Admiral William S. Sims, Rear Admiral H. T. Mayo, Captain Kenneth Whiting, then-Captain Thomas T. Craven, and then-Commander William S. Pye.[13] The conversion of the collier *Jupiter* to an aircraft carrier, the only expedient that Congress would authorize in 1919, was due to their foresight and persistence.[14]

The function of this new ship type was to provide a floating airbase for the repair, maintenance, and operation of aircraft carried aboard. The complexity of carrier design, even at that early date, made it fortunate that British naval constructor S. V. Goodall had been sent to wartime duty with the Bureau of Construction and Repair. Plans he brought of newer British designs, including carriers such as HMS *Hermes*, formed a starting point for American development.[15] Thus, in March 1922, a notable first occurred, the commissioning of the Navy's first carrier. The collier *Jupiter*, an electric-drive ship, was converted to the aircraft carrier *Langley*. It was named after Professor Samuel Pierpont Langley, a pioneer in aeronautics.[16] Shortly after the *Langley* entered service, the first U.S. Navy aircraft carrier take-off and landing occurred.

The most striking feature of the *Langley's* appearance was the great long wooden flight deck, which covered the ship nearly from stem to stern. This deck, with palisades for reducing wind velocity in certain deck areas, life nets for protection of deck personnel, catapults for launching seaplanes, elevators for hoisting aircraft to the flight deck from the hangar, gasoline piping for fueling aircraft, and arresting gear, formed the nucleus of the aircraft carrier's facilities. Improvements were also made to the engineering plant. These included the installation of a new low-pressure evaporating plant and a 6-ton ice machine. Three larger generators of 200-kilowatt capacity were installed in one of the former coal bunkers to supplement the two already-installed 35-kilowatt units. The regular Scotch boilers were retained but converted to oil burning and provided with a Howden closed ash pit system to supply air. The most noticeable engineering change was in the stack structure. The uptakes and smokepipes were led to the port side of the ship, with control dampers being arranged so that either smokepipe could be used. An experimental spray, fitted to the stack, was installed to cool combustion gases and, thus, partially eliminate the turbulence of the warm rising gases flowing over the flying deck.

The flying deck (as it was then called) extended from Frame 5 to the stern and was the width of the ship, making the dimensions 65 feet by 523 feet. It was supported by twenty-six symmetrically located towers. Access to the flying deck was through two hatches on opposite sides of the ship at Frame 156. These hatches were closed by balanced hatch covers. Forward on the center line at Frame 32, a signal hatch afforded additional access. The flying deck was wood-covered, with expansion joints located at intervals.

There was practically no change in the forecastle during conversion. Below the forecastle deck was the paint room; the lamp room, used for storage of "dope" for aircraft fabric; and the joiner shop, also used as a living space. The next lower deck contained a living compartment forward, with space for the ship's tailor and sailmaker; and the aviation machine shop, abaft the bulkhead at Frame 18. The first platform

deck contained the boatswain's stores and other storerooms for various ship and aviation stores. The well deck, just abaft the forecastle, was a continuation of the main deck, and extended to the break of the poop at Frame 139. An extension of the forecastle onto the well deck provided space for the assembly and repair officer's office on the well deck, starboard, and a printing shop on the port side. The main deck held the tower supports, operating stations for the elevator, both jib cranes, three gasoline supply stations, three lubricating oil supply stations, two motorboat platform cradles, stowage for one 24-foot motor sailing launch, and various holds for aircraft and repair parts stowage. There were twelve top-side ballast tanks under the passageways outboard the well deck. The raised poop deck was at the stern from Frame 139 aft. Above this deck was an aerological laboratory over the flight officer's quarters and the wardroom. Forward of the flight officer's quarters on the first deck was the sick bay, and forward of this, separated by the athwartship stack, was the intelligence office and the senior flight officer's office. The wardroom extended from the cabin to the poop deck to the galley spaces. The latter contained the officer's and crew's galleys, the bake shop, the butcher shop, and the scullery. Between the interior passageways leading to the galley were offices for the navigator, first lieutenant, ordnance officer, disbursing officer, and supply officer. The executive officer's office, radio room, and radio emergency battery room were forward of the galley spaces. Below the poop on the main deck level were the chief petty officer quarters, firemen's living quarters, and general crew space, containing the canteen, post office, log room, chief petty officers' room, two crew's washrooms and the steering engine room. This was the last complete deck aft. The flat forward of the aircraft engine room contained the small store issuing room, armory, radio repair room, instrument room, photographic laboratory, electrical workshop, brig, foundry, and laundry. Abaft the aircraft engine room on the stern were crew's quarters. On the flat below were storerooms for wardroom, cabin, chief petty officer, navigator, and medical issue. Between these storerooms, and what was formerly the after peak tank, was an after 5-inch magazine.

Extending from the main deck to the inner bottoms just abaft the forecastle were two voids, separated by a fore and aft bulkhead. These voids separated two forward deep oil tanks from two gasoline tanks. A water-filled cofferdam separated the gasoline tanks from the airplane stowage holds. These were followed by two aircraft holds, an elevator machinery compartment, and two more aircraft holds; the latter equipped for the stowage of wings, propellers, and lumber. Below all aircraft holds were double bottoms containing fuel oil. Below the gas tanks, cofferdam, and the void forward of gas tanks were double bottoms that contained water. An elevator compartment, between Frames 86 and 104, contained elevator machinery, gyrocompass house, air compressors and accumulators, and lubricating oil pumps. Hatches led below to a torpedo room with torpedo storage racks and warhead locker; a 5-inch magazine with shell, powder, and handling rooms; a small arms magazine; a bomb room; and four storerooms used for miscellaneous ship's stores. The elevator, when raised, was level with the flight deck; when lowered, it rested on the hatch above the main deck. The ship's motor boats, 24-foot motor sailers, dory, and two whaleboats were stowed on the main deck; the whaleboats swung outboard on davits. All other boats were nested on the same deck as flight officers' quarters.

The year 1925 was highlighted by the launching of the aircraft carriers *Lexington* and *Saratoga*. Both ships were originally authorized by Congress during World War I as battle cruisers. Early in 1922, work was suspended because of the Washington Disarmament Treaty. Later that year, the contract was modified to convert the ships to carriers as a result of the successful testing with the *Langley*. The building of these ships, however, proceeded very slowly after their 1925 launching and they were not commissioned until 1927.

The *Lexington* and *Saratoga* were unique, not only because they were the first aircraft carriers ever constructed for the U.S. Navy other than the experimental *Langley*, but also because they were propelled by the most powerful ship's machinery in history. In combined power, as well as in the power of the individual propulsion units, their shipboard machinery compared most

favorably with the largest shore power plants ever completed to that date.

These ships had an overall length of 888 feet, a beam of 106 feet, and a draft of 28 feet. The four installed turbogenerators, supplying power to electric motors on four shafts, developed a total of 180,000 horsepower for speeds in excess of 33 knots.

The large island to starboard included four smokepipes enclosed as a single unit, extended 79 feet above the flying deck, and was approximately 110 feet long. The ships carried an armament of eight 8-inch guns in four twin mounts and a number of bow and quarter anti-aircraft guns. The ship's complement comprised 169 officers, 23 warrant officers, and 1,708 enlisted men.

The hull profile of the *Lexington* and *Saratoga* resembled that of the *West Virginia* class of battleship. Other distinctive features were the fully enclosed stacks, the tripod-supported flag bridge, the anti-aircraft gun galleries, and the boat pockets set into the side of the ship under the flight deck. Turrets, bridge structure, and stacks were installed to extreme starboard with only a narrow passage outboard. The overweight to starboard was compensated for by fuel oil and other ballast to port. The port boiler uptakes were trunked to the stacks by four horizontal venturi-shaped crossovers, passing athwartship just above the third deck.

The flight deck extended the entire length of the ship, bow to stern, and ended in sloping ramps fore and aft. This deck was surrounded with appropriately placed life nets and wind barriers, and was equipped with all the necessary facilities for handling aircraft, including catapult, deck tie-downs for aircraft, illumination, an aircraft crane, and arresting gear. The flight deck was served by two hydraulic elevators from the hangar deck.

Most of the crew was berthed on the main deck from Frame 67 to the stern. This space also included the galleys, washrooms, and other crew facilities. The remainder of the crew was housed outboard of the hangar space, mainly on the port side, and on the upper half deck and middle half deck. The third deck was armored and all the machinery compartments were entered from this deck.

Air for the forced draft blowers was taken to starboard from doors opening outboard having protected spray shields, or from doors off the hangar space inboard. To port, air was taken from ducts opening into boat pockets or from doors off the hangar space inboard. The main alternators and propulsion motors had self-contained, water-cooled cooling systems.

There were seven elevators installed: one double hydraulic piston aircraft elevator with full load capacity of 16,000 pounds and speed of 60 feet per minute with 12,000 pounds; one single hydraulic piston aircraft elevator with full load capacity of 6,000 pounds and speed of 120 feet per minute with 5,000 pounds load; one electric freight-type elevator with 3,360-pound capacity and speed of 120 feet per minute; and four electric dumbwaiter elevators.

The electric-hydraulic steering gear consisted of eight 24-inch hydraulic rams connected to the rudder by thrust and connecting rods. The rams delivered a torque to the rudder of 75 million inch-pounds with 1,000 psi hydraulic pressure. At 31 knots, the rudder could be reversed in 30 seconds. In general, except for size, the equipment was similar in almost all respects to that installed on the battleships of the period. Emergency operation of the steering gear main drive motor was provided for by a 900-ampere hour storage battery installed in an adjacent compartment. Automatic relays cut the battery in and out with failure or return of ship's power. Overload conditions were cared for by overload and step-back relays. In addition to trick wheel and hand control, which could operate the steering engine directly, the ship could be steered from the pilot house, conning tower, secondary conning tower, central station, and steering control room aft.

Aviation gasoline was stored in tanks similar to the fuel-oil storage, but surrounded by ventilated voids. A saltwater exchange system was used to withdraw gasoline from these tanks. Total gasoline capacity was 163,000 gallons.

Although the ship employed electric drive, a difference existed between this installation and that of the previous battleships, partly due to the 180,000 designed horsepower. It is sufficiently significant to be covered in some depth. Four main turbogenerators, each in a separate machinery space, furnished the power for driving the main motors. As in the battleships, the boilers were in individual compartments outboard of the turbogenerator rooms. Sixteen boilers in an equal number of firerooms were outboard of the machinery spaces, eight to each side. The boilers were oil burning, Yarrow type with a heating surface of 11,250 square feet and a superheating surface of 797 square feet. The safety valve setting was 295 psi. The boilers received air from thirty-two forced draft blowers, two per fireroom for the sixteen firerooms, and had a capacity of 35,000 cubic feet per minute.

Fuel oil was distributed (via four relay tanks, two on each side) to nine service bottoms, eighty-nine storage tanks, and twenty-four emergency storage tanks. The storage tanks were outboard of the machinery spaces on both sides and in the double bottom compartments. A considerable weight of fuel oil (or water) was stored to port at all times to compensate for the extra weight on the starboard side. Total usable fuel oil was about 5,400 tons.

The propulsion turbines were rated as 32,500 kilowatts at 1,755 rpm with 265 psi steam at the throttle and 50 degrees of superheat. Being General Electric turbines, they were Curtis-impulse type. Directly connected to each turbine were main generators, rated at 40,000 kilovolt-amperes, 3 phase, 5,000 volts. Driving the propeller shafts were eight 22,500-horsepower induction motors connected in tandem pairs to the shafts to drive the four propellers.

The propeller shafting consisted of four 41-foot, 6-inch shafts, 22.5-inch outer diameter. Tube shafts were 46 feet, 10 inches long with a 22.5-inch outer diameter. Thrust shafts were 30 feet, 10 inches long with a 21-inch outer diameter. The main thrust bearings were Kingsbury horizontal, double-split, shoe-type, with six ahead thrust shoes, and six astern thrust shoes. Each shaft had two steady bearings, one at each end of the thrust bearing housing, a spring bearing, a forward and an after wood-lined stern tube bearing, and a wood-lined strut bearing.

Three-bladed propellers, approximately 15 feet in diameter, were supplied by the Philadelphia Navy Yard with a pitch of 13 feet, 3 inches and a projected area of 110 square feet.

For general electric power, six ship's service

direct current turbogenerators were used (also serving as exciters for the propulsion turbogenerators). A direct current switchboard was on the same level alongside each of three generators. Power was sent to the two distribution-room switchboards and to the direct current switchboard in the control room. There were also four main direct current switchboards and numerous smaller switchboards throughout the ship.

The ship's service generator turbines were horizontal, four-stage, Curtis (impulse) condensing type, and operated at 5,000 rpm. This type turbine was designed with a steam pressure of 250 psi gauge, 50 degrees Fahrenheit superheat. The generator reduction gear was of the single-reduction forced-lubrication type. The reduction ratio was 5,000 to 800 rpm. The generator was a shunt-wound, 8-pole, 240-volt, 3,125-ampere, 750-kilowatt unit that operated at 800 rpm. The design included commutating poles, compensating windings in the pole faces, and multiple-drum armature windings. What clearly distinguished this generator from generators previously encountered in naval service was that it was two-wire shunt wound, thus eliminating the need for equalizers in parallel operation and compensating pole face windings. Ship's lighting was obtained from two motor generators in each of the distribution rooms. The motor generators consisted of a 190-horsepower direct current motor, driving shunt-wound generators at 125 volts, 1,000 amperes (125 kilowatts) at 1,200 rpm. The motor generators transformed the 240 direct-current voltage of the ship's turbogenerators to 120 volts direct current for use in the lighting systems.

The radio installation included sending and receiving equipment, radio compasses, underwater sound capability, and a fathometer depth indicating system. This equipment was the most complete and diversified to be found on any ship of the time.

Interior communicating systems were diversified. The main equipment consisted of voice tubes, intercommunicating anti-noise telephone systems, ship's service telephones and switchboard, call bells and annunciators, general announcing system, electrical and mechanical telegraph and indicator systems, fire alarm and general alarm bells, and various bell and light alarm systems.

The ship's boat allowance was quite limited. All boats carried, except for motor life boats, were equipped with Navy V-Type engines. The stowage of a considerable percentage of these boats in boat pockets necessitated an elaborate hoisting and stowage equipment.

Thirteen motor-driven aircraft capstans mounted at various locations on the main, second, and hangar decks, and three motor-driven aircraft winches on the main deck, were all driven by compound 20-horsepower motors.

Fully equipped aircraft repair and overhaul shops were provided, as well as a general workshop and an electrical repair shop for ship's use. A woodworking shop, foundry, coppersmith shop, sheet metal shop, photographic shop, and optical repair shop were also provided.

In 1927, these carriers were completed. They underwent sea trials in 1928 and broke all existing speed records for capital naval ships.[17] The *Saratoga* maintained a speed of 33.42 knots over a measured mile course, and the *Lexington* maintained a speed of 30.7 knots for 72 hours, 34 minutes, between San Pedro, California, and Honolulu, a distance of 2,228 nautical miles. In addition, the *Lexington* broke the record for sustained speed for periods of 24, 48, and 72 hours for any class of ship. This record was formerly held by a commercial vessel, the SS *Mauretania*.

During the period 1922 through 1932, several other aircraft carrier designs were developed.[18] They ranged in displacement from just under 10,000 tons, to exclude them from treaty limitations, to about 27,000 tons. The heaviest aircraft considered for duty with these designs were usually 10,000 pounds and required 250 feet for carrier takeoff and 350 feet for landing, assuming wind speed of 27 knots or better over the deck. The area in between was to be used for handling planes on the flight deck. These criteria resulted in a requirement for a minimum active flight deck length of 600 feet, plus whatever was needed to handle returning and ready aircraft on deck. Other major design problems centered around the desire for a clear, flush deck for an aircraft carrier. That these designs did not have island structures presented many problems in both ship and aircraft handling as well as severe stack gas turbulence problems.

Commander J. C. Hunsaker, a naval engineer and constructor who helped establish American aerodynamics and who was an assistant naval attache in London in 1925, helped clear up some of the confusion by reporting on British experience.[19] The British had gotten far ahead of the United States in carrier design and operating experience in World War I and had operated aircraft carriers with both flush deck and island configurations. Flush deck design had caused such turbulence problems from stack gases that the British had been forced into major modifications. Later British carriers such as the HMS *Hermes* and *Eagle*, which were operating in 1925, had island structures, and CDR Hunsaker reported that the British aviators ". . . have learned to be no longer afraid of the island. . . ." However, the Bureau of Aeronautics (BuAer) did not give up the idea of the flush deck carrier until the 1930s when the United States decided to build a class of several new aircraft carriers.

Submarines

As discussed in the previous chapter, the first post-war American submarines were the T-boats. These were "fleet" submarines authorized before the United States entered World War I but not laid down until 1920. Although previous American submarines (except for the Navy-designed S-boats) were designed by commercial firms according to certain Navy-dictated specifications, the three T-boats and all subsequent fleet submarines were Navy-designed. The T-boats were the first American submarines with a surface displacement of over 1,000 tons. They were not particularly successful because they suffered from engine problems and poor seakeeping; therefore, they were laid up after a brief operational career and were scrapped in 1930, along with several older boats, to meet the London Naval Treaty limitations.

The trend toward larger submarines was reflected in the next three submarine classes, the first of the so-called V-boats. All were originally assigned letter-number names in the V series, but they were better known by their later names, with each class's names beginning with the same letter. The submarine V-3, *Bonita,* was launched

in 1925 as the last of the trio of fleet boats of which *Barracuda* and *Bass* were the first (SS-163 through 165).[20] These were the heaviest submarines to accompany the battle fleet on all occasions.[21] The V-3 class submarines had an overall length of 341½ feet, a breadth of 27½ feet, a draft of 15½ feet, and a displacement of 2,164 tons on the surface and 2,520 tons submerged. They were propelled by Busch-Sulzer motors of 6,500 brake horsepower and could attain a surface speed of 21 knots.[22] Their armament consisted of one 5-inch caliber gun fitted on a high-angle mounting, six torpedo tubes, and sixteen torpedoes. A key feature of this design was the great radius of action. This class had several new features: a bulbous bow, a forward engine room that was placed forward of the conning tower and control room, bow and stern torpedo rooms, and two deck levels except in way of the forward and after torpedo rooms. Another unusual feature was hatch-access trunks that could be flooded and drained to serve as escape chambers for the crew. These boats, too, had limited success, being difficult to maneuver and hampered by internal arrangement.

Construction of a still larger submarine, the V-4, was begun in May 1925. It was stated that the V-4 would displace 3,000 tons on the surface; i.e., 220 tons more than the British X-1, which at that time was the world's largest. The V-4, *Argonaut*, was the only American submarine built specifically as a mine-layer, but also with the capability to use guns and torpedoes. The *Argonaut*, launched in 1928, displaced 4,100 tons submerged (2,710 tons on the surface)[23] and was 381 feet long.[24] Two more similar to the *Argonaut*, the *Narwhal* (V-5) and the *Nautilus* (V-6), came along in 1930.

The continuing growth in size and cost of United States submarines was temporarily reversed by construction of the USS *Dolphin* (SS-169), originally designated the V-7. When she was completed in 1932, the *Dolphin* showed the characteristic clean lines and other features of the Navy's later fleet submarines. Forward, behind the *Dolphin*'s sharp bow, were the openings for four bow torpedo tubes. Another pair of tubes was fitted in the stern. The *Dolphin* set the standard for later U.S. submarines, with internal arrangement from bow to stern as follows: the forward torpedo room with reload torpedoes and bunks for the crew, "officers' country" with berthing for the officers, the control room located below the conning tower, the crew's quarters with bunks for most of the fifty-five sailors, the galley, the engine room, the maneuvering room where the engines were controlled, and the after torpedo room. Between the torpedo room and engine room there was a lower level for housing the large wet-cell batteries, stores, and auxiliary machinery. However, the *Dolphin* was not a successful submarine and was used mainly as a training platform until World War II. Later designs had the benefit of better diesel engines and other features that reduced submarine size, a trend that continued until after World War II.[25]

Submarine Tenders

The USS *Holland*, Submarine Tender No. 3, was constructed at the Puget Sound Navy Yard in Washington and commissioned in 1926.[26] The *Holland* was a single-screw ship driven by diesel engine propulsion.

Just as submarine size had increased over the years, so was the *Holland* larger than previous U.S. Navy submarine tenders. Her beam, draft, and displacement were the same as those of the destroyer tender *Dobbin*; but, the addition of a clipper bow gave her a length of 513 feet instead of 485 feet overall. On her trials, the *Holland* displaced 11,038 tons and achieved 15.87 knots.

The construction of the ship incorporated the experience from World War I in terms of watertight subdivisions of the hull to resist torpedoes and mines, the supplies to be carried, and the facilities to meet the requirements of wartime service. The USS *Holland* was designed to meet all ordinary demands of service, supplies, and repairs for a group of eighteen submarines for a period of 60 days in wartime. The necessary shop facilities for this included pattern, foundry, general machine, electrical, gyro, forge, coppersmith, sheet metal, ship carpenter, torpedo, and optical shops. The supplies carried included fuel oil, lubricating oil, fresh water, provisions, and spare parts for machinery and other equipments. The medical facilities included a ward, an operating room, and a dental department.

The main battery consisted of eight 5-inch guns. Four were on the main deck and four on the superstructure deck. Four 3in/50 anti-aircraft guns were also installed; in addition, there were two 6-pounder saluting guns on the bridge deck. Two torpedo tubes were installed in the torpedo workshop, primarily for testing torpedoes after overhaul.

There was one electrically operated torpedo hoist winch manufactured by Lenher Engineering Company on the second deck between Frames 69 and 71, port side, with a capacity of 4,000 pounds at 600 feet per minute. The winch was single geared and was fitted with a reversible drum controller. The drum controller was designed for dynamic breaking. The semi-enclosed motor was wound for 120 volts direct current and was fitted with an electromagnetic brake.

The *Holland* was equipped with an American Engineering Company steam-driven towing engine on the main deck aft to maintain a uniform tension on a towline at all times. A device was installed on the engine aft of the drum to guide the wire rope as it was coiled on, or uncoiled from, the drum.

The *Holland*'s machinery plant was similar to those in the USS *Dobbin* and USS *Whitney*, discussed later in this chapter. Three Mayflower-Lodi blower burners made by Babcock and Wilcox Company were installed on each boiler, allowing the *Holland* to operate with open firerooms up to about 14 knots. Above this speed, firerooms were closed and forced draft blowers were used to provide air to the boilers. The boilers were insulated in accordance with the new *General Specifications for Machinery* of 1925.

Main propelling turbines, manufactured by the Puget Sound Navy Yard from plans and specifications purchased from the Parsons Marine Steam Turbine Company, delivered 7,000 shaft horsepower at 105 rpm for a speed of 16 knots. The reduction gears were cut and machined in the Philadelphia Navy Yard. The propeller was manufactured in the Puget Sound Navy Yard from Bureau of Engineering plans.

To eliminate the running of tended submarine's generators for charging storage batteries, alongside, two 400-kilowatt generators were installed. Geared turbines running at 5,000 rpm drove the shunt wound generators at 1,000 rpm to produce variable power from 325 to 125 volts. Leads from a battery charging switchboard were run from ship's side, and 2,400 feet of cable were provided for charging submarine batteries in place. A motor-generator set to provide the very low voltage for a single cell charging was also installed.

Repair Ships

The *Medusa*, a repair ship designed for service with the Fleet, was commissioned at the Puget Sound Navy Yard in July 1924.[27] For primary use as a tender for battleship divisions, the characteristics of the *Medusa* were laid down, with consideration being given to steaming radius, speed, and capacity to handle battleship repair work.

The primary function of the *Medusa* was service to battleships, consisting mainly of repairs that could be classed as permanent, an entirely new concept in repair ship design.

Probably the most interesting item of this ship's installation was the extent of the repair plant for heavy machinery; the equipment in some cases being superior to that provided in Navy shipyards. The main machine shop occupied thirty-three frame spaces on the third deck and was reached through two large hatches. Two 2-ton double-beam electric traveling cranes and a 3-ton bridge crane, capable of traveling the full length of the shop, served to handle heavy materials. Several boring machines were provided, including a 73-inch Niles Bement Pond vertical boring and turning milling machine. Several large lathes capable of handling the largest forging encountered on the battleships (up to 6 feet diameter) were installed, in addition to the usual numbers of drill presses, grinders, shapers, planers, milling machines, arbor presses, cut-off saws, etc. On the second deck were a gallery machine shop and tool machine shop to supplement the main shop. Additional shops, such as the large optical repair shop on the forecastle deck, were also fitted in the ship. Two small enclosed spaces in the after end of the optical repair shop served as a laboratory and a gyro repair shop. On the third deck, abaft the machine shop, were the foundry, with its 32-inch cupola capable of melting 4 tons of iron per hour, and an 18-inch cupola having a 1½-ton capacity. Core ovens, grinding wheels, chipping

benches, tumbling barrels, weighing scales, four oil-fired tilting crucible furnaces for melting nonferrous metals, molding tubes, blowers, and traveling cranes provided the *Medusa* with a well-equipped foundry. Pattern and joiner shops, blacksmith and boiler shops, sheet metal and plating shops, pipe and copper shops, a printing shop, and an electric shop completed the ensemble.

Destroyer Tenders—
USS *Dobbin* and USS *Whitney*

The destroyer tenders *Dobbin* and *Whitney* were completed in 1924[28] and were named in honor of previous Secretaries of the Navy. They were designed to meet all ordinary demands of service, supplies, and repairs for a group of eighteen destroyers for a period of 60 days in wartime. The necessary shop facilities for this duty included pattern, foundry, general machine, electrical, gyro, forge, coppersmith, sheet metal, ship carpenter, torpedo, and optical shops. The supplies carried included fuel oil, lubricating oil, fresh water, provisions, and spare parts for machinery and installed equipments. The medical facilities included a ward, an operating room, a laboratory, a contagious ward, a prophylactic room, and a dental department. The design and construction of these tenders was delayed to ensure that experiences in World War I, such as those related to underwater protection, supplies, and facilities needed to support repair of destroyers during wartime conditions, might be incorporated.

Both the *Dobbin* and the *Whitney* had a length of 460 feet between perpendiculars, a molded beam of 60 feet, 10⅛ inches, and mean draft of 21 feet. They displaced 10,600 tons with waterline load. These ships were relatively mobile, with a full-power speed of better than 15 knots.

The refrigerating plant, consisting of the ice machines and cold storage rooms, was on the third deck. The cold storage rooms, in addition to the tenders' needs, were also for cargo, and supplied service needs for refrigerated provisions.

Electrical power was supplied by turbogenerators on the dynamo platform in the engine room. The main switchboard, located on the dynamo platform forward of amidships, distributed power throughout the ship through over twenty-five major circuits.

Two fuel-oil-burning boilers of the Bureau of Engineering express type were installed in these ships, each boiler in a watertight compartment. The smokepipe was trunked to each of the two boilers. Two forced draft blowers were provided per fireroom. Three blower burners of the Babcock & Wilcox Lodi type were installed on each boiler. A small handpump was provided for starting the burners. The blower burners were of ample capacity for normal operating conditions, but used the forced draft blowers in emergency conditions, to increase the rate of combustion.

The main propelling machinery consisted of a high- and a low-pressure turbine connected to a single propeller shaft through reduction gearing. The high-pressure turbine casing contained ahead and astern turbines, with the same arrangement in the low-pressure turbine. The ahead turbines were standard Parsons reaction-type turbines, while the astern units were the impulse wheel-type turbines. The interconnecting piping between the two turbines was so arranged that in the event of breakdown, blank flanges could be fitted and the turbine isolated. The turbine casings were made of cast iron, divided on their horizontal axes. The joint between the casings was made metal-to-metal with "fitted" flange bolts.

The identical reduction gear and pinions in the *Dobbin* and *Whitney* were manufactured by the Philadelphia Navy Yard, and were the largest marine reduction gears cut in the United States to that date. The gear was of the single reduction type and the main thrust bearing was directly aft of it.

The main shafting for the *Dobbin* and *Whitney* was also manufactured by the Philadelphia Navy Yard. Shafting could be drawn forward into the engine room through portable plates in the bulkheads. Stuffing boxes were installed where the shafts pierced watertight bulkheads. Brass sleeves were installed on the propeller shaft for bearings and to protect the shaft from corrosion.

Gunboats

The *Guam* (PG43) commissioned in 1927, and the *Tutuila* (PG44) in 1928 were built for Yangtze River service to China.[29] The earlier gunboats, the *Monacacy* and *Palso* were built at the Mare Island, California, Navy Yard, taken apart, shipped to China, and reassembled and launched at a local Shanghai dockyard. The *Guam* and *Tutuila*, however, were constructed in Shanghai at the Kiangnan Dock & Engineering Works. These two ships had a length of 150 feet, a design draft of 5 feet, 3 inches for shallow-river service, and a displacement of 387 tons. They were twin-screw, open-stern boats with three rudders and a spoon bow. They had a speed, as required by the U.S. Navy General Board, of greater than 15 knots.

At designed draft, these gunboats could carry approximately 2,200 gallons of fresh water, 7 tons of reserve feedwater in the reserve feed tank and 100 gallons of feedwater in the engine room feed tank, and 26 tons of fuel oil. Fuel oil bunker capacity at 95 percent full was approximately 78 tons.

In addition to the *Guam* and *Tutuila*, four other gunboats were launched at the Kiangnan Dock in 1927: the *Panay*, the *Oahu*, the *Luzon*, and the *Mindanao*.[30] The *Panay* and *Oahu* were 30 feet longer than the *Guam* and *Tutuila*, having a length of 180 feet, a draft of 5 feet, 6 inches, and a displacement of 474 tons. This increase in size was primarily because these gunboats had two firerooms instead of the one installed in the *Guam* class. They also had improved accommodations. The *Luzon* and *Mindanao*, designed to serve as flagships, were even larger: 198 feet in length, with a design draft of 6 feet and displacement of 615 tons.

The general specifications of the *Luzon*-class gunboat were similar to that of the *Guam*. This class was of the twin-screw, open-stern type with three rudders constructed of the lightest weight material consistent with sufficient strength for river service. All structural steel plates, and all iron and steel fittings, were galvanized using the hot dip process before installation.

The *Guam* class had two boilers in one fireroom, with fuel-oil tanks outboard on each side of the fireroom. The *Luzon* class had two separate firerooms, and, in addition to oil tanks outboard, had a tank that extended across the ship just forward of the forward fireroom.

The main deck of the *Luzon* was not a great deal different than the main deck of the *Guam*, except in its officers' quarters and in the absence of a galley. There were seven officers' staterooms on this deck, one of them double, and a wardroom twice the size of the *Guam* wardroom, together with baths and pantry. The flag facilities in the *Luzon* were on the upper deck along with the captain's quarters and one officer's stateroom. The captain's cabin was just aft of the bridge. The flag facilities included a flag office, bath and toilet, stateroom, cabin, an additional officer's stateroom, and a flag pantry. Over these quarters was the flag officer's "Palm-garden", fitted with grass rugs and wicker furniture and covered with double awnings—a delightful place to use during warm weather.

Gunboat armament consisted of two 3in/50 anti-aircraft guns, with bulletproof shields, one on the upper deck, centerline, forward of the bridge, and the other aft of the sick bay on the centerline. The forward gun had an arc of fire from dead ahead to 115 degrees aft on each side; the after gun from dead astern to 140 degrees forward on each side. There were eight machine gun mounts with bulletproof shields installed on the upper deck; a nest of three on each side at about the forward smoke pipe, and one on each side aft the main mast. The usual small arms and ordnance accessories were carried, including a 1-meter range finder.

Coast Guard Construction

Bear Class Replacement

The Coast Guard was also active in naval engineering during this period. In 1925, plans were developed for a new Coast Guard cutter for use in Arctic service.[31] This replacement for the cutter *Bear*, built with a direct-current electric drive of 1,000 horsepower, was eventually named the *Northland*. The use of electric drive was not novel; by this time, direct-current electric propulsion had made great gains and was slowly becoming the preferred method of propulsion for naval and merchant ships,[32] particularly in the United States.

To replace the *Bear*, a ship was designed by the Construction and Repair Department of the Coast Guard in Washington, D.C. In building the cutter, a procedure differing from the ordinary was followed. Contractors were called on to bid on the construction of the hull and installation only of the propelling machinery, the latter already purchased by the government, together with considerable equipment, including boats, hawsers, navigating outfit, radio outfit, china, and bed linen, to be delivered at Government expense. The Newport News Shipbuilding and Dry Dock Company won the contract for construction of the hull of the new Coast Guard cutter *Northland* at a cost of $585,000.

The *Northland* had a most unique design, quite different from any preceding Coast Guard ship. It had an overall length of 216 feet, a molded beam of 39 feet, and a designed mean draft of 15 feet. It displaced 2,050 tons and had a designed trial speed of 11 knots with 1,000 shaft horsepower. A primary hull requirement was ability to navigate in heavy ice and to withstand the enormous pressures of ice flows. To this end, the forefoot was cut away to above the waterline and all the shell plating at or near the waterline was of exceptionally heavy scantlings, with a maximum thickness of 1¼ inches at the bow. Supporting this heavy shell was a framing system of extraordinary strength and stiffness. The transverse frames, spaced 24 inches apart, were all of the "built up" or "web" type, were 16 inches in depth, and extended up to the main deck. To resist heavy transverse stresses of ice pressure, the upper, main, and berth decks were each completely plated and had heavy channel beams on every frame. The berth deck beams, which would have to withstand the heaviest pressure, were 10 inches in depth. The midship section was of particular interest because, for its size, it was the strongest and heaviest steel hull ever developed to date.

The propelling machinery of the new cutter marked an even greater departure from previous Coast Guard practice than did the hull. A diesel-electric drive was used and all auxiliaries and deck machinery were electrically driven. Steam was used only for heating, cooking, and to visually augment air whistles and horns. Even the feed pump for the two small steam boilers was electrical.

The main propelling unit consisted of two

6-cylinder, 4-cycle, single-acting, McIntosh and Seymour diesel engines, each developing 600 shaft horsepower at 200 rpm. These units were directly connected to a General Electric direct-current generator, having an output of 410 kilowatts at 350 volts. Two direct-current exciters, each having an output of 75 kilowatts at 120 volts, were directly attached to extensions of the generator shafts. The two generators drove a single 500-volt, double armature motor having an output of 1,000 shaft horsepower. This motor was connected directly to the single propeller shaft by a magnetic clutch, the latter being located between the motor and the main thrust bearing. The line and propeller shafts, 10 inches and 11 inches in diameter, respectively, drove a four-bladed, built-up bronze propeller, 10 feet in diameter.

All auxiliary machinery was electrically operated from the main or auxiliary generators. The latter two auxiliary generators had an output of 60 kilowatts at 120 volts and 500 rpm and were driven by 6-cylinder, 4-cycle Winton diesel engines of 90 brake horsepower. The principal function of these large auxiliary generators was to furnish excitation for the two main generators and the propelling motor, in emergency. In addition to the two principal auxiliary generating sets, a third set, consisting of a Hill 25 brake horsepower diesel furnished power when the larger generators were not in use. To utilize shore alternating current when in port, an 18-kilowatt motor-generator was installed.

The *Lake*-Class Cutter

In 1926, Congress authorized the construction of ten cutters and appropriated money for the first three. The resultant *Lake*-class cutters were 250 feet overall and made 17 knots on 3,000 shaft horsepower. While the U.S. Navy was shifting from electric drive to geared turbines, the *Lake* class was designed to employ steam turbines with a synchronous, alternating electric-current drive. Ship service power was also derived from the main turbogenerator as long as it was developing at least two-thirds power and turning at more than 40 cycles per second. These ten cutters were delivered from 1928 through 1931.[33] These cutters were originally intended to

break ice on the Great Lakes; therefore, they had heavy plating at the bow and waterline.

The 125-Foot and 165-Foot Patrol Boats

During the years 1926 and 1927, thirty-three 125-foot patrol boats were built for the Coast Guard by the American Brown-Boveri Electric Corporation, later known as the New York Shipbuilding Company.[34] These 125-foot patrol boats were all twin-screw, and had two 150-horsepower Winton air-injection diesel engines. These engines were nonreversing and the propellers were gear-reversed. During trials, these patrol boats made approximately 11.5 knots, a speed that made them very effective for law-enforcement work, and early in their service they were used in pursuing smugglers outside the 12-mile limit. Later, smugglers used boats of such increased speeds that some were able to outrun the 125-foot patrol boats.

In 1931, the Coast Guard took delivery of the first of six 165-foot patrol boats.[35] These boats displaced 294 tons and had a speed of 16 knots at 1,340 shaft horsepower. They had an overall length of 165 feet, a beam of 25 feet, and draft of approximately 13 feet. One of these 165-foot patrol boats, the *Electra*, became the presidential yacht, the *Potomac*, in 1935, after serving as a Coast Guard cutter for about a year. Scantlings for these boats were determined so as to make them as light as possible but with ample strength for seaworthiness under all operating conditions. Accordingly, the stiffeners of deck beams and watertight bulkheads were made of bulb-angles, the bottom and side plating was made 12.8 pounds for half the length amidships and reduced to 10.2 pounds at the ends. The deck plating on the weather deck was, in general, 7.7-pound plate with increased thickness in the stringer plates and doubling plates fitted in way of guns, ventilators, and bitts. Ample watertight subdivision was provided by six watertight bulkheads and two oil-tight bulkheads, which extended from keel to weather deck. Two forward bulkheads and one after were fitted with watertight doors for access through living spaces. There were two decks on these boats, the main or weather deck and the berth deck. The weather deck, as stated above, was all steel plated. The berth deck was wood planked and used steel bulb-angles for deck beams. The wood deck extended throughout the berthing and messing spaces, except that the galley used Alumalum tile laid atop steel plates. Engine room walking flats were of corrugated aluminum alloy plates laid on steel foundation bars.

The deckhouse was on the main or weather deck, just forward of the engine room trunk, and forward of it were the anchor windlass, a 3 in/23 anti-aircraft gun, two 1-pounder guns, and two companion hatches for crew's quarters access. The bridge was at the forward end of the deckhouse, raised about 3 feet above the main deck to ensure clear vision over the bow and abaft. In the deckhouse were the commanding officer's stateroom (just abaft the bridge); the radio room; officers' washroom, shower, toilet spaces; crew's washroom, shower, and toilet spaces; and access forward to the berth deck, to the warrant officer's staterooms, and to the engine room. Atop the deckhouse were two 18-inch incandescent searchlights and one 18-inch high-intensity searchlight. The radio direction finder loop, magnetic compass, flag lockers, two ventilation blowers, and two life rafts were also on top of the deckhouse.

The heating system consisted of a cast iron, low-pressure, steam-heating boiler and copper-fin type, extended-surface radiators. Ventilation through the staterooms, berthing spaces, and messing spaces was provided by three Sirocco motor-driven utility blowers delivering 1,200 cubic feet of air per minute. Two were located forward atop the deckhouse and one aft atop the heating-boiler hatch. The refrigerating plant consisted of two electric refrigerators, one with food storage capacity of 17 cubic feet and the other 10 cubic feet. To ventilate engine room bilges, a blower with a capacity of 320 cubic feet of air per minute drew air from the bilges and discharged it above the weather deck.

The propellers had a diameter of 62 inches and a pitch of 53 inches. The projected area ratio was 0.40. Each propeller turned outboard. The propeller shafting outside the hull was fitted with fair-waters adjacent to the shaft struts and propeller hub to minimize eddy resistance. The single-arm shaft struts were also streamlined to reduce resistance.

MERCHANT SHIP DEVELOPMENTS

1929 International Safety Convention

The International Convention on Safety of Life at Sea agreed to safety items for construction and equipment of ships.[36] Although strictly applicable only to merchant ships, the terms of the convention had clear influence on future naval designs and operations. Actually, many naval designers contributed in the development of the proposed convention.

Turbo-Electric Passenger Liners

United States merchant shipping made advances in the new Dollar liners, the SS *President Hoover* and the SS *President Coolidge*, delivered in 1933 and 1934, respectively.[37] Each was designed to carry 988 passengers, and had a 654-foot length and 31,063 ton displacement. Their 20.5-knot speed came from turbines driving alternators that supplied synchronous induction motors on twin shafts. When launched, these ships were the largest passenger liners built in the United States and part of an escalating race in the size, power, and luxury of passenger liners.

The hulls were of the complete superstructure type. On each liner, there were two masts, each fitted with cargo handling booms, and one smoke pipe. What appeared to be a second smoke pipe was a dummy used for engine room ventilation. There were nine decks in all; five of which were fully plated. Transverse framing was used throughout. The frames amidships were spaced 36 inches apart and reduced forward and aft in steps to 24 inches in the peaks. The hulls were subdivided by ten watertight bulkheads, seven of which extended to the shelter deck, two to the upper deck, and the collision bulkhead to the bridge deck. The double bottom extended from the collision bulkhead aft to Frame 200. It was divided longitudinally into eleven compartments. Those forward of the engine room were fitted for carrying fuel oil or water ballast, and those under and aft of the engine room were fitted for carrying fresh water. Sixteen watertight doors were provided in the watertight bulkheads below the main deck. They were electrically operated and controlled by the Cutler-Hammer-Newport News system. Each vessel had a slightly raked straight stem and an elliptical protected-rudder-type stern. The stern was bossed to carry the propeller shafting.

The first-class accommodations were amidships on five decks and were served by two Otis electric elevators, each having a capacity of 1,800 pounds at a speed of 200 feet per minute. There were 108 staterooms and four deluxe suites. The main dining salon was on the upper deck, adjoining the main entrance lobby. The main dining salon seated 272 persons and an adjoining private dining room seated 18 more. A writing room, lounge, smoke room, marine tea garden, and soda fountain were on the promenade deck. An open-air swimming pool, gymnasium, and children's play room were provided on the boat deck.

There were thirty-nine special-class staterooms on the shelter deck, adjoining the first-class quarters. These were arranged to be first-class accommodations if desired. The smoking room and lounge for special class were on the bridge deck and the 120-person dining salon was on the upper deck. Forward of the bridge, a deck cargo hatch was fitted for an open-air swimming pool for the special class. A deck promenade was provided abreast of the swimming pool, port and starboard.

The third-class passengers were accommodated in twenty-three staterooms on the upper deck aft. A dining salon seating 114 persons was provided on this deck. A social hall was on the shelter deck aft, and open-air space was provided on the after end of the bridge deck.

Permanent accommodations for 60 steerage passengers and portable berths for 318 additional passengers were on the main deck aft. Open-air deck space was provided for these passengers on the shelter deck aft.

Ship's company numbered about 323. Officers were quartered on the boat deck; petty officers, crew, and stewards were quartered on the shelter and upper decks forward; and the engineer's force was quartered on the main deck, amidship, port side.

All staterooms and living quarters, including crew's quarters below the boat deck, galleys, pantries, mess rooms, and machinery spaces were mechanically ventilated by means of supply and exhaust systems. The engine room system functioned through a ventilating funnel, located over the engine hatch and similar in size and appearance to the smoke pipe.

Each vessel carried twenty metallic boats, with capacity for 280 persons. The boats were handled by ten sets of Welin-McLachlan gravity davits, eight sets of hand-operated Welin quadrant davits, and two electric boat winches.

Each vessel had two 18,900-pound anchors, one 16,065-pound spare bow anchor, and one 6,825-pound stream anchor. Each main bower anchor was provided with 165 fathoms of 3¼-inch stud-link, chain cable. The windlass was on the forecastle and was of the horizontal, steam-driven, spur-geared type with 14-inch by 14-inch double-cylinder engine. An independent reversible steam capstan was on the bridge deck forward for mooring. It had a 26-inch diameter head driven by a 10-inch by 12-inch engine.

The CO_2 brine circulation refrigerating plant had four three-cylinder compressors, each driven by a 100-horsepower electric motor. Three units were sufficient to maintain the required temperatures in the cold storage spaces with seawater at not less than 85 degrees Fahrenheit, typical in the tropics. The fourth unit was used as a standby. Four brine coolers were provided, one for each compressor. They were designed to cool the seawater to a temperature of minus 10 degrees Fahrenheit. There were fifteen refrigerated cargo spaces, twelve of which were air-cooled. The exhaust air was drawn off through openings on the opposite wall of the compartment and returned to the fans through a duct. The remaining refrigerated cargo spaces and the ship's cold storage rooms were cooled by brine circulating through cooling coils mounted on the wall and overhead.

There were three steering stations, the regular station in the wheel house and emergency stations on top of the wheel house and on the bridge deck aft. Magnetic compasses were provided in the wheel house, on top of the wheel house and in the after steering station. All compasses and binnacles were Navy standard. In addition to a Sperry gyrocompass system, a double-unit Sperry gyro-pilot for automatic steering, a Sperry course recorder, a radio compass direction finder, and a fathometer were installed. Two searchlights were provided, one 18-inch incandescent type and the other a special

24-inch unit complying with the Suez Canal regulations. Both vessels were twin screw, electric drive. Each installation consisted essentially of two turbo-driven alternators and two synchronous-induction motors, together with their condensers and the usual auxiliaries.

Matson Liner SS *Mariposa*

Another merchant ship delivered in 1931 was the SS *Mariposa*, the first of three ships being constructed for the Matson line.[38] These 632-foot, 26,141-ton liners were designed to carry 1,063 passengers each. Each had 22,000 shaft horsepower power plants that produced a cruising speed of 20.5 knots.

The complete, superstructure-type hull had nine decks, four of which were almost exclusively for passengers. The framing was transverse and frames were spaced 36 inches apart amidships and gradually reduced toward the ends to 24 inches. The hull was divided into thirteen main compartments by twelve watertight bulkheads. Fuel-oil tanks and other minor bulkheads added further to the watertight subdivision. The ship was designed to remain afloat, with sufficient stability to prevent flooding undamaged compartments, when at least two major compartments were open to the sea. The double bottom was continuous from fore to after peak tank bulkheads and was fitted to carry fuel oil and water.

The general arrangements provided for two large cargo holds forward, just aft of the forward collision bulkhead and fore peak tank. Cargo space was provided well down in the ship; the upper part of these main cargo areas ("E" deck and above) being used for crew accommodations. A large block of fuel-oil tanks, above the inner bottom, followed the cargo space, followed by the forward boiler room. Another block of fuel-oil tanks separated the forward and after boiler rooms; then came an auxiliary machinery space with pumps, generators, flanked outboard by oil tanks. The main engine room came next, followed by refrigerating machinery space, and fresh and drinking water tanks. The tanks ran aft along the propeller shafts. At the after end of the hold was a trimming tank. Refrigerated cargo space, general cargo space, and refrigerated ship's

stores were located near the refrigeration machinery space. Other ship's stores, laundry, baggage, mail room, and tailor shop were located below, between the forward and after holds.

The main dining and galley spaces were amidships on the "E" deck (the first deck wholly above the deepest load water line). The "B", "C", and "D" decks were given over mainly to staterooms. The "A" deck had ten deluxe staterooms forward, eight with private enclosed verandas. The rest of the "A" deck contained public and promenade spaces, a library, a writing room, a large lounge, an extensive smoking room, a men's clubroom and bar, and a dance pavilion and palm garden across the full width of the ship, with large windows on three sides. On the boat deck (above the "A" deck) were navigating spaces, officers' quarters, the officers' mess, and radio room. A well-equipped gymnasium, whirlpool bath, and large amount of passenger promenade deck space were located aft. A tennis court was atop the main lounge and a large sport deck above the dance pavilion.

Cabin-class passengers had fine accommodations. Their staterooms were as well appointed as first-class passengers' rooms. Cabin class was provided with a very comfortable and attractive lounge; a large, excellent smoking room; a semi-enclosed veranda; and generous deck space. Each class had a large open-air swimming pool.

A major feature of the *Mariposa* was the cork insulation inboard of hull plating in way of passenger accommodations, the dining saloons, and cabin passenger space on the "E" deck. The sides of the deckhouses enclosing officers' quarters, the gymnasium, and the whirlpool bath were similarly treated. These cork slabs were an inch thick, permanently fastened to the plating, and covered by ornamental sheathing. Similar insulation, but of 1½-inch slabs, was used in way of the hospital spaces on the "E" deck forward. This insulation (together with all-white-painted weather areas and hull) ensured hot-weather comfort as well as freedom from condensation moisture.

The *Mariposa* was equipped to carry general cargo, automobiles, and refrigerated cargo. The cargo space was divided into two large, insulated holds for general cargo. Aft, there were refrigerated spaces and additional space for general cargo. Four 5-ton booms and one 30-ton were fitted on the foremast; two 5-ton booms were on the main mast. Two 5-ton booms were fitted on the forward end of the deckhouse over No. 2 hold. Aft, two kingposts with 5-ton booms at each side of the ship served the cargo hatch. Twenty-two lifeboats were carried on Welin-McLachlan gravity davits.

All cargo winches used 35-horsepower, 300-rpm watertight electrical motors with controls where operators could run two winches and still see down into the worked holds. There were two double-reduction-geared, heavy-duty winches for heavy loads on the 30-ton boom. Others were single-geared, high-speed types. All cargo gear was made in accordance with the stringent Australian cargo handling regulations. This required that each part be marked with the load to which it had been tested, that access be arranged for easy frequent inspection of all gear, and that certain steel parts be removable for periodic annealing.

The *Mariposa*'s twin screws were driven by high-pressure, high-temperature boilers, and single-reduction geared turbines, designed for 22,000 shaft horsepower at 124 propeller rpm.

In two firerooms were twelve B & W cross-drum marine boilers fitted with interdeck superheaters and tubular air heaters, six boilers in each, three abreast. A closed fireroom, forced-draft blower system was used, with four motor-driven forced-draft blowers in each fireroom (two spare). Combustion air entered between the inner and outer breeching casing near the top of the fireroom, flowed down through the air heaters, through air casings around and under the boilers, and through the double front to the oil burners. Two double smokepipes served six boilers each.

Each set of turbines consisted of three Bethlehem-Parsons turbines in series, in separate casings around a single gear wheel: a high-pressure single-flow impulse-reaction turbine with a dummy piston forward of the impulse wheel, and intermediate- and low-pressure double-flow reaction turbines. A two-stage impulse-astern turbine was in the forward end of the low-pressure turbine. The designed steam conditions were 360 psi, 650 degrees Fahrenheit at the throttle, and 28½ inches vacuum low pressure

turbine exhaust. Gears were of the single-reduction, double-helical type. The propeller thrust was taken by a 34-inch Kingsbury, thrust bearing in the forward end of the gear casing. On the forward end of each turbine shaft, 13½-inch Kingsbury bearings were fitted. The propellers were solid manganese bronze with streamline blades, 18 feet in diameter, 19 feet, 6 inches pitch, developed area of 105.8 square feet, and a projected area of 88.7 square feet. Outboard of the low-pressure turbines and connected by double exhaust trunks, were two Bethlehem main single-pass condensers, each with a cooling surface of 13,562 square feet, served by injection scoops with circulating pumps for maneuvering and stand-by.

Ship's service electrical power was generated by four Westinghouse 500-kilowatt, 240/120-volt direct current geared turbogenerators, 6000-1200 rpm, with external balance coils, each generator capable of 25 percent overload. The main switchboard consisted of ten panels and a 230-volt power bus. The lighting bus was 230/115 volts with neutral ground. All circuit breakers providing power to auxiliaries had time delay, and circuit breakers to the galleys had under-voltage trips. There were a total of forty-six electrical distribution stations throughout the ship for power and lighting. Power feeders for these stations ran directly from the main switchboard. Duplicate 3-wire lighting feeders, for all but machinery compartments, were run directly from the forward and aft lighting distribution boards, one half of the load connected to each feeder. The total connected power load was 2,600 kilowatts and the total lighting load was 230 kilowatts.

New American Transatlantic Liners

The SS *Manhattan*, delivered in July 1932, was the first of the United States Lines' two sister ships delivered for their New York-Hamburg service.[39] The second, the SS *Washington*, was launched and delivered by the New York Shipbuilding Company in the summer of 1933. The principal characteristics of these liners were 705-foot length, displacement of 33,500 tons, accommodations for 1,239 passengers, a 30,000 shaft horsepower plant, and a service speed of 20 knots. These liners were the largest commercial vessels built in the United States to date. Each met the 1929 International Convention on Safety of Life at Sea and had power and speed reserves for national defense purposes. The principal requirement for these vessels was to provide maximum comfort for cabin-, tourist-, and third-class passengers, with an option for single-class passenger accommodations for winter cruises. An additional requirement was to provide maximum fuel economy at 20 knots (consistent with conservative water tube boiler, turbine, and gear design) when fueled for a New York to Hamburg round trip, 12,000 tons dead weight.

The complete, superstructure-type hull had no expansion joints. Scantlings were determined by considering the equivalent girder as extending continuously up to the sun deck. Mild steel was used throughout. There were nine decks; four were designated exclusively for passengers. Transverse frames were spaced 36 inches apart for the greater part of the length, reduced to 24 inches in way of peak tanks, by decrements of 1 inch forward and 2 inches aft. Eleven main transverse bulkheads provided subdivision complying with the 1929 International Convention on Safety of Life at Sea. Fuel-oil tank and other secondary bulkheads provided further subdivision. Four forward watertight bulkheads extended to the "B" deck, the remainder to the "C" deck. This subdivision ensured stable buoyancy with three compartments flooded forward or aft, or four compartments amidships. Wing fuel tanks abreast of the two boiler rooms and auxiliary engine room safeguarded these spaces against all but severe damage. And, with the separation of the two boiler rooms by the auxiliary engine room, a single collision could not damage both, as had occurred in the case of the *Malolo*. With fuel amidships, only a small trim change was encountered between departure and arrival. Of nine decks, the "C", "D", and "E" extended the full length of the liner; the sun deck extended for a length of 284 feet above the officers' quarters, and the boat deck extended for a length of 300 feet above the promenade deck. The promenade deck was the strength deck for the midship portion of the hull and it extended for a length of 405 feet. The "A" deck extended for a length of 520 feet; the "B" deck extended from the bow to about 3 feet aft of the rudder post, a length of about 670 feet. The "F" deck extended forward of the machinery space, only above of No. 6 hold and aft above the after peak tank. Decks "D", "E", and "F" had no camber; deck "C" and all decks above had 6 inches camber in 86 feet.

MAIN AND AUXILIARY MACHINERY DEVELOPMENT

Propulsion Equipment

Although the treaties of this decade, as stated earlier, limited naval ship design in many areas, they caused notable advances in certain machinery and equipment. Prior to the Washington Treaty, little or no thought had been given by naval designers toward obtaining lightweight machinery for propelling naval ships, other than limited efforts for submarines and destroyers. Practically all American battleships were propelled by direct-drive turbine, turbine-electric machinery, or reciprocating engines; scout cruisers and destroyers by cross-compound geared turbines, with cruising belts or cruising turbines; submarines by diesel-battery system; and various auxiliary ships by either reciprocating engines or cross-compound geared turbines.[40] Table 5-1 shows the average total weight per shaft horsepower for various types of U.S. Navy ships and various types of propelling machinery. Companion table 5-2 shows the projected total weights and unit weight per shaft horsepower of these same types of ships if propelled by triple-divided-flow geared turbines with underneath condensers and having comparable auxiliary equipment. While it could be stated that machinery weights listed in table 5-2 were proven only for the 10,000-ton cruiser designs (with the triple-divided-flow turbines, condensers, auxiliaries, auxiliary turbine-generators and blowers), designers had calculated the weight of such naval machinery for the other types of ships listed.

It was only after limitations had been set on displacement tonnage by the treaty that efforts were made to reduce appreciably the weight per shaft horsepower of an entire machinery plant. Previously, it was commonly believed that sturdiness and reliability were necessarily accompanied by significant weight and size.

Table 5-1[41]

Ship	Type of Drive	Date Accepted	Total shp	Total Wet Weight, All Machinery (Tons)	Pounds per shp
Battleship	Reciprocating	1914	28,373	2,270	180
Battleship	Direct-Drive Turbine	1919	33,100	2,703	183
Battleship	Turbine electric	1920	29,609	2,045	155
7,500-ton cruiser	Cross-comp. geared turbine with cruising turbines	1923	94,920	1,722	41
10,000-ton cruiser	Cross-comp. geared turbine with cruising turbines	1930	106,750	2,161	45 Est
1,250-ton cruiser	Cross-comp. geared turbine with cruising turbines	1919	28,000	450	36
Airplane carrier	Turbine-electric	1928	180,000	7,075	88 Est

Table 5-2[42]

Ship	Type of Drive	Total shp	Total Wet Weight, All Machinery (Tons)	Pounds Per shp
Battleship	Triple-divided flow turbines	33,100	1,108	75
7,500-ton cruiser	Triple-divided flow turbines	94,000	1,425	34
10,000-ton cruiser	Triple-divided flow turbines	100,750	1,820	38
1,250-ton cruiser	Triple-divided flow turbines	28,000	375	30
Airplane carrier (Saratoga type)	Triple-divided flow turbines	180,000	2,500	31
Airplane carrier (new type contracted for)	Triple-divided flow turbines	53,500	960	40

It is interesting to review the advances made by experienced specialized builders in the design of central station turbines with regard to weights during a corresponding period of time. These details are noted in table 5-3.

So, while there are many opinions regarding the effects of the treaty on the numbers and tonnage of the various classes of naval ships, there can be no doubt but that the treaty limitations inspired the development of greatly improved, lightweight machinery plants. Aside from the weight savings realized by the adoption of new lighter power plants, careful analysis shows that several very important advantages

evolved in selecting such units for U.S. Navy ships. These advantages included the following:

1. Evolution of a unified and complete design responsibility for the entire propulsion system
2. Greatest possible simplicity, with resultant greater reliability
3. Greater accessibility, and less space required per unit shp
4. Greater overall fuel economy
5. Elimination of cruising turbines, gears, and clutches, as well as exhaust trunks, considerable foundation weight, and a large amount of piping and valves

Table 5-3[43]

	Date	Rating (Kilowatts)	Total Weight of Turbine (Pounds)	Speed (rpm)	Weight per bhp (Pounds)
Plant "A"	1914	60,000	1,600,000	1,200	16.00
Plant "B"	1928	65,000	600,000	1,800	5.60
Plant "C"	1915	12,000	175,000	1,800	8.70
Plant "D"	1920	12,000	89,000	3,600	4.42

6. Evolution of underneath condensers that ensured perfect drainage of turbines at all times, without the use of drain piping, valve ejectors, or pumps

7. High-pressure turbines used for cruising and up to speeds of 25 knots; above 25 knots and at full power, no idle blading in service

8. All essential auxiliaries were designed to be component parts of the main propelling machinery.

9. Development of a simple, reliable, and efficient lubricating system

10. Use of divergent scoops resulted in considerable gaining of strength and saving of weight and cost because only one hull frame was pierced.

11. Ability, because of the nature of the design, to obtain approximately 75 percent of full power on either one of the two installed turbines, a valuable asset in the case of battle casualty

12. Better protection for all main machinery from gunfire because it was located well below water line

Intrinsic qualities of ships were also improved by steadily and continually perfecting both the design criteria and the use of materials. These improvements were basically related to:

1. The use of better materials for the purpose at hand

2. The general use of welding instead of riveting where possible[44]

3. The incorporation of the protective elements of design with the required structural elements of the design.

The technical details of some of these more notable improvements are reviewed later in this chapter.

Boiler Improvements

Early in the 1920s, the Fuel Oil Testing Plant at the Philadelphia Navy Yard completed testing of the Dyson Boiler, designed by Rear Admiral C. W. Dyson, USN.[45] Test results indicated that the Dyson water tube boiler would prove a highly satisfactory steam generator for capital ships.[46] It met all the specified requirements for such a boiler, and showed a somewhat better evaporative efficiency than other boilers of its class tested. It was believed, however, that with a different boiler front, using a smaller number of larger registers and burners, improved operating conditions would be obtained, especially with respect to carbon deposits. By 1932, the water tube boiler had been definitely adopted for use in all merchant ships; few, if any, Scotch Boilers were being built.

600 PSI Steam and New Navy Fuel Oil Specifications

By 1931, enough progress had been made in the design of boilers that 600 psi superheated steam plants could be spoken of as the current standard.[47] This advancement took place because the U.S. Navy rewrote the *Fuel Oil Specification* in 1930.[48] The increasing cost of fuel oil, the advent of "cracking" and hydrogenation of crudes for a greater gasoline yield leaving a smaller yield of heavier oils, and the design of satisfactory fuel oil burning equipment for heavy oils made a complete revision of the specifications necessary. The result was the replacement of Bunker "A", "B", and "C" fuel oils with a single lower grade oil, similar to the old Bunker "C" oil, and the improvement of shipboard fuel oil and fuel oil heating systems. In addition, the earlier Navy boiler water compound of 1923 was modified in 1932 for use at the higher steam pressures and in closed-loop systems that eliminated dissolved oxygen. The new Navy boiler compound reduced the rate of scale formation, eliminated priming, decreased sludging, reduced corrosion, and controlled alkalinity.

Steam Turbine Electric Drive
in Merchant Ships

As discussed earlier, electric drives became popular in the *Maryland* and *Tennessee*-class battleships and in the aircraft carriers *Saratoga* and *Lexington* in the form of turbo-electric propulsion systems. The use of turbo-electric propulsion led to the introduction of electric drive in the first merchant ship installation of consequence, in the Panama Pacific *California*, built by the Newport News Shipbuilding and Drydock Company. This ship was followed by another for the same line, the *Virginia*, which went into service in 1929; and a third sister ship, the *Pennsylvania*, which went into service in 1930.

During this period, several other ships with similar type of propelling machinery were under construction in the United States, including ships for the Grace Line and the Ward Line.

Alternating Current in Naval
Ship Electric Plants

By specifying alternating current for the electrical installation for the 1932 destroyers, the Navy Department entered into a field of marine electrical design. Alternating current applications were not new on naval ships. They had been in use for a number of years for interior communication and fire control purposes and as part of the universally known electric drive on battleships and aircraft carriers. Alternating current also had other minor shipboard uses. Alternating current was considered for the electric plant when the 10,000-ton class of cruisers was being projected. However, after investigation of problems it then presented, alternating current was not adopted for these ships. Only with the 1932 destroyers program was the adoption of the complete alternating-current electric plant to be realized.

The advantages of alternating current generation and distribution for land installations was well recognized. Design difficulties, which had been encountered in the development of direct

current electric power drive for combatant ships, were expected to increase with the use of alternating current. There were several reasons for such expectation. The distribution system for an alternating-current ship differed in detail from previous direct-current ships, and was somewhat more complex, the complexity being more marked with ship size. For the 1932 destroyers the distribution system was more extensive than in previous destroyers. This was due to the increased size of the ships and the use of a combined generator and distribution switchboard, an auxiliary power or battery charging switchboard, an interior communication switchboard, and several fire control switchboards, all with their necessary interconnecting bus feeders and distribution feeders. For example, the 1932 destroyer combined generator and distribution switchboard was approximately 16 feet long by 6 feet, 6 inches high, as compared with switchboards in older destroyers that were 4 feet, 6 inches long by 5 feet, 8 inches high. Some of this increase was due to the electric plant increase for these larger ships. The main reason, however, was the requirement for increased switching in the alternating-current plant, and, therefore, additional panel space was required. The wiring installation, however, did not differ greatly from the previous direct-current ships. Three-phase three-conductor cable was used for the three-phase circuits, up to and including conductor size of 400,000 circular mils. Above 400,000 circular mils, single conductor cables were used. Where cables were installed for the individual phases, they were installed with a twist having a lay of approximately 20 cable diameters to neutralize inductive effect. In addition, single-conductor alternating-current cables were not grouped in the same hangers with direct-current cables.

It was known that electrolysis, due to stray direct currents from a direct-current installation, existed on naval ships, sometimes causing serious damage to hull plating. Electrolytic action from an alternating-current source was known to have generally less than 1 percent of the level produced by corresponding direct current. The adoption of the alternating-current electric plant removed this problem, although it obviously did not eliminate stray currents completely.

Standard designs of electrical fixtures, boxes, switches, and various other fittings changed appreciably for the new alternating-current destroyers. New designs of distribution panels and feeder distribution boxes were necessitated by the adoption of the 3-phase wiring system, since the earlier boxes had been developed for two-pole direct current. In addition, extensive redesign of electrical fittings was required, due both to the use of the 3-phase system and to the increased voltage. The longer 450-volt fuses replacing the 250-volt fuses required redesign of fuse boxes.

The question of comparative weights of the alternating-current ship electric plant installation versus the direct-current ship electric plant installation was one of the most vital concerns of the time. Early studies made of the actual weights of the electric plant (excluding motors and controllers) of one of the 10,000-ton cruisers, as compared with the estimated weights of the new alternating-current plant, showed that the weight of the alternating-current installation was almost 20 percent greater than the direct-current installation. However, this study had been made assuming the alternating-current installation to be identical to the direct-current installation, except for known increases for the alternating-current installation. A further study for the new class destroyer, which took advantage of weight saving in the alternating-current installation allowed by such features as increased voltage and the omission of motor generators, showed that the weight of the alternating-current installation would approach that of the direct-current installation. In general, the use of alternating current for power in the 1932 destroyer proved to be a significant improvement in the field of electrical design as applied to naval ships.

Electric Motors

Another breakthrough in technology in the 1920s was the design of electric motors that could be stalled without blowing fuses. This development led to wide use of direct-current motors for equipment such as steering gear, anchor windlasses, boat cranes, deck winches, capstans, galley appliances, air compressors, refrigerating machines, ventilation sets, engine room auxiliaries, inport fire room auxiliaries,

pumps, laundry machinery, machine tools, printing appliances, searchlight controls, gun and turret controls, ammunition hoists, shell rammers, and motor generators.

Diesel Engines

During 1926, the Shipping Board placed 2,900-horsepower diesels in the tug *Seminole*. These were the first large diesels installed in an American ship. Large diesels were also tested that year for the Shipping Board. However, it was not until 1928 that diesel-electric drive came into its own. Its use was extended into several new fields of application because of increases in diesel power limits and the flexibility of the engine for adaptation to a wide variety of ships.

One of the most outstanding installations was that of the MS *Courageous*, a converted freighter owned by the U.S. Shipping Board. This freighter, formerly 3,000 shaft horsepower turbine-driven, was re-engined in 1928 with a diesel-electric power plant of 4,000 shaft horsepower capacity. A new propeller with a designed full load speed of 60 rpm was installed in place of the former 90-rpm propeller. The bow and stern lines of the freighter were also changed. These changes resulted in an increased ship speed of from 10½ knots to more than 13 knots. Diesel-electric drive was selected in preference to diesel-direct drive because of its lighter weight, savings in space, and lower initial cost. The main power plant in *Courageous* consisted of four diesel-driven, direct-current generators, each rated 800 kilowatts, 250 rpm, 385 volts. On the end of each main generator shaft was connected an auxiliary direct-current 100-kilowatt generator for furnishing power of excitation and the ship's auxiliaries and lights. The main propulsion motor, directly connected to a single propeller shaft, was a double-motor type, rated at 4,000 shaft horsepower, 600 rpm, 1,500 volts.

In the latter part of 1928, work commenced on the construction of diesel-electric propulsion and auxiliary equipment for three lightships placed in service off the east coast of the United States, the first of their type to be so equipped. Previously, lightships were powered with steam propelling equipment for proceeding between their station and home port, and when needed to drive ahead against a storm to avoid dragging the anchor. Diesel-electric drive, because of its lower fuel consumption, permitted a much longer stay on station and provided immediate reserve power for emergencies.

There was also an extension of diesel-electric drive to propeller-type river tow boats. Two such boats were built for the Tennessee Coal, Iron and Railroad Company of Birmingham, Alabama, for transporting steel products along the Warrior River. The new boats were tunnel-stern, twin-screw type. Their main power plant consisted of two diesel-driven, direct-current generators, each rated at 335 kilowatts, 250 volts, 250 rpm. The main propelling double-type motors were coupled to the propeller shaft. Each was rated at 400 horsepower at 140 rpm. Power for auxiliaries, lighting, and excitation of the main generator and propelling motors was furnished by two 40-kilowatt, 120-volt, direct-current, auxiliary generators driven directly from the main generator shaft. Diesel-electric drive was adopted for these tow boats to obtain higher efficiency and better maneuvering capability. Maneuverability was essential since the Warrior River was relatively shallow, had sharp bends, and was quite swift. These boats could be controlled and operated from both the bridge and engine room.

The Norfolk County Ferries of Portsmouth, Virginia, also selected diesel-electric drive for their new automobile and passenger ferry boat to ply between Portsmouth and Norfolk. The power plant consisted of two diesel-driven, direct-current generators, each rated at 270 kilowatts, and a double-type propelling motor rated at 670 brake horsepower.

The combination harbor and sea tugs, *Charges* and *Trinidad*, were placed in service by the Panama Canal Authority in the early part of 1928. These were the highest powered diesel-electric tugs in the world at this time. The capacity of 108 tons of diesel fuel oil was sufficient for a cruise of 25 days at a range of approximately 7,000 miles. They could, therefore, be used in emergency for servicing or towing disabled vessels at sea. They were each equipped with a 500-watt, 100-mile night-range, radio-transmitter for use in sea service. The tugs could also be used for fire fighting because they were equipped with motor-driven pumps having a capacity of 1,000 gallons per minute at a pressure of 100 pounds per square inch. In ordinary service in the Canal Zone, these tugs were used for towing dredge barges to the dumping grounds at sea and for assisting vessels through the locks. Their auxiliary equipment was electric powered and consisted mainly of a powerful combination capstan and anchor windlass; an automatic towing machine with inhaul capacity of 75 feet per minute at 25,000 pounds; electric steering gear; and miscellaneous engine room auxiliaries, such as pumps, blowers, and compressors. Their main propelling motors were of the double type and built to deliver 900 shaft horsepower continuously at 1,450 amperes and 500 volts. Motor operating speed range at full power was 115 to 150 rpm. Both *Charges* and *Trinidad* easily passed an 8-hour dock test at 750 shaft horsepower and an "at-sea" test at 750 and 900 shaft horsepower, 180 rpm, 250 volts, shunt wound, and mounted on a single shaft.

Evaporator Improvements

The years 1922 and 1923 saw significant improvement in shipboard evaporators. Prior to 1912, shipboard evaporators usually took steam directly from the boilers and reduced it to desired working pressure. The evaporation of the sea water took place at atmospheric pressure, or slightly above, and was led to the distillers or auxiliary condensers where it was condensed into water. Great trouble was experienced in these evaporators because of scale forming on the tubes. Starting with clean tubes, it was necessary to raise the steam pressure day by day in order to make water, until the limiting pressure on the coil was reached. The plant then had to be shut down, the coils pulled out, and the scale removed. It was difficult and tedious to remove, frequently resulting in injury to the tubes.[49]

In 1912, an entirely new type evaporator, patented by S. Morris Lillie, and modified by the Bureau of Engineering, was installed experimentally on several ships.[50] The new design was known as the modified Lillie evaporator. By 1922, modified Lillie evaporators were designated as standard equipment in U.S. Navy ships. The modified Lillie used low-pressure steam and was built with double, triple or quadruple effects. A vacuum pump was used on the distilling condenser so that evaporation in the last effect took place in 26 or 27 inches of vacuum. Although such arrangements had been used before, the Lillie method of circulating the salt water feed within the shell was different. Instead of having heating tubes submerged in a large body of salt water in the shell, from the surface of which water vapor was released, the Lillie evaporator used "rain" evaporation. The salt water feed was sent through all of the effects, in series (finally being discharged overboard with a salinity of 2.5 times sea water). At each effect, a circulating pump took salt water from the bottom of the shell, and discharged only part of it to the next effect. The remainder was pumped back into the same shell, above the tube nest, where it was discharged over a perforated distribution plate. From this plate, the water was sprinkled over the tube nest. Part of each drop evaporated and the rest washed the salt deposited by the evaporation process from tubes and into the shell bottom. The water level in the shell bottom was kept just above the lower row of tubes. Such circulation caused "flash" evaporation, with sufficient extra feed so as to allow only minimal scale to form on the tubes.

The advantages of such fresh water production were many. For example:

1. All auxiliary exhaust steam was available for use.
2. By using low pressures (and thus low temperatures), deposit of sulphates on the tubes was practically obviated.
3. By using a high vacuum, the temperature range between the entering steam and the last effect vapor remained high even with pressure below 10 pounds gauge.

The Lillie evaporator temperature range permitted triple and quadruple effects; whereas high pressure, "drowned-tube" evaporators were never more than double effect. Multiple-effect evaporation economy was much better than single effect. See table 5-4.

With a constant amount of steam available, usually the condition of a ship at anchor, this multiple-effect operation greatly increased evaporating plant capacity.

Table 5-4

Evaporation Effect	Pounds of Distilled Water/Pound of Steam
Single effect	.95
Double effect	1.60
Triple effect	2.50
Quadruple effect	3.30

Pumps

The year 1927 saw the development of the Worthington single-stage, high-pressure, centrifugal feed pump.[51] This pump was designed to supply the 600 psi boilers being built for a rated capacity of 650 gallons per minute. Other manufacturers had gone to adding multiple stages to their centrifugal pumps, to using positive displacement pumps, or to installing multiple pumps in series, to satisfy this rated capacity. Worthington chose to develop a centrifugal pump with a single impeller that would fulfill the required capacity and high pressure.

By 1929, the many advantages inherent in centrifugal or rotating machinery compared with reciprocating types displaced the latter from the auxiliary machinery field, just as they had already done with prime movers.

As stated earlier, to obtain the high pressure required for boiler feed, the first centrifugal pumps were either multistage units or were made up of single stage pumps in series, the speeds of either system being relatively low. With design changes, many companies exploited the economy of using a high-speed turbine with single-stage impeller. This eliminated the complications of multistage, or multiple, series pumps. Moreover, the single-stage pump was inherently smaller and lighter, particularly desirable characteristics for marine and naval use.

The Coffin Feed Pump was a high-speed, centrifugal, single-stage, boiler-feed pump, originally developed for locomotives. Such a pump had to have minimum space and weight, rugged construction, reliability, overspeed protection, simplicity of application, high operating efficiency, and low maintenance costs. Such a unit obviously would also be ideal for marine use.

The Coffin pump was designed for 250 psi delivery pressure at 155 gallons per minute with steam pressure of 200 psi with atmospheric exhaust. Rated speed was 6,800 rpm. Actually, the pump could run at 300 pounds delivery pressure with 250 psi steam at a speed of about 7,500 rpm, which gave almost 200 gallons per minute capacity.

Shipboard Air Conditioning

In 1925, certain shipboard battle stations had to be completely closed to protect personnel and equipment from water, smoke, and chemicals, and had to be fitted with mechanical cooling. This advance in the citadel concept of ship control personnel protection involved the use, in one of the earliest forms, of air conditioning.

SHIPBOARD ELECTRONIC SYSTEMS

Gyroscopes

In 1922, the United States Shipping Board contracted to have a Sperry-designed, Westinghouse-built, gyrostabilizer installed in the 20,000-ton *Hawkeye State*. It was the first installed in a passenger liner, although the Navy had experimented with a Sperry installation in the transport *Henderson* during World War I. Such gyrostabilizers used a small control gyroscope to sense the ship's roll and then signal the main gyroscope to counter that roll. The main gyroscope operated at 880 rpm and rotated for 18 hours after being shut down. In 1930, an even more notable installation was made on the 48,000-ton *Conte Di Savoia*, but thereafter Sperry no longer promoted the gyrostabilizer and introduced a simpler gyro-controlled fin stabilizer.[52]

By the beginning of the period of this chapter, Sperry gyrocompasses had been in use in U.S. Navy ships for over 10 years and had gone through numerous modifications and improvements. These included rotor improvements, changes to the mercury-loaded "ballistic" that amplified controlling precession of the gyro, and improvements to the transmitter that sent ship's heading information from the master gyro to the repeaters throughout the ship. Sperry was very successful in converting to the needs of the peacetime market, too. Using a model based on the Navy Mark VI, more than a thousand Sperry gyrocompasses were installed in merchant ships

by 1932.[53] All gyrocompass equipments purchased for the U.S. Navy had to pass acceptance tests at the Material Laboratory, New York Navy Yard. Tests varied from time to time depending on accuracy requirements and gyrocompass improvements. The laboratory test conditions simulated, as closely as practicable, ship conditions of moderate and extreme roll, pitch, and yaw by mounting the completely assembled compass on a Scorsby test stand, which was then adjusted and operated to give the desired motions and angles in three planes. Certain tests were conducted with the stand in motion, other tests with the stand at rest.

Principle of Radar Discovered

During the course of experiments in 1922 at the Navy Aircraft Radio Laboratory at the Naval Air Station, Anacostia, Washington, D.C., Dr. A. Hoyt Taylor and Leo C. Young discovered that a steamer on the Potomac River, the SS *Dorcester*, reflected certain frequencies of radio waves. No action was taken on Dr. Taylor's suggestion that the discovery had potential to make ships " . . . aware of the presence of an enemy. . . ."[54]

In 1923, the Naval Research Laboratory (NRL) was opened, across the Potomac River from Washington, D.C., south of Bolling Field. There, in 1930, L. A. Hyland discovered that aircraft also could be detected by radio waves. Again, it was accidental, the result of reflected interference from passing aircraft during tests of a radio direction finder (like aircraft interference, today, with home television). Hyland reported it to Dr. Taylor, by now Superintendent of the Radio Division of NRL, who caused a detailed report, "Radio-Echo Signals From Moving Objects", to be submitted by the Director of NRL to the Bureau of Engineering. Shortly thereafter, the Bureau directed NRL to "investigate the use of radio to detect the presence of enemy vessels and aircraft." Further experiments led to an area-system using many transmitters, that could detect the approximate position of aircraft within 50 miles of the area center. This was not suitable for ships and was recommended to the Army. Further development of radar had to await Leo Young, in 1934, suggesting the use of pulse transmissions.[55]

Principles of Television Developed

In June 1925, seven men stood in a laboratory in Washington, D.C., watching the arms of a miniature windmill revolving on a small screen of white blotting paper. The real windmill was 5 miles away in Anacostia. The picture on the laboratory screen was being transmitted by radio. This was the first time in history that television had been demonstrated.[56] Attending the first major demonstration of this development were Mr. D. MacFarland Moore, inventor of the lamp on which the receiver depended; Mr. C. Francis Jenkins, inventor of the prismatic disc used in the transmitter; three representatives of the Navy Department; Mr. Burgess, Director of the United States Bureau of Standards; and Judge Taylor, advocate of the Department of Commerce, who presided over radio matters under Secretary Hoover. After the demonstration, opinion was unanimous that this long-sought goal was at last in sight.

In 1928, Doctor Vladimir Zworkin of the Westinghouse Research Laboratories laid the foundation for modern television systems by inventing the iconoscope, the first practical TV camera tube. In this camera, an image of the illuminated scene was focused onto a plate in the evacuated iconoscope tube. This plate was covered with a mosaic of tiny photosensitive elements, each insulated from its neighbors. The light falling on an element continuously discharged it as the light ejected photoelectrons. A beam of electrons from a gun was scanned over the plate, recharging each element by replacing the charge it had lost. This recharging current was the video signal, which was amplified, transmitted, and used to recreate the picture in the receiving television set.

Acoustic Devices

In 1930, the Navy developed an experimental steel and quartz transducer for underwater sound detection of submarines. This was the predecessor of modern echo-ranging sonar. It was adapted by the Submarine Signal Company to develop their Fathometer, a sonic depth finder, an instrument that permitted deep sea sounding as well as sounding of approaches and channels to be conducted with ease, thus eliminating the need for the laborious process of sounding by wire reel and deep sea lead.[57]

The Oscilloscope

Scientific American reported in July 1923 that the oscilloscope had become a practical instrument for observing and analyzing the operation of machinery.

> If you held your watch in your left hand in a darkened room, and held in your right hand an electric lamp which flashed exactly once a minute, and if your first flash showed the second hand upon the figure 12, the second flash and all succeeding flashes would show this second hand in the same position. Hence, it would look to you as though the watch had stopped. If, instead of giving a flash every 60 seconds, your lamp gave a flash at 61 seconds' intervals, you would see that the second hand was rotating at its normal speed of once a minute, since every flash would show the hand as having advanced one second in its regular clockwise direction. On the other hand, if the flashes came at the rate of 59 per minute, it would appear to you as though the second hand were rotating in the reverse direction, or counter-clockwise.[58]

The above quoted principles underlay the development of an ingenious and useful instrument called the oscilloscope, a device that enabled the observer to watch movement of a machine or its parts despite such rapid motion as to present a mere blur to unaided vision. Essentially, it consisted of a flash lamp and a gearbox, attachable to an appropriate moving part of a machine to be observed, with electric contacts that regulated the periodicity of the lamp flashes. When a machine is running at high speed, certain undesirable distortions and vibrations can occur. An engineer can know that they are there, his trained ear and his sense of touch can tell him so, but, because of the high speed of the machine, he cannot see their nature or extent. With the oscilloscope, the engineer was able to see these various distortions, vibrations, and other irregularities. It did this by slowing the apparent motion, as projected on the retina of the eye. Although the machine was running at 1,000 rpm, it was made to appear as though idling at only 10 rpm, 1 percent of its true speed, or even as though it were absolutely at rest.

The advantages of being able to follow

machine motion that was too fast for the unaided eye to follow were substantial. It became possible to see the extent of vibration of an unbalanced, rotating shaft about its true axis, or to assess whether internal combustion engine valves supposedly alternately raised and precisely seated, were fully seating or simply bouncing.

Radio Communications

In 1920, the U.S. government noticed that control of the domestic radio facilities was passing into the hands of a foreign corporation. The Navy Department, therefore, called in representatives of the three largest American radio manufacturing concerns, recommending to them that an American company be formed to take over these facilities. Out of this conference was born the Radio Corporation of America (RCA).[59]

Radio broadcasting had, by this time, become a regular facility, transatlantic telephone in 1923 was ensured by actual test, and commercial wireless showed a similar growth. Near the close of 1924—should any of the thousands of citizens band radio enthusiasts ever wonder where it all began—the Navy built the first mobile transmitter and receiver and installed it in the airship *Shenandoah*. The establishment of transcontinental air service stimulated commercial radio, particularly in establishing means of governing the airways and navigational facilities. When the dirigible ZR3 was brought to this country from Germany, piloting was conducted by radio, although natural interference caused somewhat bad communications. Following this event, a very thorough research into the use of "ultra" frequencies from 100 to 20,000 kilocycles was conducted. As the frequencies from 2,000 to 3,000 kilocycles were reached, a marked jump in range was noted. Experimental transmitters and receivers were built and installed on certain ships for further test. This led to the development of the first high-power, high-frequency, radio transmitter and the conduct of the first radio-controlled flight of a pilotless aircraft—a forerunner of things to come in air navigation, commercial transportation, guided missiles, and space exploration. Onboard ship, the older arc sets were disappearing fast; and spark sets were being relegated for use as emergency equipment only. Vacuum tube transmitters were replacing

the former units. By 1931, vacuum tubes had reached considerable size and capacity; and photo-electric tubes had come to stay. Among the high power tubes were pliotrons and thyratrons, which were now becoming an industrial asset through their ability to control high power; but their beginnings traced back to the old three-element vacuum tube of radio.[60]

GENERAL NAVAL TECHNOLOGY

Ship Laundries

The matter of personal laundry on Naval ships has existed from earliest times. Progress has solved many problems, but the objective continues to be the efficient removal of dirt, stains, excretions, and bacteria. In the U.S. Navy of the early 1900s, clothes were still washed laboriously by hand with cold salt water and suitable soap. Washing was necessarily performed on open decks with the possible handicap of inclement weather. Elimination of bacteria was of no particular concern if the appearance of clothing measured up to the prevailing standards.

The advent of power driven laundry washers aboard ship essentially eliminated the necessity for individual hand washing. With the addition of higher water temperatures, efficient mechanical agitation, and scheduled cycles of operation, a higher standard of sanitary efficiency was made possible within the capacity of the machines installed. By 1932, laundry aboard U.S. Navy ships was no longer performed by sailors scrubbing with cold salt soap in a bucket. "Modern" washers that handled 350 pounds of laundry used steam-heated fresh water and liquid soap. Other equipment, such as water level gages, thermometers, fresh water valves, live steam valves, soap container tanks, and quick opening drains, enabled the entire machine process to be performed by one operator.

The power driven washer, used on larger ships, was a revolving-wheel, reversing type. It consisted of an outer cylindrical shell of rust-proof nickel alloy, riveted and caulked to steel cylinder heads. These heads contained gearing and the main support bearings for the inner revolving noncorrodible wheel, which was divided into two compartments. The revolving wheel had suitable baffles, perforations in its walls, and sliding doors; when filled to capacity with 350 pounds of laundry, appropriate steam-heated fresh water, and washing soap, the washing cycle operation was ready to begin.[61] The advent of the laundry machine was another major step forward in improving the habitability of ships at sea.

Sound Movies

There were varied reasons for the Navy's 1931 adoption of sound motion pictures for shipboard entertainment.[62] For the previous 2½ years, sound motion pictures had been displayed in thousands of theaters in the U.S. with an increasing popularity and steady improvement in equipment.[63] These increasingly successful "talkies" had practically revolutionized the motion picture industry, at least to the extent of reducing silent motion picture production to a low number. Furthermore, by adopting "talkies", the Navy availed itself of a powerful medium for training both officers and enlisted men.

Shipboard equipment was not adopted because the motion picture industry produced fine theater equipment. The theater equipment was neither intended for nor suitable for shipboard use. It was fragile and subject to failure when disturbed by shock, vibration, or exposure to salt air and spray. Suitable equipment for shipboard use resulted from demand by the Navy. Practically every ship and station wanted "talkies." But before "talkies" could be supplied, it was necessary to develop equipment that would withstand shipboard conditions. The Bureau of Engineering began to investigate and study sound movie projection, seeking to adapt its use to the Navy afloat. This was difficult because there were no specifications available, no manufacturers of sound motion picture equipment had contemplated shipboard use, and no one could predict the outcome of any suggested arrangement.

The "sound-on-film" type, adopted by the Navy, used a sound track on the film. There were two methods of producing the 4-millimeter film soundtrack: the variable area method and the variable density method; either of which could have been used with the Navy equipment. The variable area sound track had the appearance of an oscillograph track. The variable density sound track appeared as a series of light and dark horizontal strips varying in width and density across the sound track.

The above technology seemed simple enough in theory, but it took well over a year to develop equipment that could withstand the rigorous conditions onboard ship. The Bureau of Engineering did not enter into this problem alone. It was assisted by the design and production engineers of the leading manufacturers of sound motion picture equipment, the material Laboratory of the New York Navy Yard, various manufacturers of radio and sound equipment, and many other sources of practical field experience with "talkies."

Every effort was made to specify an apparatus that would conform to the standard commercial equipment insofar as was practicable. The departures from standard design were chiefly in design of sound head; size and number of reproducers; design and output voltage of power amplifiers; and weight, space, and portability factors. All metal parts were required to be of a corrosion-resisting material or effectively protected against the corrosive action of salt spray, salt atmosphere, or exposure to weather. The reproducers or loud speakers had to be capable of ready portability and easy handling to facilitate use and stowage, as well as meeting shipboard requirements for sound distribution and pressure levels.

By 1932 there were three classes of equipment to be used in the Navy. Type I, Class A equipment was designed for battleship, aircraft carrier, and large shore station use. Type I, Class B equipment was designed for cruisers and auxiliary ships and consisted of a portable projector, amplifiers mounted on panels below decks but with less power output, and speakers and screen as described above for Class A equipment. The Type II, Class B equipment was designed for destroyers and small ships, as well as for small shore stations with an audience of one hundred or less. It consisted of a portable projector (the same as the cruiser type), a portable amplifier, one speaker, and a screen.

Welding

Extensive experiments conducted by the Navy Department resulted in a wide application of welding processes for fabrication structures. It may be conservatively stated that the application of welding, and of arc-welding in particular, had progressed in the United States to a greater extent than in any other country. In 1930, the Bureau of Engineering adopted arc-welded construction for the joints of the twenty-four boiler drums installed in the new heavy cruisers *Minneapolis, New Orleans,* and *Astoria.*[64] This approval of fusion-welded boiler drums by the Bureau of Engineering undoubtedly contributed to the acceptance of welded drums about 6 months later for use in the merchant navy. During 1931 and 1932, forty-seven fusion-welded boiler drums were constructed for the U.S. Navy.[65]

High pressures (1,200 psi) for steam-generating units were introduced in the central power plants of this country in 1927; the previous maximum operating pressures had been in the neighborhood of 700 psi. Earlier drums for lower pressure had been fabricated by riveting, but the higher pressures demanded drums with thicker walls, which could not be fabricated by riveting. The riveted joint's limit was about 750 psi. The advent of higher pressure steam, therefore, led to the introduction of the forged seamless drum. This approach, however, substantially increased the cost of boiler construction because it required very expensive procedures. Such drums had to be forged from extremely large ingots, required much hot working, and their finishing involved much expensive machining of the drum surface, which entailed a large wastage of material to remove all forging surface defects. The attention of boiler manufacturers, therefore, was directed to developing welding-rolled plate into a drum that had the merits of the forged seamless drum but without its high cost. Welding seemed to provide a method of joining that was equally applicable to small, low-pressure drums and large, high-pressure, thick-walled drums. Forge-and-hammer welding, electrical-resistance welding, and acetylene welding were considered and eliminated; fusion welding was tested and accepted.

Nickel-Chromium Stainless Steel Development

Among the metallurgical developments of 1925, was the increasing use of the austenitic stainless steels. It had long been known that the corrosion resistance of ordinary stainless steels could be greatly improved by increasing the chromium content; but higher chromium was not acceptable, since it led to strongly air-hardened steels. With more than 15 or 16 percent chromium, they became permanently hard and nonmachinable. They were not susceptible to ordinary heat treatment and softening, since they retained their martensitic structure, even after very slow cooling.

Development now revealed that a martensitic chromium steel could be converted into an austenitic steel by the addition of a small percentage of nickel, and that a martensitic nickel steel could be made austenitic by the addition of chromium. To produce a low-carbon austenitic steel containing 20 percent of chromium, a nickel content of at least 6 percent was required. Similarly, a 15-percent nickel steel required about 5 percent of chromium, though, unlike chromium, nickel alone, in sufficient quantity, would render a steel austenitic. There were, then, two groups of steels: the high-nickel or high-nickel low-chromium steels and the high-chromium low-nickel steels. Both classes of steel were resistant to alkalis and to many salts. The high-nickel steels were particularly resistant to the action of sulphurs, hydrochloric acids, and salts, such as magnesium chloride, that were partially hydrolyzed in solution. The addition of nickel to the 18- to 20-percent chromium steel, on the other hand, further increased its exceptionally high resistance to corrosion by nitric acid, sea water, and the atmosphere. The high-nickel steels, however, were not resistant to oxidizing agents or atmospheric oxidation in the presence of sea water and other salt solutions unless they contained a considerable amount of chromium. Thus, there was a third group: high-nickel high-chromium steels, (although the chromium content as a rule was not as high as 18 percent). These steels were more expensive than those of the other two groups, but they probably had a more general all-round resistance to the action of different media. All these noncorrosive characteristics were useful in seagoing ships.

Another characteristic of high-chromium steels, retained when nickel was added, was their resistance to high temperature scaling. However, they lost strength rapidly above 700 degrees C. In the nickel-chromium series of steels, the composition that probably retained its strength best at high temperatures was one with a combined nickel-plus-chromium content of about 50 percent, with the greater part being nickel. This indicated another application for steels of the third group above. It seemed likely, however, that these plain nickel-chromium steels were less satisfactory in this respect than more complex steels containing tungsten, or than other alloys of iron, chromium, and nickel containing 20 percent chromium and 50 percent or more nickel.

A few words may be added on the general properties of these austenitic steels. They were soft; they could be stamped, pressed, rolled, or drawn out cold; but they hardened rapidly under cold work. They were easily forged and rolled hot, and could be welded by any of the usual methods. In the soft condition they had a very high elongation and impact figure, but the limit of proportionality was low and the yield point was barely 50 percent of the ultimate tensile strength. These mechanical properties could be altered by the usual methods of heat treatment. Working at temperatures just below redness, or cold working followed by annealing within a similar temperature range, improved the yield point of these steels to a marked degree without reducing their resistance to corrosion. Most of these steels were nonmagnetic. They offered a high resistance to abrasion and they were all difficult to machine, some of them very difficult. They could be burnished, and retained a high degree of reflectivity under severe conditions of exposure; but, with regard to resistance to corrosion, they were not as dependent on surface finish as were other ordinary rustless steels.[66]

Turbine Metallurgy

In 1927, the use of chromium plating became widespread to improve wear hardness, and, shortly thereafter, was adopted by the Navy for plating of exposed metal surfaces. This use of chromium for plating led to increasing use of chromium stainless steels in turbine blading. They were found to resist the erosive effects of wet or superheated steam better than the softer alloys previously used.[67]

New Tool Steel

The year 1928 also yielded the development of a new tool steel, Carbaloy.[68] This was a special form of tungsten carbide developed in the research laboratory of the General Electric Company. Carbaloy was the trade name given to this form of metal, which was developed to overcome earlier problems of weakness and porosity in tool steels.

It was found that, by adding cobalt, tungsten carbide was made about half as strong as high-speed steel, while still retaining sapphire-scratching hardness. At the General Electric research laboratory, this carbide tool material seemed destined to play a significant part in the industrial life of the future, and, on that account, the G.E. research laboratory actively pursued their study for several years. Various forms of carbide tool materials were studied and it was this experience that led to the development of Carbaloy. The density of Carbaloy was about 14 grams per cubic centimeter and upward, depending on the amount of cobalt. This characterized it as a heavy metal, almost of the tungsten class. It did not tarnish and, when ground, resembled steel in appearance. It resisted chemical attack remarkably well and was a pleasing and satisfactory material for use in the arts.

The Momsen Lung

It was 1929 when Lieutenant C. B. Momsen, USN, began to publish his ideas on a system for escape from a bottomed submarine, ideas which he developed into a successful escape device for the submarine service. Momsen first attempted to adapt the Navy's rescue breathing apparatus (RBA) used in firefighting, but found it cumbersome and difficult to breathe with underwater.

Departing from the RBA, the first "lung" was constructed, employing a rubberized-cloth air bag of about human lung capacity, 250 cubic inches. Inside the bag was a small canister with $1/4$ to $1/2$ pound of soda-lime to absorb carbon dioxide. Two tubes led from the air bag to the mouthpiece, with mica disk valves to vent exhalation through one tube and inhalation through the other. A rubber mouthpiece fit securely and required little effort to exclude water; a nose-clip tied to the mouthpiece assisted. Retention straps passed over the shoulders and two lower clips attached to the user's trousers. At the bottom of the bag was a flutter valve that vented excess air, the heart of the Momsen lung principle.

Escape necessarily originated in a bubble of compressed air in an escape trunk (one atmosphere of pressure for every 34 feet of submergence). A lung full of air at depth amounted to many lungs full at the surface; unless the air was vented, it would fatally rupture the user's lungs during the escape ascent. Breathing into Momsen's lung vented expanding air into the rubber air bag, and sea pressure automatically vented the bag into the sea through its flutter valve.

The first tests of the Momsen lung were conducted in the Model Basin at the Washington Navy Yard in 15 feet of water. The lung was found to sustain men underwater for up to 6 minutes. The next testing phase required construction of a diving bell (simulating a submarine escape trunk) and the use of the *Crilley*, an old diving boat. Tests were conducted in the Potomac River at a depth of 110 feet. Tests in Chesapeake Bay, off Solomon's Island, in 155 feet of water were equally successful. Finally, tests conducted from the submarine *S-4* off Key West, Florida, were conducted safely from 200 feet.

These successful results led the Bureau of Construction and Repair to equip all submarines with the Momsen lung (two for each man plus 10 percent spares). Bow and stern compartments of each submarine were fitted with escape trunks and stowage of enough lungs for the entire crew. The production version's air bag was made of a specially treated rubber that resisted abrasion and tear, and that was easily laid flat for compact packaging and storage.[69]

Electric Power for Tacoma

This unique naval engineering achievement occurred because an unprecedented drought had so depleted the main hydro-electric power reservoir at Tacoma, Washington, that a power shortage appeared imminent during approaching freezing weather. In view of the situation, the Navy Department ordered the aircraft carrier

USS *Lexington* to supply power to the city, using her main propulsion generators.[70] For this power, the city of Tacoma agreed to pay to the disbursing officer at Puget Sound Navy Yard a flat rate of ¼ cent per kilowatt-hour for the connected load of 20,000 kilowatts, plus 1 cent per kilowatt-hour for the power actually received. As the total power received during the stay from 17 December 1929 to 16 January 1930 was 4,250,900 kilowatt-hours, the cost was $78,509.60 or 1.85 cents per kilowatt-hour. The cost to the ship for fuel and incidental expenses was $18,627.69, leaving for ship's repairs a surplus of $59,881.91, disregarding pay of personnel, depreciation, and loss of the ship from active service.

Power had never been supplied from a ship to a city before, and the first problem was to determine how to ensure sufficient water at a berth, not only for floating the ship, but also for the main circulating pumps. These pumps took suction from the bottom of the ship, and each of the four sets had a capacity of more than four million gallons an hour, for which a 20-foot depth beyond the draft of the ship was estimated necessary. After consulting the harbor charts and checking the soundings, the desired depth was found at Baker Dock, but required breasting-out the ship 40 feet with lighters. The dock lacked means of securing a ship as large as the *Lexington*, and required the placement of extra piles ahead and astern and use of the ship's anchors outboard on the off-dock side. A 34,000-pound anchor was placed some distance off the starboard bow and two 6,000-pound kedge anchors were carried out off the starboard quarter.

For paralleling one of the generators of the ship with the system of Tacoma, a synchroscope, synchronizing lights, a voltmeter on each system, and operating switches for the circuit breakers were installed in the control room. The operating switches were placed in a 120-volt DC circuit that energized the relays of the circuit breakers, thereby closing and opening them as desired. Since each generator aboard carried its own load, and was not designed to run in parallel with other generators, there was some doubt as to whether paralleling was possible. If it were not possible, it would have been necessary to divide the city power system so that the

Lexington could carry an independent load; but, as the surplus power of one part would not be available to the other and as the flexibility of the whole would be reduced, this arrangement was not desirable. Paralleling, therefore, was attempted. After two lines were synchronized, there was some increased apprehension as to the outcome; but when the operating switches were closed, the generator paralleled with so little line disturbance that the operator in the city controlling substation did not know that a second generator had been put on line.

To supplement the instruments of the ship, a recording kilowatt-hour meter, a recording frequency meter, and a Telechron clock (furnished later) were provided by the city. Power was generated at about 4,550 volts, 60 cycles, with a leading power factor to absorb part of the wattless current of the city. During most of the *Lexington's* stay, the ship's generator ran on the governor, took the load variations of the city, and controlled the frequency. During the first week of the power generation, the ship's frequency had evidently been a little above 60 cycles because the city electric clocks were found to be 10 minutes ahead of Western Union time. The Telechron clock, however, was furnished and thereafter correct time was maintained. During the last 10 days of the stay, the ship's generator ran on the "block", at a constant load of about 20,000 kilowatts. No casualties, power interruption, or delays occurred and the operations were as satisfactory as would have been obtained using a modern shore power plant.

Summary 1922-1932

As to this decade between World Wars, a common assumption by historians and others is that little technological progress was realized. This misconception probably arises from the lack of a separate identity for research and development in those days, and from the highlighting of spectacular shipbuilding advances in World War I and again in World War II when funds and many of the Nation's foremost scientists and engineers were mobilized for the effort. In retrospect, the achievements from 1922 through 1932 in many areas were remarkable, particularly if one considers the low funding level of the Department of the Navy as a whole after the end of World War I.

But let us not forget that the Washington Naval Conference and resulting Five Power Naval Treaty did have a significant detrimental impact on the shipbuilding industry. In February 1922 agreement was reached by the major naval powers on a plan for the curtailment of Naval construction. Work was stopped in the United States overnight on several hundred million dollars of Naval ships. Employment in the industry sank to a new low. It was probably the gravest period in the history of the American shipbuilding industry. Coupled to this, there was also another worldwide business depression in the 1923 period. Shipyards were driven to all types of work other than shipbuilding in order to remain in existence. Thirty-six ships were built during the year, but they were mostly smaller vessels for river and coastwise traffic. It is interesting to note that coal was still used for fuel in fourteen of these ships.

And, although the treaties of the decade set the stage for design and engineering improvements in ships of the U.S. Navy because of the lack of major shipbuilding programs, there were two possible peripheral reasons for this advancement. First, the Bureau of Engineering instituted the allotment system of granting funds to ships afloat in order for each ship to be able to address its needs somewhat selectively.[71] Secondly, fleet engineering competition received official recognition through publication of General Order 108 in June 1923. This order set up the Division of Fleet Training in the office of the Chief of Naval Operations. This reorganization led to healthy engineering competition between ships of similar types because of standardized and centralized management of competitive exercises.

Naval air power also showed improvements during this period in the development of flying boats and lighter-than-air ships. And no summary would be complete without citing the significant gain in sea power made by the introduction of the aircraft carrier and carrier aircraft into the Fleet.

It is doubtful, in view of the combination of ship speed, range, responsiveness, operability, and reliability, that the high standards established in the propulsion and auxiliary plants of the "Treaty" heavy cruisers, the 1,500-ton destroyers, the battleships, and the aircraft carriers of the period have been equalled by conventional systems since, although we are sure some will argue this point.

The development of radar, television, underwater acoustics, and radio communications have most likely had a more dramatic effect on our nation's future well-being than any of the inventors could have optimistically anticipated. The development of improved shipboard evaporators, laundries, and sound motion picture projectors

had its visible impact on shipboard living conditions. New advances in metallurgy and welding strengthened and lightened shipboard structures, and permitted the use of increased operating pressures and temperatures in shipboard machinery, with concomitant savings in energy use through improved operating efficiencies. Finally, the development of the Momsen lung would prove to be the forerunner of advanced submarine escape systems that would save many lives in World War II and thereafter.

Notes

1 Andrack, Ernest Jr., "The Cruiser Controversy in Naval Limitations Negotiations: 1922-1936," *Military Affairs*, Vol. XLVIII, No. 3 (July 1984) pp. 111-120.

2 Fea, L., Major, Royal Italian Navy, "Some of the Consequences of the Washington Conference with Regard to Naval Construction," *Shipbuilding and Shipping Record* (July 6, 1922).

3 Densmore, C. W., CDR, USN, "USS *Richmond*, Description and Official Trials," *ASNE Journal* (1923) p. 451.

4 Gromer, J. G. B., LCDR, USN, "USS *Omaha*, Description of Machinery Installation and Official Trials," *ASNE Journal* (1924) p. 143.

5 Alexander, J. T., LCDR, USN, "USS *Milwaukee*, Description and Official Trials," *ASNE Journal* (1934) p. 513.

6 Neuhaus, H. M., "Fifty Years of Naval Engineering in Retrospect, Part IV, 1921-1938," *ASNE Journal* (1938) pp. 527-564.

7 Keller, H. R., LCDR, USN, "USS *Raleigh*, Description and Trials," *ASNE Journal* (1925) p. 466.

8 "Warship Construction in 1929," *ASNE Journal* (1930) pp. 173-174. Also Esler, J. K., LCDR, USN, "USS *Salt Lake City*, Construction, Description, and Official Preliminary Acceptance Trial Data," *ASNE Journal* (1930) p. 223.

9 Esler, J. K., LCDR, USN, "USS *Northampton*, USS *Chester*, USS *Houston*, Construction, Description, and Official Preliminary Acceptance Trial Data," *ASNE Journal* (1930) p. 651.

10 Friedman, Norman, *U.S. Cruisers, An Illustrated Design History*, Annapolis, Maryland: Naval Institute Press, 1984, pp. 105-137.

11 Charlton, A. M., CDR, USN, "USS *Colorado* and USS *West Virginia*, Description and Official Trials," *ASNE Journal* (1925) p. 1.

12 "Electric Propulsion of Ships," *Shipbuilding and Shipping Record* (December 4, 1924).

13 Turnbull, Archibald D., Capt., USNR and LCDR Clifford L. Lord, USNR, *History of United States Naval Aviation*, New Haven, Connecticut: Yale University Press, 1949.

14 Although U.S. Naval aviation involved tremendous engineering and operational development during this era, including the evolution of fighter, bombing, observation, patrol, and torpedo aircraft; evolution of aircooled engines; and development of aircraft ordnance, it is not within the scope of this volume.

15 Friedman, Norman, *U.S. Aircraft Carriers, an Illustrated History*, Annapolis, Maryland: Naval Institute Press, 1983.

16 Keller, H. R., LCDR, USN, "USS *Langley*, Our First American Aircraft Carrier," *ASNE Journal* (1923) p. 500. Also Neuhaus, "Fifty Years of Naval Engineering, Part IV."

17 Gillette, C. S., CDR, USN, "History, Description, and Acceptance Trials of the USS *Lexington*," *ASNE Journal* (1928) p. 438.

18 Friedman, *Aircraft Carriers*.

19 *Ibid.*

20 Neuhaus, "Fifty Years of Naval Engineering, Part IV." Also Polmar, Norman, *The American Submarine*, Annapolis, Maryland: The Nautical and Aviation Publishing Company of America, 1983, pp. 39-45.

21 "Naval Construction in 1925," Notes, *ASNE Journal* (1926) p. 144.

22 "Submarine Construction," *The Steamship* (September 1924).

23 Friedman, Norman, *Submarine Design and Development*, Annapolis, Maryland: Naval Institute Press, 1984, pp. 39-41.

24 Neuhaus, "Fifty Years of Naval Engineering, Part IV."

25 Polmar, *American Submarine.*

26 Charlton, A. M., CDR, USN, "USS *Holland*, Description and Trials," *ASNE Journal* (1926) p. 777.

27 Ducey, D. F., LCDR, USN, "USS *Medusa*, Description of Vessel Designated and Built for Fleet Repair Work," *ASNE Journal* (1925) p. 377.

28 Kenney, L. H., M. E., "USS *Dobbin* and USS *Whitney*, Description of Hull and Machinery Installations," *ASNE Journal* (1925) p. 435.

29 Bruce, B., CDR, USN, "River Gunboats for Yangtze Service, USS *Guam* and USS *Tutuila*," *ASNE Journal* (1928) p. 352.

30 Bruce, B., CDR, USN, "Building Gunboats in China, Description and Trials of USS *Luzon, Mindanao, Panay* and *Oahu*," *ASNE Journal* (1929) p. 82.

31 "Coast Guard Cutter for Arctic Service," Notes, *ASNE Journal* (1926) pp. 343-346.

32 Berg, E., "Electric Propulsion of Ships," *ASNE Journal* (1926) p. 346.

33 Johnson, R. E., *Guardians of the Sea, History of the United States Coast Guard, 1915 to the Present,* Annapolis, Maryland: Naval Institute Press, 1987, pp. 114-117. Also Newman, Q. B., USCG, "U.S. Coast Guard Cutters *Chelan, Pontchartrain, Tahoe, Champlain,* and *Mendota*," *ASNE Journal* (1928) p. 673.

34 Neuhaus, "Fifty Years of Naval Engineering, Part IV."

35 Johnson, *Guardians of the Sea.*

36 Neuhaus, "Fifty Years of Naval Engineering, Part IV."

37 Gregory, H. B., "The New Dollar Liners, SS *President Hoover* and SS *President Coolidge*," *ASNE Journal* (1934) p. 610.

38 Cox, O. L., CAPT, USN, "Matson Liner SS *Mariposa*, Description Trials," *ASNE Journal* (1931) p. 66.

39 Torbert, M. W., "United States Liner, SS *Manhattan*, Description and Trials," *ASNE Journal* (1932) p. 480.

40 Lamb, C. J., LT, USNR, "The Effects of Disarmament and Treaty Limits Upon Naval Engineering," *ASNE Journal* (1930) p. 621-649.

41 *Ibid.*

42 *Ibid.*

43 *Ibid.*

44 Michel, N. L., "Ten Years of Welding Development," A.S.M.E., 1936, republished in *ASNE Journal* (1928) p. 127.

45 Dyson, C. W., RADM, USN, "Associated Notes," *ASNE Journal* (1931) pp. 181-189.

46 Cooper, H. G., LCDR, USN, "The Dyson Boiler," *ASNE Journal* (1922) p. 33.

47 Neuhaus, "Fifty Years of Naval Engineering, Part IV."

48 Hamilton, J. E., LCDR, USN, "A Short History of the Naval Use of Fuel Oil, Part IV," *ASNE Journal* (1938) p. 35.

49 Stuart, M. C., "The Continuous Flow Evaporator," *ASNE Journal* (1924) p. 55.

50 Jones, C. A., CDR, USN, and LCDR A. M. Charlton, USN, "Pressure Vacuum Evaporators," *ASNE Journal* (1923) p. 329.

51 Lincoln, J. P., "Worthington Single Stage Centrifugal Pump, U.S. Naval Experimental Station," *ASNE Journal* (1926) p. 305.

52 "The Latest Sperry Gyro-Stabilizer Installation," *The Marine Engineer and Naval Architect* (June 1922). Also, Hughes, T. P., *Elmer Sperry: Inventor and Engineer*, Baltimore, Maryland: The Johns Hopkins Press, 1971, p. 276.

53 Hughes, *Elmer Sperry.*

54 Allison, David K., *New Eye for the Navy: The Origin of Radar at the Naval Research Laboratory,* Washington, D.C.: Government Printing Office, 1981, pp. 46, 61-66. Also Howeth, L. S., Captain, USN (Ret), *History of Communications-Electronics in the U.S. Navy*, Washington, D.C.: Government Printing Office, 1963, pp. 445-446.

55 Howeth, *History of Communications-Electronics in the U.S. Navy.*

56 *Aruin, W. B., "See With Your Radio," Radio News,* (September 1925).

57 Howeth, *History of Communications-Electronics in the U.S. Navy* pp. 472-473.

58 "The Oscilloscope," *Scientific American* (June 1923).

59 Howeth, *History of Communications-Electronics in the U.S. Navy,* pp. 353-370.

60 *Ibid.,* Chapters XXXII, XL.

61 Huey, C., "The Trend in Naval Engineering, Laundry Washers," *ASNE Journal* (1932) pp. 320-321.

62 Neuhaus, "Fifty Years of Naval Engineering, Part IV."

63 Rule, H. C., LT, USN, "Sound Motion Picture Equipment for the Navy," *ASNE Journal* (1931) p. 105.

64 Neuhaus, "Fifty Years of Naval Engineering, Part IV."

65 Hodge, J. C., D. Sc., "Marine Boiler Drums of Fusion Welded Construction," *ASNE Journal* (1933) p. 149.

66 "Non-Corrodible Nickel-Chromium Steels," *The Metallurgist*—Supplement to *The Engineer* (26 February 1926).

67 *Ibid.*

68 Hoyt, S. L., Ph.D., "Carbaloy—A New Tool Material," Notes, *ASNE Journal* (1929) p. 124.

69 Momsen, C. B., LT, USN, "Submarine Escape," *ASNE Journal* (1929) p. 169.

70 White, H. L., LCDR, USN, "Naval Electrical Power in Commercial Use—USS *Lexington* Relieves Tacoma Power Shortage," *ASNE Journal* (1930) p. 311.

71 Neuhaus, "Fifty Years of Naval Engineering, Part IV.".

CHAPTER
SIX
1933–1941

The Roosevelt Resurgence

by James L. McVoy, Virgil W. Rinehart,
and Prescott Palmer

Introduction

During this period, world conditions were marked by an increasing frequency of political disorder and armed aggression in the Far East, and a breakdown of collective security arrangements in Europe and Africa. A major cause was the international economic and political disorder in the wake of World War I. This led to the rise, in Italy, Japan, and Germany, of totalitarian demagogues committed to aggressive adventures and burgeoning armaments. The Soviet dictatorship that had captured the revolution against Czarist Russia, while conducting military aggressions only toward the end of this period, engaged in widespread covert operations and agitation that contributed significantly to international political friction and instability. The League of Nations established by the European powers at the end of World War I (and rejected by American isolationism) had failed in almost every attempt to employ its good offices to mediate crises in the international scene.

Initially, American naval strength was constrained by the limits prescribed by the Washington Naval Disarmament Treaty of 1922, and below that by domestic isolationism and the great economic depression of the late twenties. The naval ambitions of first Japan, and later Italy and Germany, were increasingly revealed by building programs that tested treaty limits and that, in time, abrogated them. As a consequence, the United States began to look to its naval requirements. The first reluctant Congressional effort, implemented with enthusiasm by the Navy Department, provided the ten so-called "Treaty" heavy cruisers, discussed in chapter 5, in response to the Japanese programs of the early 1920s.[1]

The ultimate American naval response to the deteriorating international relationships was a clear expression of the leadership of President Franklin D. Roosevelt, uniquely reflecting his grasp of global dynamics and the role of sea power, and his imaginative political skills. He converted the problem of economic depression, presumably the biggest obstacle to any naval programs, into an opportunity. Naval construction was among a variety of so-called "pump priming" economic relief programs undertaken while simultaneously fulfilling specific national needs. In this case, badly needed naval strength was acquired while providing a "trickle-down" infusion into the moribund shipbuilding and steel industries. This administrative strategy was implemented with the legislative tactics of Representative Carl Vinson, who had already been on the Naval Affairs Committee for 20 years and astutely would see to the naval requirements of the nation for more than another 20. The National Industrial Recovery Act of 1933, within 6 months of Roosevelt's inauguration, provided for building cruisers and smaller vessels to treaty-permitted strengths. By March 1934, the Vinson-Trammel bill provided for the construction of 102 ships of all types, extending over 8 years, completing in early 1942. This, then, was the "Roosevelt resurgence," the brilliant economic and strategic timeliness of which even the wily "former naval person," himself, could scarcely appreciate at the time.[2]

NAVAL CONSTRUCTION

Prologue

Between wars, American naval leaders, technologically oriented by education, training, and experience in World War I, energetically pursued the potential of naval aviation (many retreaded as naval aviators), but the battleship remained the dominant capital ship. It should be mentioned that radar capability, which must be remembered as perhaps the Navy's great technological innovation in World War II, was too new to be part of the conceptual design of any pre-war ships. Radar will be discussed in the section on Research and Development.[3]

Battleships

The American battle line consisted of fifteen ships, some as old as the 29,000-ton *Arkansas*, commissioned in 1912, some as new as the three 33,000-ton *Maryland*-class ships commissioned 1921-1923. Most had 14-inch main batteries; the *Marylands* had 16-in guns, and the old *"Arky"* was the sole 12-incher.[4]

Improvement in battleships in commission was limited by the Washington Naval Treaty, budgets, and the realities of what could be accomplished through overhaul. Battleship design, however, was in as much flux as ever, under the competitive demands of big guns, propulsion, fire control systems, armor, projectile penetration, armor-piercing bombs, underwater protection, provisions for gunnery spotting aircraft, and secondary battery requirements.[5]

As mentioned previously, the Japanese abrogated the treaty limits on battleship building in 1934, and the treaty limits on size and firepower in 1935. This, coupled with past aggression in Korea, Manchuria, and China proper, and the gratuitous effrontery of dive-bombing our Yangtze River gunboat USS *Panay*, caused the United States, understandably, to feel compelled to repair its naval strength. Even then, when the two *North Carolina*-class battleships were authorized by the Act of 3 June 1936, Mr. Roosevelt felt constrained by pacifist sentiment in the United States to delay the start of the two battleships until after the 1936 elections.[6]

Numerous battleship design studies to meet a variety of requirements had been undertaken by the Bureau of Construction and Repair (C&R) during the late 1920s and early 30s. On authorization, two 35,000-ton fast battleships were laid down and built: *North Carolina* (BB-55) at the New York Navy Yard and *Washington* (BB-56) at Philadelphia. Both were commissioned in early 1941. Capable of 27 knots and equipped with nine 16in/45s in three triple-gun turrets, they constituted a substantial improvement over their World War I predecessors, the 31,000-ton, 21-knot *Marylands* with eight 16in/45s. The design was achieved with a virtual tripling of propulsion to 121,000 shaft horsepower (shp) (using the new 600 psi/850° steam systems) and addition of 80 feet of length to improve fineness-ratio for speed, and slight reduction of armor protection: sides, 12 versus 13.5 inches (but obliquely sloped 17 degrees away from impact); turret faces, 16 versus 18 inches. There were other gains, too. A 4.1-inch armored waterline-deck was constructed atop 1.5 inches of special treatment steel (STS), against aircraft bombs. Improved underwater protection combined a double-void bottom with D. W. Taylor's multibulkhead void-

and-liquid side compartmentation (and served the *North Carolina* well against a Japanese submarine torpedo). A very efficient and flexible four-director Mark 37 control system for the 20-gun 5in/38 dual-purpose (DP) battery would take a heavy toll of both Japanese aircraft and Pacific island fortifications. The automatic anti-aircraft (AA) battery of four quadruple 1.1-inch machine-cannon and twelve .50-caliber machine guns was replaced early in the war with 40mm and 20mm guns. These and all following battleships were equipped with two stern-mounted catapults used by the complement of two gunnery spotting aircraft, but no hangar space was provided. Although this class was designed and built in the pre-radar era, on availability, the U.S. Navy's first production air-search model, the CXAM, was installed on both ships by December 1941.[7]

Four 35,000-ton *South Dakota*-class battleships were ordered a year later, in 1938-39 (to be commissioned in 1942), again with 16in/45 main and 5in/38 DP batteries. Improvements included fitting a larger power plant into a smaller engineering space to provide the same high speed as the *North Carolinas*. (This was prompted by radio-intercept intelligence in 1936 revealing that the Japanese battleships, *Nagato* in particular, were having their speed significantly increased by overhaul.) The *South Dakotas'* compact design was necessitated by a reduction in waterline length from 729 to 666 feet to save weight for a unique inward-sloping 12-inch armored belt, heavier turret armor, and a 5-inch STS protective deck. These were measures against high impact-angle, long-range projectiles (now possible with aircraft spotting and improved fire-control). The armor belt's 19-degree inward slope increased protective obliqueness, and tapering to the inner bottom protected against underwater trajectory hits.[8]

The final battleships, designed and laid down prior to World War II, were the four magnificent ships of the 45,000-ton *Iowa* class, commissioned in 1943 and 1944. Their size was a consequence of a number of interrelated factors. An 860-foot length was needed to provide for a 212,000-shp engineering space and for hull fineness-ratio for 33 knots to match the Japanese fast battleships and battle cruisers. The tonnage re-sulted in part from BuOrd's requirement for three triple turrets with the new long-range (42,345 yards) 16in/50 guns, partly from providing the same sloping armor belt and protective deck of the *South Dakotas* over a ship of this size, and partly from improved and armored transverse bulkheading.[9] The recall of this class for duty in Korea and Vietnam, and again in the late 80s, is a tribute to the soundness of its design and construction.

Aircraft Carriers

USS *Ranger* (CV-4), the first American "keel-up" carrier design, was commissioned in 1934 early in this chapter's era. (The earlier *Langley* (CV-1) was a converted turbo-electric collier, and the *Lexington* and *Saratoga* (CVs-2 and -3) were converted from battlecruisers.) *Ranger* was at the low end of the design-spectrum in the fleet carrier evolution that would finally result in the very successful wartime *Essex* class. The *Ranger* was designed as a 14,000-ton flush-deck carrier, 730 feet in length, to carry about seventy-five aircraft. Her 53,500 shp provided just under 30 knots. Although provided with three folding stacks to each side for the flush-deck design, *Ranger* was completed with an island to better provide for control of air, ship, and gunnery operations. Her defensive gun battery consisted of eight DP 5in/25s controlled by two Mark 33 directors, and forty .50-caliber machine guns. She proved an unsuccessful design, however, being too slow, lacking in protective guns, with inadequate underwater protection, and being too light for rough water flight operations.[10]

It must be recognized that at that time, aircraft carriers and fleet aviation were still in an experimental stage. That is, not only were naval aviators and engineers seeking to improve and develop carrier aviation as a weapons system, they were still far from certain just what development and improvement was needed. From operational experiences with the *Lexington* class and the *Ranger*, two basic approaches were seen: heavy and light carriers. Depending on aircraft availability, heavy carriers could provide for the operation of four 18-aircraft squadrons: one of each of fighters, scouts, torpedoes, and bombers. Light carriers also provided four squadrons, but only two types: two fighters and two scouts.

Besides concern about the ability of carriers to launch, land, and cycle aircraft, there was concern about their speed for conducting flight-ops with the battle line, for operating as a detached force with cruisers, and for evading enemy cruisers. Carriers were seen to need both armor and medium-weight guns against cruisers (for night or low visibility), machine gun arrays against dive bombers, heavy AA guns against high-level bombers, a light armor deck to protect machinery and magazines against bombs, and underwater protection against torpedo attack. The problem lay in fitting all this into a carrier, most especially since the *Lexington* and *Saratoga*, at 33,000 tons each, left only 69,000 tons for additional carriers under the arms treaty. There could be five at 13,800 tons (like *Ranger*), four of 17,250, or three of 23,000.[11]

The *Yorktown* class followed with two 800-foot, 20,000-ton carriers. They carried over ninety aircraft to provide for the operation of five 18-plane squadrons. The displacement of this class provided for underwater protection, a 120,000-shp geared-turbine propulsion plant capable of 34 knots, and adequate steadiness for operations in moderately rough weather. The AA battery consisted of eight of the new, greater-range 5in/38 DPs (still Mark 33 directed), four quadruple 1.1-inch machine cannon, and twenty-four .50-caliber machine guns. About the time plans were adequately developed to build this class, however, the Great Depression had closed in, and naval building seemed unlikely. Nevertheless, newly-elected President Roosevelt found a solution. He arranged for the Navy to get the needed *Yorktown*s via a government spending program to stimulate the nation's industries, and the ships were funded under the National Industrial Relief Act of 1933. When one recalls the roles the *Yorktown* and *Enterprise*, less than 10 years later, played in the victory at Midway, this has to be recognized as rather inspired planning.[12]

Next, commissioned in 1940, came a single-ship class, the *Wasp*, in a return to a "light" carrier design, badly needed to replace the *Langley*. Built to operate seventy-two aircraft, *Wasp*'s displacement on launching was 15,400 tons, leaving tonnage to spare for another *Enterprise*. She was armed with the same eight-gun

5in/38 DP battery and Mark 33 control, as well as the four quadruple 1.1-inch machine cannon and twenty-four .50-caliber machine guns as the *Enterprise* class. *Wasp* was used to pioneer the folding deck-edge elevator, in a rudimentary tee-frame form supporting only the wheels and tail of an aircraft. Limited by size, tonnage, design, and engineering constraints, however, the *Wasp* was a disappointing ship. Her 740-foot flight deck proved crowded for handling and cycling of aircraft. In trials, it took a clean bottom and good engineering practice that delivered almost 74,000 shp to achieve 30.73 knots. The *Wasp* was deficient in underwater protection but enjoyed some degree of improved compartmentation in juxtapositioning of boiler and engineering control spaces. Her 25-pound (0.625-inch) protective decking was too light, and incomplete in covering only magazines, gasoline tanks forward, and steering gear. Her loss to three Japanese submarine torpedoes in September 1942, however, was due to gasoline explosions when hit during flight deck fueling.[13]

The 20,000-ton *Hornet* (CV-8), ordered in 1939 and launched at the end of 1940, was essentially a return to the *Enterprise* class, with minor improvements such as the Mark 37 director system for the 5in/38 AA battery. It was recognized that the *Hornet* was needed in a hurry. Indeed, she too fought at Midway, less than 8 months after commissioning.[14]

The *Essex*-class (CV-9) carrier began as the second of two ships authorized with the *Hornet* to use the remaining treaty tonnage for carriers allowed by the Vinson-Trammell legislation. Treaty abrogation and world conditions, however, led to the Two-Ocean Navy Act of 1940, which provided for three more carriers. The fall of France caused Congress to authorize further fleet expansion, resulting in still another seven carriers. The Pearl Harbor attack brought prompt order for two more, and further orders, to the total of twenty-four ships for the class, continued into the wartime era of the next chapter.[15]

The originally authorized 20,400 tons of the *Essex* was under the 23,000-ton limit for carriers of the Washington Naval Limitations Treaty, but treaty abrogation and a variety of requirements led to a final design of 27,100 tons. When commissioned in December 1942, this included flight deck area for efficient operation of a five-squadron carrier air group of larger, more powerful aircraft; 230,000 gallons of fuel for the aircraft; a lengthier, 150,000-shp propulsion plant for 33 knots (and 20 knots astern for recovery and relaunching of aircraft, despite forward flight deck damage); a 4-inch armored belt against 6-inch gunfire; a 2.5-inch STS hangar deck; a 1.5-inch secondary protective deck; and underwater protection with triple bottoms. Other features of the class were a pair of flight-deck catapults, air-conditioned ready rooms, and three aircraft elevators, one a full-sized deck-edge type. Armament consisted of twelve 5in/38 AA guns with two Mark 37 directors, eight quadruple automatic 40mm guns, and forty-six 20mm machine guns. Ultimately, the numbers of these carriers and their CVL and CVE auxiliaries would concentrate sufficient naval air power to simply overwhelm the Japanese naval forces.[16]

Although their development was somewhat out of the main line of the American fleet carrier, both the escort (CVE) and the light or cruiser-conversion carriers (CVL) played an important role in naval air operations during World War II. They owed their existence to President Roosevelt's continuing interest in providing an austere wartime supplement to the fleet carriers. Although Mr. Roosevelt early proposed conversion of already-ordered cruisers, conversions to CVLs were not ordered until 1942, and are beyond the chronology of this chapter. CVE construction and development, on the other hand, was well underway in early 1941. The U.S. Navy had long believed that treaty limits and peacetime austerity would require emergency conversion of merchant ships to auxiliary carriers to meet wartime needs. Such plans, however, had predominantly envisaged conversion of passenger liners that could fulfill size and speed needs. As it turned out, liner conversions were determined to be too complicated and expensive. In view of the *Essexes* on order, satisfactory American and British experience with converted cargo designs, the availability of cruiser hulls, and the need for troop transports, liner conversion was not undertaken. It was decided that converted cruiser hulls and converted tankers and cargo ships would fill the bill, and they did very well, indeed.

The first American conversion was the diesel-powered C-3 cargo vessel *Mormacmail*, undertaken in March 1941 by Newport News Shipbuilding. She was completed in just under 3 months as the general purpose aircraft tender USS *Long Island* (AVG-1) (just weeks earlier than an independent British project produced the similar HMS *Audacity*). Her displacement was 12,000 tons, and her 8,000-horsepower diesel propulsion achieved 17.8 knots. She was equipped to carry 100,000 gallons of aviation gasoline for a complement of sixteen aircraft. Her gun battery consisted of one 5in/51 surface gun aft, two 3in/55 AA guns forward, and four .50-caliber machine guns. She was given a 362-foot flight deck that proved inadequate and was extended to 439 feet two months later. American and British design concepts were shared to develop what would become over one hundred CVE escort carriers used for convoy support, ASW hunter-killer groups, amphibious support, and aircraft delivery. Details of this wartime development are left to the following chapter.[17]

Cruisers

As this era commenced in 1933, the heavy 8-inch gun *New Orleans*-class cruisers were being launched. The first five of these 10,000-ton ships, ordered in 1929 and 30 of slightly varied designs, were all commissioned in 1934. Their 107,000-shp propulsion plants were designed for 32.5 knots. They were each equipped with a 5-inch armor belt, 9 feet high, tapering to 3 inches and 5 feet high. The 8in/55 guns, in three triple turrets with 8-inch faces, 2.75-inch tops, and 1.5-inch sides, were controlled with two Mark 31 directors. A 1.5-inch armored deck was provided. The AA battery consisted of eight DP 5in/38s with two Mark 33 directors. Four aircraft for scouting and gunnery spotting were assigned, for which two amidships catapults and a main-deck hangar were provided. Orders for the last two of the class, the *Quincy* (CA-39) and the *Vincennes* (CA-44), were placed in 1933, with some redesign. The new design sought to optimize protection within treaty displacement limits and provided emergency diesel electrical generators. Torpedo tubes of the original design were eliminated for the entire class because of their vulnerability to explosive damage and the increased range achieved by 8-inch guns (30,000 yards). Ironically, the *Quincy* and *Vincennes* would be lost at very short range, in the Savo Island melee, to Japanese cruiser 8-inch guns and the terribly destructive 24-inch Type 93 Long Lance torpedoes (1,080-pound warhead) that, even more ironically, outranged the guns on both sides (35,000 yards at 42 knots).[18]

The *Brooklyn* light cruiser class of seven ships resulted from the London Naval Conference of 1930. There, British and American differences in cruiser requirements were reconciled by agreeing to limiting light cruisers as large as 10,000 tons to 6-inch guns and agreeing on certain tonnage totals slightly favoring the British. This eliminated future 8-inch cruisers that would threaten the many, light, 6-inch cruisers, with which the British could more thriftily defend imperial sea-lanes. (Remember the *Wampanoag* from Chapter 1.) The 10,000 tons provided for a powerful 6-inch cruiser with which the Americans felt they could cope with both 6-inch and 8-inch Japanese cruisers. This commendable professional optimism could have been more costly than it actually was had the U.S. Navy not developed its surface-search and gunnery radar advantage. Actually, caliber for caliber, Japanese and American guns were more or less equal in range, terminal velocity, and projectile weight. In the short-range night melees that eventually took place, the intensively developed Japanese skill in night tactics, their still little-acknowledged advantage in night optics, and their superb Long Lance torpedoes gave the U.S. Navy a rude shock in the early days in the South Pacific. It is far from certain that there would have been much American technological advantage, either, if long-range, daytime cruiser duels had taken place.[19]

Seven *Brooklyn*-class cruisers were laid down in 1933 and 34 and were commissioned in 1936 and 37. All displaced 10,000 tons, as did their semi-sister *Wichita*, a heavy cruiser with nine 8in/53s; however, the light cruisers were equipped with fifteen 6in/47s. Both were equipped with eight 5-inch AA guns controlled by fore and aft Mark 33 directors, but the *Wichita* was equipped with the newer and slightly longer range 5in/38 DPs and the *Brooklyn*s got the older 5in/25s. A 100,000-shp ship propulsion drove both types to 33.5 knots. As mentioned earlier,

the 10,000-ton displacement of the *Brooklyn* class was used to provide them with heavy cruiser protection—in fact, the same 3.25- to 5-inch armor belt as the *New Orleans* class. The *Wichita* had a slightly heavier belt of 4- to 6-inch armor on 1.25-inch STS. All had a wide transom stern that readily provided room for two stern-mounted catapults and a below-deck hangar for their complements of four scouting and spotting aircraft. A year following, in 1935, two modified *Brooklyn*-class ships, the *St. Louis* and the *Helena*, were laid down, to be commissioned in 1938. Their major improvements were the use of eight 5in/38s in four twin mounts, and boiler rooms separated by a boiler operating station (made possible by a compact 565 psi/700° steam plant instead of 400 psi/650°). The class as a whole stood up well to battle damage; only the *Helena* was lost, and to three Long Lances (1080-pound warheads) at that. Later, the *Savannah* took a German FX-1400 armor-piercing guided bomb in the top of No. 3 turret (the largest bomb to hit an American warship during the war), which exploded in the magazines. But in blowing out the bottom, the explosion let in water that quenched the fire in the magazines. The *Boise* took two hits from Japanese underwater-trajectory shells, one penetrating below the armor belt into No. 2 turret's handling room; but, again, flooding quenched the fires. Hits from similar projectiles failed to penetrate a turret-face and a barbette.[20]

The second London Naval Conference of 1935-36 was a final effort at treaty naval limitation. It failed, essentially, because Japan insisted on full naval parity, needed in its misguided plans for aggressive Asian imperialism. When the United States demurred, Japan walked out. There was informal agreement between Great Britain and the United States to limit light cruisers (with guns of 6-inch caliber or less) to less than 7,000 tons, and this led to the development of our *Atlanta*-class cruisers. Although later sometimes referred to as AA cruisers because of their sixteen-gun 5in/38 DP battery, this class originally was planned primarily to fulfill surface fighting needs, with and against destroyers. Not solely, however, inasmuch as a 6in/47 battery was ruled out in the end because timely development of a DP 6in/47 turret could not be ensured.

Preliminary design was completed in the summer of 1938, and President Roosevelt was interested enough to request a copy of the plans. *Brooklyn*-class hull lines were used but of a lesser 530-foot length. At 7,400 tons, the planned 75,000 shp was expected to make 32.5 knots. A wide belt of 3.75-inch armor was provided by way of machinery spaces, and a narrow belt by way of magazines (further protected by oil tanks aft and voids forward). Double bottoms curved up the sides to the 1.25-inch armor deck. Port and starboard triple torpedo tubes (changed to quadruple) were specified, and an automatic AA battery of three 1.1-inch machine cannon. The first four of this class were ordered in April 1939 (from Federal Shipbuilding Company of Kearny, New Jersey, which employed Gibbs & Cox for design). They were laid down in 1940 and commissioned in 1941 and 42. A second group of four of this class was ordered under the naval expansion program of 1940 and laid down in 1941 and 42. At Guadalcanal, in the night battle of 12-13 November 1942, the *Atlanta* took severe damage from 14-inch battleship salvos at 4,500 yards, as well as from a 24-inch Long Lance torpedo and destroyer gunfire. Losing all power except for an emergency diesel generator, she suffered progressive flooding and finally had to be scuttled, something of a tribute to the construction of such a lightly-built ship. In the same battle, sister-ship *Juneau*, hit by what was probably a Long Lance torpedo, lost a fireroom and use of one shaft, but could still make 13 knots. The next day, however, she took a submarine torpedo exactly where she had previously been damaged, and sank in 20 seconds, but that was hardly a reflection on her construction.[21]

Three more classes of cruisers were developed and laid down through 1941: the *Cleveland*-class light cruisers, the *Baltimore*-class heavy cruisers, and the *Alaska*-class heavy or so-called "battle" cruiser. The *Cleveland* and *Alaska* classes derived from the 10,000-ton *Brooklyn* class; the *Baltimore*s via the *Wichita* heavy-cruiser variant. The first two classes represented a requirement to standardize for production to achieve neglected fleet strength; the *Alaska*s fulfilled a seen need for a Japanese heavy cruiser killer. The *Cleveland*s, the numerically largest cruiser class in the Navy's history (fifty-two ordered and twenty-three built), represented an improved *Helena*. This class aimed at a reduced design displacement of 8,000 tons, an enhanced AA battery by replacing No. 3 6in/47 turret with 5in/38 mounts forward and aft of the superstructure and adding four quadruple 1.1-inch machine cannon, the improved efficiency of 565 psi/850° steam, and improved propulsion survivability from alternate boiler room groups and engine rooms. Increased emergency power was sought with paired turbo-generators in the forward engine room and abaft the after engine room. Weight and stability were continuing problems as operational requirements. Particularly, the need for increasing the automatic AA battery and the electronics installation increased topside weight.

The *Baltimore* class was an improved, larger *Wichita* class. The first four ships were ordered in July 1940 and laid down at Bethlehem Steel Yard in Quincy, Massachusetts throughout 1941. (Four more were ordered in September, but were not laid down until after the period of this chapter.) With the *Baltimore* class, increases in protection and size were chosen that pushed estimated displacement to 13,300 tons, including a longer belt of the same 6-inch armor, more rugged and extensive underwater protection, a heavier, 2.5-inch protective deck, 3-inch turret roofs, and various increased splinter protection. Propulsion, using a 615 psi/850° steam plant, was increased to 120,000 shp to provide for 34 knots. The main battery was nine 8in/55s in triple-gun turrets with 8-inch turret face armor. The AA battery consisted of twelve 5in/38 DPs in six lightly armored twin mounts, twelve automatic quadruple 40mm guns, and 26 single 20mm machine guns, reflecting the recent British experience against German *Stuka*s in Norwegian, English Channel, and Mediterranean waters.[22]

While the *Cleveland*s and *Baltimore*s were designed after the treaty restrictions had been lifted, they drew on the treaty-limited *Brooklyn*s and *Wichita* designs, and in various ways, they reflected treaty-constraint influence. However, the final pre-war class of cruisers, the *Alaska*s, being planned and designed from 1938-40, can be considered substantially free of such influences. They were designed to fulfill a requirement to overwhelm the Japanese Navy's big, fast, heavily armed *Mogami*-class cruisers (then seen as a threat to independent carrier task forces) and to deal with commerce-raiding German pocket battleships, as well as to incorporate the hard lessons of the European war dive-bombers. They demonstrated the response of American planners and builders (to say nothing of Presidential indulgence) of "going for broke." Note that the *Alaska*-class cruisers were not "battle" cruisers. The misleading type-symbol "CB" simply stood for "Cruiser, Large." And large these cruisers were—to carry their main battery of nine 12in/50s, together with an appropriate 12.8-inch armor face for their triple-gun turrets, a 9.5-inch armor belt (tapered to 5 inches) for their 808-foot hull, 10.6-inch transverse bulkheads fore and aft, a heavily armored (10.6-inch) steering room, a 1.4-inch bomb deck, a 3.25-inch protective deck on 1-inch STS, and a 150,000-shp propulsion plant (like the *Essex*-class carriers) good for 33 knots. These were major factors contributing to the *Alaska*'s 31,500-ton design displacement (comparable to the old battleship *Pennsylvania*). Heavily divided underwater protection was called for, too: heavy scantlings for double-bottoms (triple, in way of magazines), double-space sides (outboard liquid-loaded), alternate boiler and engine spaces, and separate spaces for each diesel emergency electrical generator. Additional design features included a return to an amidship, topside hangar for two aircraft, Mark 34 main battery directors, a twelve-gun Mark 37 director-controlled 5in/38 DP battery, six quadruple automatic 40mm guns, and thirty-two 20mm machine guns. Only two ships, the *Alaska* and the *Guam*, of this projected six-ship class were completed. They served effectively, during 1945, in the AA screens of the Pacific carrier task groups, their original role no longer existing.[23]

Destroyers

During the period 1933 to 1941, the Navy finally was permitted to augment and replace over 200 obsolete, flush-deck, World War I style destroyers. Although fifty were transferred to Great Britain for escort service with her hard-pressed convoys, and another fifty were converted for special duties such as mine layers, seaplane tenders, and fast troop transports, they were inadequate for fleet duties, and their replacement was overdue.[24]

The eight *Farragut*-class destroyers were laid down in 1932 and 1933 and commissioned in 1934 and 1935. They were roughly the first of a line of sixty so-called "1,500 tonners" of roughly seven classes in improving steps of destroyer design.[25] They were, at first, paralleled by two classes of somewhat heavier destroyer-leaders, the *Porter* and *Somers* classes, types of ships that went out of favor as early as 1939.

The *Farragut* class, had a 400-pound/650° steam plant design to deliver 42,800 shp for a little over 36 knots, and a range of 6,500 miles at 12 knots. Manned by a complement of ten officers and 150 enlisted men, they set a design with two stacks, a deck-higher foc's'le, 334-foot length, 35-foot beam, and two sets of quadruple 21-inch torpedo tubes. They were designed and built for torpedo attack on the enemy fleet and defense of the battle line against similar hostile torpedo attack. All the 1,500 tonners had 5in/38 DP main batteries [early classes had five guns, with protective nonballistic shields forward (against seas and weather), open mounts aft] controlled by a Mark 33 DP director, eight 21-inch torpedo tubes and four .50-caliber AA machine guns. Anti-submarine warfare was almost neglected, with a marginal performance underwater (QC) sonar and twin stern racks with fourteen slow-sinking depth-charges.[26]

The eight 1,850-ton *Porter*-class destroyers, were laid down in 1933 as destroyer squadron leaders and were provided with 381-foot hulls displacing 1,850 tons. They had an eight-gun main battery and a complement of thirteen officers and 193 enlisted. Their 400-pound/650°F, 50,000 shp propulsion plants could achieve over 38 knots and were designed for a range of 7,800 miles at 12 knots. Mark-35-director-controlled 5in/38s were in four twin mounts resembling the World War II *Sumner* class, but capable of engaging surface targets only. They had an AA battery comprised of two quadruple 1.1-inch machine cannon, although only two .50-caliber machine guns. They had the same torpedo tubes, sonar, and depth-charges as the *Farragut* class.[27]

The fourteen *Mahan*-class destroyers came down the ways next, commissioning in 1936. Their steam plants were upped to 700°F to generate 46,000 shp for 38 knots. The torpedo battery was increased to twelve tubes. Their endurance, guns, complement, sonar, and depth charges were the same as the *Farragut* class. The new 700°F steam plants involved replacing the older, British-licensed, Parsons turbine (which at the turn of the century revolutionized naval engineering by replacing the reciprocating steam engine) with the new GE turbine. General Electric had developed the Curtis in shore applications, and it was more compact, both dimensionally and in amount of blading (one-tenth). It was simpler, lighter, yet more rugged; it had higher speed, was more efficient, and introduced the Navy to double-reduction gearing. Shipbuilding's big three, Bethlehem Steel, New York Shipbuilding, and Newport News Shipbuilding, locked into manufacturing licenses with Parsons, were not enthusiastic about adopting the steam pressures and temperatures of the Curtis system. Bath Iron Works, United Shipyards, and Federal Shipbuilding and Drydock won contracts for two ships each. Gibbs and Cox of New York were chosen as the supporting designers.[28] Although Gibbs and Cox were inexperienced with destroyers, they had gained considerable reputation in the design of passenger liners with high-pressure steam systems. This ability carried over, and they were so successful as to be employed to design all subsequent destroyer classes. There was, however, criticism of crowding in the *Mahan* engineering installation, and inevitable pain in the development of a new system. Unfortunately, it provided ammunition for the bureaucratic battle that was brewing.[29]

The *Gridley* class of two destroyers, commissioned in 1937, were the first of three 16-torpedo tube classes. They were standard 1,500 tonners, with changes typical of destroyer evolution. The 600-pound/700°F plant continued the steam-pressure rise, but built by Bethlehem, had the old Parsons-licensed turbines. While lacking the efficiency of the new Curtis type, they nevertheless generated respectable power, since the *Gridley*'s sister ship *Craven* established what may be a U.S. destroyer trials record of 41.53 knots (at 1,761 tons displacement). The 5in/38 battery of all three of these classes was reduced to four guns, but enjoyed the first enclosed open mounts, forward.[30]

The second and last squadron leader class, the five *Somers* class, were introduced into the fleet next, starting in 1937. They had the *Porter*-class military characteristics (except for having only

one Mark 35 director) on a slightly shorter, 372-foot hull of the same tonnage. A move to a single stack scarcely indicated the really big change. Feisty Rear Admiral H. G. Bowen had become Chief of the Bureau of Engineering, and the *Mahan*'s engineering gains and reliability had convinced him of the value of higher steam pressures and temperatures. Never one to shrink from controversy, he directed the move to 600 psi/850°F with the *Somers* class, with additional innovations of superheat controls and air-encased boiler furnaces. The *Somers* ran trials at only 700°F but performed with 22 to 8 percent better fuel efficiency (as speed increased from 12 to 35 knots) than the comparable *Porter*-class destroyers, and indicated 21 percent increased cruising radius. Nevertheless, the Navy's Board of Inspection and Survey (I & S) was suspicious of the new-fangled system and recommended the rapidly expanding destroyer force get no further *Somers*-type boiler installations until after complete tests of the *Somers*. The techno-political struggle went on for some time, then, in the Navy Department and shipbuilding board rooms. Besides the industrial opposition and that of I & S, members of the Navy General Board also had become alarmed about "unproven and complex" engineering plants. Bowen and his technicians, however, had chosen their ground wisely. They were right, and the *Somers* was driven hard to prove them so. There were various hearings and exchanges of reports, but the Engineer in Chief of the Navy had his way, and 600-pound/850° steam increasingly, and ultimately exclusively, would be used in Navy ships (until replaced, postwar, by still higher pressures and temperatures).

The second of the 16-torpedo tube classes were the eight *Bagleys*, which moved back up to the 400-pound/700° steam and turbine system of the *Mahan* hull.

The third 16-tube class, and last 1,500-tonners, were the twelve *Benhams*. They had a 50,000-shp, three-boiler system built to operate with the 600-pound/850° steam that the *Somers* had pioneered so successfully (except for *McCall* and *Maury*, which Bethlehem built to *Gridley* specifications). The *Benham* gun installations were improved with base-ring mounts that incorporated a fuze-setting shell hoist and carried the gun crew on a platform that rotated with the gun. The *Benham* achieved 12 to 22 percent greater fuel efficiency than the *Gridley* in trials, and 13 percent better at 40.8 knots to the *Gridley*'s 38.5 knots at full power, on what must have been a very fine day for Admiral Bowen.

In the *Sims* class, commissioned in 1939 and 1940, there was a move to a slightly heavier ship, partially in response to demands for sturdier construction, and partially from a substantially enhanced Mark 37 DP gun director system, with a below-decks plotting room for the computer and stable element. The torpedo battery was reduced to twelve tubes. Unfortunately, the *Sims* ended up substantially overweight, and in her inclining test was found to have inadequate reserve stability (excessive topside weight), as well. It was a blunder on the part of the Bureau of Construction and Repair (C & R). Charged with coordinating design weights and determining stability, C & R had failed to develop adequate procedures for coordinating the inevitable weight and moment changes of initial design estimates of the other bureaus. The stability problem was remedied by the installation of 60 tons of lead ballast and the removal of ordnance material. Navy Secretary Charles Edison (son of the famous inventor) followed this up with the removal of the Chief of C & R. Earlier, from the high pressure and temperature steam controversy, he had determined a lack of cooperation between C & R and Engineering due to personalities (i.e., the Bureau chiefs). He now directed that Engineering and C & R be combined in a single "Bureau of Ships" to ensure proper coordination of ship design and construction in the future. Admiral Bowen's term of office as Chief of the Bureau of Engineering had recently expired, but a subordinate, Rear Admiral S. M. Robinson, not Admiral Bowen, was appointed to be Chief of the new bureau. Admiral Bowen won the battle of steam pressure and temperature, but found out that being right isn't always enough in bureaucratic in-fighting.[31]

A very large single class of ninety-six destroyers, meanwhile, was being planned for 1938, 1939, and 1940. Specifications called for a 1,620-ton two-stacker, with a *Sims*-size hull, four enclosed 5in/38 guns, the Mark 37 director system, a single quintuple set of torpedo tubes, and ten .50-caliber AA machine guns. The lead ship for

1938, the *Benson*, gave its name to what turned out to be a six-ship class. The specifications for all the ships had called for the efficient Curtis turbines and 600 psi/850° steam in a 50,000-shp propulsion plant. Nevertheless, several months after contract award, *Benson*'s builder, Bethlehem, asked for a contract modification. They requested and were allowed to use a low-pressure turbine for low speed, no cruising turbine, and single reduction gears. The Navy agreed because of its need for the ships and because Bethlehem guaranteed performance. The other two ships of the 1938 class, *Gleaves* and *Nilack*, built by Bath Iron Works, constituted a subclass that adhered to original specifications. The 1939 and 1940 ships, which took their class name from the 1939 lead, *Livermore*, also conformed to the original engineering specification (including twenty-four ships built by Bethlehem). Other specifications, however, particularly weapon requirements, were subject to much change as a result of operational experience with the new destroyers, and as technical intelligence flowed in from the increasingly disturbed world.[32]

The last class of destroyers developed and designed prior to World War II (of which at least thirty-six were laid down in 1941) were the wonderful *Fletcher*s, perhaps the most successful of all our destroyers, blessed even with a fine, crisp, evocative name. One hundred and nineteen were ordered in 1940, and the design continued in wartime variants to a total of 175. (The *Fletcher*s also heavily influenced the following wartime *Sumner* class.) The design began to evolve in the Fall of 1939, when the General Board became increasingly concerned about destroyer requirements to execute and survive their tactical roles in the approaching war at sea. The concept formulation continued in meetings, discussions, and exchange of information in Washington and elsewhere, and resulted in characteristics adopted by the General Board and approved by the Secretary of the Navy in January 1940. The *Fletcher* was going to have to be a big, fast, well-protected ship (for a destroyer), with a sophisticated ordnance array for offensive and defensive tasks against a variety of surface, air, and subsurface threats. This meant 2,100 tons on a longer (369-foot), beamier (40-foot) flush-deck hull, propelled by a 60,000-shp,

615 psi/850° power plant capable of 35 knots. The lead *Fletcher* design provided for the typical U.S. destroyer armament of main battery of five 5in/38 protected mounts, controlled by a Mark 37 DP director system, two sets of quintuple centerline torpedo tubes, twin-stern depth-charge racks and four throwers, a director-controlled 1.1-inch machine cannon, and four .50-caliber AA machine guns. Machinery spaces were protected by ¾-inch STS sides and a ½-inch STS main deck. The pilot house and Mark 37 director were protected with ¾-in STS. Many of these already-substantial fighting assets of the design would continue to grow in response to perceived threats and requirements, especially as the improved 40- and 20-mm AA weapons become available. The *Fletcher* class would continue to evolve and improve, even as the ships themselves began to take shape on the increasing number of building ways that were springing up throughout America.[33]

Submarines

The United States Navy entered the Thirties with a submarine force of some 120 boats, most of them the late-World War I 'R' and post-World War I 'S' classes. Gasoline engines had been replaced by diesels in the Twenties because of the greater safety and economy of diesel fuel oil, as well as the reliability of diesels demonstrated on German U-boats in World War I. Similar transitions were occurring in the navies of the other major nations of the world. Subsequent classes would be further influenced by the naval conference treaties of 1922, 1930, and 1935. These treaties set limits on the number of ships and their tonnages being built by all the major naval powers and limited both the United States and Japan to 52,700-ton totals for submarines.[34]

Strategy and Policy

Among other factors that determined the design and construction trends of submarines, the strategic policies of the era must be considered. From the American standpoint, the post-World War I threat from Europe fell to second place behind that from Japan, the major power in the Far East across the Pacific; although fascist Italy and the advent of Nazism in Germany bode ill for the future, as well. The American eye had

been on Japan's aggressive expansion in Asia for some time, as Japan had never lost a war and had won strategic victories at sea in its wars. There were 8,000 miles across the Pacific Ocean, moreover, between America and Japan, whereas in the Atlantic there were but three or four thousand at most. Thus, for both the United States, (and Japan) the design of a Pacific submarine would have to exploit the limits of submarine technology.

An American strategic "Plan Orange" had been developed for carrying a sea offensive to Japanese home waters, while ensuring defense of the Western Pacific region to the extent feasible. It assumed that Pearl Harbor, the Hawaiian and Midway chain, as well as the Inner Aleutian Islands, could be held with some certainty, while the Philippines and Wake and Guam Islands would be more questionable. Operating ranges for boats on the offensive in the Japanese waters from bases in the Philippines would only be 1,500 miles. But, realistic assessments by our Navy of the chances of holding the Philippines were grim, so the necessity for building submarines of long operating range had to be faced.[35]

Thus, the overriding strategic considerations in the Pacific helped determine the basic performance criteria of American submarines. The problem was simple: a long operating range was needed; thus, a relatively large size to accommodate both the propulsion system and the concomitant combat capability, payload and habitability, was also required. Adding the constraints imposed by the existing design practices of the 1930s, American submarine design and construction can be reviewed.

Following World War I, the American design approach, at first, emulated the 'cruiser' type submarines designed by the Germans and the British late in that great war. These were large-sized boats of over 2,000 tons displacement submerged, with heavy guns of over 6-inch caliber, and even hangars for small aircraft in some cases. The designation 'fleet-type' submarine was used for a somewhat smaller boat that would operate ahead of the fleet and use radio information from the cruiser force scouting planes for reconnaissance and location of targets. The emphasis was away from designs that emphasized submerged performance. The trend was to large seaworthy submerging surface cruisers, but always with an experimental outlook in the designs.[36]

In the mid Twenties, the United States produced the "V" class, one being a large minelaying sub, the *Argonaut* (SS-166), which was followed in 1930 by the famous *Narwhal* (SS-167) and *Nautilus* (SS-168). These were giant subs for their time, displacing over 4,000 tons submerged, with deck guns of 6in/53. Their diving depths were 300 feet. These last two fought in World War II with great combat records, but, by 1930, they were deemed too large, so size was reduced on all subsequent classes.[37]

Starting with the *Dolphin* (SS-169) in 1929, of about 2,000 tons displacement, all-welded hull technology was used, followed by two C-class boats ordered in 1931. The *Porpoise* class of ten boats, of about 2,000 tons, with four tubes forward and two aft, was ordered in 1933 and 1934 with a 3in/50 deck gun and two anti-aircraft machine guns. These boats had diesel-electric drive, and capitalized on the U.S. Navy's sponsorship of railroad industry development of 1,600-horsepower diesel engines. In 1935, six 'new' (or 'later') S-type boats (as distinguished from the large number of WWI-produced S-boats) were ordered starting with the *Salmon* class (SS-182), followed by ten more of the *Sargo* class (SS-188) ordered in 1936 and 1937, with up to four torpedo tubes forward and four aft.[38]

Next, the six T-class boats of 1938 started with the *Tambor* (SS-198), with six tubes forward and four aft, and displacement still holding at just over 2,000 tons submerged. (This "T" class used direct shaft-coupling of the diesel for surface running, a practice dropped in subsequent classes.) The twelve *Gato*-class (SS-212) boats ordered in 1939 and 1940 returned to diesel-electric drive, an evolvement from the "T" class. The year 1940 brought the twenty-two boats of the *Albacore* class (SS-218), which repeated the design of the later "G" class.

Last in the pre-World War II period, came the forty-five follow-on's of the Emergency Program of 1940, plus two additional boats ordered after Pearl Harbor. These boats were mass-produced duplicates of the *Albacore*s. Some were built at Manitowoc, Wisconsin, on Lake Michigan. The bulk of this class had improved hulls capable of a 400-foot operating depth.[39]

Hull

The submarine of the 1930s was constrained, by its evolution, to be a submerging surface ship. That is, the relatively short time a submarine of that era could operate submerged, as opposed to its very great endurance on the surface, confined submerged time on the battery to close-in tactical maneuvers when trying to sink a target. For the overwhelming proportion of the ship's operational life, the requirement was for seaworthiness in heavy seas, for high-speed transit to operating areas, and for overtaking and searching for enemy targets. As a matter of fact, since the pressure hull of the submarine was built so rigidly to constitute a submerging pressure vessel, with her streamlined fairwater for breasting the waves, she became a very seaworthy craft. She could penetrate the waves with her torpedo-like hull knifing through the seas, her round hull forming a tubular spear while the streamlined bow helped lift the hull and avoid unwanted submergence. With such performance, a submarine could make better time with equal thrust through heavy seas than a sub-chaser or a destroyer, which was lifted high by its displacement hull with each wave.

The submarine, nevertheless, was a submerging ship and required pressure vessel engineering for its hull design. A successful submarine pressure hull was the result of a combination of various aspects of the technology. For example, hull thickness had to be proportional to the shell diameter and to the stress placed on the hull (itself a function of maximum submergence depth and inversely proportional to the strength of hull material). This material had to be compatible, as well, with the seawater environment. It had to be able to withstand expected hull temperatures of the ocean waters and to resist electrolytic corrosive effects. This implied high-alloy steels right from the outset. As steels of higher quality and high tensile strength (HTS) were made available from the steel industry, submarine hulls became stronger and allowed deeper diving depth. Concurrently, information on the work done in all nations on submarine hulls was fed back to the steel industry and benefited the designers and manufacturers of steel.

Pressure-hull design technology included the objective of understanding completely all modes and effects of pressure-vessel collapse. The aim was to optimize failure mode design so that, as much as possible, no one mode of failure occurred any earlier than the others. This approach was pushed from the early days of submarine construction, especially by German design engineers. The advanced, comprehensive text by Professor von Mises,[40] for example, provided a reference for hull design theory that stood the test of several decades. There are three collapse modes of a pressure vessel: one is "shell buckling," a second is "general instability," and a third is "shell yielding." The objective in optimal spacing of the reinforcing frames, or ring-stiffeners (as demonstrated by pressure-vessel collapse tests), originally, was to trade off each of the modes against the other to minimize likelihood of one mode occurring before the other.[41] In later years, however, it was determined that "shell yielding" should be favored, and designs were made to ensure that it occurred first, using frame spacing to ensure that. (It is almost arbitrary whether frames are placed on the inside of the hull shell or on the outside. For their World War II U-Boats, the Germans used frames on the inside, whereas the Americans used frames on the outside.)

Compartmentation peaked, as far as watertight subdivision was concerned, in the World War II American fleet-type submarine. (It has since retrograded in nuclear designs, where there is less compartmentation.) This fleet-type submarine[42] had a total of eight watertight compartments, each divided from the other by compatible-pressure (to test-depth) bulkheads. The conning tower was still another separate watertight compartment (nicknamed the "Barrel"). And, any one of these compartments could be completely flooded, and the boat not necessarily lost, if all the other compartments were kept dry. (This is no longer true with the new high-speed nuclear submarines of today.)

The pressure hull for an American fleet submarine, with the adequate range desired for Pacific distances, had to house four main diesel engines, with their respective generators. Two propeller shafts were standard, which called for two main motors and, with the technology of the time, reduction gears to reduce the speed of the main motors to that suitable for propellers to avoid cavitation.[43] The boat also had to be of a size to carry sufficient batteries to provide propulsion for at least two to three whole days submerged at a few knots speed, (while still providing diesel propulsion for high-speed surface endurance for 10,000 miles transit to and from distant patrol areas). The battery's capacity also had to provide a high speed of up to 8 knots, submerged, for 1-1½ hours (at maximum battery expenditure rate). In all, an American submarine needed two main engine compartments, to house four big diesels and generators, two torpedo rooms, a motor room, a control room, and sufficient battery space.

Next of course, were the requirements for conning the ship and for crew habitation. In the past, all of these requirements had been accommodated in various submarine types by dual- or triple-purpose compartments. For example, earlier submarines would have the main battery amidships under a half deck or walking deck, and the control room above with the periscope and ship controls. A submerged conning station and crew bunks could be in the same compartment. After World War I, and following the structural characteristics demonstrated in the bigger European submarines, it became simply a matter of design to expand these functions throughout the boat. It became customary, however, in the case of the U.S. Navy, and in foreign navies, to combine the berthing compartments with battery compartments as well as to locate refrigerated food storage and deck-gun magazines in battery compartments. The control room was located in the center of a boat. Auxiliary machinery required its own space, and this was usually thrown under the walking deck of the control room, not necessarily a watertight area. The conning area, however, was located separately above the control room in later American fleet-type submarines, as it was on some of the foreign submarines. British subs and German U-boats had separate conning towers only on certain types.

The American fleet-boat design was portended by large submarine designs in the late 1920s in the case of two boats, the *Narwhal* and the *Nautilus*. This size of submarine was not attempted again until the construction of the *Salmon* and *Sailfish*, after World War II, in the Fifties. The fleet-type design settled on at the end of the 1930s, first with the *Gato* class and, secondly, the *Balao* class, was approximately 310 feet in length (about the length of a football field), with a hull diameter of about 16 feet. The designed collapse depth was determined on the basis of hull diameter, hull thickness, and yield strength of the steel (computed both theoretically and empirically) following model and full-scale collapse tests. Then, based on a safety factor of 1.5, a chosen engineering policy, the design operating depth was set at about 400 feet.

The internal machinery of the fleet submarines required nearly a mile of piping and connections for the internal seawater-circulating systems for cooling main engines, main motors, and all auxiliaries. These systems had to be designed with the most sophisticated piping technology available to take into account stresses and bending caused by the warping of the hull during dives and by the shock of collision or battle damage. For example, fundamental conversion required both a main hull closure valve for seawater systems and a backup closure valve for double protection against unwanted entry of seawater in case of a leak or rupture. (Both valves, alas, remained open and sank the *Squalus* in 1939.) The tanks around the hull and some tanks internal to the hull helped determine the shape and dimension of the ship. Open bottom ballast tanks were simply hung "saddle fashion" around the hull, into which water would flood when the vent valves in the top of the tanks were opened and the air allowed to escape. This effected what is known as a "double-hull" design, something of a misnomer, for only the inner main-hull shell was of collapse-depth strength. The outer skin of the ballast tanks was subjected to only a small pressure differential and was made of light boilerplate steel. Nevertheless, it provided a second protective cushion shell of some strength. High-pressure air (3000 psi reduced to 600 psi) was used to blow water out when the vent valves were shut. The water was pushed out the flood ports in the tank bottoms, thus adding enough buoyancy to the submarine to raise it to the surface. This air supply was contained in high-pressure air bottles housed within the ballast tanks themselves.

Fuel, of course, had to be carried in the boat, and some ballast tanks were made into fuel ballast tanks so that as fuel was consumed it would be replaced by water (differing little in density), and only slight trim compensation would be necessary. Trim tanks forward, aft, and auxiliary, were usually housed within the ship's hull, and integral to it, as were the sanitary, fresh water, lube oil, and clean oil fuel tanks.

Since all-welded hull construction and higher strength alloys were introduced in the 1930s by American submarine technologists, the operating depth was steadily increased from 200 to 400 feet. The *Balao*-class hull was 7/8-inch thick. Streamlining was not stressed for submerged travel, for at the maximum power generated by the batteries, only 8-9 knots could be attained, and streamlining would cost more in topside utility than would be gained in submerged speeds (maybe 1 knot).

In summary, the American fleet-type submarine was of the size, shape, and displacement virtually comparable to larger submarines (though not the largest) of other navies. The trend toward the even larger cruiser-type submarine, as adopted by the Japanese, was not resumed in the U.S. Navy (after the *Narwhal* and the *Nautilus*) until well after World War II. Due to the advantage realized in the *Gato* and subsequently the *Balao* classes, these became the basic designs that were mass produced for World War II. With the American design, it was not necessary to provide tanker submarines, as in the case of the German design. American subs could operate against Japan from either Pearl Harbor, with refueling stopovers at Midway, or from bases in northern Australia.

Engineering Plant

The heart of the submarine was its power source, found in the main diesel engine generator sets. Consuming near-water-density diesel oil, these prime movers fed DC electric power to the main motors when running on the surface, and charged the batteries at the same time as necessary. The batteries then supplied DC power to the propulsion motors when submerged. The batteries also supplied DC power to the auxiliary distribution board, which sent DC power to auxiliary main motors that powered diving planes, steering motors, main hydraulic plant pumps, the air conditioning pumps, fuel and lube oil purifiers, main and auxiliary circulating water pumps, the air compressors, trim and drain pumps, and the DC motors of AC generators. The AC power was used for interior communication systems, the electronics of radios, radars, sonars, and navigational and fire control systems. If AC power was lost, some emergency backup was possible using DC power; e.g., emergency lighting. Emergency plane and rudder control was also possible through the main hydraulic system when 'normal' localized power was lost. (The main vents could also be operated by hand when all power was lost.)

Weapons

The submarine's combat system consisted of guns and torpedoes. A surface gun capability was needed to engage ships not threatening enough to require diving, nor worth the expenditure of torpedoes. On the other hand, the main weapon was the torpedo, used with a stealthy approach for sinking by surprise. This called for a number of torpedo tubes and a war load of torpedoes, including their fuel and loading gear.

The space in the torpedo rooms in earlier boats allowed up to four torpedo tubes forward in two vertical nests of two tubes each. In addition, there could be four tubes in an after torpedo room. With the *Tambor* and later classes, this number went up to six and four. At sea on war patrol, live-explosive war shots would be carried; exercise torpedoes would form the inventory when in training waters. Mines could also be carried, including both moored and bottom mines (the latter are shaped like torpedoes and energized by batteries). Alcohol torpedo fuel was carried in tanks within the torpedo room. By design, a submarine is a cramped vessel, and the torpedo loading system, from the maindeck topside into the torpedo room, with its cradles, chain pulleys, and other loading gear, had to be combined with maximum efficiency with crew berthing arrangements. This meant that torpedoes were stored with crew bunks above and below them. Some torpedoes were housed both above and below the walking decks, which, of course, had to be sectioned plates for quick removal.

American torpedo tubes were fired by compressed air expulsion (typical of boats of the 30s and 40s) and would leave some bubbling at the point of ejection, although most of the air would be swallowed by what was known as a 'poppet' valve on the side of the tube. The torpedoes were propelled by a turbine driven by steam and gas from the mixed combustion of alcohol, compressed air, and water in a combustion pot. These combustion products were then exhausted behind the propeller with an unavoidably dangerous "torpedo wake" that left a visible track to the source of firing for hostile ships, especially by day. Moreover, when approaching torpedo wakes were observed, ships frequently had time to maneuver to escape being hit. One advantage, on the other hand, although less significant, was that the firing officer could observe through the periscope whether the torpedo was running straight and generally toward the target.[44]

Deck guns also were used. The ammunition load for the main deck guns, which—except for the *Nautilus* and *Narwhal*—ultimately became 5in/25 caliber, was housed in flood magazines, along with pyrotechnics and appropriate small arms for a submarine of that size. The loading crews and gun crews had to be trained to handle powder cans and shells, by hand, in the magazine below, and to provide a human chain to pass powder and shells topside during a surface engagement. The guns were not stabilized, so it was not easy to hit a target in any sea-way not mirror flat. During World War II, several American submarines were outfitted with stabilized guns, but these did not receive wide acceptance. Other navies did not even attempt gun stabilization. Gun actions were utilized mainly by German U-Boats in World War I and in the first four years of World War II, and were used by American subs throughout World War II. This was because in these periods their targets included merchant ships that were relatively defenseless.

The .30 and .50-caliber anti-aircraft machine guns with which U.S. submarines were equipped earlier, were soon replaced by more effective 40mm and 20mm machine cannon to better combat aircraft.

Fire Control

The development of fire control for torpedo firing started with basic techniques developed in World War I, leading to slightly more sophisticated methods developed in the 1930s, which then led to fire control analyzers of rudimentary types. The U.S. Navy, in time, developed torpedo fire control to a fine art and the final system was truly ingenious. It was not until the beginning of World War II, however, that the torpedo data computers (TDCs) integrated target motion information to compute firing angles and transmitted the data directly to the torpedo up to the moment of firing. Surface ship fire control used target-motion rate-control for correcting generated solutions in main and secondary battery computers; yet these were based on continually tracking the target bearing and range, visually or with radar. On a submarine, however, these inputs could only be obtained at intervals, observed when periodically raising and rapidly lowering the periscope. TDC solution, to begin with, provided a relative bearing to which the periscope could be trained when raised, giving a high assurance that the target would be near the periscope's cross-hairs and thus avoiding the need for searching around while exposed. A special periscope called the 'battle' or attack scope was used. It had a narrow, finely tapering upper portion, or neck, and a small lens, thus minimizing the chance of its detection. The other periscope, usually called the navigational scope, was of greater diameter at the top, and with the advent of radar allowed the housing of a small ranging-radar. The battle scope also had within its barrel a stadimeter for range finding. Split lenses operated by the approach officer, matched a target's masthead to its water line and determined an approximate range from masthead heights tabulated in intelligence manuals. This range was then fed into the TDC by verbal announcement to its operator. (After the first year of the Pacific war, small SJ and later ST radars were installed in the navigational periscope, which would allow short pulse ranges to be taken.) These ranges would then be transmitted electrically into the TDC along with optical bearing of the periscope, to correct the generated solution to the moment of observation. This then required almost instantaneous matching of dial pointers and counting off of incremental delta (i.e., final) corrections by the TDC operator during that brief moment the periscope was up. These range and bearing 'deltas' also were passed verbally to the adjacent assistant TDC officer (ATDC), who quickly resolved (on a vector computing board) these delta corrections into target speed and course changes. The approach officer's calling of "angle on the bow," of the target, along with the transmitted corrections, usually refined the solution to a high accuracy at the time of firing. This allowed torpedo deflection angles to be generated continually by the computer. Torpedo salvo spread spots could then be added or subtracted, by means of the spread knobs, so that the gyro setting for each torpedo would be cranked into the side of the torpedo by the gyro-setting spindle. (At the moment of firing, the spindle was retracted.) The torpedo would then run out straight from the submarine and turn to the angle of the gyro offset, finally traveling on the correct course from the submarine to intercept the target.

Habitability

Habitability is another major attribute of a submarine. In American submarines, tradeoffs in hull size, volume, and payload, discussed previously, were combined with the American knack for providing 'creature comforts,' as developed for passenger airliners, streamlined trains, and transcontinental buses. By the 1930s, the American fleet-type submarine was reaching a refined state of art, where these boats could be classified as a most comfortable type of ship. By the end of World War II, advances also had been made in the charcoal filtering for sanitary tank ventings, a traditionally objectionable process, but accepted as a way of life among submariners worldwide. (This primitive feature was simply tolerated without much attention in German U-boats to the very end of World War II.) The size and efficiency of the freezebox and cold food storage rooms, large in relation to crew size and the average duration of patrol, also contributed to crew comfort. More than ample good food was carried for extended cruises, in part due to rations allowances for submarine crews as hazardous-duty incentive. Even steel deckplates were covered with matting that cushioned the crewmen's feet, as opposed to the steel decks on surface ships. (There was another benefit, of course—silence when submerged.) The efficient spacing of bunks, conveniences in the crew's galley, the comfort of the officers' wardroom, and the liberal use of stainless steel all made the World War II American submarine unique in its habitability.

The air conditioning technology available by the end of the 1930s from the widespread development of commercial air conditioning in the United States, made for straightforward application to the fleet-type submarine. Freon compressors were simply added to the auxiliary machinery array, already comprised of air compressors and electric pumps for the boat's many auxiliary systems. Unfortunately, air conditioning had to be secured when running silent in combat, allowing interior humidity, temperature, and discomfort to rise steadily. Such conditions, in combat, actually were limited by breathing-air endurance, which could be no more than two or three days. So it became a matter of training for submariners to withstand such discomfort.

The air sealed within the submarine upon diving became the reserve for human consumption during that submergence. If the submarine was held down to the limits of its air endurance by enemy forces, the survival tactic often was to stay quiet, stay deep, and run judiciously on battery until the enemy was eluded. If the enemy held contact, this became discouraging. It was necessary in many cases to stay submerged until dark and attempt a high speed escape on the surface. Accordingly, methods to extend air endurance were essential. When ambient carbon dioxide (CO_2) rose to the hazardous level of 3%, men could not survive for long, much less stay awake, or perform reliably. Carbon dioxide absorbents, such as soda-lime, were spread on the plastic bunk covers, while keeping the crew as inactive as possible. Also, oxygen was bled from storage flasks to raise the partial pressure of oxygen in the air. The Momsen escape lungs could also be used to scrub CO_2 from an individual's exhalation, but were limited in their endurance. All things considered, submarine submergence time from the standpoint of air breathing by the crew was about 72 hours.[45]

Communications and Electronics

By the 1930s, communication with ships far around the world was well developed. Similarly, while on the surface, the submarine could listen with a low-frequency antenna, and transmit when necessary on a low-frequency antenna, as well. Usually, submarines did not communicate when in a war-patrol status. At the time of the daily and nightly worldwide fleet broadcasts, they could copy while submerged or while surfaced at night charging batteries. They were equipped with decoding machines and carried predated key lists. The submarine's call sign could be quickly spotted among the messages and the coded message processed appropriately by the decoding machine. During the dramatic chase of the new Japanese giant carrier *Shinano* by the *Archerfish* (SS-311), Lieutenant Commander Joe Enright, USN, her captain, found it necessary to transmit his sighting of such a very large target to the Submarine Force Commander. Admiral Lockwood personally responded that it was probably the *Shinano* and to stay after it, which Enright did until it was sunk.[46]

Summary

The evolution of the American submarine, from the post World War I "R" and "S" classes to the later S classes *Porpoise, Gato, Balao, Albacore*, and *Tench* that fought WWII, was due to the extremely well-managed, positive feedback of experience and hard lessons. The result was one of the most remarkably successful and effective warships of naval history. Some 250 boats totaling about 500,000 tons of compact machinery and steel accounted for the destruction of over 4,800,000 tons of enemy shipping—a credit to both the engineers and technicians who designed and built these submarines, and to the men who operated them.

THE SHIPBUILDING INDUSTRY

What the Future Would Bring

The story of naval engineering in the preWorld War II era requires a review of the changes in the naval shipyards and the private shipbuilding and ship repair industry in the United States. In fact, the ability of the industry to adapt, expand, and produce in response to the demands put upon it by rapid and cataclysmic changes in the state of the world is one of the marvels of modern industrial achievements. Starting in 1933 from a quiescent state, it grew to an amazing production machine that by 1945 had produced the largest and most powerful navy and merchant marine the world had ever seen. America was not only the "Arsenal of Democracy", it also built the ships that carried the supplies, ammunitions, tanks, planes, and sometimes other ships to all parts of the world.[47]

Status of the American Shipbuilding Industry

At the beginning of this era, the shipbuilding industry, like the rest of the country, was mired in depression. The period between 1923 and 1935 saw only modest naval construction in most countries, including the United States. Writing in 1945, H. E. Rossell noted that "In the 1920s the tempo of naval construction was slow, for most peoples of the world, exhausted and impoverished as a result of World War I, were more inclined to reduce armaments than to increase them." (Japan was a notable exception.) The Washington Treaty Limiting Naval Armaments, signed in 1922 by representatives of the United States, Great Britain, Japan, France, and Italy, was an attempt first to maintain the relative *status quo* of capital ships, including aircraft carriers, between the signatories. To some degree, the effect was to shift the emphasis to construction of lighter vessels. The overall effect, however, was a reduction in naval construction during this period.[48]

Constraints on Merchant Ship Construction

Similar forces inhibited the construction of commercial vessels. In reality, the maritime industries of the United States had been in a long slide downward since the middle of the previous century, interrupted only periodically by fits of resurgence, such as that which accompanied the Spanish American War and World War I. Absorbed in its internal affairs—the Civil War, the subsequent Western expansion, and its non-maritime industrialization—America increasingly turned abroad for the satisfaction of its shipping needs. One notable exception was the construction and operation of vessels engaged in the domestic trade of the United States, vessels which by law (the so-called Jones Act) had to be built in yards in the United States, registered in the United States, and manned by U.S. citizens. Construction of passenger liners, supported by Government mail subsidies, also continued to provide some business for American yards. On balance, however, commercial construction in 1933, like naval construction, was at a low ebb.[49]

Naval Shipyards

While naval construction was slowed, it nonetheless was steady during most of this decade, with nine yards engaged in building destroyers, submarines, cruisers, auxiliaries, and some heavier vessels. During the period 1934-40, Boston Navy Yard completed twelve destroyers. Charleston built a number of destroyers, submarine chasers, and Coast Guard cutters. Mare Island completed three destroyers, five submarines, and a submarine tender. New York completed two destroyers, a gunboat, a Coast Guard cutter, and two light cruisers (*Brooklyn* and *Helena*). By the end of the decade, it had under construction three modern battleships (*North Carolina, Iowa*, and *Missouri*), as did Norfolk. Philadelphia had had all along as its primary mission the construction of heavy ships and by the outbreak of World War II had three battleships (*Washington, New Jersey,* and *Wisconsin*) building and three more authorized. In addition, it delivered the heavy cruiser *Minneapolis* in 1933 and the *Wichita* in 1938, the light cruiser *Philadelphia* in 1937, and five destroyers, four Coast Guard Cutters, and several smaller aircraft in the period 1933-39. Portsmouth, New Hampshire, was dedicated to submarine construction and delivered thirteen of these vessels from 1933-40, with two more under construction. Construction of sixteen more was undertaken in the 1940-43 period. Puget Sound during the period completed the cruiser *Astoria* (building since 1929), eight destroyers, and two seaplane tenders. In 1940, Pearl Harbor added two graving docks.[50]

From the above listing, it is clear that as the decade ended, not only did production increase but also there was a shift of emphasis in certain yards from lighter vessels, mainly submarines and destroyers, to heavy vessels, especially battleships. These developments also required major improvements in facilities and increases in manpower, especially during the latter part of the period as war drew nearer.

Samples of Activity

The following selected statistics give some idea of the magnitude of this process. In 1937, Mare Island had one drafting room of eighty-six men. By May 1941, it had three buildings accommodating over 400 naval architects, engineers, and draftsmen. Its working force of 5,593 at the beginning of 1939 expanded to 18,500 by May 1941. At Pearl Harbor, two new graving docks (drydocks No. 2 and No. 3) were added in 1940. In addition, a new power plant, dredging and mooring facilities, and new base facilities at Ford Island were all added. Employment increased from 3,300 on 30 June 1940, to 7,300 on 30 June 1941. Philadelphia, already one of the nation's largest shipyards, underwent radical expansion. With the President's declaration of a state of Limited Emergency, over $100,000,000 was invested in new facilities, which included the following: two of the largest building drydocks in the world; two large capacity marine railways; a new turbine-testing laboratory with facilities to test marine propulsion equipment up to 83,000 shaft horsepower; new piers, cranes, shops, storehouses; 300 acres of new storage space; 50 miles of railroad; and hundreds of miles of steam piping, sewage, electrical circuits, and compressed air lines. With the completion of this work in the early 1940s, the plant valuation stood at approximately a quarter of a billion dollars, a huge sum at that time.[51]

New England Private Yards

The private shipyards of the nation also contributed to the buildup of Naval forces during this period, and, to many, the Naval buildup contributed importantly to their return to economic health. The Bath Iron Works, which rose out of the ashes of its predecessors in 1927 and began again almost from scratch, was able to build ninety-eight ships by 1943, including several well-designed and built destroyers. Credit for much of these achievements is given to John H. Hyde, president; Charles P. Wetherbee, chief engineer; John McInness, hull superintendent;

and W. S. Newell, who succeeded John Hyde as president.

Further down the coast, Bethlehem Steel Company's Fore River Yard had been building Naval combatants since 1898, including the airplane carrier, *Lexington*. In the late 1920s it delivered the cruisers *Northampton* and *Portland*, and the Matson liners *Mariposa, Monterey*, and *Lurline*. By 1933, it was suffering from the general world depression when it received a contract for two heavy cruisers, the *Quincy* and *Vincennes*. Other contracts that followed helped build this yard into a strong facility capable of producing many ships for the war effort, including the second *Lexington*, launched 26 September 1942. Important contributors to Bethlehem Steel's efforts were S. Wiley Wakeman, Arthur B. Homer, H. E. Gould, and W. H. Collins.[52]

Cramp Shipbuilding

In 1830, William Cramp had started a small shipyard in Kensington, Pennsylvania, on the Delaware River, which by the early 1900s had grown into a great establishment known as the William Cramp and Sons Ship and Engine Building Company of Philadelphia. In addition to transatlantic liners, the Cramp Company built warships of all types, from battleships to gunboats, principally for the U.S. Navy, but also for the Imperial Russian Navy, the Imperial Ottoman Navy, and the Imperial Japanese Navy. In 1927, however, faced with a continuing lack of new business, the company decided to give up the marine business. Fortunately, for the war effort, enough of the facilities remained in 1940 so that, revamped and retooled by a new organization known as the Cramp Shipbuilding Company, it could once more build a wide range of vessels, including cruisers and submarines.[53]

Newport News Shipbuilding

The year 1933 represented the lowest ebb in shipbuilding for Newport News Shipbuilding and Drydock Company in many years, with employment dropping below five thousand; although, in that year, contracts were entered into for the aircraft carriers *Yorktown* and *Enterprise*. Between 1933 and 1940, the yard was busy building twenty-eight ships, including two light cruisers, large freight vessels for private owners, and thirteen vessels for the United States Maritime Commission (the first of which was the *America*, the largest passenger liner constructed in this country until then). In February 1941, Newport News built a subsidiary yard at Wilmington, North Carolina, for the United States Maritime Commission, and during the year 1942 fifty-one Liberty ships were completed and delivered by that yard.

Commenting on the great publicity being given at the time to the construction of the Liberty ships and the wartime merchant vessels and the contrasting secrecy accorded the construction of naval vessels, Homer Ferguson, president of the yard during those years, later lamented the lack of recognition accorded to those who "have done during this war the greatest job of shipbuilding that has ever been done in the world. They have built more ships," he went on to say, referring to Naval vessels, "higher-grade ships and finer ships, and on account of the secrecy surrounding our war movements, no one has been able to say anything about it." He specifically praised Charles F. Bailey, William Gatewood, F. P. Palen, S. L. Wood, W. T. Dimm, James Rowbottom, Matt Doughty, and James Plummer for their efforts on behalf of Newport News.[54]

New York Shipbuilding

The New York Shipbuilding Corporation (originally planned for Staten Island) was founded in 1899 and built shortly thereafter on the banks of the Delaware River in Camden, New Jersey. The yard was laid out based on the ideas of its first president, Harry G. Morse, a man with structural and steel fabrication experience. One of Mr. Morse's ideas was the use of extensive prefabrication, thought by many to have originated under the 1941-42 emergency shipbuilding program. From its founding, to the early 1940s, the yard had 446 ships built and building, including eleven battleships, ten aircraft carriers (including *Saratoga*), twenty-six cruisers, forty-three destroyers, thirty-seven passenger and cargo ships, forty-four oil tankers, and thirty-six colliers and cargo ships. The best known passenger ships built at the yard during this period were the *Manhattan* and *Washington*, in 1932 and 1933, respectively. During 1941, the yard's outfitting

basin and the five original ways were extended riverward some 250 feet to enable ships up to 850 feet in length to be built on all ways. Capacity of overhead cranes was increased to 300 tons. The space occupied by merchant ships and destroyer ways built in World War I was rebuilt to provide five additional ways for building large ships. A notable addition to the yard was a turret shop, which first produced (in 1941) completed 16-inch turret structures for a battleship. Other shop facilities were expanded accordingly. A new drafting room, accommodating 650 draftsmen and necessary supervisory engineers, was added in 1939 to permit use of the yard by the Navy as a design yard for preparing detail designs for all classes of naval vessels built in the yard.[55]

Pusey and Jones

Pusey and Jones, established in 1848 in Wilmington, Delaware, by two well-known mechanics of the day, had a long history of successful shipbuilding prior to the 1930s, including the construction, in 1854, of the *Mehlon Betts*, the first iron-hull sailing vessel attempted in the United States. The yard produced the U.S. Army mine planter *Ellery W. Miles* in 1937, a 310-foot seagoing dredge *Chester Harding* for the U.S. Engineer Department in 1939, and a half dozen cutters and lighthouse tenders for the Coast Guard and Lighthouse Service. In addition, in 1939, the yard had delivered the two fastest American cargo carriers built to date, the 19-knot, 5,500-horsepower *Quaker* and *Cavalier*, later taken over by the Navy. These successes, plus the addition of new 550-foot side-launching ways by the company, encouraged the Maritime Commission to award contracts in 1940 and 1941 for the construction of C1-A type ships, eighteen of which were built by 1944.[56]

Sun Shipbuilding

The Sun Shipbuilding and Drydock Company of Chester, Pennsylvania, was another private yard that contributed to and benefited from the war buildup. Commenced by the Sun Oil Company of Philadelphia in 1916 to compensate for the scarcity of ships in World War I, the yard had excellent facilities, including eight ways for building tankers. Even so, when the Maritime Commission awarded it a contract on 27 May

1941, for ninety-two large oil tankers, it began a drastic expansion of its facilities. In 1941-42, under Maritime Commission contracts, twenty new building ways were added in three separate yard groupings. As of this writing, the yard has been purchased and is operated as the Pennsylvania Shipbuilding Company.[57]

Bethlehem San Francisco

The final yard to be mentioned in this section is the Bethlehem's San Francisco Yard. The earliest predecessor of the yard was the Union Iron and Brass Foundry started by two blacksmiths at the corner of First and Mission Streets, San Francisco, California, a year after the discovery of gold at Sutter's Mill. By 1924, the Union Iron Works Company (its name dating from 1905) was operating three separate yards in the San Francisco area: the Portrero works (with five building slips where vessels up to 500 feet long could be built), the Hunter's Point works (with a concrete graving dock 1,000 feet long by 110 feet wide on the blocks with 40 feet of water over the sill), and the Alameda works in the Oakland Estuary across San Francisco Bay (with six building slips capable of building vessels up to 550 feet in length). In that year, the yards were purchased by the Bethlehem Steel Company, Shipbuilding Division. On 15 November 1938, the name of the Portrero yard was changed to the San Francisco Yard. On 29 December 1939, the Hunter's Point property was sold to the Navy Department. By the early 1940s, the various yards constructed a total of 420-odd vessels of a wide variety of types, including the battleship *Oregon* and cruiser *Olympia*, both of which distinguished themselves in the Spanish-American War in 1898. In later years, the emphasis was on smaller vessels, including destroyers and tankers.[58]

The Kaiser Yards

Despite the head start provided by the Maritime Commission's shipbuilding program stemming from the Merchant Marine Act of 1936, existing shipbuilding capacity was not able to keep up with losses at sea once the United States entered World War II. U-boat wolf packs roaming the Atlantic coast destroyed more than 7 million tons in 1942 alone. A spectacular and controversial solution was provided by an innovative industrial entrepreneur, Henry J. Kaiser, who had already achieved a reputation as a builder of roads, bridges, and dams, including the Hoover and Grand Coulee dams. Backed by President Roosevelt and armed with contracts from the Maritime Commission, Kaiser quickly built seven shipyards, a steel mill, and an engine plant on the Pacific coast. He also perfected a new cargo ship design, a 10,500-ton Liberty ship that was engineered for rapid production. Using his new yards and innovative production techniques, Kaiser launched the first Liberty ship, SS *Patrick Henry*, in 1941. As the yards and workers gained experience, vessels were built at a faster and faster rate. In November 1942, one of them, the SS *Robert E. Peary*, was launched 4 days, 15 and one-half hours after the keel was laid, and delivered in 7 days, 14 hours, and 29 minutes, a record that still stands. In all, he produced more than 1,400 vessels during World War II, including light aircraft carriers. Asked for the secret of his amazing ability to succeed, Kaiser replied: "Success in anything depends upon three things. First, you must visualize what the need is. Second, you must visualize the how and when the need can be met. And third, you must visualize the organization that can meet it." It was the last of these in which Kaiser excelled. Parts and subsections were identified, produced, and delivered in a logical sequence. Workers were organized and assigned specialized tasks to allow relatively unskilled people to do their jobs rapidly and well. He was especially adept at developing and maintaining workers' incentives.

Kaiser was not universally loved and respected. Liberty ships were sometimes called "ugly ducklings" for their ungraceful lines, and they had little chance of surviving a U-boat attack, or even a severe storm at sea, because of poorly welded joints. Some sailors dubbed his light carriers "Kaiser's Coffins." Ashore, he was attacked by older shipyards and conservative Navy people who accused him of not only unorthodox methods but also questionable business practices. Congressional inquiries failed to produce any legitimate basis for these charges. Despite the limitations of his ships and the criticisms of the shipbuilding establishment, Kaiser met a real need of the country at the time. Ironically, he may have contributed to the larger term decline of the shipbuilding industry by contributing to a false sense of complacency. According to F. Harvey Evans, Professor Emeritus at the Massachusetts Institute of Technology, "There is a feeling that if we could turn ships out in five days, then we could do it again if we needed to." Even more seriously, while many established American shipyards scorned and ignored Kaiser's innovative methods, Japanese (and later Korean) yards were to embrace his methodology and improve on it. Since World War II, they have built the bulk of the world's freighters and tankers, while American yards have concentrated on small numbers of expensive and sophisticated ships, like missile cruisers.[59]

Small Boat Yard Mobilization

In anticipation of the United States' entry into World War II, already raging in Europe, demand increased for construction of vessels and more and more industrial capacity was enlisted in the effort to meet the demands. The construction of small landing craft, subchasers, and torpedo boats in East Coast yacht-building yards is illustrative of the construction these yards made during this period and subsequently.

Since the Civil War, the United States and other countries had made many attempts to utilize relatively small, fast boats to launch torpedoes at naval and other targets with indifferent success. In 1938, the British bought two more new motor torpedo boats, one of them a 77-foot boat capable of 70 knots in smooth water. In 1940, Erwin Chase of the ELCO yard in Bayonne, New Jersey, obtained rights to build these Scott-Paine designed vessels. The U.S. PT "mosquito boats" based on this design carried four fixed torpedo tubes and two 50-caliber anti-aircraft guns, and, by leaving off two of the torpedo tubes, could carry fifteen depth charges. These boats, capable of a wide variety of naval missions, became famous because of the exploits of Lieutenant John S. Bulkeley, USN, in the Philippines. They were the boats which took General Douglas MacArthur out of the Philippines in 1942.[60]

Captain Richards T. Miller, USN (Ret), in recent correspondence, provides some interesting observations on the contributions of the Annapolis Yacht Yard (successor to the Chance Marine Construction company and forerunner to Trumpy's) and other small boat yards. Having designed an aluminum-hulled PT to the Bureau of Construction and Repair requirements as his senior thesis at Webb Institute of Naval Architecture, Richards as an Ensign, CC-V(S), USNR, was one assigned to duty as Resident Supervisor of Shipbuilding, Annapolis, in September 1941. The following account is based on his recollections.

> Following the lead of ELCO, Chris Nelson of the Annapolis Yacht Yard had gone to England in early 1941 to negotiate for rights to build Vospers-designed PTs for the British Purchasing Mission. With the passage of the Lend-Lease Act, contracting was actually done through the U.S. Navy Bureau of Ships, headed by Rear Admiral E. L. (Ned) Cochrane. The first contract, signed July 16, 1941, provided for the construction of eight 70-foot Vosper motor torpedo boats (BPTs 21-28) for the British. Subsequent contracts to the Annapolis Yacht Yard provided for the construction of four British PTs in November 1941, sixteen British PTs in July 1942, thirty Russian PTs in March 1943, and seventy Russian PTs in March 1944. In addition, the yard served as lead yard and central purchasing agency for similar PTs being built by Robert Jacobs of City Island, New York; the Herreschoff Yard in Bristol, Rhode Island; and Harbor Boat in Long Beach, California.
>
> One of the most interesting developments was a provision in the second Russian contract for the construction of fourteen of the PTs in "knock-down" or "kit" form. The plan was to ship the components across Iran to the south shore of the Black Sea, where they would be assembled for use against the Germans, who then held the north shore. The effort required a great deal of revised planning and development of a detailed assembly book, which included hundreds of pages of instructions, drawings, and photographs. Due to changes in the war situation, only three of the boats were sent in kit form, these being assembled in Leningrad by crews of Russian women, with assistance of Annapolis Yacht Yard advisors.[61]

Shipyard of the Rockies

An even more dramatic example of the use of component and subassembly construction for assembly at a remote site occurred on the opposite side of the country during the period 1941-

1943 in connection with the building of destroyer escorts in the Mare Island Navy Yard. By mid-1941, it became clear that a severe manpower shortage in West Coast shipyards was fast approaching. Naval shipyards had gone into high gear a year earlier, building new ships, fitting out fleet vessels, reactivating World War II four-stackers for transfer to England, and repairing battle-damaged British cruisers. Civilian yards, such as Kaiser, were soaking up manpower for merchant ship construction. When on 1 November 1941, it was announced that Mare Island Naval Shipyard would build twenty-four small destroyer-escort type ships for the British (BDE 13-37) under Lend-Lease, all to be delivered within 30 months of that date, it was clear that it would be necessary to find new sources of labor. The answer was the "Shipyard of the Rockies."[62]

Faced with this task, and already committed to a submarine construction program, yard management immediately undertook the construction of ten new building ways at the north end of the yard. Earlier in the year, in anticipation of its needs, yard representatives had surveyed appropriate firms in the Denver, Colorado, area as possible sources of assistance. Now it moved actively to follow up. Rear Admiral John H. McQuilkin, later to become Assistant Chief of BuShips for Research and Development and an innovative force in the private engineering sector, was then a young Naval officer recently graduated from MIT with a Master of Science degree in naval construction and assigned to the DE construction program. He describes the activities as follows:

> Serious negotiations with a number of companies in Denver, Colorado, were initiated. These included outfits engaged in structural steel work, machine and welding shops, etc, the idea being that they would receive steel and plans, do all structural fabrication possible (envisioned as hullplating, frames, foundations, bulkheads, gun tubs, deck houses, etc), and supply such fittings and other parts as their facilities and those of local subcontractors permitted, then ship the material to Mare Island for assembly on the ways . . . contracts (cost-plus type) with 12 such firms were signed on December 2, 1941. Thus was born "the shipyard of the Rockies", a venture which proved most timely.[63]

A steel mill in nearby Pueblo furnished plates and shapes in accordance with orders received directly from Gibbs & Cox of New York, the design agent. A local transfer and storage company with a large open area served by the railroads was selected to handle incoming steel and outgoing assemblies, including pickling and painting. One incident, typical of the many problems encountered by an inland company responding to unfamiliar demands, resulted in the collapse of the pickling tanks in only 2 weeks due to the use of cold-rolled steel assembly bolts instead of the corrosion-resistant steel (CRES) bolts specified. Dedication to the war effort, a willingness to learn, and hard work soon overcame this mistake and many others.

Denver shipped its first carload on 22 February 1942, "with all due ceremony including a 'launching'." Keels for the first two ships were laid simultaneously on 28 February, and the lead ship, scheduled to be named HMS *Bentinck* (BDE-13), was launched on 22 August, christened by a bottle of water from melted Colorado snow. A week later, BDE-14 was launched and the others followed quarterly. With the United States now actively involved in the war, the decision was made to commission all twenty-four vessels into the U.S. Navy. Commissioned the USS *Brennan*, the erstwhile *Bentinck* was the first DE completed and commissioned of some 300 ships of the basic class being built in shipyards around the country.[64]

U.S. COAST GUARD

The Coast Guard Comes Of Age

The Roosevelt era, which eventually resulted in the greatest expansion the Coast Guard has ever seen, actually began with a threat to its continuation as a separate service. Faced with reduced appropriations resulting from the Great Depression, the Coast Guard had implemented plans in January 1933 to close six bases and fifteen lifesaving stations and to decommission seven destroyers, 111 75-footers, and fifty-eight picket boats assigned to prohibition enforcement. Congressional measures looking to the reorganization of Executive departments in the interest of increasing economy and efficiency, promised further scrutiny of its affairs.[65]

Earlier Governmental Scrutiny

Coast Guard officials must have been reminded of the 1912-15 period, which began with a recommendation to abolish the Revenue Cutter Service. This time, however, the service, which had more than 400 commissioned officers, 500 warrant officers, and 9,000 enlisted men, did not seem to be threatened with extinction.[66] A more likely possibility was its transfer to the Department of the Navy, a move favored by newly-elected President Roosevelt since he had served as Assistant Secretary of the Navy a decade earlier. His views were not without precedent.

In Alexander Hamilton's report, which led to the establishment of the Revenue Marine, he had recommended to Congress that the officers of the service "be commissioned as officers in the Navy. This will not only induce fit men the more readily to engage," he wrote, "but will attach them to their duty by a nice sense of honor."[67] Although Congress specified in the resulting legislation that the men in charge of the revenue cutters be known as Officers of the Customs, rather than as Naval officers, the Treasury fleet soon was pressed into Naval service to oppose French privateers, which were preying on American merchant seamen. Until the newly authorized Navy could build up its own fleet, these vessels were armed and authorized to defend the seacoast and repel attacks on commerce under "an Act providing a Naval Armament" passed by Congress on 1 July 1797. With the commencement of hostilities on 7 July 1798, eight of the cutters found themselves under Naval orders, establishing a precedent that continues to this day.[68]

Early Roosevelt Years

President Roosevelt's planned transfer of the Coast Guard to the Department of the Navy with a position analogous to that of the Marine Corps failed to materialize. Perhaps it was due to the opposition of maritime interests. Perhaps it was due to the urging of Congressmen from coastal states not to carry out the transfer. Perhaps it was the influence of newly appointed Treasury Secretary Henry Morgenthau, Jr., who had a personal relationship with the President. For whatever reasons, the plans were quietly dropped, and not until the Executive Order of 1 November 1941, were Coast Guard vessels once more formally transferred from the Treasury Department to the Department of the Navy on a temporary basis. In the intervening years the service expanded and modernized its capabilities in many areas.[69]

Coast Guard Mission and Duties

Before examining the developments in fleet composition and technology during this period, it is appropriate to examine the duties of the Coast Guard. These duties, and the areas in which they are carried out, have a critical effect in the types of vessels (and aircraft) in the Coast Guard fleet (some of them unique), their configurations, and their salient features. Enforcement of laws that regulate or prohibit importation of certain contraband materials remains one of the primary duties of the Coast Guard to this day. Over the 200 years of its existence, it has always been engaged in the enforcement of customs laws. From time to time it has mounted major efforts against specific contraband materials. From 1920 to 1933 it was the primary seagoing agency for the enforcement of the National Prohibition (Volstead) Act, which forbade the import of so-defined intoxicating beverages. It is presently heavily involved in efforts to reduce the flow of illegal drugs into the United States. In addition to these well known duties, it has been responsible for prevention of the foreign slave trade (after its prohibition in 1807), enforcement of health and quarantine laws in support of the Public Health Service, and enforcement of immigration laws. Other duties have involved suppression of piracy, protection of fur seals and otters, regulation of fishing and whaling, and destruction of abandoned ships.[70]

Categories of Ships and Craft

The wide range of mission responsibilities, and operations where the forces of nature rather than opposing armed forces were the principal menace to overcome, have resulted in the evolution of types of Coast Guard vessels that are distinct from both Naval and merchant vessels. Two of these types of vessels in which the 1930s saw major developments are described here: multimission cutters and icebreakers.[71]

Multimission Cutter Requirements

Concerned that too many revenue cutters built during the Civil War had been designed with an eye toward naval use, Secretary of the Treasury Hugh McCulloch expressed the opinion that

> cutters should be of light draught, manned by a small crew, and able to navigate the shoal waters and penetrate the inland bays, rivers, and creeks with which our sea, lake, and gulf coast abound, but of sufficient tonnage to enable them to perform efficiently and safely the duties of a Coast Guard at sea and to furnish succor to vessels in distress.[72]

While the cutters in the Coast Guard fleet in 1933 were undoubtedly larger than the ones Secretary McCulloch had in mind in 1865, they reflected quite well his concern that they should be capable of performing a multiplicity of missions. Capability for independent operations, extended range without refueling, reliability under adverse conditions, and shallow draft to allow operations in restricted waters took preference over speed, armament, and high performance.

Along with some miscellaneous older vessels, the Coast Guard multimission cutter fleet in 1933 consisted of several classes of vessels built from 1926 to 1931, ranging in length from 100 to 250 feet. The largest class, in terms of numbers, was the 125-foot class, or "buck and quarters," of which thirty-three were built. Designed for reliability and endurance for trailing rumrunners, the steel-hulled vessels were driven by diesel engines (top speed 10 knots) and mounted a 3-inch, 23-caliber gun. They were considered to be very seaworthy whether heading into the sea or running before it.[73]

The *Lake* Class

The largest class, in terms of size, was the 250-foot *Lake* class, of which ten were built. Authorized by Congress in June 1926, five were completed in 1928-29 by the Bethlehem Shipbuilding Corporation at Quincy, Massachusetts, and five more (of nearly the same design) were completed by 1931, four by the General Engineering and Drydock Company in Oakland, California, and one by United Drydock at Staten Island, New York. Drawing on 5 years' experience

with the earlier 240-footers, Constructor Frederick A. Hunnewell had designed the new vessels with a cruiser stern to reduce shocks from stern or quartering seas. He also incorporated a raked stem, a flared bow, and increased freeboard to keep the forward area drier in bad weather. To increase power and endurance, they were longer and beamier than their predecessors. Likewise, the armament suite was heavier, calling for three 5-inch, 51-caliber and two 3-inch, 50-caliber guns (only one of each in peacetime). Their designers were well pleased by their performance and predicted they would last for 50 years. On 30 April 1941, four of the vessels were transferred to the British Navy under the Lend-Lease Act, and the remainder followed within a month. Six of the seven cutters survived and were returned to the United States at the war's end.[74]

Two additional classes deserve brief mention. The lead vessel (*Thetis*), of the 165-foot A-class cutters, was launched in November 1931, the first of eighteen cutters designed to track rumrunners. They were handsome in appearance, had good maneuverability, and served their purpose well; however, they were lightly built, crowded, and uncomfortable at sea. A second series of six 165-footers, known as B-class cutters, were for icebreaking in Lake Michigan and elsewhere. They had moderately cutaway forefoots, heavy plating at the bow and waterline, and were driven by geared steam turbines. Launched in the 1931-34 period, they prepared the way for the next class of larger cutters using similar propulsion systems.[75]

The *Campbell* Class

The vessels that did become the 40-year cutters envisioned when the 250-foot *Lake*-class cutter was built were the 327-footers built from 1933 to 1936. In May 1933, Rear Admiral Harry G. Hamlet, then Commandant of the Coast Guard, submitted a vessel requirements list, which included nine 300-foot high-speed cutters capable of carrying airplanes, to be funded as Emergency Public Works under the National Industrial Recovery Act. During the design of these vessels, it was realized that they would be similar to gunboats being designed for the Navy. Constructor Hunnewell was directed to use the same propelling machinery and underwater lines as those for the gunboats *Erie* and *Charleston*, and to modify the rest of the design to meet Coast Guard needs. The resulting vessels were longer, slimmer, and of relatively lighter draft than previous cutters, required the use of longitudinal framing, and had heavier scantlings than the gunboats. They were the first all-welded Coast Guard cutters. In another departure from traditional cutter designs, they had twin screws, driven by geared turbines. During the period 1933-36, seven of these vessels were built, all in Navy yards (two in New York, four in Philadelphia, and one in Charleston), and named after former Secretaries of the Treasury. The first, *Campbell*, was commissioned on 16 June 1936, followed shortly by *Bibb, Duane, Hamilton, Ingham, Spencer,* and *Taney.*

These 327-foot vessels, 41-foot in beam and displacing 2,216 tons, were good-looking ships with raked bows, cruiser sterns, and a single stack. Initial armament consisted of two 5-inch 51-caliber guns and three 6-pounders, later increased for wartime service. While their size precluded the installation of a hangar on deck, the vessels had king posts aft that served as a crane to handle an aircraft to provide search and rescue services for commercial aircraft that were beginning to fly over the oceans. While more vulnerable to ice damage than earlier cutters because of their twin-screw design, extremely wet in a heavy seaway, and less suitable for towing service than the *Lake*-class cutters, they were highly maneuverable and proved to be extremely tough and versatile in service. Early in their life, with the war situation deteriorating in Europe, Roosevelt directed that Coast Guard vessels be fitted out for weather patrol duty in the Atlantic. In early 1940, the *Bibb* and *Duane* took up stations between Bermuda and the Azores, thus commencing service that Coast Guard vessels would provide for nearly 40 years. Meanwhile, the *Taney* had been stationed in Honolulu. Moored at Pearl Harbor on 7 December 1941, she was the first Coast Guard vessel to fire on the enemy after the United States formally entered World War II. The remaining six vessels were soon actively engaged in the Battle of the Atlantic. They proved to be highly suitable for protecting merchant convoys against German

U-boats, having greater endurance and being more sea-kindly than destroyers, while possessing adequate speed and armament. The *Alexander Hamilton* (renamed to distinguish it from the USS *Hamilton*) was the only vessel of the class not to survive, falling victim to a torpedo attack on 29 January 1942, and sinking the next day. All the rest not only survived the war, but continued in service for over 40 years in a wide range of duties, including action in Vietnam.[76]

The 225-Foot Class

The next class of multimission cutters was the 225-foot class. The lead vessel *Owasco* was not laid down until July 1943 nor completed until May 1945, too late for service in World War II. However, the class had its origins in Hunnewell's design of the early 1930s, which had been overtaken by the decision to pattern the 327-footers after the *Erie* gunboat class. In addition, their authorization was based on a need to replace the relatively new 250-foot *Lake*-class cutters transferred to Great Britain in 1941. It seems fitting, therefore, to discuss these vessels as part of the Roosevelt expansion. Rumors persisted for years that the Coast Guard had been directed by Congress to shorten these vessels from the 316-foot design Hunnewell had prepared earlier. It was a rumor easy for those who sailed in these crowded ships and those who were disappointed in their stubby appearance to believe when compared to the sleek 327-footers. However, it is more likely that the Coast Guard cutters were a reversion to a more traditional cutter configuration. Also, operations in ice had become a more important design factor for Coast Guard vessels, and the shorter cutter could be made stronger and more maneuverable in ice. The hulls were designed with a combination of transverse and longitudinal framing and were unusually strong, with an ice belt of heavier plating at the waterline.

The propulsion system of these vessels was especially interesting. Engineer-in-Chief Harvey Johnson shared Quincy Newman's preference for electric drive, and the resulting design featured a turbine-driven generator, which powered a single 4,000 shaft horsepower synchronous motor. (These vessels proved to be the last Coast Guard vessel using either steam or electric drive.) To provide pilot house control, boilers were redesigned and elaborate control systems were developed. In practice they were seldom operated in the remote control mode. To reduce length of steam lines and, hence, to increase efficiency, all machinery was packed into a single crowded engine room. Operators were to complain in future years that "the only way to get into some spaces for maintenance was to be born there." In trials, the *Owasco* was found to vibrate so badly that it was impossible to attain full power, a problem that was solved by replacing the three-blade screw with a five-bladed design having similar efficiency based on tests at the Navy's David W. Taylor Model Basin.

Conditions topside and in the berthing spaces were crowded. Original armament consisted of two 5-in/38 dual-purpose mounts, three automatic quadruple 40mm AA guns, six 20mm machine guns, and depth charge racks and projectors. A combat information center (CIC), fire control radar, and various other electronics equipment required both space and additional manpower, which worsened the crowding. There was no room for the seaplane originally envisioned, and it was necessary to ballast empty fuel tanks in severe weather to maintain stability.

Even with their faults, however, these vessels proved to be highly successful in the postwar period. Drastic reduction of armament and peacetime manning halved the size of the crew and made living conditions tolerable. Their efficient power plants permitted nearly the same speed as that of the 327-footers at only two-thirds the shaft horsepower and a greater cruising range. While rough-riding in heavy weather, with an infinite variety of unsettling motions, they were extremely reliable and served well in a variety of missions, including ocean station duty, law enforcement, fishing patrols, and combat duty in Vietnam.[77]

Icebreakers

From its early years, the Coast Guard (and its predecessor, the Revenue Cutter Service) had been involved in operations in ice-covered waters, including long service in Alaska. In addition, winter operations on the Great Lakes, in New England waters, and in the Hudson River, frequently required icebreaking services, and

vessels had been designed or strengthened for this purpose. When the old *Bear* completed her last Alaskan cruise in 1926 after 40 years of service, the Coast Guard set about designing a replacement. Opinions of a wide variety of experts were solicited, and the resulting vessel, *Northland*, reflected the variety of opinions. Commissioned in 1927, she had an extremely strong, 216-foot steel hull, constructed by riveting supplemented by electric arc welding, with a sharply cutaway forefoot and a broad U-shape forward for ice breaking. Two efficient 600-horse-power diesel generators, driving a 1,000-horse-power motor directly coupled to the shaft, drove her at a top speed of 11 knots. Additional propulsive power was provided by a hermaphrodite-brig sail rig. She carried a 4-inch, 50-caliber single-purpose gun on either side forward. She was the most expensive cutter built to date, and presumably the most advanced, yet her performance was disappointing. She was slow, handled poorly, had numerous engineering problems, and was ineffective as an icebreaker.

Roosevelt's executive order of 21 December 1936, which directed the Coast Guard to assist in keeping channels and harbors open to navigation by means of icebreaking operations, breathed new life into the Service's commitment to icebreaking. Earlier in the year, Lieutenant Dale R. Simpson had published a paper on "Bow Characteristics for Icebreakers," predating by some 30 years the work of Commander Roderick White, who was to be honored by the American Society of Naval Engineers for his contributions to icebreaker bow design. Reacting to Roosevelt's order, Captain Harvey Johnson, Engineer-in-Chief, immediately selected one of his subordinates, Lt. Edward H. Thiele, to make a survey of northern European icebreakers. (Thiele himself was, in time, to be promoted to Rear Admiral, succeeding Rear Admiral K. K. Cowart as Engineer-in-Chief in 1958.) The young lieutenant was an especially likely choice, being in Denmark on leave at the time with his Danish wife, whom he had met on a cadet cruise while he was an instructor at the Academy. While he was well-received and gained valuable information, especially from the Swedes and the Finns, it is ironic that he found that one of the most advanced Swedish icebreakers, the 258-foot

Ymer built in 1932, had been designed using the bow form of the Great Lakes car ferry *St. Marie* and Quincy Newman's electric drive! When Thiele returned to the United States, he joined with Hunnewell and Lieutenant Commander Rutherford B. Lank, Jr., to design a class of highly successful 110-foot icebreaking tugs, the first completed in 1939.

Another large icebreaking vessel was authorized in 1941 and completed in September 1942. First designated the *Arctic*, and later the *Eskimo*, and finally comissioned as the *Storis*, this vessel was an enlarged 230-foot version of 180-foot buoy tenders. Designed to serve as a light icebreaker and supply ship in Greenland waters, the *Storis* was to gain a certain amount of fame in 1957 when she and two 180-foot tenders became the first American vessels to travel the Northwest Passage from the west to the east.[78]

All the foregoing designs proved to be prologue for the design of the nation's first true icebreakers, the *Wind* class. Roosevelt's pervasive influence is demonstrated by Johnson's account of the initiation of this effort.

> President Franklin D. Roosevelt seemed to have been directly responsible for this development. Forty years later, Rear Admiral Edward H. Thiele, USCG (Ret), remembered that in March 1941 he had obtained orders to the *American Sailor* as executive officer, believing that too much Washington duty might affect his career adversely. While the ship was fitting out at Baltimore, he was recalled to the Coast Guard Headquarters by Engineer-in-Chief Harvey Johnson, who took him to the Commandant's office. There Waesche handed him a note that the President had written to Treasury Secretary Morganthau, 'I want the world's greatest icebreakers.' Thiele speculated that these ships were to support in the construction of an air field at the head of Greenland's Sondre Stromfjord, and to aid in the shipment of lend-lease supplies to Archangel, the Russian White Sea port.[79]

The Coast Guard Depot and Yard

Since its founding in 1899, the Coast Guard Depot at Curtis Bay, Baltimore, Maryland, had provided extensive repair and alteration service for, first, the Revenue Cutter Service, and, when it was established, the U.S. Coast Guard. By 1934 the Depot's industrial plant had become outmoded and Congress appropriated funds to mod-ernize the facilities. In 1940, as the possibility of world war became apparent, Congress saw the need for greater shipyard capacity, and an extensive program of expansion was authorized and appropriated. New buildings, piers, shipyard, and equipment were installed, and channels and waterways were dredged. When this broad program had been fulfilled Curtis Bay was comparable to a medium-sized navy yard and the depot was appropriately designated the U.S. Coast Guard Yard. Based on these facilities, the Coast Guard even undertook building its own larger size vessels during later years.[80]

Salvage Engineering

Naval rescue and salvage engineering skills and knowledge were tested during this period with the successful effort to recover the submarine USS *Squalus* (SS-192) in 1939. In training for preliminary trials on 23 May, the newly completed fleet-type submarine USS *Squalus* suffered indicator-light failure to her hull-closure status board. As a consequence, the main outboard engine-air induction valve and four inboard valves remained open during a quick dive. This allowed seawater to directly flood the two engine rooms and after battery space, and to progress into the after torpedo room through an open bulkhead door. Quick-acting crewmen closed off further flooding, forward of the after battery space, but the disabled *Squalus* sank to 240 feet, south of Isle of Shoals, near Portsmouth, New Hampshire, with thirty-three survivors.[81]

Once the *Squalus* was overdue, an immediate search of her operating area located her submarine-emergency buoy, which the trapped survivors had released to the surface. Communication was then established with survivors in the three forward hull compartments, by means of the buoy telephone. Escape using a "Momsen Lung" was precluded by the protracted decompression that would be required of escapers after inhaling high-pressure air from a rescue breathing device exposed to sea pressure of 240 feet. Rapid deployment, however, of one of the Navy's new McCann rescue chambers aboard the submarine rescue vessel *Falcon* (ASR-2) enabled this device to effect rescue. Divers secured a down-haul line to the forward torpedo-room escape hatch of the *Squalus*, and the operator of the large, cylindrical bell that constituted the rescue chamber, veteran diver Chief Machinist Mate William Badders, was able to winch it down and attach it to the hatch. In four trips, then, the twenty-eight crewmen, civilian technician, and four officers were successfully extracted from the bottomed submarine. A fifth trip was made, to the after torpedo room escape hatch to determine that there were no survivors. Salvage of the *Squalus* then proceeded.[82]

Ashore at Portsmouth Navy Yard, canny submarine constructor then-Commander Andrew McKee, had already evolved a salvage plan. In a quickly assembled conference with representatives of the Navy bureaus (Construction and Repair, Engineering, and Medicine and Surgery) and the New London submarine base, McKee's plan was soon recognized to fulfill all requirements, and was put into effect.[83] The plan for raising the *Squalus* involved standard U.S. Navy procedure using salvage pontoons, 13½-foot diameter steel tanks, 32 feet long, protectively sheathed with wood.[84] A number of these would be flooded down to the submarine, made fast to chain slings under the hull, and then pumped buoyant with compressed air. Together with buoyancy in the *Squalus*, they would lift the sunken sub.[85]

Squalus's salvage was made difficult immediately by the 240-foot depth, substantially greater than considered feasible, until then, for the necessary divers' work. This was confirmed in initial dives. Divers became confused and disoriented from nitrogen narcosis by the time they reached bottom and could do little useful work (but fortunately avoided the accidents prevalent in salvage diving). In addition, bottom time for divers was minimal before having to start the long, slow decompression ascent necessary to release nitrogen (dissolved by the pressure) from the blood, slowly and safely without bubbling, to avoid crippling injury from "the bends."

Fortunately, a helium-oxygen breathing system permitting deeper diving was being developed at the Experimental Diving Unit of the Navy in Washington, D.C. Helium was substituted for the nitrogen component of atmospheric air. Light and inert, helium dissolves less readily in the blood under pressure, and when pressure

is released (as in surfacing after diving) it is released from solution more easily and safely. Developmental equipment was brought to Portsmouth, pressed into service, and further improved during operations. (An uncomfortable chilling of divers from breathing helium was offset with electrically heated underwear, and the "Donald Duck"-like distortion of divers' voices from more rapid vibration of vocal cords in helium, was remedied with a vacuum-tube telephone system, used instead of sound-powered phones.)

Besides use of pontoons for lift, *Squalus*'s main ballast and fuel tanks were blown buoyant. This left a requirement for two pontoons forward and five at the stern, to break *Squalus* from the bottom mud. At this point, salvage experience indicated that the effective buoyancy would suddenly exceed what was needed for the rest of the lift. Equally inconvenient, the decrease from almost eight atmospheres of bottom pressure at 240 feet, as the lift proceeded, would progressively expand the air in the pontoons and blown tanks of the sub, to further increase buoyancy and lift. To prevent a runaway lift, two of the pontoons aft and one forward were rigged to be 85 to 90 feet above the others on the lift cables. Although these pontoons were needed for breaking the hull free, they were in excess for the rest of the lift. The rig, therefore, caused them to surface first, and the act of surfacing then ended their lifting effect, thus neatly reducing total lift to the residual needed.

Another problem was posed by the task of passing a reeving line under the stern of the *Squalus* with which to haul a chain sling for lifting, since the stern was almost completely buried in mud. A fire-hose powered curved pipelance with a waterjet-propelled head was fabricated for the task. Telescoping sections enabled divers to push it through the mud under the *Squalus*'s stern. Back-slanting holes in the sections ejected water under pressure to maintain the tunnel made by the self-propelling head. Before the lance had been pushed entirely around the hull, the hose was disconnected and the hollow lance was used as a guide to pass a quarter-inch "snake," which served as a messenger for a series of reeving lines of increasing diameters. (The lance was retrieved by the first line of larger diameter than that of the interior of the lance.)

Typically of salvage, the rigging of chain slings, wire-rope lifting cables, pontoons, and compressed air lines involved a variety of complications and snarls. The rigging was progressively accomplished, however, over several weeks, together with the extraction of diesel oil from the fuel tanks of the sub preparatory to their being blown buoyant. (The Navy was environmentally sensitive as early as this, and wished to avoid any pollution of New Hampshire beaches.) Three slings were rove under the stern for low- and intermediate-depth pontoons on one sling, intermediate- and upper-level pontoons on a second, and an upper-level pontoon on the third. A reeving wire was readily swept under *Squalus's* bow, which was well clear of the bottom, a chain sling pulled in place, and attached by lifting cables to intermediate- and upper-level pontoons.

The stern lift of the configuration, aided by blowing all after-main ballast tanks of the *Squalus* and all but one of her fuel tanks, was successful in breaking her stern from the mud. Pivoting the bow into the bottom, the stern swung upward with a great boil of air and settled finally, suspended about 85 feet under the surfaced upper stern pontoons. The bow phase of this lift, unfortunately, then failed. After blowing all bow main ballast tanks but No. 2, blowing of it pulled the bow from bottom mud and it surged to the surface with both bow pontoons. This feared runaway lift was produced by the following: sudden release of mud suction, expansion of air in ballast tanks and pontoons (as lift reduced sea pressure), draining of free water from bow compartments as the bow slanted upward, and momentum. Worse yet, the sling of the lower pair of after pontoons broke, releasing *Squalus's* stern to the bottom again. Held in this position momentarily allowed the main ballast tanks to spill most of their air, *Squalus* became bow-heavy, and sank again to the bottom, with pairs of pontoons still tethered at bow and stern.

There was a 2-week delay clearing away the welter of cables, chains, hoses, damaged pontoons, and other wreckage. For the second lift attempt, the precaution was taken to reeve three slings under both *Squalus's* bow and stern. Likewise, to avoid another runaway, three high

pontoons were rigged bow and stern to ensure early lift cutoff when the pontoons surfaced. In further preparation, No. 4 main ballast tank was blown, as well as all upper pontoons but one at the bow.

Suitable weather arrived on 12 August and the lift was started at dawn. First, the remaining bow pontoon was blown, then No. 3 main ballast tank, followed by the lower pontoons at the stern. The stern lifted after a little more than 3 hours, while pumping the last stern pontoon, and the upper stern pontoons surfaced slowly. Next, the lower pontoon at the bow was blown, followed by No. 1 fuel tank. As that was being finished, the bow lifted, surfacing the bow pontoons, and the *Squalus* was suspended about 160 feet below the surface. The *Falcon* took up position ahead of the *Squalus*, took aboard a prepared towline and, assisted by the tug *Penacook* and a Coast Guard dispatch boat, got underway slowly. The tow proceeded toward port, for over an hour, moving *Squalus* into ever-shallower water, until she grounded on an uncharted mudbank at the 160 feet where she was suspended below the surface by the pontoons. Here she was then deposited, by venting and flooding all pontoons, in preparation for the next lift.

In the new location, *Squalus* was found to be on a sloping bottom with her bow 20 feet lower than her stern. Here, after a typical delay of a day due to rough seas, pontoons were re-rigged for a second lift. The upper, stern pontoon group was rigged with three pontoons 80 feet below the surface, and two more pontoons at about 120 feet, only slightly above the bottomed submarine. To allow for the sloping bottom, the upper, bow, pontoon group was set with three pontoons 100 feet below the surface, and an additional pontoon at 140 feet. (When both upper pontoon groups surfaced, they would level *Squalus* fore and aft.) This work took 5 days.

August 17th dawned clear, and the pumping of air to pontoons and ballast tanks began. With the weather remaining favorable, pumping was continued until both sets of upper pontoons surfaced, indicating that the *Squalus* was suspended, something over 80 feet below the surface. The *Falcon* tow got underway as before, proceeding slowly toward port and into shallower water until, in late afternoon, *Squalus* again grounded on hard sand in what proved to be 92 feet of water.

The next phase of operations aimed at bringing the *Squalus* virtually to the surface for the final tow into port and dry dock. All previous rigging was cleared, and as much water as possible was removed from flooded compartments aft for a lift attempt using only a pair of stern pontoons and buoyancy produced in the *Squalus*. This work took 10 days, and pumping for the lift was started early on 27 August. Beginning with the bow, two main ballast tanks and two fuel tanks were blown by mid-morning when *Squalus*'s bow surfaced. Unfortunately, lifting on her rudder skeg as her bow slowly rose, she listed over on her beam-ends as her bow swung slowly up. This increasingly spilled the air from her ballast tanks, allowing them to reflood, and the *Squalus* sank back on the bottom, but losing some list.

Stern-lift was now quickly undertaken, and although the stern lifted in less than an hour of pumping air (along with losing most of the list), free water in the *Squalus* ran forward, making her bow too heavy to lift with internal buoyancy. This called for rigging two pontoons on the bow (close to the deck as at the stern), but weather prevented installing this rig for 11 days.

Wind finally moderated on 9 September and the day was spent reeving two bow slings and setting the pontoons. There were then further delays, first from weather and then to repair damages before a final lift could be undertaken on 13 September.

Preliminary blowing started the night before, and was completed early the morning of the 13th. Pumping for a stern-first lift commenced about dawn, and about mid-morning the stern surfaced with its two pontoons. Following this, blowing forward main ballast tanks and bow pontoons was started. In less than an hour the bow surfaced, but with excessive internal buoyancy that overpowered the pontoons. Again this caused listing that spilled air from the blown ballast tanks and at noon the *Squalus*'s stern sank, which again required bottoming of the bow.

The blowing procedure was restarted immediately and finally success was achieved. Although the stern still proved stubborn, persistent effort was successful in raising both it and the bow, and at mid-afternoon the tow again got underway and the *Squalus* was brought into Portsmouth harbor in early evening. With *Squalus* barely awash and tide at low slack, her excessive draft caused her to ground three times in the channel before she was finally grounded as desired off Berth 6 in Portsmouth Navy yard.

Subsequently, the task of de-watering and re-floating commenced. This final aspect proved to be as difficult as any of the earlier problems of salvage, exacerbated as it was by the wide New England tidal range. First the bow was made buoyant by blowing No. 1 ballast tank, and a 100-ton sheer-legs crane took a strain on *Squalus*'s periscope support to keep her on even keel, surfacing. When the forward torpedo-room hatch was well above water, it was opened, and submersible pumps were taken below to de-water spaces, starting forward, aft through the forward battery room. During this work, *Squalus*'s stability under conditions of mixed buoyancy, with flooded spaces and tanks, again proved troublesome. In addition, de-watering the submarine's hull with the original induction system casualty still in effect (as well as other breaks in watertight integrity) was a constantly challenging process. It continued around the clock until *Squalus* was well afloat, and 30 hours after being brought into port, she entered dry dock.[86]

This was undoubtedly the Navy's both most demanding and most successful single salvage operation, to date. Efficient emergency procedures and equipment quickly identified and located a lost submarine. An imaginative and effective safety device was quickly mobilized to minimize loss of human life. Salvage resources were available to commit to an effective plan to rapidly and safely (only minor personnel accidents) recover a valuable asset for the Pacific submarine campaign just two years away.[87]

RESEARCH AND DEVELOPMENT

In these critical years leading up to World War II, much of the Navy's research and development was conducted, quite appropriately, by the Naval Research Laboratory (NRL) in Washington, D.C., at Bellevue on the Potomac, just south of today's

Bolling Air Force Base. Much of the work was unimaginative—useful, but it brought only modest improvement of materials, equipment, or process. Three major developments, however, demand attention. Two, radar and sonar, were important because they contributed so significantly to the Navy's success in combat. The third, nuclear energy, was taken from Navy auspices early in the war for development as a national project. But, because of the Navy's early alertness to and investment in the potential of this profound discovery, the development of nuclear energy merits more attention and appreciation here.

Radar

The directivity and reflection of radio signals had been variously observed and studied by scientists and engineers in the early twentieth century. This study resulted in what we know today as radar being developed independently (and secretly) during the 1930s by the United States, England, France, Germany, and Japan. (The term radar was not coined until much later by then-Lieutenant Commanders Frederick R. Furth of the Office of CNO and Samuel M. Tucker of the radio section of the Bureau of Engineering.)[88] Chapter 4 discusses radio phenomena observations (in 1922 by Dr. Hoyt Taylor and Leo C. Young, and in 1930 by L. A. Hyland) that led these American Naval researchers to recognize a radar potential, and to persuade the Bureau of Engineering to pursue further research. Radar research dwindled, however, after Hyland, Taylor, and Young's first continuous-wave area-radar research in 1931 and 32, a consequence of depression-shrunk development budgets and competition for funds.[89]

The NRL had been taken over in a resource grab by the Bureau of Engineering (BuEng), orchestrated by Director of Naval Communications, then-Captain Sanford C. Hooper. Hooper convinced himself and others that NRL research should be minimized, that research was best left to industry, and that NRL's assets should be devoted to engineering test and support (more useful, of course, to the immediate needs of Naval communications.)[90] NRL's director, Captain Edgar G. Oberlin, understandably affronted by the secretly engineered coup, fought a desperately gallant but losing defensive action. In fact, his career ended in fighting this decision on which the Bureau chiefs were already committed. However, he did force policy to be established that precluded research from being emasculated to the extent envisioned by Hooper. Most importantly, it allowed radar research to continue, although it attenuated research liaison with the Navy as a whole.[91]

This precarious research relationship is well revealed in the frustrating efforts of then-Commander William S. Parsons,[92] a graduate of the Navy ordnance postgraduate program, assigned to NRL in July 1933 as the BuOrd liaison officer. He was uniquely qualified, intellectually and professionally, to recognize the potential of radar for gunfire control. Nevertheless, Parsons was surprised at the lack of such recognition at NRL, and appalled by resolute indifference at BuOrd ("Such research was adequately pursued commercially!") Deake Parsons may not have realized it, but he had joined the historic naval company of Isherwood, Sims, Chambers, and Bowen, innovators frustrated in their day.[93]

Meanwhile, Leo Young was involved in unrelated research into eliminating transmitter-key clicks. Using cathode-ray tube (CRT) analysis, he found not only that they had very short signals, but also high power spikes, consonant with the ranges involved in the continuous-wave detection research. While this was suggesting an approach to transmitter circuits to Young's receptive mind, the radial range presentation he saw on a CRT being used by the NRL Sound Division in sonar research suggested similar handling of range in a radio pulse receiver. The rest is history, and a monumental amount of development. Dr. Taylor (head of NRL's Radio Research Division), was soon convinced by Leo Young of the feasibility of the pulse approach. He backed it vigorously and shifted roles—from a midwife to radar, to that of impresario—seeing to proper funding, administration, manning, and high-level recognition.

In March 1934, direction of the development of the pulse-radar system project was assigned to newcomer Dr. R. M. Page. His scientific knowledge, combined with great inventiveness, made him a good choice. In time, Dr. Taylor would credit him with more ideas in the radar field than any other single person. In 1934, Dr. Page first built a 60-megahertz (MHz) pulse set. When put on the air in December and tested, this system was able to receive pulse-echoes from aircraft, but only to a distance of 1 mile, and the narrow bandwidth gave unsatisfactory signal resolution.[94]

A second pulse-radar was built during 1935 despite drying-up of funds and support from BuEng, which initially delayed work. (Young directed Dr. Page to design the receiver needed, with as large a frequency range as possible, so that the work could be charged off to a high-frequency communications project.) (In contrast, in England, early in 1935, Sir Robert A. Watson-Watt, Superintendent of the National Physical Laboratory, was sought out by the Air Ministry on development of locating aircraft by radio. He then organized a group of three scientific officers and six assistants who were then "seconded" to the Air Ministry. The British Treasury gave permission for approximately $60,000 to be allocated to the project during its first year. By July they were detecting unknown aircraft at up to 33 miles.)[95] Dr. Taylor went up to Capitol Hill, where engineer Appropriation Committee member, Representative Scrugham of Nevada, was persuaded to back the radar project, and an additional $100,000 was made available. Equally importantly, dynamic Rear Admiral Harold G. Bowen became Chief of BuEng. His commitment to technological innovation was discussed earlier in relation to improved propulsion plants for destroyers. Now under his aegis, NRL was freed from BuEng's Radio Division and linked directly to his office as Bureau Chief, and radio detection would be given top priority.[96]

Part of the additional funding was used to provide an additional researcher, Robert C. Guthrie, to assist Dr. Page. He joined the project in November 1935, about the time the new receiver finally was delivered from the shop. Guthrie developed and built a self-keying transmitter from an idea suggested to Dr. Page by Laverne Philpott, who also would soon join the project. Meanwhile, Dr. Page busied himself modifying his cathode-ray scope from a circular time sweep to a linear time/distance plot. This presentation scheme would become the popular

"A-scope" used to depict range in many early operational radar sets. As work on the second system was being completed, it was decided to drop to a frequency of 28.3 megahertz to use an antenna already at NRL. Trials were conducted in April 1936, and using seven kilowatts of power, echo patterns were excellent, and ultimately ranges of 27 kilometers were obtained on aircraft. Page and Guthrie knew that they had produced the basic invention of radar. Demonstrations were conducted up through NRL, Bureau, and the Naval staff, including CNO and the Assistant Secretary of the Navy, all resoundingly successful and impressive. A place for radar in the Navy's arsenal was ensured.[97] And even as demonstrations were being conducted, a new member, A. A. Varela, was added to the team and put to work developing a 200-megahertz system.[98]

Dr. Page decided on the move to 200 megahertz for several reasons: he believed that it was about the limit of the vacuum tubes on the market, the higher frequency allowed smaller antennas, and the National Bureau of Standards had developed a 200-megahertz radio receiver whose design would simplify the building of the new radar receiver. Dr. Taylor then relayed an intuitive requirement to Dr. Page, via Leo Young, that, if possible, a single antenna should be used for transmission and reception. Page's initial reaction was that this was impossible. Once again, however, he drew on his inventive genius to produce what would become a basic element of all radars, a duplexer, that alternately connected and disconnected the radar transmitter and receiver and made the single antenna possible. The 200-megahertz system was quickly readied and tested in July 1936, work to increase power and reliability continued into 1937. By late 1936, however, there was a call for a fleet demonstration of radar. Within the project, qualms about the status of development led to simple shipboard tests of the system aboard the old flush deck destroyer *Leary* during 1937. The tests were moderately successful, but shipboard performance was considerably inferior to that regularly attained at NRL. The problem was recognized to be the limitation on the pulse power that could be developed with the electronic tubes available to date. Work continued unremittingly to solve this problem, and some improvement was obtained with a new Eimac tube, designed to withstand the rigors of use by radio amateurs.[99]

Early in 1938, the demand by CNO for a fleet test had to be met, and a prototype model of the 200-megahertz system, designated the XAF, was constructed for installation on the battleship *New York*. The equipment was exhaustively tested in winter Caribbean maneuvers in January through March 1939, and proved more than satisfactory. Reliability and availability was high, aircraft were detected out to 48 miles, ships to 10 miles; buoys were detected at 4 miles; projectiles were followed in flight, and their splashes (essential for gunnery spotting) were observed at up to 8 miles. The Commanding Officer of the *New York* was prompted to recommend that XAF be installed on all our aircraft carriers, and the Atlantic Squadron Commander, Rear Admiral A. W. Johnson, stated, "The XAF is one of the most important military developments since the advent of radio itself."

In May, based on the glowing operational reports and NRL's technical assessment, CNO was disposed to order twenty exact copies of the XAF. BuEng demurred on the number in the interests of performance improvement thought possible, and the order was cut to six, in a contract let to RCA. They went to the carrier *Yorktown*; the heavy cruisers *Chicago, Chester, Pensacola*, and *Northampton*; and the battleship *California*. After test-use had proved the value of the radar, and some modifications made, the remaining fourteen sets were ordered as the CXAM. Placed on all carriers, three cruisers, five battleships, and a seaplane tender, almost all were in place when America entered the war, and proved tremendously useful during the first two years of the war. They were cited by Fleet Admiral E. J. King for their contribution to such victories as Coral Sea, Midway, and Guadalcanal.[100]

Earlier in this chapter, it was noted that as Chief of BuEng., Rear Admiral Bowen's energetic drive to enhance steam propulsion technology had caused friction with the Bureau of Construction and Repair. Bowen was right, but Acting Secretary of the Navy, Charles Edison was reluctant to renew Bowen's appointment as Bureau Chief, and instead made him Director of NRL,

reporting directly to the Secretary as his "Technical Aide." It identifies Edison as a most sophisticated administrator, for it not only smoothed some internal Navy political difficulties but also solved problems that Edison saw to be troubling Navy research. It focused research directly under the office of the Secretary and put it under the direction of an experienced officer of Bowen's competence and dedication to innovation. It contributed significantly to the effectiveness of research in the development of the vital weapon of radar in the approaching naval war.[101]

With the XAF success, radar development began to burgeon in the United States as the technological developments were disclosed to American industry. Among the leaders in the field, besides already-mentioned RCA, were Bell Telephone Laboratories, General Electric (GE), Western Electric, and Westinghouse. Many other firms, too numerous to mention, participated increasingly as subcontractors as World War II approached and continued. NRL next developed a 200-MHz search radar of higher power and smaller antenna for smaller vessels. Designated the XAR, it was produced by GE as the SC, along with the similar RCA-developed SA. Admiral Bowen soon got into the act in pressuring Dr. Taylor to do something about a radar to warn submarines of approaching aircraft. The ever-competent Taylor selected Guthrie again to investigate the possibilities of a nondirectional 114-MHz radar in March 1940, and the project was brought to completion as the SD (produced by RCA) to serve usefully in the submarine campaign against Japan.

In England as in America, radar development started well within the radio frequencies being used for communications, and improved performance was quickly seen to require higher frequencies and power. Extensive effort in both countries went into seeking to improve the performance of triode tubes for this purpose. The big improvement, however, was to be achieved by the development of a magnetron oscillator with an ingeniously shaped cathode, and the British researchers achieved it. By this time, September 1940, the Tizard Mission had come to Washington to commence the sharing of all military technology for mutual defense. The following month, one of the first of twelve "multicavity magnetrons" was made available to Bell Laboratories for test and reproduction by their advanced tube production facilities.[102] Microwave radar, with its superior power, range, and resolution would now get under way on both sides of the Atlantic.

In noting the radar contributions of Dr. Page, his creation of the plan-position indicator (PPI) type of presentation for a radar scope deserves mention. This is the widely used "polar-chart" type of format, with a rotating sweep that "paints" (on the CRT face) all radar targets detected by the system, at the appropriate bearing and scale range from the center. (Like radar itself, it also was invented independently elsewhere.)[103]

Gunfire control radar was the last type to be developed (a delay that might have been avoided, had BuOrd been responsive to Deake Parson's efforts in 1933, mentioned earlier). Western Electric Company, the manufacturing subsidiary of AT&T, was the pioneer. They had been kept advised of the NRL radar project since as early as July 1937, when the 200-MHz pulse system had been disclosed to them and Bell Labs, the AT&T research facility. Bell began its own development late that year and by mid-1939 demonstrated a 500-MHz radar with a compact, 6-foot square antenna and a 15-mile range. This led to Navy acceptance in April 1940 of a Western Electric proposal for a 500-MHz shipboard fire control radar, designated the CXAS. In December 1940, tests met required performance specifications and were followed by a contract for ten CXAS-1 production models (later designated FA radars) for cruiser main batteries. The FA had drawbacks in the way of short oscillator-tube life (75 hours) and the limitation to fixed target bearings by a primitive mechanical equivalent of what later was called "lobing," which required the operator to hand-oscillate the antenna while observing the radar scope. In the meanwhile, conference with BuOrd had led to the request to modify the FA to a continuous tracking radar for both main battery and AA fire, and the suggestion that the radar controls be co-located with the optical controls in the gun director. Development was in progress for such an FB radar when magnetrons became available and a new transmitter was developed. The new unit was retrofitted

in the FAs, made the basis of an FC for main batteries and an FD for AA and destroyers, later known as the Mark 3 and Mark 4 fire control radars, respectively, and the FB was dropped. A breadboard model of the FC was tested in June 1941, proved superior in all details to the FA, and the first production FCs started going aboard cruisers and battleships in October. By 7 December, ten had been delivered and were being installed. The first FD was tested in August and tracked aircraft to 24 miles. The following month it was installed on the first of the Mark 37 directors for 5in/38 dual purpose batteries, being installed on the USS *Roe* (DD-418) of the new *Sims* class. In tests, range and bearing performance was good, as with the FC, but the new requirement for elevation angles was poor at long ranges, although it improved as targets closed. In time, it was determined to be caused by sea-surface echoes at low elevation angles, and remedial technology was developed in subsequent AA radars. The FD/Mark 4 was fitted to all Mark 37 systems and retrofitted to the predecessor Mark 33 director until replaced by improved follow-on fire control radar systems.[104]

Sonar

Research in acoustic detection of submarines during World War I had indicated the need both to exploit supersonic frequencies (to minimize ambient noise) and to use active transmission of acoustic signals for search. British research, shared with the U.S. Navy, suggested the use of the piezoelectric property of quartz, with a steel and quartz sandwich used as a sound source. By 1918, work had begun for both navies on supersonic echo-ranging gear, but sharing of research information discontinued at war's end.

Any discussion of U.S. acoustic research for anti-submarine warfare (ASW) must indicate the continuing, prominent role played by Dr. Harvey C. Hayes. Prior to World War I, as a professor of physics at Swarthmore College, his interest in underwater sound had led to experiments using the college swimming pool. This led to his services being sought for ASW research at the Naval Experimental Station established at Ft. Trumble near New London, Connecticut. Postwar, this work moved first to the Naval Engineering Experiment Station at Annapolis, Maryland, and subsequently, in 1923, to NRL. Here, the underwater sound group had completed a number of experimental quartz-steel echo ranging sets. This 20- to 40-kHz system, designated the QA, detected echoes to several hundred feet, but only at ship speeds of 3 or 4 knots. By 1931, a more sensitive JK receiver was developed, using piezoelectric Rochelle salt crystals. Crystals were used for transmission, as well, in a QB system for submarines, otherwise similar to the QA. By 1933, the Washington Navy Yard produced about twenty of the quartz-steel sets; approximately sixty of the JK devices were under construction. The Submarine Signal Company received a contract to produce thirty QBs. Working in collaboration with Goodrich Tire and Rubber Company, a spherical rubber cover also was developed to reduce turbulence noise that drowned out target sounds and echoes at speeds above 5 knots, and allowed up to 10 knots, which at the time was suitable for ASW.[105]

In 1934, a device using an array of miniature nickel-alloy core electromagnets, or "magneto-striction-tubes," was developed, replacing the quartz and crystal systems. The tubes were force-fit into a steel diaphragm that transmitted pings when the array was pulsed with electric current, and conversely, detected sound vibrated the diaphragm to alter the magnetic flux in the magnetostriction-tube windings, and generate processable signals. A QC sonar system utilizing this technique was designed by NRL and the Bureau and put into production by the Submarine Signal Company. An improved 24-kHz QC went into service in 1934. Typical results with a QC-1A in 1936 show sub contacts at 3,000 to 3,500 yards at 5 knots, and 1,750 yards at 15 knots destroyer speed. The 14-degree sonar beam did not provide for very efficient search, hampered by the relatively slow ping travel time. Moreover, its large vertical diameter meant that it could only provide target bearing and range, not depth.[106]

The QC was the primary destroyer sonar in World War II. Sixty were installed by 1939. The slow production rate of fourteen sets per year was improved in 1940, and by the time the war started, 170 destroyers were equipped with sonar.[107]

In 1940, military technology exchange with England was resumed and underwater acoustic development was found to be rather parallel. The Royal Navy was still using quartz-steel transducers, but had developed a steel dome for them that permitted search at 15 knots. In addition, the British system employed a recorder that substantially improved attack tactics. Both dome and recorder were quickly adopted by the U.S. Navy. For the war, sonar was quite effective as an attack aid, not defensive search or screening. A submarine that revealed its presence, however, was likely to be hunted down and destroyed. Effective search sonar was not to arrive until 1946.[108]

Nuclear Power

In March 1939, nuclear scientists at Columbia University arranged through Assistant Secretary of the Navy Charles Edison for Nobel Laureate Enrico Fermi to give a briefing at the Navy Department on the potential of nuclear fission. Rear Admiral Stanford C. Hooper (now technical assistant to CNO) assembled an audience of Naval officers, Army ordnance officers, and two NRL scientists. Fermi sensed condescension and the brush-off, but one of the NRL scientists, Dr. Ross Gunn, already interested in fission, was impressed by Fermi's information. Dr. Gunn, a physicist and Technical Advisor to the Director of NRL, also was concerned with submarine propulsion. It says a lot for NRL and BuEng that Dr. Gunn was able to quickly lead the Navy into the nuclear field, the first government agency to conduct such research. Less than 2 months later, he got the Chief of the Bureau (again the progressive Rear Admiral Harold Bowen) to allot $1,500 to conduct exploratory research into the use of nuclear energy as a power source. In June, NRL submitted a memorandum on the use of atomic power in submarines.[109]

Research started with R. R. Miller of NRL's Chemistry Division and Dr. T. D. O'Brien, hired specially from the University of Maryland, undertaking modest production of uranium hexafluoride. This was seen as a likely route to the isotopic separation of uranium 235, the potential fissile energy source.[110]

The use of U_{235} for power was even the subject of an article in the November 1940 *ASNE Journal*: "Uranium 235–Power Fuel of the Future?" It discussed sources of uranium ore, difficulty of isotope separation, neutron bombardment and chain reaction, use for heat in steam generation, and factors in power plant operation.

In 1940, NRL contracted with the University of Virginia and Columbia University for high-speed centrifuge separation of U_{235}, and with the Carnegie Institution's Dr. Philip Abelson, who was developing a liquid thermal diffusion process. In July 1941, Dr. Ableson moved to NRL to develop his thermal diffusion separation process, in conjunction with Dr. Gunn.[111]

In 1942, Abelson and Gunn built and operated a series of pilot diffusion plants at NRL, and in 1943 built a large thermal diffusion plant at the Philadelphia Navy Yard (to exploit steam available gratis from the Naval Turbine and Boiler Laboratory). NRL had been visited as early as January and February 1942 by a Manhattan Project advisory committee whose members reported favorably on the NRL process. The Manhattan Project was unable to settle on its use, unfortunately, at that time, apparently preferring to continue exploration of other methods. By June 1944, however, only magnetic separation (for final enrichment) was really panning out,[112] and NRL's plans were requested to facilitate construction of an industrial-size Abelson-Gunn type installation at Oak Ridge, Tennessee. NRL also participated in training operators for the plant, which was then used to achieve initial U_{235} enrichment in series with subsequent magnetic separation, which produced the final bomb-grade fissile U_{235}.[113]

Thus, the Navy and NRL contributed significantly to recognizing and harnessing nuclear energy, which was used to convince a fanatic adversary of the futility of continuing war.

SUMMARY

The pattern of engineering production and development growth set forth in this era make "The Roosevelt Resurgence" an appropriate title for this chapter. The naval engineering establishment produced 102 badly-needed ships for the U.S. Navy—and just in time. Nevertheless, these vital elements of American sea power would have been unavailable had it not been for the astute global awareness, imaginative political leadership, and wonderful strategic deviousness of Mr. Roosevelt.

It should, nevertheless, be emphasized that the resurgence in Naval strength was barely adequate, and that the era was characterized by a sadly irresolute drift into war. Although naval engineering was permitted to produce enough of a fleet to hold the treacherous adversaries at bay, it was only marginally adequate to the task. (Many brave men died well, making do with worn and obsolete weapons.) It was a fleet that earlier had even been denied treaty parity, in the fatuous belief that "restraint" would be encouraged by example. The fleet was quite inadequate to deter aggression, and instead seemed to display a lack of national resolve, which encouraged arrogant ambition.

Few wars are fought in just the way the participants expect. Nevertheless, it does appear that the U.S. Navy had anticipated the adversary, the geography of the war, and the ships and weapons needed. The newer ships were battle-strong and in most respects well-weaponed. The naval engineers had identified the appropriate technology, and designed and programmed the resources needed to produce the ships and weapons (including new technologies of radar and sonar) that far outstripped such effort by the adversaries. Substantial groundwork was even laid for the production and further development that would eventually win the war. (See Chapter 7.)

It would be unreasonable to conclude that the naval engineering community should have tried harder to sell the preparedness it clearly saw as necessary. It is reasonable to suggest, however, that those charged with providing our technological strength in the future should be alert to challenge those who always find reason to urge the minimum for defense.

Notes

1 Potter, E. B., editor, *The United States and World Sea-power*, Englewood Cliffs, New Jersey: Prentice-Hall, Inc., 1955.

2 *Ibid.* Also Friedman, Norman, *U.S. Aircraft Carriers: An Illustrated Design History*, Annapolis, Maryland: Naval Institute Press, 1984.

3 Bowen, Harold G., Vice Admiral USN, *Ships, Machinery and Mossbacks*, Princeton, New Jersey: Princeton University Press, 1954.

4 Breyer, Siegfried, *Battleships and Battle Cruisers 1905-1970*, Garden City, New York: Doubleday & Company, Inc., 1978.

5 *Ibid.* Also Friedman, Norman, *U.S. Battleships: An Illustrated Design History*, Annapolis, Maryland: Naval Institute Press, 1984.

6 Potter, *United States and World Seapower.* Also Bowen, *Ships, Machinery and Mossbacks*; Breyer, *Battleships and Battle Cruisers*; Friedman, *U.S. Battleships.*

7 Dulin, R.O., and W. H. Garzke, *Battleships: United States Battleships in World War II*, Annapolis, Maryland: Naval Institute Press, 1976. Also Bowen, *Ships, Machinery and Mossbacks*; Breyer, *Battleships and Battle Cruisers*; Friedman, *U.S. Battleships.*

8 Breyer, *Battleships and Battle Cruisers.* Also Friedman, *U.S. Battleships*; Dulin & Garzke, *Battleships in World War II.*

9 *Ibid.*

10 Friedman, *U.S. Aircraft Carriers.*

11 *Ibid.*

12 Potter, *United States and World Seapower.* Also Friedman, *U.S. Aircraft Carriers.*

13 Friedman, *U.S. Aircraft Carriers.*

14 Potter, *United States and World Seapower.* Also Friedman, *U.S. Aircraft Carriers.*

15 Friedman, *U.S. Aircraft Carriers.*

16 Potter, *United States and World Seapower.* Also Friedman, *U.S. Aircraft Carriers.*

17 Friedman, *U.S. Aircraft Carriers.*

18 Friedman, Norman, *U.S. Cruisers: An Illustrated Design History*, Annapolis, Maryland: Naval Institute Press, 1984. Also Eliot, Samuel Morison, *The Two-Ocean War*, Boston, Massachusetts: Little, Brown & Company, 1963; Dull, Paul S., *A Battle History of the Imperial Japanese Navy*, Annapolis, Maryland: Naval Institute Press, 1978; Campbell, John, *Naval Weapons of World War Two*, Annapolis, Maryland: Naval Institute Press, 1985.

19 Friedman, *U.S. Cruisers.* Also Campbell, *Naval Weapons;* Jentschura, J., D. Jung, and P. Mickel, *Warships of the Imperial Japanese Navy 1869-1945*, Annapolis, Maryland: Naval Institute Press, 1986.

20 Friedman, *U.S. Cruisers.* Also Eliot, *Two-Ocean War.*

21 *Ibid.*

22 Friedman, *U.S. Cruisers.*

23 Breyer, *Battleships and Battle Cruisers.* Also Dulin & Garzke, *Battleships in World War II*; Friedman, *U.S. Cruisers*; Eliot, *Two-Ocean War.*

24 Bowen, *Ships, Machinery and Mossbacks.* Also Friedman, Norman, *Destroyers: An Illustrated Design History*, Annapolis, Maryland: Naval Institute Press, 1984.

25 Two of the *Farragut*-class destroyers capsized and were lost in the typhoon that struck the U.S. Third Fleet in December 1944. (See Chapter 7 regarding the stability controversy.) Calhoun, C. R., *Typhoon: The Other Enemy*, Annapolis, Maryland: Naval Institute Press, 1981.

26 Friedman, *Destroyers.*

27 *Ibid.*

28 A peripheral expertise at Gibbs and Cox was the fabrication of very precise scale models, as a type of three-dimensional blueprint. These mock-ups were essential in design and development of the new, compact and highly crowded destroyer engineering spaces. Now, they are valuable historical artifacts, as unique and useful in preserving the technological history of their era, as the Admirality models instituted by Samuel Pepys with ship purchases of the Restoration Navy. (Bowen, *Ships, Machinery and Mossbacks.*)

29 Bowen, *Ships, Machinery and Mossbacks.* Also Friedman, *Destroyers.*

30 Friedman, *Destroyers.*

31 Bowen, *Ships, Machinery and Mossbacks.* Also Friedman, *Destroyers.*

32 *Ibid.*

33 Friedman, *Destroyers.*

34 Lenton, H. L., *Navies of the Second World War, American Submarines*, Garden City, New York: Doubleday & Co., Inc.

35 Friedman, Norman, *Submarine Design and Development*, Annapolis, Maryland: Naval Institute Press, 1984. Also Polmar, Norman, *The American Submarine*, Baltimore, Maryland: Nautical & Aviation Publishing Company of America, 1983.

36 *Ibid.*

37 Bagnasco, Erminio, *Submarines of World War Two*, Annapolis, Maryland: Naval Institute Press, 1973.

38 *Ibid.* Also Friedman, *Submarines;* Polmar, *American Submarine;* and Von Mises, Richard and Von D. B. Tuebner, Druck and Verlag, *Elemente der Technischen Hydromechanik*, Leipzig and Berlin (In German), 1914.

39 *Ibid.*

40 Von Mises, et al, *Elemente der Technischen Hydromechanik.*

41 Heller, S. R., "A Personal Philosophy of Structural Design of Submarine Pressure Hulls," *Naval Engineers Journal* (May 1962) p. 223.

42 *The Fleet Type Submarine*, NAVPERS 16160, Bureau of Naval Personnel, 1946.

43 Gabler, Ulrich, Prof. Dipl-Ing, Wehr and Wissen, *Unterseebootsbau*, Darmstadt, West Germany: Verlagsgesellschaft Publication-6426, 1972.

44 Subsequent to World War II, there was evolution to hydraulic ejection, whereby the torpedo was ejected by a waterslug behind it, rather than by an air bubble under pressure. This was a German innovation, and in their design, air pressure was used in a separate tube to push a ram, which, in turn, would force water under pressure behind the torpedo to eject it without the escape of tell-tale air bubbles. (See note 43.)

45 No one knows to this day how many of the fifty-two U.S. submarines lost in World War II were lost because of their air becoming too foul for human endurance. New technologies, however, have pushed forward the life support capacities of the nuclear submarines of today. Systems for sustaining the air environments within submarines have become so advanced that 'atmospherics' have been virtually removed as a factor in constraining the time submerged for a submarine.

46 Beach, Edward L., *Submarines*, New York, NY: Holt Publishing Co., 1952.

47 Potter, *United States and World Seapower.*

48 *Historical Transactions 1893-1943*, The Society of Naval Architects and Marine Engineers, New York, NY, 1945. Also Potter, *United States and World Seapower.*

49 *Ibid.* Also Whitehurst, Clinton H., Jr., *The U.S. Shipbuilding Industry*, Annapolis, Maryland: Naval Institute Press, 1986.

50 *Historical Transactions 1893-1943*, SNAME. Also Fahey, James C., *The Ships and Aircraft of the United States Fleet*, New York, NY: Ships and Aircraft, 1942.

51 *Historical Transactions 1893-1943*, SNAME.

52 *Ibid.* Also Fahey, *Ships and Aircraft.*

53 *Ibid.*

54 *Ibid.*

55 *Historical Transactions 1893-1943*, SNAME.

56 *Ibid.*

57 *Ibid.*

58 *Ibid.*

59 Chiles, James R., "The Ship That Broke Hitler's Blockade," *Invention and Technology*, Winter, 1988.

60 Friedman, Norman, *U.S. Small Combatants: An Illustrated Design History*, Annapolis, Maryland: Naval Institute Press, 1987. Also Kelbaugh, Jack, "Notes on Annapolis Torpedo Boats," *The Public Enterprise*, Annapolis, Maryland: The Public Enterprise, Oc-

tober 1987; Miller, Richards T., Private correspondence dated 26 October 1987.

61 Miller, Richards T., Private correspondence, 26 October 1987.

62 McQuilken, John H., Rear Admiral (USN Ret.), Private correspondence, 12 January 1987.

63 *Ibid.*

64 *Ibid.*

65 Johnson, Robert Erwin, *Guardians of the Sea: History of the United States Coast Guard, 1915 to the Present*, Annapolis, Maryland: Naval Institute Press, 1987.

66 *Historical Transactions 1893-1943*, SNAME, p. 128.

67 Johnson, *Guardians of the Sea*, p. 5.

68 Johnson, *Guardians of the Sea.*

69 *Ibid.*

70 *Ibid.*

71 *Ibid.*

72 *Ibid.*, p. 11.

73 *Historical Transactions 1893-1943*, SNAME. Also Johnson, *Guardians of the Sea.*

74 *Ibid.*

75 *Ibid.*

76 *Ibid.*

77 *Ibid.*

78 *Ibid.*

79 Johnson, *Guardians of the Sea*, p. 214.

80 Nachtwey, Donald P., *U.S. Coast Guard Yard*, U.S. Coast Guard, Department of Transportation, Curtis Bay, Baltimore, Maryland, 1985.

81 LaVo, Carl, "The Short Life of the *Squalus*," *Naval History*, Vol. 2/2/3 (Spring 1988). Also Tusler, Floyd A., Lieutenant Commander (CC) USN, "The Salvage of the *USS Squalus*," *ASNE Journal*, Vol. 52, No. 2 (May 1940).

82 LaVo, "Short Life of the *Squalus*."

83 Shratz, Paul, Captain USN, "In Contact," *Naval History*, Vol. 2/3/4 (Summer 1988).

84 Salvage of the Royal Navy's submarine HMS *Thetis*, lost in sad coincidence within weeks of *Squalus*, is in interesting contrast. It was conducted almost concurrently, using tidal lift, by means of cable slings from a freighter, moving into successively shallower inshore locations. See Notes: "The Salvage of HMS *Thetis*," *ASNE Journal*, Vol. 52, No. 4 (November, 1940).

85 LaVo, "Short Life of the *Squalus*." Also Tusler, "Salvage of the *Squalus*."

86 Tusler, "Salvage of the *Squalus*."

87 *Ibid.* Also LaVo, "Short Life of the *Squalus*;" Shratz, "In Contact."

88 Bowen, *Ships, Machinery and Mossbacks.*

89 Allison, David K., *New Eye for the Navy: The Origin of Radar at the Naval Research Laboratory*, Naval Research Laboratory, Washington, D.C.: U.S. Government Printing Office, 1981. Also Howeth, L.S., Captain USN, *History of Communications-Electronics in the United States Navy*, Washington, D.C.: U.S. Government Printing Office, 1963.

90 Rear Admiral Sanford C. Hooper, USN must, in all fairness, be recognized at the same time for his tremendous role in the technical, operational, and administrative development of U.S. Navy radio communications. From the earliest days of shipboard radio, when Hooper was a young lieutenant, he brilliantly and single-mindedly contributed in innumerable ways to the U.S. Navy's preeminence in radio communications. See Howeth, *History of Communications*, 1963.

91 Allison, *New Eye for the Navy*.

92 Later, Rear Admiral Parsons, one of the Navy's most distinguished officer technologists, played a major role in many aspects of the Manhattan Project, including explosives engineering of implosion, altimeter-radar triggering, and airborne arming of "Little Boy", personally. See Baxter, James Phinney, *Scientists Against Time*, Boston, Massachusetts: Little Brown and Company, 1946; Rhodes, Richard, *The Making of the Atomic Bomb*, New York, N.Y.: Simon and Schuster, Inc., 1986; see also Chapter 7.

93 Allison, *New Eye for the Navy*.

94 Gebhard, Louis A., *Evolution of Naval Radio-Electronics and Contributions of the Naval Research Laboratory*, Naval Research Laboratory, Washington, D.C.: U.S. Government Printing Office, 1979. Also Allison, *New Eye for the Navy*; Howeth, *History of Communications*.

95 *The Origins and Development of Operational Research in the Royal Air Force*, Air Ministry, London: Her Majesty's Stationery Office, 1963.

96 Gebhard, *Evolution of Naval Radio Electronics*. Also Allison, *New Eye for the Navy*; Howeth, *History of Communications*.

97 NRL demonstrated the 28.3 megahertz pulse radar to the Army Signal Corps Laboratory director, Colonel William R. Blair, and his staff in June 1936 and passed information on subsequent developments. This and further cooperation contributed to successful development of the Army SCR 268 air search and AA fire control radar, subsequently used in all theaters of war.

98 Bowen, *Ships, Machinery and Mossbacks*. Also Allison, *New Eye for the Navy*; Howeth, *History of Communications*; Gebhard, *Evolution of Naval Radio Electronics*.

99 Allison, *New Eye for the Navy*; Howeth, *History of Communications*; Gebhard, *Evolution of Naval Radio Electronics*.

100 Bowen, *Ships, Machinery and Mossbacks*; Allison, *New Eye for the Navy*; Howeth, *History of Communications*; Gebhard, *Evolution of Naval Radio Electronics*.

101 Sapolsky, Harvey M., "The Origins of the Office of Naval Research," *Naval History—The Sixth Symposium of the U.S. Naval Academy*, ed. Daniel M. Masterson, Wilmington, Delaware: Scholarly Resources, Inc., 1987. Also Bowen, *Ships, Machinery and Mossbacks*; Allison, *New Eye for the Navy*.

102 The tube's anode gave the name to this "multicavity magnetron." It consisted of a copper cylinder with a large cylindrical central cavity, surrounded by a concentric ring of much smaller holes connected by slits to the central cavity. An oxide-coated wire-spiral anode ran down the axis of the central cavity. (Howeth, L. *History of Communications*.)

103 Bowen, *Ships, Machinery and Mossbacks*; Allison, *New Eye for the Navy*; Howeth, *History of Communications*; Gebhard, *Evolution of Naval Radio-Electronics*.

104 Friedman, Norman, *Naval Radar*, Annapolis, Maryland: Naval Institute Press, 1981. Also Baxter, James Phinney, *Scientists Against Time*, Boston, Massachusetts: Little, Brown and Company, 1946; Allison, *New Eye for the Navy*; Howeth, *History of Communications*; Gebhard, *Evolution of Radio-Electronics*.

105 Klein, Elias, *Notes on Underwater Sound Research and Applications Before 1939*, Office of Naval Research, Washington, D.C.: U.S. Government Printing Office, 1976, Also Bowen, *Ships, Machinery and Mossbacks*; Howeth, *History of Communications*.

106 *Ibid.* Also Friedman, *Destroyers*.

107 Friedman, *Destroyers*.

108 *Ibid.* Also Bowen, *Ships, Machinery and Mossbacks*; Howeth, *History of Communications*.

109 Rhodes, Richard, *The Making of the Atomic Bomb*, New York, NY: Simon and Schuster, Inc., 1986. Also Bowen, *Ships, Machinery and Mossbacks*; Allison, *New Eye for the Navy*; Baxter, *Scientists Against Time*.

110 Bowen, *Ships, Machinery and Mossbacks*.

111 *Ibid.* Also Rhodes, *The Making of the Atomic Bomb*.

112 This applied only to U_{235}. In parallel to U_{235}, the program to produce fissile plutonium by carbon-moderated uranium pile was proving quite successful.

113 Bowen, *Ships, Machinery and Mossbacks*; Baxter, *Scientists Against Time*; Rhodes, *The Making of the Atomic Bomb*.

The *Holland* (SS-1) was built at the Crescent Shipyard in Elizabethport, New Jersey.

John P. Holland and Simon Lake were the "big two" in submarine development and were fierce competitors. Holland was first to strike gold when the Navy accepted his *Holland* (SS-1) in 1900. In 1912, the *Seal*, renamed SS-19½, was Lake's first sale to the U.S. Navy. Earlier, both Lake and Holland had sold five submarines each to Russia and Japan, respectively, but these submarines did not figure prominently in the Russo-Japanese War.

The *Tarantula*, another Holland design, was built by the Fore River Shipbuilding Company, for the Electric Boat Company.

USS *Grampus*, launched in 1902, was one of six of the same design developed by Holland. Like all early boats, they were powered by gasoline engines.

Submarines *Grampus* and *Pike*, each only 63 feet, 4 inches in length, share dry dock with USS *Lawton* in 1906.

USS *Thrasher*, 1912. The inscription on the stationary crane in the background identifies the yard as "Cramp and Sons Ship Building Co."

Launching of the S-43.

Left, above. Hull sections of *Picuda*, (SS-382) and *Pampanito* (SS-383) rest side-by-side on the keel blocks as building begins at Portsmouth Naval Shipyard in 1943. At right, USS *Redfish, Ronquil*, and *Razorback* prior to triple launching in 1944.

USS *Albacore* (SS-569) in building ways, 1953. *Albacore*'s teardrop-shaped hull would be refined and applied to later nuclear powered submarine designs.

USS *Menhaden* (SS-377) begins sea trials following overhaul at San Francisco Naval Shipyard in 1957.

USS *Tunny* (SSG-282) was Guppy conversion with Regulus I missile hangar and launching gear added.

Engineering problems do not stay at home when ships deploy. Here, left to right, submarines *Bream, Pomodon, Stickleback, Bluegill*, and *Bashaw* enjoy brief upkeep in Yokosuka, Japan. This is the yard that spawned *Shinano*, the Japanese battleship-turned-carrier, in World War II.

USS *Grayback* (SSG-574) was first missile firing submarine designed specifically for that purpose. Her Regulus II missile was victim of a budget cut.

USS *Nautilus* (SSN-571) was world's first nuclear-powered submarine. Her water-cooled reactor set precedent for almost all future reactors. The liquid sodium reactor tried in *Seawolf* was never replicated.

Then-Rear Admiral Hyman Rickover, renowned as "Father of the Nuclear Navy," in a reflective moment on deck of USS *Nautilus* in 1958.

The engineer officer and watch personnel of USS *Skate* (SSN-578) control reactor power during Arctic voyage of exploration in 1959.

USS *Skate* logged over 3,000 miles during 12 days under the ice pack. On 17 March 1959, *Skate* became the first submarine to surface at the North Pole. A year earlier, *Nautilus* had visited the Pole, but remained deep.

USS *Sargo* (SSN-583) on the surface at the North Pole, 1960.

Technological advances in submarine design and construction include both hull form and materials, as well as propulsion systems.

Even submarines need tender loving care! Here, USS *Ulysses S. Grant* (SSBN-631) spends a quiet evening alongside USS *Proteus* (AS-19). Nuclear power plants, missile systems, and complex electronics require a high order of engineering support.

Vice Admiral William F. Raborn, USN. His Special Projects Office master-minded Polaris.

Polaris A-3 missile takes flight after sub-merged submarine launch.

The business end. The USS *Sam Rayburn* (SSBN-635) shows off her 16 Polaris missile tubes. A multitude of engineering problems had to be solved to permit underwater launch and transition to airborne flight of the Polaris missile.

Artist's concept of the SSN-21, the proposed attack submarine of the future.

CHAPTER

SEVEN

1942–1945

World War II Development and Expansion

by Edward M. MacCutcheon

INTRODUCTION

Wounds inflicted on the United States during the weeks preceding New Year's Day 1942 portended a dismal national future. On the twenty-fourth day after the attack on Pearl Harbor, our nation was reeling under successive onslaughts by the Japanese. One day later, Manila fell and the nearby U.S. naval base at Cavite was taken. Resentment, frustration, and fury were the prevailing emotions. Rancor from treachery fueled the resolve of the nation. We had been ambushed and were committed to the greatest war of all time.

World War II was a maritime war. It was symbolic that the first shot was fired by a German battleship, the United States' baptism of fire began with the attack on the fleet at Pearl Harbor, and the Japanese signed the final capitulation on a U.S. battleship in Tokyo Bay in November 1945. Almost every war strategy depended on the use of the sea for operations or logistics.

The saga of World War II is one of surprising threats, innovative countermeasures, and new counterthreats. It featured a medley of firsts, as science and technology were pressed to develop new weapons systems and deploy them in battle. Every type of combat saw major innovations. Time was compressed. Basic science was enlisted, and new technology was developed, engineered, evaluated, manufactured, and placed in the fleets in 2-year time intervals; the period of this chapter, 1942-1945, was one of extremely rapid movement in naval engineering. This chapter embraces the saga of World War II, and it highlights the technical innovation successes and disappointments that to a large extent governed the direction and outcome of the war's combat operations.

CAMPAIGNS AND LOGISTICS

War In Europe

Until the entry of the United States, the British had been fighting a valiant, but lonely, and probably losing struggle. Our peacetime help was not enough. The German U-boats were strangling the supply lines and the larger British warships were tied up blockading Germany to prevent its fast battleships and battle cruisers from getting out to destroy convoys.[1] When America entered the war, most major U.S. Navy fleet units were assigned to the Pacific. Later, a few units augmented bombardment and helped to screen landing forces in the European campaigns. In contrast, the escort capability of the United States predominantly was used in the Atlantic sea-lanes to ease the U-boat pressure.

Meanwhile, the war at sea continued. The entry of the United States as an active belligerent in 1942 caused the balance of sea power, both militarily and logistically, to tilt in favor of the Allies. The substantial British domestic ship production program and the stupendous ship production of the United States were beginning to turn out ships faster than the enemy could sink them, and the predations of the U-boats were more and more curtailed by larger anti-submarine warfare forces and improved tactics.

Operation Overlord culminated on D-Day, 6 June 1944: every type of combat operation known to man was put into full swing in the greatest amphibious operation of all time. In spite of the adverse weather that increased the difficulty of the amphibious assault, the months of careful preparation and patience paid off. The landings in Europe succeeded.

The great war on land following the invasion was accompanied by a new technological aspect of warfare; two days after D-Day, the German V-1 "buzz-bombs" (pulse-jet cruise missiles) commenced to fall on southern England. The United States got into this technological area on 3 September 1944 with radio-controlled explosive-packed bombers, but was upstaged when the first V-2 rockets landed in London. The V-1 and V-2 attacks on London were among the last gasps of a dying Third Reich, and on 7 May 1945 Germany surrendered.

Supply By Sea

Supplies from the United States were critical to the friendly combatants, Britain and Russia. Cargoes featured petroleum products, food, and supplies. Later, they included munitions and other warfare material. After the United States became a combatant, major cargoes included

troops, wounded, and prisoners of war. Major supply lines encompassed the entire world. They ran across the Atlantic to Britain and to Murmansk in the Soviet Union. Other Atlantic routes extended around the Cape of Good Hope to secure Middle Eastern oil, to supply the Soviet Union from the South, and to support the China-Burma-India Theater. Across the Pacific, the supply lines ran to Australia, New Zealand, and again to the Soviet Union via Vladivostok.[2] These long routes provided easy prey for the U-boats and surface raiders of the Third Reich, especially in the Atlantic.

War In the Pacific

Pearl Harbor was only one of many attacks attracted from a weak air defense. Three days after Pearl Harbor, the British battleship *Prince of Wales* and the battle cruiser *Repulse* were sunk by Japanese aerial torpedo attacks near Malaya.[3] Nothing was going well for the Allies, and, in late February 1942, the cruiser *Houston* (CA-30) was sunk in the Java Sea.[4] On 7 May 1942, during the Battle of the Coral Sea, the aircraft carrier *Lexington* (CV-2) was crippled by air attack and had to be sunk by our own forces.

However, not all news was gloomy. Prior intelligence at the Battle of the Coral Sea brought success; similarly, at the Battle of Midway, a United States carrier force was able to surprise the Japanese and a victory ensued that historians consider to be one of the more decisive in U.S. Naval history.[5]

From the beginning, American submarines took the offensive. By the closing days of the war, coastal shipping around Japan was throttled by torpedo losses and mining denial, almost to the point of extinction.[6]

The first great advance in the Pacific was in the Solomon Islands at Guadalcanal. A small technological bonus occurred early in the sweep, in August 1942, when the U.S. Marines landing on Guadalcanal captured a shore-based Japanese sea-search radar. This capture was the first positive evidence that the Japanese were using radar, and it provided an opportunity to examine and evaluate it.

The Navy's Southwest Pacific campaign entailed a series of major amphibious operations, interspersed with island hopping and some major naval engagements. The heavy losses on both sides attest to the violence of the many actions, but a ship-loss count obscures the point. These were real victories for the United States because its troops on the beachheads and its supply lines were protected from the Japanese fleet.

The clearing of the central Pacific continued in 1943 with defensive operations in the Aleutians; landings on Tarawa, Kwajalein, and Eniwetok; and carrier strikes on Truk. These were followed by the Marianas landings at Saipan, Tinian, and Guam. Finally, when two years of the U.S. Army campaign up the New Guinea coast was completed, it was time to tackle the Philippines.

The early landings at Leyte had little opposition. But later, major Japanese fleets appeared, and in the waters off Leyte, engagements commenced covering 3 days. In January 1945, landings in Lingayan Gulf were mostly unopposed, and on 24 February 1945, Manila was reoccupied. Both sides had realized for some time that Japan was losing the war. By March 1945, the Japanese desperation began to show when they introduced widespread kamikaze attacks, many of which seriously damaged our ships.

Two important Pacific steppingstones remained: Iwo Jima and Okinawa. Fixing our flag on top of Mount Suribachi on Iwo Jima was a most appropriate symbol of the long and arduous series of campaigns during the Pacific sweep. The United States forces were now poised for the greatest of the operations, the invasion of Japan. Everyone knew from bitter experiences on the islands of the Pacific that this enemy did not yield easily.

The greatest American technological advance of this period, the atomic bomb, was revealed when President Truman approved a drastic step to end the war. Our arsenal contained only two atomic bombs, but the drops on Hiroshima and Nagasaki forced Japanese capitulation and ended further loss of life on both sides. On 2 September 1945, Japan signed the surrender documents on the deck of the battleship *Missouri* (BB-63) in Tokyo Bay to end World War II.[7]

Naval Engineering

A review of the chronicle of World War II reveals enough fascinating and important naval engineering problems and opportunities to fill a thousand-volume description. Naval engineering activities during World War II constituted the translation of results of basic and applied research into the designs, machines, and doctrines required to conduct warfare operations. At the end of World War II there still were plenty of problems and opportunities left over for the naval engineers to tackle; it is hard to select a single area of development as a standout for importance. Some of the major areas of development have been selected for discussion to illustrate the impact of selected naval engineering activities during this period. The major impact of all of this innovation on the prime platform, the ship, is given separate attention.

The major technological advances of World War II were no accident. They were derived from a strong American technological base stemming from decades of active research and development. But, equally important were the production and operating organizations that further exploited the technology base and orchestrated the concert of workers and managers who brought about the naval technological revolution of this period. Above all, this story of naval engineering is about the dedicated and creative people who developed the innovations in the warfare systems and who energized the organizations. Those who are named here are a sample and a symbol of the hundreds whose dedication moved the Allies to victory in the war.

SHIP DESIGN AND CONSTRUCTION

World War II challenged United States industry with its severest test in all history. The demand for ships, weapons, and material of all kinds heavily taxed the capacity of the prevailing industrial base. In the case of shipbuilding, all the shipbuilding ways in the United States could not satisfy the ship construction rate required to meet the Allies' shipping needs as they expanded by the attrition caused by U-boat sinkings. The need for both warships and merchant vessels was matched by three equally pressing needs, especially applicable to the warships: to modify ships in response to the new enemy weapons, to convert them to meet changing strategic needs, and to maintain and repair them.

Ship Technology

For 20 years before World War II, the navies of the world had been subject to arms limitations. This resulted in strong technical competition because it was necessary to pack as much punch as possible and still remain within the tonnage and other limitations. Many of the technical advances were exchanged through technical literature, through the open press, and through intelligence. Ships have a long life, however, and the shared technology was not introduced by all navies at the same time. As a result, the ships of the large navies, although having different mixes of combat attributes, reflected similar levels of technology. Moreover, the ships that entered the war on both sides were not all new. Some had been in World War I. Hence, hulls and propulsion systems of many older ships were basically World War I technology. The United States and Germany had introduced higher steam conditions and double reduction gears in their newer ships, whereas the others had not. These advantages provided fuel economies and power that gave an advantage to the two fleets throughout World War II.[8] Air conditioning and ventilation was another area in which the United States was a leader. Hospital ships and sick bays received early attention. Another notable application of American technology was in the "fleet-type" submarine, which sustained a good health record for its crews in spite of the warmer climates of the South Pacific, its primary operating area. By contrast, German U-boat crews suffered from cold, heat, and foul air.[9]

During World War II, warships, and to a lesser extent merchant ships, were subject to repeated modification. Part of this was in response to new weapons and part due to the changes in basic operational requirements. In the case of new weapons, there was a double impact. They had to be mounted on shipboard with a complete support system. If the enemy was using them, we had to respond with active or passive countermeasures. All of these changes and the related technology usually were classified for security reasons during the war, so they did not appear in the open literature. A survey of the technical literature from 1942 through 1945 revealed a series of rather prosaic papers. The reader would receive few clues that these papers had been presented during the greatest war of all time. The few references to the war were in respect to the benefits of welding, novel designs to facilitate construction, novel shipyard techniques, novel designs, or ship salvage.[10]

The Bureau of Ships (BuShips) was the center of naval engineering and ship production. BuShips was created 20 June 1940 by combining the Bureau of Construction and Repair and the Bureau of Engineering. At the same time, the Naval constructors were made line officers with an engineering duty designation. Rear Admiral S. M. Robinson, chief of the Bureau of Engineering, became the first BuShips chief. On 31 January 1941, he was replaced by Rear Admiral A. H. Van Keuren, and on 2 November 1942, Rear Admiral Edward Lull Cochrane became chief, remaining until September 1945. All of these officers were well-known naval engineers.

BuShips was also the center of much research and development, operating the Experimental Model Basin, the David Taylor Model Basin, the Engineering Experiment Station, the Naval Research Laboratory, the Naval Electronics Laboratory, and several others.[11]

Battle Damage and Control

Early in the war, there was a recognition of the need to understand the precise threat posed by enemy weapons. Extensive reports were required by BuShips for each incident, and each battle damage report was reviewed, analyzed, and summarized. War damage report summaries were an invaluable aid to ship designers and operating forces.

For instance, gunfire and torpedo damage reports revealed lessons having to do with arrangement of redundant systems to avoid their simultaneous destruction, as was the case with the auxiliary power on the USCGC *Alexander Hamilton* (PG-34), torpedoed near Iceland on 29 January 1942.[12] Kamikaze attacks revealed the need for topside protection, especially for gun crews. Kamikazes striking our carrier decks penetrated the wood and light steel. In contrast, the kamikaze attacks on British aircraft carriers were less damaging because of their armored steel flight decks.[13]

By 1941, American ships were well subdivided and provided with effective damage control. The operational information input for these and other designs and procedures was primarily based on World War I experience, coupled with intelligent projection and, later, the hundreds of battle damage analyses performed during World War II.

Capital ships were protected against torpedo attack and mines by protective bulkheaded sides that sandwiched longitudinal tanks containing liquid (oil or water) and voids. The proper disposition of liquids and voids is critical to system effectiveness and requires pumping water into fuel-oil tanks as they are emptied of oil. Engineering officers dislike this because water tends to pollute fuel and cause burner malfunction. In peacetime it was easy to fall into the practice of ballasting for operational convenience rather than for maximized resistance to torpedo attack. The importance of proper ballasting was preached by representatives of BuShips to the fleet from time to time, but it took actual torpedo damage experience early in the war to make true believers of the operating forces. The *Lexington* and *Saratoga* shared a special problem. Having been designed as battle cruisers, the asymmetric location of the added island required asymmetric ballasting, and the desirable liquid loading of the side protective system was frequently compromised. The solution was a starboard blister.

On 11 October 1942, in the Battle of Cape Esperance, the cruiser USS *Boise* (CL-47) received a shell hit that started a magazine fire. The hit, however, almost simultaneously, flooded the magazine and no explosion occurred. This led to an extensive set of experiments on improved sprinkler-flooding systems for magazines, and to shipboard installation of such systems in the fleet.[14]

New weapons promised new problems and new resolutions. For instance, the magnetic-influence mines and torpedoes sought detonation beneath ships where the hulls were more vulnerable. Even the heaviest ships, the battleships, had relatively much less protection on their bottoms and required greater passive defense. In addition, the need for better internal shock protection was revealed. In contrast, bombs and kamikazes placed a premium on topside deck armor. Now even more projectiles could strike at a high angle to penetrate decks designed to protect magazines and sensitive machinery.[15]

Another spectacular example in the damage control arena was the fire on the *Lafayette* (AP-53), the former French liner *Normandie*. A fire occurred during conversion at her pier on the Hudson River in New York City. Overzealous municipal firefighters put too much water in her upper decks and she capsized between two piers. A similar fate befell the gunboat USS *Erie* (PG-50) in the Caribbean after being struck by a U-boat torpedo. During repairs in Curacao, she too capsized at the pier, the result of ignorance and inattention to stability control.[16]

Typhoon Losses and Damage

The tactical exigencies of war taxed the judgement of the decision makers and often compromised prudent seamanship. One consequence was the large number of groundings. Many gambles were made with Mother Nature, such as the landings on the beaches of Normandy with a high surf. Other such instances occurred in the Pacific when the fleet attempted to fight in restricted waters, or maneuver through typhoons.

The Third Fleet was supporting the invasion of the Philippines in December 1944, at a point about 300 miles east of Luzon, when it was enveloped in such a typhoon. The destroyers of one particular class were least able to stand the storm and two of them, the *Hull* (DD-350) and the *Monaghan* (DD-354) [as well as the *Spence* (DD-512) of another class] capsized and were lost. Nine other vessels, including four cruisers, were seriously damaged, and nineteen had lesser damage. The ensuing Navy investigation examined all facets of the disaster, including command decisions, weather forecasting, and vessel stability.

Stability of capsized destroyers is a naval engineering issue. Naval ships are designed with a margin of weight reserved for lifetime growth in warfare systems. The usual margin was allowed in the design of the *Farragut* class, including the *Hull* and the *Monaghan*, launched in 1935. During the nine years between 1935 and 1944, the weight reserve was heavily pushed by addition of more anti-aircraft guns, automatic gun directors, and radar, all high up on the ship. To permit continued safe operation of these ships, BuShips issued stability instructions calling for saltwater ballasting of each fuel oil tank as it was emptied. Saltwater ballasting is unpopular with operating forces because of the danger of fuel contamination leading to oil burner flame-out during a crucial moment, as in combat. The destroyer skippers faced a difficult choice between inadequate stability and the chance of boiler fire malfunction. On 18 December 1944, this problem was further compounded when many of the destroyers were enroute to rendezvous with fleet oilers and tanks were dewatered in anticipation of fueling when the typhoon hit.

It is easy to condemn the stability of the *Farragut* class, but another capsized destroyer, the *Spence*, was of the later *Fletcher* class. Probably we shall never know the degree to which stability was the factor in the loss of the *Hull* and the *Monaghan*. In the end, no sole cause was blamed, but the weather forecasting promptly improved and the *Farragut*-class destroyers were soon retired. The fleet command did not change, but the aftermath involved a considerable verbal wind storm.

Six months later, in the Okinawa campaign, the fleet was operating near the Ryukyu Islands when the weather struck again. Although damage to the ships was again heavy, none were lost. The thirty-six ships damaged included four battleships, eight carriers, and seven cruisers. On 4 June 1945, the *Pittsburgh* (CA-72) fought the typhoon in 100-foot seas spurred by 70-knot winds. Her starboard aircraft had just been lifted off its catapult by the wind when her second deck buckled. Promptly, 105 feet of her bow bent upward and broke off. Damage control parties worked to shore up the bulkhead now exposed to the sea. For 7 hours the *Pittsburgh*'s complement continued outstanding seamanship and damage control before the storm abated. As a result of the crew's skill, the *Pittsburgh* was able to make its way to a harbor of refuge at Guam, under its own power, at a speed of 6 knots.[17]

Structural Failure

An ominous series of events began in 1942 as the war-built merchant ships went into service. Cracks appeared in main hull structures, including many that endangered the survival of the ships. Occasionally these cracks were short, but not always. Each month the number of casualties grew: five in October, seven in November, and twenty in December 1942. Finally, in January 1943, the event that electrified these industries was the breaking in two of the brand new T-2 tanker, the *Schenectady*. The *Schenectady* had completed her sea trials and was tied up at a builder's berth at Swan Island near Portland, Oregon. Suddenly, she just broke in two with a crash heard at least a mile away. The air temperature was 26°F, but the water surface had not a ripple.[18] The whole shipbuilding and ship operating communities of the United States were shocked by this serious and threatening new problem in the war-built ships.

Fractures in the main structure of steel ships, previously, had been rare events, but the frequency of the new wartime problem seemed one or two orders of magnitude higher than in the prewar-built ships. It appeared that some unforeseen anomaly was in the structural equation. The war-built ships were different in several respects. They were mainly welded, and, with the welding, many structural design features were changed to exploit welding advantages. The welding also fostered a greater use of large prefabricated subassemblies. Finally, adjustments had been made in steel alloy composition because of wartime manganese importing problems. The validity of blaming wartime construction methods was partly reinforced by the lower-than-average cracking record experienced by the one builder who continued to rivet most of the longitudinal hull seams in Liberty ships. Perhaps the answer was that the cracks tended to stop at riveted seams, but in the welded ships they ran far enough to make news.[19]

In a war world, with the Allies depending on American ship production, the possibility of a major fracture epidemic was chilling indeed. Preliminary surveys resulted only in mystery. The best naval architects were immediately sought. They gave little comfort. It appeared that the traditional standards had been met and that no obvious clues existed. As no recognizable cause emerged, the deep concern became tinged with panic. There was fear of the war effort grounding on a reef of crippled ships, further heightened by the discovery of cracks in warships as well. Was this a pandemic ailment? The question quickly assumed strategic proportions.

From lack of evidence of nonstandard practice, it was concluded early that the real problem was worse than at first suspected. Much wild speculation followed. Fingers were pointed in all directions. The targets of blame included unknowledgeable shipbuilders, careless or greedy workers, politics, and foreign agents. Meanwhile, the engineers responsible, realizing that difficult technical problems lay at the source of the trouble, sought research and development help. The national emergency gave research and development a blank check. Funding and talent soon flowed through the Office of Scientific Research and Development. In addition, the Secretary of the Navy, pursuant to Coast Guard responsibility for merchant vessel safety, established a board of investigation. Every aspect of the design, construction, and operation of the war-built ships was suspect. Potential culprits included loading, severe sea conditions, air and water temperatures, locked-in welding stresses, poor welding, inadequate structural detail, and the steel. Research was initiated immediately on all reasonable aspects of the problem, guided by the best scientific and engineering talent from the War Metallurgy Committee of the National Academy of Sciences. In parallel with the research and development, casualty data were gathered using a tailor-made system. The Coast Guard, responsible for merchant marine safety, directed the technical collection from field inspectors. Every major casualty received a post mortem, including steel tests and analysis at the National Bureau of Standards. The Navy, Coast Guard, Maritime Commission, and American Bureau of Shipping cooperated. Under the aegis of the Navy's General Board, Rear Admiral Harvey F. Johnson, USCG, Engineer-in-Chief of the Coast Guard, was the center of the coordination. There was strong and continuous cooperation with the British Admiralty. Also, the Soviet Union was an interested observer, operating several Liberty ships on the Murmansk run where the low temperatures increased the risk of fracture.[20]

The war and the U-boats did not pause to await the research results. Surely the Germans were applauding the Allied ship structural problems. Interim remedies were sought and came in three major areas. First, shipyard inspections

and training were improved. Second, offending structural elements were modified. And third, riveted "crack arrestors" were built into the hulls.

Liberty ship hatch corners being major crack generators (especially number three hatch), several improvements were made to hatch corners and other structural details. The crack arrestor consisted of a riveted seam. In the all-welded ships, a longitudinal cut was made near the gunwale, and a riveted strap or gunwale angle was fitted to restore structural integrity. Similar devices were devised for the numerous T-2 tankers and other ships. Remedies were applied on the basis of the probable jeopardy. Hospital ships, troop ships, and prisoner-of-war carriers received priority. Different types of modifications were provided for new construction, for ships still being outfitted, and for ships in service. On 1 February 1946 there were 2,212 Liberty ships in United States operation. Of these Liberties, 2,047 had had hatch corners modified and 1,854 had had crack arrestors added.

The modifications greatly reduced the frequency of cracking, and the crack arrestors limited the gravity of the cracks. This proved effective in most cases. The modifications, however, failed to stop crack initiation. One inspector claimed that he would wager every ship operator a drink if he failed to find a crack in the operator's ship. He never lost his bet, and would have become alcoholic if he had not abandoned the wager.[21]

Research soon revealed that the record of cracking casualties and research went back as far as 1884, and involved several types of steel structures, including ships, bridges, and storage tanks. The decks of the famous ocean liner *Leviathan* had cracked, and the cracks were arrested by riveted seams. Examples also included spectacular failures of storage tanks. All fractures shared one element: steel was at low temperature (also increasingly apparent in the ship failures).[22] Fracture statistics for Liberty ships, in port, soon confirmed the cold steel effect. Below 20°F, fracture incidence was thirty or more times that above 70°F.[23]

After 3 years of research, the programs began to reveal underlying problems, and the delays and the expenses of the remedial measures were vindicated. Poor design detail and poor workmanship had contributed by providing crack sources. But, the biggest problem turned out to be the steel itself. The shipbuilding steel of World War II was found to crack at a higher temperature than prewar steel. In fact, some "heats" (batches) of steel cracked at temperatures as high as 90°F. It appeared that short of manganese, the steel makers substituted carbon. While this maintained the strength, it made the steel more brittle and there was no required test for ship steel brittleness. This news hit hard because there was no way of replacing the hull steel of any ship. New steel alloying specifications were to be a solution only for future ships.

When the report of the Navy Board of Investigation came out on 15 July 1946 it bore the ponderous title *To Inquire Into the Design and Methods of Construction of Welded Steel Merchant Vessels*, and it contained 164 pages of technical information.

The happy technological ending to this episode is that the temporary remedies and design changes worked. In March 1944, the casualties had climbed to 138 per month on 2,700 ships in operation, but by January 1946 they were down to 28 on 4,400 ships. A change in the steel alloying specifications essentially eliminated the problem from post-World War II ships. The logistic impact had been grim. The hundreds of ships laid up for repair and modification had a major impact on ship availability during a crucial phase of U-boat attacks. The structural failure problem, while not of the same order as the U-boat attacks, seriously constricted the wartime supply pipeline.[24]

Construction Programs

The main shipbuilding task of the United States was to produce ships, merchant and naval, faster than Allied ships were being sunk. No other Allied nation had the industrial capability to stem the growing shortage of ocean shipping. A major new technology had entered shipbuilding since World War I. It was electric arc welding. It produced stronger joints, resulted in a lighter structure, and required fewer workers than riveting. Welding, however, presented some problems. Weld shrinkage when cooling caused distortion, which made it more difficult to fit subsequent parts into the structure. As an example, the hull of a cruiser under construction could warp so as to raise the bow a foot or so above the building ways as topside welding was completed. Another problem of welding was to train new welders to practice the care required for sound welds and to realize the consequences of defects.

Welding facilitated prefabrication of shipyard subassemblies. It moved work into open areas where workers could function more effectively and speeded final shipway assembly. The large numbers of identical ships permitted more detailed instruction of workers (many of whom had never seen a ship before), including training models and detailed subassembly perspective drawings.[25]

Multiple production permitted the provision of assembly jigs, repeatable procedures, and material-supply planning so the building of ships could be more efficient and rapid. The term "multiple production" was preferred (rather than mass production) because the quantities were much less than in typical mass production of such items as washing machines and automobiles, which involve tens of thousands of identical units. To achieve the required ship-production rates, a large number of shipyards was needed. The size and location of new yards depended partly on availability of labor pools. Thus, the number of identical subassemblies for each yard was measurable in hundreds and the production of ships from each shipway in dozens. One ship launched from each shipway of a shipyard was said to be a "round" of output, this as a unit measure of the shipyard's production. Typically, shipyards produced twenty "rounds" in the World War II program.[26]

When construction programs "took off" in early 1941, the Maritime Commission could count on only fifty-three building ways in nineteen American shipyards.[27] All other facilities were occupied by naval construction, which had had an earlier start and a higher priority. The only solution was new yards designed specifically for multiple production. By the time construction programs reached their peaks, the total U.S. shipways had climbed from 130 to 567 in eighty commercial shipyards. In addition, there were thirty-eight building basins (plus the twenty-nine shipways in the eight naval shipyards).[28] The total employment in the shipyards had risen from about 170,000 to 1,500,000 workers, not including an almost equal number of workers in the supply of components and materials.[29] (See also U.S. Maritime Commission and War Shipping Administration under ADDITIONAL NAVAL ENGINEERING ACTIVITY section of this chapter.)

Both the Navy and Maritime Commission sought to exploit all possible resources. The Maritime program farmed out portions of propulsion systems; for instance, for Liberty ships, 2,710 identical engines could be contracted to machine shops all over the United States. All parts were interchangeable, so the dispersion could pay dividends in flexibility. This, however, required a strong central control-and-scheduling system. In contrast, the Navy decentralized work to prime contractors, especially for naval shipyards. Sections of DEs, landing craft, and PT boats came through the inland waterways and down the Mississippi River as deck cargo on barges, and submarines built in Manitowoc, Wisconsin, floated down the same route on special floating docks.[30]

Dennett K. (Deke) Ela mentions creative examples of efforts to utilize the far corners of industry. Deke was a lieutenant, just out of naval construction post-graduate school at the Massachusetts Institute of Technology. He was assigned as a ship superintendent at the Charleston Navy Yard, which concurrently was building a DE and an LST on a continuous flow. They planned the construction so some subassemblies could be produced by a garage in South Boston, Massachusetts. He also recalls that new cruisers and naval cargo ships, completed at the Bethlehem yard in Quincy, Massachusetts, were moved to Boston Navy Yard for modification with combat-generated alterations before they joined the fleet.[31]

The multiple units offered new possibilities for efficiency through well-planned worker training and on-the-job experience. The benefits were reflected in production-record learning curves. Two measures were used to examine the productivity: time on the shipbuilding ways and man-hours per ship. With successive "rounds" of ships the time decreased. Usually, the tenth round took about one-fifth of the time required for the first round. The overall average time on

the ways for Liberty ships was 28 days, but the Oregon Shipbuilding Corporation managed to sustain an average of 17 days! In fact, Oregon Shipbuilding Corporation launched one ship after 10 days on the ways, and Richmond Yard No. 2, not to be outdone, launched a ship in only 4 days. Obviously, these short assembly times could not be maintained. They were stunts that even delayed other production. On the other hand, they were pretty remarkable demonstrations. The first round of ships required much training and instructional material. Production jigs and other facilities had to be built. Many of the first rounds started before the shipyard was completed. These factors are reflected in the man-hours per ship, which dropped by about two-thirds from the first to the tenth round. This reduction was believed to indicate a 100 percent increase in worker productivity. The efficiency benefit applied, not just to the Liberties, but to all classes of ships where the numbers of identical units required several rounds per shipyards.

The ships constructed under the two major programs, Maritime Commission and Navy, constituted almost one-quarter of all munitions produced by the United States during World War II. The Maritime Commission program came to about $13 billion, and the Navy's to about $18 billion. Including ordnance, the Navy program was about $26 billion.

The Maritime Commission program included 2,708 emergency ships, labeled Liberties. Appropriately, the first Liberty launched was the SS *Patrick Henry*, at Baltimore, Maryland, on 27 September 1941. Also included in the tabulation are 682 LSTs and other military types, 65 for foreign consignment, and 104 vessels of concrete construction. In peacetime, this would have been a major effort. In the wartime competition for resources, it was little short of a miracle. Merchant ship construction was about four times that of World War I, and it was about six times the British merchant-ship program of World War II.[32]

The Naval ship construction program was even larger than the Maritime program in both dollars and man-hours. Mr. Owen H. Oakley, a member of the preliminary design branch in BuShips during World War II, and later its technical director, summarized the situation.

The U.S. entered WWII with a fleet of ships of mixed ages. Half the battleships were of pre WWI vintage. Most were built [or rebuilt] during the treaty years, 1920 to the mid-1930s, to conform with the limitations of the several treaties of that period. When, in the mid-thirties, the treaties were abrogated, the rearming of Germany and the aggression of Japan in the Pacific clearly required a considerable increase in our Navy's strength. The Navy intensified its design and construction program in all major fleet categories. This was a period of development that laid the groundwork for the wartime building programs. The ships laid down in the late 1930s and early 1940s were just beginning to enter the fleet when we became a belligerent in the conflict. The ships constructed in the wartime programs were mostly designs that had been earlier developed in that time frame. Emphasis was on speed of production and to this end, designs had to be standardized and limited in number. In fact, only a few new designs of major fleet elements were carried out during the war. This, of course, did not apply to landing craft, a family of ships and craft virtually invented during WWII.

A full accounting of all of the Navy's ships acquired during the war would be a monumental task. Besides the major combatants there were the auxiliaries: the tenders, fleet oilers, repair ships, transports, cargo ships, and so on, numbering in the thousands. Patrol and mine craft ranging in size from the DE-size 'frigates' to the 110-foot wooden hull sub chasers and the PT boats represent several thousand more. Construction of all of these was in addition to the staggering merchant shipbuilding program. Small wonder, then, that all possible facilities, human skills and sources of components were sought out and put to work. A builder of greenhouses in New York turned to building LCCs (landing craft control), and a metal fabricator in Colorado built sections of DEs and submarines for assembly at the Mare Island Naval Shipyard. Main propulsion units of all descriptions, triple expansion and Uniflow steam engines, direct drive diesels, diesel-electric, and turbine-electric were utilized.

Although the DEs were designed for mass production, and to this end structure was simplified, utilizing a minimum of plate and shape sizes, they were also designed to make use of available manufacturing capacity not normally engaged in shipbuilding. This was particularly true in regard to propulsion machinery.[33]

Four basically different power plants were used in the DEs and this fact was identified in the classed designations: WTG for geared turbine, TE and TEV for turboelectric, DET and GMT for diesel electric, and FMR for geared diesel.

By late 1943, the tide had turned against the U-boats. With the imminent invasion of France and the demands of amphibious operations in the Pacific, the DE building was cut back in favor of landing craft. In all, some 500 DEs were constructed and saw service, mainly in the Atlantic.[34]

The Navy was increased from 400 to 10,000 ships during the period.[35] From 1942 through 1945 the following ships were delivered:[36]

Type of Ship	Number	Displacement Tonnage
Steel combatant naval vessels	1,321	3,363,210
Steel auxiliary naval vessels	175	1,109,449
Landing craft	4,099	
Small self-propelled vessels, of auxiliary and combatant types	3,282	

These totals include the military types tabulated in the Maritime Commission program, and they include the following major construction:[37]

    8 Battleships
   29 Aircraft carriers
   48 Cruisers
  361 Destroyers
  505 DEs
  206 Submarines
  102 Escort aircraft carriers

In addition to all the aforementioned ship construction, the same ship yards, along with the U.S. ship repair yards, managed to maintain, modify, and repair 67,902 ships.[38]

The shipbuilding programs of World War II were remarkable examples of industrial enterprise.

SURFACE WARFARE AND RADAR

Background

Often it is said that the major engagements between naval capital ships ended with the Battle of Jutland. Actually, there were quite a few important surface engagements during World War II.

A number took place at night with little or no air involvement. During World War II, 184 major warships, destroyers, or larger, were lost to ships' gunfire and surface-ship torpedoes, and that included six battleships and three aircraft carriers.[39] But the fleets of World War II were far superior to those of World War I. Aside from World War I ships retained or called back into service, there were better ships in all of the fleets and a new capital ship, the aircraft carrier. Ships were better compartmented, mostly faster, and with many major innovations, not the least of which was superior gunfire control. Power plants were more economical and all burned oil rather than coal.

Major Ship Types

Owen H. Oakley reports that "At the time of our entry into WWII our battleship force consisted of seventeen ships of which ten were commissioned before or during WWI." He continues:

> Five more were commissioned shortly after WWI, the most recent of which was *West Virginia* (BB-48). She entered service in 1923. In the years between the World Wars, these ships were extensively modernized. *North Carolina* and *Washington* (BB-55 and 56) were completed and commissioned in 1941, thus making up the seventeen BBs. Eight of the older battleships were in Pearl Harbor on 7 December 1941. Of these, *Arizona, California, Oklahoma,* and *West Virginia* were sunk and the rest damaged. The damaged ships were rapidly repaired and returned to the fleet. *California* and *West Virginia* were ultimately salvaged, refitted, and served in the Pacific. The *South Dakota* class (BB-57 through 60) and the *Iowa* class (BB-61 through 64) were completed during the war, to participate in hostilities.

Although carriers proved to be the decisive element in engagements with the Japanese fleet and in providing essential air support for amphibious assaults, battleships remained a potent threat to surface ships, and by their very presence influenced the nature of fleet engagements. They were also highly effective in providing shore bombardment support for amphibious operations.

At the time of Pearl Harbor, the U.S. Navy had eighteen heavy and nineteen light cruisers in service. These were a mix of 'treaty' [see Chapter 5] and post-treaty ships. Wartime construction included production of the *Baltimore*-class 8-inch heavy cruisers, *Cleveland*-class 6-inch light cruisers, and *Atlanta*-class 5-inch anti-aircraft cruisers. Additionally, two of six projected 'battle cruisers' with 12-inch guns, *Alaska* and *Guam* (CB-1 and -2) built during the war, were completed in time to participate in the closing battles in the Pacific. During the war, twelve CAs of the *Baltimore* class, thirty CLs of the *Cleveland* class, and eight *Atlanta*-class AA cruisers were completed.

Approximately 200 DDs were in commission at the end of 1941 including over one hundred 'four-pipers' of WWI vintage. The remainder were the raised forecastle DDs that evolved from the *Farragut* class of the early 30s with standard displacements ranging from 1,500 tons for the *Farragut*s to 1,630 for the *Benson* class.

The immediacy of the war in the Atlantic prior to Pearl Harbor and our commitment to supply Britain in the face of the German U-boat threat, led to an accelerated destroyer building program. The design of the 2,100-ton flush-deck *Fletcher* class was the base for this program, although over seventy of the earlier *Benson*s also were constructed. Following closely on the *Fletcher* design came the *Sumner* class. They were the same length but, at 2,200 tons slightly heavier than the DD-445s. These mounted six 5in/38 guns in twin mounts vice the five single 5in/38s on the *Fletcher*s. Cruising range was a problem for destroyers, particularly when engaged in screening fast task forces. In the broad Pacific, refueling had to be accomplished every few days. To reduce the refueling needs of later DD-692s, the *Gearing*-class ships were built with fourteen feet added amidships. This was devoted primarily to tankage for added fuel capacity. By war's end the Navy had about five hundred DDs in service and more in the 'pipeline.'[40]

Superior Radar

A standout difference among the fleets, was the superior radar of the Allied fleets. Since most of the surface combat took place at night, it added importance to the development of radar, a new device in which, at sea, the United States led development and use throughout the entire war. In a broad sense, the Allies had radar, but our major naval surface warfare adversary, the Japanese Navy, did not.

Tizzard Mission

Since the beginning of the war in England, Henry T. Tizzard, a distinguished British defense scientist, maintained that the cause of British interests would be advanced if American production capabilities were applied to many of their secret military devices. He proposed offering the United States access to recent British technical developments. Churchill sent an *aide-memoire* to Roosevelt advocating the proposal, and, supported by his top military advisors, Roosevelt accepted the concept. The final agreement called for an open exchange on all technical matters of interest to either nation. This remarkable agreement was signed by the British on 25 July 1940. The British technical mission, subsequently called the Tizzard Mission, arrived in the United States in September 1940. After a short month of testing the water, it was clear that both sides had much to offer the other, and the intended full disclosure on both sides ensued. One of the many benefits from this exchange was the availability of the newly developed British multiple cavity magnetron tubes, which thereafter became the foundation of our microwave radar.[41]

Search Radar

The demand for radar grew as soon as the Naval Research Laboratory's first experimental ship installation, the 200 mc. XAF was tested in the USS *New York*. Its merits were very apparent. As early as 1938, this experimental unit had detected aircraft and taken bearings at a 100-mile range.[42] In 1939 and 1940, RCA received contracts to manufacture the experimental XAF as the CXAM, which was fitted on twenty ships before Pearl Harbor. The next step was the XAR, which was lighter in weight but also operated on 200 mc. This set became operational as the SC and was widely used during World War II. When the United States entered World War II, there were only the twenty ship-mounted CXAM installations plus a couple of experimental installations; but, production of the SC units was growing, and by December 1942, they were being produced at the rate of fourteen per week.[43]

Development continued with efforts focused on packing more power into the system, while at the same time employing higher frequencies to gain better resolution. During 1941, radar had advanced additional strides. One step was the development of an airborne microwave radar set, the ASV, for aircraft detection of surface vessels. This had the potential of vastly extending the range at which it was possible to locate enemy

ships. The advent of radar, however useful, also posed a problem of target identification, especially in the dark or fog. A positive identification had to be provided for all friendly planes of the Allies. British research served as a basis for American development of identification equipment for both ships and aircraft. With this equipment the ships' radar automatically interrogated aircraft contacted and the aircraft transponders would return coded signals. A hostile contact returned no coded signal. The system became known as IFF (identification friend or foe).[44]

Radar Controlled Gunfire

The first radar gun-control unit had resulted from combining the research work of the Naval Research Laboratory and Bell Telephone Laboratories. In 1940, BuShips ordered ten production units to be manufactured by the Western Electric Company, and the first was placed in the USS *Wichita* (CA-45) in July 1941. It was designated the FA ("F" for fire control). Other units were installed on one heavy and eight light cruisers. They proved effective also for search and detection out to the design-range of 10 miles.

The development of the so-called "strapped" magnetron (performance-enhancing busbars in the cavity region) by the British offered high power at higher frequencies. This allowed the United States to develop the 700 mc. Model FC for surface targets and FD for air targets. The two models were much superior to the FA. The FC (later designated Mark 3) was put into production as a main battery fire control radar for battleships and cruisers, and twenty-seven were installed by the end of 1941. The FD (later labeled Mark 4) used lobe switching to give more accurate elevation angles, and by the spring of 1944, 600 units had been installed in the dual-purpose batteries of battleships, cruisers, and destroyers. The value of the FD-equipped Mark 37 gun director system was demonstrated by the *South Dakota* (BB-57), which on 16 October 1942 claimed thirty-eight out of thirty-eight attacking planes.[45]

In early 1944, the newer Mark 12 radar replaced the FD in fleet installations with the Mark 37 director systems, with the Mark 22 add-on helping to home on low-flying planes. The development rate of the wartime equipment was phenomenal. Often there was only a two-year interval spanning development, production, and fleet application; and the obsolescence interval was also about two years. Even so, heavy-machine gun control was not significantly aided by radar during the period.[46]

Japanese Radar

In the early months of the war, American forces found no evidence of Japanese radar use. Finally, in August 1942, Marines landing on Guadalcanal found a shore-based search radar. It was a Japanese Mark I Mod 1 with a huge antenna, similar to our XAF in 1938. The set was promptly crated and shipped back to the United States and carefully examined. Lt. Ralph Clark of the Bureau of Aeronautics reported it was built of Japanese copies of standard U.S. commercial parts, and, in his judgement, the unit reflected at least a two-year lag behind American radar technology.[47]

By September 1942, a response to the threat had been developed and NRL Countermeasure Project #1, Cast Mike #1, got underway. This team entered the Pacific arena equipped with radar intercept equipment and jammers. They were all ready for work, but it was many months before they had much to work on.[48]

In March 1942, the first Japanese radar, a Mark II Mod 1, was placed aboard the battleship *Ise* for test and evaluation. Later, in the spring of 1942, a Mark II Mod 2 went to sea for test on the battleship *Hyuga*. These radars were for search and main battery fire control. There were no systems at that time for anti-aircraft gunnery or searchlight control.[49] By October 1944, the Japanese had fitted sixty Mark II Mod 2 radars on their ships. They operated at 3,000 MHz, but with only 2 kilowatts of power they were not very effective.[50]

Radar in Battle

The radar equipment in United States warships entering the Pacific war in early 1942 has been described. Not all ships had radar and not all of the sets were equal to the tasks faced. The Japanese had no shipborne radar, but they earned a reputation for skillful night fighting. They had excellent optical equipment, including powerful, mounted, night binoculars with which they frequently spotted our ships before being detected by our radar.[51] The following descriptions of two Pacific surface warfare engagements are selected to chronicle the introduction of radar in the United States and later in the Japanese fleet.

On the night of 9 August 1942, during the Marine landings on Guadalcanal, the destroyers *Blue* (DD-387) and *Talbot* (DD-390) of the surface support force were on picket duty, equipped with SC radar with a range of at least 10 miles. They were on either side of Savo Island, some dozen miles to the northwest of the rest of the surface support force of six destroyers and five cruisers, which was deployed closer to the partially unloaded transports. The pickets were right in the path of an oncoming Japanese surface attack force, but their radar detected only two aircraft, misidentified as friendly. Actually, the aircraft were reconnaissance float planes of the Japanese force, efficiently scouting the American ship deployment. The Japanese ships sighted the *Blue* and adjusted course to avoid her. Seven Japanese cruisers and the destroyers sailed by, some as close as 14,000 yards, and were not detected by the *Blue*. The Japanese float planes then illuminated the Allied fleet with flares, so any advantage of the inefficient U.S. radar was further offset, and the Japanese targeted our ships, silhouetted by their flares. Three U.S. cruisers were sunk by gunfire, and the Australian *Canberra* was sunk by gunfire and a torpedo. The cruiser USS *Chicago* took a torpedo and three destroyers were damaged by gunfire. The Japanese force then retired without any damage, but neglected the vulnerable transports. The Battle of Savo Island has been marked as a successful defense of the landing troops, who were not molested; but, for the U.S. Navy, it was a tactical and technical disaster.[52]

The chronicle of radar in Pacific surface action had turned full circle by October 1944. In the Battle of Surigao Strait, an imposing Japanese force of two battleships, four cruisers, and eight destroyers encountered an even more powerful U.S. surface force of five battleships, eight cruisers, twenty destroyers, and thirty PT boats. It was the 24th of December 1944 and the enemy sought to disrupt the landings in Leyte Gulf, approaching through Surigao Strait to the south. By this time, some of the Japanese ships were equipped with their Mark II Mod 2 radar. It operated at 3,000 MHz, and only 2 kilowatts of power, so it was not very effective. The U.S. force, on the other hand, was equipped with highly effective search and fire control radars. In addition, the U.S. fleet had improved its night fighting tactics immensely over the preceding 2 years.

The lead Japanese force stood north into Surigao Strait, seemingly unaware of the peril into which they were steaming. The strait was lined with torpedo launchers: first thirty PT boats, and then U.S. destroyers in divisions to port and starboard. The northern end of the strait was closed by two lines of cruisers and finally a line of six battleships. The approach of the Japanese was detected by radar at 36,000 yards and it was signaled by the PT boats as they launched their torpedoes. All firing was by radar; there were neither searchlights nor star shells. The groups of destroyers made their attacks with radar-controlled torpedo launches. First, the battleship *Fuso* took several hits, commenced to burn, and later broke in two. The night became brighter and brighter as the Japanese ships were lighted up by the fires from the torpedo hits. The battleship *Yamashiro* was hit by torpedoes, as were several destroyers, two sinking. The *Yamashiro* then came under the fire of the heavy guns of the USS *California*, USS *Tennessee*, and USS *West Virginia*, which were firing from a range of 22,800 yards into a pitch black night, using the new Mark 8 fire control radar. The other three U.S. battleships could only partially participate, because, at the great range, their older fire control radar could not distinguish the targets. The cruisers joined in the shooting and the *Yamashiro* capsized and sank. Of the lead force of the attacking fleet, only the destroyer *Shigure* and the damaged cruiser *Mogami* survived. The second section of the attacking force got far enough into Surigao Strait to have the cruiser *Abukuma* torpedoed, and then they retreated. The *Mogami* and the *Abukuma* fell to aircraft next day.[53] The only U.S. casualty, the USS *Albert W. Grant* (DD-649), was badly damaged when she was caught in the crossfire, but, the Japanese losses were staggering: two battleships and three destroyers sunk, one cruiser crippled and one cruiser damaged in a collision.[54]

The battle had been fought entirely by radar. The only illumination came from the dying Japanese ships. The gunfire was at ranges that could be considered long for daytime battle. Radar surface gunnery had come of age in history's last surface fleet engagement.

AIR WARFARE

Air warfare includes air-to-air combat for fleet defense, as well as air attack against enemy ships and installations. As World War II progressed, it became evident that this would be the way of future naval operations. There probably would be few Jutland-type slugging matches among battleships. Aircraft carriers had become the capital ships of the fleet. The naval fighters and torpedo bombers with which the United States entered the war were inferior in a number of respects to their Japanese counterparts. However, there ensued a period of development of American propeller-driven aircraft, which by war's end eliminated most of the Japanese technical advantage. In addition, our fighter pilots developed successful tactics for dealing with the more maneuverable Japanese Mitsubishi A6M Zeros.

Aircraft Carriers
Owen Oakley reports:

The design of the *Essex* class of carriers (CV-9 *et al.*) had been completed, and construction of this class was underway. They were basically an evolution from two previous classes, and larger, 872 feet long. The first of the class entered the fleet in 1943, and in all, twenty-three *Essex*-class carriers were constructed; they formed the backbone of the task forces in the Pacific for the rest of the war.

All of these ships could pass through the Panama Canal, which was important because most of the shipbuilding capability existed on the East Coast and, as it turned out, most of the carriers wound up being deployed in the Pacific.

For all except *Lexington* and *Saratoga* the hangar deck was the strength deck. For all other carriers, especially the escort carriers, the flight deck strength had become marginal by 1945 to handle the heavier, faster planes coming into service.

The naval war in the Pacific was dominated by the carriers. Six of our seven carriers were committed to the Pacific early in the conflict; only *Ranger* remained in the Atlantic. Fortunately none was in Pearl Harbor on 7 December 1941. By the end of the war only *Enterprise* (CV-6) and *Saratoga* (CV-3), of the original seven, remained afloat, but their potent presence held the line until the new *Essex*-class ships entered the fray in 1943. The critical role of the carriers was evident early in the war in the Pacific in which air strikes by the opposing forces largely dictated the outcome.[55]

Fighter Control

The merits of radar for fighter control became apparent early in the war. In the major battles of the Coral Sea and Midway, the CXAM-1 radar detected enemy aircraft as far away as 76 miles, and in both battles, fighters were vectored to intercept them. Similar radar operations occurred in the other two great carrier battles, the Battle of Eastern Solomons and the Battle of the Santa Cruz Islands. In all four battles, however, and throughout much of the war, the capability of the intercept tactics was limited by the lack of adequate radio-communication circuits to meet the demands of vectoring multiple fighter groups.[56]

Assault Drones

These unmanned craft might well be called radio-directed bombs or humanitarian-style kamikazes. Whatever the name, the concept had origins during World War I. The early aim of the "drone" project was to provide targets for anti-aircraft training. In the late thirties, successful radio controls were developed. It was possible to take off, fly, and land the drone craft using control stations either on the ground or in control planes.

In May 1942, the drones were tested for a new role. They demonstrated that they could be used successfully to impact moving targets, and, in March 1943, it was recommended that they be brought to operational status. Admiral E. J. King directed that a plan be prepared to use the drones as guided missiles in combat, and insisted that the project be made large enough to have a significant impact when first introduced in combat. The plan included 10,000 Naval personnel, including 1,000 aviators, and cost about $235 million (1942 dollars). The size of the plan went up and down as it competed with the ongoing wartime production demands.

Admiral King recognized that this project would have an impact on other fleet priorities, so in September 1943, Captain Oscar Smith was dispatched to Headquarters, Pacific Fleet. Captain Smith's purpose was to discuss this still very secret project with Fleet Admiral Chester W. Nimitz. Admiral Nimitz felt it would be unwise to upset prevailing successful operations by allocating operating forces to introduce an untried weapon. Thus, under the circumstances, the project was retrenched to a developmental status, but the technology was completed and ready for other uses.[57]

Rockets

The use of rockets as an aircraft weapon had been suggested to the Navy during World War I by Dr. Robert Goddard, the rocket pioneer, who offered some patents, but got no response. Early in World War II, years after Goddard's original suggestion, the Navy moved to establish a rocket program. The Office of Scientific Research and Development had been set up to sponsor and coordinate research outside the Federal Laboratories. With its help, California Institute of Technology (CIT) was named contractor in September 1941. With incredible speed, CIT established its rocketry program, and a first test missile was developed, fabricated, and test fired at Aberdeen, Maryland, by July 1942. The rocket developed was a forward-fired aircraft-to-ground weapon. Leaning on many related developments, CIT was able to establish regular production lines and produce over 100,000 rounds in less than 1 year from the initial request.[58]

The Atomic Bomb

On 25 June 1942, President Roosevelt and Prime Minister Churchill agreed to a combined U.S.-British effort on an atom bomb.[59] This agreement added adrenaline to the project.

Despite the Navy's early and independent nuclear research energy program dating back to 1939, the Navy's association with the atomic bomb was in the form of technical support rather than responsibility. Navy support started in early 1943 with the selection of Captain William S. (Deake) Parsons to be deputy to Dr. Robert J. Oppenheimer at the secret Los Alamos Laboratory in New Mexico. Here, Parsons was involved in the early efforts at bomb design, and assisted with his engineering knowledge and his contacts with Navy laboratories. He collaborated in the development of the high explosive "implosion" technique to squeeze the uranium into a "critical" fissioning mass, assisting in the procurement of the implosion explosives for the Fat Man model and in coordinating the manufacture (by the boiler experts of Babcock and Wilcox) of an adequate casing to contain the force of implosion. Later, he worked out the arrangements for supporting projects at the Naval Ordnance Test Station in Inyokern, California, and with the Navy Salton Sea test range in Southern California for Army Air Corps experimental drop testing. Finally, it was Captain Parsons who rode the *Enola Gay* to escort the Little Boy bomb to Hiroshima. He arranged to arm the plutonium gun-weapon after the B-29 was airborne, to avoid a low-order but contaminating detonation in event of crash on take-off. He then witnessed the attack, and saw the complicated and dreadful weapon he had helped to create perform as intended to terminate the war.[60]

AIR DEFENSE

Air attack was by far the greatest threat to the naval combatant ships and craft during World War II. The first defense of the fleet depended on the success of strikes on the source: enemy carriers and airfields. The second line of defense was interception of enemy aircraft by friendly fighters. In the end, however, many attacking aircraft penetrated the first two lines of defense, so all fleet units had to have a self-defense capability. During World War II, this defense consisted almost totally of anti-aircraft (AA) gunfire.

Guns

The Bureau of Ordnance (BuOrd), established in 1842, exerted its powers to the limits during World War II keeping the fleets and our allies supplied with guns, fire control equipment, and munitions. This material was produced within BuOrd's own establishments and vastly expanded under wartime production contracts with American industry.

FIGURE 7-1—Typical 5" 38 caliber single mount.

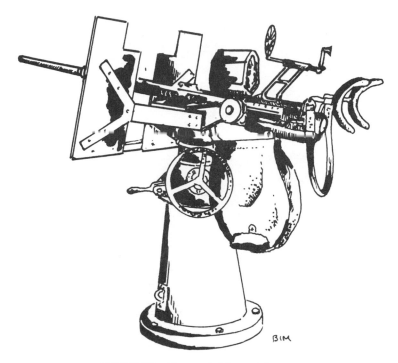

FIGURE 7-2—20mm pedestal mounted gun.

Increasingly, the backbone of fleet air defense, after its introduction in 1934, became the 5in/38 caliber dual-purpose gun. It was dependable because it had been completely debugged through use. Other air defense was provided by the 1.1-inch automatic cannon and the .50- and .30-caliber machine guns. The 1.1-inch gun was not totally reliable and the machine guns provided inadequate AA against modern aircraft.[61]

New light rapid-fire guns were needed to fill the gap below the 5in/38. A Navy Department Anti-aircraft Defense Board was appointed 9 August 1940 to study the problem and recommend remedial measures. The board reported in December 1940 that lack of adequate close-range AA defense was the most serious weakness in the Navy's readiness for war, and the implementation of a solution started with a survey of existing internationally available guns. The 20mm Swiss Oerlikon was selected as the lighter of perhaps two guns. The British were already using the Oerlikon with great success. Initially, there were legal problems with manufacturing the gun in the United States for export to Britain and not using it in our Navy. This was especially distressing because the British were already using it, and standardization of parts and ammunition was an important goal. Soon, the exigencies of war prevailed, American production commenced in the summer of 1941, and the U.S. Navy had a fine new heavy machine gun.[62]

For the heavier gun, several candidates were considered and the Bofors 40mm gun was selected. This gun had an excellent reputation. It was basically a Krupp design, manufactured in Sweden (and used by both sides). In 1939, the York Safe and Lock Company had been exploring the possibility of a licensing agreement. It was a close call. The working model shipped to the United States had to be diverted via Finland because Norway was overrun by the Germans. In spite of the fine reputation of the gun, the projectile fuses were unsatisfactory. Bofors and the British both proposed fixes. The British fuse did not lend itself to mass production, but with some trepidation it was chosen, and mass pro-

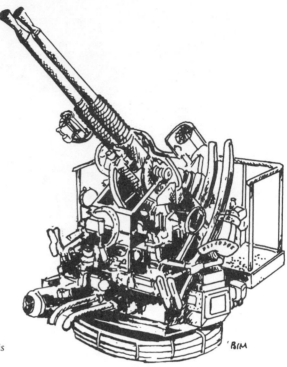

FIGURE 7-3—40mm twin anti-aircraft gun mount. This
gun was also installed in quad mounts.

duction commenced. At this point, R. L.
Graumann of the Naval Ordnance Laboratory
devised a new fuse, so superior that our Army,
Navy, and the Royal Navy accepted it immediately. Production was stopped and the new
fuse started through the production lines. It was
called the Mark 27 and is estimated to have
saved much grief and $250 million during the
war. Deliveries of the 40mm gun commenced in
1942.[63]

The 20mm fired 450 rounds per minute, the
40mm 150 rounds per barrel per minute, and
gun crews could be trained to load and fire the
5in/38 at up to 15 rounds per minute. All three
guns fired explosive projectiles. Proximity-fuses
would be fitted for 5-inch projectiles when they
became available.

Doctrine for opening fire varied over time but
usually the 5in/38s opened fire as soon as approaching enemy air targets could be tracked (as
far as 10,000 to 12,000 yards). "Open-fire" range
was, however, greater than "effective" range at

which an acceptable kill rate can be expected.
Thus, the procedure of early open fire was used
to get the guns operating and trained so that
when the enemy aircraft reached the effective
range, the whole system would be focused actively on the target. Similar doctrines applied to
the use of the 40 and 20mm guns. As the enemy
aircraft approached, the 40s would open up at
around 3,000 yards. Finally at 1,500 yards the
20mms opened fire. Attack on American ships
was tough duty for Japanese aviators. They could
expect defensive fire as far away as 5 to 6 miles
when the 5in/38s opened up. The intensity of
fire would increase when the 40mms commenced,
and finally, the airspace would be saturated with
projectiles when the 20mms let go.[64]

Both 20 and 40mm guns proved to be excellent selections. The 40mm even guns proved
very useful during the kamikaze attacks of 1944
and 1945. The close-in protection of the 40mm
guns was estimated to account for 50% of the
kills. There was a big demand for the 40mm as

40-MM ASSEMBLIES

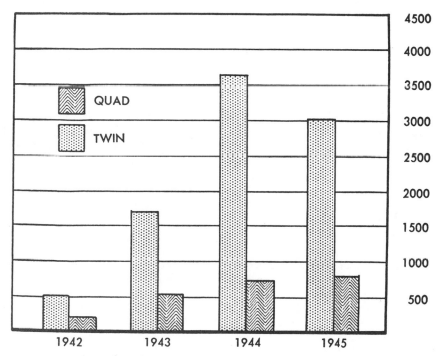

FIGURE 7-4—40mm gun assembly production, 1942 through 1945.

it became available, and, in time, there was a strong trend to replace the 20mm with 40mm. However, the 20mm had been the lead gun from December 1941 to September 1944 when it accounted for 32% of the kills. The 20mm survived because it was lighter and easier to install on shipboard, it could be brought into action faster, and it could operate without ship's power.

The combined effect of more guns, more ships, and more rapid fire was calculated to increase the total fleet anti-aircraft fire power from 411 to 4,479 tons of projectiles in a 15-second interval.[65]

Gunfire Control

As World War II approached, control of the anti-aircraft batteries was further improved with, first, the Mark 33 and, later, the Mark 37 director for 5in/25 and 5in/38 guns. The stabilization system was improved, transmission of target bearing and range measurements to computers became fully automated, and gunmounts became electrically or hydraulically powered and automatically controlled by signals from an electromechanical gunfire computer. This type of gunfire direction was good, except for two important weaknesses. First was the difficulty of setting mechanical time fuses accurately so as to detonate the shells as they passed near the target,[66] and second was the degradation with poor visibility, especially at night. Once the target was acquired and tracked optically, the Mark 33 or Mark 37 gun director did the rest of the aiming. Shortly before World War II they were improved by the addition of radar. This solved the problem of firing in low visibility and increasingly gave a more accurate range measurement than could be obtained optically.

The main problem with the Mark 33 director was its weight. The Mark 33 weighed in at 20,000 pounds and had to be mounted so high on the ship that it was often called "apple on a stick." Consequent ship stability and mast vibration problems, however, were not prohibitive and many units remained in use until late in the war.[67]

In 1936, development had started on the Mark 37, a more reliable and accurate director. While heavier than the Mark 33, it presented less of a ship stability problem because the heavy computer and stable elements were below decks. All major combatant ships used the Mark 33 or Mark 37 systems to control the 5in/38 guns. The number of these directors ranged from four on the battleships to one on destroyers and some auxiliaries. Both directors proved effective, although at close range, accuracy and target selection fell off unacceptably.[68]

Procurement of the new 20mm Oerlikon and 40mm Bofors anti-aircraft machine guns presented a new problem. Gun directors were not a part of the procurement package and they were needed before the guns entered the fleet in 1941 and 1942. The first-developed director, the Mark 44, was too difficult to manufacture and only eighty-five were produced. A hiatus prevailed during July 1941 when the new gunsight invented by Dr. Stark Draper was under evaluation. It involved a small, gyroscopically-precessed sight that generated lead angles by measuring the angular motion of the gun as the target was tracked.[69] After some development, it proved effective for the 20mm guns, which were additionally aimed by the use of tracer bullets. The Draper sight was labeled the Mark 14 and went into service in the autumn of 1942.

The Draper sight was incorporated in the Mark 51 gun director, a simple yet highly effective handlebar-manipulated director for 40mm guns. The Mark 51 also could be hooked up as an alternate director for the 3-inch and 5-inch dual-purpose guns for close-in firing.

Wartime development of the Draper system led to the Mark 52 director, built around the Mark 15 gunsight, an improved version of the original Mark 14 Draper sight. The Mark 52 coupled range-only radar with optical tracking, for the 3-inch and 5-inch guns. Mark 52 deliveries started in the spring of 1944.

Development continued, and toward the end of World War II, two new gun directors, the Mark 57 and Mark 63 came on the scene. Their capabilities spanned the ballistics of the 40mm, the 3-inch, and 5-inch guns. Their radar input provided for "blind" firing of the 40mm guns and divided firing for dual-purpose mounts.

The VT Proximity Fuses

In December 1944, a U.S. Coast Guard officer shared a compartment on a train to London with two British Army ratings. They were attached to an anti-aircraft battery engaged in shooting down V-1 missiles to protect London. They thanked the Yank for new ammunition they recently had received from the United States, explaining that for the last month they had been blasting away at the V-1s, throwing up everything they could, but often failing to stop the V-1s. With the new ammunition, two or three rounds would destroy the missiles. The trio on the train did not know it, but the British gunners were now using proximity-fused shells in an ideal application.[70]

The proximity fuses had been in use for 2 years, but only at sea. The secret of their design was considered so crucial that they were banned for use over land, for fear that a dud might lead to enemy facsimiles or countermeasures. (The security on the development and production of these fuses was so tight that the terms "influence" or "proximity" were classified, thus the name variable-time (VT) fuse.) In 1944, however, the V-1 threat to London was considered to transcend the embargo. The subsequent statistics against the V-1s over an 80-day period showed kill percentage rise from 24 to 79 with the use of proximity fuses.

Matching target ranges with the correct time settings for projectile fuses had always been a most inaccurate part of AA gunnery. A top priority scientific goal was stated to be " . . . to detonate the projectile at a moment when the shell fragments would embrace the target." In August 1940, a new section and committee were established by the National Defense Research Committee (NDRC) to tackle this problem. The committee was chaired by Dr. Merle A. Tuve of the

Carnegie Institution of Washington, D.C. The problem it accepted was difficult because the fusing device had to withstand 20,000 "g" (the acceleration force of gravity) produced by the linear acceleration when fired from a 5-inch gun, as well as a centrifugal acceleration to 500 rps of projectile rotation. Moreover, the lethal burst range of the 5-inch shell (about a 70-foot radius from the target) had to be triggered.[71]

After discarding other possible approaches, a tiny radar was tried, and in January 1942, only 1½ years from problem assignment date, test firings were performed. In test firings of 5in/38 anti-aircraft projectiles, 52 percent of the projectiles detonated as they approached seawater at the end of a 5-mile trajectory.[72] As the program evolved, organizational control was needed and The Johns Hopkins University assumed management. In August 1942, test firings were conducted from the *Cleveland* (CL-55) on Chesapeake Bay. Several days of planned testing collapsed into just a part of a day because all three available target drones were destroyed by four rounds of the new ammunition.[73]

Production of the minute electronic tubes for the radar began promptly, and by October 1942, they were being turned out at the rate of 500 per day. By the end of 1944, this number had risen to 40,000 per day. Only one company, Sylvania, met both the quality standards and mass-production quotas for tubes. On the other hand, some eighty-seven companies were doing the assembly in 110 plants. In all, some 22 million fuses were manufactured, and as experience was gained, the cost dropped from $732 to $18 per unit.[74]

BuOrd applied proper production quality control, devising a realistic but nondestructive test applicable to sample rounds from production lots. The method used during research was continued into production.[75] Mr. Arne D. Yensen, formerly with the Naval Ordnance Laboratory, described the tests on three plowed fields leased from a monastery at Newtown Neck, Maryland, on the Potomac River.

> A battery of old 5-inch guns was aimed straight up. At beginning of the day's tests a couple of dummy shells would be fired to check the prevailing wind drift. Then the test shells were fired a few at a time. The shells would rise to the apogee of their trajec-

tory and then, gyroscopically held vertically, would drop base first into the plowed fields. Spotters in shacks with 10-inch reinforced concrete roofs would listen and watch for the impact at the predicted time. At each pause in the firing, shells were dug up to be shipped back to Eastman Kodak or other manufacturer for a post mortem of fuse performance.[76]

The triggering radius of the fuse was 70 feet and (depending on target size) effectively made an aircraft target up to over one hundred times as large as a contact fuse profile. More importantly, destructive air bursts (close enough to the target) no longer depended on time fuses. Time fusing, until then the only system for air bursts, was inescapably inaccurate and detonated most AA shells too soon or too late. With VT fuses, an AA shell had only to be fired to pass close enough; the VT fuse did the rest. Its little radar sensed proximity to the target and detonated the shell at the right instant for a kill. On 5 January 1943, the *Helena* (CL-50) "splashed" a Japanese plane with two salvos in the first operational use of the VT fused shell. Subsequently, a task group in the Pacific knocked out 91 of 130 enemy attackers using the VT fused shells, which proved to be three to four times more effective than time-fused shells and up to fifty times more effective than contact-fused projectiles.

The research, development, design, and production of the proximity fuse was one of the great examples of technological success in warfare. Following the lifting of the use-over-land restriction, the shells were next used in the defense of Antwerp against the V-1 bombs, and finally by Army artillery for deadly air bursts against German infantry during the Battle of the Bulge. The shells detonating above the ground made fox holes and slit trenches virtually useless for protection and damaged the morale of the German soldiers. General Patton probably summed it up best when he wrote, "The new shell with the funny fuse is devastating. . . . "[77]

Air Defense Summary

By the time the Japanese surrendered, every ship in the American fleet bristled with anti-aircraft guns. Further, to augment the air defense of the fast task forces, nine *Cleveland*-class light cruisers under construction were completed as light carriers: the *Independence* class (CVLs-22 to 30). These ships were fast enough to keep up with the large carriers, and they were used to provide fighter protection for the large carriers while the air groups of the latter were off attacking the enemy. Thus, air defense was immeasurably better than at the beginning of the war.[78]

It is impossible to put a number on the combined anti-aircraft impact of the improvements on each ship. The increase in caliber and quantity of fire power, improved gunfire control, enhanced air search, radar-directed gunfire, and the use of the proximity fuse varied with prevailing threats. Whatever the improvement, it was clearly very high when compared to 1941.

By the end of the war, problems with target designation and acquisition remained, but the fleet air defense against the best conventional aircraft had reached the point that air attacks were costing the attackers more than the U.S. defenders.

However, the game of measure, countermeasure, and new measure played on. The Germans first used guided bombs and missiles in 1943, and the Japanese human guided missiles, kamikazes, in 1945. A German guided bomb, the FX 1400 with a 600-pound explosive charge, hit the *Savannah* (CL-42) on 11 September 1943. It penetrated turret number 1, detonated in the lower barbette, and blew out the bottom. (The resultant flooding extinguished magazine fires almost immediately.)[79] In 1945, the Japanese kamikaze attacks commenced in substantial numbers. The carriers were the primary targets of the attacks. Flight decks and hangar sides of U.S. carriers were lightly constructed and highly vulnerable to kamikazes or bombs. (The *Midway*-class carriers with 3½-inch armored flight decks and heavy special-treatment steel hangar and protective decks for bomb protection, deployed too late in 1945 to see action.) In part because of this vulnerability of carriers, kamikaze attacks were disastrous. Of 13,000 American sailors killed in 1945, three quarters were killed by kamikazes.[80]

Coming over the air warfare horizon in 1945 were jet aircraft, which would introduce new levels of attack speed. Thus, as World War II ended, the technological contest continued.

ELECTRONIC WARFARE

Electronic Countermeasures (ECM)

Soon after American entry into the war, radar jamming was introduced by the United States in the Pacific. Similar jamming was already occurring in the European theater. New methods of electronic warfare also were invoked. In February 1942, the Harvard Radio Research Laboratory was established to research, develop, and ultimately manufacture a variety of countermeasures. One of the products of the laboratory was an improved Chaff, or Window (already in use by the British). Chaff consisted of thousands of small strips of aluminum foil cut to radar wavelength. Dropped from aircraft, their reflections cluttered enemy radar to conceal attacking ships and aircraft. Chaff, for example, was used to blind the German radars during the Normandy invasion.[81]

Radio Direction Finding

World War I added a new element to reconnaissance when aircraft came into use along with balloons and blimps. In World War II, new "eyes in the sky" radar and improved radio direction finders (RDF) were added. RDFs were used long before the United States entered World War II.[82] One of the primary uses was to locate U-boats by signal-triangulation as the U-boats regularly broadcast reports to their headquarters. Receiving stations on both sides of the Atlantic recorded and targeted the U-boat signals. The bearing data were plotted daily and issued to the fleet and convoy escorts. As the war progressed, the convoy escorts themselves were fitted with effective radio direction finders so they could obtain close-range bearings in the vicinity of U-boat transmissions.[83]

Cryptography

Ingenious electromechanical engineering provided the U.S. Navy and Army with secure means for encipherment to protect radio messages from being read by our adversaries.

Based on principles that he evolved early in a brilliant career of Army cryptanalysis, Colonel William Friedman developed a series of alphabetic rotors, which were the heart of an electromechanical device that suitably scrambled any messages typed into it. These scrambled messages could not be deciphered without both the machine and knowledge of the initial rotor settings used. The device was widely employed during the war by both the U.S. Army and Navy to securely encrypt classified messages for radio transmissions. The Navy called it the electrical coding machine or "ECM" (actually, it enciphered), and the Army called it the Sigaba.[84] Widespread use was also made of variants of a mechanical ciphering machine developed by the Swedish inventor, Boris Hagelin. This was used by both Allied and German forces when its compact (cigar box) size was desirable and its less secure systems were acceptable.[85]

Cryptanalysis

With the development of radio communications, the major navies of the world moved rapidly to devise means of intercepting and interpreting enemy radio transmissions. By World War II, it was a natural development to site mobile intercept units aboard ships for this purpose. Major ships were often used for such intercept support, and carried specialized electronic equipment to execute these duties. The effort invested in such intelligence gathering yielded a huge payoff during the war, and the necessary supporting tasks were carefully and diligently executed.

For several years prior to World War II, the United States had an important advantage over the Japanese. Colonel Friedman and his cryptanalysts had broken the code of the Japanese "Purple" machine that encrypted their diplomatic messages, and U.S. Navy cryptanalysts had broken Japanese naval ciphers.[86] By 1943, they also had broken part of the Japanese Army cipher. The collaboration of skilled cryptanalysts with electromechanical engineers produced suitable devices for the job. In the successful attack on the Japanese "Purple" encryption machine, a team led by Colonel Friedman used the assistance of Washington Naval Gun Factory technicians to build an analog of the Japanese device to facilitate the cryptanalysis.[87]

In May 1942, deciphered messages revealed that the Japanese planned to seize Port Moresby, and Admiral Nimitz was able to send an intercepting task force. Thus, it was no coincidence that the *Yorktown* and *Lexington* were able to engage the Japanese in the Battle of the Coral Sea. Soon after, COMINT (communications intelligence) revealed a Japanese intent to invade Midway. Again, the fleet was deployed to meet the threat and the Battle of Midway ensued. This battle, one of the greatest naval engagements in our history, would never have occurred without COMINT. COMINT's other services included securing ship-by-ship records of additions to and losses from the Japanese naval order of battle. These were obtained so promptly by COMINT, that the United States possessed a continuously updated inventory of the enemy fleet. Finally, throughout the Pacific island campaigns, COMINT repeatedly indicated where the Japanese had deployed their air, sea, and land strength in the expectation of attack. Thus, our attacks could be planned for spots of least resistance.[88]

American forces, as well as the British, benefited tremendously from the latter's penetration of the Enigma machine ciphers used by all the German armed forces. Exploitation was based on copies of Enigma originally produced by the Poles, prewar. Additionally and increasingly, use had to be made by the Poles of linked Enigmas to beat the Germans' increasingly varied initial settings of their machines. In time, a series of early computers were developed by the British for this purpose. The famous computer mathematician, Allen Turing, figured significantly in this work.[89]

Of equal importance to cryptanalysis was the continuous sharing and synthesis of intelligence from all sources. As skills increased and coordination improved, the Allies were able increasingly to fill in the intelligence mosaic, with pieces from reconnaissance, prisoners of war, espionage, captured equipment, technological analysis, and, of course, COMINT.

During World War II the cost of COMINT ran about one-half billion dollars per year. However, the ranking officers felt it was probably the most cost-effective system in the armed forces. Vice Admiral Lockwood estimated that the United States submarines sank 30 percent more Japanese shipping because of COMINT. Admiral Chester Nimitz believed that its worth in the Pacific was equal to that of another whole fleet.

In Europe, General Thomas T. Handy claimed that it shortened the war by one whole year.[90]

ANTI-SUBMARINE WARFARE (ASW)

Submarine Threat in the Pacific

The Japanese entered the war with seventy-five seagoing submarines and thirty or more midgets. Almost from the beginning this submarine fleet averaged about ten Allied ship sinkings a month in the Pacific and Far East, but the rate soon dropped. By 1943, Japanese submarine attack was limited to targets of opportunity because a substantial number of their submarines were diverted to acting as transports.

The Japanese submarines had trouble evading the American sonar, and it often appeared that they did not know they were being attacked. Twenty-two Japanese submarines were destroyed in 1944, but with new construction, the Japanese Navy was able to maintain their total above seventy boats. However, in 6 months in 1945, twenty-six Japanese submarines were sunk. This depleted their fleet by war's end to forty-three submarines, most of them tied up.[91]

Japanese submarines posed a serious threat but nowhere near as serious as their surface ship and naval air operations.

Submarine Threat in the Atlantic

The initial absence of U-boat activity in the Atlantic was explained in part by Hitler's complete surprise by Pearl Harbor. He had been trying to get the Japanese to strike at Russia, not the United States. None of Admiral Doenitz's U-boats were in the Western Atlantic, and deployment required about 2 weeks. When the U-boats finally arrived off the United States, they found easy pickings. The only American ships at that time with sonar were destroyers, mostly employed as convoy escorts in the Northern Atlantic.[92] The U.S. Navy's East Coast anti-submarine fleet consisted of three 110-foot wooden subchasers, two 173-foot patrol craft, about twenty Eagle Boats from World War I, and four U.S. Army Air Corps airplanes. These defensive units did not have to wait long for the U-boats. Admiral Doenitz was quick to appreciate the opportunity for a killing. In a short time, the Germans had twelve U-boats on patrol off the East Coast. The results were devastating to the United States' war effort. In the first half of 1942, the U-boats sank 585 ships, and in July through September they sank another 302 ships.[93] By early 1943, the numbers of submarines in the "wolf packs" hunting the convoys exceeded the numbers of convoy escort vessels by as much as two to one. The situation could not be tolerated for long because losses exceeded new construction. By June 1942, the situation had became so serious that General Marshall sent a note to Admiral King stressing the impact on the war effort. He pointed out that of seventy-four ships allocated to the Army, seventeen had been sunk, 22 percent of the bauxite fleet was lost, 20 percent of the Puerto Rican fleet was lost, and tanker losses were running 3.5 percent of the available fleet every month.[94]

The Cryptographic War

One of the great achievements of British cryptanalysis was breaking the German cipher for communicating with its U-boats. By December 1942, the British had successfully decrypted the Triton (or Shark) U-boat cipher, so the regular messages between the U-boats and their headquarters could be read. Analysis of these German messages revealed the U-boat schedules for rendezvous with each other and with tanker submarines. This permitted locating many of the submarines. Another type of cryptographic victory was achieved when it was ascertained in June 1943 that the Germans had broken the British Admiralty convoy cipher as early as February 1942 and the British changed the cipher system to cut off this costly leak of intelligence.[95]

In addition to cryptanalysis, any transmission longer than 30 seconds permitted RDF bearings to be taken at stations on both sides of the Atlantic. The resulting RDF fixes were communicated regularly to the anti-submarine forces. One of the best illustrations of the effectiveness of the RDF system came in June 1942, with an exceptionally good fix on a U-boat north of Bermuda. The fix was signaled to Lieutenant Richard E. Schreder, USNR, who was patrolling in a Mariner PBM aircraft only 50 miles from the U-boat. He flew directly toward the fix and found U-boat 158 surfaced with the crew sunning themselves on deck. He dropped a depth charge and made

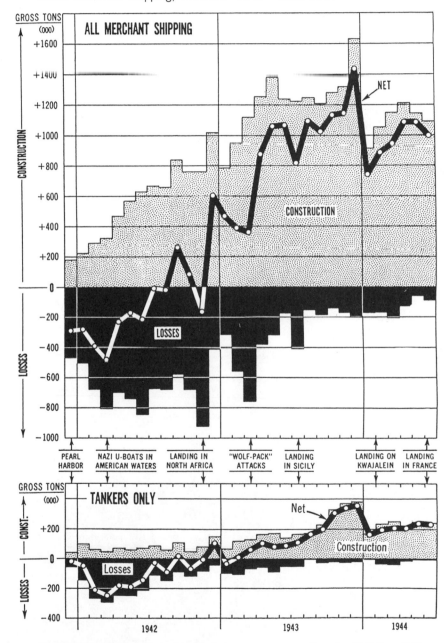

LOSSES vs CONSTRUCTION
Allied Merchant Shipping, December 1941 — June 1944

FIGURE 7-5—Allied merchant shipping: losses vs. construction, December 1941-June 1944.

a direct hit. The charge stuck to the U-boat, but having no impact fuse, did not detonate. The boat was in a crash dive by then, and, on reaching the depth setting on the charge, U-158 terminated its service to the Third Reich.[96]

In 1943, RDF capability was extended to convoy escorts. These mobile sets, tuned for high frequency direction finding of U-boat communications, permitted local fixes far more accurate than those of distant shore stations. They became available on two or three ships of each convoy. The British called this system "Huff-Duff." The United States developed a similar system at about the same time.[97]

Radar and Sonar

Air search was one of the most important factors in locating submarines. Land based aircraft covered an increasing portion of the major convoy routes. Airborne radar was fitted early in 1942 and permitted detection of the U-boats at night when they were surfaced charging batteries. In May of 1942, the British added a powerful airborne searchlight, the Leigh Light. Their bombers could home on a target by radar and as they closed, turn on the light, inspect the target, and bomb it as required. This system worked fine until August, when new U-boat radar detectors gave them time to dive before detection. The

countermeasure to the radar detector did not come until 1943 when the Allied aircraft were fitted with microwave radar, which the Germans did not learn to detect for a considerable time.

Passive underwater sound detection sonars had been available in primitive form for undersea detection since World War I. Active "sonar" was developed between the wars by the Naval Research Laboratory and concurrently by the British as ASDIC, the code name taken from the initials of the Anti-submarine Detection Investigation Committee. In 1943, passive sonar capability was extended to aircraft by the development of the expendable sonobuoy. This device could be dropped by an aircraft in search patterns in a likely area of search. The buoy's sensitive microphone picked up underwater noise from a submarine and radioed it to the aircraft.[98]

Anti-submarine Weapons

One of the problems in attacking a submarine using sonar was that sonars lost contact passing over the target. Deploying a pattern of depth charges astern an ASW ship, therefore, was a somewhat speculative procedure. The course and speed of the quarry probably was changing and his whereabouts were uncertain. One solu-

FIGURE 7-6—Hedgehog launcher being loaded.

tion was the British ahead-thrown weapon, Hedgehog. In early 1942 the United States produced its version of this British weapon. It had more than one advantage. Not only did it permit attack while in sonar contact, but also offered a large circular pattern of small, quick-sinking missiles that exploded only on contact. Thus, it did not disturb the listening environment with minutes of echoes and sound-reflecting turbulence from depth charge explosions. If the projectiles failed to hit, there was no explosion and the sonar search could continue, once the ASW ship passed over the target submarine. One problem was that the Hedgehog could not be fired from small craft that could not sustain its recoil of 40 tons. The solution to this problem was the development of Mousetrap, a launcher that used 7.2-inch rockets with no recoil, and thus was usable on small craft and ships.[99]

An important development associated with Hedgehog was the attack plotter, an ASW fire control computer. The maneuvers of the target were fed in, the characteristics of the weapon were built-in, and the plotter advised the attack-vessel commander when and where the Hedgehog pattern should be placed. This device measurably increased the kill potential.

We entered World War II with the Mark 6 depth charge. It was a cylindrical casing containing 600 pounds of TNT and had a sinking speed of 8 feet per second on a meandering path. It could be set to detonate at one of seven depths from 50 to 300 feet. Late in 1942, the Mark 9 was developed with a teardrop-shaped container, holding 200 pounds of TNT, that could be used in existing racks and K guns. The streamlined casing and canted fins permitted a fairly straight underwater trajectory with a terminal velocity of 14.2 feet per second.[100]

Captain William Mac Nicholson, USN (Ret.) recalled an evaluation of the Mark 9 off Charleston, South Carolina. In 1942, he was assigned the job of determining a safe-ship-speed-versus-depth-setting envelope for the new weapons. The fleet was concerned because of the relatively quick sinking and detonation of these new depth charges as compared to the Marks 2 and 3. Nicholson proceeded to Charleston accompanied by engineers from David Taylor Model Basin (DTMB) and BuShips. He reports:

We fitted the *Bell* (DD-587) with strain gauges and an assortment of special instruments, such as accelerometers. For each of successive trials, both ship speed and depth setting of the charge were reduced until damage to the ship resulted. Damage was undefined and the skipper of the *Bell* took a dim view of this. He was a grey haired commander with a brand-new ship, a totally green crew, and all the worries of taking his new command into the war. It did not suit for a young EDO to be telling him to do significant damage to his new ship. The weather really kicked up for the trials and about eighty percent of the crew both of the ship and of DTMB were actively ill. We carried out the job eventually, knocking out a lot of light bulbs, dumping lockers, and recording yards and yards of instrument records.

I was never able to follow up with the experience of the *Bell* when she left Charleston, but I suspect that while we were shaking up the ship, we were of significant help in shaking down her crew.[101]

By the end of 1944, Mark 9 depth charges Mods 2, 3, and 4 were in use, with an even higher sinking speed and hence a problem for slow ASW craft. With these new depth charges, Hedgehog, and the attack plotter, however, the U-boat kill rate had increased to 20% of the attacks.[102]

Operations Research

Improved tactics and doctrine had as much to do with success of the anti-submarine warfare efforts as did technological improvements. By improved doctrine, all new and old technology was brought to bear with greater efficiency. It started on 2 March 1942 with an ASW unit commissioned in Boston to perform post-mortem on all anti-submarine actions. This was followed by the ASWORG (Anti-submarine Warfare Operations Research Group) on 1 April 1942. ASWORG was a spinoff from the National Defense Research Committee and had several centers. It sought to use scientists directly in operations research (OR), or operations analysis of ASW, to facilitate rigorous assessment and development. ASWORG was heavily seeded with physicists and mathematicians, and their OR studies resulted in superior search and attack patterns for both aircraft and ships. They provided search and attack patterns applicable to broken contacts with the quarry, and are even credited with offering a countermeasure for the German acoustic torpedo before it was placed in operation. New doctrines reached the fleet promptly via the Submarine Chaser Training Center, commissioned in Miami in March 1942. New ASW doctrines were a part of the center's curriculum for more than 10,000 officers and 38,000 enlisted men, including many from foreign navies.[103]

Escort Carriers

Aircraft are the particularly effective adversaries of submarines, and it was soon apparent that aircraft carriers were needed in Atlantic convoys and in ASW hunter-killer groups. Escort carriers, utilizing merchant ship hulls and machinery, were devised. Among the most numerous were the Jeep carriers of the *Casablanca* (CVE-55) class, produced from keel up in quantity by the Kaiser shipyards. Other CVEs were converted from merchant ships, notably the CVE-105 class, converted from 20-knot T-2 tankers. Although the CVEs were intended as escort carriers and not fleet units, they provided air support for Pacific landings and were even involved in an unexpected engagement with major Japanese surface fleet units off Cape Engano where they rendered a good account of themselves.[104]

By the spring of 1943, there were sufficient escort vessels to add convoy support groups to the screens of threatened convoys and to hunt down the submarines contacted.[105] By this time, almost all of the major technological advances in detection and weapons described became operational. Finally, a completely interlocking convoy system was provided for the East Coast.[106]

Coping with Acoustic-Homing Torpedoes

In dreary, drizzling Scottish weather, a tanker, the *Niso*, newly completed at a Clydeside shipyard less than a week earlier, and manned by an all-British crew, lay at anchor off Gourock in the River Clyde. Also on board was an Admiralty research team of three Admiralty engineers and a U.S. Coast Guard officer (naval architectural advisor to the team). Their research was to consist of measuring strains, deflections, accelerations, and wave profiles as the tanker crossed the winter North Atlantic on her way to New York.

The team's goal was to evaluate equipment for more elaborate tests of the reaction of a ship's hull to the forces of the sea. The latter studies would help solve the pervading problem of hull fracture in war-built ships. To measure wave profiles, bow, stern, and amidships water-level detectors had been fitted. Under wartime construction pressures, the amidship contacts inadvertently were omitted, but ingenious Admiralty engineers jury-rigged flatbars, port and starboard, for mounting the water-level detectors. The flatbars were strapped on by running a steel cable around the girth of the ship's underwater body.

In late December 1944, the *Niso* commenced her maiden voyage, underway to join her convoy for the voyage across the Atlantic. Entering the more open waters of the Firth, the *Niso* gained speed, and the flatbars containing the water-level detectors began to strum against the hull. The greater the speed, the louder the strumming. Approaching cruising speed, the flatbars produced a fierce din. Every known audio frequency was excited to an intensity that would intimidate the hardest rock band today. In a very short time, Captain Jackson, C.B.E., *Niso*'s skipper, summoned the research team leader and announced that the strumming of the cable was beckoning every U-boat and every German acoustic-homing torpedo in the Irish Sea.

In September 1943, the Germans had introduced their new acoustic-homing torpedo *Zaunkoenig* ("Wren"), designed to home on the underwater noise of a ship's propellers. Warned in advance by signal intelligence, the British were quick to react. By March 1944, they had developed and introduced a towed underwater noisemaker, based on the strumming steel bars as they were towed astern the ship. They made much more noise than the propeller and lured the torpedoes far astern. The very principle of the noisemaker was at work in the strumming of the flatbars on *Niso*, but the device on *Niso* was far more elegant and much, much louder. The skipper had strong praise for the power and effectiveness of this noisemaker but aside from the unbearable din, he had only one complaint. It would decoy the torpedoes right to his amidships. The boatswain's crew removed the cable, and *Niso* proceeded to the relative tranquility of the winter North Atlantic. Thus ended another chapter in research at sea.[107]

Additional ASW Challenges

Had the war lasted longer, German Admiral Doenitz had other nasty surprises ready for the Allies. The Germans had completed 119 of the Type XXI and XXVI and class submarines, but only three were operational. The Type XXI boats displaced 1,500 tons and were equipped with *snorkel*. They had much larger batteries; that, with a more streamlined hull, permitted 17½ knots submerged. The other surprise was the Walther closed-cycle powered Type XXVI boat. This boat was driven by a turbine using hydrogen peroxide fuel. It could run 158 miles underwater at a speed of 35 knots.[108] Fortunately, the collapse of Germany as a fighting power precluded deployment of these submarines, thus saving the Allied navies from the problems of coping with a renewed German submarine offensive.

SUBMARINE WARFARE

Even as Pearl Harbor burned, the astonished local naval command observed that the submarine base and the tenant submarines were untouched. It was difficult to believe that they had been ignored in such a well-executed raid. Admiral Nimitz, himself an officer with duty in submarines, later expressed amazement and satisfaction that the single force that immediately could be brought to bear on the enemy was still intact. He saw to it that the reaction was prompt and sustained. The American submarine force in the Pacific, commanded by Vice Admiral Charles A. Lockwood, was one of the most effective attack forces. It quickly became the leading cause of Japanese merchant ship loss, and ranked third after air attack and surface gunfire in destruction of Japanese warships.

In the Atlantic, the situation was quite different. The American submarine force consisted mostly of older and smaller boats, and the major attack action was being carried out only by the British. Nevertheless, our Atlantic submarines were kept very profitably employed in crew training and the solution of ASW problems to support all fleets.[109]

Submarines

More than half the 106-boat active American submarine fleet on 7 December 1941 consisted of World War I design approaching 20 years in age. Twenty-five were remnants of World War I; thirty-six were of the "S" class commissioned in 1920-1925. Most of the older boats were comparatively small and even the S-class boats at 790-850 tons standard displacement were not designed for long Pacific patrols.[110]

The attack submarines of the United States in World War II were dominantly of the "fleet" type. The term "fleet" comes from the pre-World War I concept that these boats were to fight with the fleet. Between the wars, the missions of the submarines were greatly enlarged. They coordinated in some fleet actions as they did at Midway, but their dominant use was for independent action against Japanese commerce and warships, as well as for other duties such as blockade runners. They also performed aircraft lifeguard rescue duty in target areas during air strikes, and conducted photo-intelligence and other reconnaissance missions. One submarine, the *Argonaut*, was converted to carry 120 marine atoll raiders and bore the unique designation (APS-1).[111]

From 1920 through April 1941 fifty new fleet-type submarines were commissioned. There were about thirteen classes reflecting a variety of design features. Some were very large and some were small, almost coastal types. The power plants also varied widely. It was a period of experimentation, and the designers exploited heavily the German U-boat technology of World War I. Because of the war in Europe and other threat evidence, Congress early released funds for major naval construction increases, and the construction program of World War II submarines was underway at the time of Pearl Harbor.[112]

The design of the fleet type submarine of World War II was based on a synthesis of the experience with the fifty boats built since World War I. (Refer to Chapter 6.) Some very famous naval constructors were involved directly in submarine design between the wars. These included Vice Admiral Emery S. (Jerry) Land and E. L. (Ned) Cochrane, Captain H. E. (Savvy) Saunders, and Admiral Samuel M. (Mike) Robinson. All made major personal contributions to the between-wars designs that later flowed into the fleet-type designs.[113] Each later rose to major responsibilities and after retirement to important roles in government, industry, and education.[114]

Essentially, the World War II fleet boats involved three different but very similar classes:

Class	Number of Boats Completed
Gato	77
Balao	119
Tench	25
Total	221

All of the above were about 311 feet, 9 inches long overall, with a standard displacement of about 1,525 long tons. Crews consisted of ten officers and seventy men. They were capable of 20 knots on the surface and about 9 knots submerged. Surfaced, they could travel 11,000 miles or more at 10 knots by diesel. Submerged, they could go 48 hours at 2 knots on batteries. They had capacity for provisions sufficient for a 75-day cruise. All had six torpedo tubes in the bow, and four aft. The *Gato* and *Balao* class could carry a total of twenty-four torpedoes, and the *Tench* class twenty-eight. All boats could carry forty mines with two in the torpedo tubes.

There were two other differences between the classes. The *Gato* class had a diving depth of 300 feet, whereas the *Balao* and *Tench* classes had heavier pressure hulls and were rated for 400 feet. The second difference was in the deck armament. The *Gato* class originally carried one 3in/50 gun. The *Balao* class had one 4in/50 and one 5in/25. The *Tench* class had one or two 5in/25. Actually, the armament was modified for various boats as missions required; thus, the only significant difference was the diving depth.

The primary design process for the *Balao* class consisted of removing every source of marginal weight from the *Gato* class, and putting the saved weight into a heavier hull steel. In addition, the steel of the *Balao* class was stronger. The pressure hull went from the *Gato* class' 11/16 inch of medium carbon steel to 7/8 inch of high tensile steel, and the conning tower was increased to 1-inch STS. The latter change was to

reduce casualties from gunfire, especially aircraft strafing.

Among the weight-saving removals authorized by the Navy's General Board were the large Kingston valves at the bottoms of ballast tanks. U-boats that surrendered after World War I were found to have no main ballast-tank flood valves. They were "riding the vents" to facilitate crash diving. Most American submarine skippers also rode the vents in hazardous waters. Eliminating the Kingstons and employing other system improvements reduced the time to submerge from 50 to 30-35 seconds.[115]

Sonar

As we entered World War II, American submarines were equipped with 3-foot-long magnetostriction hydrophones on deck. (Refer to Chapter 6.) These were capable of excellent passive reception, and directional determination up to 10 miles. These submarines also had superior active sonar with good operative range at submerged speeds. The listening capability permitted recording target propeller-beat to estimate target speed. During the war, a special high-resolution mine-detection sonar was developed to enable submarines to conduct missions in the Yellow Sea and around the Japanese islands.

Much oceanological mapping had been done between wars. The characteristics of important thermoclines and high shrimp-noise areas had been charted. This knowledge was exploited by the U.S. submarine skippers seeking refuge from attack or stealth in approach.

In contrast to the American sonar, the hydrophones on Japanese escorts were unable to track our submarines during the opening months of the war. In 1943, they started to have echo-ranging equipment, but they had much less success than the United States in its use. Overall, we did much better with sonar than did the Japanese.[116]

Torpedoes

Technologically speaking, our torpedoes produced a stark contrast with the effectiveness of our sonar, giving trouble from the very beginning in the defense of the Philippines. A 2-year nightmare ensued, and problems were not resolved until the autumn of 1943.

The torpedo most used on the fleet-type submarines was the Mark 14, 21 inches in diameter with two speed settings. At 46 knots it had a range of 4,500 yards and 9,000 yards at 31.5 knots. The warhead contained 668 pounds of torpex detonated by a Mark 6 exploder. The Mark 6 was a double-triggered device, intended to respond to a direct hit or to a variation of the earth's magnetic field. The Mark 6 exploder embodied several complicating features including arming the warhead about 450 yards into a run by moving the detonator into the booster cavity. At this point another control prevented premature detonation from nearby explosions.[117]

After April 1943, the Mark 18 electric torpedo began to satisfy a major portion of the fleet demand. It had the advantage of wakelessness, but it was slower, reaching only 28-30 knots. Another torpedo model, the Mark 10, also had a 21-inch diameter and was equipped with the Mark 3 exploder. This torpedo was a veteran and its exploder was a simple contact device. It had less speed, less range, and less charge than the Mark 14, and was used on the R- and S-boats because it was short enough to fit in their torpedo tubes.[118]

The Mark 14 torpedoes exhibited almost every form of malfunction, including: circular runs, porpoising, too-deep runs, premature detonation, triggering failures, and other misbehavior.[119] The torpedo was a very complicated and expensive weapon, costing in 1941 about $10,000. With such complicated equipment, occasional misfires might be expected, as well as hydrodynamic antics and erratic prematures. Not so with the deep-runs and the duds. Accordingly, our submarines went to sea with half their ammunition blank and no idea of which half.[120]

Misbehavior such as porpoising can in wartime be fatal. The World War II failures caused many disasters, including two involving the submarines *Tang* and *Salmon*. On 4 October 1944, the *Tang* (SS-306) was north of Formosa, completing her cruise. She had an outstanding record. She had sunk twenty-four ships, which put her in second place among the whole submarine force. She lined up on a good target, and fired her last torpedo. To the consternation of

the skipper, Commander Richard H. O'Kane, who was on the bridge, the torpedo turned, porpoised, and continued to turn. The *Tang* tried to maneuver clear, but she could not act quickly enough. The torpedo ran in a circle and hit the *Tang*. This time the exploder worked. On 30 October 1944, the *Salmon* (SS-182) fired a salvo of four torpedoes. Three broached! The broaching helped to reveal the *Salmon's* position and the enemy escort vessels filled the seas with depth charges. The damage control efforts in the *Salmon* are a fantastic yarn of determination, knowledge, and discipline. At one point, the boat settled to about 600 feet, far below her rated operating depth of 250 feet. Finally she had to surface and fight herself free, using the cover of a rain squall. When she reached port she was found to be damaged beyond repair. Her fame stems from the severity of the damage that her design and construction survived.[121]

As a society, we have learned to live with imperfection in machines. We accept and expect some erratic behavior in automobiles and aircraft, even in peacetime and even when the consequences are serious. However, the failures must be rare and this was not the case with the Mark 14 torpedo. Its repeated failures were frequent enough to jeopardize the mission of the submarine strike forces in the Pacific (and some claim to have even permitted Japanese invasion of the Philippines).

The problems of the Mark 14 had a tendency to obscure each other. For instance, it was not until after the depth control problem was remedied that the torpedoes consistently hit the targets and revealed that the contact trigger of the Mark 6 exploder was frequently failing to operate. The depth control problem was discovered in 1942. Actually it was a rediscovery, because evidence, as far back as 1938, had indicated that torpedoes were running too deep. Finally, tests in the summer of 1942 showed that the Mark 14 was running 10 feet deeper than set. This fact was obscured in many earlier attacks because the magnetic trigger sometimes worked and an explosion resulted. In January 1942, BuOrd had issued an advisory indicating that the Mark 10, as well, was also running 4 feet too deep. The problem was handled primarily by directive to the fleet.[122]

When hits without detonation became more consistently obvious, it was clear that the exploder was not functioning. The problem, however, was blamed on the magnetic-influence fuse because its malfunction would seem to explain both premature detonations as well as duds. Prematures were a very dangerous type of defect because the explosion alerted the enemy to the presence of our submarine and aided in location.[123] The Mark 6 exploder had been so secret that almost nobody in the fleet knew about it until it was issued. It was complicated and there was little time for training in its use and maintenance. BuOrd, of course, blamed the failures on handling and operational procedures; the fleet blamed BuOrd; and both blamed the torpedo builders. Within the fleet, the failures produced loss of confidence among the skippers, the torpedomen, and the control center. Months of repeated frustration took a serious morale toll, especially of the skippers, who blamed themselves for a problem that they did not know was beyond their control.[124] The submarines began to request and to receive authorization to deactivate the magnetic triggers. This practice was made official for the Pacific Fleet by order of Admiral Nimitz on 24 July 1943.[125] However, by this time, deactivation of the magnetic triggers increased the number of duds instead of decreasing them.[126]

On 24 July 1943 the *Tinosa* (SS-283) sighted the huge tanker *Tonan Maru* No. 3, converted from a whale factory. This dream target was unescorted and within reach of the *Tinosa*. The *Tinosa*'s skipper, Lieutenant Commander L. R. "Dan" Daspit, tried to close, but the closest he could come was 4,000 yards. He fired a spread of four torpedoes. Two hit near the stern of the tanker, exploded, and brought her dead in the water. He promptly fired two more torpedoes, which hit and exploded. The target was helpless but still afloat. With no escort force, Commander Daspit had only to avoid the fire of the guns on board the tanker. To do this, he remained submerged and took a position at 875 yards squarely abeam the *Tonan Maru*. He fired one torpedo. At the end of the run he saw a splash but no explosion. He then realigned his position and fired another torpedo. Again no explosion. Twice more he carefully realigned and fired. Each time

an echo of total silence, four duds in a row. Daspit's exasperation must have been monumental. His wonderful chance for a dream kill was being frustrated by a load of blanks. He decided that the best thing he could do would be to gather irrefutable evidence of the Mark 14's malfunctions. He continued to fire, before each shot withdrawing the torpedo from its tube to check all adjustments. In all, eight shots were fired from close range on the beam of the huge ship. The torpedoes could not miss the target and in a couple of cases were seen to create a splash as they hit. Eight hits and eight duds. With one torpedo left, Daspit decided that it should be brought home for a thorough examination. In return for the escape of the *Tonan Maru*, Daspit brought back evidence that would solve the torpedo problem and lead to the sinking of dozens of other Japanese ships struck by Mark 14 torpedoes that had been rectified to explode on contact.[127]

The remaining *Tinosa* torpedo was carefully examined in Pearl Harbor and was found to be in excellent condition. The warhead (torpex removed) was elevated by a crane at Pearl Harbor to a height where the terminal velocity of a drop would equal the attack speed setting. It was dropped onto solid concrete and it was a dud. A sister torpedo was fired at an underwater cliff and proved a dud. These tests at Pearl Harbor convinced all levels of command that the problem was in the torpedo exploder. The drop tests were continued, and it was found that with a direct hit, square to the target surface, the 5-g load on the firing pin created a 190-pound frictional force and jammed the pin. On the other hand, a glancing blow allowed the pin to set off the detonator. That explained why the *Tinosa* had stopped the *Tonan Maru* with its angular shots but failed to score with shots directly from the beam station.[128] Several competing trigger designs were immediately developed by the Pearl Harbor submarine base and the submarine *Holland*. On 30 September, the *Barb* (SS-220) left with the first new firing pins in all torpedoes on board.[129]

Important lessons were learned. Lack of communication between developers and users of equipment can be a fatal flaw.[130] Moreover, no new development should go to sea until it is exhaustively tested ashore. Conservative testing procedures of shipbuilders are confirmed by this torpedo disaster. In 1944, the Chief of BuOrd summed it up when he said:

> Even with the relatively meager funds available in time of peace, much of the work now being done after more than a year and a half of war, could and should have been accomplished years ago . . . That the work was not accomplished during peace or earlier during this war, or, so far as the Bureau records disclose, that no one either in the Bureau or at Newport apparently questioned the inadequacy of the design without such tests, shows a lack of practical appreciation of the problems involved which is incompatible with the Bureau's high standards, and reflects discredit upon both the Bureau of Ordnance and the Naval Torpedo Station, Newport. The Chief of the Bureau therefore directs that as a matter of permanent policy, no service torpedo device ever be adopted as standard until it has been tested under conditions simulating as nearly as possible those which will be encountered in battle.[131]

Electric Torpedo

After April 1943, the Westinghouse Mark 18 electric torpedo became available to the fleet. It was slower and had less range, but it was wakeless and therefore almost impossible to evade. During the last year of the Pacific war, the electric torpedo constituted 30 percent of those used, and the expenditure rate rose to 500 per month. Besides its relatively slow speed, this "fish" had two other shortcomings. Battery gases of the earlier models were inadequately vented, causing some rather harrowing shipboard hydrogen fires. Aboard the *Flyingfish* (SS-229), a fire made the torpedo so hot that the torpex melted and ran out. The hydrogen-venting problem was promptly solved. No real solution, however, was found for the other problem of the batteries becoming weak in the colder waters and the torpedoes becoming very sluggish.[132]

Submarine Warfare Record

It can be seen that although the U.S. submarine campaign, in the end, played an eminently successful part in strangling the seaborne shipping of the Japanese empire, and took a critical toll of major vessels of the Japanese fleet,

significant technical problems had to be solved from the beginning. Although fifty-two U.S. submarines were lost, with 374 officers and men, the damage wrought by the submarines was tremendous. During the war Japan lost 686 warships and 2,346 merchantmen of over 500 gross tons. More than half of these losses were attributed to submarine attack, which played a key element in the outcome of the war.[133]

AMPHIBIOUS WARFARE

It was clear that any plausible Allied strategy would require many major amphibious assaults in both Atlantic and Pacific theaters, as well as major moves into Europe more immense than anything ever before contemplated. Amphibious assault operations are very difficult. The attacker is highly visible and most vulnerable as he nears the beach and must shift from water to land transport. Even after the attacker is ashore, his bombardment and resupply vessels continue to be vulnerable. The Allies were little experienced for the amphibious tasks they foresaw. Their officers lacked the tactical experience, troops were not trained for amphibious operations, and most of the equipment needed had yet to be built. Winston Churchill dreaded a repeat of Dunkirk, and Allied preparations for amphibious operations commenced in an atmosphere of determination mixed with caution and concern.

Among the many needs was that for ships to carry the heaviest tanks, guns, trucks, and other cumbersome material to the beach. Also needed were smaller craft to provide fire support to land infantry. Finally, it was clear that covertly or by force, the beachhead must be cleared of mines and obstructions, and the firepower of the defenders must be minimized. In recognition of these requirements, Admiral Ernest J. King established the U.S. Naval Amphibious Forces on 20 February 1942. Force structure focused on development, planning, mobilization, and operational needs. During the first years of the war, a large share of the effort was devoted to developing and producing the required material while tactics were being developed and tested, and troops were being trained. Many amphibious assaults were made in the Mediterranean and Pacific, but it was not until 1944 that the Allies were ready for Normandy, primarily due to lack of sufficient amphibious ships and craft.

The problems had priority attention right to the very top. President Roosevelt even drew his own sketch of a landing ship, including a realistic plan and profile.[134] The chronicle of planning, resource allocation, training, and deployment preceding the major amphibious operations contains many fascinating tales. The stories of the creation of the landing ship, tank (LST), the design of smaller landing craft, the enhancement of beach bombardment capability, and the development of the pontoon causeway are among the most interesting.

Landing Ship, Tank (LST)

The U.S. Navy began the development of landing craft as early as 1936, aiming to handle a light tank of 16 tons. By 1941, the available design could handle only one such tank, and tactical trends indicated that this was insufficient. So development was continued for a lighter to carry a 30-ton medium tank. The resultant craft was too heavy for expeditionary ship loading. Furthermore, the progress of the war indicated that some of these same craft would have to be capable of carrying heavy equipment, as well.

The British had had by far the greater experience, but their ready amphibious craft had either excessive draft for beach delivery or inadequate capacity for heavy equipment.[135] British shipyards, moreover, were already overloaded and were in no position to undertake the building of hundreds of large ships capable of delivering numbers of the heavy tanks to the beach. The Americans and British, therefore, concluded that an entirely new program should be handled by the United States, and the British came to Washington to help arrange it. They arrived early in November 1941 with barebones performance criteria, which included speed, range, slope of beach, and bow draft at beaching.

On 4 November 1941, British officers and engineers met at BuShips with Mr. John Niedermair, head naval architect for preliminary design. It was recognized that the design operation required a ship with two loading conditions. An oceangoing ship was needed, with sufficient draft for long voyage seaworthiness. Such a ship also had to operate as a shallow-draft landing craft capable of beaching with full vehicle load. Meeting both conditions required extensive liquid ballast tankage for the ocean voyages. Mr. Niedermair prepared a quick conceptual study including a simple sketch crystallizing basic characteristics such as open ocean draft, as well as draft and slope of keel for beaching. That very day the study was sent to England.[136]

The British prepared "staff requirements" and their naval mission consulted with the designers. They arrived three weeks after the preliminary sketch was prepared. By then, BuShips had determined basic characteristics, but many important problems remained unresolved, including bow door and ramp operation, tank engine ventilation for the tank space, and main-to-lower-deck vehicle-transfer to permit bow ramp use from both decks.[137]

The ships had to be easy to fabricate. Common structures and simple shapes were necessary for speedy production, and lightness mandated maximum use of ⅜-inch steel plate. In spite of these constraints, preliminary design was completed in a month, and a lines plan was sent to David Taylor Model Basin for hydrodynamic test in January. Also in January, a contract was let with Gibbs and Cox, Inc., New York, for working drawings while contract plans were being prepared. Finally, on 23 January 1942 the first construction contract was let. Project urgency and importance increased as work proceeded. A need to increase the delivery requirements occurred more than once, and the recognition of the need was shared at the highest levels of the Allied governments.[138]

The LST was large, 328 feet long with a lightship weight of 1,625 long tons. In the quantity contemplated, the program was a major overload on the shipyards.[139] The scarcity of building ways was overcome by the construction of new shipyards, some operated by firms that had never built ships before. National-level adjustments to materials priorities were made to facilitate progress, and a large Materials Control Agency was established in New York City.[140] The first LST was delivered 23 October 1942, less than a year from Niedermair's first rough sketch, and from 1942 through 1945 the United States delivered 1,026 LSTs,[141] plus 3,073 other landing craft.

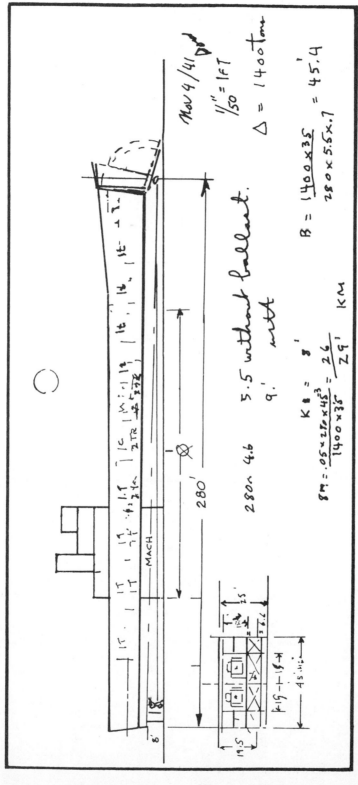

FIGURE 7-7—*Original pencil sketch of the LST by John Niedermair, head naval architect, Preliminary Design, Bureau of Ships. 4 November 1941. [Note: this sketch by Niedermair is to naval engineers what a Rembrandt sketch is to the art world. Regardless of its graphic quality, it is a classic to the engineer.]*

The first LST in the Pacific arrived in March 1943, followed promptly by sister ships, as they commenced hauling supplies. First combat use occurred when Admiral Halsey's forces landed on Rendova Island on 30 June, and shortly thereafter, in July, the LSTs supported the occupation of Sicily. Although intended initially for heavy tanks, their versatile design soon made them the workhorse of the fleet. They carried just about everything everywhere.[142] Winston Churchill is reported to have said, "The destinies of two great empires . . . seemed to be tied by some goddamned things called LSTs, whose engines themselves had to be tickled on by . . . LST engine experts of which there was a great shortage."[143]

With a speed of about 10 knots, the LSTs were slow, and fondly dubbed by their mostly non-professional crews, "Large Stationary Targets." The need for higher speed craft capable of carrying heavy tanks led to the LSM (landing ship, medium). Smaller than the LST, at 203 feet length overall, these ships had open vehicle wells, bow doors, and ramps similar to the LST. They were about half again as fast as the LSTs, but because they came along late in the war, not many saw action as landing craft. A number were converted to or completed as rocket ships. About 500 LSMs and LSM(R)s were built. The perceived need for a fast infantry landing craft spawned the LCI(L)s (landing craft, infantry, large). About 900 of these craft were built, of which a number were converted to or finished as gunboats or rocket support craft.[144]

Landing Ship, Dock (LSD)

The LSD was designed with the same rapid competence as the other ships and craft of the amphibious program. Planning for detailed design construction also commenced on the basis of preliminary plans, before contract plans were completed. At one point in preliminary design, there was a decision for riveted construction to make use of a supposed excess of qualified riveters. The midship section design was already well along as a welded structure. This was frantically converted to a riveted design, but before that could be completed the decision was again reversed back to welded construction. These were substantial ships, 457 feet length overall, displacing about 8,000 tons loaded. The LSDs were

essentially high-speed floating dry docks, to carry loaded landing craft in the large docking wells, and flooded at the landing site to float out the landing craft. The LSDs also served as repair and service bases for PTs and other small craft. Some twenty-seven LSDs were constructed during the last three years of World War II.[145]

Landing Craft, Tank (LCT)

The smallest of the larger landing craft were the LCTs. These were lightly constructed barge-like craft, about 120 feet in length overall, capable of carrying three medium tanks or about 200 tons of cargo. Not fast and unsuited to long ocean voyages, they nevertheless served well in the landings at Sicily and Normandy. A number were made into rocket barrage ships.[146] One of the many loads that could be carried by the LST was an LCT. The LCTs were mounted on the long open LST decks, supported above greased skids, ready to launch. The task consisted of knocking out the wedges so that the LCT would drop to the greased skids. With LST ballasted for a 10- or 11-degree list, the restraining lines were then cut to launch the LCT with a magnificent splash. The task was simple and quick. It was easy to keep up with the arrivals, so no backlog existed.[147]

The LCTs were designed to be built in three sections to allow transport on cargo ships, and most were so shipped. Once afloat, the three sections were ballastable to allow the sections to be aligned and bolted together. The process was easier on paper than in practice, so various ingenious schemes were devised for assembly overseas.[148] The first LCT assembled by the British took 65 days. This was gradually improved to 50 days, and finally a marine railway in Plymouth assembled some in 5 days. This, however, still was not satisfactory. It was February and D-Day was fast approaching. A large backlog of unassembled LCTs was on hand. Lieutenant Mario Andrea, USNR, was a member of an amphibious repair unit that arrived in Glasgow, Scotland, in January 1944. As a naval architect, he was sent to Plymouth to help unload the LCTs from arriving LSTs. Lieutenant Andrea was transferred from launching to speeding up the assembly of the LCTs.[149]

Andrea found a graving dock, but with no

caisson. Nevertheless, the tidal range flooded and drained the dock every tidal cycle. The problem was aligning the three sections for assembly. Floating independently, their trim were such that they could not be connected. But, a way was found. Near the graving dock was a usable crane, and at the nearby U.S. receiving station it was easy to secure a detail of fifty seamen standing by for assignment. The three LCT sections were floated into the graving dock and grounded as the tide went out. The sailors red-leaded all flanges to be joined, and tied canvas gaskets in place with string. As the tide came in, the sections were floated together. Ballasting was unnecessary because the crane could adjust the trim sufficiently to achieve alignment at the main deck, and long bolts were inserted to pull the sections together. This juxtaposed the lower flanges. The hull joint was not tight, but with three pumps in both holds, water level could be kept below 1 foot. The detail swarmed in with drift pins and bolts, and with all hands at work, in no time all bolts were tight, leakage was reduced to a trickle, and the holds were pumped dry. The assembled LCT was then floated out on the rising tide and moved to an outfitting pier for connection of piping and electrical circuits. Meanwhile, three more sections were floated in to repeat the process on the next falling tide. The tides provided an assembly rate of two LCTs per day, ten times the rate on the marine railway and the backlog soon dwindled.[150]

Pontoon Causeways

The first phase of amphibious operations establishes a beachhead on which larger forces and material can be landed. The second phase of support, supply and resupply, involves the landing of thousands more troops, hundreds of tanks, trucks, munitions, supplies, and heavy construction equipment. This period of over-the-beach traffic may last for weeks before proper piers can be constructed. Meanwhile, the volume requires effective temporary terminal facilities to cope with the traffic. The solution in World War II was the Navy lightered pontoon causeway (NL).

Bureau of Yards and Docks (BuDocks), established in 1842 to take care of the Navy's shore establishment, is the center of the activities of the officers of the Civil Engineer Corps. BuDocks

records going back to 1933 included speculation on the use of such standardized pontoon units. They covered the problems of design and transportation to advanced bases, along with the problems of on-site assembly and utilization. In 1935 and 1936, the Bureau had received proposals provided by Lieutenant Commander Haines of the Bureau of Construction and Repair. Haines's designs were based on a steel company's sectional barges whose buoyancy units were joined by fasteners piercing the sides of the floats.

When Commander John Noble Laycock (CEC), USN reported to BuDocks in mid-March 1939 as war plans officer, he discovered the modular pontoon information in his office files. As a naval officer and a civil engineer, he became doubly fascinated by the possibilities of the concept. With the help of other BuDocks engineers, the subject was given an intensive and innovative review, and two important changes were made. First, the corners of the rectangular pontoon modules were chamfered diagonally, and heavy extending pad-eyes were welded on to permit corner connections without piercing the watertight pontoon. Second, overall structural strength of pontoon assemblies was ensured with a strong external structure. These changes greatly improved the strength, simplicity, and versatility of the causeway units and greatly eased assembly under operational conditions. After considerable study of buoyancy needs and operating conditions, initial dimensions of the flotation pontoons were standardized at 5 feet by 5 feet with lengths of 7 feet or 9 feet 6 inches.

Cigar-box and kite-stick models used in developing the structural concept were reused to demonstrate the concept to operational and material decision makers. The great need motivated commitment, and three full-scale experimental assemblies were authorized. They were a 100-ton drydock, a 50-ton barge, and a seaplane ramp. Pittsburgh-Des Moines Steel Company received the construction contract on 18 February 1941. Tests proved these units successful, and an order was placed for 3,000 pontoons. The tests of simplicity, producability, and usability were being completed rapidly, and an example of versatility was illustrated by the early search for large outboard motors to propel the causeway units as ferries. The NL pontoon causeway was made up of a number of buoyancy modules held together by structural elements. These modules were joined with large structural angle "irons" and 1½-inch steel bolts. These irons were as large as 8 by 8 inches of ½-inch gauge weighing a ton or more. Collectively, the units made up a sort of "erector set" from which all sorts of floating causeways and piers could be assembled. The assembly gear, including the 1½-inch bolts and the 1-ton steel angle iron, was affectionately called "jewelry."

Specially trained teams were needed to assemble and employ the causeway units. So by December 1942 the Construction Battalion (CB or Sea Bee) Center at Davisville, Rhode Island, organized by Admiral Ben Moreel, head of BuDocks, became a proving ground to test causeway concepts and to train Seabees (members of naval construction battalions) in their operational assembly and use.

On 10 July 1943, the causeways were used in the landings on Sicily. The Germans were prepared to repulse the assault, but unprepared to cope with the quantities of heavy tanks and artillery promptly brought ashore at unlikely landing sites over the causeways. The causeways proved to be an outstanding success, and they became an integral feature of future landing operations.[151]

Standard "jewelry" permitted causeways of various sizes. A typical unit would employ thirty-six pontoons in a three wide by twelve long configuration. For long journeys, the causeway sections could be carried fully assembled and secured to the sides of an LST, from which they were unloaded by dropping them into the water. Locally, the sections were towed like a barge.

At Kwajalein in 1944 an LST could not get close to the beach so the Seabees invented another type of pontoon ferry. A causeway section was used to move the LST cargo by a typical Seabee-invented "propulsion" system. It consisted of two bulldozers, one at each end of the ferry route, operating their winches to haul the ferry back and forth. In another case, an LST grounded 60 feet from shore on falling tide. Causeways were floated in to bridge the space and the LST was promptly unloaded.[152]

When motors were added, pontoon units became warping tugs and self-propelled ferries. The variety of uses for this super Erector-set was endless. The pontoons and "jewelry" were used to build drydocks for PT boats, bridges, barges for fuel or water, and even temporary shelters ashore. The big event for the causeways came with the Normandy invasion, and their service there was far from mundane. Because of the large Normandy tidal range, it was advisable to keep the LSTs farther from shore. One solution was "Rhino" barges, towed across the English Channel. These were large self-propelled causeway segments, each unit carrying a bulldozer and a small landing craft. As the LST approached the beach, the bulldozer pushed the landing craft into the water where it became a warping tug. Then the "Rhino" barge was warped and lashed to the front of the LST ramp for loading. After loading, the "Rhino" barge proceeded to the beach. First ashore was the bulldozer, which bulldozed a beach ramp for unloading of the barge, and later helped to push the barge off the beach to return for another load.[153]

Seldom has an innovation spawned so many satellite innovations. Creative application of solid engineering pyramided into a major amphibious development. Captain Laycock was repeatedly honored for his part in the innovation and for his imaginative leadership in bringing the embryo pontoon concept to a practical amphibious system.[154]

Bombardment

Danger on beaches crossed by the Allied amphibious forces was much reduced by bombardment. It destroyed defensive strong points, obstructions, and mines, and suppressed the firepower of the defenders. In the Pacific, shore bombardment was a major activity of naval gunfire. It was especially helpful in destroying identified heavily protected bunkers and gun emplacements. Because ships had to stay offshore in deeper water, they became less effective in providing support as the troops progressed inland.

Vice Admiral Wilson Brown suggested rockets to the National Defense Research Committee (NDRC) for the needed bombardment. The problem was assigned to a group of rocket enthusiasts at CIT. As an interim response, they provided rockets using the 2.25-inch Mousetrap motor and a 20-pound projectile containing 6 pounds of TNT, with a range of about 1,100 yards. The CIT development continued, and by 25 August 1942 a 4.5-inch barrage rocket was tested on Chesapeake Bay. Within 4 days, BuOrd asked CIT to supply fifty launchers and 3,000 rockets, and 2 months later they were used at Casablanca.

The British fitted rocket launchers in the bays of some of their LCTs, initiating a progression of successively more powerful rocket support craft and ships. In early 1943, LCI(L)s also were fitted with forty launchers containing 480 projectiles in a single loading. These are what greeted the Germans on 10 July 1943 when they tried to defend the beaches of Sicily against the Allied assault.[155]

Rocket barrages became an essential stage of all subsequent World War II amphibious assaults. By 1945, both rockets and launchers had been greatly improved. Spin stabilized rockets (SSR) having more predictable trajectories were introduced. Launchers now could be trained and the rocket's impact point controlled. The LSM(R) (landing ship, medium, rocket) was selected as the craft and Mark 102 launchers were installed on 40 mm gun mounts so Mark 51 gun directors could aim the launchers.[156] The two tubes on each mount were capable of launching thirty 5.0-inch SSR rounds per minute. As the ship approached the target area, it could launch 1,020 rounds in the first minute—then it would take 45 minutes to reload. The 5.0-inch SSR had a range of 10,000 yards, or about ten times the range of the earlier rocket installations, and was far more accurate.[157]

During World War II, the amphibious operations ranged from a Marine raid in August 1942 on Makin Atoll from the submarines *Argonaut* (APS-1) and *Nautilus* (SS-168), to Operation Overlord, the invasion of Europe at Normandy. The first large-scale landing was on Guadalcanal on 7 August 1942. The experience in the early landings was crucial to the success of the greatest amphibious assault of them all, Overlord, which involved 702 warships, 25 minesweeping flotillas, and 9,000 landing craft and support ships.

MINE WARFARE

Mining

Mining is an important form of warfare because it is so effective, and very cost-effective, at that. Mines can be set to detonate immediately, or can be a delayed threat because they can lie dormant for months waiting for a victim. Mines, also, are easier to use surreptitiously than many other forms of armament. They can be laid by aircraft, patrol boats, or submarines. Mines were used by the United States in World War II to cause major attrition to the Japanese naval and maritime fleets. The direct impact of mining is only a part of the cost, and not necessarily the highest cost, to the defender. A major impact of mining is the dislocation of shipping, including the total closure of ports and channels selected, even when only suspected of being mined. The impact and cost can be crucial to a maritime nation like Japan, heavily dependent on sea imports.

In all, American submarines laid 658 mines in thirty-six mine fields as part of the "Outer Zone" mining. Surface ships laid another 2,829 mines in seventeen other fields, and the rest of the job was done by Army and Navy air. The aircraft planted 9,254 mines in 108 different mine fields in the Outer Zone. After Guam, Iwo Jima, and Okinawa were captured, airfields were established close to Japan and the "Inner Zone" plan was activated. This campaign concentrated on the harbors and critical passages for shipping around the Japanese islands. In all, 24,876 mines were planted. They sank 515 ships, severely damaged 560 more, and brought Japanese ship traffic to a virtual halt. This fierce mining onslaught on the Inner Zone started in March 1945 and ended in mid-August, completing the strangulation of Japan.[158]

Mine Countermeasures

The advent of the magnetic mine meant a new minesweeper design and complete overhaul of minesweeping equipment was necessary. In addition, magnetic mines required installations called "degaussing gear" on all major ships to neutralize the magnetic "signature." The knowledge for neutralizing the magnetic field of the ships was

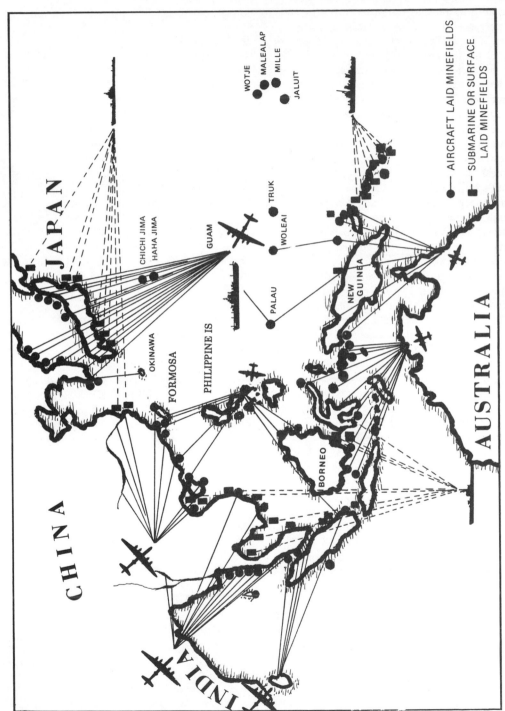

FIGURE 7-8—Offensive mine laying against Japan, October 1942-August 1945.

in hand, but the cost and time loss were significant, and the certainty of success was less than 100 percent. Magnetic mines had a considerably larger lethal radius than contact mines. Also, they could discriminate, by their sensitivity setting, between large and small ships. Finally, if the setting happened to be right, they would explode beneath a ship and wreak destruction throughout by generating shock waves that traveled from end to end.[159]

During World War II, many of the smaller minesweepers were built of wood to reduce their magnetic signatures. This led to a revival of the art of building wooden ships; however, questions regarding the ability of wooden ships to survive an exploding mine were also raised.[160]

A final countermeasure to the mine fields deserves repetition. It was the previously mentioned high resolution sonar developed to detect and evade mines. It was especially important to the American submarines operating in and around the Japanese harbors near the end of the war.[161]

RESEARCH AND DEVELOPMENT (R&D)

The United States technological and industrial bases were crucial to the outcome of World War II. The term "Arsenal of Democracy" was deserved. Not only did the United States command most of its necessary raw materials, but it had an unequalled industrial base, an educated population, and an innate drive toward achievement. We next need to highlight the R&D foundation that provided the basis to the naval engineering achievements that contributed to winning the war. The new technology flowing into the fleet in 1941 strongly reflected the nature of Navy-controlled R&D then underway. Much of this work was conducted in laboratories operated by the Navy as the United States entered the war. These laboratories had established a strong base in the science and technology important to the Navy and other maritime activities. Thus, the wartime expansion in naval engineering technology was built on a strong foundation of science and technology stored in the minds of the Navy's own workforce.

Existing Organizations

National Academy of Sciences — On 7 December 1941, the scientific and technological structure of the United States was already coordinated by a well-established national organization, the National Academy of Sciences and its National Research Council (NAS/NRC).

According to its charter, the National Academy of Sciences is a nongovernment institution established to ". . . investigate, examine, and report upon any subject of science or art, . . . whenever called upon by any department of the Government, ..." The actual expense of such investigations is ". . . to be paid from appropriations which may be made for the purpose, but the Academy shall receive no compensation whatever for any service to the Government of the United States." Its charter was passed by Congress and approved by President Lincoln in 1863. Thus, it provided technical and scientific advice during the Civil War.

The National Research Council is organized by the National Academy of Sciences to implement its advisory services through conferences, technical committees, surveys, sponsorship of scientific publications, organizations for research, and the administration of research projects and fellowships. The War Metallurgy Committee was one of the many groups assembled by the NAS/NRC to assist during World War II. Among its tasks was to study the ship fracture problem.

Experimental Model Basin — At the beginning of World War II, the oldest of the major laboratories of the Navy was the Experimental Model Basin at the Washington Navy Yard, established in 1899 under the Bureau of Construction and Repair. The facility was established after years of advocacy by the famous naval officer-scientist-engineer David Watson Taylor, at the time, Commander, USN. This testing station was the site of the experiments leading to Taylor's Standard Series and his world-renowned book, *The Speed and Power of Ships*. It continued in operation throughout the war to pick up the overload of work from its successor, the David Taylor Model Basin at Carderock, Maryland.[162]

Engineering Experiment Station (EES) — In 1908, another useful naval laboratory was established.

It was the Engineering Experiment [sic] Station (EES) on the Severn River at Annapolis, Maryland, near the Naval Academy. At the time of its establishment, EES was under the Bureau of Steam Engineering. This laboratory was the center for testing and research on ships' propulsion systems. At the end of World War II it was engaged with closed-cycle propulsion for submarines until the advent of nuclear power provided a superior alternative.[163]

United States Naval Radio Telegraphic Laboratory—The first application of electronics in the U.S. Navy was in radio communications. In 1908, the United States Naval Radio Telegraphic Laboratory was established at the National Bureau of Standards. Cognizance of this laboratory was transferred to the Bureau of Steam Engineering in 1910.[164]

Naval Ordnance Laboratory—The Naval Ordnance Laboratory (NOL) was established in the Washington Navy Yard in 1918. (Postwar, a new facility was built at White Oak, Maryland.)

Naval Research Laboratory (NRL)—In response to the need for a home for broader-based basic science, NRL was established in 1923 at its present site at Belleview, District of Columbia, on the Potomac River, and became the source of many electronic marvels used by the United States fleet during World War II. Its success with radar had tended to eclipse its other important contributions in such fields as metallurgy, optics, nuclear energy, shock, and vibration.[165]

New Organizations

David Taylor Model Basin (DTMB)—The first new Navy laboratory to go on line during World War II was not an emergency response to wartime needs. It was the David Taylor Model Basin (DTMB), which fortuitously had been in the planning and construction stages long before the beginning of the war. Its technical activity was an extension of the work of the Experimental Model Basin in the Washington Navy Yard, but physically it was clearly the largest and finest hydrodynamics facility for ship model testing in the world. The new laboratory also offered facilities for the study of structural mechanics of ship hulls, aerodynamics, and underwater explosions. But the main thrust was hydrodynamics.

DTMB was dedicated on 11 April 1939 as a laboratory under the direction of the Bureau of Construction and Repair. The first technical director was another gifted scientist-engineer, Captain Harold E. Saunders, USN, who had been instrumental in the design of the facility.[166]

National Defense Research Committee (NDRC)—By 1940, the importance of new technology to our war effort was widely recognized, and the need to provide a better focus of national capabilities was being pressed by renowned scientists, including Dr. F. B. Jewett of the National Academy of Sciences. Under Dr. Jewett's urging, President Franklin Delano Roosevelt issued an executive order on 27 June 1940 establishing the NDRC, "to correlate and support scientific research on the mechanisms and devices of warfare."[167]

M.I.T. Radiation Laboratory—At the suggestion of the British, the United States undertook two related projects: microwave airborne intercept radar, and microwave anti-aircraft fire control radar. To prosecute these projects, a new laboratory, the Radiation Laboratory at the Massachusetts Institute of Technology, started operations in November 1940 under the direction of Dr. Lee A. DuBridge.[168]

Office of Scientific Research and Development (OSRD)—To provide for the necessary overall sponsorship, guidance, and coordination of scientific research outside of the Federal laboratories, OSRD was established as an independent agency on 28 June 1941.[169] The new agency was headed by Dr. Vannevar Bush and received guidance from the NDRC. The OSRD was viewed as a wartime operation and was terminated at the end of the war.[170]

Harvard Radio Research Laboratory—Another laboratory established to address wartime needs was the Harvard Radio Research Laboratory. This innocuous sounding title merely obscured the function of the laboratory, which was to study radar countermeasures, codes, and enemy surveillance—electronic warfare, that is. The laboratory was opened in 1942 and closed in 1946 after a short, but useful, career.[171]

Office of Patents and Inventions/Office of Research and Inventions/Office of Naval Research—An advisory committee under the chairmanship of R. J. Dearborn, on 10 March 1944, recommended that the Navy establish centralized management for its scientific activities. This recommendation resulted in the establishment of the Office of Patents and Inventions on 19 October 1944. It was in the Office of the Secretary of the Navy, with Vice Admiral Harold G. Bowen as the first director. One of the factors in this action was the need to provide a home for Navy science management as the war drew to a close and the end of the OSRD became imminent. The Navy's research coordination was strengthened, and, on 19 May 1945, the organization became the Office of Research and Inventions. Just after the war, on 1 August 1946, by Act of Congress, Public Law 588, it became the Office of Naval Research.[172]

Other Laboratories

Three other important laboratories established during World War II became a permanent part of the Naval establishment. In 1942, the Bureau of Ships established the Naval Electronics Laboratory (NEL) in San Diego, California, to work on shipboard electronics problems. In August 1943, the Bureau of Ordnance established the Naval Ordnance Test Station (NOTS) at Inyokern, California, to provide a test site for its growing rocket developments, and, on 1 March 1945, the Naval Research Laboratory opened a branch in Orlando, Florida, the Underwater Sound Reference Division. The latter provided a site for precision testing of the ever more elaborate sonar equipment for shipboard use.[173]

ADDITIONAL NAVAL ENGINEERING ACTIVITY

In addition to the Bureau of Ships, there was much other significant naval engineering. The activities of the Bureau of Yards and Docks, founded in 1842, and headed in World War II by Admiral Ben Morrell, CEC, the "King Bee of the Seabees," included extensive and varied naval engineering such as drydocks and pontoon causeways. BuOrd, also founded in 1842, strained to keep the fleets and our allies supplied with munitions, weapons, and fire control equipment. A younger organization, the Bureau of Aeronautics, formed in 1921, was vital to the war

effort in many ways as carrier aviation became paramount.

U.S. Coast Guard

The U.S. Coast Guard, ordered on 1 November 1941 to operate as part of the Navy, made outstanding contributions, both operationally and technically. The shift of the Coast Guard to the Navy was a statutory shift; we were not even at war yet. The regular duties of the Coast Guard continued and were added to as activity in shipyards, ports, and off the coasts increased. The duties included patrolling coastlines, providing navigational aid, lifesaving, and ensuring merchant marine safety. The latter entailed inspecting ship construction and repairs and taking the lead in solving the ship fracture problem.

U.S. Army

At the beginning of World War II, the U.S. Army was said to have more ships and boats than the U.S. Navy. The Army Corps of Engineers surveyed and maintained all the inland waterways. They operated dredges, tow boats, and survey launches. In addition, the Army Transportation Corps operated all troop transports.

When the United States entered the war, the Army's fleet of transports was inadequate to meet predicted war needs. They immediately sought to charter passenger vessels and to prepare them for the troop loads they would have to carry, many times the peacetime passenger load.

The problems of troopship conversions are illustrated by the USAT *John L. Clem*, a passenger ship under conversion at the Army base in New Orleans. For defense, on the wings of the lower bridge, two small field artillery guns were installed and could be seen as painters were busy covering the gay paint of the liner with more somber colors while the ship was being readied for a stability test. The test revealed a difficult problem. The large number of troops and their gear added considerably to the topside weight. Also, this large number of passengers would be aboard long enough to consume all fresh water. Since the water tanks were in the ship's inner bottom, the stability would be further reduced. Large seawater distillation units were planned as the solution. It typified costliness of the troop-ship conversions.[174]

U.S. Maritime Commission

The Maritime Commission was created under the Merchant Marine Act of 1936 with the duty to enhance the United States Merchant Marine through research and development and various ship construction and operating benefits. The new chairman of the Commission, appointed by President Roosevelt in April 1937, was Rear Admiral Emory Scott Land, recently retired from the Navy. Land was an exceptionally able and well-respected naval constructor. He had completed the graduate program at the Massachusetts Institute of Technology, and had held important billets, including Chief of the Bureau of Construction and Repair. Admiral Land assumed responsibility for the ship design and construction activities of the Commission, and began to strengthen the organization as war loomed. He was a longtime friend of the President, from the days when Roosevelt was Assistant Secretary of the Navy. To strengthen the technical staff, he recruited a most capable ship designer, James L. Bates, who had worked for the Navy for 30 years, most recently as head of the Bureau of Construction and Repair preliminary design branch. Bates was named director of the Technical Division. Admiral Land guided the Commission through the greatest shipbuilding program ever seen. He was an excellent choice. He was made a Vice Admiral in July 1944 by a special act of Congress.[175]

War Shipping Administration

Many emergency ship construction activities were removed from the Maritime Commission by Executive Order on 7 February 1942, and along with ship operating functions, they were established in the War Shipping Administration. Admiral Land assumed the added duty of administrator of this new organization and named Captain Howard L. Vickery, also formerly with the Bureau of Construction and Repair of the Navy and of the Maritime Commission, to be his deputy director for ship construction.[176]

American Bureau of Shipping

The American Bureau of Shipping (ABS), formed in 1862, is governed by a board of shipbuilders, ship operators, and insurance underwriters. This agency sets standards and checks merchant and passenger ship construction plans. Its surveyors inspect construction, repair, and maintenance. The ABS surveyed all of the wartime merchant ship construction, and as a part of this duty was deeply involved in the ship fracture problem. The chief surveyor during the war years was Mr. David Arnott.[177]

U.S. Naval Technical Mission in Europe

According to the recollections of Captain Henry Arnold, USN (Ret):

> As the pages dropped from the calendar of 1944 and the eventual outcome of WWII came into focus, three senior naval officers, Commodore Henry A. Schade, Captain Albert G. Mumma, and Captain Wendell P. Roop, perceived an incipient problem and, to solve it, conceived a novel task for naval engineers. The German Navy had developed some new and outstanding technology in certain fields (e.g., rockets, sonar, submarine design and construction, fast planing boats, and propulsion machinery). In the chaos that would mark the dissolution of the Third Reich, this technology might be lost, destroyed or otherwise denied to the Allies—or, worse—fall into the hands of the Japanese. (VJ day was still a year away.) To uncover, capture, and preserve this technology—key people as well as documents, machinery and equipment—for the exclusive use of the United States and its allies became the mission of a unique organization called the Naval Technical Mission to Europe, or more often, NavTechMisEu.[178]

Recognition of the problem and proposal of the novel solution occurred early in 1944, and a plan had been waiting on the desk of Vice Admiral Cochrane, Chief of BuShips. When the opportunity came, a naval technical party joined an Army mission in the fall of 1944, but the group soon outgrew its Army parent, and NavTechMisEu was commissioned in January 1945. The main headquarters was established in Paris. The scope of the mission is illustrated by the titles of its five sections: Ship, Ordnance, Air, Yards and Docks, and Electronics.[179]

When Germany surrendered in May 1945, the many parts of NavTechMisEu began to assemble their hoard of valuables into reports and packages that were forwarded to the various Navy control centers in the United States. Near the end of 1945, most of the mission had returned home and the operation was dovetailed into "Project Paperclip," which helped move interested scientists and engineers from Germany to the United States.[180]

Conclusions

Leadership

The Allied nations were fortunate to have two great leaders, President Roosevelt and Prime Minister Churchill. These two were compatible in the conduct of war, and moreover, were statesmen who knew how nations work and had a considerable understanding of the armed forces and how they operate. The two leaders recognized the United States as the most productive nation in the world. They felt that it was capable of almost unlimited production magic. Their view, shared by much of the rest of the world, was that the United States was the "Arsenal of Democracy." The hope of the leaders and of the Allied nations was realized by fine organization and management. The productive magic worked; the Allied strategies and tactics were effective and well supported by the American material.

Innovation and Dedication

The ships and fleets emerging from World War II were a different breed from those that entered. The aircraft carrier had superseded the battleship as the capital ship, and air defense was a major characteristics of every fleet unit. Aircraft and missiles were on their way to supplanting the "big guns," and the variety of special-purpose ships seemed to have no end. Ship complexity had multiplied. The dominant aspect of complexity was electronics in every system, from navigation to proximity fuse. The post-World War II fleet totally outclassed the pre-World War II units in every area of naval warfare.[181]

There had been technical innovation in earlier wars, but more frequently the contest had been between men, tactics, and strategies, with little or no change in the weapons during the course of the war. In contrast, during World War II, almost every naval combat system saw major

innovation. Major advances in combat systems resulted from utilizing modern science as a basis for technical innovation. Other features of World War II were the exchange of technical information among the Allies, the coordination of the utilization of resources, and the rapid introduction of novel combat systems. A notable attitude was the willingness to take risks, with a consequent telescoping of the normal research and development gestation period. This procedure permitted new ideas and science to move from the committee rooms to production in as little as 2 years. The Americans and British were favored by a substantial reservoir of up-to-date science that was exploited from the beginning of the war. On the other hand, little science discovered during World War II saw combat. On 8 December 1945, Fleet Admiral E. J. King, USN, reported to the Secretary of the Navy:

> It had often been predicted that in a national emergency the totalitarian countries would have a great advantage over the democracies because of their ability to regiment scientific facilities and manpower at will. The results achieved by Germany, Italy, and Japan do not bear out this contention. Studies made since the close of the war indicate that in none of these countries was the scientific effort as effectively handled as in the United States. The rapid, effective and original results obtained in bringing science into our effort are proof of the responsiveness of our form of government to meeting emergencies, the technical competence of American scientists, and the productive genius of American Industry.[182]

It is natural to be fascinated by the exotic new combat systems that saw action in World War II. It is appropriate, even an obligation, to feel respectful and thankful toward the creators of the systems, which shortened and helped to win the war for the Allies. Value attaches to the achievements of the naval engineers because their achievements made it possible for the United States to prevail over its enemies and to limit human suffering by hastening the end of combat. The ships, aircraft, torpedoes, and guns were only one part of the system. Each system included men who accompanied the systems into combat, and these men deserve an even greater measure of our respect and gratitude. The scientists and designers loaned their brains to save the nation, but the seamen and operating officers risked their lives to operate the systems in combat. In October 1987, at the dedication of the Navy Memorial in Washington, D.C., the Secretary of the Navy, James H. Webb, Jr., had this to say: "We don't send a naval force into a crisis, and we don't send ships. We send people. . . ."

Notes

1 Sims, A. J., "Warships 1860-1960," *Transactions of the Royal Institution of Naval Architects*, Vol. 102, London, 1960.

2 Billings, John Shaw and Daniel Longwell, *Life's Picture History of World War II,* Time Incorporated, 1950.

3 *Naval Chronology, World War II,* Naval History Division, Office of Chief of Naval Operations, U.S. Navy Department, Washington, D.C.: Government Printing Office, 1955.

4 Morison, Samuel Eliot, *Two-Ocean War, A Short History of the United States in the Second World War,* Boston, Massachusetts: Little, Brown and Company, 1963.

5 Bamford, James, *The Puzzle Palace,* Penguin Books, Houghton Mifflin Co., 1983.

6 Johnson, Ellis A. and David A. Katcher, *Mines Against Japan,* Silver Spring, Maryland: Naval Ordnance Laboratory, White Oak, 1973.

7 Billings and Longwell, *Picture History.* Also, *Naval Chronology,* 1955; Morison, *Two-Ocean War.*

8 Sims, "Warships," p. 658.

9 Sims, "Warships." Also, Schade, Henry A., Commodore, USN, "German Wartime Technical Developments," *Transactions,* Society of Naval Architects and Marine Engineers, Vol. 54, New York, 1946, p. 83.

10 MacCutcheon, Edward M., unpublished notes of author's personal recollections.

11 Johnson, Robert S., "The Changing Nature of the U.S. Ship Design Process," *Naval Engineers Journal,* Vol. 92-2, April 1980. Also, "Edward Lull Cochrane, Obituary," *Transactions,* SNAME 1959, New York, 1960.

12 *Naval Chronology,* 1955.

13 Morison, *Two-Ocean War.*

14 Nicholson, William Mac, Captain, USN (Ret), Anecdotes, 19 March 1987.

15 Sims, "Warships."

16 Nicholson anecdotes, 1987.

17 *Naval Chronology,* 1955. Also "The Navy's Need for New Destroyers," *Washington Post,* 26 August 1986; Calhoun, C. Raymond, Captain, USN (Ret.), *Typhoon: The Other Enemy,* Annapolis, Maryland: Naval Institute Press, 1981.

18 Secretary of the Navy—Board of Investigation Final Report, "To Inquire Into The Design and Methods of Construction of Welded Steel Merchant Vessels, 15 July 1946," Washington, D.C.: GPO, 1947.

19 *Ibid.*

20 *Ibid.,* Also, MacCutcheon notes.

21 MacCutcheon notes.

22 Shank, M. E., "Brittle Failure in Carbon Plate Steel; Structures Other than Ships," Ship Structure Committee Report SSC65, National Academy of Science, National Research Council, Washington, D.C., 1 December 1953.

23 *Ibid.,* Also, "To Inquire Into Design and Methods of Construction of Merchant Vessels, 15 July 1946."

24 "To Inquire Into Design and Methods of Construction of Merchant Vessels, 15 July 1946." Also, Jonanssen, Finn, "A Summary of the Research Work Conducted Under the Direction of the Ship Structure Committee," *Transactions,* SNAME, Vol. 57, New York, 1949, p. 556.

25 MacCutcheon notes.

26 Lane, Frederic C., *Ships for Victory, A History of Ship Building Under the U.S. Maritime Commission in World War II, Historical Reports on War Administration,* United States Maritime Commission No. 1, Baltimore, Maryland: The Johns Hopkins Press, 1951.

27 *Ibid.*

28 Fassett, F. G., Jr. Professor, (editor), et al., *The Shipbuilding Business in the United States of America,* Vol. 1, SNAME, New York, 1948.

29 Lane, *Ships for Victory.*

30 Scher, Robert and Cy Barnes, *Naval Architecture and Marine Engineering at the University of Michigan, 1881-1981,* Ann Arbor, Michigan, 1981.

31 Ela, Dennett K., Captain, USN (Ret), Anecdotes, 26 January 1987.

32 Lane, *Ships for Victory.* Also, Fassett, et al., *The Shipbuilding Business.*

33 Oakley, Owen H., Notes especially prepared for chapter 7, unpublished, 14 July 1986 and subsequent dates.

34 *Ibid.,* Also, Fahey, James C., *The Ships and Aircraft of the U.S. Fleet,* Victory Edition, Ships and Aircraft, New York, 1945.

35 "Edward Lull Cochrane, Obituary," *Transactions,* SNAME, Vol. 67, New York, 1959, p. 789.

36 *Ibid.,* Also, Fassett, et al., *The Shipbuilding Business.*

37 Fassett, et al., *The Shipbuilding Business.*

38 *Ibid.*

39 Sims, "Warships."

40 Owen Oakley notes, including citings from Fahey, *Ships and Aircraft of the U.S. Fleet.*

41 Howeth, L. S., Captain, USN (Ret), *History of Communications—Electronics in the United States Navy,* Washington, D.C.: Government Printing Office, 1963. Also, Allison, David Kite, *New Eye for the Navy: The Origin of Radar at the Naval Research Laboratory,* Naval Research Laboratory, Washington, D.C.: Government Printing Office, September 1981.

42 Harrison, Charles W., Jr., Commander, USN, and James E. Blower, "Electronics—Your Future," *ASNE Journal,* Vol. 62, No. 1, February 1950, p. 99.

43 Howeth, *History of Communications.*

44 *Ibid.,* Also, Harrison and Blower, "Electronics—Your Future."

45 Howeth, *History of Communications.*

46 Rowland, Buford, Lieutenant Commander, USNR, and William Bn. Boyd, Lieutenant, USNR, *U.S. Navy Bureau of Ordnance in World War II,* Bureau of Ordnance, Dept. of the Navy, Washington, D.C.: Government Printing Office, 1954.

47 Price, Alfred, *The History of Electronic Warfare,* The Association of Old Crows, USA, 1984.

48 *Ibid.*

49 *Ibid.,* p. 29.

50 Hezlet, Vice Admiral Sir Arthur, K.B.E., C.B., D.S.O., D.S.C., *Electronics and Sea Power,* New York, N.Y.: Stein and Day, 1975.

51 Morison, *Two-Ocean War.*

52 *Ibid.,* Also, *Naval Chronology,* 1955; Hezlet, *Electronics and Sea Power;* Roscoe, Theodore, *United States Destroyer Operations in World War II,* Annapolis, Maryland: Naval Institute Press, 1953.

53 Morison, *Two-Ocean War.*

54 *Ibid.,* Also, Billings and Longwell, *Picture History; Naval Chronology,* 1955; Morison, *Two-Ocean War.*

55 Owen Oakley notes.

56 Hezlet, *Electronics and Sea Power.*

57 Howeth, *History of Communications.*

58 Christman, Albert B., *Sailors, Scientists, and Rockets,* (History of the Naval Weapons Center, China Lake, California, Vol. I), Naval History Division, Navy Dept., Washington, D.C., 1971.

59 *Naval Chronology,* 1955.

60 Ashworth, Frederick L., Vice Admiral, USN (Ret), "Rear Admiral William S. Parsons, USN and the Atomic Bomb," *Shipmate,* July-August 1986, Annapolis, Maryland: U.S. Naval Academy Alumni Association, p. 24.

61 Rowland and Boyd, *U.S. Navy Bureau of Ordnance in World War II.*

62 Roscoe, *U.S. Destroyer Operations in World War II.*

63 *Ibid.,* Also, Rowland and Boyd, *U.S. Navy Bureau of Ordnance in World War II.*

64 Dulin, Robert O., Jr. and William H. Garzke, Jr., *Battleships, United States Battleships in World War II,* Annapolis, Maryland: Naval Institute Press, 1976. Also, Reilly, John, Naval History Division, Navy Dept., telephone conference with author 17 February 1988.

65 Rowland and Boyd, *U.S. Navy Bureau of Ordnance in World War II.*

66 *Ibid.*

67 *Ibid.*

68 *Ibid.*

69 *Ibid.*

70 MacCutcheon notes.

71 Howeth, *History of Communications.* Also, Rowland and Boyd, *U.S. Navy Bureau of Ordnance in World War II.*

72 Howeth, *History of Communications,* p. 497.

73 *Ibid.,* Also, Rowland and Boyd, *U.S. Navy Bureau of Ordnance in World War II.*

74 Rowland and Boyd, *U.S. Navy Bureau of Ordnance in World War II.*

75 *Ibid.*

76 Personal interview with Arne D. Yensen regarding proximity fuse tests, 12 April 1987.

77 Rowland and Boyd, *U.S. Navy Bureau of Ordnance in World War II.*

78 Owen Oakley notes.

79 Hezlet, *Electronics and Sea Power.*

80 Billings and Longwell, *Picture History.* Also, Owen Oakley notes.

81 Price, *History of Electronic Warfare.*

82 Sims, "Warships."

83 Hezlet, *Electronics and Sea Power.* Also, Gordon, Don, E., *Electronic Warfare Element of Strategy and Multiplier of Combat Power,* New York, N.Y.: Pergamon Press, 1981.

84 Clark, Ronald, *The Man Who Broke Purple,* Boston, Massachusetts: Little, Brown & Co., 1977.

85 Kozaczuk, Wladyslaw, *Enigma,* University Publications of America, Inc., 1985; Also, Layton, Edwin T., Rear Admiral, USN (Ret), *And I Was There,* New York, N.Y.: William Morrow and Co., Inc., 1985; Lewin, Ronald, *The American Magic,* New York, N.Y.: Farar Straus Giroux, 1982.

86 Hezlet, *Electronics and Sea Power.*

87 Clark, *Man Who Broke Purple.*

88 Bamford, *Puzzle Palace.* Also, Owen Oakley notes.

89 Lewin, Ronald, *ULTRA Goes To War,* New York, N.Y.: McGraw-Hill, 1978. Also, Kozaczuk, *Enigma*; Layton, *And I Was There*; Lewin, *American Magic.*

90 Bamford, *Puzzle Palace.* Also, Owen Oakley notes.

91 Howeth, *History of Communications.*

92 *Ibid.* Also, Morison, *Two-Ocean War.*

93 Johnson and Katcher, *Mines Against Japan,* pp. 228, 231.

94 Morison, *Two-Ocean War.*

95 Hinsley, F. H., et al., *British Intelligence in the Second World War,* New York, N.Y.: Cambridge University Press, 1981. Also, Hezlet, *Electronics and Sea Power.*

96 Morison, *Two-Ocean War.*

97 Hezlet, *Electronics and Sea Power.*

98 *Ibid.,* Also, Morison, *Two-Ocean War*; Baxter, James Phinney, *Scientists Against Time,* Cambridge, Massachusetts: The M.I.T. Press, 1968.

99 Sims, "Warships." Also, Rowland and Boyd, *U.S. Navy Bureau of Ordnance in World War II.*

100 Rowland and Boyd, *U.S. Navy Bureau of Ordnance in World War II.*

101 Nicholson, anecdotes, 7 April 1987.

102 Rowland and Boyd, *U.S. Navy Bureau of Ordnance in World War II.*

103 Morison, *Two-Ocean War.*

104 *Ibid.*

105 Hezlet, *Electronics and Sea Power.*

106 Morison, *Two-Ocean War.*

107 MacCutcheon notes. Also, Morison, *Two-Ocean War.*

108 Morison, *Two-Ocean War.* Also, Schade, "German Wartime Technical Developments," SNAME, 1946.

109 Sims, "Warships." Also, Roscoe, Theodore, *United States Submarine Operations in World War II,* Annapolis, Maryland: Naval Institute Press, 1949.

110 *Naval Chronology,* 1955. Also, Fahey, *Ships and Aircraft.*

111 Alden, John D., Commander, USN (Ret), *The Fleet Submarine in the U.S. Navy, A Design and Construction History,* Annapolis, Maryland: Naval Institute Press, 1979.

112 *Ibid.*

113 *Ibid.*

114 *Ibid.*

115 *Ibid.*

116 Howeth, *History of Communications.*

117 Roscoe, *Submarine Operations.*

118 Rowland and Boyd, *U.S. Navy Bureau of Ordnance in World War II,* p. 95.

119 Johnson, *Mines Against Japan.*

120 Roscoe, *Submarine Operations.*

121 *Ibid.* Also, Beach, Edward L., Commander, USN, *Submarine!,* New York, N.Y.: Henry Holt and Company, 1946.

122 Rowland and Boyd, *U.S. Navy Bureau of Ordnance in World War II.* Also, Roscoe, *Submarine Operations.*

123 Roscoe, *Submarine Operations.*

124 *Ibid.* Also, Johnson, *Mines Against Japan.*

125 Rowland and Boyd, *U.S. Navy Bureau of Ordnance in World War II.*

126 *Ibid.*

127 Roscoe, *Submarine Operations.*

128 *Ibid.*

129 *Ibid.*

130 Hooper, Edwin B., Vice Admiral, USN (Ret), "Over the Span of 200 Years—Technology and the United States Navy, *Naval Engineers Journal,* August 1976, p. 17.

131 Rowland and Boyd, *U.S. Navy Bureau of Ordnance in World War II.*

132 Roscoe, *Submarine Operations.*

133 *Ibid.*

134 Roosevelt, Franklin Delano, undated "Sketch of Landing Ship," at the Franklin D. Roosevelt Library and Museum, Hyde Park, New York.

135 Sims, "Warships."

136 Owen Oakley notes.

137 *Ibid.,* Also, Johnson, "Changing Nature of Ship Design Process.

138 Owen Oakley notes.

139 *Naval Chronology,* 1955.

140 Sims, "Warships."

141 Fassett, *The Shipbuilding Business.* Also, Owen Oakley notes.

142 Owen Oakley notes.

143 Billings and Longwell, *Picture History.*

144 Owen Oakley notes.

145 *Ibid.*

146 *Ibid.*

147 Andrea, Mario I, Ph.D., unpublished anecdotes regarding the launching and assembly of LCTs, Bethesda, Maryland, 8 May 1987.

148 Owen Oakley notes.

149 Mario Andrea anecdotes.

150 *Ibid.*

151 Matthews, Charles, "John Laycock CEC, USN Patron of the Pontoon," *The Navy Civil Engineer*, August 1968.

152 Unassembled notes from Bureau of Yards and Docks Archives, Port Hueneme, California.

153 *Ibid.*, Also, Mario Andrea anecdotes.

154 Mario Andrea anecdotes.

155 Rowland and Boyd, *U.S. Navy Bureau of Ordnance in World War II.*

156 Nicholson anecdotes, March 1987.

157 Rowland and Boyd, *U.S. Navy Bureau of Ordnance in World War II.*

158 Johnson and Katcher, *Mines Against Japan.*

159 Sims, "Warships." Also, Miller, Richards T., Captain, USN (Ret), "Minesweepers," *Naval Review, 1967*, Annapolis, Maryland: U.S. Naval Institute, 1966.

160 Miller, "Minesweepers."

161 Howeth, *History of Communications.*

162 Allison, *New Eye for the Navy.* Also, Rock, George H., Rear Admiral, (CC), USN (Ret), editor, *et al.*, *Historical Transactions, 1853-1943*, Society of Naval Architects and Marine Engineers, New York, 1945; Hovgaard, William, *Biographical Memoir of David Watson Taylor, 1864-1940*, Presented at Annual Meeting of National Academy of Sciences, Vol. XXII–Seventh Memoir, Washington, D.C., 1941.

163 Allison, *New Eye for the Navy.*

164 *Ibid.* Also, Howeth, *History of Communications.*

165 Allison, *New Eye for the Navy.* Also, Bowen, Harold G., Vice Admiral, USN (Ret), Ships, *Machinery and Mossbacks*, Princeton, New Jersey: Princeton University Press. 1954.

166 Saunders, Harold E., Captain, USN, "The David W. Taylor Model Basin," *Transactions*, Vol. 48, SNAME, New York, 1940.

167 Allison, *New Eye for the Navy.* Also, Baxter, *Scientists Against Time.*

168 Allison, *New Eye for the Navy.* Also, Howeth, *History of Communications.*

169 Allison, *New Eye for the Navy.*

170 *Ibid.* Also, Brinckloe, W. D., Captain, USN, "Research Navy," *Proceedings*, U.S. Naval Institute, Annapolis, Maryland, 1958.

171 Allison, *New Eye for the Navy.* Also, Brinckloe, "Research Navy;" Price, *History of Electronic Warfare.*

172 Brinckloe, "Research Navy." Also, Bowen, Harold G., Vice Admiral USN (Ret), "Reminiscences," *ASNE Journal.* May 1957.

173 Christman, *Sailors, Scientists, and Rockets.* Also, Howeth, *History of Communications.*

174 MacCutcheon notes.

175 Lane, *Ships for Victory.*

176 *Ibid.*

177 Rock, *et al., Historical Transactions, 1893-1943*, SNAME, 1945.

178 Arnold, Henry, Captain, USN (Ret), *A Different Kind of Naval Engineering*, unpublished anecdotes, 20 April 1987.

179 Schade, "German Wartime Technical Developments."

180 *Ibid.*, Also, Arnold, *A Different Kind of Naval Engineering.*

181 Sims, "Warships."

182 Howeth, *History of Communications.*

CHAPTER
EIGHT
1945–1950

Search for a Mission

by Robert L. Scheina

INTRODUCTION

The defeat of Germany and Japan completely changed the goals of the U.S. Navy, thus altering the direction of naval engineering in this country. Prior to and during the war, the U.S. Navy envisioned its primary role to be seeking out and destroying the enemy's fleet. But during the years immediately following the war, there was no significant naval threat. Admittedly, the Soviet Navy rapidly built up its submarine force, enhanced by German technology, but the impotency of the Soviet submarine force during World War II lent little credibility to this threat. With no enemy fleet to immediately confront, the Navy sought new missions in the context of potential conflicts.

A land war with the Soviet Union was envisioned to be the most likely future conflict. The Navy projected two potential roles in such a war. First, the Navy began to develop the capacity for attacking targets *deep inland*, or strategic bombing. The ability to even conceive of such a role for the Navy was made possible by the tremendous acceleration of technology that had taken place during World War II. Prior to the war, navies could fleetingly influence events only a hundred or so miles inland—the operational radius and time over target of carrier aircraft of that day. Second, since such a war was envisioned as being a lengthy rerun of World War II, and one which could not be won by the use of the atom bomb (even by 1950, many military leaders believed that not enough nuclear weapons existed to force a successful end to such a war, an opinion apparently not shared by most of the public), the Navy had to be prepared to protect convoys resupplying Europe and project amphibious forces far from safe havens. The advent of the atomic age did cause doubt that large-scale amphibious landings would take place in the future; the submarine would become an increasing threat to the resupply and amphibious convoys.

National economic priorities changed almost overnight on V-J day. America was tired of war and all that was associated with it. Americans had the mind-set that now that Nazi Germany and Imperial Japan had been defeated, the world was safe for democracies. Few remembered the tensions that had existed with the Soviet Union and Stalin prior to the war. The American public, in part, was a victim of Allied wartime propaganda re-forming the Soviet image. Also, America was the sole possessor of the atom bomb and it was backed by the greatest arsenal of weapons ever produced. Therefore, it should not come as a surprise that any new initiatives for programs that would result in significant military spending were not favorably received, and that the few approved were approved reluctantly. One need only review the Navy's budget in the post-war years to appreciate its plight. Between 1945 and 1947 the budgets were $30, $15, and $6 billion; and by 1948 to 1950, it was only $4 billion. This was the political and economic realities within which the Navy had to live.[1]

INITIAL POST-WAR DESIGNS

Given the large number of warships on hand of all types, the Navy could, at best, expect to get only a few new units, whose purpose, at least in the eyes of Congress, would be to stimulate the evolution of technology at as little expense as possible. The reality of the situation was that the projected needs for the most part would be filled by redesigning existing units.

On top of this, the Navy was confronted with the problem of preserving the large numbers of surplus warships. The limited budget had to be stretched to include the "mothballing" of these ships, a program from which the Navy could only benefit in the long term. In early 1944, the office of Demobilization and Post War Planning was created. This office was responsible for preserving some 3,000 ships in an inactive status. This had to be accomplished at a minimal cost, primarily by the regular crews assisted by a specialist. These ships had to be able to be returned to duty within 30 days. Therefore, all ship's records, equipment, bedding, galley equipment, plans, instructions, manuals, and other items necessary to permit the ship to be ready for

service within the needed time were left on board. The Navy chose to preserve its most important mothballed units through dehumidification. First, the ships were given pre-deactivation overhauls. Spare parts were brought up to prescribed allowances. After dehumidification equipment were installed, the ships were then sealed. Machinery was coated with preservatives. Open-mount gun mounts had their barrels removed, then the mounts were cocooned with a desiccant placed inside. At regular intervals, these ships had to be drydocked and painted topside. The estimate for mothballing the ships was $12,000,000—the construction cost of a destroyer.[2]

The introduction of new warship classifications shortly after World War II symbolized the new missions envisioned by the Navy. The immediate post-World War II surface warship development, whether new construction or conversions, could be placed into three categories: carriers for strategic bombing, task force escorts to protect the carriers, and ocean escorts to protect the convoys. However, the traditional nomenclature, such as cruisers and destroyers, persisted on paper and in the minds and hearts of all. Among other steps taken by the Navy to help give direction to future efforts was the establishment of the Office of Naval Research in 1946.[3]

THE EVOLVING SURFACE NAVY

The key to the Navy's strategic bombing role would be a new breed of aircraft carrier. This carrier was not to be just the usual evolution of bigger and better. It was to be a whole new animal. Between 1945 and November 1948, some seventy-eight different carrier designs were considered before one was accepted for the 6A Carrier Project. The new carrier was authorized under the 1949 Naval Appropriations Act and the contract was awarded to the Newport News Shipbuilding and Dry Dock Company.

The carrier United States was specifically designed to accommodate a new generation of long-range bomber capable of delivering nuclear weapons. A smaller carrier design of between 35,000 and 40,000 tons was studied. A ship this size, however, could not accommodate the large aircraft needed to handle nuclear weapons, which at this time were huge.[4] The *United States'* design possessed what now are seen as some radical features. The earlier designs did not incorporate a hangar deck; the aircraft would be much too large to be stowed below decks. (A hangar deck was added to subsequent designs, but apparently this was intended only for use by the fighter escorts.) Less space was devoted to magazines than in later classes due to the subordination of nonstrategic missions. A flush deck design without an island was selected to simplify flight operations, but this did create significant exhaust disposal problems. The unusual shape of the flight deck was the result of the desire to be able to launch two bombers and two fighters simultaneously. However, the ship was not designed to be able to launch and recover aircraft at the same time. Among the innovations was a new type of internal combustion cylindrical catapult.

A four-ship class was projected. Funds were approved by the House of Representatives on 13 April 1949, and the *United States* was laid down at Newport News on the 18th. The development of a carrier designed to carry strategic bombers brought the Navy and Air Force into conflict. The Navy argued that it needed such a carrier to be able to attack enemy submarines at their bases. Obviously, the Navy had other targets in mind as well, but these would have been even less well received by the Air Force. The Air Force argued that the new carrier would merely duplicate its capability at a cost of $500 million. The Navy estimated the cost to be $189 million. The Air Force won out. On 15 April, even before the carrier had been laid down, the Secretary of Defense, Louis Johnson, again asked the Joint Chiefs of Staff to review the project amid renewed criticism. After reviewing their reply, the Secretary canceled the construction on the 23rd. The next day, the Secretary of the Navy, John L. Sullivan resigned in protest. Construction on the *United States* stopped 5 days after it had begun and the funds for the program were transferred to the Air Force for bombers. At least for the moment, the fate of the large aircraft carrier within the U.S. Navy was very much in doubt.[5]

In spite of the fact that the backbone of the carrier force, the *Essex* class, was less than 5 years old by 1945, these ships needed to be modernized. In April of that year, carrier task force commanders had requested heavier and larger aircraft to prosecute the war with Japan. This could only be viewed as a long-term proposal because it could only be achieved by developing new aircraft and reinforcing existing carriers. When proposed, neither atom bomb had yet been dropped and many military planners projected that the war with Japan would last until 1948.

This call to improve the ability to carry heavier aircraft was reinforced by numerous experiments that took place soon after the war. In July 1946, an FD-1 Phantom jet took off from the carrier *Franklin D. Roosevelt*. In March 1948, an FJ-1 Fury jet operated from the *Boxer*. A month later, a Jato-assisted P2V Neptune took off from the deck of the *Coral Sea*. And on 5 May 1948, the first all-jet squadron became carrier-qualified on board the light carrier *Saipan*.[6]

The first existing carriers to receive alterations were the members of the new, and substantially heavier *Franklin D. Roosevelt* class. In April 1947 the lead ship was given a "special weapons" (i.e., nuclear weapons) capacity under Ship Improvement Program No. 1. She was followed by sisters *Midway* and *Coral Sea*. Post-war requirements also necessitated rebuilding the *Essex* units so that they could accommodate heavier aircraft. On 4 June 1947 the Chief of Naval Operations approved the plans for the reconstruction of the *Essex* class. Known as Project 27A, its principal goal was to give the reconstructed carriers the capacity to operate aircraft up to 40,000 pounds gross weight. This was achieved by replacing the H4-1 catapult with the H-8 model, strengthening the flight deck, increasing the deck space available for aircraft, increasing the elevators' capacities and dimensions, adding jet blast deflectors, and increasing their aviation fuel capacity. Space and weight savings were accomplished primarily by removing four twin 5in/38 mounts from the flight deck. The hotel facilities on board the *Essex* carriers also were altered. Pilot ready rooms were moved from directly under the flight deck to spaces below the hangar deck to increase the protection afforded to the pilots. An escalator was installed abreast the island to get the equipment-laden pilots from the ready rooms to the aircraft via a dedicated expeditious route. The first *Essex* to receive the Project 27A work was the *Oriskany*. She entered the New York Navy Yard in October 1947 and was followed by eight of her sisters, the last leaving the yard in October 1953. In fact, Project 27A was to be extended to nine more carriers in a desire to adopt the British-designed angled flight deck, but due to the development of the steam catapult and the continuing weight growth of aircraft, a new program was needed.[7]

The post-war task forces were to be built around the new strategically oriented *United States* class and the reconstructed *Franklin D. Roosevelt* and *Essex* types. When complete, the new strategically oriented *United States*-class carriers would need to be protected by task force escorts. Unique among these requirements was the need for a command ship equipped with a long-range air-search radar. During World War II, this role was met by the carriers themselves. However, as noted, the *United States* was to have a flush deck with no masts, a design that precluded carrying air-search radars. A flagship possessing long-range radar and capable of controlling air defenses was essential. Accordingly, the *Northampton*, an incomplete heavy cruiser, was redesigned around the massive SPS-2 air-search radar, and she was fitted with an exceptionally large combat information center (CIC). This 17,049-ton ship was armed with but four 5in/54s and eight 3in/50s—no more than a self-defense armament. The *Northampton* was a unique warship. The evolution of her projected role in life illustrates the uncertainty of the times. She was laid down as a *Baltimore*-class heavy cruiser; she was redesigned during the war to become one of the *Oregon City* class; she was then to be completed as an amphibious force flag ship (AGC); and, finally, she evolved into a command ship (CLC).[8]

Additional escorts were needed to protect the new strategically-oriented carriers. The most likely threat would come from the air. During the 1945-50 era, the carrier task force could still count on its speed advantage to elude submarines, and the Soviets had few surface warships. A prime requirement for the task force escorts was that they had to be able to maintain station even in relatively heavy seas. Given the

large number of modern light and heavy cruisers on hand, and the fact that no technological breakthroughs had yet occurred in anti-aircraft missiles, it should come as no surprise that few new task force escorts were built during this era.

One new class of task force escorts was constructed during this 5-year period, the *Mitscher* class. The most striking features of these four ships were their large size, high speed, and heavy anti-aircraft armament. Their full load displacement was 4,855 tons as compared with 3,460 tons for the wartime *Gearings*. The *Mitscher* developed 34.84 knots on 75,862 shaft horsepower at 4,550 tons during trials. These were the first ships in United States service to have 1,200-psi propulsion plants. Increasingly, higher performance was being demanded of power plants. For example, the immediate pre-war *Gleave* class developed 580 psi at 825°F. The *Mitschers* were 1,200 psi at 950°F. Not surprisingly, the innovative power plants had teething problems and two of the units had to be rebuilt later in their careers.[9]

Numerous armaments were projected for this class. This seeming indecision was caused by the fact that numerous weapons were under development at that time. Initially, the class was to be armed with a twin semi-automatic 5in/54, which never became operational. Then it appeared that their gun battery would be made up entirely of the new 3in/70. But at the insistence of Fleet Admiral Chester Nimitz, the 5-inch gun in the form of the new single 5in/54 was retained. Apparently, the admiral believed that the 3-inch gun lacked range and weight for use against surface targets. As completed, the ship was armed with two 5-inch guns, and four 3-inch guns. However, since the 3in/70 was not yet operational, the class carried the 3in/50. A most important part of the *Mitscher*'s anti-aircraft defenses were her large CIC and heavy AN/SPS-8 air-search radar. The war against the kamikaze had demonstrated the need for these systems. Her anti-submarine warfare (ASW) weapons were guided torpedoes, Weapon Alfa, and depth charge tracks.

Ships were also modified to improve their usefulness as task force escorts. Among the most important modifications were those changing the twenty-four *Gearing*-class destroyers into radar picket destroyers. The principal change was the removal of the quadruple 21-inch torpedo tubes and the addition of an air-search radar. These ships were intended to serve with the task force. The 1949 Program provided for twelve radar picket destroyers equipped with the scarce SPS-6 air-search radar to serve as the seaward barrier for the United States Continental Air Defense System.

Only one ocean escort was constructed during this 5-year period. The "hunter killer ship (CLK)" *Norfolk* was the prototype of the new ocean escort flagship. She, in fact, became a "one and only." The potential enemy was projected to be large numbers of Soviet submarines based on the German Type XXI boats, which came out in very late World War II. The *Norfolk* was a bold combination of new offensive and defensive systems and, as a result, had many teething problems. The *Norfolk* was armed with new ASW homing torpedoes. She was fitted with eight 21-inch torpedo tubes in her aft superstructure. A new intermediate-range weapon was fitted, Weapon A or Alfa (automatic rocket launcher). Even her planned anti-aircraft battery was innovative, four 3in/70 guns, although she completed with the traditional 3-inch, 50-caliber guns.

The *Norfolk*'s hull design was based on that of the *Atlanta*-class light cruisers. The tremendous increase in size over past escorts was needed to give the ship the capacity to maintain high speeds during severe weather. Review of World War II operations showed that in heavy weather the Coast Guard 327-foot cutters rated at 20 knots were faster than destroyer escorts rated at 27 knots because the former were better sea ships. If the projected land war with the Soviet Union materialized, northern Europe would once again need to be reinforced, which would mean North Atlantic convoys.

The *Norfolk* was the first warship completed in this country that drew on the lessons learned at the Bikini nuclear tests. Her decks were kept as uncluttered as possible to facilitate the washing of fallout from her decks. Her bridge was entirely enclosed to afford greater protection. She was fitted with large-diameter, slow-turning propellers to improve quietness.

The *Norfolk* was laid down on 9 January 1949 and was commissioned on 4 March 1953. Although the *Norfolk* played an important role in the development of systems, she did not serve as a prototype for an ocean escort as intended. First, by 1950, the submarine threat had not materialized. Although the Soviet Union did begin production of the Soviet "Whiskey" class, in fact, by 1950, they were not available in sufficient numbers to threaten the sea lanes. Second, the *Norfolk* proved to be too expensive to be able to duplicate in sufficient numbers; the *Norfolk* spent most of her career as a test and evaluation platform.[10]

One important factor in the defeat of the U-boat during World War II had been the large number of ocean escorts that were available. The backbone of this force had been the mass-produced destroyer escorts and patrol frigates. Hundreds of these ships had been built to meet the threat. However, at the close of the war, a new generation of submarine was introduced that more than doubled the 8-knot underwater speed of the opponent, thus greatly reducing the value of the existing ASW escorts. The new submarines had been too little, too late to influence the outcome of the war. But, they did spell the end of the 20-knot ocean escort. Submarines were now fast enough to escape from sonar range, given their superior turning radius and immunity to surface conditions. To restore the superiority of the escorts, their speeds needed to be raised to at least 30 knots. To meet this need, fast ships would need to be converted to this mission.

The first step in the program was to reconfigure *Fletcher*-class destroyers into escort destroyers—DDE—another new category. Nine were converted under the 1948 Program, three under the 1949, and seven under the 1950. Armament varied among these ships; typically they retained two 5in/38 guns and four fixed ASW torpedo tubes. To this was added four 3in/50s and Weapon Alfa or a trainable Hedgehog. It was hoped that all surviving *Fletchers* would undergo this modification and many were retained in reserve for this eventuality. In fact, this program was not carried on beyond these 3 years. Instead, it was decided to improve the ASW capability of the general-purpose destroyers.[11]

Next, seven *Gearing*-class destroyers were converted to escort destroyers. They sacrificed the superfiring twin 5in/38s forward for a Weapon Alfa. They also received improved sonars. These ships (and subsequent planned conversions), along with *Essex*-class carriers, were to form ASW hunter-killer groups.

Yet another new ocean escort category was created in the Hunter-killer destroyer (DDK). Eight *Gearing*-class units received more extensive ASW weapons and sonars than the DDE conversions. Typically, they were armed with four 3in/50s, two Weapon Alfas, and two Hedgehogs, and carried sono-buoys to aid in locating the submarine.[12]

The Navy also had to assume its share of the strategic defense of the United States. The memory of Pearl Harbor was fresh in the people's minds. The broad oceans that were once seen as broad shields now could hide the approach of an enemy. Accordingly, conversion of the twelve previously mentioned *Gearing*-class destroyers to radar picket destroyers (DDR) began under the 1949 Program, and an additional twelve were begun the following year. They served in the United States Continental Air Defense System. The priority assigned to these ships is underscored by the fact they were among the first to receive the new and scarce SPS-6 air-search radar.

SUBMARINES

The United States Navy also had to find new missions for its submarines. Unlike Japan, the principal target of U.S. submarines in World War II, the Soviet Union possessed neither a significant surface fleet nor a merchant marine in 1945. Therefore, the U.S. submarine force received the same tasks as the surface fleet, strategic warfare and anti-submarine warfare. The outcome of World War II had an even larger impact on the design of U.S. submarines than it did on that of the U.S. surface fleet. Not only did the initial projected enemy not possess maritime targets requiring submarines (as was also the case for the surface fleet), but developments in Germany had made the U.S. submarine obsolete. Almost immediately following World War II, United States submarine design followed one of three lines of development: strategic missile submarines, fleet submarines, and ASW submarines.

As to be expected, the boats that were introduced prior to the Korean War were modifications of ones already in some stage of development when World War II ended.

The potential of using a submarine to launch a strategic weapon was apparent by the closing days of World War II. The Navy acquired German plans for a submarine-towed submersible barge containing a V-2 rocket at the close of the war. Paralleling this development, the Navy was working on the Loon missile, the American counterpart to the German V-1 pulse-jet. The Loon was launched from the deck of the submarine *Cusk* on 18 February 1947. Given the complexity of the systems involved in developing a strategic missile submarine, the first, the *Grayback*, would not commission until 1958.[13]

Another new breed of boat was the ASW submarine (SSK). These boats were designed to lie in wait outside enemy harbors to ambush the enemy's boats. Their principal quality was stealth, achieved through their small size, quietness, and a powerful passive sonar. Because it was hoped that this design could be mass produced, efforts were made to keep the design simple and inexpensive. Three members of the *Barracuda* class were laid down in 1950 and completed in 1951-52. Later, the class was criticized as being too small and uncomfortable. These boats were half the displacement and over 100 feet shorter than the fleet boats of World War II.

The backbone of the U.S. submarine force remained the general-purpose, or fleet, submarine. The first new class built after the end of World War II, the *Tang*, included so many innovations that it might more accurately be considered an experimental class and not a general-purpose fleet type. The *Tang* design was an attempt to incorporate all of the wartime technology, both domestic and captured, into one class. In fact, the class was composed of two competitive designs, one being built by the Portsmouth Navy Yard and the other by Electric Boat Company. The initial Ship Characteristics Board requirement specified that these boats have the potential to be re-engined with a closed-cycle or nuclear power plant at a later date.[14]

The first four of this six-member class were propelled by a new compact radical diesel. The

Tangs were given a much greater battery capacity than their World War II predecessors. This doubled their underwater speed as compared to the wartime fleet boats. They had a streamline superstructure, snorkel, and improved sonars. Their new hull form allowed for a relatively short hull (269 feet as compared with 311 feet for fleet boats) without reducing interior volume. The new shape did reduce the number of torpedo tubes to eight (six bow, two stern), as compared with ten (six bow, four stern) for fleet boats, and also the number of reloads carried.

But, the requirement to immediately update the U.S. fleet submarine could not wait the evolution and construction of new designs. In fact, it was achieved through a series of reconstruction programs known as "Guppy" (Greater Underwater Propulsive Power) conversions. The "Guppy I" conversion consisted of increasing the battery capacity and streamlining the superstructure. To achieve this, space for four torpedo reloads, fresh water tanks, and magazines had to be sacrificed within the boat. To help accomplish the streamlining, the deck gun had to be removed. The conversions were highly successful. The *Pomodon* (the second prototype) made 18.2 knots submerged at half battery rate. This first conversion was followed by the "Guppy II" version. This added a snorkel to the improvements. The *Pickerel* snorkeled for 505 hours during a 5,200-mile passage between Hong Kong and Pearl Harbor. Also, the II version employed an advanced battery, which yielded one additional knot of speed but proved to be very costly. The 1947 Program provided for the conversion of twelve boats to the "Guppy II" design. These proved to be the only boats converted to the II design. During the next two decades additional boats were converted to the IA design (the A variant included a snorkel) and "Guppy IIIs."[15]

NAVAL ANTI-AIR
WEAPONS AND SENSOR SYSTEMS

The success of these classes, from the super carrier to the submarine, was dependent on the evolution of new weapon and sensor systems. In many cases, a class combined a variety of new systems that had been tested in the laboratory but lacked the trials of operational experience.

Given the fact that from concept to commissioning, the first unit of a major new class could take as long as a decade, to some degree the design had to be based on anticipated developments in the multitude of systems used. This was even truer for the planners in the years immediately following World War II due to the acceleration of technology during the war.

Of all of the systems in existence in 1945, the sensor had the greatest impact on ship design during the next 5 years. Probably for the first time in the history of naval engineering, major warships were being designed around sensors. During the immediate past decades, the history of naval architecture had been dominated by the evolution of weapons and defensive systems, primarily armor. For centuries, the sensor for surface (and later air) targets was human vision aided by increasingly powerful optics. However, with this method about 30 miles was about as far as one could see from a mast head; beyond that distance, the target was lost over the horizon due to the curvature of the earth. The only way the range of that sensor—the eye—could be improved was to place the observer higher and higher, which obviously had practical limitations. The advent of radar revolutionized a warship's capacity to surveil its environment.

Two general categories of radar evolved out of World War II: search and fire control. The search radar, in particular, influenced the development of surface warship design during the 1945-50 period. Search radar was most needed if the Navy was to be prepared for its projected strategic role. The naval engineer had to contend with two inescapable truths related to radars, in general, and to the air-search type, in particular: the higher the antenna is placed, the less electronic interference to contend with, and the larger the radar, the more power it demands. Placing large, heavy antenna high in a ship created stability challenges, and the electrical power demands had to compete with other ship systems.

It is difficult to segregate radar development that was achieved in the 5 years immediately following World War II because it was such an evolutionary process. The three most important goals related to radar development during that era were to make the radars more durable and thus more reliable; to reduce their weight, particularly that of the antenna; and to improve their accuracy. The first two goals heavily influenced ship design.

The Navy's strategic initiative did give impetus to air-search radars, which were in various stages of development when the war ended. Important among these was the AN/SPS-2 radar, a stacked-beam, L-band height finder. This system was being developed during the war as a land-based, long-range detector for high-altitude targets such as the German V-2 rockets. While under development, the SPS-2 exhibited the potential to serve as the long-range, air-search radar, which became a priority in the post-war years for the new task force built around the *United States*-class carrier. The SPS-2 had a range of 300 nautical miles against a high-flying heavy bomber and about 150 nautical miles against a small target such as a V-1 rocket. The set proved to have adequate accuracy for its day. Altitudes could be determined within one-quarter of a degree and a range of 400 yards could be achieved. As to be expected, the SPS-2 was very complex and very heavy. The pulses were produced by a single 6.5-megawatt magnetron, the most powerful of its day. This placed great demands on the ship's generating capacity. The entire system weighed almost 50 tons. The 40-by 20-foot stabilized antenna accounted for more than half of its weight. Given these characteristics, one can appreciate why the set was not adaptable to the projected bridgeless carrier and why only two sets were built. A cruiser-size ship, specifically designed to carry the radar, was needed. Thus, the design of the command ship *Northampton* was heavily influenced by this system.

Another radar that received accelerated development during this period due to the Navy's new strategic mission was the AN/SPS-6. This was another air-search set, but one with broader applications, due to its smaller size and power demands. This set could use a variety of antennas, thus making it somewhat adaptable to a specific circumstance. Although the range of the set varied greatly, due to the size, altitude, and speed of the target and the antenna used, in general, it could detect a bomber at about 150 nautical miles and a fighter at about 60. The SPS-6 was tested on board the heavy cruiser *Macon* in late 1948. The A and B2 models were tested the following year on board a variety of warships. The radar picket destroyers and the Essex units undergoing Project 27A were among the first to receive these sets.[16]

Although research and development was continuing on fire control radar, particularly that related to missile control, developments were not sufficiently advanced to influence naval engineering in the immediate post-war period.

ASW SENSOR AND WEAPON SYSTEMS

Like radar, sonar development was still in its infancy in 1945. Due to the potential submarine threat, this research received continued attention, but advances were limited by the technologies then available. One development that did profoundly affect the work of the naval engineer was the realization that the size, shape, composition, and location of the protective dome could significantly improve the efficiency of sonar. These fluid-filled domes, slung from the bottom of the ship, influenced maneuverability, displacement, and other ship-design concerns. In fact, the *Mitschers* experienced poor sonar reception because sonar was interfered with by bow-entrailed bubbles. The first major postwar sonar, AN/SQS-4, did not enter the fleet until 1954.[17]

A major gap in ASW was the absence of an effective underwater fire control system. The Mark 100 was developed and became operational in 1948; it was superseded 3 years later by the Mark 102. This system was able to assimilate target data and weapon capability. It could accommodate all ASW weapons in the fleet and those under development.

In 1945, it was believed that the Soviet submarine fleet would rapidly expand, and it was logical to assume that the Russians would take full advantage of captured German technology. If this forecast proved accurate, American ASW forces needed to be rearmed with more effective weapons. In April 1945, the Chief of the Bureau of Ordnance began a program to develop new, more effective ASW weapons. The performance goals for the new weapons were a range of 800 yards and a high rate of fire and sinking rate for the charge. The new weapon, a mortar, was to be fitted in a 360-degree trainable mount. Two systems evolved, differing only in the size of the charge that they fired (Weapon Alfa, 250 pounds; Weapon Baker, 50 pounds). In the final analysis, Weapon Baker was considered to be only a modest improvement over the existing Hedgehog and not able to defeat the projected new generation of Soviet submarines. Due to the immediacy of the perceived threat, Weapon Alfa was rushed into production without a thorough testing and evaluation. The system became operational in 1949. Although it was the prime ASW weapon of the late 1940s and early 1950s, being fitted in the *Norfolk* and the reconstructed ASW-oriented *Gearing*s and *Fletcher*s, Weapon Alfa suffered from mechanical problems and never lived up to expectations.

One notable spin-off from the research phase of Weapon Baker was the development of a trainable and stabilized spigot mortar, Hedgehog. This was conceived by the Operational Development Force as a means of studying the use of weapons firing small contact charges. The trainable Hedgehog proved valuable in its own right. To bring the wartime untrainable Hedgehog into firing position, the ship's heading had to be brought to bear in the direction of the contact before firing the weapon. Making the weapon trainable gave the attacker much greater flexibility in the angle of attack. The first trainable Hedgehogs, the Mark 14s and 15s, began to appear in the fleet during late 1947, and soon they became standard features on ASW-oriented ships, both new and reconstructed ones. Research continued on improved Hedgehog systems throughout the 1950s, but none of the products became operational.

Most appreciated that the ASW mortar was an interim measure for combatting new, high-speed submarines and that the best long-term solution would be a homing torpedo. To increase the effectiveness from a ship, the torpedo would have to be propelled to some distance from the ship. In November 1945, the Pacific Fleet called for the development of such a weapon. The first ASW conference, in April 1946, recommended the development of a rocket that would carry an ASW homing torpedo. A rocket was developed and various torpedo payloads suggested; a

number of potential payloads were under development at that time. However, the evolution of technology had not kept pace with imagination of the designers. During the late 1940s, sonars were not yet capable of detecting targets at a sufficient range to employ such a weapon, even if the other technological challenges could be overcome. The development of such a weapon would have to wait for the future. When the war came to an end in 1945, the U.S. Navy had fifteen torpedos under development. Research continued on six of these, and three ultimately entered service. The Mark 16 was a submarine-launched, anti-surface ship weapon; the Mark 32 was a surface-ship launched ASW torpedo; and the Mark 34 was an aircraft-launched ASW torpedo. The Mark 32 began a new era for the U.S. Navy because it was the first active acoustic torpedo; it entered service in about 1950. The Mark 32 was a short, squat torpedo, the tailfins of which protruded beyond the main body. As a result, it could not be launched from a standard torpedo tube. Instead, a thrower, known as "a poor boy," was developed to launch the torpedo.

NAVAL GUN SYSTEMS

In addition to ASW weapons, the Bureau of Ordnance concentrated on anti-aircraft development. Although missile research was being pursued, operational results were still years away. Improved anti-aircraft guns were needed in the interim. Immediately after the war, there was renewed interest in a heavy caliber anti-aircraft gun. Some research was done on developing a twin 6in/47. One thought was to replace the 6in/47, single-purpose guns then on board the *Cleveland*-class light cruisers, with this anti-aircraft weapon, thus converting these ships into long-range (for their day) anti-aircraft ships. There was even talk of converting the incomplete *Kentucky* into an anti-aircraft battleship by mounting the 6in/47 or some other heavy anti-aircraft gun, yet to be developed. However, this weapon, and other efforts to develop a heavy caliber anti-aircraft gun, did not progress much beyond the planning stage.

The Bureau of Ordnance preferred to concentrate on developing the more versatile medium-caliber anti-aircraft gun. Much effort went into the 3in/70, projected to be the principal anti-air-craft gun of the next decade or so. This weapon was developed in cooperation with the British Navy; each navy was working on its own mount for the weapon. This gun was designed to be radar controlled and to have a 90-rounds-per-minute rate of fire. For an anti-aircraft gun, which could elevate to 90 degrees, to reach this high rate of fire, the weapon required a complex, and heavy, loading system given the technology available. In fact, the twin 3in/70 mount out-weighed the standard twin 5in/38 mount and weighed about the same as the new single 5in/54. The 3in/70 was very late coming into service, not joining the fleet until 1956. As noted, this weapon had been projected to be an impor-tant part of the weapons suite for the *Norfolk* ocean escorts and the *Mitscher* task force escorts, which commissioned in 1953. Even the super carrier *United States* was to have carried the 3inch/70 in six twin mounts. At least for the interim, the Navy had to find a substitute.

Paralleling the development of the 3in/70 was the development of an automatic 3in/50. This gun, as a nonautomatic weapon, had long been in the fleet and done yeoman service. Once it was realized that the 3in/70 would be very late entering the fleet, work was speeded on the less complex 3 in/50. This weapon joined the fleet in 1947 as an interim measure, but due to the continued problems with the 3in/70, the 3in/50 became the mainstay. To a lesser degree than the 3in/70, the 3in/50 was overweight. When in-stalled, it was common for the ship to lose a barrel or two to compensate for the heavier mount. However, the fact that the replacement was an automatic weapon made up for this loss.

The development of the 5in/54 had begun during the war, first as a twin mount and later as a single. Work continued on this weapon immediately following the war and it became operational in the 1950s. Like the other anti-aircraft guns, it was overweight and complex, both limitations a result of the technology then available. Little consideration was given to 20mm and 40mm guns during this period. It was be-lieved that the need was for the medium-caliber guns, particularly the 3-inch gun, and that the 3in/50 would replace the 40mm in particular. Due to weight problems discussed above, this never came about.

In September 1945, the Chief of Naval Opera-tions standardized the fire control requirements for each class. During the preceding decades, a wide variety of fire control systems had crept into service, particularly those that were dedi-cated to anti-aircraft fire. The systems in the inventory were able to meet the needs for all weapons due to be introduced into the fleet for the immediate future.

MISSILE DEVELOPMENT

Missiles were the weapons of the future and in 1945 this future was still more than a decade away. Therefore, missile development research during the years immediately after World War II improved the "data base" but did not produce any operational weapons in the short term. The late 1940s were but the beginning of serious missile development by the United States Navy. The Naval Air Missile Test Center, Point Mugu, California, was established in October 1946. In early 1948, the *Norton Sound* was equipped as a mobile missile launch platform. The need to add missiles to the Navy's weapons inventory created new challenges for the naval engineer. And often new construction and conversions had to be designed on the basis of what was expected to become available.

The Navy had evolved an interest in anti-aircraft missiles during the war, stimulated in the last few years by German rocket success and the successes of kamikazes. The Navy em-phasized the development of two categories of anti-aircraft missiles: those that could be fired from an aircraft—and due to their size limita-tions would be short range—and those that would serve in the fleet. The Navy also had an interest in other types of missiles, even though these were given a lower priority than the anti-aircraft missiles. Tests were conducted with cap-tured German V-1 and V-2 rockets; in October 1947 a V-2 was fired from the deck of the *Midway*. Surface-to-surface missile development still pre-sented rocket engineers with enormous obstacles in guidance and payload size. Therefore, ramjet and turbojet propulsion was selected by the Navy. Immediately after the war, work started on the ramjet-powered Rigel. This surface-to-surface missile was to fly at Mach 2 and have a 100-nautical-mile range. It was canceled in 1953 due to the very large size and weight of its launcher. Research and development began for the turbo-jet Regulus immediately following World War II. The first missile to be fired from a submarine occurred in July 1953.

Air-to-air missile research pursued a number of avenues. The Navy's first post-war anti-aircraft guided missile, the Lark, was test fired in early 1949. Although this missile did not warrant developing into an operational weapon, the work on this missile provided significant information that was used in the development of subsequent missiles. Another missile that suffered a like fate was the Oriole. Although it offered promise, escalating costs and a shrinking budget proved its demise. The Sparrow ultimately led to an operational type in 1956. Unlike the other missiles, it was designed as a beam rider, thus eliminating many of the technical problems and higher cost of its competitors. Research during the late 1940s made it clear that adequate aeronautical and rocket technology existed to produce a successful anti-aircraft weapon; the principal problem was guidance.[18]

The surface-to-air missile program was an outgrowth of the wartime Bumblebee program. Propulsion relied on the ramjet principle. Because little expertise had been developed in this area, much rocket research was necessary. Bumblebee employed a solid fuel rocket motor and a radar beam-controlled guidance system. A contract was awarded to Consolidated Vutlee Aircraft Corporation (General Dynamics) to build a prototype in February 1949. The missile was tested at the Naval Ordnance Test Station, China Lake, California, in February 1950. Talos evolved out of this research. The first successful test flight of Talos took place in October 1952, although it did not become operational until 1959. Talos was not suited to frigate-sized ships due to the weight and size of the system. A smaller missile, the Terrier, evolved out of the Talos program. This missile became operational in 1955.[19]

U.S. COAST GUARD

The technological explosion that occurred during World War II influenced a dramatic change in the direction of the United States Coast Guard, and thus, its naval engineering needs. Prior to the war, the Service was occupied by a monumental law enforcement effort, prohibition of alcoholic beverage smuggling. On the eve of the war, the Coast Guard absorbed the Lighthouse Service, which included some 5,000 employees, 750 lighthouses, 50 lightships, 50 tenders, and 35,000 aids to navigation of all shapes and sizes. During the war, the Coast Guard's principal tasks were cold weather operations (including icebreaking), high seas search and rescue, manning landing craft during invasions, and port safety and security. But, much like the role change for Navy, the focus of the Coast Guard's attention before the war, law enforcement, was no longer a prime concern afterward. The Coast Guard had matured into a multimission service, whose roles would evolve with the needs of the nation. Safety at Sea was the task emphasized immediately following the war. This, in part, was the result of technological advances during the war.

The Coast Guard's immediate task was to make available to the civilian community those aids to navigation that had evolved during the war. To extend Loran (Long Range Aid to Navigation), a radio navigation system that could reliably provide longitude and latitude positions, new transmitting stations needed to be built throughout the world. As early as mid-1946, the Coast Guard had forty-nine stations in operation in such faraway places as the Marshalls, Marianas, Palau-Morotai, and Okinawa. And by 1950, the number of stations had doubled.[20]

Radar was increasingly being used by merchant ships and many questions needed to be addressed. For example, how effective was radar for detecting icebergs? Some were surprised to find that although radar was of some use, it was not a substitute for the work being done by the International Ice Patrol, which was a product of the *Titanic* sinking and was administered by the Coast Guard. Ice tended to absorb radar emissions, and sea-clutter tended to hide the almost submerged bergs. Therefore, the returning signal was weak and was frequently misleading. Also, the Coast Guard had to determine how radar and other electronic aids affected the rules of the road.[21]

Automation of lighthouses was restarted during these years. This required the development of reliable automatic devices for changing bulbs in lenses, detecting change in light conditions, and providing reliable backup systems. Due to the high costs of initial automation and a shortage of funds, little progress had been made by 1950.

The Coast Guard played a leading role in convening the 1948 Safety at Sea Conference. This developed a new set of safety standards for merchant ships that replaced those that had been adopted in 1929. Among the new regulations adopted were stronger bulkhead standards, standards requiring double lifeboat boatage on all vessels, and improved standards for carriage of dangerous cargoes. Increasing technology brought new challenges to naval engineering. Safety measures were developed for the handling of ammonium nitrate and other hazardous cargoes following the Texas City disaster in 1947.[22]

Also, in 1948, Congress authorized the expansion of the Ocean Station Program to seven and a half ships (half was a jointly-manned station with Canada) in the Atlantic and two ships in the Pacific. These mid-ocean stations had two primary duties: to serve as emergency rescue sites for the rapidly growing international air service and to provide weather information. The program had begun during World War II, but due to lack of funds, had been greatly reduced after the armistice.[23]

No new ship construction was undertaken by the Coast Guard during this era. The 255-foot *Owasco* class did commission during the 1946-47 period. These ships incorporated many innovative technologies but were, in fact, a wartime product. The 255s had been designed in 1941, but due to their low construction priority, were completed well after the war. Most of the Coast Guard's naval engineering energies went into reconverting its cutters to peacetime service. For the most part, this meant reducing armaments and installing a limited amount of special equipment, such as balloon hangars for ocean station duty. In fact, the service had to lay up many brand new cutters because of a lack of personnel and funds.[24]

U.S. MERCHANT MARINE

The United States merchant marine faced challenges no less traumatic than those faced by the Navy and Coast Guard. The merchant marine had expanded to extraordinary proportions during World War II. Two-thirds of the world's tonnage was flying the American flag; there were 4,500 new vessels, and the United States outranked Great Britain (the traditional world leader) three to one in terms of tonnage. The abrupt end to the war brought the greatest shipbuilding program in history almost to a standstill. Wartime production had left the U.S. merchant fleet enormous but unbalanced. There were not enough specialized types such as passenger, refrigerated, and coastal ships. Much like the U.S. Navy, the U.S. merchant marine would have to make due with what it already had. If specialized types were needed, they would have to be converted from existing ships. In addition to the large fleet of merchant ships, there were hundreds of military auxiliaries that required conversions if they were to enter merchant service. Each of these ships presented unique problems; no two conversations were the same. There was also the challenge of correcting problems in wartime construction. The most notable of these was the tendency of T2 tankers to break in half, a particular problem because of the shortage of tanker-type vessels, but an immediate problem because the danger involved risk of lives.[25] Due to wartime expediencies, many of the former military auxiliaries had been built at variance with the rules and regulations of peacetime regulatory bodies; the U.S. Maritime Commission had to arrange compliance.[26]

The Maritime Commission faced many challenges in addition to those related to engineering. One problem was the transformation of this almost entirely government-owned, government-controlled merchant fleet into a private American industry in accordance with the Merchant Marine Act of 1936. Privatization and foreign sales were the order of the day.

The first task was preserving, or mothballing, those ships that had no immediate utility but were valuable national assets. The Merchant Marine Commission was faced with the prospect of mothballing over a thousand ships with a limited amount of funds; it was not about to succeed in getting additional money where the Navy had failed. The ships had to be preserved so that they could be returned to service with a minimum of time and expense. Two preservation methods existed, dehumidification of a ship's interior and the more traditional coating of oil and grease. Dehumidification was a relatively new procedure in 1945 and the preferred method used by the Navy. The Merchant Marine Commission contracted Todd Shipyards to carry out the 6-month experimental dehumidification of the Liberty ship *John Stevenson* at Hoboken, New Jersey.

Greasing a ship requires that all machinery other than electrical be opened and grease or oil applied to all moving parts. Also, the interior of the vessel is sprayed with a preservative compounded to penetrate rust and prevent further corrosion. It was necessary to spray the interior every fourth year. The exterior of the hull above the waterline was sprayed with a mixture of preservative oil and paint, and resprayed every third year. The windings of all electrical installations such as motors, generators, and controls were treated with an insulating varnish containing a fungicide.

A comparison of the cost between the two methods resulted in the adoption of greasing because it was satisfactory and far less expensive than dehumidifying. The project of greasing all of the ships that were laid up took a number of years to complete. By 1950 there were 2,277 ships in the reserve fleet.

Much research was undertaken to extend the lives of those ships in mothballs. Numerous compounds were tested for possible use in preserving ships' bottoms, the one area that was most vulnerable to corrosion. Experiments were also carried out to improve the fungicidal compound used to preserve electrical installations.

After mothballing, conversions presented the most pressing issue. There was a demand for passenger ships and practically all of them, new or old, had been converted into troop and attack transports (APs and APAs). Not surprisingly, the modern liner *America* was among the first to undergo conversion to peacetime service. Even though the ship required only minor structural and machinery repairs, her interior and decorations—essential trappings of a passenger liner— had suffered badly. They were restored in the best way possible, given the materials on hand in 1946. The need for passenger ships even justified

the austere renovation of a grand old lady, the *Washington*. Even the *Argentina, Brazil*, and *Uruguay*, the youngest of which was 18 years old, were restored for service to South America. Ships that had been built as transports during the war took longer to introduce into merchant service than those that had seen previous service as passenger ships, due to the extent of work necessary. For example, the *General W. P. Richardson* underwent conversion between 1948 and 1949 and entered the merchant service in May 1949 as the *La Guardia*. Three other "Generals" also entered service the following year.[27]

Advances in marine engineering continued within the merchant service in spite of the gloomy shipbuilding environment. These were evident in both new construction—what little there was—and renovations. Tankers and passenger ships received the most attention. The late 1940s marked the introduction of the supertanker with the commissioning of the 26,555 dead weight tons *Esso Zurich*. She was soon surpassed in size by a succession of American-built tankers. In addition to being big, this ship introduced a number of innovations. The *Esso Zurich* was equipped with a portable deck sprinkling system designed to spread a film of water over the upper deck in way of all cargo oil tanks to reduce the vapor tensions of grades A through C petroleum products. Her turbines could deliver steam up to 850 psi and over 850°F. By the end of the decade, marine propulsion turbines were using temperatures over 1,000 degrees.[28]

The *Del Norte* and two sisters, built in 1946-47, used aluminum for the riveted upper house and stack installation. Numerous post-war innovations could be found in the *President Cleveland* and *President Wilson*, combination passenger-cargo ships built for the American Presidents Line. They were the first American merchant ships to make extensive use of aluminum in their superstructure. These liners were air conditioned. Two more liners were laid down in 1949. These were the *Constitution* and the *Independence* for the American Export Lines. These ships incorporated many new safety features, in part the result of lessons learned during World War II. This was all leading to one of America's greatest naval engineering achievements, the liner *United States*. On 7 April 1949 a contract was awarded to the Newport News Shipbuilding and Drydock Company for the largest ship to be built in this country. Her keel was laid down on 8 February 1950;[29] more is said on her in the next chapter.

A number of research projects were supported by the Maritime Commission. An improved type of cargo-handling gear was developed to reduce costs of loading. This side-port gear was installed in the *President Cleveland* and *President Wilson* and proved very successful. This led to improved versions that were in operation before the Korean War. Also, the possible use of gas turbines on ships received serious research in these years and numerous shore-based facilities became operational.[30]

SUMMARY

The years between 1945 and 1951 were difficult for the sea services, in general, and the United States Navy in particular. One might liken the Navy's dilemma to a well-fed football lineman who has just won the Super Bowl and now is forced to go on a crash diet. On top of that, the coach has told him that he might now be a quarterback or perhaps a receiver. Should he develop his arm or his legs while on a diet? For the Navy, the questions became what role should it play in a future war and what would it choose to develop with its limited resources? The Coast Guard evolved out of World War II with the clear self-image of what its future should be. In large measure, this was due to the outstanding leadership of its longest serving (1936-45), and possibly greatest Commandant, Admiral Russell Waesche. The merchant marine knew what its future role should be, it simply could not convince others. The era of 1945 through 1950 was more than the years between World War II and the Korean War. It was a very dynamic time filled with great challenges, many of which were solved by advances in naval engineering.

Notes

1 U.S. Department of Commerce, Bureau of the Census, *Historical Statistics of the United States*. Part II, Washington, D.C.: Government Printing Office, 1975, p. 1114.

2 Epstein, Leon, "The Inactive Mothball Fleet," Manuscript preserved by the American Society of Naval Engineers, Washington, D.C.

3 *Conway's All the World's Fighting Ships 1947-1982*. Part I, The Western Powers. London: Conway Maritime Press, 1983, pp. 182-190.

4 Ibid. Also MacDonald, Scot, *Evolution of the Aircraft Carrier*. Washington, D.C.: GPO, 1964. Friedman, Norman, "The U.S. Fleet Carrier Design of 1945," *Warship*. Vol. 10, pp. 100-106.

5 *Conway's Fighting Ships*. Also MacDonald, *Evolution of the Aircraft Carrier*; Friedman, "U.S. Fleet Carrier Design;" and Friedman, Norman, "The First of the Super Carriers, USS *United States*," *Warship*. Vol. 12, pp. 218-223.

6 Bauer, K. Jack, *Ships of the Navy 1775-1969*. Troy, New York: Rensselaer Polytechnic Institute, 1970. Also *Conway's Fighting Ships*; Friedman, "U.S. Fleet Carrier Design;" and *Dictionary of American Naval Fighting Ships*. 8 Vol., Washington, D.C.: GPO, 1959-1981.

7 *Conway's Fighting Ships*. Also "Navy Commissions Aircraft Carrier," *Marine Engineering and Shipping Age*. (November 1950).

8 *Conway's Fighting Ships*. Also *Dictionary of Fighting Ships*.

9 Warren, G. B., "Development of Steam Turbines for Marine Propulsion of High-Powered Combatant Ships," *Transactions*. SNAME (1946), pp. 268-316.

10 *Dictionary of Fighting Ships*. Also *Jane's Fighting Ships 1949-1950*. London: Sampson, Low, and Marston, Co., 1950.

11 Bowen, Harold G., "Reminiscences," *ASNE Journal*. (May 1957), pp. 291-294. Also Miller, Richards T., "Sixty Years of Destroyers, A Study in Evolution," *Proceedings*. Annapolis, Maryland: U.S. Naval Institute, November 1962.

12 *Jane's Fighting Ships 1946-47*. London: Sampson, Low, and Marston, Co., 1947. Also *Jane's Fighting Ships 1947-1948*. London: Sampson, Low, and Marston, Co., 1948. *Jane's Fighting Ships 1949-50*.

13 Schade, Henry A., "German Wartime Technical Developments," *Transactions*. SNAME (1946), pp. 83-111.

14 Friedman, Norman, "The U.S. Navy's 1945 Submarine Design," *Warship*. Vol. 4, pp. 42-49.

15 "Two New Classes of Submarines Under Construction by Navy," *Marine Engineering and Shipping Age*. (July 1950), pp. 49-50.

16 Friedman, Norman, *Naval Radar*. Greenwich: Conway Maritime Press, 1981. Also Sherwin, Sidney A., Jr., and Richards T. Miller, "The Impact of Electronics on Warship Design," *Transactions*. SNAME, Vol. 61 (1953), pp. 635-671.

17 Friedman, Norman, *U.S. Naval Weapons*. London: Conway Maritime Press, 1983. Also Sherwin and Miller, "Impact of Electronics."

18 *Evolution of a Missile Family*. Produced by General Dynamics.

19 *Ibid.*

20 Bureau of the Census, *Historical Statistics*. 1975. Also U.S. Department of the Treasury, *Annual Report*. Washington, D.C.: GPO, 1947-1951 (Reports for 1946 through 1950); Johnson, Robert Erwin, *Guardians of the Sea: History of the United States Coast Guard, 1915 to Present*. Annapolis, Maryland: Naval Institute Press, 1987.

21 "Postwar Radar Installations on Commercial Vessels," *Marine Engineering and Shipping Age*. (January 1950), p. 61. Also, Harvey, H. Franklin and Frederich P. Coleman, "Electronics on Shipboard," *Transactions*. SNAME (1947), pp. 170-201.

22 Farley, Joseph F., "The 1948 International Conference on Safety of Life at Sea," *Transactions*. SNAME (1948), pp. 95-103.

23 U.S. Dept. of the Treasury, *Annual Report 1948*. GPO, 1949.

24 "Trouble-Free Operation of Steam Generators on Coast Guard Cutters," *Marine Engineering and Shipping Age*. (July 1950), pp. 46-48.

25 U.S. Department of Commerce, *United States Maritime Commission Report to Congress*. (Reports of 1946, 1947, 1948, 1949) Washington, D.C.: GPO, 1947-1950. Also _____ , *Annual Report of the Federal Maritime Board and Maritime Administration 1950*. Washington, D.C.: GPO.

26 "American Merchant Fleet Is Badly Unbalanced," *Marine Engineering and Shipping Age*. (November 1949), p. 72.

27 U.S. Dept. of Commerce, *United States Maritime Commission Report to Congress*. (Reports of 1947 and 1948.) Also, *Annual Report of Federal Maritime Board and Maritime Administration 1950*; Braynard, Frank O. and William H. Miller, *Fifty Famous Liners*. 3 volumes, New York, N.Y.: W. W. Norton, 1982-1987; Fox, William A., *Always Good Ships*. Norfolk, Virginia: The Donning Company, 1986; Miller, William H., *Transatlantic Liners 1945-1980*. New York, N.Y.: ARCO Publishing, Inc., 1981.

28 "World's Largest Tanker Launched at New York Ship," *Maritime Engineering and Shipping Age*. (July 1950), p. 74. Also Ireland, M. L., Jr., M. D. Wheeler, and L. E. Spencer, "The Performance and Design of Machinery for the 26,800-Ton Esso Supertankers Built by the Newport News Shipbuilding and Dry Dock Company," *Transactions*. Vol. 59, SNAME (1951) pp. 897-932; Luce, H. and W. I. H. Budd, "The Design of a Class of 28,000-Ton Tankers," *Transactions*. Vol. 58, SNAME (1950), pp. 423-477.

29 "Structural Model Tests Comparing Aluminum-Alloy and Steel Superstructures," *Maritime Engineering and Shipping Age*. (March 1950), pp. 58-61. Also "Aluminum for Ship Superstructures," *Maritime Engineering and Shipping Age*. (March 1950), pp. 52-56; Holden, Donald A., *Men, Ships and the Sea. The Story of Naval Architects and Marine Engineers*. Newcomen Address (1968); Bates, James L., "Aspects of Large Passenger Liner Design," *Transactions*. SNAME (1946), pp. 317-373; Forrest, Mathew F., "Applications and Use of Aluminum Alloys in Ship Construction," *Transactions*. SNAME (1947), pp. 305-331.

30 "G. E. Starts Large-Scale Gas Turbine Production," *Marine Engineering and Shipping Age*. (October 1950), p. 40. Also, Holly, Hobart and James A. Pennypacker, "Economic Aspects of American Merchant Ship Design," *Transactions*. Vol. 61, SNAME (1953), pp. 635-671; *The History of American Bureau of Shipping on Its One Hundred and Twenty-fifth Anniversary*. New York, N.Y.: American Bureau of Shipping, 1987; Vasta, John, "Structural Tests on Passenger Ship SS *President Wilson*—Interaction Between Superstructure and Main Hull Girder," *Transactions*. SNAME (1949), pp. 253-306.

CHAPTER
NINE
1950–1972

Korea and Vietnam

by Willis C. Barnes

INTRODUCTION:
PROFOUND AND RAPID CHANGES

In 1956, Rear Admiral Albert G. Mumma, Chief of the U.S. Navy's Bureau of Ships (BuShips) and later (1957) President of ASNE, wrote:

> Evolution equivalent to a revolution is taking place in the Navy. The engineers' dream of atomic power has become a reality in the *Nautilus*. Now, only one year after her trials, the Navy has in its current and proposed building programs an atomic fleet of 14 other submarines, a cruiser, and designs and preliminary component work on an aircraft carrier.
>
> Far-ranging missiles are just as rapidly supplanting guns. Two submarines and five cruisers already have guided missile capabilities, and current and proposed programs provide for the construction or conversion of a whole fleet of guided missile ships.
>
> These two developments, as historic as the introduction of steam and the rifled gun, are being integrated with other developments which, taken collectively, are also revolutionary.[1]

In retrospect, Admiral Mumma understated the situation. The period 1950-72 saw an unprecedented explosion of technology in every scientific and engineering discipline. Almost every one of these developments made a significant impact on some aspect of ship design and naval engineering. The innovations were by no means limited to hardware—that is, new weapons, sensors, propulsion, materials, and hull forms. Equally dramatic changes took place in the very character of naval engineering—not only in ship design, but also in other aspects, such as acquisition and maintenance.

The profusion of these developments poses the difficult task of providing an orderly description of what was a most disorderly process. Technological innovations appear in a random and unplanned way, and their adoption is often haphazard. Tracing the effect of the myriad of new technologies on ship design and engineering is an elusive exercise, at best. So also is the establishment of a logical, coherent thread linking the changes that transpired in the character of naval engineering. In an attempt to bring order to these complexities, this chapter will first describe some of the specific, significant technological advances during this period, and their implications with regard to ship design. Then, it will describe the trends in design of various kinds of existing naval ships and the evolution of new ship types, showing how the designs were affected by (or made possible by) the previously cited innovations. Developments in the Coast Guard and the merchant marine will also be covered. In conclusion, the narrative will cite some of the institutional changes to the profession of naval engineering.

NUCLEAR PROPULSION

Admiral Rickover's Achievement

Obviously, the developments cited by Admiral Mumma in 1956 had begun some years earlier. It may also occur to some knowledgeable readers that in those days the process of converting technical innovation into practical military hardware was much faster than it was two decades later. The prime example was the development of nuclear propulsion, with the concurrent evolution of the nuclear submarine. Never has a naval engineering project of such complexity been accomplished successfully in so short a time. As is well known, the vision, drive, and technical genius responsible for this result were embodied in one of the great naval engineers of all time, Admiral Hyman G. Rickover.

The story of nuclear propulsion has been told by a number of authors and will not be repeated here. Some of the accounts were sanctioned by Admiral Rickover; some were not. In any case, readers will note that the chronicles dwell largely on the personalities involved, the management and leadership processes, the development and interplay of the technical and political institutions, and the conflict between Admiral Rickover and the many leaders of industry and government who opposed him.

The Missing Technical Chronicle

What readers will not find, however, is a *technical* history of nuclear propulsion. Nowhere is

there a detailed account of the dozens of engineering alternatives considered and the technical basis for the choices made, or the criteria used to decide among the choices. Nor is there any in-depth description of the kinds of research, engineering development, and testing that supported those decisions. Although this same observation is true for many other naval engineering developments, it is ironic that the most far-reaching and successful propulsion innovation in naval history is almost totally lacking a documented technical account of how it was done.

Engineering Decisions

An example of the difficult engineering choices that had to be made was the fundamental choice of the type of reactor to be used. When the naval nuclear propulsion program began, the Navy was leading the entire world in the development of nuclear power; there was no experience upon which to base the selection. Two different approaches were selected, not as alternatives that would be compared in order to select "the best," but simply because it was not certain at the time that either one would work at all. One was the water-cooled submarine thermal reactor to be developed by Westinghouse at the Bettis Plant near Pittsburgh for the USS *Nautilus*. The other was the liquid-sodium-cooled submarine intermediate reactor to be designed by General Electric at the Knolls Atomic Power Laboratory in Schenectady, New York, for the USS *Seawolf*.

The Organic Coolant Reactor

These choices were made out of dozens of possible combinations and variations of coolants, moderators, fuels, power cycles, and other variables of largely uncertain characteristics. Many of them were subsequently tried by the (then) Atomic Energy Commission (AEC), and almost all failed. An example was a reactor cooled by an organic liquid, an idea that was of interest because this coolant could be operated at low pressure and it acquired very little induced radioactivity while passing through the reactor. As a consequence, the coolant piping outside the reactor could be thinner and would require little shielding. The naval reactors program pursued this idea briefly in the late 1950's, concluded that it was impractical because of chemical changes in the organic coolant, and abandoned the effort. However, the AEC considered the organic reactor one of "the big three" for future commercial power production, along with pressurized water and boiling water reactors. The AEC continued to support its development until its Organic Reactor Experiment in Idaho failed some years later, putting an end to the idea. The episode exemplifies the sound engineering judgment that was, and continues to be, the hallmark of the naval reactors program.

Naval Reactor Systems

Both types of naval reactor worked, although not with the same degree of success. The pressurized water reactor was very successful and was developed in many variations and sizes to be the Navy's mainstay for nuclear propulsion in both submarines and surface ships. It also served the nation as a major pillar of the commercial nuclear power industry, along with the boiling water reactor. The naval reactors program laid the cornerstone for this development by designing and supervising the construction of the world's first commercial nuclear power plant at Shippingport, Pennsylvania. As for shipboard reactors, although the sodium-cooled reactor itself worked nearly flawlessly, liquid sodium at high temperatures proved difficult to contain. Leaks in the superheater heat exchangers eventually resulted in having to bypass them, and hence, to operate the plant on saturated steam. The *Seawolf* plant operated extremely well in this mode for two years, but the advantage of superheated steam in reducing the size of the secondary machinery had been lost. Furthermore, the success of the pressurized water plant made unnecessary the expense and effort of developing an alternative. A final negative factor for sodium was its inherent danger in a sea environment, since it reacts violently and spontaneously with water. In view of this situation, Admiral Rickover recommended that development of sodium-cooled reactors for naval propulsion be terminated.

Termination of the Sodium-Cooled Reactor

Such action was virtually unprecedented. Scientific and technical developments usually tend to perpetuate themselves, regardless of merit. In the case of sodium-cooled reactor de-

velopment, its termination proved almost as difficult as its initiation. There were a number of forces at work—some political, some economic, and some technical. General Electric had been working on sodium for over 10 years and was understandably reluctant to acquire the stigma of "failure" as well as to lose financial support. Furthermore, the company believed the problems could be solved and that sodium had great potential for a lightweight plant for a destroyer. The *Seawolf's* commanding officer, Commander Richard Laning, strongly opposed cutting off the development. The AEC wanted to pursue sodium technology particularly for fast breeder reactors and, in fact, subsequently did so through other projects. It took a great deal of professional and personal courage to recommend canceling a project on which a quarter of a billion dollars had been spent. It also took some uncommonly persuasive technical exposition. It should be instructive for today's technical writer to know that the cover letter of the final report that recommended termination was a mere one and a half pages long. The final sentence was one that should be drummed into the minds and consciences of engineers everywhere: "For what has happened, the responsibility is entirely mine.—(signed) H. G. Rickover."

In lieu of further sodium reactor research, General Electric was assigned the development of a new pressurized water plant specifically designed for destroyer propulsion. This was to become the basic plant for the USS *Bainbridge* and, in later variations, for other surface ships and submarines. The prototype was built on the site of the original sodium reactor plant, and the *Seawolf's* sodium plant was replaced by a pressurized water system, thus ending the Navy's involvement with liquid-metal-cooled reactors. In spite of many proposals and outside pressures to develop other types of reactors, as the Soviets have done, the Navy has adhered exclusively to pressurized water for all applications.

Nuclear Propulsion Program
Impact on the Navy

The nuclear propulsion program had a major impact on the size and shape of both submarines and surface ships, as will be described later. Beyond this, and of even greater significance, is the fact that few developments in naval engineering history have exerted a more profound influence on the Navy as an institution. This influence permeated every aspect of the Navy's business, including ship design, acquisition, maintenance, and logistic support, the selection and training of engineers and operators, contract management, and the education of midshipmen. The crux of this influence was the nuclear Navy's uncompromising engineering excellence, which set a standard for all other technical endeavors. This standard exerted pressure on the Navy to achieve the same kind of equipment reliability, quality of operation and maintenance, and management effectiveness with regard to the non-nuclear aspects of ships. As more and more officers became trained in the program, and as they rose to greater seniority, they oriented the entire Navy toward the standards they had learned in the nuclear program. As an example, the growing base of nuclear experience generated an increasing awareness of shortcomings in the material condition of the fleet as compared to nuclear standards, and a concomitant thrust toward restoring all ships to those standards. The effort often borrowed nuclear program methods, such as propulsion examining boards, to ensure safe material condition of machinery plants and operator competence, prior to operation. Land-based versions of conventional propulsion plants became common for training operators, and standard procedures for operation and casualties were emphasized. In one particularly unpopular move, senior officers were sent to Idaho ("Sagebrush U") for several months of hands-on propulsion plant training, in an effort to inculcate a more intimate understanding of operation and maintenance.

As the period covered by this chapter ended, many different classes of nuclear submarines had been built or authorized, using several variations of pressurized water reactor. Eight nuclear guided-missile cruisers were in the fleet or authorized, one nuclear carrier was at sea, and two more under construction. Although the U.S. Navy had led the world in developing nuclear propulsion, and had shared its know-how with Britain, the Soviet Navy was quick to grasp and exploit the new technology, and had built a formidable nuclear fleet of its own. France was also reported to have a number of nuclear ships in service or under construction.

Conservative Design

Admiral Rickover and his nuclear propulsion colleagues have been accused of extreme conservatism or, more bluntly, stodgy thinking, as regards "new" or "advanced" kinds of reactor plants. The proponents of such plants invariably claimed light weight, small space, high power, simple operation, minimal development effort and low production cost, all of which—like all propulsion plants that exist only on paper—were unarguably "factual" at that stage. One of these fanciful plants was alleged to be small enough to be dropped down the stack of a merchant ship, a fate which struck some experienced nuclear engineers as being entirely appropriate. Contrary to popular misconception, the nuclear propulsion program studied many alternatives to pressurized water reactors, and knew more about their potentials and pitfalls than any other agency, government or private. Opposition to these alternatives, many of which were little more than crackpot ideas, was based on solid technical fact and engineering analysis, always tempered by the experience of naval engineers who had operated machinery in real ships, and with the overriding considerations of safety. If the resulting technical decisions were conservative, they were well-founded.

USS *Narwhal* Propulsion Plant

Nevertheless, the development of the USS *Narwhal* (SSN-671) propulsion plant in the early 1960s flew in the face of conservatism; in many ways it was the most developmental nuclear propulsion plant ever built. Although it was a rule in the nuclear propulsion program (and a good rule anywhere) not to combine several developments in one project, the caution in this case was ignored.

The design of the *Narwhal*'s machinery plant started with a simple question: "What would a submarine nuclear propulsion plant look like if quietness were the *only* design criterion?" With this premise, every piece of machinery was scrutinized with the following objectives in mind: if possible, eliminate it; if it cannot be eliminated, slow it down or find a new quieter design; if it cannot be eliminated or redesigned, sound-isolate it.

For the reactor, natural circulation was a logical approach, since it immediately eliminated the powerful and noisy main coolant pumps that forced pressurized water through the reactor. Of course, there was a major problem of redesigning the reactor and the entire primary system to minimize pressure drop of the circulating water, while still keeping the size of the primary system within reasonable bounds. Even as eminent a scientist as Nobel Laureate Dr. Willard Libby, then an AEC Commissioner, wanted to know how it would work. To confirm feasibility, labora tory test loops, with simulated heat sources and sinks, were mounted on rock-and-roll platforms, acquired from obscure sources, to test response to roll and pitch. Some seemingly simple features under consideration were found to lack basic engineering data. So revolutionary was the approach, that serious consideration even was given, with sound technical justification, to eliminating the reactor's primary isolation valves (until then, sacrosanct), a step which would have enhanced the natural circulation.

Even more radical was the approach to the secondary plant. The two primary contractors, General Electric and Westinghouse, were each asked whether the *fundamental* approach to re ducing machinery noise should be speeding the machinery up or slowing it down; not surpris ingly, the answers were diametrically opposed. To eliminate reduction-gear noise, a direct-drive turbine was considered. When prospective tur bine manufacturers were called in to discuss feasibility, they arrived with reference manuals looking like parchment—the last direct-drive turbine had been built 50 years earlier. The thought of a turbine 20 feet long boggled minds. Starting with saturated steam, the lower stages had such a high moisture content that it was said they could almost be called water wheels. Need less to say, erosion posed an unusually serious problem, as did differential expansion, rotor clearances, and other turbine details. On the positive side, the low turbine speed suggested the possibility of bearings without forced lubrica tion; that is, like line shaft bearings, thus eliminating lubricating oil pumps. To eliminate main condenser circulating water pumps, the unthinkable (at least for submarines) was thought: scoop injection.

That was not all. Noisy air conditioning com pressors could be eliminated if steam-jet air conditioners could be used. Only three manufac turers had any practical experience with such machinery, and only one system was in operation in the entire country. Serious thought was given to reciprocating main feed pumps, for the simple reason that they had been observed to be excep tionally quiet in the propulsion plant of the Norfolk-Newport News ferry. In short, no ra tional proposal was rejected without good en gineering reason.

The land-based prototype reactor plant re quired unusual features of its own. As the first real test of full-scale natural circulation cooling, it was highly desirable to ascertain the effects of ship motion. Since there was no practical way to mount an entire reactor plant on a movable platform, the prototype hull was designed to float in a basin in the middle of the Idaho desert. To make it roll, gyro stabilizers were mounted in the hull, operating in reverse to impart motion instead of opposing it. When model tests pre dicted that synchronous sloshing of the basin water might occur, "beaches" were built in it to dampen the waves. And since it was clearly im practicable to pipe cooling water to a rolling condenser, the basin water had to be used to cool the condenser, and then be cooled itself. If there was a lack of innovative spirit in the naval nuclear program, it was not evident in the de velopment of the *Narwhal*.

Non-Nuclear Propulsion

The Unconventional *Timmerman*

"The impossible happens regularly on the *Timmerman*."[2] So wrote the ship's Engineer Of ficer, Lieutenant Commander Robert J. Knox, in 1956 in one of the few reports available on this unique, controversial ship devoted to experi mental machinery. "The Twentieth-Century *Cler mont*," as Knox affectionately dubbed her, was "completed" by Bath Iron Works as EDD-828 in 1952 at a cost of $93 million. Her hull and arma ment were essentially those of a World War I *Gearing*-class fleet destroyer. However, by decree, there was nothing conventional about her machinery. On the contrary, the machinery was designed and built (as related by Knox) "on the premise that if an individual piece of equipment did not fail then that piece of equipment was not designed close enough. Manufacturers were requested to give only a guarantee of good workmanship, good intentions, and their best technical brains." The developmental features included high-pressure, high-temperature steam (2,000 psi, 1,050°F), but with one plant more than twice the pressure of the other (thus prohibiting cross connection); 400-hertz, 1,000-volt electrical generators and motors; a planetary reduction gear; shaft roller bearings; three different boiler designs (including forced circulation and integral superheat) with automatic combustion controls; one gas-turbine and one diesel-powered emergency generator of a novel design; and vertical forced-draft blowers hung from the overhead. The net result was a plant of some 100,000 shp (shaft horsepower) with a specific weight about half that of a conventional destroyer.

Unusual steps were taken to test the propulsion plant, and to select and train the engineering officers and crew. LCDR Knox was an experienced steam engineer and was, therefore, assigned to the Naval Boiler and Turbine Laboratory during the test phase, and to the Supervisor of Shipbuilding, Bath, during the ship's construction. He and a carefully picked core of junior officers and petty officers lived with the machinery, from the factory, through prototype testing and installation, to shipboard testing and operation at sea. These innovative and useful procedures became common two decades later.

Results from the *Timmerman*

Whether the *Timmerman* was a success depends on one's point of view. According to LCDR Knox in 1954, "the vessel has been 99% a success because 99% of the equipment has failed in one way or another." From her commissioning in September 1952 until June 1953, she was at sea for only 3 days, for a total of 23 hours, with a maximum speed of 31 knots on two boilers. In Boston Naval Shipyard she was known as "Building 828." The machinery plant never achieved full power. In 1954, in realization of the ship's inability to serve both as a fleet destroyer and an experimental platform, her guns were removed and the ship was redesignated EAG-152; she was decommissioned in 1956. The *Timmerman's* design and performance history were cloaked in secrecy. Some reports on the machinery innovations and results were written in the Bureau of Ships, but many were classified and limited to a

few copies. No definitive engineering analysis was ever published in the open literature on the lessons learned, the limitations experienced, and the advantages and disadvantages of the various design concepts. Some innovations, such as higher steam temperatures and pressures, continued to be used, as will be discussed. Although 400-hertz power was adopted for certain uses on board ship, it was never again attempted for general ship service power. Planetary reduction gears were never again used for main propulsion. In any event, few naval engineers ever learned the answers the *Timmerman* was designed to provide, and in many ways did provide, on the frontiers of naval machinery. For better or worse, the Navy will not see her like again.

1,200-PSI Steam Plants

Nevertheless, machinery of reduced weight and space and greater thermal efficiency remained a worthy objective. The *Timmerman* set the stage for the adoption of 1,200 psi, 950°F steam conditions as the norm for naval warships, succeeding the 600 psi, 850°F standard of World War II. As often happens with innovations, the transition was not limited to a simple change in steam conditions, but was accompanied by a number of ancillary trappings that greatly complicated and confused matters. Among these were automatic combustion controls, integral superheaters, higher fuel oil pressures, vertical forced-draft blowers hung from the overhead, and boiler feedwater pumps and deaerating feedwater tanks located in the fireroom. This last feature was a classic example of design oversight: fireroom personnel traditionally had nothing to do with, and knew nothing about, operating and maintaining the feed system. Thus, a few simple strokes of the drawing pen in the Bureau of Ships' machinery arrangement section created a significant problem in the operation and maintenance of 1,200-psi propulsion plants at the floor plate level. Also, the severe steam conditions were less forgiving of steam leaks and water chemistry, the blowers were difficult to maintain (as the machinery plant was, in general, because of excessively compact layout and high temperatures), and automatic combustion controls posed problems, as described elsewhere. Training of engineering personnel for the new system never seemed to catch up with demand, and the Navy suffered from a chronic shortage of qualified and experienced petty officers to cope with the newer technology. In some instances, the problems were compounded by other novelties, such as controlled-circulation boilers and pressure-fired boilers. Operating and maintenance problems continued to plague 1,200-psi steam plants throughout the period, giving rise to myriad "get-well" programs. Among these were Propulsion Examining Boards, Boiler Assistance Teams, Engineering Operational Sequencing Systems, Personnel Qualification Standards (PQS), and type commander Mobile Training Teams, all intended to help ships' forces maintain and safely operate their machinery. Special appropriations were sought from the Congress for the express purpose of restoring ships' 1,200-psi steam plants to their as-built condition during ship overhauls. Finally, Naval Sea Systems Command found it necessary to establish a project manager organization dedicated solely to technical and logistic support of 1,200-psi steam plants. This troublesome history should be considered in any debate on the role and future of innovation in naval engineering. The difference between great expectations versus real world results has seldom been better manifested.

New Steam Turbines

In short, as noted by one observer, higher-pressure steam conditions "opened up a whole new galaxy of problems and techniques."[3] An example of the impact can be seen in the design of steam turbines.

Late World War II destroyers had separate cruising and high-pressure turbines, used in series for high efficiency at low power and with the cruising turbines bypassed at high power. Higher pressures aggravated casing sealing problems at the turbine inlet ends. They also dictated higher rotative speeds, which aggravated windage heating of the cruising turbine when bypassed. The solution was a return to a "series-parallel" concept, or "HP-IP combination." In this arrangement, steam enters a HP-IP (high pressure-intermediate pressure) turbine at its center; at high power, it divides and flows in parallel through both groups of blades. At cruising power, it flows in series through first one set

of blades and then the other. This arrangement reduces steam pressure and leakage where the shaft penetrates the casing, eliminates the windage problem, and simplifies the transition between the cruising and high-power modes. Low-pressure turbine design, although not fundamentally changed, was affected by reducing standard condenser vacuum from 27.5 inches to 25 inches. This considerably reduced the size of the last stage. The total number of turbine stages remained essentially constant, thus requiring higher rpm to extract the greater pressure and temperature drop from the steam. The combination of all these factors yielded a significant decrease in specific turbine weight, although little improvement in efficiency.

These basic advances were accompanied by myriad improvements in such details as interstage seals, rotor and casing materials, moisture removal in lower stages to alleviate blade erosion, and oil and steam seals. Thus, even in a technology as seemingly prosaic as steam turbines, significant advances were made.

Gas Turbines

Although the gas turbine concept predates the twentieth century, and gas turbines were built in Europe prior to World War I, it was only after World War II that they began to find wide acceptance and application in power generation and propulsion.[1] At first, their development and growth were largely spurred by the aircraft industry, since their characteristics of compactness, high power per unit weight, and fuel efficiency (with cheaper fuel) offered major advances in aircraft performance. However, other uses soon evolved, such as for pumping gas in pipelines. (As will be seen, an adaption of such a unit provided the propulsion plant for the first U.S. gas-turbine-propelled merchant ship, the *John Seargent*.) As a result of the early orientation of gas turbines toward aircraft propulsion, almost all marine power plants were "marinized" versions of aircraft engines.

Early interest on the part of the U.S. Navy was heavily oriented toward the need for lightweight power plants for small craft, and for novel vehicles such as hydrofoils and air-cushion craft. As late as 1966, BuShips experts observed that "This preoccupation with weight has tended to obscure the fact that the gas-turbine, power-plant system has many advantages in shipboard applications based on criteria other than weight and volume."[5] By 1965, the Navy had installed over 500 gas turbines for electric power generation and 400 for auxiliary power, but only 78 for propulsion, of which all but 3 were for small craft. However, by that time, the Navy had committed to a combined-diesel-or-gas (CODOG) propulsion plant for the patrol motor gunboat (PGM), using diesel engines for cruising and a GE LM1500 gas turbine at 14,000 horsepower for the boost mode. By the end of the period, the GE LM2500 rated at 20,000 horsepower had been developed, and the Navy was well on the way to using it extensively for main propulsion of both frigates and destroyers. These and other installations are noted subsequently in the discussion of specific ship developments.

Naval Boilers

The never-ending quest for reduced weight and space of machinery led the Bureau of Ships inevitably to pressure-fired boilers, also called supercharged steam generators. In these boilers, combustion air was provided to the furnace at about 65 psi and 490°F from a turbine-driven compressor, powered by furnace exhaust gas.[6] The elevated pressure required less space for combustion and gas flow, and improved heat transfer. About 50 percent reduction in overall boiler size and weight resulted. The wide-range burners fired downward from the top of the firebox. Natural convection circulation was employed for steam generation.

The first (and only) Navy ships equipped with this type of steam generator were the *Garcia*-class frigates (DE 1040), operating at 1,200 psi, 950°F. These ships experienced the typical problems of other 1,200-psi ships. In addition, the compactness of the boilers made them difficult to maintain. When problems with the superheaters required a redesigned replacement, they had to be removed rather inelegantly through the bottom of the ship.

Another attempt to reduce boiler size focused on forced internal circulation, by pumps, a technique that was first employed in the *Timmerman*, with unpublished results. More definite results, mostly bad, derived from the installation

of "controlled" circulation boilers in the *Mitscher* (DL-2) and three follow ships. Plagued with problems, they were so unreliable that they were replaced with conventional boilers. This experience, along with the *Timmerman*, fomented some skepticism, if not hostility, in the fleet with regard to Bureau of Ships innovations.

Reduction Gears

Progress in the design and manufacture of reduction gears was characterized more by methodical evolution than by dramatic technical breakthrough. Even before the end of World War II, the Bureau of Ships had decided to explore whether gear designs were too conservative, and, if so, what the real limits were.[7] In 1944, a Navy Gear Industry Committee was established, and the Naval Boiler and Turbine Laboratory (NBTL) in Philadelphia embarked on an extensive series of gear tests. Included were tests of Swiss-manufactured hardened and ground gears that were known to operate at much higher loading than comparable U.S. Navy gears. Many combinations of gear material, hardening and shaping processes, and basic tooth design were compared.

This test program confirmed that gear design had, indeed, been conservative, and pointed the way to a number of approaches to smaller gears without sacrificing reliability. As described by Commander Ivan Monk, then Head of the Bureau of Ships Turbine and Gear Branch,[8] these developments included harder teeth to resist pitting; stronger teeth, achieved by coarser pitch and shot-peening the gear roots against breakage; more accurate gear cutting and shaving; modified tooth profiles to reduce scoring; and improved forging and heat treating, all of which might be summed up as attention to detail.

By the early 1950s, naval propulsion gears were being built and operated at two to three times (and even greater in the *Timmerman*) the loading of World War II gears. Refinements continued throughout the period, including later emphasis on fine-tooth gears for quieter operation. However, the Swiss techniques of hardening and grinding, although proven in many foreign ship applications, and offering quieter operation, never took root in the United States, perhaps because the demand never justified the invest-ment expense.

Propulsion Shafting

After World War II, the Bureau of Ships began to look for higher strength steels for propulsion shafting to reduce weight.[9] Alloy No. 4, with a minimum tensile strength of 120,000 psi was selected and allowable stress was increased as compared to the conventional steel. In 1954, the USS *Norfolk* suffered a disastrous shaft fracture at the forward face of a propeller hub, at nearly full power. The failure was attributed to fretting corrosion. The Navy had been plagued for years by these corrosion fatigue cracks in external shafts in the vicinity of the steel waster rings commonly installed at the ends of bronze bearing sleeves. In most cases, repairs had been made by grinding out or welding the cracks. However, the *Norfolk* shaft failure led to replacement of all external Alloy No. 4 shafting.

These problems led to several other develop-ments in shafting design. Cold rolling of shafts, in way of the hub and strut bearings, was used to increase corrosion fatigue strength. More conservative estimates of the maximum bending moment were mandated, and shaft designs were predicated on lower allowable bending stresses and higher torque. Concurrently, safety factors were slightly reduced. Rubber covering replaced the steel waster rings. All these factors and im-proved cathodic protection virtually eliminated the corrosion fatigue problem.

Automatic Combustion Controls

Combustion controls for naval application were first tested by the NBTL in 1940, and shortly thereafter in the USS *Robinson* (DE-220), with unpublished results.[10] The next tests took place at NBTL in 1948, followed by the first installation in a large combatant, the USS *Northampton* (ECLC-1). The system proved suc-cessful, the only significant problem being related to purity of the compressed air that ac-tuated the system. Combustion controls were incorporated during the mid-1950s into the *Forrestal, Saratoga,* and subsequent carriers, as well as smaller combatants with 1,200-psi steam propulsion plants. As with many innovations, growing pains abounded. Lack of training in the

use and maintenance of the systems was a major problem; at one time the *Forrestal* had a specially trained, five-man team dedicated exclusively to maintaining the system and training other crew members. Air compressors continued to pose problems of contaminated air. However, by 1956, the Navy had 253 ships of 19 different types equipped with automatic combustion controls. By 1972, combustion controls had become a reliable standard feature of all steam plants.

Controllable Reversible Pitch (CRP) Propellers

According to one chronicler, a patent for a controllable pitch propeller was granted as early as 1844.[11] Several ships were fitted with them between 1850 and 1860, including the USS *Merrimac* (later the ironclad CSS *Virginia*). De-velopment of mechanically-operated CRP propel-lers continued for some 90 years, but it was the application of hydraulic power to the mechan-ism, in about 1934, that triggered their wide-spread use. Their advantages of reversible thrust, without reversing the prime mover, improved maneuverability. Also, their greater efficiency through adjustability to operating conditions led to a number of applications in diesel-propelled ships such as tank landing ships (LSTs).

The emergence of the high-powered gas tur-bine as a prime mover changed the CRP propel-ler from a desirable option to a virtual necessity. Thus, they were employed in the PG-84-class patrol gunboats with CODOG propulsion plants, driven in the boost mode by gas turbines of 7,000 horsepower. Other applications included the Coast Guard's *Hamilton*-class cutters, pow-ered by FT-4 engines rated at 20,000 horsepower, the Maritime Administration's *John Seargent* at 6,000 horsepower, and numerous other domestic and foreign ships up to about 20,000 horsepower per shaft.

The general success of CRP propellers in those power ranges led to confidence that scaling them up to the power required for destroyer propul-sion—40,000 horsepower per shaft—would be straightforward. As stated in 1954 by one group of engineers, "The reliability of this equipment will soon be established sufficiently to permit reversing at higher powers."[12] However, it was 1962 before BuShips undertook development of a high-power CRP propeller,[13] and, it was not until 1972-73, another 10 years, before the Navy had CRP propellers rated as high as 35,000 horsepower, nearly double the power rating of any existing design, available for shipboard testing. Two different designs were developed. One was installed in the USS *Patterson* (DE-1061) and the other in the USS *Barbey* (DE-1088) for at-sea evaluation under realistic conditions (although with steam-turbine drive instead of gas turbines). The propeller in the *Patterson* eventually suffered a minor control system malfunction, but otherwise proved structurally sound. The *Barbey*'s propeller operated satisfactorily for a time, but then, without warning, shed all five blades at once during a reversal from full power ahead. This was a matter of some concern, since by that time the Navy was committed to two whole classes of ships (thirty *Spruance*-class destroyers and fifty *Oliver Hazard Perry*-class frigates) driven by propellers of similar, although not identical, design. An intensive effort was launched to analyze the cause of failure and prescribe an appropriate fix. The program included elaborate strain gage instrumentation and sea test of a *Spruance*-class propeller. This test, plus others carried out by the Naval Ship Research and Development Center, not only pointed to the potential problems and appropriate modifications, but also provided some surprises regarding the location and magnitude of stresses. One of these was that the maximum stress occurred not during a crash-back (full power reversal), according to conventional wisdom, but during a crash-ahead or full power turn. In any event, modifications were made and the *Spruance* and *Perry* propellers performed satisfactorily. The episode was a lesson in the potential pitfalls in scaling up machinery to bigger sizes and higher powers.

Diesel Engines

Diesel engine development proceeded in two almost diametrically-opposite directions. For naval applications, the keynotes were small, high-speed, and lightweight; for merchant ships, the trend was toward large, slow-speed engines of higher power and efficiency.

The trend in post-World War II submarine design toward greater submerged speed provoked a demand for diesel engines of greatly

(44%) reduced weight, capable of snorkeling and resisting high shock.[14] To meet a goal of 4,000 horsepower in one engine room, one engine contractor, Fairbanks Morse, developed a 1,335 horsepower at 1,335 rpm opposed-piston engine, which was installed in the *Harder*, the *Gudgeon*, and later, three other boats. The other contractor, General Motors, developed a 16-cylinder, 1,000-horsepower, "pancake" design, which was installed in the *Trigger* class (SS 564-6) and the *Albacore* (SS-569). Both types of engines immediately demonstrated a greater propensity for trouble than for performance. The pancake engines were eventually removed from the *Trigger* class. The Fairbank Morse model underwent numerous design fixes and alterations. The unfavorable outcome was attributed to venturing beyond the state of the art and the lack of a commercial application (to attract greater engineering and financial support). It might also have suggested inherent incompatibility between diesel engine reliability and "high-speed, lightweight."

These engines were by no means the last high-speed diesels in naval application. The USS *Dolphin* (AGSS-555) was equipped with 2,300-rpm, 900-horsepower, 12-cylinder, Curtis-Wright engines with specific weight of 4½ pounds per horsepower—less than half the specific weight of the engines cited above. Some 160 minesweepers were built with a special design of Packard nonmagnetic engines of comparably low specific weight, so casualty-prone that they eventually had to be replaced. This episode was a classic case of pushing orderly development into premature production under pressure of war—in this instance, the Korean conflict.[15] Another lesson lurked in the fact that these engines, like the high-speed submarine engines, had no commercial market. Thus, even though their faults were in time largely overcome, they lacked spare parts and other logistic support. It is interesting that when they were superseded by commercial, automotive engines of greater weight and less horsepower, the propulsion characteristics of minesweepers were such that their top speed was only slightly affected.

These problems were by no means typical of all diesel developments during the period. For example, a highly imaginative British design, the

Napier Deltic, used opposed pistons in cylinders arranged in the form of an equilateral triangle, with a crankshaft at each apex. With eighteen cylinders, these engines were rated at 2,500 bhp (brake horsepower) maximum at 2,000 rpm and 1,875 bhp continuous at 1,700 rpm. They were successful in patrol boats, minesweepers, and other applications. Other diesels of foreign and American design, with lower rpm, proved reliable and were adopted for propulsion of smaller warships such as frigates, either alone or in combination with gas or steam turbines. They also found widespread acceptance as prime movers for electric power generators.

In merchant ship propulsion, diesels became more and more predominant, even before the oil shortage overshadowed all other considerations in machinery selection. An idea of the pace of growth in diesel engine size for merchant ships can be gleaned by two reports from *The Motor Ship*.[16] At the end of 1958, this source noted that no marine diesel engine above 15,000 bhp was in service, but cited plans for engines up to 24,000 bhp. By 1968, an article in the same publication listed several "super-large-bore" (over 1,000-mm) diesels producing up to 44,000 bhp with twelve cylinders, at slightly over 100 rpm. Although smaller, higher-speed, geared diesels continued to be used in some commercial ships, the major trend was toward large, slow-speed, direct-coupled engines because of their simplicity, "carefree operation on boiler-fuel," lower maintenance costs, lower fuel and lubrication oil consumption, less noise, and simpler remote control.[17]

Submerged Chemical Plants

Prior to nuclear propulsion, submariners avidly sought a propulsion plant capable of much greater endurance at high speed while submerged. The search led to a number of exotic and complex schemes such as Projects Alton, Ellis, and Wolverine.[18] These power plants were essentially partially closed cycles, using internal combustion with oxygen or hydrogen peroxide as oxidants and with partial recirculation of the working fluid, the rest being discharged overboard. Two of the plants used gas turbines for power, while the Ellis plant employed a steam boiler and turbine. Experimental versions of all

three were built and tested to some degree by the U.S. Navy. Significant problems included gas discharge and regeneration, storage and handling of the oxidants, corrosion, complexity, control, and the extremely high cost of hydrogen peroxide. A 10-hour run on one of the plants was projected to cost $147,000 just for the oxidant. Interest in such schemes waned with the advent of nuclear propulsion, at least in the United States.

Navy Distillate Fuel

One of the truly great boons to Navy operating engineers of all ranks during this period was the change from the heavy, black Navy Standard Fuel Oil (NSFO) to a distillate fuel: first, Navy Distillate (ND), and later, marine diesel. It was not only cleaner burning in boilers but also could be used for all fuel purposes except aircraft engines. The impetus for the change was that, in the mid-1960s, the fleet identified boilers as its most aggravating maintenance problem, particularly the fouling of firesides and the mandatory cleaning thereof every 600 hours.[19] An early suggestion to change to aircraft fuel, JP-5, which would have reduced aircraft carrier fuel requirements to a single type, foundered on the fact that private industry lacked the necessary production capacity. Steam atomization of the fuel was also considered, but the final choice was a distillate fuel.

Trial conversions were made in a variety of ship types, with favorable results. Fireside inspections were needed only every 1,800 hours, which coincided conveniently with waterside inspection. Other advantages included longer refractory life, reduced soot-blowing, cleaner topsides and firerooms, more time for other maintenance, and better morale. Accordingly, the Navy undertook to convert all oil-fired ships to a single fuel, ND, by 1973 (later shifting to the more common and available marine diesel fuel.)

Lest it be wondered why this had not been done long before, it should be pointed out that the conversion was neither simple nor cheap. Most fuel oil pumps had to be replaced, rebuilt, or modified. Tanks and piping systems had to be cleaned, sprayer plates changed, fuel oil heaters blanked off or bypassed, seals and gaskets improved, and adjustments made to combustion control systems. Also required were new technical manuals, training, and other logistic support. There were times the fleet doubted it was all worthwhile. Fortunately, it was.

COMBAT SYSTEMS

Guided Missiles

The development and naval application of guided missiles evolved concurrently with, and at the same rapid pace as, nuclear propulsion. In 1944, the Bureau of Ordnance initiated the Bumblebee program to develop a ramjet-propelled guided missile, Talos, together with supporting fire control and launching systems.[20] The technical effort was centered in Johns Hopkins University's Applied Physics Laboratory, where expertise in advanced weaponry would continue to flourish. By 1949, a "test vehicle" called Terrier was being used to test the Talos guidance systems. Terrier worked so well that a decision was made to make it an operational weapon.

At this same time, according to the referenced account, two other related developments influenced the outcome. One was the discovery of the feasibility of a "zero-length launcher" instead of long, cumbersome launching-rails. The other was the concept of the Weapons Direction System (WDS). Whereas the gun fire control systems of World War II had performed a relatively simple function of directing fire at a single selected target at a time, the WDS was required to perform multiple functions to cope with the increasing speeds, numbers, and varieties of targets, and the consequent need for faster reaction time. Accordingly, the WDS was to track all targets, evaluate their relative threats and the priority of countering them, assign targets to fire control radars, assign weapons, and initiate firing orders. Obviously, the faithful old Mark 37 gun fire control system that had directed the 5-inch guns of World War II would not be up to the task.

In 1951, the ex-battleship *Mississippi* (EAG-128) was converted into a tactical prototype Terrier missile ship, and ultimately was to fire over 400 missiles in support of both the technical and tactical developments of guided missiles. The same year, it was decided to convert the USS *Boston* and *Canberra* (CAG-1 and 2) to the world's first surface-to-air missile (SAM) ships. This was to be done by removing the after 8-inch gun turret and installing two Terrier twin-launchers. The installation was to include a WDS and a rapid, automatic, launching system. The complexity of the task can be inferred from the fact that the *Boston* was not recommissioned until 1955.

Thereafter, "firsts" abounded: the USS *Gyatt* was converted to the first guided-missile destroyer in 1957, the USS *Galveston* converted to the first Talos ship in 1958, and the *Dewey* delivered as first of a class of Terrier frigates (later classified as cruisers) in 1959. In 1961, the world's first nuclear-powered cruiser, the USS *Long Beach*, carried both Talos and Terrier, and the latter was installed for the first time in a carrier, the USS *Kittyhawk* (CVA-63). In 1962, the *Albany* became the first of three conventionally powered cruisers to be converted to carry both Talos and Terrier. Meanwhile, in 1960, a third and smaller member of the "3-T" family of missiles, Tartar, appeared as the main weapon of the new DDG-2-class USS *Adams*. Also, Regulus I surface-to-surface cruise missiles (SSM) had been installed several years previously in four heavy cruisers and two submarines.

Missiles profoundly affected the design of naval ships, as did the concurrent development of nuclear propulsion. There were several reasons.[21] The weapons direction system was more than a concept: it comprised a great deal of electronic hardware in the form of sensors, computers, data processors, information displays, and power supplies, all of which were heavy. An increasing proportion of weapons systems' weight was devoted to detection and fire control, equipment that is located high in the ship. Missiles required much more space than guns. Gun ammunition was smaller and could be stored compactly in low-level magazines. Missiles were much larger, more fragile, and needed to be stowed close to their launcher—that is, higher in the ship. Their greater size and weight, per unit, required large, powerful handling equipment, as well as more room for handling and maintenance. Topside, their size and rocket blast also demanded more space—that is, a longer ship. The handling equipment and electronics required a dramatic increase in electric power, and more ship's fuel to produce it. Environmental considerations also obtruded on ship design: electronic equipment needed temperature and humidity control; missiles imposed new demands for weather deck dryness, shock protection, and magazine sprinkling. Service systems such as special power supplies and dry air supply for waveguides began to proliferate.

Missile-carrying ships became "volume controlled" instead of "weight controlled." That is, their size was determined primarily by the space required for their contents, rather than the weight of the contents. The required spacing of topside weapons and sensors dictated ships' lengths, and the higher center of gravity of their weapons system components augured increased beam for stability. Below decks, the bulky missiles demanded more internal space, as did their support functions. Stability problems were offset to some extent by substituting aluminum superstructures for steel, by lower specific weight of machinery, and by greater weight of required fuel load. In a sense, this latter requirement was an asset; by the time the ship was big enough to carry its weapon system payload and machinery, it needed and could easily accommodate the required fuel, and, in fact, needed the weight low in the hull for stability.

Ironically, this feature to some degree counteracted the salability of nuclear propulsion, which was predicated largely on the unlimited cruising range it provided for destroyers and cruisers. By the time the USS *Bainbridge* (DLGN-25) was completed in 1962, conventionally powered ships of comparable or even greater firepower, such as the *Leahy* (CG-16), were capable of cruising 8,000 miles at 14 knots. This was a reasonably competitive capability when combined with other practical limitations on ship endurance, such as food and (in wartime) ammunition supplies, limitations which apply to nuclear and conventional ships alike.

Other nations were, of course, developing and deploying shipboard missile systems of their own, and some even anticipated this country in the adoption of SSMs, notably in small craft. It would be impossible to recount all these developments in this brief chapter. However, certain dramatic events served to remind a world that

might have forgotten the buzz-bombs of World War II that there was emerging a new and sobering dimension to naval warfare. Notable among the attention-getters was the sinking in 1967 of the Israeli destroyer *Eilat* by Soviet-made Styx missiles fired from a Soviet-supplied Egyptian Navy fast gunboat (PGM).

In this regard it is interesting that while ships were being radically redesigned to accommodate missile-firing capabilities, they remained virtually unchanged during this period with regard to defense against such weapons.

Polaris

The development of the Polaris ballistic missile system has been compared with that of nuclear propulsion in the speed and efficiency with which enormous technical problems were overcome. Equally fascinating to some historians was the difference in the personalities and management techniques between Polaris' project manager, Rear Admiral William F. Raborn, and Admiral Rickover. Whatever the relative merits of their methods, Admiral Raborn conclusively demonstrated that there is more than one way to accomplish great engineering feats.

While SAMs were being developed and deployed, as described above, great energy was also being directed toward surface-to-surface missiles (SSM, or bombardment) for attack on both ships and land targets. The initial effort grew naturally from the German V-1 pilotless aircraft-bomb of World War II. A radio-guided American version of the V-1, called Loon, was installed in launching ramps on the decks of two fleet submarines, the *Cusk* and *Carbonero*, with the *Cusk* also being provided a hangar. The *Cusk* made the first launch in early 1947. Later that year, a German V-2 was successfully launched from the deck of the carrier *Midway*. Subsequent Loon firings proved the feasibility of the concept, and provided a solid technical basis for a successor having greater speed, range, and payload—that is, a nuclear warhead (at that time, about 4,000 pounds).

The successor, under development since 1946, was the radio-guided Regulus I, 33 feet long, with folded wings and, in improved versions, a speed of Mach 0.9, altitude of 35,000 feet, and range of 575 miles, with nuclear-warhead capability. As related later, it was quickly installed (by 1953) in the converted fleet submarine *Tunny*, and later in other boats. It was also installed in four heavy cruisers (the *Toledo, Helena, Macon*, and *Los Angeles*), and ten carriers were fitted out to carry it, as well. On surface ships, Regulus storage and launching facilities had only a small impact. The inevitable follow-on, Regulus II (although it was a completely new design), was capable of Mach 2 speed at 60,000 feet and a range of 1,200 miles, with twice the weight of Regulus I. First tested in 1956, its first U.S. submarine launch was from the *Grayback* in 1958. Although the Navy had plans for its installation in numerous submarines and surface ships, the program was canceled in 1958 in favor of the promising Polaris development.

In 1955, President Eisenhower formed the Killian Committee to study missile developments. Among other things, the committee recommended a 1,500-mile ballistic missile for both land and sea basing. This resulted in orders for the Army and Navy to develop with top priority an intermediate range ballistic missile, Jupiter. The Navy immediately created a Special Projects office to develop a surface ship version of the liquid-fueled Jupiter by 1965, with submarine capability to follow. However, the Navy, with strong technical support from the National Academy of Sciences, the Secretary of Defense's Science Advisory Committee, and its own Office of Naval Research, wanted a solid-fuel rocket, and withdrew from the Jupiter program in 1956. By early 1957, the target date was set ahead to 1963, but Soviet missile programs injected even greater urgency into the work. The result was an all-out effort to complete and integrate the missile design, warhead design, and ship design by 1960, a herculean engineering effort.

By April 1959, the first successful flight of a test vehicle was accomplished. The first Polaris submarine, the *George Washington* (as told later, a *Skipjack* with a parallel middle-body "plug" for the weapons) was commissioned in December, and in July 1960 fired its first missiles. With sixteen single-warhead, 1,200-mile missiles, the *George Washington* ushered the Navy into a new role as the "third leg of the strategic deterrence triad." In the following years, improved versions of the missiles provided greater range and multi-

ple warheads, but even when the missiles grew in size and weight, shipboard retrofits were possible because the engineers had wisely allowed design margins for growth. Eventually, however, limits were reached and new submarine designs were required, for these and other reasons.

The Polaris project, under Admiral Raborn and his outstanding staff, including Technical Director then-Captain Levering Smith and Chief Engineer J. B. B. Buescher, has been praised as a model of management effectiveness in the pursuit of engineering development. Observers were particularly fascinated by management "tools" such as the Program Evaluation Review Technique (PERT), the Critical Path Method (CPM), and the Management Information Center (MIC). These devices purported to define all critical technical developments, identify problems for resolution and display up-to-the-minute status of every facet of the program. An alternate view was that these trappings were not so much used in the actual execution of the project as they were to bedazzle potential critics and meddlers into keeping their hands off it. To the extent that this gambit succeeded, it was a significant accomplishment in its own right. (Admiral Rickover often complained to the Congress that he spent more time fending off meddlers than doing technical work.)

A much greater and more technical key to the program's success was the definition and control of the interfaces between the various pieces of the whole system, for example, between the missile and the launch, navigation, and fire control systems; and between the weapons complex and the supporting ship systems. Also, interfaces had to be defined, in engineering terms, between the numerous contractors. The object was, of course, to pinpoint responsibilities and ensure that all the pieces would fit. "Dick" Buescher, as Chief Engineer, directed this work with great technical insight and rigorous discipline, as evident by the results. His methods served as models for the development of other complex weapons systems.[22]

Navy Tactical Data System (NTDS)

One of the most successful developments of this or any other era, and one of tremendous importance to naval ships, was the Navy Tactical

Data System (NTDS). Few projects of such complexity have gone from concept to successful hardware in 5 years as the NTDS did. As is usual in such cases, the impetus was talented, dedicated people, working under an effective organization, and directed by a technically competent, hard-driving professional. In NTDS, the leader was Captain E. C. Svendsen, U.S. Navy.

In World War II shipboard combat information centers (CIC), the tactical situation was displayed by marking up plotting boards with grease pencils, based on telephoned information from individual sensors (i.e., lookouts, radar, sonar) or voice communications from other ships. In the multithreat, high-speed combat environment of the post-war era, it became clear that this would no longer do. Fortunately, the high-speed, compact, digital computer opened up a whole new world of information processing capabilities.

By the early 1950s, several development programs were underway to solve the problem, but none offered an overall system encompassing the multiple sensors and multimission requirements of U.S. Navy ships. In 1954, the Chief of Naval Research, Rear Admiral Rawson Bennett, initiated Project Lamplight at MIT, a large, tri-service, NATO study on air defense. He skillfully used the Navy portion of this study to develop a unified Navy position for a fleet data system. His project officer, Commander I. L. McNally, with the help of E. E. McCown of the Naval Electronics Laboratory (NEL), wrote the system concept, which recommended the development of a tactical data system using digital equipment.

In 1955, BuShips undertook NTDS development to implement the Lamplight recommendations. Commander McNally, an expert in radar and displays, was assigned to BuShips to write the specifications, and he recruited then-Commander Svendsen to assist in the computer area.[23] Although it would be impossible in today's bureaucratic climate, those two officers, with little help, wrote the full technical requirements of the system during the summer of 1955. The feat was particularly remarkable in the light of the system's complexity, novelty, and dependency on electronic hardware not even available at the time. Equally incredibly, they got their report approved by a Navy Committee on Tactical

Data Processing and by the Chief of Naval Operations that same year, with support for the necessary funding.

The project organization was simple and effective. In the Bureau of Ships, Svendsen headed a project management team of four Engineering Duty Officers (EDO) with prior fleet experience, each a specialist in a related electronics field such as computers, communications, displays, and administration. They were supported by many highly competent BuShips civilians, notably Donald L. Ream, whose computer expertise was invaluable in solving technical problems as well as monitoring the work of the computer contractor. The NEL was designated as lead laboratory for "in-house" technical support and development of a shore-based test and evaluation center. By mid-1956, three contracts had been let for the development: to Remington Rand Univac for solid state digital computers, to Hughes Aircraft for the displays, and to Collins Radio for the communication link between ships. The project got strong support from the Office of the Chief of Naval Operations, and also enjoyed uncommon continuity of personnel.

The core of the development was a new, compact digital computer, the most capable for its size ever built up to that time (1961). With this computer integrated into a system with the displays and communications links, the resulting NTDS revolutionized tactical analysis and control for fleet and ship commanders. It did this by an orders-of-magnitude increase in the volume of data that could be continuously digested from sensors and communications links, and in the speed and accuracy with which the information could be interpreted and displayed for decision making. A vital feature of the system was modular construction in both hardware and software so that it could be easily expanded or changed to accommodate new and different functions.

By 1958, a prototype, experimental NTDS was being delivered to NEL for evaluation. By 1961, an NTDS was installed in three ships for service test (two guided-missile frigates, the *King* and *Mahan*, and a carrier, the *Oriskany*), with successful completion in 1962. Concurrently, an NTDS was installed in the USS *Enterprise* and USS *Long Beach* to handle the digital output of the SPS-33, a large, phased-array radar. Ten years later, fifty U.S. Navy ships had the system, and a number of foreign ships as well.

In 1966, the NTDS and the WDS MK 11 were installed in the USS *Wainwright*. The coordinated design of these systems for this class of ship achieved a new level of system integration and interface definition for the CIC and weapons control systems. This was the first integrated combat system.

With the new digital technology of NTDS came requirements for computer programming and training facilities. To meet the schedule for the service test in 1961, it was necessary to establish interim programming and training activities at NEL. Concurrently, Navy construction projects were initiated for permanent programming and training facilities. A remarkable achievement by all of the naval activities involved was the completion and commissioning of the first Fleet Programming Center, in San Diego in July 1961, 2 months before the start of the shipboard service evaluation.

Among its many pioneering achievements, the NTDS project produced:

1. The first shipboard tactical data system in the world to use stored-program, solid-state digital computers. Also, the first to use multiple computers in a distributed tactical data processing system.
2. The first shore-based test site (NEL San Diego) to check out and evaluate a complete tactical data system.
3. The first shipboard system in the world to use automatic computer-to-computer data exchange between ships and aircraft. The message structure for the data links became the basis of a Canada-United Kingdom-United States (CAN-UK-US) standard and a NATO standard, which is still in use.

Digital Computer Impact on Naval Engineering

The ascendency of digital computers greatly affected the character of both naval engineering and naval ships. In naval engineering, they made calculations speedier and more accurate and, as will be seen in the case of the FFG-7, permitted more design options and "what-ifs" to be explored. A whole new industry blossomed within the ship research and engineering community, dedicated to generating new computer applications programs such as CADCAM (Com-

puter-Aided Design, Computer-Aided Manufacturing), CASDOS (Computer-Aided Structural Design of Ships), and to computerized ship synthesis models such as ASSET (Advanced Surface Ship Evaluation Tool). Computer-generated graphic displays and drawings became common tools in ship design, performing almost instantly such erstwhile time-consuming tasks as drawing ships' lines and making layouts of carrier flight decks. In shipyards, hull steel could be laid out and cut by computer, and many other tasks of detail design and fabrication were similarly facilitated. Computers also simplified the storage and retrieval of technical data and, for better or worse, provided the backbone for proliferation of the management information systems subsequently discussed.

While computers in many ways made ship design easier, they also created a virtually limitless workload of their own. This consisted of developing software that would organize existing and newly generated data in a form that would facilitate its use in future ship and weapons design and engineering. In other words, the capacity to "crunch numbers" created a vacuum for more numbers to crunch. In some cases, research and development programs seemed to focus more on generating computer programs than on removal of technical barriers to engineering progress.

Much has been said about the increasing complexity of modern ships. The digital computer was unquestionably a key factor in this trend in that it permitted the comprehension and analysis of complex hardware far beyond the capability of former computational methods. Moreover, it also provided vastly improved means for predicting the performance of complex systems, both in isolation and in relation to one another. The computer thus became the foundation for emphasis on *systems integration* or the even more esoteric concept of *systems architecture*. These elusive concepts rose to a status approaching a religion, particularly in the world of 'combat systems,' the automated control systems integrating the operation and control of sensors, decision equipment, and weapons. Whether they made design any easier can be debated, but they provided employment for a new breed of specialists among naval engineers: systems integrators and systems architects.

Electronics

Revolutionary developments took place in electronics, many of which had significant effects on naval ship design. The tiny transistor replaced the bulky and energy-consuming vacuum tube; the compact, mass-production, printed-circuit board, about the size of a playing card, incorporated all the functions of a hand-wired console radio; solid state devices were developed, particularly "microchips"—electronic circuits the size of a thumbnail—that could outperform circuits that had previously weighed a hundred times as much. These developments spearheaded a trend toward "miniaturization" of electronic components. At the same time, the urge to increase the effective range of active sensors, such as radars and sonars, demanded an increase in power and, for sonar, lower frequency, both of which led to increased size of the equipment and its power supplies. Development of phase-shifting, a means of electronically steering radar and sonar beams without actually rotating the antenna, changed the configuration of these antennas and the design of both surface ships and submarines. The impact of phased-array radar can be seen in the box-like superstructures of the USS *Long Beach* and USS *Enterprise*, the first U.S. Navy ships to be specifically designed to incorporate such radars.

At the same time, the functions of these and other sensors became more complex by orders of magnitude. They were required to not only detect and report targets, but also to analyze the targets' character, motion, and intentions, and provide data for attack, if warranted. The sensitivity of all sensors increased tremendously, owing considerably to techniques of "signal processing" that became possible with the concurrent development of digital computers. The expanding capabilities to accomplish these complex functions accurately, and virtually instantly, naturally led to a phenomenal increase in the number and complexity of electronic components in naval ships. Electronics come to play an increasingly vital role in almost every ship function: detection, evaluation, information display, fire control, command control, navigation, communications, and control of machinery from main propulsion to deck winches.

As an example, electronics developments profoundly affected naval communications. Higher-power radio transmitters, more sensitive receivers, and other advances in circuitry permitted the use of higher frequencies, which permitted more circuits, or channels, within a given frequency band. On-line encryption and decryption of coded messages eliminated the laborious and time-consuming manipulation of coding machines. Later, geostationary satellites provided the means to communicate practically instantly, even by voice radio, between two stations almost anywhere on the planet. The capability to "issue rudder orders from the Pentagon" was not lost on proponents of centralized control of military operations. All in all, these new capabilities triggered a revolution, not only in communications but also in concepts of intelligence handling and command control, related endeavors that acquired the collective label of C^3I.

Electronics provided the means for great advances in navigation, as well. Shore-based navigation systems such as Loran and Omega became more accurate and more automated. Earth-orbiting satellites became beacons to submarines (and other ships) through the predictability of the satellites' orbits and the sensitivity of the ships' radio receivers to doppler shifts in frequency as the satellite approached and receded. As the period ended, satellite systems capable of defining a ship's position within a few yards, with little more effort than pushing a button, were a looming reality.

Electronic warfare naturally prospered. Greater receiver sensitivity, sophisticated circuitry, and the digital computer combined to greatly enhance the ability to detect, classify, and analyze electromagnetic emanations and, if desired, to counter, or "jam," them. As time went on, electronic warfare capabilities became more and more integrated into ships' combat systems, providing threat warnings and countermeasures in addition to intelligence.

In electronics, as in other technologies, gains did not come without problems, many of which affected ship design. Electronic equipment generated heat, but was also sensitive to high temperature. This characteristic required air conditioning or other cooling to prolong the life of the equipment. On the other hand, the new techniques of electronic circuity greatly increased reliability, so much so that determining the mean time between failure (MTBF) became difficult when the time exceeded several years.[24] Electronic circuits became so small that replacement of individual components was practically impossible. Instead, a whole circuit, typically a circuit card or (later) microchip, would be replaced. The result was a revolution in the logistic support of electronic equipment, both ashore and in ships. The change was not only in the number and character of spare parts and their storage requirements, but also in the way people were trained to diagnose and correct problems.

But more importantly, the proliferation of electronics created its own formidable monster in the form of electromagnetic interference (EMI), and a curative industry aimed at electromagnetic compatibility. As forests of antennas sprouted in ships, mutual interference, both electronic and physical, became a formidable problem. The EMI so degraded performance of the equipment that antenna location became a serious consideration in the topside design of ships.[25] For example, by 1966, a typical aircraft carrier had eighty transmitters and 150 receivers, employing seventy antennas.[26] Obviously, attenuation of interference by simply increasing the distance between antennas was no longer practical. An extreme, but dramatic, example of the problem was a hydrofoil ship whose electronic foil control system failed whenever a certain radio transmitter was activated, causing the ship to "crash" from its foilborne position. With such incentives, the search for means to predict and minimize EMI became a significant and very difficult endeavor in ship design.

Other problems arose. As ships' "senses" became increasingly dependent on electronics, so did they become more vulnerable. A serious threat was an electromagnetic pulse generated by a high attitude nuclear explosion, a burst of energy that could theoretically destroy electronic equipment in a fashion similar to a lightning strike. Another threat was the destruction of delicate antennas and waveguides by shrapnel from close-aboard explosion of a missile warhead. Such an event actually occurred, and rendered the ship virtually helpless, even though structurally intact. These threats began to affect the design of antennas and the topsides of ships, as defensive measures such as internal routing, or external armoring, of waveguides were incorporated.

As might be expected, radiation hazards also became a serious consideration in ship design. High-powered radar, particularly, posed a physiological threat to personnel, making antenna location and beam pattern important factors in topside arrangements. Ungrounded topside equipment posed two problems. One was a tendency to act like an antenna, absorbing and re-emitting radiation, sometimes at a different frequency (the "rusty bolt effect"). The other was the tendency of the equipment to store up energy, with the threat of a nasty electric shock to anyone who might unwittingly "ground" the equipment. Internally, inadequately grounded electronic gear could allow the inadvertent propagation of radiation outside the hull, with the potential of compromising classified information. These problems led to design emphasis on nonmetallic materials for topside rigging, lifelines, handrails, ladders, and stanchions, and on avoiding corroded and loose joints between appendages and the basic ship structure. Typically, the attack on deficiencies in existing ships involved specially-trained teams of experts, dedicated to inspecting ships and correcting the faults.

In summary, during this period electronics became a new and serious factor in ship design. One observer estimated that the percentage of ship cost traceable to electronics could be as high as 40 percent.[27] In any case, the growth of electronics unquestionably affected ship design in requirements for greater space, increased weight (often high in the ship), increased power and cooling, special support systems such as dry air supply for waveguides, greater space for repair parts, and more people for operation and maintenance (and space and weight for their support), in addition to the other impacts cited above.

SUBMARINES

Revolutionary Design

One of the world's foremost submarine designers, Captain Harry A. Jackson, USN, has described five revolutionary innovations in submarine design.[28] Only the last took place during the era of this chapter. This was the transition from a submersible surface ship to a true submarine, epitomized by the marriage of nuclear propulsion to the high-speed, tear-drop hull form, most ideally exemplified by the USS *Skipjack* (SSN-585). However (according to Jackson), the emphasis on submerged performance at the expense of surface performance had been presaged by the fourth revolution: the 1944 German technology Type XXI boat, capable of snorkeling and high-speed submerged attack. In any event, submarine design was also affected by many other influences, as will be seen.

Primarily Submerged Operation

Nuclear propulsion provided the conclusive argument for the design of submarines as primarily submerged vessels. Nevertheless, the USS *Nautilus* was essentially a World War II design for the simple reason that it was all that was available at the time. Surprisingly, data on the optimum hull shape for submerged speed were sparse. Following an intensive research program, the tear-drop form evolved in the diesel-powered experimental USS *Albacore* (AGSS-569) and was quickly incorporated in the nuclear *Skipjack* (SSN-585) and the diesel-powered *Barbel* class. It should not be overlooked that the concomitant adoption of single-screw propulsion for submarines was a drastic departure from conventional practice and, considering the novelty of nuclear power, a remarkably bold one. The propeller, axially-mounted behind a body of revolution, constituted an ideal combination for propulsive efficiency and high submerged speed. However, while this hull shape eventually became the norm, several other nuclear submarines were produced. These included one-of-a-kind designs such as the high-power, twin-reactor, radar picket submarine USS *Triton* ("Around the World Submerged"), the low-power, hunter-killer, turbo-electric-drive USS *Tullibee*, and the first submarine designed and built specifically to fire missiles (Regulus I), the medium-power USS *Halibut*. For a number of reasons not necessarily related to these boats' specific capabilities, none of them found a niche in submarine warfare that attracted further support. The same was true of the USS *Skate* ("Surface at the Pole") class of four medium-power boats; these were smaller versions of the *Nautilus*, superseded by the *Albacore*-type hull.

Fast Attack Requirements

Eventually, the Navy settled on two basic types of submarines, both nuclear powered. One was the fleet ballistic missile submarine (SSBN), capable of submerged launching of long-range, strategic nuclear missiles. The other was the fast attack submarine (SSN), optimized for detection and destruction of enemy submarines and surface ships. The *Skipjack* hull form served as a prototype for both kinds. However, the ideal tear-drop shape gave way to less perfect forms under the pressures of urgent, competing requirements, which, in the final analysis, combined to make submarines bigger, longer, and of less optimum shape for speed. This trend continued and was reflected in the design of many foreign submarines, notably those of the Soviet Navy. One influence was the change from the double-hull design of American World War II "fleet boats," with the pressure hull externally framed, to a single hull with internal frames. This structure somewhat complicated the arrangement of equipment and tended to require more internal volume. Another influence was the urge to go deeper. Since the necessary increase in hull thickness and weight would be further aggravated by increasing the hull diameter, the latter tended to remain relatively constant, with the additional weight balanced by lengthening the hull. Increased volume was required for other reasons, too. The capability to remain submerged for long periods created a need for greater creature comforts than submariners previously had required; improved habitability became a conscious design factor. Although living accommodations would still appall landlubbers, they offered amenities unimaginable in the old boats. Crew spaces became bigger, better lighted, air conditioned, better decorated, and better equipped with recreational equipment. Prolonged submergence also demanded longer-lasting and more reliable life support systems for oxygen generation and atmospheric purification. Adequate, reliable air conditioning was a must. Requiring redundancy, this equipment not only added space and weight for itself but also for the extra power generation to support it.

Weapons, sensors (especially sonar), communications, and command and control systems grew bigger, heavier, more numerous, and more sophisticated. For example, large, spherical, bow-mounted sonars in some boats displaced the torpedo tubes farther aft, requiring outward angling for launching. As these systems grew, more crew was needed to operate and maintain them. Quiet operation became a major, if not predominant, design objective. Designing machinery for quiet operation usually added weight, as did sound isolation devices and acoustic insulation. New safety features, such as an emergency main ballast tank blow system, all contributed to growth. As submarine size grew to accommodate the increasing burden and its support, the power plant also had to grow, further promoting the upward size-and-cost spiral.

Diesel Submarines

The advent of nuclear submarines did not by any means stop development of diesel-electric boats. Earlier, the German, late World War II Type XXI design spurred the United States and other countries to develop submarines of similar high-speed submerged capabilities. An early step was the "Guppy" conversion of some of our World War II fleet submarines to increase submerged speed and incorporate a snorkel.[29] This entailed removal of deck guns, life rails, and propeller guards; a smaller superstructure; an enclosed, faired bridge; housed cleats and chocks; and other refinements to decrease resistance. With a larger battery of twice the former voltage and a greater discharge rate, this conversion achieved much increased submerged speed and endurance. A new *Tang* class was built, with characteristics similar to the Type XXI.[30] These were the first United States submarines specifically designed to use the German "snorkel" for air intake while submerged. They were also the first (and last) fleet boats equipped with the previously mentioned lightweight "pancake" diesel engines, disastrously unreliable and eventually removed.[31] Britain and France also built *Tang* equivalents.

Other designs included conversion of ten World War II fleet boats to radar pickets, and three small hunter-killer boats (SSK), neither of which prospered, although they spawned nuclear counterparts in the *Triton* and *Tullibee*, respectively. The last diesel boats were three of the *Barbel* class built in the late 1950s, with *Albacore*-type hull forms and SSN-type sail planes (a conversion). These three remained in service to the end of this period. A particularly novel foreign design during the period was the Dutch *Dolfijn*-class submarine, a triple-hull design of three separate, nonintersecting cylinders, with the machinery mounted in the two lower hulls.

The experimental *Albacore* was completed in 1953, as previously mentioned, to confirm the predicted efficiency of the tear-drop form and to try out other new approaches to submarine design, such as the single axially-mounted propeller, stern planes forward of the propeller, and bow planes located in the fairwater, all of which proved successful and were incorporated into the *Skipjack*. Capable of 26 knots submerged, as built, the *Albacore* later attained 33 knots with silver-zinc batteries and contra-rotating propellers.

The imperative to go deeper necessarily fostered a search for stronger hull materials. By the late 1950s, HY80 steel had been accepted and incorporated in the *Skipjack* and the *Thresher* classes, increasing operating depth. Still higher-strength steels were investigated, such as HY100 and HY130. Such new materials involved a host of potential problems such as weldability, producibility, fabricability, corrosion resistance, creep resistance, and—new with nuclear submarines—fatigue resistance, all requiring lengthy and costly development to resolve.

Missile Submarine Requirements

Finally, the incorporation of missiles in submarines presented a whole world of new considerations to the ship designers. By the addition of a missile hangar and launcher on deck, and internal supporting systems, two fleet boats, the USS *Tunny* and USS *Barbero*, were converted to launch the subsonic, jet-powered, radar-guided Regulus. Their successes prompted redesign of two more boats under construction, the *Grayback* and *Growler*, for guided missiles (SSG).[32] This dramatically illustrated the design impact of the missiles, increasing length by 50 feet, displacement by 1,000 tons, and causing a major internal rearrangement. A nuclear-powered variant, the *Halibut*, was also built. These boats operated successfully until the nuclear ballistic missile superseded Regulus. Even then, the Navy found use for these boats. The missile hangars of the *Tunny* and *Grayback* were converted into compartments capable of carrying sixty people, eight boats, and four swimmer-delivery vehicles (or equivalent combinations). In this configuration, they supported numerous special operations, including assault and reconnaissance in Vietnam.

The ballistic missile imposed different and even more pronounced changes in submarine design. The first Polaris missile submarines used the *Skipjack* bow and stern, with a cylindrical middle body "plug" to carry the missiles and ancillary equipment. This added 135 feet of length and 3,200 tons of displacement. Subsequent, improved versions of the missiles and their fire control, support, and sensor systems demanded increasing space. The result was that the third-generation *Lafayette* class (SSBN 616), with no change in hull diameter, was over 40 feet longer with 1,500 tons greater displacement than the original *Skipjack*-derived versions.

AIRCRAFT CARRIERS

Our Debt to British Innovation

Just inside the entrance to the British Admiralty's ship design establishment in Bath, England, an American visitor in 1976 was pleased to see a model of a modern United States aircraft carrier. Then he observed a nearby plaque that succinctly pointed out that the ship's major design features had originated as British innovations. Duly humbled, the visitor had to concede that the British pride was justified. With the armored flight deck, angled flight deck, steam catapults, mirror landing system, and other inspirations translated into workable hardware, the British set the style, if not the pace, for aircraft carrier design in the post-war era.

Post-World War II Carrier Requirements

As related by naval technology historian Norman Friedman, 2 weeks after North Korea attacked South Korea on 25 June 1950, Secretary of Defense Louis Johnson offered Chief of Naval Operations (CNO) Admiral Forrest Sherman a new carrier.[33] Only a year earlier, Johnson had

canceled construction, a week after keel laying, of what the Navy had hoped would be its first post-war carrier, the USS *United States* (CVB-58). Its successor and direct descendent, although scaled down, would be the USS *Forrestal* (CVA-59). The design of the *United States* had been agonized over at least as much as that of post-war destroyers, whose evolution is described later. Based on World War II experience, the "wish list" for carriers included an armored flight deck, other armor (including modest side protection, the thickness and distribution of which was argued *ad infinitum*), better torpedo protection, deck-edge elevators, larger aviation fuel capacity, greater rearming speed and flexibility (faster, bigger ammunition elevators), and improved self-defense capabilities (possibly guided missiles). Other concerns were the location of CIC out of the vulnerable gallery deck, improved firefighting capability, better ventilation, more air conditioning, and alternate sources of air intake (to help reduce smoke induction from fires). A major impact was the requirement to handle a bigger, heavier, attack aircraft capable of carrying an 8,000-pound bomb (or 12,000 with sacrifice of fuel and range). This was to be the A3D, which dictated all aircraft handling capabilities of both the *United States* and *Forrestal*.

However, the *Forrestal* was anything but a copy of the *United States*. By the time the construction contract was let to Newport News Shipbuilding in 1951, the carrier had changed in concept from a heavy attack (nuclear) role to a tactical air warfare role with a mix of smaller, more numerous planes and weapons. Design time for the ship, in spite of this major revision, was compressed to a year as compared to 32 months for the USS *Midway*. Meanwhile, other upheavals were in the making. In 1951, the angled-deck concept emerged in Britain, soon followed by successful tests there and in the USS *Antietam* (CV-36). Accordingly, in 1953, 10 months into the construction, CNO ordered an angled deck for the *Forrestal*. Concurrently, the British had convincingly demonstrated the practicability and advantages of steam catapults, which also were adopted for the *Forrestal*. The angled deck revived the efficacy of a full, conventional island, with uptakes, in lieu of the original, flush-deck, retractable-island configuration that had been planned.

The number and magnitude of the changes were enormous. Fortunately, the ingenuity and energy of BuShips' and Newport News' engineers were equal to the task. In spite of the drastic redesign, the *Forrestal* was completed in less time than her immediate successor, the *Saratoga*. After the *Forrestal*, no major, fundamental changes in attack carrier design took place, with the exception of nuclear propulsion. However, the U.S. Navy did design and build a new class of amphibious-assault helicopter carriers. Throughout the period, there was agitation from various sources for smaller, cheaper carriers. Dozens of conceptual designs were studied, but none ever refuted the premise that payload and effectiveness per dollar invested decrease as carrier size decreases, and no "small" carrier was ever authorized. However, other nations settled for smaller carriers, some with VSTOL capability (that is, operation of aircraft capable of vertical or short take-off and landing), incorporating some of the hull and armament characteristics of cruisers. No other nation ever ventured into "big decks" even remotely comparable to the 80,000-ton *Forrestal*.

CRUISERS, DESTROYERS, AND FRIGATES

As can be seen in the earlier chapters, warships tended to grow in size, particularly during World War II, as a result of the effort to increase firepower.[34] After the war, the trend continued, and the nomenclature of ship types became more confusing than enlightening, as frigates and destroyers grew larger than World War II destroyers and cruisers, respectively, and the concept of what constituted a cruiser (compared to a big destroyer) grew more elusive. The distinction was sometimes more political than nautical.

The seemingly inexorable growth stemmed from several factors. One was the guided missile, the influence of which was described earlier. Longer-range detection of targets by radar and sonar demanded more power, bigger "black boxes," and bigger antennas and transducers. Radar antennas grew so large that their support pedestals and rotating mechanisms became major engineering problems and their wind

resistance a ship stability factor. Sonar transducers, because of lower frequencies and higher power, ballooned from a minor appendage to a fairing the size of a 40-foot landing craft. As electronic systems and computers proliferated, such as in the Navy Tactical Data System, so did their support needs: cooling water, electric power, and climate control, to say nothing of people to operate them. With regard to the people, habitability gradually superseded survival as a design criterion for living spaces, a requirement that also translated into more volume. The introduction of helicopters, first remotely controlled, later piloted, required landing and hangar space as well as support facilities. Features to reduce noise became more common and more influential in ship size.

Concurrently with these developments, confusion and controversy reigned over what a destroyer was supposed to do. Again, historian Norman Friedman has described the arguments in detail.[35] Disagreements abounded among the Navy's General Board and the Bureaus of Ships and Ordnance regarding the requirements for, and feasibility of, more speed, cruising range, anti-surface-ship weapons, anti-aircraft weapons, anti-submarine weapons, and other characteristics. The disagreements stemmed from indecision about the post-war role of destroyers, the best way to fulfill that role and, of course, what the budget could support. Much of the chaos revolved about the "big destroyer" design, which was to culminate in the *Mitscher* (DL-2) class. Scheme A was succeeded by scheme B and a bewildering assortment of other permutations and combinations through at least scheme L. Many schemes had variations within themselves: the *Mitscher* approximated Scheme J-13. The outcome was a class of four ships that, because of their size (492-foot length, 5,000 tons), were classified as destroyer leaders, powered by the first 1,200 psi, 950°F steam plants and, as noted elsewhere, notoriously unreliable controlled-circulation boilers.

The *Forrest Sherman* (DD-931) class were the first and only post-war destroyers to evolve from (and bear some resemblance to) World War II designs. At 4,000 tons, they were an outgrowth of the *Sumner* (DD-692) design. These were the last all-gun destroyers during this period, and, for all practical purposes, the last general-purpose destroyers, as their increasing size and cost impelled the Navy toward specialized missions to limit ship size.

Similar uncertainties characterized the evolution of destroyer escorts (later redesignated frigates) and cruisers. Although numerous designs of each type were built, converted, and constantly modified or modernized in a profusion that is beyond the scope of this chapter to describe, there were few dramatic developments other than nuclear propulsion. Most new designs proved successful, but some fell so far short of expectations as to cause concern about the efficacy of the elaborate interaction process between operators and the engineers. Among these were the *Mitschers*; the USS *Norfolk* (DL-1), intended to be a new type of submarine killer, but ultimately relegated to duty as an experimental platform; and the diesel-powered *Claud Jones*-class escorts, too slow and lightly armed to be useful.

Some areas of ship engineering seem to have received little emphasis. Seaworthiness was a consideration in the "large destroyer," but the engineers' approach to its improvement was to increase hull size and strength rather than to make fundamental changes in hull geometry. Active fin stabilizers were installed in two classes of escorts, but proved unreliable and unpopular with many commanding officers. Although almost every foreign navy was using active fin stabilizers at the end of the era, the U.S. Navy still did not have any policy for their use. Seakeeping, or seakindliness, was more a subject of interesting academic research than an urgent military characteristic, until operators began to notice the superior seakeeping capabilities of Soviet warships.

AMPHIBIOUS SHIPS

The emergence of the helicopter, dramatically demonstrated in the Korean war as a useful, versatile aircraft, inspired for the Marine Corps the vertical envelopment concept for amphibious warfare.[36] In 1957, the Marine Corps set high priority for transport helicopters, as well as amphibious vehicles and amphibious ships, to support this concept. This initiative provided the

impetus for a whole new look in amphibious ships.

The validity of the concept was confirmed by conversion in 1956 of a World War II escort carrier, USS *Thetis Bay*, as the first United States amphibious assault ship, helicopter (LPH), capable of carrying 1,000 combat troops and twenty helicopters. Soon two World War II *Essex*-class carriers were also converted to LPHs, followed in 1961 by the first of seven *Iwo Jima*-class LPHs designed from the keel up. These ships provided the foundation for the ensuing 20-knot amphibious force, a major advance from World War II capability.[37] Meanwhile, the size and capabilities of helicopters also increased dramatically.

The new amphibious warfare ships included two amphibious command ships, loaded with facilities and equipment for external and interior command control and communications. New attack cargo ships were designed for much greater speed and cargo handling flexibility, as well as the required 20 knots. The amphibious transport, dock (LPD) combined the features of the LPH with the World War II landing ship dock (LSD), carrying a balanced load of vehicles, supplies, and troops to be landed by its own embarked landing craft and helicopters. New LSDs deferred to the ubiquitous helicopter by having a "portable" landing platform over the dock. Perhaps the most dramatic and innovative new design was the *Newport* class of landing ship tank (LST). With fine hull lines forward for speed, off-loading was accomplished by a long bow-ramp deployed by means of two built-in derrick arms extending far beyond the bow. The design of all these ships incorporated advances in cargo stowage and handling equipment, internal arrangements, and habitability, as well as the constantly evolving capabilities of new sensors and electronics.

FLEET AUXILIARY SHIPS

The most striking development in this category of ships was "one-stop replenishment." The goal was to replace the single-product oilers, ammunition ships, and stores ships of World War II with multiproduct ships that could deliver all these stores in one "stop" alongside. Potential advantages included a reduced number of replenishment operations, which would reduce total replenishment time and time alongside, reduce vulnerability to attack, reduce the time for mishaps during replenishment, and significantly reduce numbers and total costs of replenishment ships.

In spite of these seemingly irresistible enticements, enthusiasm was far from universal.[38] However, in 1954, an ex-German ship was converted to a test ship, the *Conecuh*, and favorable trial results sparked support for design studies that confirmed the practicability and affordability of such ships. In 1961, the first of four *Sacramento* (AOE-1)-class, fast combat-support ships was authorized, capable of 26 knots at 54,000 dead weight tons (dwt); with a mixed cargo of 177,000 barrels of fuel, 2,150 tons of ammunition, and 750 tons of provisions. During a deployment in the Western Pacific, the *Sacramento* surpassed the normal performance of three conventional single-product ships, with half their total personnel.[39] Five years later, construction of seven *Wichita* (AOR-1)-class replenishment oilers was initiated. Also authorized in 1961 were seven new *Mars* (AFS-1)-class combat stores ships, carrying a mix of dry and frozen provisions plus spare parts. The capabilities of these ships were enhanced by various advances in cargo handling, including helicopters for "vertical replenishment," constant-tension winches, lightweight fuel hose, fuel hose probes for rapid, spill-free hookup and disengagement, and internal cargo elevators and transfer devices. Another unconventional ship design during this period was the catamaran submarine-rescue ship USS *Pigeon* (ASR-21). The separated twin hulls provided a wide beam (86 feet) to reduce roll, and permitted handling of heavy (60 tons) diving and salvage equipment between the hulls, with minimum effect of ship motion on handling operations, and vice versa. A primary mission was to transport and support a deep submergence rescue vessel (DSRV, discussed elsewhere), launched and retrieved by an elevator between the hulls. These ships experienced structural problems, a reminder to naval architects that Murphy's Law flourishes in the realm of the unconventional, even when the problems are recognized and sound engineering methods applied.[40] Although five DSRVs were

planned, only two were built, and only two ASRs of this type were constructed.

NEW SHIP TYPES

Hydrofoils

Hydrofoils offered two major advantages over the motor torpedo boats of World War II: high speed with less power, and superior seakeeping at high speed. In 1947, the Navy Department initiated research and feasibility studies of the concept. These investigations culminated in the *Sealegs*, an experimental 5-ton, 29-foot stock Chris Craft hull, fitted with a submerged, canard foil system designed by Gibbs & Cox, and electronic controls designed by the MIT Flight Instrumentation Laboratory.[41] The success of this craft, in 1960, led to an accelerated Navy hydrofoil research program.

By this time, the Navy was already designing its first naval hydrofoil vessel, the USS *High Point* (PCH-1), an anti-submarine patrol craft of 110 tons displacement and 40-knot speed, powered by two 2,800-horsepower Bristol Proteus gas turbines. Its role was to test various weapon and sensor payloads to assess the ship's potential as an effective fleet unit. Construction was authorized in 1960. Only 2 years later the Navy obtained authorization for a much larger experimental ship, the USS *Plainview* (AGEH-1), designed by Grumman for 320-ton displacement and a speed of 50 knots, powered by two General Electric LM 1500 gas turbines rated at 14,000 horsepower each. This was, and remained during this period, the world's largest hydrofoil.

The experience and technology acquired from these two ships provided the basis for the Navy to contract in 1966 for two patrol-gunboat hydrofoils of different design, one by Boeing and one by Grumman. Both powered by gas turbines, the USS *Flagstaff* (PGH-1) was propelled while foil-borne by a single, variable-pitch, supercavitating propeller through a right-angle gear transmission. The USS *Tucumcari* (PGH-2) was propelled by a waterjet. Both were capable of operating in sea states up to five and at speeds up to 50 knots. They operated for a time on patrol off Vietnam, supported by a dedicated maintenance facility and crew. Later, the *Tucumcari* operated in the Mediterranean as a demonstration for other

NATO navies, with the objective of stirring interest in a joint venture to build a larger, missile-firing vessel (later the PHM). Subsequently, the *Tucumcari* was assigned to the Atlantic Fleet, where, in 1972, she was badly damaged in a grounding and never repaired.

As is common in the genesis of new types of ships, there were visionaries who foresaw "flying ships" of all sizes, up to aircraft carriers. As is also common, practical limitations eventually prevailed, and the hydrofoil settled into a useful niche of small vessels, where its advantages could be realized without excessive cost or technical complications.

Air Cushion Vehicles (ACV)

The idea of supporting vehicles on a cushion of air has been traced back as far as 1717, long before the existence of suitable engines.[42] In the intervening years until 1950, many inventors explored the concept, generating numerous patents and a variety of experimental craft, some of which were remarkably successful. However, it was not until the 1950s that such vehicles progressed from the realm of interesting experiments to the realm of practical commercial and military vessels.[43]

In 1950, British engineer Christopher S. Cockerell became interested in the air cushion idea and became a vigorous and effective proponent. By mid-decade, he had generated support for its development in the British government, in United States technical circles, and particularly, in the Saunders-Roe Division of Westland Aircraft, Ltd., which became the pioneers of the British Hovercraft industry. By 1959, the company had built the SR.N1, a test-bed vehicle of 4 tons and 25 knots. This was followed in 1962 by the SR.N2, a 27-ton vehicle designed to carry seventy passengers or 8 tons of freight at a speed of 70 knots, powered by four Nimbus gas turbines of 815 horsepower each.

Other companies and countries soon joined in the development and utilization of hovercraft, mostly for commercial purposes. These early activities resulted in a great variety of designs and capabilities, although the craft generally displaced less than 30 tons. By 1967, however, a 150-ton SR.N4 was under construction, designed for a maximum (calm sea) speed of 77 knots.

Vickers-Armstrong was also building a VA-4 craft of similar size and speed capability. In the United States, the U.S. Navy took the lead and, in 1963, together with Bell Aerosystems, produced the SKMR-1, an experimental ACV of about 22 tons and 70-knot capability, powered by four, 1,080-horsepower Solar gas turbines. This rapid evolution of ACVs owed considerably to the increasing availability of reliable, high-power, lightweight gas turbines. As for incentives, the inherent capability of hovercraft to negotiate marshland, beaches, and other "marginal terrain" was a considerable inducement for military planners and for some commercial operators as well. For the Navy, the ACV held out the prospect of a great leap forward in amphibious assault landing craft.

Nevertheless, the further evolution of ACVs was anything but smooth. After Navy and Marine Corps tests were completed on SKMR-1 and two British hovercraft, funding was cut off.[44] For a time, such development as continued was related to surface effect ships—that is, ACVs with rigid, surface-piercing sidewalls. Their evolution is described later in this chapter. Interest was also sustained, indirectly, by Navy acquisition and militarization of three British SR.N5s. These were evaluated in Vietnam and led to a follow-on effort by the U.S. Army.

The ACV development was revived in 1965 by a Navy operational requirement for a better landing craft. There followed several years of feasibility studies, competitive designs, reviews of requirements, and twists and turns of project organization and funding, culminating finally in 1969 with an approved technical development plan. By 1971, the Naval Ship Systems Command had sorted out some fifty-seven design concepts that had been seriously considered, and had awarded contracts for two JEFF-boats that would be the world's largest military hovercraft. These boats were to be functionally equivalent but technically different. The contracts provided for design, construction, test, and trials support of a JEFF (A) by Aerojet General Corporation and of a JEFF (B) by Bell Aerosystems Company.

Each craft was to be about 90 feet long, 48 feet wide, and 23 feet high, capable of fitting into well-deck ships and carrying a 150,000 pound payload of tanks, trucks, or troops in its own well (some 80 feet long and 27 feet wide). Design speed was 50 knots in sea state two against a 25-knot head wind. Gas turbines totaling almost 18,000 horsepower were designed to drive a combination of lift fans for the cushion and aero propellers for propulsion. Despite these common features, the two designs differed widely in structure, cushion, design, propulsion-lift arrangements, and control.

As this era in naval engineering history drew to a close, design and construction of these craft were proceeding, and planning for tests, trials, training, and logistics support were also underway. The groundwork was being laid for a future, highly successful, landing craft, air cushion (LCAC) program. Nevertheless, considering how long the basic idea of ACVs had been around, it is hard to disagree with ACV program veteran James Schuler's assertion that "It takes a long time to develop technology."[45]

Surface Effect Ships (SES)

As previously indicated, the surface effect ship (SES) is a form of ACV characterized by rigid, surface-piercing sidewalls, with flexible seals at the bow and stern. It is supported while underway by a combination of the cushion air pressure and the displacement of the catamaran-like hulls.

An early application of the principle can be traced to 1929 when D. K. Warner pressurized the air between the hulls of his catamaran to increase its speed in races on Lake Compounce, Connecticut, and filed a patent application.[46] As with ACVs, various design configurations were considered in subsequent years. In the early sixties, the U.S. Navy tested a landing craft vehicle and personnel (LCVP) hull modified with solid sidewalls, fore-and-aft seals, and supported on a cushion of air. This craft failed to exceed the performance of a conventional LCVP with the same installed power. About this time, the Maritime Administration (MarAd) was investigating the feasibility of multithousand-ton SESs for transoceanic service at speeds up to 100 knots. This speed target was to acquire a mystical quality that associated it almost automatically with any SES of any size or purpose. MarAd's report on its study of various configurations of air-supported ocean vehicles favored development of the SES type of hull for large displacement

vessels. The U.S. Navy had been working closely with MarAd in these evaluations.

In 1969, the Navy awarded two construction contracts, with a common performance specification, for 100-ton SES test craft. One was to Aerojet General Corporation for a waterjet-propelled craft (SES-100A) and the other to Bell Aerospace Company for SES-100B, propelled by supercavitating propellers. The specification called for a top speed over 80 knots, a payload of 10 tons, and a range of 1,500 miles. According to one prominent participant, "It was recognized that if such a test craft could be developed, it would demonstrate that the larger SES (in the 2,000–4,000 ton displacement class) would be a viable ship of tomorrow's Navy."[47] In an equally hopeful vein, CNO Admiral Elmo Zumwalt envisioned that SESs, ferrying troops and supplies, "could go a long way toward neutralizing Russia's lead over the U.S. in submarines." Hindsight suggests that there are pitfalls in overly optimistic prognostication of the extent to which new technology will solve strategic problems.

By 1972, both craft had been delivered and were undergoing tests and trials that generally confirmed design procedures and targeted performance. The SES-100B was later to achieve a speed of 100 statute miles per hour. The success of these craft provided the technical base for further Navy development toward a 2,000-ton SES design, later to be escalated to 3,000 tons as the "3K SES." However, as projected construction costs approached $300 million, the 3K SES died on the drawing board.

Outlook for Advanced Vehicles

As the era 1950-72 approached its end, the potential of "advanced" vehicles such as hydrofoils, air cushion vehicles, and surface effect ships seemed virtually unlimited, in the minds of many Navy enthusiasts. In 1970, a seminar was held at the Naval Ship Research and Development Center (NSRDC) attended by representatives of NavShips, NSRDC, both fleets, the CNO's Ship Characteristics Board (SCB), and industry. After presentations on the state of the art and on a variety of notional vehicles, group workshops convened to deliberate on possible missions for each type. Advocates of each type, often unfettered by quantitative engineering data, conjured scenarios of almost every conceivable mission, for vessels of almost any size up to thousands of tons. Visions of a 100-knot Navy danced in some heads. In many instances, engineering reach far exceeded engineering grasp.

Nevertheless, Rear Admiral J. H. King, chairman of the SCB, concluded that "steady as you go" seemed appropriate with regard to the scope and space of then-current development programs. Viewing the relatively well-developed hydrofoil technology, one observer remarked prophetically that, "The hydrofoil is a solution looking for a problem." Nevertheless, extravagant claims for the potential of each vehicle eventually led to a "hold" on further development, pending the outcome of an Advanced Naval Vehicle Concept Evaluation study, intended to sort out the most practical concepts for fleet application. In time, practical engineering problems inexorably imposed their constraints on the development and employment of advanced vehicles. Even when technology was not a problem, other impediments—political, economic and bureaucratic—often prevailed to limit, or even extinguish, the great hopes of advanced-vehicle advocates.

Naval Engineering Innovation

Innovation is one of the most controversial aspects of naval engineering; during this period, the controversy flourished. There was continuing argument over whether there was too much or too little innovation, whether it was too slow or too fast, and how to bring it about in the face of budget limitations and other obstacles that always seemed to rear up most formidably at the point of transition from research to real hardware. The subject was of particular interest in this period of technology explosion. Many naval engineers pondered the problem. Writing in 1977, Dr. Reuven Leopold analyzed the situation in the light of two cases wherein technology was well developed and in use elsewhere long before it was adopted by the U.S. Navy—namely, roll stabilizers and gas turbines.[48] He proposed several reasonable actions to foster innovation, none of which have come to pass. Dr. Alan Powell, also using roll stabilization as an example, postulated underlying causes that inhibit

innovation, all of which were operative during this period, and persist today.[49]

One statement about innovation would probably be accepted by all: Everybody is for innovation as long as it works. On the other hand, most proponents of greater innovation insist that risk is its inseparable companion. The Navy's problem with this latter postulate is that the fleet's primary mission is not to develop technology. Fleet commanders have strategic and operational commitments to meet with all too few ships. They have little time for, nor patience with, ships that do not work and equipment that will not operate until "fixes" are devised to correct defects. A similar attitude prevails among commercial ship operators, where their mission is to operate profitably.

All too often, undue haste and inadequate testing resulted in passing the risks, prematurely, on to the fleet. In 1959, then-Captain Nathan Sonenshein related the history of a number of innovations that had proven troublesome and, in come cases, even abortive.[50] Although not specifically included, the destroyer *Timmerman* was a prime example. The fleet never accepted the ship for what is was—an experimental "shot for the moon." What the fleet wanted was a fully operational greyhound of the Atlantic destroyer force. Other problematic innovations included controlled-circulation boilers; alloy shafting; high-speed, lightweight, nonmagnetic diesel engines for minesweepers; nonparalleling forced-draft blowers; missile-handling systems; radar-antenna drives and pedestals; and even such a seemingly simple modification as aluminum deckhouses instead of steel. Other problems such as 1,200-psi steam have been noted herein. Lest it be concluded that failure was the norm, Sonenshein went on to cite some forty major developments, most of which, as noted elsewhere in this chapter, were successful. Nevertheless, in accordance with Shakespeare's aphorism, the failures were often better remembered than the successes.

Institutional Barriers

Whatever reasons one may favor for reluctance to adopt new technology, it can be argued that the Navy's management structure had become inimical to innovation. For one thing, ships were now being acquired for the Navy by Ship Acquisition Project Managers (SHAPMs), who were not inclined to take risks. The last thing a senior captain, looking toward flag rank, needed was a technical fiasco on his hands. This sensitivity became especially acute because some reports of defects in new ships, by the Board of Inspection and Survey, found their way into the media and the halls of Congress. Naysayers, seeking a reputation as crusaders, routinely cited the deficiencies out of context and exaggerated them. Caution on the part of the SHAPM was also operative for the Office of the Chief of Naval Operations (OpNav) sponsor, especially the Deputy CNO for the particular ship being acquired. Furthermore, innovations tended to add costs that SHAPMs were reluctant or unable to bear; a typical example was the deferral, under the pressure of "design to cost," of fin-stabilizer installation in the FFG-7 frigates. Finally, a prerequisite for innovation, cited by Leopold, was missing: there was no mechanism for the formulation of top-level policy on innovation, as opposed to ship-by-ship tradeoffs. Where was that brave decision-maker who was willing to stand up and say: *I* declare that Innovation X is an acceptable risk, *I* authorize it for installation in Ship Y, and *I* will accept full responsibility for the consequences?" Unfortunately, his identity (and position) remained as elusive as the solution to the problem.

OTHER DEVELOPMENTS

Deep Submergence

Disaster is often a spur to new developments. Such was the case in the loss of the USS *Thresher* in 1963. The resulting developments took two major forms: one was the devising of vehicles, systems, and methods for rescue, salvage, exploration, and operations in the deep ocean; the other was the development and widespread application of more stringent quality control and quality assurance over materials and fabrication for hazardous naval applications. The naval nuclear propulsion program had already established high standards for reactor plant material and personnel; the *Thresher* loss provided the impetus for their adoption on a wide scale.

Rear Admiral William Brockett, Chief of BuShips, set the tone for the Navy: "Specifications are not to be considered as desirable goals, but rather as minimum standards which must be met or exceeded." Under his direction, strong quality assurance organizations were set up in the Bureau, in the naval shipyards, and in the Navy's organizations for supervising ship construction in private shipyards. A rigorous material identification and control system was established for critical materials. "Level I" pipe, for example, could be traced from receipt in a shipyard all the way back to the chemical analysis of the poured metal ingot from which it was fabricated. Obviously, this kind of control, necessary as it might be, did not come free of time, cost, and paperwork. New and more accurate means of nondestructive testing (NDT) were implemented, together with the training and qualification of the NDT operators. Qualification and certification of craftsmen, such as welders and pipe brazers, were required for work on Level I systems. Elaborate procedures were established for controlling "entry" into (starting work on) vital systems and for controlling their cleanliness, integrity, repair, testing, and certification. "Subsafe" became the norm for submarine work—the term meaning that these and other prescribed controls and inspections had been completely and satisfactorily carried out, with *documented proof*, before the ship could go to sea. Such measures were by no means so widely applied to surface ships.

For deep submergence developments, the Navy convened a technical review group, which culminated in the establishment of a special project, initially under the temporary direction of John Craven, a noted ocean scientist. He was soon succeeded by Captain W. M. Nicholson, an EDO experienced in ship design. Although the immediate goal was to develop a means to rescue the crew from a sunken submarine, the project gradually assumed a broader role in deep ocean technology. This project and related developments in naval and commercial salvage, diving, and oceanographic research resulted in many novel vehicles and new capabilities. Among them were the DSRVs, designed with limited mobility, to mate with submarines and rescue as many as twenty-four people at a time from a depth of

3,500 feet. Typically, the pressure hull was of high-strength steel spherical construction. A nuclear-powered research submarine, NR-1, was completed in 1969, a highly versatile vehicle of 700 tons, with wheels for moving on the ocean bottom. Perhaps most famous, although not *per se* a product of the deep submergence project, was the U. S. Navy bathyscaph *Trieste* (purchased from August Piccard), which in 1960 dived to a record depth of 38,500 feet. The navy's *Sea Cliff* and *Turtle* were initially capable of ocean exploration by three operators down to 6,500 feet and later, with a spherical titanium hull, to 20,000 feet. Meanwhile, research and innovations in the equipment, techniques, and physiology of individual diving greatly extended the time and depth capabilities of divers. There were also great advances in deep-diving, remotely controlled vehicles equipped with sophisticated sonars and other sensing equipment, capable of locating, photographing, and even manipulating objects on the ocean floor.

The flourishing offshore oil industry also sparked and refined numerous innovations related to exploration, drilling, and oil production. Seagoing drilling rigs were built in the form of semisubmersible platforms, floating platforms, and monohull ships, capable of drilling wells at ocean depths of thousands of feet. These vessels often incorporated extremely accurate navigation equipment, together with highly effective positioning and mooring devices. The most dramatic development in this vein was the Hughes *Glomar Explorer*, a vessel built along the lines of a drill ship but specially configured and equipped to handle and retrieve heavy loads from great depths. The ship recovered parts of a sunken Soviet submarine from the bottom of the Pacific, over 3 miles deep, a fantastic engineering achievement.

Firefighting

The U.S. Navy continued to lead the way in the development of more effective firefighting materials and techniques, motivated by the disastrous consequences of fires on board ships during World War II and even afterward. Fires in engineering spaces, although not frequent, were usually fatal to some of the occupants. In 1967, the USS *Forrestal* suffered a colossal topside fire,

augmented by bomb and other ammunition explosions, when an aircraft missile accidentally ignited on the flight deck crowded with airplanes. The investigation report by Admiral James S. Russell contained dozens of recommendations for improved fire protection and firefighting capabilities. His report served as an agenda for such developments for years.

Among the innovations was the flight deck sprinkling system, designed to deluge the deck, from sprinkler heads embedded in it, so as to prevent ordnance attached to airplanes from "cooking off," a phenomenon which had greatly aggravated the *Forrestal* catastrophe. A major development during the period was the twin-agent firefighting system. One agent was "light water," a chemical detergent having high surface tension. When mixed with water in the right proportions, it formed a film over fuel and oil that prevented the escape of flammable vapors. The other ingredient was "Purple K," a powdered potassium compound with excellent fire extinguishing properties. When both ingredients were delivered simultaneously from a dual nozzle, they were very effective in fighting fuel fires, especially in machinery spaces. Another and later advance was the use of Halon, a gas that, when released into a compartment under the right conditions, would snuff out a fire almost instantaneously. Halon had the added advantage that it was nontoxic, so that the atmosphere in the compartment was still breathable for a time. It was installed first in the engineering spaces of minesweepers and later in aircraft carriers.

In 1953, the port hydraulic catapult in the USS *Leyte* exploded, followed by a massive fire that killed thirty-seven people.[51] The cause was diagnosed as compression ignition of the flammable hydraulic fluid in the catapult air-oil system. Seven months later, the USS *Bennington* suffered a similar casualty, also with major damage and great loss of life. These accidents spurred a search for a nonflammable, or at least less flammable, fluid for high-pressure hydraulic systems. In 1956, the Navy selected a phosphate ester fluid called cellulube to replace conventional hydraulic oil. Although the new fluid solved the explosion problem, it brought new problems of its own, including cost, toxicity, corrosiveness, lubricity, stability at high temperatures, and viscosity-temperature variations. Special safety instructions were issued for handling it. Although the steam catapult eliminated the hazard of hydraulic catapults, the search for a perfect substitute fluid continued for the many other shipboard hydraulic systems.

U.S. COAST GUARD

Naval engineering developments in the Coast Guard, as reflected in engineering journals and in the reminiscences of its Engineers-in-Chief, were characterized by steady progress rather than dramatic innovations. Midway through the period, the statutory Congressional appointment of engineer-in-chief was abolished in favor of a position to be filled as directed by the Commandant. The move was but one more subtle step in the gradual erosion of the prestige and influence of naval engineers, a trend observed in the Navy and in other maritime circles as well.

The Coast Guard pioneered, in the United States, the use of the CODOG propulsion plant in its twelve *Hamilton*-class high-endurance cutters, first built in 1967. These 378-foot, 3,000-ton ships utilized two 3,500-horsepower diesel engines or two 18,000-horsepower FT-4 gas turbines driving two CRP propellers for a designed top speed of 29 knots and a maximum range (on the diesels) of 14,000 miles at 11 knots. The CRP propellers were the largest in any American ship up to that time. Maneuverability for docking was enhanced by a Schottel retractable bow propulsion unit of 350 horsepower, trainable through 360 degrees. The hull design emphasized seaworthiness first and speed second. These ships remained until 1974 the largest United States military vessels powered by gas turbines, and thus provided at-sea experience for their adoption by the U.S. Navy in destroyers and frigates. They were also the largest ships ever built for the Coast Guard, except for icebreakers. Other notable features included an aluminum superstructure, use of the deckhouse overhead (the 01 level) as part of the hull girder, and unprecedented attention to habitability for the crew.

The Coast Guard also led the way with CODAG propulsion in the first five of its sixteen medium-endurance cutters, built between 1964

and 1969. In this application, CODAG proved unfavorable and was abandoned in favor of diesels only, with the same total horsepower.

THE MERCHANT MARINE

Ship and Management Evolution

Merchant ship developments in the United States continued to be influenced by the Merchant Marine Act of 1936, which provided subsidies for construction and operation of United States flag ships, funds for research and development, and national defense features (such as those in the SS *United States*, described later).[52] In 1950, the independent Maritime Commission created by the Act merged into the Department of Commerce as MarAd. Its first Administrator was one of the nation's most distinguished and respected naval engineers of all time, Vice Admiral E. L. Cochrane, wartime Chief of BuShips and later Dean of Engineering at MIT. An immediate and important development under his direction was the *Mariner* design, the first 20-knot, general-purpose, dry-cargo ship capable of numerous variations for both military and commercial purposes. The propulsion plant incorporated many World War II Navy machinery characteristics, with 600 psi steam at 865°F driving geared turbines into a single shaft with a normal output of 17,500 shaft horsepower, and two 600-kilowatt, 440-volt AC turbo generators; this design was so successful that it served basically unchanged as a standard for the next 20 years. A fine example of the *Mariner*'s design versatility was its conversion to the passenger ships SS *Monterey* and *Mariposa*, the first post-war U.S. ships to use active fin roll stabilizers.

In the 1960s, stiff competition and rising costs of ship construction and operation provided the impetus for several trends and innovations. Generally the trends were to bigger and faster ships, reduced manning, and reduced time and labor for cargo handling. At that time, fuel was cheap and its cost was not a major consideration in propulsion plant design, a fact that, at least partly, accounted for the persistence of steam plants in United States ships in contrast to otherwise worldwide emphasis on diesel engines. The notion of supertankers as 30,000 dwt ships was quickly revised upward as they grew to over

200,000 dwt. Break-bulk cargo ships were designed with quick-opening hatch covers and a host of innovative (and not always successful) cargo handling equipment. Containerships were probably the most dramatic development of the period, facilitated by the standardization of containers as to size and handling characteristics, a remarkable achievement of trucking magnate Malcolm McLean. Early ship designs were encumbered with cranes and other container handling equipment, but as ports acquired the necessary handling and storage facilities, many ships were built without self-loading capabilities. Another approach to rapid cargo handling was the roll-on, roll-off (RO/RO) ship, with vehicle ramps arranged internally and from dock to ship, permitting cargo to be driven on and off the ship with no need for conventional shipboard or dockside lifting gear.

A whole new concept of cargo transfer was developed by J. L. Goldman as the LASH (Lighter Aboard Ship). LASH is essentially a container ship capable of handling and stowing either standard 20-foot containers or 61- by 31-foot, 500-ton barges. This ingenious scheme obviously provides for cargo transfer to and from locations otherwise inaccessible to a large ship, such as shallow-draft ports and canals. However, this concept would not have been feasible without some solid analysis of the dynamics of picking up a 500-ton barge in a seaway, and some fine engineering of the lifting equipment to do it. As the period ended, many LASH ships were in operation in both United States and foreign service. These included the follow-on SEABEE, designed by J. J. Henry to carry barges up to 1,000 tons, with several pioneering weight-handling methods.

Other trends in merchant ship engineering included use of aluminum in superstructures (notably successful in the United States), the use of high strength steels in parts of the hull, and the use of computerized design and construction techniques. Steam conditions increased until they stabilized in the range of 850 psi and 950°F, with some plants employing reheat or air preheaters in addition to fuel heating. However, the low cost of fuel during this period provided little incentive for the increased capital outlay and maintenance costs of complex cycles. Rising labor costs sparked progress in automation, particularly in propulsion plants but also on the bridge. Other labor-saving measures included corrosion-resistant materials and coatings, navigation aids, bow thrusters to aid maneuvering, automatic data loggers, remote sensing and alarm systems, and highly efficient cooking and messing arrangements. Meanwhile, as was the case in the Navy, habitability continued to improve.

The infrastructure of merchant ship design and engineering during the period, unfortunately, followed the trend of its naval counterpart. The size and expertise of MarAd's engineering staff dwindled. So, inevitably, did its capability and responsibility for ship design, which shifted gradually to independent design agents and later to shipyards marketing their own proprietary designs. MarAd's role was reduced to research and development, conceptual design, design approvals related to government subsidies, and secondary observation of shipbuilder performance and trials.

SS *United States*

The liner *United States* could be called a keynote to naval engineering progress during the period 1950-72. Laid down in 1950 at Newport News, she represented a longtime dream of her eminent designer, William Francis Gibbs, to create the world's fastest oceanliner. The United States government also wanted a fast ship, which in wartime could be converted into a troop transport that could match the performance of the British "Queens" in this role during World War II. Accordingly, the ship was subsidized by the government and designed to have special subdivision, stability, fireproofing, and damage control. At a length of 990 feet overall, a length-to-beam ratio of 9.26, and a 32-foot draft, the ship displaced a maximum of 47,000 tons (45,400 tons design). The hull had fine lines, a slightly bulbous bow, and an aluminum deckhouse to save weight. The propulsion power was far beyond that of any existing liner—240,000 shaft horsepower. The machinery plant comprised eight boilers delivering steam at 925 psi, 1,000°F to turbines driving four shafts, with a mix of four-bladed and five-bladed propellers. The plant was essentially a transition between the naval machinery of World War II (600 psi, 850°F) and that of the 1950s (1,200 psi, 950°F). The merchant marine had never seen anything like it.

The ship's horsepower and maximum speed were cloaked in secrecy until 1978, when it was revealed that during final trials "a top speed of 38.32 knots [was] established while developing 241,785 total shaft horsepower at the trial displacement" (39,900 tons).[53] On her maiden transatlantic voyage, the *United States* averaged 35.05 knots for the round trip, beating the British-held record by 4 knots, while using only two-thirds of her power. The British magazine *Punch* lamented: "After the loud and fantastic claims made in advance for the liner *United States*, it comes as something of a disappointment to find them all true."

During the next 17 years, the *United States* crossed the Atlantic 400 times at an average speed of over 30 knots, using essentially half of her propulsion plant for each transit. She established an "outstanding reputation for seakindliness, dryness, and speed in adverse weather; and for consistently meeting schedule."[54] Succumbing to high costs and the malaise of transatlantic ship travel, the ship was laid up in Norfolk in 1969, a sad end to a triumph of naval engineering.

Nuclear Ship (NS) *Savannah*

In 1956, the President convened a blue ribbon panel on the "Peaceful Uses of Atomic Energy." The success of the Navy's nuclear submarine, *Nautilus*, suggested that nuclear-powered merchant ships might be prime candidates for such peaceful use. In a classic example of bureaucratic trickle-down, the task of writing a learned dissertation on this topic eventually sank to the level of two of Admiral Rickover's junior naval officers, neither of whom knew the first thing about merchant ships. Unfazed, with the aid of some hasty library research and the burning of midnight oil, they wrote an analysis that survived virtually unchanged in the panel's "authoritative" final report.

The technical and political climates being right for a nuclear merchant ship, the Congress in 1956 authorized construction of the first and only United States version, the cargo-passenger

liner NS *Savannah*. At 581 feet in length and 21,800 tons displacement, the *Savannah* was designed to make 21 knots at a maximum of 22,000 shaft horsepower, powered by a pressurized-water nuclear reactor. A contract for the propulsion plant was let to Babcock and Wilcox in 1957. The reactor fuel was slightly enriched (4.7%) stainless-steel-clad uranium oxide, with a thermal output of about 70 megawatts. Unlike naval reactors, the primary plant was surrounded by a containment vessel. Although the ship was launched in 1959, she did not undergo final acceptance trials until April 1962.

In the next 8 years, the *Savannah* logged some half million miles, with one refueling, visiting fifty-five ports in fourteen countries, with a reported 99.88% at-sea availability of her propulsion system. In 1970, MarAd retired her from service as having fulfilled her "Atoms for Peace" mission.[55] She did indeed demonstrate the myriad problems of nuclear merchant ships—not only the technical difficulties, which can be overcome, but more importantly the many other opposing forces, which, collectively, seem to pose an impenetrable barrier to further development. These forces—political, legal, economic, bureaucratic, administrative, labor, and safety—made the outlook for nuclear ships at the end of the period dim, at best. Nevertheless, hope springs eternal, and in 1970, MarAd, still seeing a future for nuclear merchant ships, embarked on a study of a "standardized" nuclear propulsion system of 120,000 shaft horsepower for large, twin-screw, high-speed container ships and tankers. In the meantime, few other countries had ventured into nuclear propulsion for nonmilitary ships. The Soviets had built the icebreaker *Lenin*, the Germans (in 1968) a 26,000 dwt ore carrier, the *Otto Hahn*, and the Japanese had laid the keel in 1968 for a freighter-training ship.

Gas Turbine Ship *John Seargent*

Early in this period, the Maritime Administration's Office of Ship Construction and Repair under Chief Engineer John J. McMullen, a retired Navy commander, embarked on an imaginative program to test the marine application merits of four different advanced propulsion plants. The set comprised a regenerated gas turbine, a free-piston gas generator turbine, a steam turbine and a geared diesel.[56] The program was undertaken with a view to upgrading World War II Liberty ships from 10 to 15 knots.

The regenerated gas turbine installed in the *John Seargent* was an adaptation of an existing General Electric design used for gas pipeline pumping. It was a two-shaft machine, with a 1,450°F-inlet high-pressure turbine driving a 4.9-to-1 ratio compressor, and a 6,000-horsepower low-pressure power-turbine driving the CRP propeller. The exhaust gas preheated the compressed air in the regenerator and then passed to the waste heat boiler to generate steam for the ship service generator turbine.

By early 1959, the ship had logged some 7,000 hours on the engine, covering 95,000 miles of almost faultless commercial operation in the North Atlantic, with a fuel rate of less than 0.53 pound per shaft horsepower hour. A fuel treatment system was installed to permit burning residual fuels, a process that generally worked satisfactorily. Some deterioration in plant performance did occur during each voyage from ash buildup on the turbine blades, but these deposits were easily removed by water washing.

A counterpart to the *John Seargent* installation was a gas turbine plant installed in the *William Patterson*, coupled with a free-piston gas generator. However, this mode of gas generation did not prove attractive.

Although the *John Seargent* demonstrated the practicality of gas turbines for merchant ship propulsion, with fuel rates comparable to steam plants, it fell far short of diesel ship performance, and was never replicated. However, it did encourage the building of other merchant ships with gas turbine drives, particularly the 20,000-horsepower Pratt and Whitney FT-4. These ships, like the *John Seargent* were technically successful but not competitive with diesel-driven ships in the world market.

Gas Turbine Ship *Adm William M. Callaghan*

Although gas turbine propulsion for merchant ships was not destined to play a major role in the maritime industry, the *Callaghan* represented perhaps the best that could be achieved in gas-turbine-powered commercial vessels. Built for the Military Sea Transportation Service (MSTS) to transport military vehicles and equipment, she was basically a RO/RO merchant ship to be operated on MSTS charter. At 624 feet and 24,000 tons, powered by two Pratt and Whitney FT-4 gas turbines delivering a normal total of 39,000 shaft horsepower to two shafts, the *Callaghan* was, in 1967, the world's largest and probably fastest RO/RO ship.[57]

Trial speed was 26½ knots, with a service speed of 25 knots and cruising range of 6,000 miles. Unlike most other high-powered gas turbine ships, the *Callaghan* did not have CRP propellers. Instead, her designers, Sun Shipbuilding, selected reversing gearboxes and clutches built by Falk and Fawick Airflex. These gearboxes provided excellent service and maneuverability, with capability of full power, both ahead and astern. Single lever control was provided for the engine throttle and clutch engagement sequence, with remote control from the bridge.

By 1971, the *Callaghan* had completed 3 years and one hundred crossings in transatlantic service, with impressive records for speed and availability. That same year, the port FT-4 engine was removed and replaced by a General Electric LM 2500 so that the ship could serve as a test bed for this type, which was slated for main propulsion of the U.S. Navy's *Spruance*-class (DD-963) destroyers and *Oliver Hazard Perry*-class (FFG-7) frigates.

THE INSTITUTIONAL CHANGE TO NAVAL ENGINEERING

Profound Bureaucratic Change

It would be almost futile to attempt to detail all the changes that took place in the character of naval engineering in terms of the numerous bureaucratic reorganizations. The focus of naval engineering in the United States, the Bureau of Ships, typically underwent almost constant changes, some big enough to warrant description as "reorganizations." Also typically, there was never a traceable connection between organizational upheavals and subsequent performance. Fortunately, in spite of all the management manipulations, the engineering professionals in the trenches, fighting the day-to-day engineering technical problems, managed to carry on. However, there were some changes in the governmental framework that did have a significant impact.

Management versus Engineering

One of these was the emphasis on management that accompanied the accession of Robert McNamara as Secretary of Defense. Almost overnight, *management* supplanted *leadership* as the *sine qua non* of successful pursuit of all Defense Department endeavors. Any attempt to trace all the manifestations of this management syndrome would be controversial. Nevertheless, some impacts were clear. For one thing, the emphasis on management diverted attention away from professional engineering skills in favor of managerial techniques. In the operating Navy, this led to a diminution of officers' knowledge of, and attention to, the details of their ships' equipment and its operation. Engineering, in general, and propulsion plant operation, in particular, came to be viewed increasingly as unrewarding assignments for unrestricted line officers. In the engineering community, this atmosphere fostered a decline in technical proficiency in favor of management expertise. It was not until 1976 that this situation was finally recognized and addressed by the Engineering Duty officers, and steps taken to reverse the trend.

Organization By Project

Another example was the emphasis on Project Managers for the acquisition of new ships. In the nuclear propulsion program, project management consisted of a project engineer (and a secretary) coordinating the functional elements of the organization toward achievement of the desired new technology. In Naval Ship Systems Command (NavShips) (and other naval engineering activities), project organizations evolved into large staffs of people representing every technical and administrative discipline involved in ship design, acquisition, production, and logistic support. A ship acquisition project manager could have a staff of several dozen people. The insidious aspect of this development lay in the fact that in a period of fixed or declining numbers of personnel, this staff had to be drawn almost exclusively from the functional organizations of NavShips. Thus, the best and brightest of the "doers" often became nonproducing staff coordinators looking to the functional organizations whence they had come for the technical expertise and products that they had themselves been providing.

Dispersion of Engineering Expertise

Nowhere was the effect of this inhouse manpower drain more severely felt than in the naval ship-design organization. In the face of budget-dictated declining numbers of engineers, and an increasing workload (discussed elsewhere), the solution was to "farm out" more and more of the engineering work to contractors. As a consequence, engineers spent less and less time performing actual engineering, and increasingly greater time as contract administrators. By 1972, almost two-thirds of the Naval Ship Engineering Center's work was being contracted out. This loss of in-house engineering capability and, perforce, engineering control, was replicated in varying degrees throughout the naval engineering establishment. By 1973, the role that BuShips had played in 1950 as the ultimate authority in naval ship engineering matters had seriously deteriorated. There were other contributing factors, as will be seen.

Preoccupation With Administrative Devices

The fascination with management gave rise to obsessive preoccupation with systems, standards, plans, procedures, and integration. Thus, when the Naval Material Command was created in 1966, BuShips (and other bureaus, similarly) became the Naval Ship *Systems* Command (NavShips). Dissertations appeared to the effect that ships should be viewed as weapons systems, and seemed to imply that this would somehow simplify the complex compromises and difficult choices involved in ship design. The solution to every technical, management and leadership problem was a management system, frequently a management information system (MIS). The Department of Defense led the way in all this with the Program, Planning, and Budgeting System (PPBS) that governed its entire operation, with a blizzard of plans and procedures. In the world of ships, new systems sprang up like weeds. If preventive maintenance in the fleet was not being performed, then the solution was a Planned Maintenance System (PMS) and a

Maintenance Data Control System (MDCS). If ships' forces were ineffectively employed during overhauls, the answer was a Ship's Force Overhaul Management System (SFOMS). If naval shipyards were inefficient, it was assumed that the reason was simply that their leaders lacked sufficient information; the response: a Naval Shipyard Management Information System. High efficiency of all Department of Defense industrial activities was to be achieved by a Defense Industrial Management Engineering System (DIMES!), in which "engineered" work standards would be established for all jobs, for purposes of planning, estimating, and cost control. MISmanagement often became self-fulfilling.

There was a widespread notion that such systems would, of and by themselves, solve problems and improve management. Many people mistook them for the end rather than the means. The confusion was akin to mistaking power steering for automatic steering. What these systems did, for certain, was divert the attention and efforts of many talented people toward creating and administering management systems instead of concentrating on their functional engineering jobs. Once again, many engineers who had been doers became, at best, system administrators and, at worst, paper shufflers. Every facet of naval engineering—ship research, design, acquisition, production, maintenance, and logistic support—was affected by this trend. For example, every aspect of a ship acquisition project had to be covered by a plan—management plan, design plan, procurement plan, integrated logistic support plan, test and evaluation master plan, *ad infinitum*. Profuse instructions and standard procedures were issued for every conceivable managerial and technical endeavor, especially in response to some human error or any material failure. In shipbuilding and ship repair, elaborate procedures and manuals were generated for scheduling and "progressing" work, for material control, quality assurance, control of ripout and reentry of systems, control of testing and trials, and 'Certification' that all had, thereby, been rendered perfect.

Overstructuring The Design Process

The Navy ship design process also became highly structured, with formal documents like the "Top Level Requirements" (TLR) provided by OpNav (in concept, anyway), and responding Top Level Specifications (TLS) by NavSea. Exotic terms like Tentative Conceptual Base Line (TCBL) were invented to describe the events and products of the process. For major ship acquisition programs, elaborate administrative reviews were conducted up the chain of command to the Defense Systems Acquisition Review Council (DSARC), resulting in some cases in major design changes. Naval ship design also became a victim of bureaucratic expediency in other ways. To meet a mandated reduction in the size of headquarters, the engineering and related logistic functions of NavShips were designated as a field activity, the Naval Ship Engineering Center (NavSec), and moved to Hyattsville, Maryland, a half hour from the center of NavShips action. Then, to reduce the number of people on the Navy's direct payroll, NavSec was designated a "modified industrial fund activity." This meant that all NavSec's engineering work had to be separately funded by, and therefore directed by, individual "customers" in NavSea. The impact of this was that, for all practical purposes, NavSec could not work on a fleet problem (or anything else) without authorization and funding from some NavSea manager. Proliferation of bookkeeping and administration chores naturally went hand in hand with the work orders. The Navy's ship engineering organization became a job shop, complicated by its role both as a contractor (to NavSea and other "customers") and as a customer to the numerous ship engineering contractors who, as related earlier, now did two-thirds of the design work.

Birth and Growth of the Naval Material Command (NavMat)

Still another influence on naval engineering was the creation of the Naval Material Command (NavMat) in 1966. Heretofore, the Navy's technical bureaus had reported directly to the Secretary of the Navy. Under the new setup, the bureaus became Systems Commands reporting to NavMat, which reported to the Chief of Naval Operations. Foreseeing the obstacles to efficient ship engineering and acquisition that such an arrangement could pose, the Chief and Deputy Chief of BuShips, Rear Admirals Brockett and

Curtze, resigned in protest. Although NavMat was chartered to function as a coordinator of the various technical commands, and intended to make the old "Bureau" functions more responsive to the Chief of Naval Operations, it quickly and predictably became just another management level through which all communications and decisions had to filter. For this and other reasons, its abrupt elimination 20 years later by the Secretary of the Navy was enthusiastically received. In the interim, however, NavMat had a similar impact on engineering talent that NavShips' project organizations had had. NavMat created a number of project organizations of its own. These and other technical elements of the NavMat staff also recruited their technical personnel largely from the subordinate commands, thus converting still more doers into coordinators, further absorbing and reducing the technical expertise available to perform design engineering. NavMat also gathered under its wing all of the Navy research laboratories that had been "owned" by the engineering systems commands. As a consequence, NavShips lost control of its key research facilities, the David Taylor Model Basin at Carderock, Maryland, and the Marine Engineering Laboratory at Annapolis (eventually combined as the Naval Ship Research and Development Center). Like NavSec, these laboratories became Navy Industrial Fund activities, funded and tasked by whatever customers (within certain guidelines) they could find or wished to work for, and therefore no longer efficiently responsive to NavShips.

New Role for the Board of Inspection and Survey (InSurv)

One of the positive influences during this period was the emergence of the Navy's Board of Inspection and Survey (InSurv) as a strong voice against ship design deficiencies. In 1967, Rear Admiral John D. Bulkeley, as the new President of InSurv, began to revitalize it with competent, enthusiastic people and more frequent, realistic inspections. One of his most effective techniques was to report the major deficiencies he found, during inspections and trials, in personal letters to senior officers. These letters, uncompromising and often colorful, were hard to ignore and began to get attention (sometimes in unwanted places

such as the Congress and the media). Admiral Bulkeley also reported summaries of his findings quarterly to the CNO Executive Board. As time went on, InSurv increasingly became a valuable and welcome partner in ship design, pointing out past mistakes to be avoided. InSurv also provided excellent feedback for engineering improvements needed in existing ships.

Design-To-Cost

"Design-to-cost" was another management concept that affected naval engineering. Often more honored in the breach, its most literal application in ship design was probably the FFG-7-class frigate. Intended as a "low mix" ship, the overriding criterion was cost limitation: whatever military capabilities could be had within the designated cost would have to suffice. The ship design was rigorously confined within the dollar limit. In the process, over 200 design permutations and variations ("what-ifs") were considered. Without the digital computer and ship synthesis models, the effort would have been impossible. Although the outcome was generally considered successful, significant alterations (including crew augmentation), had to be made after completion, a common occurrence in the ship acquisition business.

Ship Acquisition

"Total Package Procurement"

The emphasis on management inspired a host of new management initiatives. The most far-reaching of these in the ship acquisition world was the concept labeled "total package procurement" coupled with "concept formulation/contract definition." The basic objective was to increase industry participation in naval ship acquisition, not only in the design phase but in analyzing and planning logistic support of a ship's total, life-cycle support. Under this concept, the Navy would forego its traditional role in preliminary and contract design. Instead it would only conduct cost and feasibility studies to provide to potential builders a ship concept "in terms of ranges of performance characteristics."[58] Commercial shipbuilders would then submit proposals to build a ship capable of meeting the required performance, using optimized production techniques and minimizing lifetime, logistic-support costs. Competitively selected shipbuilders would then perform "Contract Definition," comprising proposals for total ship procurement. These proposals included ship drawings and design specifications, together with plans for management, production, facilities, training, and logistic support for the life of the ship, all with price tags. The Navy's role would then only be to choose that contractor whose technical design and planning, when matched with his proposed total life-cycle cost, proves the most cost effective to execute the proposed contract. The winning contractor in the case of major ship programs would be awarded a multiship, multiyear contract (another innovation).

The abortive fast deployment logistics ship project was the first attempt to apply this new scheme to naval ship procurement. Chartered in 1965, the project set a target of mid-1967 for selection of a contractor for detail design and procurement of the ship. However, no funds were forthcoming for construction. Nevertheless, the project manager, Rear Admiral Nathan Sonenshein, judged that the experience had pointed the way toward several improvements in ship acquisition, such as increased industry input, improved standardization, encouragement of industry modernization, and lower average ship costs.[59] The concept was viewed by the Navy hierarchy as attractive enough to apply to the acquisition of the Amphibious Assault Ships (LHA) and *Spruance*-class (DD-963) destroyers, the results of which will be covered in the succeeding chapter.

Ship Maintenance

Ship maintenance, particularly in the Navy, underwent great changes in concept, organization and performance during this period. Major trends included: (1) a progressive transfer of responsibility for knowledge of ships' material condition, and for performance of shipboard maintenance, from the fleet to the material establishment; (2) a concomitant creation of numerous new organizations and procedures aimed at determining ships' material condition and assisting ships in correcting deficiencies; (3) an increase in the number and kinds of inspection and certifying agencies; (4) proliferation of computer-oriented management systems aimed at simplifying, or at least automating, information on maintenance problems, spare parts availability, and other related data; (5) increasingly earlier planning for ship overhauls and an order of magnitude increase in the planning effort; (6) a phenomenal increase in overhaul and other costs; and (7) increasing application of sound engineering to the planning and execution of fleet maintenance and modernization.

An early development by the Bureau of Ships was the Planned Maintenance System (PMS) and its counterpart the Maintenance Data Collection System (MDCS). PMS provided ships for the first time a plan for preventive maintenance of every piece of equipment in the ship, in terms of what to do, when and how to do it, and the tools and time required. The MDCS was designed to catalogue needed repairs, with the aid of automated data processing, so that they could be planned and scheduled for later accomplishment. This automated system was intended to ease the burden of generating and keeping up to date the traditional Current Ship's Maintenance Project (CSMP), which had been a laborious manual chore. The MDCS also provided for recording spare parts usage, the time required for the repairs, and other data, with the noble objective that all this data would be analyzed by BuShips engineers to identify the fleet's most troublesome equipments and take corrective engineering action. Although preventive maintenance and corrective maintenance were both being poorly executed in the fleet, these new maintenance systems met with resistance and poor compliance at the shipboard level. Many fleet leaders viewed them as mere bureaucratic impedimenta, and BuShips abetted this reaction, for too long, by showing little results from the paperwork-intensive MDCS. Earnest efforts were made to improve and simplify both systems, and compliance gradually improved through a combination of better salesmanship, greater acceptance, more rigorous supervision, and sometimes brute force. Nevertheless, progress was slow. On the other hand, many merchant ship operators adopted versions of one or the other of these systems and employed them with both success and enthusiasm, a fact worthy of thoughtful reflection by engineers interested in Navy ship maintenance.

Although neither system was created on the basis of solid engineering analysis of maintenance requirements, engineering gradually became a prominent feature in both. BuShips finally set up aggressive procedures for analyzing MDCS data and for identifying problem equipments and necessary engineering modifications. As for PMS, its procedures were originally derived mostly from manufacturers' recommendations, of varied reliability, or even pure guesswork. The burden they put on ships' crews demanded a hard engineering look at what really needed to be done, and how often. Eventually, this effort led to a study of commercial aircraft maintenance and adoption of its approach, Reliability Centered Maintenance. This approach considered such factors as redundancy of equipment, and the consequences of failure, in deciding the frequency of inspection and repair. Thus, preventive maintenance became progressively less arbitrary and more solidly founded on engineering need, as it should be.

A major advance of the period was the Extended (or Engineered) Operating Cycle (EOC), a concept from the submarine community for increasing the interval between overhauls. There, it was in response to longer reactor core lives and the need for more operating time and reduced overhaul costs. The EOC concept embodied a rigorous engineering analysis of all required maintenance, and the assignment of every maintenance operation either to the ship, an intermediate maintenance activity (IMA), or a shipyard, according to their capabilities. The maintenance was accomplished during a series of scheduled interim maintenance periods between major overhauls, assisted by specifically assigned inspection teams, in liaison with special headquarters engineering teams tasked to monitor progress and continuously update the plan.

This concept was adopted for almost all ship types in some form. Carriers employed a series of shipyard Selected Restricted Availabilities (SRAs)—actually abbreviated overhauls—and increased IMA help to sustain them between regular overhauls. The destroyer community set out to emulate the submariners' format, albeit with fewer resources. A particularly interesting

variation evolved for auxiliary ships in the form of a Phased Maintenance Plan in which the total maintenance was to be accomplished in a series of shorter, planned availabilities in lieu of a long regular overhaul. This approach leaned heavily on merchant marine practice, especially its concept of a port engineer. Rather than having repairs prescribed by the ship's force, with their penchant for wanting to overhaul everything, the determination would be made by a dedicated, expert port engineer motivated (ideally) by a desire to do nothing not absolutely required to ensure continued safe, reliable, and effective operation of the ship. All these efforts were supported by special BuShips field activities called PERAs (Planning and Engineering for Repairs and Alterations), one for each type of ship.

Engineering input to fleet maintenance took other forms. At the depot level, the use of Technical Repair Standards to define the criteria and procedures for overhaul of components was initiated. At the shipboard level, engineers and technicians from myriad government and contractor field activities participated in countless inspections and "tiger" teams dedicated to helping ships to diagnose and correct their own deficiencies. This hands-on experience provided unprecedented opportunity for design engineers to perceive at the working level the culmination of their efforts at the drawing board. No account was rendered as to subsequent benefits, but one likes to think benefits would indeed materialize in the form of more reliable, operable, and maintainable equipment.

In spite of all the well-intentioned engineering initiatives noted above, the material condition of the fleet continued to decline throughout the period, illustrating the nebulous relationship between engineering and maintenance, and the importance of that key ingredient, discipline: unless maintenance routines, however faulty and cumbersome, are actually carried out, neither their faults nor their effects can be accurately assessed so that improvements can be made. Considerable engineering effort was wasted in such esoteric pursuits as putting a meaningful "number" on the "readiness" of individual ships, or on their material condition. The events of 1950-72 could well serve as a model of the difficulty of influencing ship maintenance by design engineering initiatives alone. For one thing, engineering depends on data, as should maintenance. However, even as the period ended, there were no means of collecting data at the primary source—that is, shipyards —on the actual condition of things being overhauled. Thus, information as to whether the repairs performed were actually required was nonexistent. Also largely lacking was credible confirmation that the prescribed planned maintenance was actually being performed. In any event, there remained at the end of the period an increasing urgency for rapport between the fleet and the design engineers. If the lament is familiar, the solution remained obscure.

Conclusion

This chapter has attempted to relate briefly the major events and trends in naval engineering from 1950-72. It was not intended to be an encyclopedia of every significant development. Many developments, such as those in auxiliary machinery, while recognized with admiration, are not covered. No attempt has been made to give equal treatment to developments by foreign naval powers. That others made noteworthy advances in naval engineering during this period is readily acknowledged, if not recounted in detail.

The narrative has deliberately emphasized the technical aspects of the various engineering developments. Obviously, such developments do not, in real life, take place in a purely technical atmosphere. Rather, they occur in a complex, competitive, and hostile world of political, bureaucratic, and economic influences, which, as earlier observed, can defeat even the best ideas. (They can also, if cleverly manipulated, serve to support development of some innovations to an extent that greatly exceeds their intrinsic technical merit. But that is another story.) Regardless of technical merit, engineering developments can come to fruition only if their proponents can overcome these obstacles and obtain the necessary funding, people, and political support for their project. Whole books have been written about this aspect of some engineering feats, such as the development of nuclear propulsion and the Polaris missile. To some, the politics can be a more important part of the story than the technology. This facet of engineering history, in this chapter, has been left to other historians.

Finally, one regrets the impracticality of incorporating all the personal reminiscences and anecdotes submitted by engineers who were key players in these events as they unfolded. Their stories greatly enriched the recollection, if not the telling, of these events. They served to remind that the real story of engineering progress lies in the people—their character, motivation, skills, and industry. For obvious reasons, it was not possible to mention the thousands of competent engineers involved in this story, much less to analyze their characters and its impact on the various events. Suffice to say that a rich store of poignant memories resides in the minds of those who participated, and to hope that it may find expression in another account.

Notes

1 Mumma, A. G., RADM USN, "Managing a Revolution," *ASNE Journal.* (August 1956).

2 Knox, Robert J., CDR USN, "Twentieth Century 'Clermont's' First Cruise," *ASNE Journal.* (May 1956) p. 245.

3 Young, Harold L., LT USN, "Techniques and Practices in Recent Naval Steam Turbine Construction," *ASNE Journal.* (November 1959).

4 Warren, G. B., "The Gas Turbine—The Versatile Power Unit," (Speech to ASME March 1958), *ASNE Journal.* (August 1958).

5 Brockett, W. A., RADM USN, et al., "U.S. Navy's Marine Gas Turbines," *Transactions.* ASME. (March 1966).

6 LiCausi, Anthony C., "The Supercharged Steam Generator," *Naval Engineers Journal.* ASNE (May 1963).

7 Monk, Ivan, CDR USN, et al., "Recent Developments in Naval Propulsion Gears," *Transactions*. Vol. 60, SNAME (1950).

8 Meigs, Charles H., CDR USN, "Comment by Commander Ivan Monk on Recent Naval Steam Plant Design," *Transactions*. Vol. 62, SNAME (1945), p. 273.

9 "A Quarter Century of Propulsion Shafting Design Practice and Operating Experience in the U.S. Navy," *ASNE Journal*. (February 1959).

10 Schirmer, J. E., "The Navy's First Combustion Control Systems," *ASNE Journal*. (February 1956).

11 Neilson, Christian K., "A Summary of Controllable Pitch Propeller Systems Employed by the U.S. Navy," *Naval Engineers Journal*. ASNE (April 1974).

12 Fowden, W. M. M., et al., "The Gas Turbine as a Prime Mover on U.S. Naval Ships," *ASNE Journal*. (February 1954).

13 Boatwright and Strandell, "Controllable Pitch Propellers," *Naval Engineers Journal*. ASNE (August 1967).

14 Reinertson, et al., "The Submarine Propulsion Plant—Development and Prospects," *Naval Engineers Journal*. ASNE (May 1963).

15 Miller, Richards T., "Mine Sweepers," *Naval Record*. Vol. II, No. 2 (March/April 1967).

16 "Marine Diesel Engineering in 1958," *The Motor Ship*. (January 1959).

17 Kinchelmann, Walter A., "Slow Speed Versus High Speed Diesel Engines for Ship Propulsion," *Naval Engineers Journal*. ASNE (June 1964).

18 Reinertson, et al., "The Submarine Propulsion Plant—Development and Prospects" . ASNE (May 1963).

19 Sigal, Edward B., "The Navy Distillate Fuel Conversion Program," *Naval Engineers Journal*. ASNE (December 1971).

20 Van Dusen, William B., "The Ship Launched Projectile," *Naval Engineers Journal*. ASNE (February 1963).

21 Ferris, Lawrence W., Richard A. Frey, and James L. Mills, Jr., "The Ship Launched Projectile," *Naval Engineers Journal*. ASNE (February 1963).

22 *Modern Warfare*. New York, N.Y.: Arco Publishing, Inc., 1985. Also Friedman, Norman, *U.S. Naval Weapons*. London: Conway Maritime Press, Ltd., 1983.

23 Graf, R. W., *Case Study of the Development of the Navy Tactical Data System*. Report for the National Academy of Sciences, 1964.

24 Boehm, W. R., CAPT, "Microelectronics—Its Impact on Naval Ships," *ASNE Journal*. (June 1960).

25 McEachen, John C. P., and H. Kent Mills, "The SEMCIP—A Program for the Operating Fleet," *Naval Engineers Journal*. ASNE (October 1976).

26 DeJarnette, H. M., CMDR and H. J. DeMattia, "Electromagnetic Interference Considerations of Shipboard Electronics Systems," *Naval Engineers Journal*. ASNE (June 1966).

27 Sherwin, S. A., Jr., CAPT, "Coordinated Ship Electronics Design," *Naval Engineers Journal*. ASNE (May 1962).

28 Jackson, Harry A., CAPT USN, et al., "ASW: Revolution or Evolution," *Proceedings*. U.S. Naval Institute, September 1986.

29 McKee, A. I., "Recent Submarine Design Practices and Problems, *Transactions*. SNAME, 1959.

30 Arentzen, E. S., CAPT, and Philip Mandel, "Naval Architectural Aspects of Submarine Design," *Transactions*. SNAME, 1960.

31 Friedman, Norman, *Submarine Design and Development*. Annapolis, Maryland: Naval Institute Press, 1984.

32 Bryan, C. R., CMDR, and J.R. Wakefield, "The Effect of Weapons on Submarine Design," *Naval Engineers Journal*. ASNE (February 1963).

33 Friedman, Norman, *U.S. Aircraft Carriers*. Annapolis, Maryland: Naval Institute Press, 1983.

34 Miller, Richards T., "Sixty Years of Destroyers, A Study in Evolution," *Proceedings*. Naval Institute, 1982.

35 Friedman, Norman, *U.S. Destroyers, An Illustrated Design History*. Annapolis, Maryland: Naval Institute Press, 1982.

36 Berkeley, J. P., "Modern Concept of Vertical Envelopment," *Naval Engineers Journal*. ASNE (June 1965).

37 Larson, et al., "Ships of the Twenty Knot Amphibious Force," *The Naval Engineers Journal*. ASNE (June 1965).

38 Brooks, R., "Acorns and Ideas, How Today's Multi-Product Replenishment Ships Started," *Naval Engineers Journal*. ASNE (December 1968).

39 Weintraub, S., "Replenishment at Sea," *Naval Engineers Journal*. ASNE (June 1967).

40 Lankford, B. W., Jr., "ASR Catamaran Cross-Structure," *Naval Engineers Journal*. ASNE (August 1967).

41 Miller, Richards T., CAPT USN, "Hydrofoils for Naval Purposes," *Naval Engineers Journal*. ASNE (October 1963).

42 Hayward, L. H., *The History of Air-Cushion Vehicles, Hovering Craft and Hydrofoils*. Vol. 2, No. 3 (December 1962).

43 Nakonechny, Basil V., "Survey of Present State of Technology and Practical Experiences With Air Cushion Vehicles," *Naval Engineers Journal*. ASNE (August 1967).

44 Schuler, James L., "The Amphibious Assault Landing Ship Program," *Naval Engineers Journal*. ASNE (April 1973).

45 *Ibid.*

46 Mantle, Peter J., "Development of the USN Surface Effect Ship, SES-100B," *Naval Engineers Journal.* ASNE (October 1973).

47 Wachnick, Z. George, "Air Cushion Vehicles—New Technology in the Navy," *Naval Engineers Journal.* ASNE (April 1973).

48 Leopold, Reuven, PhD., "Innovation Adoption in Naval Ship Design," *Naval Engineers Journal.* ASNE (December 1977)

49 Powell, Alan, PhD., "To Foster Innovation in Naval Ships," *Naval Engineers Journal.* ASNE (April 1982).

50 Sonenshein, Nathan, RADM USN, "The Costs and Risks of Engineering Progress," *Naval Engineers Journal.* ASNE (November 1959).

51 Bigsby, V. L., CAPT USN, "The Development of a Safety Type Hydraulic Fluid for Naval Shipboard Use," *ASNE Journal.* (August 1958).

52 Dillon, et al., "Forty Years of Ship Designs Under the Merchant Marine Act, 1936-1976," *Transactions.* SNAME, 1976.

53 "The Speed of the SS *United States*," *Marine Technology.* (April 1978).

54 Payne, Stephen, "From Flier to Floatel: SS *United States*," *The Naval Architect.* (January 1987) p. E11.

55 Kalmanson, A. G., "Nuclear-Powered Merchant Ships: Some Legal and Regulatory Considerations," *Transactions.* Vol. 83, SNAME (1975).

56 Jackson, Robert L., "Operating Experience with the GTV *John Seargent*," *ASNE Journal.* (February 1959).

57 "The Gas-Turbine Powered 26½ Knot *Admiral William M. Callaghan*," *Motor Ship.* (August 1968).

58 Sonenshein, Nathan, "The Fast Deployment Logistics Ship—A New Approach to Ship Procurement," *Naval Engineers Journal.* ASNE (April 1966).

59 Sonenshein, Nathan, "Results of FDL Contract Definition," *Naval Engineers Journal.* ASNE (October 1967).

Crew of USS *Bunker Hill* (CVA-17) battles fire after being hit by Japanese suicide plane in 1945. The realm of the naval engineer includes technology applicable to damage control and fire protection.

San Francisco Naval Shipyard hosts carriers *Ranger* (CVA-61), *Kitty Hawk* (CVA-63), and *Bon Homme Richard* (CVA-31).

USS *Valley Forge* (LPH-8) is highly specialized platform for helicopters.

The Navy's first nuclear-powered attack aircraft carrier, USS *Enterprise* (CVAN-65), at Newport News Shipbuilding and Dry Dock Company, where she was built.

USS *Enterprise*, shown returning from Vietnam duty in 1967, displays a sampling of the many aircraft types she must be capable of supporting.

USCGC *Dependable* (WMEC-626) investigates fire on oil rig in Gulf of Mexico. Helicopter on landing pad stands by to assist.

Stern view of USS *Forrestal* (CVA-59) shows angled deck from the perspective of a pilot about to land—without, of course, the parked aircraft!

Oiler, USNS *Taluga* (TAO-62), plows through heavy seas while transferring petroleum products to USS *Constellation* (CVA-64).

USS *Sacramento* (AOE-1) and USS *Haleakala* (AE-25) are vital elements in the operational and support cycle of combatant ships.

USS *Missouri* (BB-63), shown firing 16″ salvo at Chong Jin, Korea, in 1950, was retired thereafter, but later recalled to active duty during the Vietnam War. Reactivation and modernization of "mothballed" ships presents many unique engineering challenges.

USS *Iowa* (BB-61) in shipyard. Personnel remain at attention following hoisting of colors. Right-hand picture shows *Iowa* at sea following reactivation.

USS *Turner* (DDR-834) appears to imitate a submarine as her bow disappears in a heavy swell during refueling operation. Naval engineering must provide a wide margin of safety to enable ships to withstand a harsh environment.

USS *Bunker Hill* (CG-52) fires SM-2 missile from forward Mk 41 vertical launching system, part of Aegis system. This photo was taken during 1986 sea trials.

Nuclear tests in the Pacific provided data vital to the development of ships and systems that might survive nuclear attack.

U.S. Navy river patrol boats like this one had to be able to withstand a hostile environment as well as enemy action.

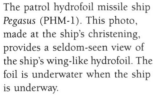

One of the Coast Guard's latest cutters is the *Hamilton* (WHEC-112).

Patrol air cushion vehicle (PACV) is tested in continuing search for high performance weapons platforms and delivery systems.

The patrol hydrofoil missile ship *Pegasus* (PHM-1). This photo, made at the ship's christening, provides a seldom-seen view of the ship's wing-like hydrofoil. The foil is underwater when the ship is underway.

The *Highpoint* (PCH-1) is an experimental hydrofoil assigned to the David Taylor Research Center's Hydrofoil Special Trials Unit. The *Highpoint* is shown firing a Harpoon missile.

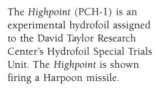

USNS *Hayes*, the Navy's first seagoing catamaran. So far, the program has yet to prove that two hulls are better than one.

CHAPTER
TEN
1973–1980

Decline of the Seventies

by Joseph F. Yurso

Introduction

Decline in Ships, Yards, and Building

The period from 1973 to 1980 can be labeled as one of decline, turmoil, and conflict in the field of naval engineering. The numbers of ships built during the early part of the period gave hope that shipbuilding would once again become a robust industry in the United States. The U.S. Navy would suffer its largest loss of ships in this short period of history, but none as a result of enemy fire. Naval shipyards once again would come under politico-economic pressures resulting in the closing of two yards and reducing the total number to eight. Large dollar claims against the U.S. Navy by the shipbuilders would crest and be resolved in the period.

Areas of Progress

However, there were some bright spots that glimmered during these years. The positive effects of the Merchant Marine Act of 1970 were felt. There were new merchant ship designs, such as liquefied natural gas (LNG) tankers and ultra large crude carriers (ULCC), and innovation in naval ship designs, such as nuclear aircraft carriers, cruisers, and submarines. There were also significant improvements in the fields of firefighting, pollution abatement, and shipbuilding productivity. Much credit goes to the talented marine engineers, naval architects, and other dedicated and innovative people who found a way to be productive during hard times.

Assaying the Decline in Naval Strength

Historical Fleet Strength

Perhaps a brief review of some key information concerning the U.S. Navy will reveal a true perspective of this period. In 1945, at the height of World War II, we had approximately 5,700 ships in the Navy. In the Korean War, and later during the Vietnam War, we had just over one thousand ships. Some people may not realize how much the U.S. Navy was weakened in the years following the Vietnam War. The total number of active ships at the end of fiscal year 1980 was 492 ships. Statistically, our country had been reduced to one-tenth of the ships that we had needed the last time we fought and won a war at sea. How did this deterioration of our maritime power come about? What were the circumstances that precipitated such a reversal of national policy?

THE NATION

Background Economy

Richard Nixon was re-elected President in November 1972 by a landslide vote, carrying forty-nine states. This apparent continuity and stability of government did not provide any indication of our maritime industry's tumultuous

future. Annual increases in the consumer price index had been running approximately 3 percent. History tells us that 10 years would pass before these increases would be again as low. Reviewing figure 10-1 provides insight into the "roller coaster" effect of the soaring inflation rate.

Political Turmoil

The "roller coaster" was also in effect, politically, at the highest levels of government. On 10 October 1973, the Vice President of the United States, Spiro Agnew, resigned after pleading "no contest" to a charge of income tax evasion. Representative Gerald R. Ford was approved as Agnew's successor by Congress on 6 December 1973. Less than one year later, Vice President Ford would become President when Richard Nixon resigned the Presidency. The lack of order

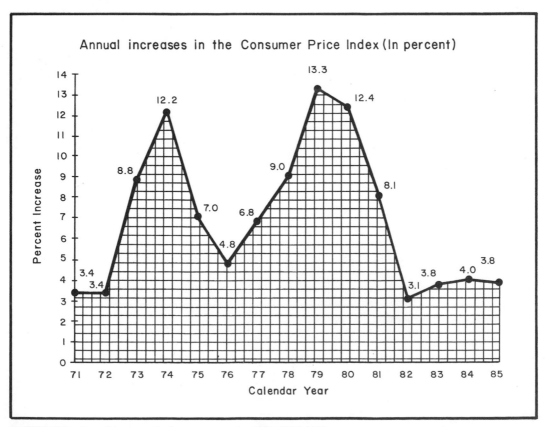

FIGURE 10-1—Annual increases in the consumer price index, 1971-1985.

and stability had an impact on every branch of our government.

THE DEPARTMENT OF DEFENSE

Shipbuilding Funds

During the Johnson administration and the early years of the Nixon administration, defense dollars went to fight the Vietnamese war, and money for building ships was scarce. Unfortunately, this was followed by a steep decline in construction of naval ships and the placement of new orders. New naval vessels ordered from private yards are depicted in figure 10-2. Note the dramatic decline from 1970 to 1973.

Military Installations

The United States pared its military forces to 2,231,908 troops as of 30 September 1973, the lowest level in 23 years. On 16 April 1974, Elliot L. Richardson, then the Secretary of Defense, announced the largest reduction in domestic military bases in nearly 25 years. The reductions affected 274 installations and were scheduled to eliminate 42,818 military and civilian jobs by June of 1974. The impact on both mercantile and naval ship construction was devastating. Figures 10-2 and 10-3 provide some insight as to the impact of cost reductions. These cuts were spurred by turmoil in government and attempts to curtail a soaring inflation rate. A quick review of figure 10-1 confirms the inflation concern.

The Shipyards

The maritime and naval environments had changed considerably during this period. In the two decades preceding the 1970s, the Navy had undertaken an ambitious shipbuilding program. In the 1960s, the program was spread to over

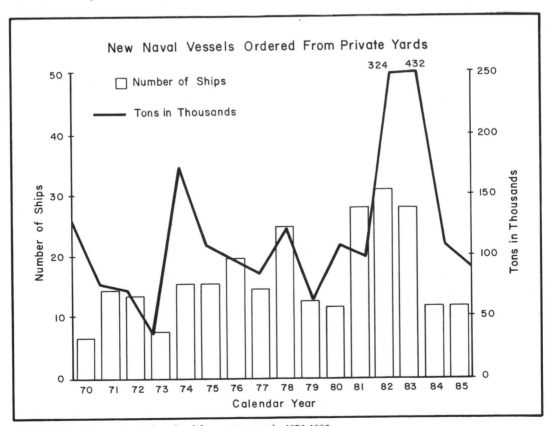

FIGURE 10-2—New naval vessels ordered from private yards, 1970-1985.

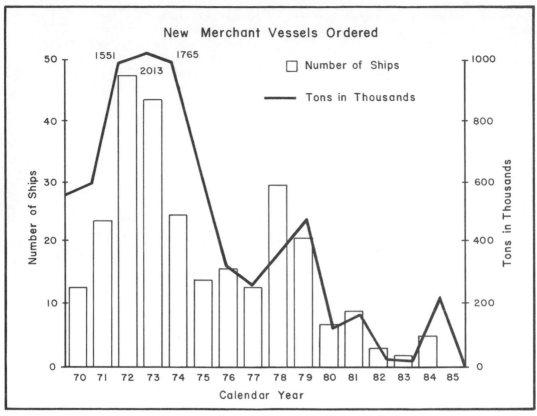

FIGURE 10-3—New merchant vessels ordered, 1970-1985.

twenty private shipyards, as well as naval shipyards. By the 1970s, however, with the increased acquisition of nuclear ships and the reduced number of ship types, only nine private shipyards were building naval vessels. Three of these yards, Electric Boat Division of General Dynamics Corporation (hereafter called Electric Boat), Newport News Shipbuilding and Drydock Company (hereafter called Newport News Shipbuilding), and Ingalls Shipbuilding Division of Litton Industries (hereafter called Ingalls Shipbuilding) were performing over 75 percent of the work. All ship construction was phased out of our naval shipyards during the 70s. The shipbuilding industry was plagued with inflationary cost increases, material shortages, and labor instability. Substantial problems were encountered with specifications and drawings provided by the Navy. Working under contracts with escalation clauses that did not fully compensate for soaring inflationary costs, the major shipbuilders experienced large cost overruns that could not be settled by normal means. The result was major shipbuilding claims that, by the end of 1977, totaled 2.7 billion dollars.

Shipbuilding Leadership

This period has been most appropriately identified as "the decline of the 70s." Almost the entire period was plagued with great pressures for retrenchment and cutbacks. In this gloomy environment, there were notables in the industry of shipbuilding and ship maintenance who persevered and performed well under difficulty. James Goodrich, President of Bath Iron Works (and later Chairman of the Board), was one of the many remarkable contributors to the marine field in this period. The following naval personnel made many contributions and are listed in the order in which they served in key offices: Vice Admirals Robert C. Gooding and C. Russell Bryan as Commanders, Naval Sea Systems

Command (NavSea); Rear Admirals David H. Jackson, C. Russell Bryan, Lee W. Fisher, and James K. Nunneley as Directors, Ship Maintenance and Modernization, Office of the Chief of Naval Operations (OP43); Captains Emera S. Bailey and Charles L. Mull as Supervisors of Shipbuilding (SupShip), Bath, Maine; Captains Patrick G. O'Keefe, Robert K. Reed, William L. Martin, and Joseph F. Yurso as SupShip, Groton, Connecticut; Rear Admirals Clarence M. Hart and Robert J. Eustace, and Captain Vincent J. Manara, Jr. as SupShip, Newport News, Virginia; and Rear Admirals Charles N. Payne, Cabell S. Davis, Jr., William E. McGarrah, Jr., and William C. Wyatt as SupShip, Pascagoula, Mississippi. A notable group of private industry personnel included: Joseph D. Pierce, General Manager, Electric Boat; Ned Marandino and following him, Leonard Erb, President, Ingalls Shipbuilding; and John P. Diesel, Ralph Cousins, and Edward J. Campbell, serving consecutively as Chief Operating Officers, Newport News Shipbuilding.

Department of Defense Leadership

In spite of the decline in Navy shipbuilding during the early 70s, and the primary environment of planned reduction, there were some bright spots. Melvin R. Laird, Secretary of Defense, repeatedly pressured Congress until it funded development of the Trident missile submarine, which immediately improved our strategic posture. However, the incumbent Secretary of Defense changed several times. Melvin Laird resigned in January 1973 and was replaced by Elliot Richardson; on 30 April 1973, Richardson was named Attorney General. He was replaced by James R. Schlesinger, former director of the Central Intelligence Agency. These were only a very few of the key changes taking place.

AMERICAN MERCHANT MARINE

Status of the Merchant Fleet and Merchant Shipbuilding

American shipbuilding and shipping needs had drastically changed during the 1950s and 60s. While tonnage of bulk cargo being shipped was constantly growing larger, this market had become almost completely monopolized by the use of foreign flag vessels and foreign flags of convenience. In addition, while most foreign trading nations embarked on an aggressive shipbuilding program, ship construction in the United States went to such a low level that replacements were not being built for the overage tonnage that was being retired. A bright spot of this period was the recognition, by both the legislative and executive branches of the federal government, that previous federal maritime programs had seriously neglected the development and maintenance of an American merchant marine. The merchant fleet increasingly failed to meet both the United States' commercial needs and national security requirements. The Merchant Marine Act of 1970 was an outgrowth of this recognition of the situation of the U.S. merchant fleet and an attempt to correct those deficiencies by bringing federal maritime policy in conformance with U.S. merchant fleet needs.

The Merchant Marine Act of 1970

The Merchant Marine Act of 1970 provided the keystone for growth and stability of all segments of the maritime industry. This act committed the federal government to an expanded shipbuilding program for the 1970s, encouraged shipbuilders and operators to upgrade their facilities and equipment, and extended the full benefits of construction and operating aid to bulk carriers.

The U.S. Department of Commerce officially reported to Congress in the annual Maritime Administration Report of 1973 that substantial progress had been made in implementing the maritime program as embodied in the Merchant Marine Act: "An unprecedented level of shipbuilding activity was generated by the aid of the construction differential subsidy program." The volume of shipbuilding reached 2.4 billion dollars, covering construction of forty-seven new vessels and sixteen container ship conversions, and generating almost 120,000 man-years of work. As of June 1973, eighty-three ships, aggregating 5.4 million dead weight tons, were on order or under construction. Included in the orders for new vessels were tankers ranging in size from 38,300 to 390,770 dead weight tons. Contracts were also included for the construction of two versatile oil bulk carriers and LNG carriers.

Largely because of those orders and those generated by the Maritime Administration's (MarAd's) indirect assistance programs, American shipyards were enjoying the largest boom in their peacetime history. Some yards were expanding their facilities. Newport News Shipbuilding not only modernized its existing yard but, in addition, invested more than 150 million dollars to build a "North Yard." Newport News later built two 25,000-cubic-meter natural gas carriers, the *El Paso Southern* and *El Paso Arzew*. In addition, the *UST Atlantic* and the *UST Pacific*, delivered by the yard in 1979, are still the largest ULCCs to be built in the Western hemisphere. Each was 1,187 feet long and reckoned at 397,140 dead weight tons.

Subsidy Arrangements

The order book of MarAd had provided the impetus for American shipbuilders to modernize their yards, construct new yards and facilities, and improve efficiency through increased productivity. These advances in the maritime field had been accomplished at the same time that federal subsidy rates were dropping. Prior to the enactment of the new maritime program, subsidy rates were averaging about 54 percent of the domestic costs of constructing a new ship. This meant that United States taxpayers were funding more than one-half the cost of an American vessel. The 1970 Act prescribed an annual declining subsidy rate until a 35 percent maximum would be reached in 1976. Productivity improvements, combined with international economic factors, were decreasing subsidy rates to about 33 percent for conventional ships, and as low as 16.5 percent for LNG ships. As previously mentioned, the climate was very bright for American merchant ship construction during the early years of this period. A quick review of figure 10-3 shows that there had been increases in both the number of merchant ships and the total tonnage of ships ordered.

NAVAL SHIPBUILDING

Great Reduction in the Early 1970s

For the U.S. Navy, the picture was considerably different. A review of figure 10-2 will reveal that new Navy ships ordered had declined signifi-

cantly for the years leading up to 1973, both in numbers and tonnage. The Department of Defense had closed several naval shipyards as a result of pressure by private industry because of a perceived idea that there was excess capacity in shipbuilding.

Competition for Residual Building Capacity

This decline of naval shipbuilding, coupled with unprecedented growth in merchant ship construction, created an unusual situation. The Navy was being squeezed out of the industry. Congress was authorizing naval ships to be built, but merchant ship construction had used up most of the building capacity of private industry. The Navy found itself unable to award contracts for all the ships authorized. The U.S. Navy, the U.S. merchant marine, our naval shipyards, and private shipyards by 1974 had all jumped into what would be a free-swinging competitive donnybrook of mammoth proportions. This fracas would not crest until several years later. Simply stated, there was not enough new construction capacity in private and public yards combined to build all the new ships needed; and, there was an abundance of ship repair capacity, but not enough ships in need of repair to provide work for all yards and lesser facilities bidding for the business. The several-years-old conflict reached a critical state in 1974 and was waged like open warfare. The Navy had shut down three naval shipyards, Boston, Brooklyn, and Hunters Point, and one major repair facility at San Diego as a result of past politico-economic pressures. For two years, the Navy had been unable to place contracts for all the ships authorized in the budget. On 23 January 1974, Vice Admiral Robert C. Gooding, in his capacity as the Coordinator of Shipbuilding, reported to the Secretary of Defense that ten ships authorized in fiscal years 1972 and 1973 had not been awarded to any shipbuilder.

1974 Congressional Committee Hearings

On 9 July 1974, the House Armed Services Committee opened hearings to review, and hopefully reconcile, the differences between naval and private shipyards. Vice Admiral Gooding, Commander NavSea, testified on plans to assign some of the Navy's new construction work to Mare Island, Puget Sound, and Philadelphia

Naval Shipyards. An exchange had taken place just a few weeks earlier before the House Appropriations Committee that featured some of the most acrimonious language it had heard in recent years. Edwin Hood, President of the Shipbuilders Council of America, had spoken about the "needlessly expensive penchant" of those government officials "responsible for the apportionment of repair, alterations, and conversion work" on the Navy's non-nuclear surface ships, and about "favored, unfair, and costly government competition with private enterprise." Hood's language was extreme, but he was reeling from harsh criticism by numerous witnesses. Obscured by the charges, countercharges, and rhetoric that had dominated the congressional hearings, facts slowly emerged to indicate that after years in the doldrums, the larger private yards were beginning to enjoy an unprecedented peacetime boom. The combination of merchant marine contracts, U.S. Navy ship construction, and the burgeoning requirement for large, ocean, oil-drilling rigs strained the capacities of private yards to their limits.

Decreasing Private Yard Naval Construction

The picture in 1974 was that the boom in new construction was likely to continue for the indefinite future. Unfortunately, the improved shipbuilding outlook was spread inconsistently throughout the industry. Only a limited number of shipyards were capable of building the sophisticated surface warships and submarines needed by the Navy or had the capacity to build the similarly sophisticated LNG or jumbo tankers. During this erratic boom period, some of the larger shipbuilders turned away from the Navy. Newport News Shipbuilding let it be known that every effort would be made to reduce the impact the Navy had on its workload. This builder went so far as to testify to the U.S. Congress that if the Navy wanted more supercarriers built, they would have to develop another source, since his company would no longer build such ships.

Decreasing Responsiveness to Navy Building Business

In addition to private yards making it difficult for the Navy to place shipbuilding contracts, the last two remaining yards capable of building nuclear submarines were not responsive to bid requests for the new Trident submarines. It is easy to understand why Newport News Shipbuilding was unresponsive. With all their commercial and other Navy work, they lacked a strong desire to invest in new submarine facilities. But Electric Boat, a 100-percent submarine facility, was something else. They had the lead in the submarine design business, and had even designed the proposed Trident submarine USS *Ohio* (SSBN-726); yet, they resisted bidding to build it. Why did they not bid? One can only surmise that they already had a fairly adequate workload (constructing 688-class nuclear attack submarines), and they wanted to hold out for something better than the "fixed-price" contract being offered by the Navy. Electric Boat finally decided to bid after the Navy was forced to offer a much more generous and innovative contract.

THE FINANCIAL PLIGHT OF AMERICAN SHIPBUILDING

Hiring of Unskilled Personnel

The following analysis gives an insight into what the future would bring to the entire shipbuilding industry. The saga was similar for all the large shipbuilders: an expanding workload forced rapid expansion of work forces. When experienced workers were no longer available, shipbuilders hired untrained personnel, many of whom were not even potentially trainable. The resulting situation was just short of chaotic. Gross inefficiencies were created, costs skyrocketed, and the work did not get accomplished either in quantity or quality. The average turnover rate of a production worker was estimated at something approaching 75 percent per year. (A newly hired worker is estimated to be only 50 percent efficient in the first two years.)

Additional Cost Claims

The shipyards could no longer manage the workloads and the inefficiencies they created, nor pay the increased numbers of workers, and stay solvent, so they attempted to solve these problems by submitting huge cost claims. Who was really responsible for these gross inefficiencies and who should have paid for these massive costs? There is no conclusive answer to this question. The yards had obviously made some bad decisions on hiring personnel. Also, from a business view, the Navy could have taken the position that a contract was signed in good faith and should have been followed. Both parties knew the risks in entering a business contract. Unfortunately, that approach was much too simplistic.

The Navy's demands for more ships, combined with the commercial shipbuilding business, had created work far beyond the capacity of the existing experienced work force. Animosity between the Navy and the shipyards increased when management of the yards began to realize that contracts did not have provisions for the costs of labor escalation beyond ship delivery dates. The lack of this provision created massive cash flow problems. For example, the contract for construction of the nuclear carrier *Eisenhower* was written for Newport News Shipbuilding in the 1960s, but did not keep up with inflation. In the mid 1970s, the company was being reimbursed for labor at 1960 rates. This created hard feelings and bitter business relationships. The yards had to borrow funds to make payrolls. The claims picture reveals the magnitude of the problem facing the shipbuilders. Early in this period, claims by all shipbuilders against the Navy were less than 300 million dollars. However, by 1978, the value of the claims had grown to 2.7 billion dollars. The problem became so severe that the Secretary of the Navy convinced the Administration and the Congress that it was prudent to invoke Public Law 85-804 and 'bail out' the shipbuilders with government funds. This action was necessary because claims were not upheld by the Claims Review Board headed by Rear Admiral F. F. Manganaro, USN. But, in an effort to save the American shipbuilding industry, the Secretary of the Navy negotiated generous settlements with all major shipbuilders with large dollar-value claims. He used as his authority a seldom-invoked law that provides for compensating private industry when the defense of the country is at risk. In addition, major changes were effected for future shipbuilding contracts. Today, as a result of lessons learned, the cost escalation provisions of all shipbuilding contracts are much more generous and protect the shipbuilder against these types of cost overruns, especially when ships under construction go beyond their contract delivery dates.

Difficult Times at Electric Boat

Unprecedented Expansion

The engineering and facility advances at Electric Boat were impressive. It is, at first, difficult to comprehend why an organization that was so advanced, from an engineering point of view, ran into so many difficulties in the areas of economics and people. Electric Boat more than doubled its work force between 1973 and 1977. This unprecedented expansion resulted in dilution of experience levels throughout the organization. Managers and workers, alike, were hard put to cope with the dynamics of such a rapid expansion. A simple analysis would reveal that even if the expansion had been accomplished easily and smoothly, the yard would still have been in a difficult position from a profit standpoint.

Peter Drucker's Pessimistic Prognosis

Three years earlier, Peter Drucker, the famous industrial consultant, made a rather simple financial analysis and reported to Electric Boat's General Manager, Joseph D. Pierce, that the company was facing trouble. Financial records notwithstanding, it was losing money or barely breaking even. The following are extracts from Peter F. Drucker's letter to Joseph D. Pierce 11 August 1970:

> . . . My first question would relate to the productivity of the entire Electric Boat operation and of its two component parts, the construction work and the design engineering. You have total sales of around $240 million a year and spend about $90 million to purchase parts, supplies and sub-assemblies. This leaves around $150 million as value contributed. Of this, design engineering bills $60 million so that the construction operation accounts for around $90 million. You have a total of 12,500 employees of which there are about 7,000 directly employed in construction with about another 2,000 indirect employees in various support operations including engineering, and you have about 3,000 people in two engineering operations. This means that your total value contributed per employee runs around $12,000; yet each employee costs you around $11,000, everything considered, so that your margin per employee is less than 10 percent. In your yard operation with 7,000 to 9,000 employees, you have a value contributed of $90 million so that you come out at around

$10,000 per employee which must be somewhat lower than your actual cost per employee. I cannot see any profit in your yard operation no matter how you keep your books. . . .

I am perfectly aware of the fact that my figures are crude and, at best, approximate, and prone to all the ills accounting figures and accounting allocations are prone to. . . .

For even if you change the figures—and you should of course do that to conform to your own internal figures—the result would remain the same: your margin, if any, is wafer-thin. Yet, your competitors manage to underbid you and do so, apparently, with a profit, even though they have new yards rather than the fully depreciated facilities with which you operate. If I go by what Mr. McPherson told me, and assume that your competitors operate on the basis of a capital investment that is ten to twelve times what you show in your books for your facilities, and that, further, your competitors aim at least 7½% profit after taxes, it would seem to me that your productivity is about 20 percent or so below theirs. Clearly, this is a serious matter . . . .

Either Drucker's perception of the problem was uncanny, or else the competitors' bids were unreal—or both.

Shipbuilder-Navy Relations

Shipbuilders such as Newport News Shipbuilding and Electric Boat have had a strong organic association with the Navy. Electric Boat had been building submarines for the U.S. Navy for many years—generations actually. They had essentially no commercial business. The Navy's submarine design and acquisition organization was inclined to look at Electric Boat as an extension of its own capabilities, facilities, and productive manpower. In this environment, strong trusting relationships built up over many years. The Electric Boat-Navy team, civilian and military, shared the accomplishments of submarine design, innovation, and creativity, and also the heartbreak when efforts failed. Electric Boat was a dedicated professional organization, responsive to Navy needs. This close relationship, however, developed strains as the nuclear propulsion era extended into decades.

Coercive Atmosphere Develops

Organizations within the Navy, especially the Nuclear Power Directorate of the Bureau of Ships

(later NavSea), assumed ever-stronger control of the nuclear yards. Strong-willed officers and civil servants were inclined to coerce shipbuilders to react and perform as desired. These yards were even dissuaded from venturing into non-Navy activity. Attempts to develop new markets or facilities encountered deliberate discouragement. Such influence was unprecedented, but the shipbuilders became more and more accommodating. In fact, the organizational structures of some yards even started to reflect the complicated Navy organizations that dealt with them. Frustration and resistance began to grow among the shipbuilders. Differences in interpretation of contracts and specifications were to be expected, but as industrial leadership in the Navy became increasingly domineering, the relationship between producer and customer became increasingly antagonistic.

The relationship policy became more one-sided in response to Admiral Rickover, and the collegiality deteriorated. For example, when the shipbuilder uncovered a potentially serious problem, it was not only required that the shipbuilder notify the Navy, but also that the shipbuilder describe the steps taken to correct the problem and the action taken or planned to prevent recurrence of similar problems. Moreover, the Navy used this provision repeatedly against shipbuilders, who found that it put them in the awkward position of increasingly having to acquiesce to increased Navy demands. For years, Electric Boat had been a very open company, all levels sharing data, information, and ideas with the Navy representatives. But in this era, they came to realize that the system was using their own information against them. The resident SupShips recognized that, inevitably, overharsh criticism of the shipbuilder would lead to withholding of information about shipbuilding problems. A delicate balance was required to ensure that enough concern and pressure was exerted but always in an atmosphere of professionalism and courtesy. Increasingly, however, SupShip Groton was chastised by Admiral Rickover's headquarters as too close or too sympathetic to the contractor. In time, the environment became so intense that no officer could survive as SupShip.

The SupShip Groton billet had been recognized in years past as significant in the design, construction, and maintenance of our submarine force, a stepping stone for talented and ambitious submarine engineering duty officers. Now, several potential flag officers were to have their careers fatally damaged from the constant conflict between the Navy and Electric Boat. This was unprecedented in the history of the Navy and the nation's shipbuilding.

New Electric Boat Management

By late 1977, with the arrival of a new and ruthless Electric Boat manager, Takis Veliotis, and his "Quincy Eight," the situation became worse. Veliotis, desiring to "fix" Electric Boat, made drastic changes in pursuit of his goal of cutting 100 million dollars from the shipyard's overhead. He also removed 4,000 workers from the rolls, including Electric Boat's design group, paid almost entirely on cost-plus-fixed-fee contracts. The members of this group would have made money for Electric Boat even had they performed no useful work; and, quite to the contrary, many were performing important work for the Navy. Veliotis, however, had decided to fire workers, and these people were removed from the rolls throughout the company. The firings, in particular, added a special chill to the environment that discouraged any dialog with the Navy.

Uneasy Navy–Electric Boat Relationship Resolved

Veliotis created a situation where mature professionals had to fear for their jobs and livelihoods. Very capable people were discharged in a most unpleasant manner. The signals were clear: if you cooperated with the Navy, you could lose your job. The engineering atmosphere became extremely unhealthy. Open and honest exchange is essential to design ships, especially ships as complex as ballistic missile nuclear submarines. Fortunately, this situation moderated in time as channels, albeit unofficial, were re-established between the professionals of the Navy and Electric Boat, who realized that shipbuilding had to continue. People such as Navy Commander Robert Traister and Electric Boat design engineer Bob White were able to communicate and solve many problems. Lieutenant Commander Ken

Carroll was another successful Navy representative. Through his dedication and professional integrity, he was able to work with Electric Boat during the most difficult times of the Trident program (construction of the USS *Ohio*). Fortunately for the Navy and the country, many others, too, made concerted efforts to keep necessary information flowing.

Improved Groton Facilities

Electric Boat had realized the importance of modernizing their submarine facilities in the late 1960's and early 1970's. By 1973, construction had started on the Groton renovation officially called the Land Level Submarine Construction Facility (LLSCF). The complex covered eight acres and was completed in 1976 for an approximate cost of 140 million dollars. This facility completely replaced an antiquated submarine fabrication area.

Electric Boat, under Joseph D. Pierce's leadership, had begun developing concepts that would permit the construction of modern nuclear submarines in Groton on extremely limited land. The detailed development of the LLSCF was a good example of the cooperative atmosphere among certain shipbuilders at that time. In addition to developing plans with their own talent, Electric Boat had the benefit of visiting the Ingalls West Bank facility in Pascagoula, Mississippi. Litton had just completed a land-level facility for surface ships. One of the lessons learned and applied in Groton was not to use conventional, raised rails for transporting the submarines or portions of the submarines. Raised rails created havoc and interfered with vehicles such as fork lift trucks. Electric Boat quickly adopted flush rails or recessed rails for the transport system. This flush roadway permitted complete freedom and passage of any type of vehicle or crane on the ground or floor level. The facilities added at the Groton yard were superb and permitted significant flexibility for the construction of both attack submarines and fleet ballistic missile submarines. The latter were too large to launch into the restricted waters of the Thames river. These boats were assembled at the LLSCF and then moved to the outdoors and prepared for launch by a transfer system. (See figure 10-4.)

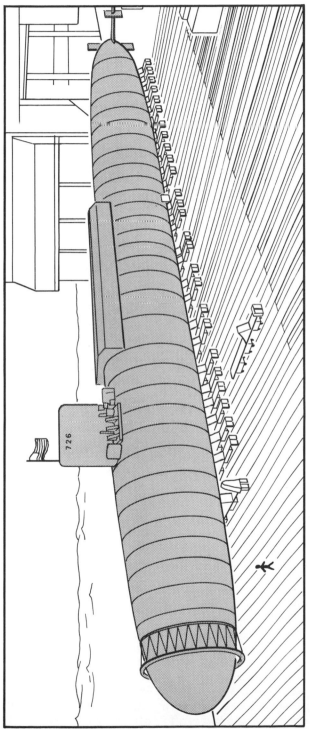

FIGURE 10-4—SSBN roll out, land-level submarine construction facility.

New Quonset Point Facility

Approximately 45 minutes north of Groton, Electric Boat acquired land at Quonset Point, Rhode Island, by negotiating a bargain with the state of Rhode Island for the area vacated by the closing of the Naval Air Station. On this site, Electric Boat built a very modern submarine hull facility. The automated submarine frame and cylinder manufacturing facility was an engineering marvel. Figures 10-5 and 10-6 show, in a small way, the scope and nature of the capabilities of the facilities. When the Quonset Point facility became fully operational, it gave Electric Boat a tremendous competitive advantage.

Industrial Advantages of the Quonset Facility

The Quonset yard was not unionized and enjoyed great flexibility of worker trade assignments. In addition, more and more of each submarine was manufactured and assembled at Quonset. Fritz Tovar, the Manager of Electric Boat, Quonset Point Facility, was an aggressive shipbuilder and fabricator who continually pursued construction of hull sections that were ever more complete.

The modern equipment at Quonset consisted of thirty-three welding machines and fixtures, including ten hull-form-fabrication fixtures, twelve hull cylinder-assembly units, and three hull-cylinder pairing fixtures. This facility was capable of constructing 27- to 42-foot hull cylinders and of handling two different classes of submarines simultaneously. Hull sections built on the automated facility were then thoroughly outfitted with decks, machinery, piping, etc. In addition, these sections were preserved and painted internally and externally. Systems were flushed, tested, and capped or sealed. These extremely complete hull sections were then barged to Groton for final assembly. This resulted in a large portion of the submarine actually being constructed in a facility external to the already crowded and busy Groton facility. (The Germans had pursued a similar course in the later stages of World War II, constructing various compartments of the world's first high speed 'true' submarine, the Type XXI class, at widely dispersed locations, to escape the heavy bombing raids. These completely outfitted hull sections were then shipped to submarine building yards

to be quickly assembled in minimum time in the old building ways.)

NUCLEAR SUBMARINES

Ohio-Class Ballistic Missile Submarine

The *Ohio* was a traditional design, but extremely large by U.S. Navy standards. Unlike the Soviet missile submarine *Typhoon*, the *Ohio's* missile tubes were behind the sail area. The *Ohio*, essentially, was a very large *Lafayette* (SSBN 616) class but with many unique, sophisticated features. She incorporated lessons learned from previous ballistic missile nuclear submarines (SSBNs). The boat was incredibly large: 560 feet long with a 42-foot diameter pressure hull. Larger than a World War II surface cruiser, she displaced 18,750 tons submerged. The *Ohio's* sail bore the traditional diving planes. Fifteen feet up sail, which towered 25 feet above the hull, were located huge diving planes, control surfaces approximately 16 feet long and 12 feet wide. The sail also featured periscopes, masts, radio transmitting antennas, and radio receiving antennas, as well as radars, electronic countermeasure masts, and snorkel induction and exhaust masts. The stern of the *Ohio* provided solid visual evidence that it was a unique submarine. Here, a single 26-foot diameter propeller drove the ship from the extreme stern! Figure 10-7 provides a stern cross-section view from astern.

Ohio-Class Design Concepts

When the Navy first considered a boat to replace the Polaris submarines, it established a number of design objectives. The most obvious were survivability, noise reduction, and hull strength. But, unlike previous submarines, the *Ohio* hull was designed to allow maximum room for future components, such as new weapons systems and new sonars, while simultaneously providing maximum shock resistance. In addition, a program for detailed "logistic replacement paths" for equipment was developed and recorded. This concept permitted the maintenance or replacement of all operating equipment without the necessity of cutting holes in the pressure hull. This meant the entire submarine might never require a complex overhaul since all in-

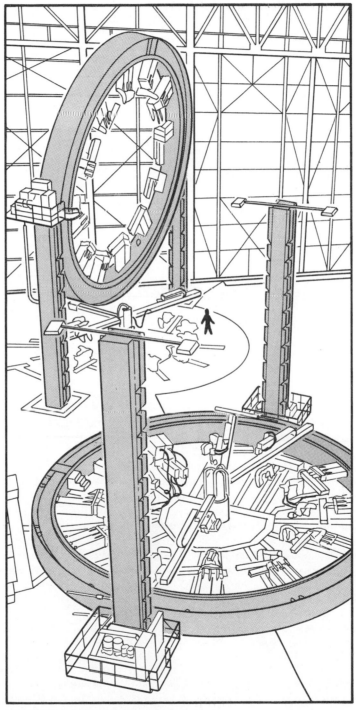

FIGURE 10-5—*Sketch of automated frame facility.*

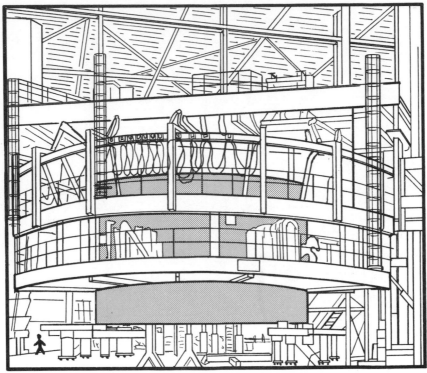

FIGURE 10-6—Sketch of automated hull facility.

stalled equipment could be progressively maintained. (Submarine engineers, in particular, can appreciate the significance of this evolution.) Furthermore, even the cylinders making up the entire pressure hull were, for the most part, uniform cylinders permitting a much easier hull fabrication process than for submarines such as the *Skipjack-*, *Permit-*, or *Sturgeon*-class designs. Except for the tapered bow and four stern cylinders, the entire submarine was made up of forty-one uniform-diameter hull cylinders. This hull design permitted and encouraged the application of automated fabrication, with tremendous savings in time and money without sacrificing quality. In fact, the quality was improved with the elimination or significant reduction in manual welding on these hull cylinders. Automatic welding, once perfected, could consistently produce hull cylinders of superior quality.

Los Angeles-Class Attack Submarine

The *Los Angeles*-class nuclear-powered fast attack submarine came to reality during this period. The detail design was accomplished by Newport News Shipbuilding under the specific direction of Arnold H. Medbury. This submarine was a capable, anti-submarine/anti-surface ship warfare platform and was vital to countering the threat posed by the Soviet's unprecedented, multimission, nuclear submarine construction program. The *Los Angeles*-class submarine had an allaround capability that was superior to any single Soviet submarine class. A formidable addition to the capability of these ships is the planned deployment of the Tomahawk cruise missile. This vertical-launch missile system has been designed and was in the detailed planning stage as of 1987.

Los Angeles-Class Shortcomings

Unfortunately, the *Los Angeles*-class submarine violated the submarine "holy trinity" of speed, depth, and stealth. Although her design was adequate in the stealth area, speed and depth were inferior to the best Soviet designs.

Critics of this class have claimed that while

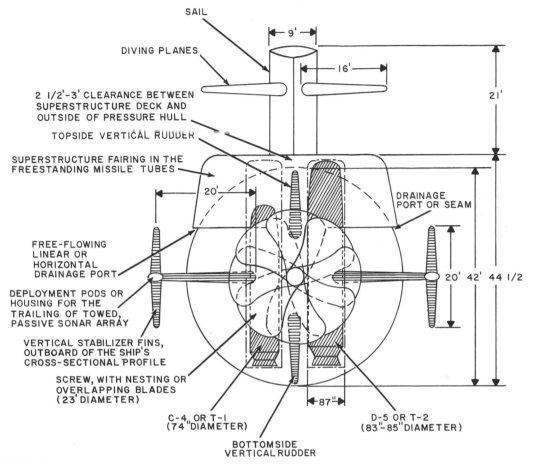

FIGURE 10-7—Stern view of USS Ohio (SSBN-726).

the U.S. Navy had the capability and technical knowledge to produce a better design, internal squabbling prevented the best design from emerging. They further claim that new submarine designs were not permitted to occur, pointing to the many ship designs developed in earlier years as opposed to the few from the 1970s. Numerous submarine designs were conceived and brought to reality in the 1960s such as the *Albacore, Nautilus, Dolphin, Barbel, Skipjack, George Washington, Ethan Allen,* and *Lafayette.* Since the end of that decade, the Navy has limited itself to two new classes of submarines, the *Los Angeles* and the *Ohio.*

Aircraft Carrier Programs

Newport News Shipbuilding Carriers

Newport News Shipbuilding was less dependent on the Navy than Electric Boat, in view of its extensive commercial business. In fact, as previously mentioned, in the mid-1970s, Jack Diesel, chief operating officer, was making considerable progress toward a predominantly commercial workload. His stated goal was a workload mix in which Navy contracts played a minor role. As trends seemed to show that this plan might succeed, the shipyard's management became increasingly more resistant to the Navy's direction. This was a most ominous turn of events. Newport News was a leader in aircraft carrier design and construction. By the mid-1970s, they were the only shipyard in the United States capable of building supercarriers. New York Naval Shipyard in Brooklyn, which had built and maintained supercarriers, had been closed. New York Shipbuilding Corporation in Camden, New Jersey, was bankrupt and no longer in a position to build ships.

Since Newport News Shipbuilding was the only remaining builder of carriers, the Navy had no choice but to be flexible. There was a period in which the atmosphere became tense, and the business of designing, building, and repairing ships was as difficult as it had ever been and probably even more so. As with the other shipyards, there were claims (requests for equitable adjustments to existing contracts) and litigation.

In spite of the difficulties of this period, the team of Newport News Shipbuilding and the Navy was able to deliver numerous ships of good quality. SSBN conversions, the nuclear carriers *Nimitz* and *Eisenhower*, and several *Virginia*-class nuclear cruisers were completed.

The 1970s became the age of the nuclear carrier. The USS *Nimitz* (CVN-68) was delivered in 1975 and the *Eisenhower* (CVN-69) in 1977, but the Navy was totally dependent on one shipbuilder for these large, complex ships.

Service Life Extension Program

The Aircraft Carrier Service Life Extension Program (CV-SLEP), was conceived in the mid-1970s as an alternative to new construction. At this time, the Navy foresaw the need for fifteen carrier battle groups (around which the 600-ship Navy objective would subsequently be established). All conventionally powered carriers were projected to reach the end of their nominal thirty-year service lives in the late 1980s and early 1990s. These ships were built when there were three new-carrier construction shipyards. With only one shipyard remaining (Newport News Shipbuilding), the timely replacement of *Forrestal*-class carriers was impossible. The desired force levels could not be attained through new construction alone. Consequently, the Chief of Naval Operations (CNO), Admiral James L. Holloway, requested that the Commander,

NavSea look into the possibility of extending the service life of the *Forrestal* (CV-59)-class carriers from 30 to 45 years.

SLEP Goals

The CV-SLEP had to ensure continued capability for full operation and support of first-line aircraft. Particular emphasis was given to structural repairs, rotating machinery repair or replacement, and upgrading ship habitability. Several alternatives were considered: from extending ship length by inserting 50 feet of parallel midbody (requiring an availability of more than 3.5 years), to options requiring no special scheduling but incrementally providing for service life extension. The CNO approved the SLEP concept in March 1976 and provided the following guidelines:

1. The fleet modernization program and SLEP will be integrated to require no more than 24 months for CV-SLEP.
2. A carrier will enter SLEP every two years starting in 1980.
3. There will be no ships-force work; the ship is to be manned at minimum levels for training requirements and for conducting the shipboard test program.
4. Funding will be provided in the Shipbuilding and Conversion, Navy appropriation, with advance planning funded in research and development.

Based on the analysis and assessment of carrier deck professionals, such as Captain Francis L. Gerow, USN, Robert Christiansen, Marsh Hendrickson, and Larry Guzik, NavSea concluded that achieving the SLEP objective in a single yard-availability of only 24 months would not be attainable under the CNO's constraints. Accordingly, an alternative program of 28 months was recommended. The plan was presented to Congress in August 1976 and given final Naval approval by the CNO Executive Board in March 1977.

SLEP Implementation

The *Saratoga* (CV-60) was selected to be the first carrier to undergo SLEP. Philadelphia Naval Shipyard was announced as the SLEP site. As conceived, the CV-SLEP would provide about one-half the service life of a new construction carrier at about one-fourth the cost. Captain Raymond Pierce was selected to head the Philadelphia Naval Shipyard during the build-up and preparation phase. This immense task involved more than doubling the work force; conducting necessary training; and developing production, planning, and control systems to cope with the effort. The shipyard had to be ready for the complex task of repair and modern-ization of an aircraft carrier when the ship ar-rived. The public visibility of such a large pro-gram, coupled with sensitivity of the politico-economic relationships, resulted in the involve-ment of the White House and Congress. The combined efforts of numerous people in the highly visible program led to many planning, production, and control improvements in execut-ing an industrial package of 1.5 million man-days for each carrier. The CV-SLEP became a proven, cost-effective supplement to new construction.

Small Aircraft Carrier Concept Explored

The realization had grown by the early 1970s that the *Midway* class, the first post-World War II carrier, would soon be 30 years old and due for replacement, and that, in addition, the *Forrestal* class, the first supercarrier, would also be approaching replacement age by the early 1980s. The advent of the vertical short take-off and landing (VSTOL) aircraft (which had the potential to facilitate significant reduction in carrier size), caused anticipation and interest in smaller aircraft carriers to grow markedly. With nuclear supercarriers costing over a billion dol-lars, both Congress and the Executive Branch were interested in a less expensive approach. In this environment, several administrations during this period endorsed and directed efforts toward designing and building a smaller type of carrier. The concept became known as the CVV. Naval authority in favor of the medium carrier began with Admiral Elmo Zumwalt, a CNO strongly in favor of a reverse of the ominous slide in naval strength, and a reduction in the unit-costs of ships to provide for increased numbers. The CNO had support in the highest levels of govern-ment. Nevertheless, the large carrier ultimately remained the winner due to a combination of reasons.

As confirmed by such review boards as Rear Admiral Forrest Petersen's Ad-Hoc Committee, considerations such as aircraft payload, weights, and volumes, dictated deck weights and magazine and elevator sizes that simply would not fit into smaller carrier design. Other factors, such as congressional pressure and our Navy's experience with carrier operating requirements in the Arabian Sea and Indian Ocean, led to the conclusion that the CVV was not a viable con-cept for the U.S. Navy's missions.

Nuclear-Powered Supercarriers

The strengths of a nuclear-powered aircraft carrier, and the weaknesses of a conventionally powered ship of the same size and air strength became painfully obvious during the energy crisis of the early 1970s. The political unrest in the Middle East and the requirement of maintain-ing a presence in the Indian Ocean made this even more clear.

The *Nimitz* Building Program

The construction period of a ship as large and complex as the *Nimitz* was approximately 7 years. The USS *Nimitz* [CV(N)-68], designed by the Navy and built by Newport News Shipbuild-ing, was delivered on 11 April 1975. Tens of thousands of people were involved in her crea-tion. During a portion of the time of this great ship's construction, Newport News Shipbuilding employed more than 30,000 people. The collec-tive talents of people in NavSea, Naval Ships Engineering Center (NavSec), SupShip Newport News Shipbuilding (NNS), the shipbuilder, and thousands of contractors made this project a success.

The *Nimitz*-Class

The *Nimitz* design consisted of two reactor plants and represented a dramatic increase in reactor power, ordnance, and aviation fuel over prior carrier designs. The F-14, the most ad-vanced fighter aircraft, was made a part of the carrier air group, with ship support facilities incorporated prior to ship delivery. The *Nimitz*-class carriers were huge ships, over 1,000 feet in length, 134 feet at the beam, and displacing over 90,000 tons. Although they were not the world's largest ships (some supertankers displaced over

400,000 tons), they were beyond doubt the most formidable warships.

The *Nimitz* class' large size permitted operation of an air wing with a four-dimensional target capability. Action could be taken against air, land, surface, and subsurface adversaries. The ship could operate the entire range of tactical aircraft, both conventional and VSTOL. The *Nimitz* design provided enormous operational safety and flexibility in high seas by having a large and stable deck.

Of course, the *Nimitz*-class nuclear carrier was expensive and time-consuming to build and to maintain, but the judgements of its influential advocates, including Admiral Hyman Rickover, were respected. The capability, adaptability, and flexibility for projecting air power and weight of ordnance made a convincing case that one supercarrier might be less expensive than several small ones. To project the same power, it would have taken several smaller carriers, at unit-costs not much cheaper than a supercarrier. (Subsequent British experience in the Falklands seemed to bear out this premise.) The result was that all future carriers for the forseeable future were to continue essentially as duplicates of the 1960s-designed *Nimitz* class.

SHIPBUILDING PRODUCTIVITY IMPROVEMENTS

Foreign Mercantile Techniques

A 1980 study of merchant ship construction sponsored by the Maritime Administration concluded that: "Productivity in the best Japanese and Scandinavian yards is of the order of 100 percent better than in good U.S. or U.K. shipyards. Thus, whereas a typical U.S. yard might be able to produce four medium ships per year, it can be shown that a good foreign yard could produce of the order of eight ships per year with a labor force the size of the U.S. yards."

There has not been any lack of study of these shortfalls. Various studies in the early 1970s supported the productivity differences and confirmed the values, with some qualifications. Foreign yards achieved a 35-40 percent improvement in productivity by using a better layout of facilities and techniques and a 30-35 percent improvement by introducing better systems and a more effective work force.

Comparative Naval Building Productivity

While United States merchant ship construction productivity compared with foreign has been studied extensively, studies comparing construction productivity of Navy ships is sparse or nonexistent. Limited information appears to support the conclusion that no major differences exist. The best foreign productivity rates were achieved on multiple, almost identical type merchant ship production. It may be safe to assume that the low volume and complexity of military ships kept the productivity gap narrow in this area.

Productivity Enhancement

The end of World War II certainly found American shipbuilding industrial capacity at its greatest. Between 1945 and 1970, American shipbuilders did little to improve their technical capability to produce ships. Most yards, by 1970, had abandoned all pretense of carrying on research and development to improve productivity. The yards remaining in 1970 were trying to survive. The health of the American shipbuilding industry received national attention with the passage of the Merchant Marine Act of 1970. The act authorized MarAd to collaborate with the shipbuilding industry to improve shipbuilding in the United States.

Merchant Shipyards
Improved to Offset the Decline

The 1970s brought forth substantial improvements in American shipyards' capabilities with the investment of 2.0 billion dollars to upgrade facilities. This upgrading of facilities, in some cases, included the transfer of foreign technology to the American shipyards. Under MarAd sponsorship, some American shipyards adopted Japanese production techniques. Improvements occurred in various areas: workflow, computer-aided design (CAD) and computer-aided manufacture (CAM), quality of engineering and management personnel, capital formation, government contracting, quality assurance, and employee safety and health. The American shipbuilding industry did not completely recover in the period of 1973-80, but progress was made.

OTHER NAVY BUILDING PROGRAMS

In addition to the submarines and aircraft carriers, there were other significant ship construction milestones accomplished during this period. The following sections highlight concurrent ship design and construction efforts.

The FFG-7 Class[1]

Faced with an aging fleet of World War II destroyers, Admiral Elmo Zumwalt, CNO, embarked on a program to build a large number of "lo mix" ships to replace them. These were to have a guided missile launcher and some anti-submarine warfare (ASW) capability.

The overriding design philosophy was that the Patrol Frigate (PF), as it was then called, be a relatively austere ship using state-of-the-art technology and off-the-shelf equipment. Ship manning was to be kept to the absolute minimum, utilizing automation and off-shore maintenance and repair.

The overriding design constraint was acquisition cost, which, for the purpose of controlling the design, was converted to a list of payload items and a ship displacement constraint during the Concept Exploration Phase of the design.

The *Oliver Hazard Perry* (FFG-7)-class frigates resulted from the PF and were the first ships to be built to the "fly before buy" concept. Developed in the early 1970s, the concept was to produce a tested lead ship and the second one of the class; there was ample time to factor learning into the follow-on ships.

In addition, the plan included a deliberate effort to design a ship that could be built by any destroyer-capable shipyard in the United States. Participants in the original design included the Naval Ship Engineering Center, Bath Iron Works, Gibbs and Cox, and Todd Shipbuilding Corporation. The Todd-Seattle yard had very different capabilities than the Bath yard in Maine. If yards with wide variations in capabilities, facilities, and capacities could build the FFG, then almost any yard could compete. History now shows that the approach was correct, with several yards successfully participating in the FFG construction program.

The FFG Construction Program

The lead ship, *Oliver Hazard Perry*, was awarded in October 1973 to Bath Iron Works. Captain Edward J. Otth was the Ship Acquisition Project Manager, and Anthony D. Ditrapani his deputy. This program, in addition to initiating the "fly before buy" concept, was also the Navy's first "design to cost" ship program. "Fly before buy" was a misnomer in many ways. If the Navy truly built a ship and tested her completely before contracting for the subsequent ships in the class, the transpired time would have made their technological gap so large as to render them obsolete immediately. In shipbuilding, the gestation period is extremely long. Experience has shown that it takes four years to build an FFG-7 class ship, from signing the contract to delivering the ship. The post-shakedown period following delivery takes almost another year. The Navy could not wait that long before awarding follow-on ship contracts.

The lead ship of this class was delivered on 17 December 1977, and the first Todd-Seattle ship was delivered in February 1980. The entire program was well managed by men like Captain Edward J. Otth and Rear Admiral James Lisanby. As always, Bath Iron Works was a dedicated and capable shipbuilder. James Harvie, the patrol frigate (PF-109) class project manager of Bath Iron Works, represented the shipbuilder, and served the fellow shipyards, too. Other important figures in the program were Robert H. Link, director of procurement, planning, and production; Commander Thomas J. Miklos, director of integrated logistic support; and Captain Charles L. Mull, technical director. Captain John D. Beecher succeeded Captain Otth as program manager. Commander R. Bruce Woodruff was trials officer and hull technical director during most of the trial of the class. Supporting the program managers was the early design effort of the Naval Ships Engineering Center (NavSec). Following the abrogation of early design responsibility in the cases of the *Spruance* (DD-963)-class destroyer and the Amphibious Assault Carriers (LHAs), the Navy reasserted its historic role in the design process. Captain John E. Rasmussen, USN, displayed a strong role in this successful transition.

Amphibious Assault Ship (LHA)

The commissioning of the USS *Tarawa* (LHA-1) in May 1976 and her exceptional operational evaluation constituted a large step in development of a modern amphibious capability for the United States. Moreover, her conception, design, construction, and delivery incorporated a major change in shipbuilding. This class was truly a worthy creation of the American shipbuilding industry. The *Tarawa* had an 820-foot-long flight deck, 106-foot beam, and displaced almost 20,000 tons, fully loaded. When compared to earlier amphibious designs, such as the LPH, the *Tarawa* was a major advance in operational capability. Her flight deck had a 41 percent capacity increase over that of the LPH design, and the 265-foot-long hangar deck could accommodate thirty CH-46 helicopters. The flight deck was also capable of handling VSTOL aircraft. The LHA helicopter carrier incorporated an LSD-type well deck for landing craft and considerable cargo capacity. She could squeeze through the Panama Canal, and, at a top speed of more than 20 knots, could deploy rapidly to nearly any place in the world. The two boilers that drove the steam turbines were the largest in any U.S. Navy ship. Each boiler could provide two-thirds of the steam required for the operation of the ship.

Surface Effect Ships (SES)

There was excitement about the potential of ships riding on a cushion of air.[2] After more than 50 years of only trivial increases in the speed of ships, a tripling or even quadrupling of the maximum speed was within the U.S. Navy's grasp. Two testcraft, the SES 100A built by Aerojet General Corporation, and the SES 100B built by Bell Aerospace Company, were products of the early 1970s. While expectations of this period (i.e., for large ships capable of speeds up to 200 knots) ran high and included projections of building SES aircraft carriers, the craft grossed at approximately 100 tons and were comparatively small. They were capable, however, of speeds in excess of 80 knots.

The experiments showed that major reorientation of thinking about research and development (R&D) costs for ships was needed. For example, R&D costs for airplanes, which are orders of magnitude greater than the total cost of a single airplane, were widely accepted. Ships, however, have R&D costs that are only a fraction of the cost of one ship. Because the seemingly high cost of designing the SES carriers was new to ship designers, the dollars for R&D were not allocated, and therefore, the potential of surface effect ships has been scarcely realized.

DD-963 *Spruance*-Class Destroyers

This program was initiated in the mid-1960s as a DD/DDG development, wherein a common hull and power plant design could be utilized with either general purpose or anti-aircraft warfare combat system configurations. The *Spruance* class procurement plan committed the U.S. Navy to design and build thirty identical ships.

The ship was a large destroyer of the following dimensions:

> Length: 563 ft., 4 in.
> Beam: 55 ft.
> Draft: 29 ft.   Amidships: 19 ft.
> Displacement: 7,800 tons

The ship was powered by four General Electric LM-2500 marine gas-turbine engines rated at 20,500 horsepower each. The engines were arranged so that two drove each of the two shafts through a conventional double-reduction gear, with reversing provided through controllable reversible-pitch propellers. The hull form was characterized by a large bulbous bow housing the sonar transducer. The maximum draft at the bow was approximately 10 feet greater than amidships.

The contract to build these ships was awarded in June 1972 to Ingalls Shipbuilding Corp. The design and construction of these destroyers was accomplished at the Pascagoula, Mississippi, facility. The basic concept utilized a modularized system, wherein, as far as possible, functional entities were completely contained within a set volume or "module." The West Bank yard, which was built on an assembly line concept, was a naval engineer's delight. Managing this modern shipyard was Ned J. Marandino, President, assisted by John Serrie, Vice President of Production.

The early years of this construction program resulted in a spectacular growth at the new facility. Creating a shipyard on the Mississippi Gulf

Coast of the size required to construct thirty large destroyers was a tremendous challenge.

Geographically dispersed construction facilities brought the modules and sections together in a logical sequence from both an engineering and shipbuilding perspective. Ease of fabrication and access, coupled with optimization of the construction process, were the achievements of this program.

The yard had well learned how to build *Spruance* destroyers and had become proficient, but, unfortunately, with the completion of that program and the LHA program, there was little to keep the yard fully utilized and Ingalls was not awarded sufficient government contracts for future years. As a result, the Ingalls rolls dropped precipitously in 1979 and 1980. The yard work force had grown to nearly 20,000 people and then had to be reduced to about 5,000. It was during this turbulent period that Leonard Erb replaced Marandino as president. It was truly an unfortunate event that the Ingalls work load had to lapse after the yard had reached such a high level of efficiency in shipbuilding.

Ship Maintenance

Up to this point, the principal focus in this chapter has been on the construction of ships for the U.S. Navy and some merchant ship construction. There is, of course, another world of naval engineering: maintenance. Ships operate in a very difficult environment; they are exposed to hostile elements and operate continuously for long periods of time.

Submarine Force Origins of the Overhaul Work Package (OWP)

Just as the new construction environment was one of cutbacks or of achieving economies, similar pressures existed in ship maintenance. Others in the U.S. Navy frequently accused the submarine force of being bloated with money and of solving any problem by pouring money on it. The fact is that the submarine maintenance people conceived many of the innovations that improved overall Navy maintenance, with resulting economies. Such was the case in the early 1970s. This was the era of refining the overhaul work package (OWP) as a management tool for

the planning of ship overhauls. Lieutenant Commander Victor Peters, a career Naval officer, was the "father" of the OWP and had authorized the first one in the early 1970s. The OWP was a major step forward in overhaul planning. Previously, the engineering officer of each ship entering the overhaul would submit a stack of repair requests to be accomplished for each work-item he felt appropriate. Because the engineering officer was rotated often, perhaps every two years, he did not have the benefit of the repair history of his ship. The OWP changed that to include a data bank of history of repairs, not only to that ship, but to others of its class. In addition, it utilized the input of many people, combining the knowledge of Planning, Engineering, Repair and Alterations for Submarines [PERA (SS1)]; NavSea; and the Commander, Submarine Forces, U.S. Atlantic Fleet (ComSubLant) Material Staff. The OWP for each submarine was initially designed by reviewing each boat's Current Maintenance Project (CSMP), a compendium of all repairs that might be required, and the list of applicable, but unaccomplished alterations for that boat.

The OWP provided for a consistent approach to overhauls. Equally important, it shifted much of the administrative burden for overhaul planning from the submarine's engineer and crew to support staffs ashore. The concept is now in use for all types of U.S. Navy ships and provides the formal structured approach to maintenance.

Overhaul Cycles

In 1973, the issue of extending operating cycles was very topical. Prior to this time, much of the submarine force had operated on a 4-year overhaul cycle. There was pressure from the fleet then, as there is now, to operate more and overhaul less. Captain Kenneth Fox, Assistant Chief of Staff (Code N40) of ComSubLant, had negotiated a "22 and 2" concept for the nuclear submarines (SSNs). Under this concept, a submarine would operate for 22 months following "post-shakedown availability" (PSA) overhaul, and then enter a 2-month restricted availability (RAV), which would include an interim dry docking. The cycle would then be repeated, 22 more operating months, another 2-month RAV, followed by the final 22-month operating period before entering overhaul. This concept would result in a 70-month period between overhauls. This represented a major departure from the past practice of sending a submarine into overhaul every 48 months. It made maintenance more efficient and economical and increased the operating time for the submarines between overhauls.

Extended Refit Program

In the nuclear ballistic missile force, similar influences were at work. In 1970, when the USS *Madison* (SSBN-627) completed overhaul and conversion to the first Poseidon-missile-capable submarine, Rear Admiral Robert L. J. Long started a monitoring program expressly to determine how to extend the operating periods for SSBN submarines. The Submarine Maintenance Monitoring and Support Office (SMMSO) was established within the Naval Ships Engineering Center (NavSec) for this purpose. At that time, the *Madison* and some of her sister submarines had been equipped with a new reactor core, which was predicted to have a 9-year life. Therefore, there was pressure to keep the boats out of the shipyards for the life of the core. As something of a parallel to the SSN "22 and 2" concept, the "extended refit program" (ERP) was devised to have the SSBN operate on normal refit cycles for 4 years following overhaul completion. The submarine would then receive an "extended refit" of 60 days in lieu of the normal 28, and then the cycle would be repeated. Following the second ERP, the submarine would operate until the end of useful core life and then enter the shipyard for overhaul and refueling.

Today, all of this may appear a little mundane, but in 1973 the issue was hotly debated. There was discussion as to where the ERPs should be conducted: in the shipyards or in the submarine bases. The major difference was that at a shipyard, weapons had to be off-loaded before entering and on-loaded on departure. All this, of course, added to the "off-line" time for the submarine. Accordingly, there was a strong lobby for taking the shipyard to the submarines at their bases simply to eliminate the off-load/on-load overhead. The lobby prevailed.

Floating Dry Dock Refurbishment

One of the first questions in preparing for the ERPs was whether the existing dry dock in Holy Loch could support the 45-day dry docking. One purpose of the ERP was to do maintenance that could not be done during a regular refit due to time constraints. Therefore, there were two issues related to the dry dock. The first dealt with basic safety. What was the construction of the structure? Could it safely support a nuclear submarine for 45 days while that submarine underwent major maintenance? Clearly an in depth material inspection was in order.

A fiscal year 1973 planned overhaul of the floating dry dock had been canceled. Pressure on the budget was a major factor in this decision; however, it was also argued by the squadron commander that the intermediate maintenance activity (IMA) was capable of maintaining the dock and there was no real need to send it off to a shipyard for refurbishment. This decision, in light of the subsequent decision to proceed with the ERPs, made the safety question seem even more pertinent.

The second issue related to the dry dock was whether it could support the more than 200 shipyard workers that would be deployed to help execute the ERP. Were the available services adequate? Was the power available compatible with the shipyard's welding machines? Was there adequate compressed air, staging material, weight-lifting capability, power-generating equipment, and salt-water cooling?

Electric Boat was designated to do the ERP work, so they were told to hold an INSURV-like inspection of the dry dock. This inspection was to answer two specific questions: Was the dock sound enough for 45-day dry dockings, and could it support the required industrial work force?

In correspondence in 1986 with the author, Frederick Richmond reported that in the process of tasking Electric Boat, he (then Commander Richmond) talked to an individual in the Office of Chief of Naval Operations (OpNav) who was trying to obtain funding for a new floating dry dock to support the SSN-688 program. The CNO officer's comment was, "You must be careful not to spend too much on those dry docks because some day you will have a 45-year-old dry dock on your hands." Richmond asked himself, "Why was a 45 year-old dry dock bad? Was it not already 35 years old and still in usable condition? Was it not simply a steel tank with machinery to dewater the tank and other machinery for 'hotel' services? If the tank was structurally sound, its age was meaningless. The machinery would age, but it could be replaced or otherwise modernized." There was no problem with a 45-year-old dock as long as it was in good condition. As it turned out, there must have been other people with the same thoughts because today, the dock at Holy Loch is 45 years old and there are no plans to replace it in the near future.

The results of the Electric Boat dry dock inspection were revealing. The major finding was that the 36-inch dewatering pipe, which was required to be 0.375 inch thick, was in certain places less than 0.0625 inch. The basic concerns for safety were well founded. Based on these findings, the dock was repaired and upgraded to provide all necessary support for the ERPs. Unfortunately, the bill exceeded the projected cost of the canceled overhaul by over a factor of two. Nevertheless, the first ERP and all subsequent availabilities were completed successfully and countless dollars and valuable submarine operating time have been saved.

Although Electric Boat performed the initial ERPs, it was soon determined that naval shipyards were more flexible to perform overseas availabilities. Also, the ERPs were disruptive to a stable Electric Boat workload stateside.

Naval Shipyard ERP

Charleston Naval Shipyard had proven its ability several years earlier with overseas submarine battery renewals in record times. In addition, the mission of the naval shipyards was much more closely allied with these ERPs. Gradually, Charleston and Portsmouth Naval Shipyards took over the responsibility of all SSBN maintenance ERPs for the SSBN maintenance program. These concepts, developed by the submarine maintenance people (i.e., a disciplined ship maintenance approach), extended

operating cycles and increased utilization of intermediate activities (IMAs).

IMAs were an intermediate level of organization, either ashore or afloat, with a specific maintenance responsibility for overhaul. [The lowest level of maintenance (organizational) was performed by the ships' crews; the highest level of maintenance (depot-level) was major repair work performed by public or private shipyards.] IMAs were manned by military personnel and usually had lesser capability for major repairs than depot-level facilities. The increased use of IMAs was practical because the facilities and personnel were already in place and worked directly for the submarine commanders. They were also much less expensive than depot-level maintenance activities.

The largest contributors to ship maintenance were, of course, the shipyards that performed depot-level repairs. There were eight naval shipyards employing approximately 75,000 people. In addition, there were ship repair facilities both in the United States and overseas, such as on Guam, at Subic Bay, P.I., and at Yokosuka, Japan, as well as numerous private yards performing maintenance. The spectrum in the private area ranged from a yard as large as Newport News Shipbuilding (approximately 30,000 people) to small activities possessing a limited master ship repair (MSR) contract employing a handful of people.

Repair Ship Activity

IMAs, afloat or ashore, perform a vital service for the ships they repair and maintain. To give an insight into the workings of a repair department on such a ship, the following account was relayed by Frederick Richmond to the author, in correspondences cited earlier, as he remembered his days as repair officer on a submarine tender:

> I remember the day I checked aboard. Everyone I met, including the commanding officer, executive officer and squadron commander told me the same thing, 'Do something about Shop 38; those guys can't do anything right.' (Shop 38 is the outside machine shop on a tender.) I found my way to the Shop, where a single member of the duty section was reading a paperback. I introduced myself, looked around, and asked this young sailor where

the tool crib was. He walked over to the workbench and pulled open a drawer half full of broken screwdrivers, 19/32 wrenches, and a couple of hammers with sawed off handles. 'This is it,' he said. I asked him how Shop 38 did any work with these tools. He replied that, when sent out on a submarine to 'fix something,' they had to borrow ship tools. If this was not possible, they could not do the work!

It was not hard to figure out what was wrong with Shop 38! The next day, I instructed the division officer to start building a tool crib and to purchase any tools required to do the job. Two years later, I was normally transferred, after the ship had won the 'E' for having the best repair department in the Atlantic Fleet. Shop 38 had a fully outfitted tool crib with the correct tools needed for any job the shop might do as they were carefully guarded by the shop members, especially by those who could remember how it was before the crib existed.

OTHER GOVERNMENT SHIPBUILDING

At this writing, the Coast Guard is in the process of acquiring a fleet of thirteen 270-foot medium-endurance cutters. The first flight of four cutters has been completed by Tacoma Boatbuilding Company, and the cutters have been in service since 1984. The second flight of nine cutters was awarded to Robert E. Derecktor of Rhode Island, a new shipyard located at the former site of the Navy destroyer piers at Newport. Several cutters of the second class have been delivered to the Coast Guard, and the last is expected in 1989.

The 270-foot cutter's armament reflects the close cooperation that exists between the Navy and the Coast Guard. In addition to one Mk 75 76-mm dual purpose gun and Mk 92 fire control system, the class has either installed, or has provisions to install, a towed array sonar, SLQ-32 electronic countermeasure system, Mk 36 RBOC, Phalanx, Harpoon, and LAMPS-1. This armament is funded by the Navy and would be required by the Coast Guard to perform its wartime responsibilities as part of the Navy.

To reduce the manning requirements of the 270-foot cutters to a minimum, the Coast Guard developed a Command, Display, and Control (COMDAC) System that has the capacity to automate bridge, navigation, and communications functions. Through the use of digitized charts, an optical sight, and radar inputs, navigational functions, including collision avoidance, have been simplified.

The Coast Guard also bought a new class of 110-foot patrol boats, the *Island* class. When Vice President George Bush directed that the level of operations against drug traffic be increased, the Coast Guard decided to request bids for an existing design in the expectation that this would speed up the delivery of the boats. Marine Power and Equipment won the contract, but it was challenged by Bollinger Machine Shop and Shipyard Company because the engine proposed was not identical to that in the parent. Bollinger won the contract after the court redirected the re-evaluation of proposals. The winning design was the Vosper-Thornycroft 110-foot boat powered by two Paxman Valenta 16-cylinder 4,000-horsepower engines derated to 3,000 horsepower to match the torque limitation of the propeller shafts. (The engines had been up-rated as initially specified for the design.) Bollinger is the licensee for U.S. production of this design, and Vosper engineers assisted in establishing the production. Initial reports stated that the hull plating forward needed additional stiffening for service in the Caribbean, and a second fleet of boats currently under construction have been strengthened to overcome this problem. Although the boat's performance is generally satisfactory, the hull strength problems, coupled with potential logistical support difficulties of a projected 40-year-old engine, make off-the-shelf procurements of boats for demanding Coast Guard use an open issue. The design of these patrol boats has been the subject of an article in the *Naval Institute Proceedings*, February 1986, and two papers delivered at the ASNE/Coast Guard Patrol Boat Symposium.

The Coast Guard has completed the contract for a replacement polar icebreaker. Although funds have not yet been appropriated for construction, they are expected at a later time, particularly since the icebreakers *Northwind* and *Westwind* have recently been decommissioned.

The Army Corps of Engineers built a replacement for the dredge *Essayons* at Bath Iron Works on subcontract at Sun Shipbuilding. The ship is a diesel-propelled hopper dredge with extensive automation. Side dragarm suction dredges contain 1,080-kilowatt electric motor-driven dredge pumps. The design began on 1 July 1976 and was completed 1 June 1979. The ship was delivered in 1983.

Research and Development

Firefighting Experience

Fires aboard the USS *Forrestal* in 1967, the USS *Oriskany* in 1967, and the USS *Enterprise* in 1969 highlighted the inadequacy of fire protection on the flight and hangar decks of aircraft carriers and the need for individual escape devices for crewmembers in smoke environments. As a result, great improvements were made in shipboard fire protection in a relatively short period of time.

The collision of the USS *Belknap* (CG-26) with the carrier USS *Kennedy* in 1975 and its resultant fires focused further attention on deficiencies in shipboard firefighting equipment and escape devices. USS *Belknap*'s fire was the most devastating shipboard fire of this period. Although the masts and some of *Belknap*'s aluminum superstructure were sheared off by the overhang of *Kennedy*'s angle deck sponson, much of the damage to the superstructure resulted from the melting of the aluminum structure above the steel 01-deck level during the collision. The fire was fed by JP-5 fuel from the *Kennedy*'s sheared flight-deck fuel-risers. These fire disasters generated R&D efforts and provided the impetus for increased funding.[3]

Prior to the *Belknap-Kennedy* incident, survival support devices were developed to permit escape from smoke-filled compartments. Flight deck washdown systems, which were originally installed on carriers to wash down chemical or biological-attack contamination, were converted to an aqueous film forming foam (AFFF) dispensing system. Owing to the self-sealing foam blanket it formed, which had its origin in a high surface tension, this foam was much more effective in suppressing fires than the previously used protein foam. A greater number of water and foam monitors, which streamed AFFF at great distances and with great force, were installed on flight and hangar decks. New vehicles that were equipped with twin-agent systems and could close burning aircraft in seconds were developed

for the flight deck. Twin-agent hose lines mounted on reels were installed in the machinery spaces of all ships, allowing the firefighter the choice of a Purple K powder nozzle (especially for use against oil-spray fires) or the AFFF nozzle for use against all other fires.

The Advent of HALON

A fluorocarbon gas of the Freon family, specifically bromotrifluoromethane, or Freon 1300, had been commercially developed at the beginning of the 1970s, and primarily used for the protection of computer spaces in its earliest applications. It could be discharged in an essentially sealed compartment and at a concentration of a few percent, and could suppress the hottest burning fires, even the oil-spray fires on ships. Human beings could function without harm in that concentration; although some of the products of the suppressive reaction of HALON with the fire were toxic, they added little more toxicity than the products of combustion from the fire itself. Although the HALON did not bring 'cool down' and was, therefore, less effective against a deep-seated fire, it was nevertheless useful in that case if it were applied in time to preclude the fire's growth and the sources of reflash.

The Survival Support Device

An example of how naval engineers can improvise when they have to was seen in the development of the Survival Support Device (SSD). Although NavSec had been working for some years on developing a 10-minute emergency escape breathing device (EEBD), employing the same principle as the oxygen breathing apparatus (OBA) (i.e., a demand process potassium hydroxide oxygen generator), the cumbersome mechanics of putting it on, plus concern for the possible explosive reaction of the chemicals in oily water when a crewman wore it on his chest, caused the Navy to look at the compressed gas reservoir concept. The Lear-Siegler Corporation, experienced with high-pressure aviation life-support systems, offered an intriguing idea: oxygen-enriched air would be stored in tightly would steel coils and when released by a toggle would flow into a transparent plastic hood and provide at least 8 minutes of breathable mixture. Captain John Iarrabino, USN, who had been commanding officer of the *Oriskany* during her awful fire off Vietnam, with many lives lost due to smoke inhalation, picked up on this concept and pressed for its rapid development and production. Unfortunately, although there was enthusiasm for this approach, there was no budget authorization for such a device. Nevertheless, Admiral Isaac B. Kidd, USN, then CNM, directed that the Naval Material Command push this device into production as a matter of life-saving urgency.

There were still problems to solve, especially involving the containment of high-pressure gas and then the effect of carbon dioxide build-up in the hoods. Admiral Kidd assigned a newly arrived CNM staff officer, Captain Richard B. Jacobs, USN, the responsibility of riding herd on the new device's development. Rear Admiral Nathan Sonenshein, USN, then ComNavShips, arranged, via Rear Admiral Frank C. Jones, USN, ComNavSec, for Captain James L. McVoy, USN, to be assigned technical coordinator with NavSea and to work closely in support of Captain Jacobs. These two officers decided very early that oxygen enrichment should be dropped and plain compressed air used, because of its intrinsic safety. The use of air, however, made liaison between the Material Command and the Bureau of Medicine (BuMed) important; the questions of carbon dioxide build-up in the final minutes or so of the device's use had no precedent nor other immediate answers, in spite of extensive data from diving and SCUBA (Self-contained Underwater Breathing Device Apparatus) medicine. Then Lieutenant Commander Richard Daster, one of BuMed's health physicists, made himself constantly available to assist in resolving the physiological problems. Once the medical go-ahead was given for an 8-minute flow, the SSD was placed in production. Over 300,000 units were ordered, the bulk destined to go aboard aircraft carriers for the entire ship's company. When the first units rolled off the production line, they were found to be leaking-off after being charged at 7,500 psi. There was consternation among all parties involved. A rush meeting was held in the Pentagon and gloomy looks were exchanged between the Navy's officers and the Lear-Siegler representatives. The attitude of the OpNav officers who made up the plan for distri-

bution of the one-third million units to the fleet was, "You Material Command guys cooked up this program, so, what are you going to do now?" Captains Jacobs and McVoy had, by this time, come to know the Lear-Siegler project engineer well and recognized him to be a highly competent engineer. They opted in their own minds to show confidence in him and announced to the group that, "We should not lose our heads, but give Dave Shonerd a chance." He was given that chance and quickly resolved the problems. The SSDs made their way into the Fleet and, within a year, cases were reported to the Navy Safety Center of lives being saved by the device. Problems remained in the way of some units leaking-off and an initial unreliability of the air recharging machines, but these were resolved for the most part. The introduction of this survival device bought time for a parallel R&D program to be pursued in a more methodical manner. The result was a new Escape Breathing Device (EBD) based on the generation of oxygen by a chlorate candle. This EBD is now aboard all ships of the Fleet. Such individual devices have caught on in other navies, in airlines, and in hotels.

In fact, most developments in shipboard fire protection pioneered by the U.S. Navy expanded to other industries. AFFF became commonplace at all American commercial and military airports. Purple K powder and AFFF twinned-agent units, large-scale HALON applications, and lightweight refractory felt were used to protect aluminum superstructures and were adopted for use commercially.

Metallurgy and Welding

A broad spectrum of metallurgical research addressing high-strength steels, titanium alloys, aluminum alloys, copper- and nickel-based alloys, and superalloys was conducted by the Navy in the latter half of the 1960s. A comprehensive program to evaluate HY-130 steel, including weld metal and heat-affected zone performance, stress-relief embrittlement, and low-cycle fatigue, was completed. An initiative to develop weldable steel systems in the range of 180- to 200-ksi (thousands of pounds per square inch) yield strength commenced, and the research focused on the stress corrosion cracking performance of high alloy maraging steels.

During this period, a key research area was the study of the stress corrosion performance of high-strength aluminum alloys to provide crack-resistant hydraulic system components. Alloy development and studies of the physical metallurgy of high-strength titanium alloys began. Fundamental phase equilibria, structural response, stress corrosion cracking, and nonlinear deformation development of high strength copper-nickel alloys for seawater piping and nickel-aluminum bronze castings for seawater systems were accomplished. Corrosion research included evaluation of the cathodic protection aluminum alloys, and corrosion performance of metals in the deep ocean environment. Due to increased interest in naval gas turbine drive, research in hot corrosion research was expanded to include development of corrosion-resistant alloys, mechanistic studies, and coatings.

In the early 1970s, the metallic materials research continued on steels, aluminum, titanium, and other systems, but focused on fewer alloys and more detailed characterization and fabrication of structural models. The HY-130 steel exploratory development program was completed, and the advanced development program intended to ready this steel system for certification was initiated. A broad series of tasks was performed to fully develop procedures for all fabrication processes, demonstrate welding procedures in full-scale fabrication models, and evaluate full-scale fatigue performance. Investigations of HY-100 steel plate and heavy-section forging performance were completed. Research for the selection of an optimum candidate for a 180-ksi yield strength steel system resulted in thorough investigations of HP 9-4-20 and 10-Ni dual-strength steels.

To focus on selection of an alloy system to meet U.S. Navy requirements for a weldable structural material, titanium research expanded to study a broader matrix of properties. Project Titanes, the design, construction, and nondestructive inspection of a high-strength titanium pressure hull for the Deep Submergence Research Vehicle *Alvin*, was accomplished. This successful alloy production and fabrication effort doubled the depth capability of this vehicle without increasing its weight. To provide for the design of high-performance ships (hydrofoils,

air cushion vehicles, and surface effect ships), exfoliation-resistant tempers for marine-grade aluminum alloys were developed, and a program to investigate welding, long-term corrosion performance, and fatigue properties was completed.

Gas-turbine materials research in this period addressed ceramics, sputtered metal coatings, and thermal barrier coatings. Corrosion research programs were initiated to study stray current phenomena, cathodic protection for SES and hydrofoil craft, and improvement of nickel-aluminum bronze corrosion performance. Other development programs included improved high-velocity corrosion resistance in copper-nickel piping alloys, improved properties of high-strength alloys in gaseous hydrogen, and titanium alloys for seawater pumps.

From 1975 to 1980, high-strength steels research focused largely on certification of HY-130 steel for warship construction. Major problems related to stress corrosion and fatigue performance of this alloy were solved. Welding consumables were developed and the full spectrum of welding processes necessary for large-scale construction were specified and validated in shipyards. Important steel welding research initiatives were directed at improved process efficiency. HY-80 flux cored electrodes were developed for cost reduction. Advanced high rate processes, including narrow gap welding, and electron beam, laser, and high frequency resistance welding, were successfully developed for component fabrication. Investigations into welding process control and automation were conducted, leading to major shipyard innovations and opportunities to reduce costs.

A major initiative in high-strength titanium alloy characterization was undertaken that included evaluation of fatigue, fatigue crack growth, creep, stress corrosion cracking, and dynamic structural performance of plate, weldments, and other high-strength alloy product forms. Extensive work resulted in the development of all position gas metal arc welding and repair procedures for titanium alloys. A modification of DSV *SeaCliff* was undertaken at this time, using a titanium pressure hull and auxiliary components to achieve 20,000-foot depth capability with this submersible and recovery vehicle.

In response to service failures, sulfide-induced

corrosion and corrosion control for copper-nickel alloys were investigated. Accelerated hull corrosion-control techniques, shaft seal materials, and inspection procedures for de-alloying were developed during this period. Extended-life cathodic protection systems were successfully developed and implemented. Test procedures were developed to duplicate and model low-temperature marine gas-turbine corrosion, leading to evaluation of precious-metal aluminide coatings to extend service life between overhauls. Major new initiatives in dynamic fracture mechanics and elastic plastic fracture mechanics were initiated, and proved to provide effective methodologies for assessment of structural integrity. Late in this period, the High-Strength, Low-Alloy steel development program was initiated, and by 1980, had identified promising alloys that were eventually certified for surface ship construction in the mid-1980s.

Structures

The structural design of the *Trident* submarine provided many challenges.[4] Meeting these challenges included developing analytical techniques and formulating guidelines for simplified design of the missile compartment, design of the reinforcement for the large opening access hatch, and the design of the sandwich holding bulkhead. The sandwich bulkhead, which permitted improved arrangements and a reduction of submarine length, and the large access hatch, necessary for improved logistics and increased time-on-station, are structural concepts that found initial use on *Trident*. The missile compartment structure was a major problem with the early *Polaris* boats, where the design was necessarily developed and refined, based on engineering judgement and subsequent experimental data from models and sea trials. For *Trident*, design and analysis methods were developed to arrive at an adequate baseline design without resorting to time-consuming and costly experimental programs. Design procedures were developed based on computer parametric studies using new analytical techniques and small scale-model tests. Tests of a single validation model demonstrated the adequacy of the initial design. In 1974, a large-scale verification model of the *Trident* missile compartment, including a logistic

hatch, was tested to collapse under hydrostatic pressure. The collapse of the model, as predicted, demonstrated the adequacy of the design. The use of these design analysis techniques in conjunction with validation models and deep submergence trials resulted in safe and efficient structures at reasonable cost.

Submarine structural efforts at the David Taylor Naval Ship Research and Development Center (now David Taylor Research Center) were not confined solely to the *Trident*, but also included the development and acceptance of promising configurations and structural concepts for future combatant submarines. A Ti-100 titanium hull was designed and certified for the manned spherical hull of the *Alvin*, a deep diving submersible. Complementary to the structure itself was the need for lightweight buoyancy material, critical in the design of modern deep-diving submersibles. New foam, along with other innovations, was used to modify the submersible *Seacliff* to increase its operating depth from 6,500 to 20,000 feet.

In response to a premature failure of the CRP on USS *Barbey* (FF-1088), a comprehensive laboratory and sea trial investigation on CRP propeller attachment design loads, stresses, and material applications was begun. CRP propellers are used on ships outfitted with single-rotation gas-turbine engines to provide these ships with a reversing capability. Results of the investigation raised serious questions concerning the adequacy of CRP propellers being installed on the lead ships of the USS *Spruance* (DD-963), USS *Oliver Hazard Perry* (FFG-7), and USS *Ticonderoga* (CG-47) classes. Engineering Change Proposals regarding the blade attachments, including blade fillet shapes, crank rings, blade bolts, and cover plates, were issued for these ship classes. The knowledge gained was applied in the evaluation of CRP propeller problems that became apparent on the USCG *Polar*-class icebreakers and the ships of the Royal Saudi Navy PCG-1 and PGG-511 classes.

In the early 1970s, a need existed to develop large-scale, life cycle experimental techniques for naval applications and to provide a validated technology base for aluminum-hulled, ocean-going ships. To achieve these goals, the Navy fabricated an all-aluminum ship model and began extensive large-scale evaluation of the ship's 85-foot structure. Tests were performed in 1978 to evaluate cyclic rates and to resolve software and hardware problems. The lessons learned from ASEM (Aluminum Ship Evaluation Model) showed that an integral aluminum superstructure with attachment details and an overall geometry like ASEM would be unreliable during a ship's lifetime. Fatigue cracking in the ASEM deckhouse proved to be formidable. On the other hand, the primary hull of ASEM behaved in a totally reliable way. Minor cracking was easily explained and properly corrected. The testing depicted a 20-year life for ASEM. Analytical methods validated through the ASEM effort, combined with the supporting data base, provided the Navy with the capability to properly design and analyze aluminum ship structures.

These few examples highlight the diversity of structural development during the 1970s.

Surface Ship Machinery

Machinery system development in the 1970s was influenced by many different objectives. The items on the list probably had not changed from that of previous decades—performance, energy efficiency, weight, size, cost, reliability, maintainability, and logistics burden, to name the more obvious ones. However, the emphasis on each varied, and was dependent on many factors.

Energy efficiency was elevated in importance after the 1973 OPEC oil embargo on the United States. The U.S. Navy responded by establishing R&D lines under the exploratory, advanced, and engineering development categories. One effort looked at the availability of distillate fuel worldwide for combustion in its gas-turbine ships. Ship mobility would be compromised if suitable fuel was not available. As the civilian population of the United States grappled with its gas shortage and became exposed to "gasahol," the U.S. Navy, in conjunction with the Department of Energy, developed, refined, and successfully tested at sea a distillate fuel derived from oil shale. Another facet of the energy conservation program looked at the efficiency level being achieved as oil was being consumed. This effort not only included the mechanical efficiency of different machinery items, but also looked at total systems, including the architecture of the

ship itself. Concepts for more energy-efficient propulsors, rudders, hull lines, and coatings were developed. Hull cleaning techniques were provided and implemented by the Fleet. Systems for both automated and semi-automated recording of shipboard energy consumption were developed to-assist the Fleet engineers in monitoring and achieving minimum fuel consumption under real-time performance requirements. Thus, the oil embargo sparked an exhaustive effort for improving the efficiency of the ship systems that carried over into the decade of the 1980s.[5]

A technology that again began to obtain serious U.S. Navy interest and support was the application of electrical machinery as the transmission in the main propulsion shaft lines. Flexibility in machinery arrangements and in system operation had long been recognized as an attribute of electric drive systems. The ease with which electric systems could be reconfigured with switch gear could enhance survivability. Cross connection at cruise power levels (e.g., one engine powering two shafts), together with speed ratio control, could additionally permit propulsion engines to be operated at favorable load and speed conditions, an important factor, since simple cycle gas turbines had poor part-power fuel economy. The other side of electric transmission systems were higher cost, lower transmission efficiency, and greater weight and volume compared with mechanical drives.[6]

Most notable of the electric drive efforts of the 1970s was the development and demonstration of superconductive excitation and liquid metal current collection in a direct current (dc) system at the David Taylor Research Center. With direct conductor liquid cooling, these technologies would provide dc motors and generators, which are smaller, more efficient, and easier to control than their alternating current (ac) counterparts. A 40,000-hp, 180-rpm conventional ac air-cooled motor was estimated to weigh 320,000 pounds with a diameter of 20 feet—its advanced dc electric motor was projected to be 80,000 pounds and 6.5 feet in diameter. A 300-kW acyclic dc system, consisting of a superconducting generator and motor, was demonstrated at the Annapolis Laboratory of DTRC. (Subsequently, the system was installed on the *Jupiter*

II, a 65-foot crew boat, and demonstrated at sea.) This effort set the stage for acquiring 3,000-kW components incorporating this new technology.[7]

In 1972, the Chief of Naval Operations directed that a study be conducted to investigate ways to reduce ship's bridge manning requirements. Based on results from the seventeen ships participating in the program, it was determined that a significant reduction in bridge manning could be achieved by consolidating and integrating communications and displays into a centralized work station and automating certain piloting, navigation, collision avoidance, and logging functions. The evaluation, which commenced on the USS *McCandless* (FF-1084) in January 1977, was designed to collect data in four general areas: manning, operational effectiveness, operational availability of the equipment in a Navy environment, and detailed design features required for possible follow-on efforts in bridge design. The at-sea evaluation of the Integrated Bridge System design demonstrated that bridge watch functions can be performed as effectively, or more effectively, with significantly fewer people. It was a step toward achieving what Vice Admiral Metcalf called for almost a decade later as "Revolution at Sea" and the challenge of a bridge no larger than the cockpit of a 747.[8]

The decade of the 1970s saw a broad range of machinery development efforts, illustrated by the preceding examples. It was a decade of diversity and challenge.

Pollution Abatement Program

The early 1970s, through legislation and government-developed standards, provided some real challenges to the Navy in the development of solutions to the environmental pollution problem. The Secretary of the Navy acknowledged that treating ship sewage was one of the greatest environmental problems facing the Navy. The Navy pursued several systems; biological, mechanical, electrical, and chemical treatment methods were considered for shipboard use. Paralleling these efforts, the Navy developed collection, holding, and transfer systems that retain wastes aboard for disposal to a barge or shore-based treatment system. During this era, the Navy was faced with limited shipboard storage capacity and inadequate shore-based facilities, but much progress was made toward being in compliance with the Environmental Protection Agency (EPA) standards. At every port where ships were stationed, the Navy initiated major efforts to abate shore pollution. Sewage disposal systems; collecting, holding, and transfer systems; and oily water separating systems became common terms with the operating forces, and especially with the ship maintenance personnel. Extensive ship alteration programs for pollution abatement were developed and implemented.

Oil Spill Abatement

Oil spills and discharges have plagued the nation's water for years, contaminating shorelines and beaches, coating floating structures and watercraft, and causing taste and odor problems in municipal water supplies. Since human error accounts for 90 percent of oil discharges, preventive measures are vital to any oil pollution abatement program. Much effort has been expended to upgrade the methods for fuel transfer to minimize the casualties. When a spill does occur, every effort must be made to contain oil at its source. Considerable progress was made in the development of quick-response clean systems. These included standby equipment, trained response teams that were always on call, and skimming and containment equipment. The effectiveness of these systems was greatly enhanced during this period.

NAVY ENGINEERING LEADERSHIP

Admiral Rickover's Outlook

Returning now to shipbuilding and the Navy's leadership, it is interesting to reflect on the viewpoint of the Navy's most influential leader in the post-war era. In 1974, Admiral Hyman Rickover, in a speech to a society of former special agents of the FBI, addressed the role of engineering in the Navy. He focused on engineering as it dealt with warship design, construction, and operation. His speech was an indictment of the system that was instituted during the Kennedy-Johnson Administration by Robert McNamara. Admiral Rickover's assessment was that the proven system that resulted in great success during World War II had been completely and foolishly scrapped. Formerly, in-house technical specialists had been in charge of all aspects of ship design, construction, and maintenance, but under the new management philosophy, technical specialists were no longer required or desired. In Rickover's words, "Many of our naval leaders are actually 'cheerleaders' making heroic attempts to keep the Navy together with endless exhortations and lectures on the values of leadership. Yet, they themselves are not knowledgeable enough to instruct or to see that the work has been done properly." One of Rickover's controversial suggestions did, however, come to fruition years later. In his 1974 speech, Rickover stated, "The entire Office of the Chief of Naval Material with its huge staff should be recognized as the huge burden it is, and disbanded."[9] In 1986, this suggestion was fulfilled when Secretary of the Navy Lehman took steps to eliminate the office of the Chief of Naval Material.

"Upgrading" of Engineering Personnel

There *were* naval leaders during the period of 1973-80 who were tuned into some of Admiral Rickover's thoughts and suggestions: Admiral James Holloway (CNO); then-Vice Admiral James Watkins, Bureau of Personnel (BuPers); and Vice Admiral C. Russell Bryan, Ship Material and Readiness Division, OpNav. "Russ" Bryan had a special talent for finding ways to encourage the industrial establishment to perform. During this period, he conceived the idea that the engineering specialists of the U.S. Navy needed a review and upgrade. A special task force was formed at the request of the CNO under the auspices of the Bureau of Naval Personnel. This group reviewed the professional qualifications of the "upgrade." A small percentage who did not meet the criteria were allowed to complete their careers but were made aware of their special status. The measures taken were a sound approach to revitalizing the technical arm of the Navy. The prestige and professional quality of the engineering duty community depends on the maintenance of these positive measures. Unfortunately, this plan has not always been followed in subsequent administrations. Many of the successes that have taken place in the decade of the 1980s were the

direct result of the professional upgrading of the engineering duty community. In addition, many of the key personnel assignments in the field of design, acquisition, and maintenance were made as a result of an administration that had devoted great effort and resources to understanding and developing strong engineering talent. Many benefits have accrued to the U.S. Navy because of strength in both the civilian and military personnel as a result of Vice Admiral Bryan's foresight and innovative style of management.

DECLINE OF THE SEVENTIES

A Period of Problems

The United States Navy celebrated its 200th birthday in 1975. The naval service is actually older than the nation, as the Navy was founded by the Continental Congress in October 1775, nine months before the Declaration of Independence was signed. The year 1975 should have been a very proud one in United States naval history, a birthday year when a powerful new aircraft carrier joined the fleet. However, the Navy had its problems. While trying to carry out its missions of protecting the sea-lanes for transport of critical imports and rendering a political and diplomatic presence in the world in support of our national policy, the U.S. Navy in 1975 had the fewest number of ships in the active fleet since a year and a half before the attack on Pearl Harbor.

Fleet Capability and Strength

Ships of this period had greater capabilities than their World War II counterparts, of course. These ships, such as the carrier USS *Enterprise* (CVA-65), with its air group of sophisticated aircraft, packed a much more potent punch than her World War II predecessor, *Enterprise* (CV-6). However, just a few years prior to this, in 1969, the U.S. had an active fleet of nearly 1,000 ships. Much of the fleet, however, had been constructed during World War II. In 1968, as a consequence, the average age of the active fleet was over 18 years. It became unmistakably clear that the United States had to reduce the number of its older ships and build new ships if it was to maintain naval supremacy. Reducing the number of older ships in the inventory seemed feasible and easy. Building new ones was a different story.

Shipbuilding Funds Diverted

From 1963 through 1967, the Navy had programmed 250 new ships, fifty per year. Then came the physical demands of the Vietnam War, with its requirements for operating funds at the expense of shipbuilding. The United States also undertook an expensive conversion of thirty-one Polaris-missile submarines to carry the Poseidon missiles, which, although substantially upgrading the nation's strategic deterrence capabilities, further bit into the Navy shipbuilding budget.

Obsolescence Overtakes Replacement

The result was that the Navy received authority to build only thirteen ships per year. That slow rate of shipbuilding meant that the U.S. Navy, in the not-distant future, would not be able to sustain a fleet of even fifty active ships unless substantial increases were made in the number of ships being built annually in future years. The Navy, in this period of the 1970s, found itself forced to a course of action amounting to unilateral naval disarmament if left uncorrected. Perhaps some of the comments by key officials during this period illustrate this point. The CNO, Admiral Zumwalt, on 19 February 1974, testified before the Senate Armed Services Committee, "We stand now at our point of greater weakness and, in my estimate, in our greatest jeopardy." This was not a very comforting position for the CNO to be expressing with such concern to Congress. Admiral Zumwalt later stated on 13 May 1974, in an interview with the *New York Times*, the "United States has lost the control of the sea lanes to the Soviet Union."

Perhaps a quote from the official periodical of the Navy League of the United States, *Seapower*, in March 1975, says it best of all:

> That ships are needed, desperately and immediately, is simply beyond question to those unafraid to face the facts of international life and to realize and accept that national security cannot be bought on the cheap, that it has to be the first priority of any nation, and that it would be foolish, dangerous and perhaps eventually suicidal to cut U.S. naval and military strength further in order to save additional funds for what are eloquently, but

not very intelligently termed "higher domestic priorities."

The Nadir of Shipbuilding and Repair

Naval shipbuilding was seeing some rough times. There was rampant inflation; relationships between shipbuilders and the Navy were strained and there were extensive claims backlogs. John Diesel, president of Newport News Shipbuilding, told the House Armed Services Subcommittee on Seapower on 6 August 1974 that the problem in warship construction developed from Navy cost-estimates, Navy delivery dates, and Navy arrogance. He told Congress that the Navy chronically underestimated ship costs so that it could get shipbuilding dollars from Congress. On 30 August 1974, Admiral Rickover, in a speech, charged that Navy ships were in the worst material condition in 50 years.[10] Just a few months later, Gordon Rule, a civilian procurement specialist for the Navy, in writing to the chairman of the House Armed Services Subcommittee on Seapower on 4 October 1974, called the new Trident shipbuilding contract ". . . one of the most imprudent [he ever saw], with built-in overruns and assurances to bail out the shipbuilder. . . ." Morale was at an all-time low and things seemed to be getting worse instead of better. We had become accustomed to bad news and were expecting more of the same in the future.

Congress Awakens to Need for Reform

Sometimes, however, adversity produces improvements, and this was now the case. In fact, the House Armed Services Subcommittee on Seapower, in 1975, made three cogent recommendations: 1. That Congress adopt a firm 5-year shipbuilding program. Congress should retain the authority for annual review, but with minimum necessary changes in the already approved plan. 2. That within the 5-year program, ships be built at the rate of thirty-five per year. 3. That U.S. naval shipyards once more be assigned "some new naval vessel construction."

That panel was chaired by Charles E. Bennett, Democrat of Florida, and Bob Wilson, Republican of California and the senior GOP member. They held extensive hearings on the "current status of the shipyards" over a 4-month period in 1974. They concluded that the status, in a word, was "horrendous." Simply reporting the facts, and without casting blame or seeking scapegoats, the Bennett subcommittee included in its report the following "long list of complaints," many against the Navy itself, but some against conditions, in general, which representatives of the United States shipbuilding industry had made clear during the hearing:

1. Lack of a steady shipbuilding program
2. Lack of profitability on Navy contracts
3. Too much oversight by the Navy
4. Too many change orders
5. Change orders on claims not quickly settled
6. Defective Navy drawings and specifications
7. Inability to get and train employees
8. Inability to keep employees
9. Problems with steel priorities
10. Inflation
11. Navy contracts less attractive than building merchant ships, which are simpler, have fewer changes, and provide a profit.

In spite of this unhealthy atmosphere, some ships were delivered. On 17 August 1974, USS *Parche* (SSN-683) was commissioned in Pascagoula, Mississippi, a product of Ingalls Shipbuilding Corporation. In October 1974, the USS *Philadelphia* (SSN-690) was launched at Electric Boat. On 14 December 1974, the USS *Virginia* (DLGN-38) was launched at Newport News Shipbuilding. On 21 December 1974, the *Glenard P. Lipscomb* (SS-685) was commissioned in Groton, Connecticut, a new super-quiet nuclear submarine that had been strongly supported by Admiral Rickover. In addition, the U.S. Coast Guard accepted delivery of the *Polar Sea* in 1978, an icebreaker of 60,000 shaft horsepower, with the capability of breaking more than 6 feet of ice at 3 knots speed.

CONCLUSION

The period from 1973 to 1980 was a difficult and complex one in the history of naval engineering. The Navy experienced a serious decline in numbers of warships, and business relationships with shipbuilders were "rockier" than ever. Although there were successes in that some new ship designs were introduced, the active Navy really suffered. Shipbuilding claims were larger than ever before. The government had to invoke a public law to save some shipbuilders from ceasing naval construction. Merchant ship construction rebounded early in this period and then fell into serious decline.

Although the Navy maintained its lead in technological achievements with ships like nuclear supercarriers, quiet nuclear submarines, and new amphibious assault ships, our adversaries were outspending and outbuilding us at a tremendous rate. The situation would not begin to turn around until late 1980 with the change of administration in government and a recognition that a strong Navy and shipbuilding were vital to this nation.

Notes

1 Beecher, John D., "FFG-7: The Concept and Design," *United States Naval Institute Proceedings*, 104 (March 1978) p. 148. Also Beecher and Anthony R. Ditrapani, "The FFG-7 Guided Missile Frigate Program — Model for the Future?" *Naval Engineers Journal* (June 1978) p. 93

2 Butler, Edward A., "An Advanced Concept for Propeller-Driven Surface Effect Ships," *Naval Engineers Journal* (October 1973) p. 55. Also Truax, R. C., "Surface Effect Ships in the Surface Navy," *United States Naval Institute Proceedings*, 99 (December 1973) p. 50.

3 Pohler, C. H., J. L. McVoy, H. W. Carhart, J. T. Leonard, and T. S. Pride, "Fire Safety of Naval Ships — An Open Challenge," *Naval Engineers Journal* (April 1978) p. 21.

4 Dalgleish, Douglas and Larry Schweikart, *Trident,* Chicago, Illinois: Southern Illinois University Press, 1980.

5 Krolick, C. F., "U.S. Navy Shipboard R&D — An Overview," *Naval Engineers Journal,* Vol. 93 (April 1981). Also, Ganthey, J. Richard and Joseph P. DeTolla, "The Energy Crisis and Naval Ship Research and Development," *Naval Engineers Journal* (June 1977) p. 27.

6 Doyle, T. J., R. W. Kornbau, and A. L. Smookler, "Surface Ship Machinery — A Survey of Propulsion, Electrical, and Auxiliary System Development," DTNSRDC Report 87/044.

7 Doyle, T. J. and H. O. Stevens, "Development and Demonstration of a 300 kW Advanced dc Ship Drive System," *Transactions,* UK Institute of Marine Engineers, Vol. 97 (1985).

8 Puckett, L. J. and R. A. Sniffen, "Integrated Bridge System 'At Sea' Evaluation," *Naval Engineers Journal,* Vol. 90 (April 1978).

9 Rickover, H., ADM USN, "The Role of Engineering in the Navy." Speech given to the National Society of Former Special Agents of the FBI, 30 August 1974.

10 *Ibid.*

CHAPTER
ELEVEN
1981–1988

The Six Hundred Ship Navy and Merchant Marine Doldrums

by John R. Baylis

INTRODUCTION

This period commenced renewed interest in national defense, under national leadership that recognized the great strides made by the Soviet Navy and began to build to meet the threat of the much strengthened Soviet Navy. This is the era of the gas turbine ship, and of guided missile systems of sophisticated capability. This is the period when the research and development gains of the past two decades began to appear in the ships of the fleet. This period is also a nadir of the commercial shipping business for the United States.

HISTORICAL MARITIME BACKGROUND

Defense-Oriented Administration

The Six Hundred Ship Navy era got underway with the first inauguration of Ronald Reagan. His administration believed that the Soviet Union understood and respected strength; consequently, his administration supported a strong defense policy. The previous administration had announced a plan to achieve a 550-ship Navy. This was increased to a plan for a 600-ship Navy by the new administration, and supplemental appropriations were enacted to begin the build-up.

To direct the revitalization of the Navy, President Reagan appointed John F. Lehman as Secretary of the Navy. Lehman studied foreign affairs at St. Joseph's College and at Cambridge University. He was a member of the Foreign Policy Research Institute at the University of Pennsylvania and a senior staff member of the National Security Council. He served at the Vienna arms reduction negotiations and as deputy director of the U.S. Arms Control and Disarmament Agency. His dynamic and forceful leadership changed the organization of the Navy Department to respond to the needs of the expansion program. A major change was the disestablishment of the Naval Material Command (NavMat) headquarters, viewed by many as an unnecessary layer in the bureaucracy whose coordinating function had declined following the merger of the Naval Ship Systems Command (NavShips) and the Naval Ordnance Systems Command (NavOrd) into the Naval Sea Systems Command (NavSea). The Material Command procurement review function was transferred to the Office of the Chief of Naval Operations. The Naval Electronics Systems Command (NavElex) was redesignated the Space and Warfare Systems Command (SPAWARS), giving the Department of the Navy air, sea, and space-oriented material commands.[1] Perhaps the greatest achievement of Mr. Lehman's administration lies in personnel matters. This has little to do with the engineering history *per se*, but the morale of the services improved greatly, and with improved morale comes improved material readiness. Ships' crews of this period were better trained and motivated to operate the fleet than those of the preceding decade. Six years after his appointment, John Lehman had the Navy well on the way to 600 ships.

Battleship Reactivation

The appropriations supplement added funds for CG-47 class and for the Light Airborne Multi-Purpose System (LAMPS).[2] The supplement also included funds for the reactivation of the Navy's four mothballed battleships, and this sparked controversy. The Marine Corps had been strident about the need for major caliber gunfire support after the big gun cruisers had been put out of service, and the battleships would furnish such support. The press asserted that the ships were vulnerable to air attack. Many in the Navy were more concerned about the manpower demands of these old designs. Reactivation required the replacement of much of the electronics and the installation of Tomahawk and Harpoon cruise missiles, Phalanx close-in weapons systems, and electronic warfare equipment. The *New Jersey* was rushed through conversion to provide major-caliber gun support at Lebanon, and once the battleships were back in service, they no longer drew the attention of the press.

Iranian Rescue Failure

The Iranian seizure of the United States embassy in 1979 and the continued holding of American personnel resulted in an ill-fated secret operation to free the hostages. The carrier-based helicopters used were not equipped to operate in dust storms, and the luckless force was disabled by such a storm in the Iranian desert and discovered there by the chance passage of a bus load of Iranians. The Iranian operation failure, and the expanding Russian overseas operations, led to a build-up of U.S. military force in the Indian Ocean. Support for these forces was established on the island of Diego Garcia. Basing agreements also were negotiated in Oman, Kenya, and Somalia, but these bases were negated by Russian basing activity in the vicinity and were never put in service.[3] Deploying ships to the Indian Ocean put a premium on cruising range, adding to the need for greater propulsive efficiency. This and other incidents demonstrated the need for a rapid deployment force.

Rapid Deployment Force

A Rapid Deployment Force was created to provide trained and equipped U.S. Marine Corps and Airborne troops on short notice anywhere in the world. Sea lift for heavy equipment and other support for this force required the conversion of merchant shipping to Military Sea Transport Service (MSTS) auxiliaries. The ships of the Rapid Deployment Force are to be loaded with vehicles and supplies and maintained in a ready condition. The cargo (T-AK) ships were converted from hulls that were originally ordered for the Waterman shipping lines, and the vehicle cargo (T-AKR) types were converted from the Sea-Land SL-7 high-speed container ships that became uneconomical following increased fuel costs. The U.S.-flagged merchant fleet had been in a steep decline—to the point that there was concern for the availability of sea-lift to support an amphibious operation. But the fleet has changed character and is now mostly container ships. These will need special appliances to be utilized where there are no special port facilities or where the container port is destroyed. Crane ships configured to provide this support are included in the new types.[4]

Soviet Union Overseas Activity

The Soviet Fleet had increased the numbers of ships deployed abroad, and by 1985 there were about fifty ships in the Atlantic, fifty in the Mediterranean, twenty-five in the Indian Ocean, and forty-five in the Pacific, according to Rear

Admiral Butts, U.S. Director of Naval Intelligence. The Soviets moved into the Indian Ocean filling the void left when Britain announced its withdrawal in 1968. They moved into Cam Ranh Bay following the U.S. withdrawal from Vietnam and established a major naval base there. Their naval forces operated from Cuba and Ethiopia. Soviet naval aircraft frequently operated out-of-area, independently, and in major fleet exercises that were carried out in the Atlantic or off the North Cape every year since 1978 (except 1982).[5]

Soviet submarines have been detected within the territorial waters of Scandinavian nations; one was caught hard aground in 1982. Tracks of bottom-crawling Spetznaz mini-subs have been found in Swedish and Japanese waters. In Sweden these brazen violations of territorial waters have awakened a public concern for anti-submarine warfare (ASW) capability after years of apathy.[6]

Soviet Fleet Expansion

The Soviet Fleet had been expanding and assuming a more worldwide character for a number of years without provoking much response in the United States. Beginning in September 1981, the Department of Defense began publishing *Soviet Military Power*,[7] a detailed, frank, and authoritative report that provides information that not only has not been available before but that, according to the Secretary of Defense, was also unavailable to the Soviet people. At the same time, more of the intelligence briefing from the Congressional appropriations hearings was published. Several new submarines were reported in the hearing records and repeated in the press: *Oscar*—a 14,000-ton cruise-missile submarine; *Typhoon*—a 25,000-ton SSBN; *Mike*, *Sierra*, *Yankee*, and *Akula* classes of attack nuclear submarines. The *Yankees* are attack submarines converted from SSBNs in observation of the Strategic Arms Limitations Treaty. *Alfa*, a class of six SSNs, has been credited in the press with 43 knots, an operating depth of over 1,000 meters, and a titanium hull. Most Soviet subs are credited with under-ice operating capability. The USSR has been working to achieve submarine designs superior to those in the west by producing a large number of designs while the United States produced but one attack

submarine design and one ballistic missile submarine design. If it were not for a number of accidents that have been witnessed by western observers, one might conclude that the Soviets have succeeded (October 1986, SSBN explosion in a missile tube; SSN disabled off North Carolina; SSN fire off Japan).[8]

In 1986 there were four *Kiev*-class VSTOL carriers afloat armed with Forger aircraft, Helix helicopters, SA-N-4 surface-to-air missiles, and SS-N-12 anti-ship missiles. A new 65,000-ton, nuclear-propelled carrier with angled flight deck and forward "ski-jump" ramp will probably join the Soviet Fleet before 1989. It is expected that this carrier will be capable of air operations similar to those of the U.S. carriers.

The lead ship of a new class of guided missile cruisers, the *Slava*, was deployed to the Northern Fleet Area in 1983. This ship has sixteen SS-N-12 anti-ship missile launchers. The *Kirov*-class cruisers are the first Soviet nuclear-powered surface warships. They have a vertical launch system and carry anti-ship cruise missiles and anti-air missiles.

A new destroyer, *Udaloy*, appeared with improved ASW weapons. This class has a bow-mounted and a towed sonar and can support two Helix ASW helicopters.

Two *Ivan Rogov* LPDs (landing transport, dock) have been built. These ships employ air cushion landing vehicles, of which there were about eighty in service (compared with twelve in the United States) in 1986.

New ships have been built for the KGB, which operates a large maritime border guard Fleet that is analogous to the U.S. Coast Guard. Two new space event support ships have also appeared. Two new *Arktica*-class icebreakers were being built in Finland for Russia, and will have nuclear power installed in a Russian yard. Ice-breaking LASH ships (container ships with special stowage gear) and SSBN support ships are also being constructed. Clearly, naval engineering is still booming in the USSR.[9]

Falklands Campaign

There have been only a few naval actions since World War II and most were one-ship affairs. The Falklands (Malvinas) War between England and Argentina is the most notable exception. Argentine commandos landed on 1 April 1982 from a destroyer. The next morning an Argentine LST disembarked 19 LVTs, 600 marines, and 279 army and air force troops, and the islands were under Argentine control. Great Britain declared a war zone extending 200 miles from the Falklands, and began requisitioning ships to support the campaign. The SS *Atlantic Conveyor* was converted to an "air capable" ship by the installation of Arapaho, a hangar and flight deck assembled from containers and modules to fit the standard container lashings. This was a development initiated in the United States by the Naval Air Systems Command. The Arapaho conversion and load-out took one week. A total of three container ships were converted this way. These ships operated Sea Harriers and Harrier VSTOL aircraft, as well as Chinook, Wessex, and Sea King helicopters. On 5 April, the Royal Navy Task Force sortied to retake the Falklands and South Georgia, a 7,000 mile deployment, arriving on 29 April. The second leg of this route, 3,300 miles from Ascension Island, was the route required for the ASW and bomber aircraft for each mission. The length of these sorties was fatiguing for the air crews and has been blamed for the lack of success of British ASW and bombing missions. In contrast, the Argentine radius of action was about 400 nautical miles, and there were many heavy raids on Royal Navy ships in confined waters. The British defense was adequate, and the Argentine offense was perhaps a little thin and dispirited.[10]

The ship and aircraft losses were as follows:

Argentina

ARA *General Belgrano*, Torpedoed
ARA *Sante Fe* (SS), captured
ARA *Islas Malvinas* (WPB), captured
ARA *Rio Iguazu* (WPB), strafed
ARA *Rio Carcarana* (AK) Harrier
ARA *Islas de Los Estados* gunfire
ARA *Monsumen*, (AK) grounded
MV *Narwhal* (AGI), bombed
ARA *Alfred Sobral*, damaged
84 fixed wing aircraft
   17 by Sidewinder missile
    6 by 30mm A/C gun
   55 by SAM
10 Helicopters

Great Britain

HMS *Sheffield*, Exocet, fire
HMS *Coventry*, 3 1000# bombs
HMS *Ardent* (FF), Bombs, fire
HMS *Antelope* (FF), 500# bombs
SS *Atlantic Conveyor*, Exocet
RFA *Sir Galahad* (LST), bombs
2 ships damaged, dud bombs
10 Harriers
24 Helicopters

While much of the damage can be attributed to missiles, some Exocet missiles and a large number of bombs did not explode. The major overall damage mechanism was fire. When attacked, HMS *Sheffield* lost all firefighting capability immediately. The fire produced much acrid smoke and destroyed the aluminum superstructure. It appears that in the years since World War II, warships have accumulated much combustible material. Aircraft, their fuel, and weapons are still a serious fire hazard. *Sheffield* was hit while in the vicinity of *Hermes*, as was *Atlantic Conveyor*. There is some belief that the missiles were fired at *Hermes* and that the missiles were decoyed by electronic warfare and then acquired the nearest alternate target.

The lessons of the Falklands were presented by Captain John Walker at the 1983 ASNE Day.[11] The first lesson was reported as "modern wars are going to be 'come as you are,' there will not be an extended mobilization time. Losses will not be regenerated, but must be replaced from reserves." The second lesson was that today's friend may be tomorrow's enemy. Any nation must be able to defend against weapons in every inventory. The enemy may have your weapons in his inventory. Naval ships must have air defense, anti-submarine, surface warfare, and shore bombardment capability in multimission hulls. The Royal Navy found shore bombardment extremely effective. Captain Walker noted that the centralized control placed vital functions at the radar and visual centroid (aim point) of the ship. He suggested that in the future it may be prudent to disperse these vital functions, and the power and auxiliary functions as well.

The *Naval Institute Proceedings*, January 1986, carried an article based on the Soviet military press that presented the Russian lessons distilled from the Falklands campaign. They are:

- At sea, nuclear-powered submarines are pre-eminent among offensive weapons.
- Amphibious reconnaissance-diversionary teams are highly effective.
- Commercial ships have wartime usefulness.
- Attacks by large numbers of aircraft are effective.
- Passive electronic warfare defense systems work, and electromagnetic incompatibility contributed to the loss of *Sheffield*. (Radar interfered with communications and was turned off at the time of the attack, according to the Russians.)

Iran-Iraq War

In September 1980, Iraq sent troops into Iran as the two governments attempted to overthrow each other. Eight years later, the war continued, with occasional attacks on oil ports and tankers. While there has been concern over the passage through the Straits of Hormuz, the flow of oil has not been curtailed.

On 17 May 1987 the USS *Stark*, an FFG 7-class frigate, was hit by one or two Exocet missiles launched from an Iraqi Mirage fighter aircraft, killing thirty-seven men. A Congressional investigation determined that the ship was capable of defending itself but did not. The ship was severely damaged but the fire was extinguished, a credit to the damage control effort of the ship's force.[12]

President Reagan announced that the United States would keep the Persian Gulf open to oil traffic and would protect Kuwaiti tankers re-flagged to U.S. registry.

Iran was reported to have mined the waters near Kuwait and several tankers were damaged by mines. American minesweepers took several weeks to transit to the Persian Gulf. Iran also installed Chinese Silkworm anti-ship missiles near the Straights of Hormuz and began operating Swedish small 70-knot patrol boats said to be loaded with explosives to conduct suicide attacks on American ships.

Grenada

In March 1979 a Communist group led by Maurice Bishop seized power in Grenada. In May 1980 his government signed a treaty with Cuba and shortly thereafter Cubans began building a long airstrip on Grenada. The United States and several Caribbean governments saw this as a base for further Cuban adventures in the Caribbean basin. In November 1983 a U.S. Joint Task Force with elements from Jamaica and under the command of Vice-Admiral Joseph Metcalf, invaded Grenada, deposed Bishop, and restored the former government. This short action was marked by communication difficulties between elements of the force that resulted in U.S. losses to U.S. weapons. Later this led to a new effort to unify communications systems. The Grenada action was the first in a new active defense policy for the United States.

Libya and Terrorist Activities

Beginning in July 1984, there were nineteen explosions in the Red Sea. At the request of the Egyptian government, the United States joined a multinational mine-sweeping effort and one mine of recent Russian manufacture was recovered. Analysis of Red Sea traffic disclosed a Libyan RO/RO ship to be the probable minelayer. No clear motive for the mining was apparent other than to embarrass Cairo.[13] This episode demonstrated that mining requires simple assets while mine defense takes more equipment and more time.

In October 1985, the Italian cruise ship *Achille Lauro* was hijacked and an American citizen was murdered. The hijackers escaped, but later in the month American intelligence pinpointed them aboard an Egyptian airliner bound for Tunis. The aircraft was intercepted by F-14s from the *Saratoga* and forced to land in Sicily, where the hijackers could be apprehended.[14] An Aegis radar system was used to control the interception.

Shipbuilding Decline

Oil was pretty much at the root of shipbuilding problems. There was a world-wide glut of tanker capacity resulting from a decline in consumption and the introduction of new sources following the Organization of Petroleum Exporting Countries (OPEC) cartel price escalation beginning in 1973. Refiners got more high-grade product from each barrel of crude oil, which caused a decline in the quality of residual oil and an increase in price of bunker fuel for ships. The market for high-speed commercial ships disappeared. New ships were diesel-propelled with longer stroke, high-efficiency engines typified by the *Exxon Valdez*, a 209,000-ton diesel-propelled tanker built by National Steel in San Diego. Most of the older tankers were laid up or scrapped. The Naval Institute *Proceedings* noted that eleven shipyards closed in 1984.[15] In 1987 there were no new orders for commercial ships in American shipyards.

American shipbuilding centered on the Navy and Coast Guard programs. As mentioned earlier, the conversion of excess merchant capacity to the Rapid Deployment Force put idle ships to use and provided needed work for the shipyards. The Coast Guard ordered a new class of 1,000-ton medium-endurance cutters.[16]

Economic Environment

During this period, a changing world economic environment became evident. The United States had been the pre-eminent world industrial power up until 1970, then saw its share of industrial production fall from 40% to 22%. United States' exports fell to second place behind those of the Federal Republic of Germany in 1986. Most alarming was the fall in high technology production from 70% to 50% of the total world output.[17]

A change in government policy, in which "Buy America" was phased out and replaced with a policy that required that only half of any procurement be of United States origin, opened the doors to foreign equipment in U.S. Navy ships. Some segments of the shipbuilding infrastructure were hard hit. The electrical machinery business, already suffering from a lack of public utility orders, found most of the large machine orders going to foreign suppliers. Only in gas turbines did the United States find an export market for marine equipment. These actions, which opened the American defense market to foreign competition, caused a loss in the ability of American enterprises to compete.

Industry in the United States was competitive at home for products with wide application and mass production technology, but an alarming amount of the manufactured products that were developed in the United States were rapidly copied by foreign competitors or were deliberately consigned, by American business management, to off-shore manufacture.

The Reagan administration attempted to stem the flow of technology by enforcing export controls and by limiting access of foreign nationals to advanced technology meetings and installations. A number of cases of illegal export of computer technology were found and prosecuted. In 1987, Toshiba of Japan and Kongsberg of Norway were found to have sold equipment that would allow the Soviet Union to manufacture precise, quiet propellers, an advantage to their submarines. *U.S. News and World Report* stated that these companies, for a small profit, did irreparable damage to the ASW capability of the United States, and their violations of laws were ignored by their governments. The Congress began action to bar Toshiba from selling to American customers.[18]

MARITIME ENGINEERING AND TECHNICAL HIGHLIGHTS

Cruise Missile Development

The development of the Tomahawk cruise missile began in the last decade as a stand-off anti-ship missile for submarines. The development was managed by a Joint Cruise Missile Project that was staffed by NavAir and NavSea personnel. The prime contractor was the Convair Division of General Dynamics. The guidance system contractor was MacDonnell-Douglas, who was also the developer of an earlier cruise missile, Harpoon. In this application, the missiles are loaded in the torpedo tubes in canisters and are fired from the canister when the submarine is at shallow submergence. The weapon was first added to surface ships in a fixed-box launcher that evolved from the submarine launch method. The first successful firing of a Tomahawk from a Navy ship was on 30 June 1986, from the USS *Long Beach* (CGN-9).

The Vertical Launching System (VLS) that is now installed on the CG-52 can launch Standard Missile, Harpoon, Tomahawk, and a modified ASROC. The VLS was developed by Martin Marietta and is manufactured by Martin and FMC. It is described in the April 1981 issue of the *Naval Engineers Journal*.[19] All missiles that can use the VLS come certified, in sealed canisters, and do not need servicing while in the launcher. Missiles that need no more attention than display models—this is the "Wooden Round" concept that has been so long desired for missile systems. The VLS is built in eight-cell modules and is suitable for the modular concept of warship design. The Mk41 VLS was developed to fit the footprint of the Mk26 missile launch system so that the VLS could be a direct replacement for the dual arm launcher and could be used as a replacement for the ASROC launcher on the *Spruance* class. The VLS provides increased missile storage in the volume allotted and greater mission availability; a failure in any cell or missile will not impact the ability of another cell to fire. (Other launchers require some effort to jettison a dud before another round can be fired.) The VLS also increases the maximum firing rate. The first ship launch of a missile from the VLS, other than the development firings from the USS *Norton Sound*, was from the USS *Bunker Hill* (CG-52) on 20 May 1986. The vertical launch development started in the early 1970s, after the development of high specific-impulse missile propellant and agile missile control systems. The high specific-impulse propellant requires protection of the launcher and ship structure from the effects of an accidental ignition of a restrained missile and management of the missile exhaust.

Following the vertical launch development for surface ships, a vertical launch system was developed for submarines. It is installed on some of the SSN 688-class submarines.

Aegis Air Defense System Development

The modern air defense system has been under development for many years. The need for improved air defense was recognized in 1955. The Typhon missile system was started in 1957, under the able direction of Admiral Eli T. Reich, as an integrated anti-aircraft warfare (AAW) system. A development model of the radar was installed in the *Norton Sound* in 1963, the year that Typhon was terminated. In 1964, Secretary of Defense McNamara authorized the Advanced Surface Missile System (ASMS). Captain Bryce Inman was an early advocate of the multifunction phased-array for ASMS, and both the *Long*

Beach and *Enterprise* had phased-array search radars. In August 1964, seven contractors—Boeing, GE, Hughes, RCA, Raytheon, Sperry, and Westinghouse—were funded to prepare proposals for ASMS. These seven contractors submitted twenty-eight weapons system proposals that were evaluated by a group of 126 experts. The contractors recommended a system with phase-phase radar, slaved illuminators, a digital system compatible with the Navy Tactical Data System (NTDS), dual rail launchers, and the Standard Missile with mid-course guidance. Many of these concepts traced their origins to Typhon. This was a system that would achieve the performance with low technical risk. There was a delay in the program when John Foster, Assistant Secretary of Defense for Research & Development, Test and Evaluation (RDT&E), sought to combine the ASMS with the Army's SAM D program. In 1969, RCA won the engineering development contract and about this time the system was named Aegis, after the mythical shield of Zeus and Athena.

The Development Concept Paper called for a risk reduction plan and simplification. Three engineering development models were planned: EDM-1, a single array and illuminator for land based test in 1973, and test in *Norton Sound* in 1974; EDM-2, for missile development (but canceled to save money); and EDM-3, for installation at the Combat System Engineering Development Site (CSEDS) at Moorestown, N.J., in 1978. (The CSEDS is a replica of the superstructure and combat system spaces of an Aegis ship, a surprising sight for travelers on the New Jersey Turnpike.) Production was authorized on 2 March 1978. Then-Commander Wayne Meyer was assigned as the project manager in 1974, and at about that time the Navy was directed to adapt the *Spruance* class to carry Aegis. Later, Rear Admiral Meyer brought the development to a successful conclusion with the installation in the USS *Ticonderoga*.

The Ship Qualification Test, the first test of the system installed on an Aegis cruiser firing missiles at target aircraft, was held on 4 April 1983. News media loudly reported a failure. There were initial problems with computer software that were soon corrected to allow the system, on 7 April, to engage the required number of targets simultaneously. In September there were problems with radar performance that were quickly repaired. Congressman Denny Smith challenged the adequacy of testing, and in April 1984 the system was successfully tested against multiple low-flying targets. Since then, each cruiser has been delivered, on schedule, with fully functional Aegis systems.[20] Full-scale shock trials conducted on the *Ticonderoga* revealed some problems that were later corrected. *Mobile Bay* successfully completed shock trials and demonstrated full capability in 1987.[21]

This system has produced the largest real-time computer program known to exist, and is an outstanding example of "top-down" engineering. This project was 26 years from the requirement determination to Initial Operational Capability (IOC). Admiral Meyer notes that this required extraordinary devotion on the part of the team because there are always detractors and raiders with whom to contend. He observes that nobody *gives* the manager money or authority to accomplish his responsibilities, he must take the authority and go get the money.

Aegis development is a prime example of disciplined engineering. New technology was introduced without risk to the program by the process described by Admiral Meyer and Mr. W. V. Goodwin, the RCA Aegis Vice President, as "Build a little, test a little, learn a lot."

ASNE initiated combat systems symposia that kept the ship and weapons systems community informed on the development of Aegis and other combat systems. Admiral Meyer's superb communication skills were demonstrated at these symposia.

Gas Turbine Propulsion

The early successful gas turbine propulsion systems were based on the Pratt and Whitney FT4A and the General Electric LM1500 aircraft-derivative engines. In 1970, the FT4A was the choice for the DD-963 class, but during the detail design, the LM2500 was qualified for naval service following tests on USNS *Admiral Callaghan*. The improved fuel rate made the change to this engine very desirable. Since that time, the LM2500 has been the predominant engine for warships. In 1987 there were 235

ships committed to this engine, and 607 engines sold worldwide for marine service. As experience with this gas turbine has grown, the maximum rating for shipboard service has increased from 20,000 to 25,000 shaft horsepower and the time between overhauls has increased according to plan. These engines are now in service on the PHM-1, DD-963, FFG-7, and CG-47 class ships and are planned for the DDG-51, AE-36 and AOE-6 classes. Today, steam is used with nuclear propulsion; all other new ships are diesel or gas turbine-propelled.

The simple-cycle gas turbine has served the Navy well, but the part-load fuel rate is a matter of continuing concern. Operationally, the twin-shaft ships can improve fuel consumption by running with one shaft powered and the other "free wheeling" (shades of the 1930s Chryslers). One improvement that has been under development is the combined-cycle Rankine Cycle Energy Recovery (RACER) system. This will use a Rankine steam cycle to extract heat from the gas turbine exhaust and add to the propulsion power. Such systems have been used for a number of years in stationary electric power plants with good success. For Naval ships the RACER is a complex system that may introduce problems in control and will introduce the training and support problems of two power technologies on one ship. The weight of the RACER system is considerable, but the promise of about 30% saving in propulsion fuel has kept this concept alive.[22]

One of the problems facing naval engineers is the political reaction to a failure. This reaction always brands the concept as a failure when more often than not the problem is defective engineering. Such is the case with the heat recovery boilers and steam system in the DD-963 class. The poor engineering of this system resulted in a call for the elimination of all steam from diesel and gas turbine ships. The good engineering is reported in the May 1987 *Naval Engineers Journal*, which says the system for the Aegis ships was designed with the faults of the DD-963 in mind, and tested in a Land Based Test Site (LBTS).[23] The increasing use of LBTS for the pre-production testing of hull, mechanical, and electrical equipment is a characteristic of this era. The Naval Ship Engineering Center at

Philadelphia is the Navy's primary LBTS for this class of equipment.

A better concept for propulsion energy saving in gas turbine ships was the development of an intercooled regenerative gas turbine. The regenerative gas turbine is another old idea whose time may have come. The first installation in GTS *John Seargent* was reported in the 1955 *Transactions* of the Society of Naval Architects and in the February 1959 *ASNE Journal*.[24] In the 1960s, the United States and Canadian Navies funded a small regenerative gas turbine project that was unsuccessful. In these early attempts, the pressure drop in the heat exchanger caused a loss in efficiency about equal to the thermal gain. The addition of the intercooler and the high pressure ratio (16:1) of modern gas turbines has made this concept viable. Today there are two developments, one led by the Allison division of General Motors and based on the Rolls Royce engines, and one based on the General Electric LM1600, a third-generation engine to be produced in the 1990s. Rolls Royce is also said to be developing a series of regenerative gas turbines for marine service. Caterpillar has tested regenerative engines in the low horsepower ranges. These engines promise about 28% fuel savings with the usual ship operating profile, fuel savings over the entire operating speed range, negligible complexity, less increase in machinery weight than the RACER, easy control, and reduced infrared signature compared to the simple-cycle engines. Figure 11-1 shows the comparison of fuel rates for simple cycle and intercooled regenerative gas turbines. Maurice Hauschildt can be credited with the revival of

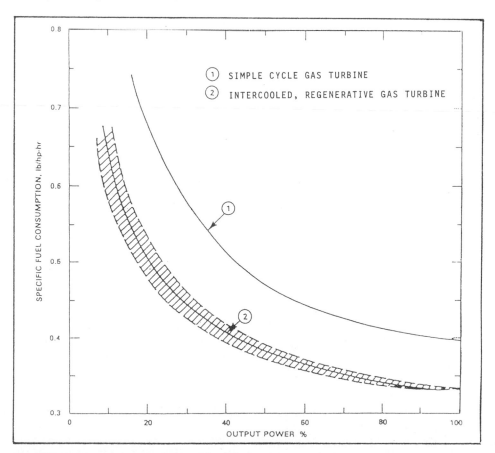

FIGURE 11-1. *Comparison of partial-load fuel rates.*

interest in regenerative gas turbines, and Daniel Groghan has presented a paper recording the development.[25]

The development of a gas turbine is very costly, and this expense conflicts with our national understanding of costs in heavy industry. We all expect turbines for public utilities and marine service to evolve from prior technology without any development cost. Therefore, any gas turbine for marine service must have been developed for another market (aircraft) where these costs are expected. The LM2500 and FT4A development and support costs were mostly borne by the aircraft applications. The regenerative intercooled gas turbine will probably be successful if it can be developed using proven components from aircraft or industrial gas turbines. It will not get very far if the marine application development costs are more than nominal.

Another fuel saving idea is propulsion-derived ship service electric power. Power-take-off (PTO) generators are in service on several commercial ships and are being built into new fleet auxiliaries using foreign-built generators. They are well suited to ships that operate at a large fraction of their installed propulsion power for long periods. (See figure 11-2.) Warship application, where the range of speeds is greater, requires more development.[26]

Such a ship service electric power generator is included in an electric-drive propulsion program that is now in the works. This program will develop and test electric generators, frequency changers, and motors to transmit and control power from gas turbines to the propellers. Electric drive will allow the propulsion gas turbine to operate at its best speed, will allow one gas turbine to drive two shafts to the limit of its rating, will allow more freedom in the arrangement of machinery, and will permit reversing the shafts, thereby eliminating the need for controllable reversible-pitch propellers. The ability to operate the gas turbine at its most efficient speed, and the ability to operate the minimum number of gas turbines for the required power will reduce fuel consumption 10% to 14%. The propulsion-derived ship service power will also save between 10% and 14% as compared with the existing generators. The new electric machinery will be water-cooled and much smaller than the equivalent air-cooled machines. James Jolliffe and David Green presented a prize-winning paper on electric drive at ASNE Day 1982[27].

Advanced Marine Vehicles

In the 1970s there was a large effort devoted to surface effect ships (SES) and air cushion vehicles (ACV). An ACV is supported on a fan-

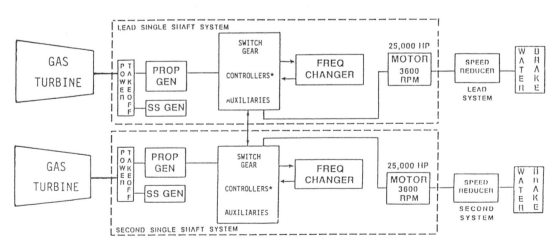

* INCLUDES TWIN SHAFT CONTROL

FIGURE 11-2 — Typical DD/DDG propulsion system.

generated air cushion contained by flexible skirts around the ACV periphery. The air cushion and flexible skirts give the ACV mobility over water, dry land, swamps, and ice. The air cushion vehicles have found a place in the military inventory; the Navy LCAC (landing craft, air cushion) is the direct descendent of the R&D "Jeff" craft. The Army operates LACV-30 air cushion lighters and is building a higher capacity LAMP-H. The Soviet Union has AIST, a 120-ton payload ACV, and LEBED, a 50-ton payload vehicle. The LEBED can be carried as deck cargo and operate from the well deck of the *Ivan Rogov*-class amphibious warfare ships. The *Pomornik* class is a 350-ton air cushion landing craft.

The first LACV-30 was delivered in 1981. The first LCAC began testing in 1984, following the AALC "Jeff" R&D program, which started in 1970 under the direction of James L. Schuler. The AALC program took a long time because the funds were repeatedly used to accelerate the surface effect ship program.[28]

The United Kingdom demonstrated the ability of the BH-7 craft to survive a mine explosion, thus the United States developed an interest in hovercraft for mine sweeping and hunting. The Bell Aerospace division won a contract to design and build the MSH, the first ACV mine hunter in the United States. This was to be fabricated of glass-reinforced plastic, a first in the United States for a vehicle of this size and type. By 1986, the MSH development was in trouble, mostly due to weight growth and the failure of a test section. In 1987, interest in glass-reinforced plastic ships shifted to the conventional displacement-hull Italian minesweeper that is discussed later in this section.

ACVs are in regular service crossing the English Channel, and many designs of small ACVs are shown in Jane's *Surface Skimmers*.

Surface effect ships are also supported on a dynamic air cushion, but the containment is by rigid structure at the sides and flexible seals at the bow and stern. The rigid sidewalls reduce the required cushion fan power and make screw propulsion possible. The U.S. Navy SES program has dwindled down to one prototype, SES-200. This is a Bell Halter 110 that has been lengthened to increase displacement to 200 tons. It is used in a continuing research program. The Coast

Guard placed two Bell-Halter 110s in service as patrol boats.[29] Another SES derivative, the Special Warfare Craft, Medium (SWCM), was under construction by RMI when they filed for bankruptcy. This was a small rigid-sidewall craft, about 73 feet long, designed to deliver SEALS (Navy frogmen). While the requirement for the vehicle remains, the future of this program is uncertain.[30]

Small Waterplane Area Twin Hull (SWATH) ships are another type that has had a slow emergence. A SWATH ship has an above-water platform supported by struts with a small waterplane cross section from two submarine-like bodies. A well-designed SWATH ship should be comfortable in rough weather and will have a lot of usable deck area. A SWATH ship could have reduced high-speed resistance, but the structural weight will be higher than an equivalent monohull.[31] As of 1987 there is a design for a SWATH T-AGOS (civilian-manned ocean surveillance ship) that is under contract to be built as the first of a new flight in the T-AGOS program. The monohull T-AGOS is known to be very uncomfortable in winter in northern latitudes, and the SWATH is expected to do better in this environment. The design manager for the SWATH T-AGOS, Philip Covich, has written about the design in the May 1987 *Naval Engineers Journal*.[32] The Army Corps of Engineers has built a SWATH survey craft that is in service in the Pacific northwest. The Coast Guard produced a SWATH cutter design in 1985 and the Navy had a concept of a SWATH frigate, but there was no acquisition program for these types. Designs for SWATH ships abound, but the acquisition programs are scarce. There were four commercial applications of this technology in operation as ferries and research ships.

Hydrofoils are a waterborne analog of airplanes; they have a displacement hull analogous to landing gear, and submerged foils that support the ship when up to speed. Hydrofoils are out of favor in the western world. One company proposes hydrofoils for ferries, but the Navy has no procurement or design effort for hydrofoils. Boeing stopped marketing their commercial Jetfoil in 1985. The Royal Navy was testing a Boeing hydrofoil HMS *Speedy*, for their service but discontinued the tests because of trouble with modifications to the Boeing design to meet Royal Navy requirements.[33] Israel built the *Snapirit*, a hydrofoil based on the USS *Flagstaff* design, in 1985. The Soviet Union built *Kollchida* beginning in 1981 as a replacement for the 20-year old *Kometa* class. A history of the U.S. Navy hydrofoil program emphasizing the role of the *High Point* was published in 1987 by the David Taylor Naval Ship R&D Center.[34]

For detailed descriptions of all of the advanced ship type technology, see the February 1985 Special Issue of *Naval Engineers Journal*.

Electronic Warfare

Electronic Warfare (EW) utilizes most of the methods of signal collection, information processing, and tactical deception practiced in modern naval warfare. Ship EW systems tend to be more general purpose and adaptable than aircraft EW systems. Ship EW systems consist of threat warning equipment, signal analysis equipment, and electronic countermeasures, including chaff and decoys. Systems such as the AN/SLQ-32 were widely installed by the end of the 1980s, and were available in large ship suites and systems for small ships. Aircraft systems have been battle tested in the many small wars that have occurred, but ship systems have been tested recently only in the Falklands war. As an adjunct to electronic warfare, the Israeli *Reshef*-class corvettes were reported to have reduced radar cross section on certain target angles. This was done to increase the effectiveness of EW and decoys.[35] The United Kingdom used some radar absorptive materials for this purpose in the Falklands, but little is said about its utility, except in sales brochures.

Command and Control

Electronic systems for command and control have recently come to be recognized for their capability. Until recently, the commanding officer considered that his battle station was on the bridge. The CIC was recognized as a great resource, and was placed near the bridge. Now his battle station is in the CIC and CIC can be put in a protected location. Secretary Lehman, speaking at the 1986 ASNE Day luncheon, recounted the success of operations in the Mediterranean, the intercept of the *Achille Lauro*

pirates, and the operations near and against Libya, noting that, in these operations, command and control and electronic warfare systems performed flawlessly.[36]

Global command and control probably had its beginning in the Cuban Missile Crisis of 1962, when the Chief of Naval Operations exercised close control of the naval forces in the Caribbean. With the communications capability provided by satellite, this kind of close control can be applied anywhere in the world and is applied when the politics demands. The delay caused by the need for permission for any action must be a concern at all levels of command. Conversely, the temptation it provides for high-level tampering with operational matters has not been sufficiently recognized.

Integrated Circuits (IC) and Microcomputers

The IC has become ubiquitous. IC microprocessors are imbedded in engine controls, steering, navigation, interior communications, exterior communications, fire control, guided missiles, command and decision, and in the computers and terminals for all the administrative functions of the ship. It is changing the architecture of the combat systems. When digital computers were first introduced, they were relatively large and expensive and were confined to the center of the command and decision system. Then they were used in fire control, but still in a central location. As the microprocessor gained in capabilities and power, computers based on it began to appear in weapons and sensors and some of the functions previously performed in the central computer complex were delegated to these subsystems. As the subsystems gained power and capacity, they have been designed to perform more of the functions, particularly in degraded mode operations when a unit has failed or been damaged. Now, concern for the survivability of microprocessor-based systems is responsible for increased emphasis on electromagnetic compatibility, the exclusion of electromagnetic noise and nuclear electromagnetic pulse effects from shipboard equipments and their interconnections.

The reliability of shipboard computer-based systems has increased greatly. While much of this increase was due to the computer, the improved reliability of interconnections from improved shipyard processes and the development of fault-tolerant software also are major factors in the ability of systems to run for months without failure.

In commercial ships, microcomputers have been introduced in controls for unmanned engine rooms, in navigation systems, in satellite communications, and in loading control systems.

Computer-Aided Design and Manufacturing (CAD/CAM)

An amazing innovation in American industry was the advent of computer-aided design and manufacturing (CAD/CAM). Where in the previous decades there was little capability to custom manufacture items, in the 1980s there was a resurgence in this type of factory. Traditionally, American businesses had concentrated on expensive mass-production tooling that required a long production run to be economical. Custom manufacturing was so labor intensive that such business was left to foreign suppliers. With computer-aided design and manufacturing, engineering changes may be readily entered into production and so are much more acceptable to business. A resurgence in competitive position of American heavy machinery industries is possible in the next decade. The prognosis is not certain because foreign producers also have been quick to adapt CAD/CAM methods. The General Electric Company invested heavily in CAD/CAM, both for internal use and for sale to others. In 1987, GE management was reported to be disappointed with the slow domestic market for CAD/CAM and robot tools.

The Navy took an early lead in applying computer-aided design (CAD) and manufacturing (CAM) to the marine industry. The Navy sponsored the installation of numerical lofting in some yards, and developed a large library of design aids beginning in the 1960s. By the 1980s the library was large and in constant use. Captain L. D. Ballou, Mr. John Nachtsheim, Mr. W. Dietrich, Dr. Robert Johnson, Mr. Ralph Mills, and Mr. Philip Anklowitz are some of the people associated with the early development of ship design programs. Later, the names associated with design programs became too numerous to mention.

The Navy Manufacturing Technology Program developed numerically controlled machines and methods to produce fixed-pitch ship propellers, and the controllable reversible-pitch propeller blades for the DD-963 class were manufactured on numerically controlled machines. The rest of the ship propeller business has been slow to follow because of the investment cost. It is noted that the Soviet Union bought numerically controlled machines to produce quiet submarine propellers.[37]

Shipbuilding Productivity

There was a general effort to improve shipyard productivity that involved a Navy manufacturing technology program directed by Raymond Ramsay. Louis D. Chirillo was a power behind a shipyard innovation program. The Society of Naval Architects and Marine Engineers (SNAME) began publication of the *Journal of Ship Production* in May 1985, and a National Shipbuilding Research Program was started by the Maritime Administration (MARAD) to promote cooperative research by the industry.

Fiber Optics

Fiber optics became a preferred method of long distance telephone and data communication ashore. The U.S. Navy became interested in fiber optics as a method for reducing the weight, moment, and size of electrical signal cables in warships. The Aegis project made trial ship installations to gain experience with fiber optics. The Navy established a Fiber Optics Program Office under the direction of James H. Davis to develop standards and accelerate the shipboard application. Fiber-optic communications are expected to contribute to the survivability of shipboard combat systems and interior communications by providing redundant data paths that are immune to radio frequency interference and electromagnetic pulse damage. The program seeks to provide for the future growth of data transfer with the design of the initial installation.

Auxiliary Machinery

Titanium has been introduced in seawater systems, in cooler tubes and water boxes, in valve seats and discs, and in fire pumps. Titanium was selected because of its resistance to erosion. The fire pumps are standardized and were ordered in large quantity (over 100) for a big savings in price.[38]

High-efficiency electric motors are now specified for U.S. Naval ships. The higher efficiency results in reduced motor cooling requirements and reduced fan noise of the motors. High-efficiency air conditioning and high-efficiency fluorescent lighting also were introduced.

Improved Performance Machinery Program (IPMP) for Submarines

NavSea initiated a program to develop new lightweight submarine machinery. The objectives included improved efficiency and reduced noise. This machinery appears destined for the *Seawolf*, the SSN-21 class design that is in progress at Electric Boat and Newport News.

Hydrodynamics

The program for ship energy efficiency improvement initiated several hydrodynamic studies. Stern tunnels, asymmetric stern lines, bulbous bow, bulbous skeg, stern wedges, propeller inflow controls, vane wheels, contrarotating propellers, and large-diameter, low-rpm propellers have been included in commercial designs and in U.S. Navy studies. These are not all applicable to all designs, but the numerous approaches indicate the increased interest in economy. By 1985, a comprehensive program for hull cleaning afloat was in effect, and a program to develop improved hull coatings was underway.[39] A wax to prevent fouling of propellers also was announced. In contrast, the use of highly effective organo-tin toxicants in anti-fouling paint was severely restricted because of expected damage to marine life.

Foreign Developments

During this period there was much submarine design activity in Europe, both nuclear and diesel powered. Tyssen Nord See Werke designed and built three TR1700s for Argentina. The Australians funded a design modification of that submarine for their service, but bought a version of the Swedish *Vastergotland*. Holland has a new *Walrus* class building. The United Kingdom has a new diesel-electric submarine, the *Upholder*, and a new nuclear submarine, the *Trafalgar*.

China was reported to be building submarines, some believed to be nuclear. France has a new small nuclear submarine, the *Rubis* class. Canada has a program to replace her aging *Oberon* class with under-ice-capable submarines. The U.S. Navy is reported to be opposed to the transfer of nuclear power technology from the United Kingdom to Canada, blocking a Canadian *Trafalgar*, one of the likely sources of under-ice capability. Another candidate for Canada is the French *Rubis*. Israel also was shopping around for a new class of submarines and a number of American yards were interested. The U.S. Navy, fearful that U.S. technology would leak out, would not permit construction in the United States, so an IKL design was built in Germany for Israel. Many observers believe that the real reason for U.S. Naval opposition was that diesel-electric technology would leak in.[40] In any case, the policy resulted in lost design and construction experience in the United States. Captain Harry A. Jackson, in a 1988 presentation to the Flagship section of ASNE, pointed out the many features of foreign submarine designs that are traceable to U.S. Navy submarine developments.

NATO nations began a design program to define the frigate of the 1990s.[41] This was done by a multinational company that was situated in Hamburg, Germany, and composed of employees of the share-holding companies of the multinational. The nations participating were Canada, France, Germany, Italy, the Netherlands, Spain, the United Kingdom, and the United States. Earl Barondes, representing Canada, was selected as the General Manager of the joint-venture company.

NAVY SHIPBUILDING AND CONVERSIONS

Aircraft Carriers

The aircraft carrier program contains both new construction segments and a ship life extension program (SLEP). The decade began with consideration of the reactivation of the *Oriskany*, decommissioned in 1976. The Navy found that the cost would be excessive and she was scrapped instead. The *Saratoga* life extension program completion was delayed by faulty workmanship on the boilers. To extend the life of the *Midway*, blisters were added to compensate for the weight and moment she had accumulated over the years. In an attempt to improve resistance to damage however, the blisters gave too much additional metacentric height and then needed more alteration to restore her seakindliness. In this, the naval architects relearned a lesson that had been learned with battleships more than 50 years before and documented in Bureau of Construction and Repair Bulletin No. 1. The *Forrestal* and *Independence* also were "SLEPed." In addition to the SLEP, the older carriers are scheduled to have upgrades to their combat systems to make them equivalent to that of the *Theodore Roosevelt*.

New construction carriers were all nuclear propelled and built at Newport News Shipbuilding. They were essentially repeat designs of the *Nimitz* (CVN-68) with protection against missiles added for the *Theodore Roosevelt* (CVN-71), *Abraham Lincoln* (CVN-72), and *George Washington* (CVN-73). They are 90,944-ton full-load displacement, 1092-foot length overall (LOA) ships.

Submarines

Only two classes of submarines were being built during this period, the *Los Angeles* (SSN-688)-class attack submarines and the *Ohio* (SSBN-726)-class ballistic-missile submarines. The 688s were still being ordered when the design was more than 20 years old. Some Congressmen questioned the wisdom of continued procurement in the face of the progress made by the Soviets with the *Akula*-class submarines. Admiral DeMars, Director of Submarine Warfare, affirmed that the 688s were being improved and were still marginally better than the *Akula*. In 1986, the pattern of awarding half the SSN 688-class contracts to each of the submarine new construction yards was broken. All were awarded to Electric Boat. This was a surprise, because Electric Boat had been barred from bidding as a result of a dispute over the propriety of some charges on earlier contracts.[42] The Navy planned to continue buying four SSN 688s per year for the rest of the decade.

In 1986, the design yard responsibilities for the next class of SSN, the *Seawolf*, were assigned, but the construction of this submarine was not authorized. Electric Boat was assigned the design of the propulsion spaces, and Newport News Shipbuilding was assigned the rest of the design. Details of this design were not available, but the objectives were for a faster, deeper diving, and quieter submarine than the 688 class. A display model showed the same mostly cylindrical lines that have characterized all recent U.S. Navy submarine designs. Recently, Anthony Battista, a House Armed Services Committee staff aide and Navy gadfly, attacked the SSN-21 design as inadequate to meet the undersea threat. At the same time, he decried the lack of skilled naval architects. It is amazing that the lack of new design construction and the lack of naval architectural experience are seen as separate items in Congress.[43]

Battleships

The contract for the reactivation of the battleship *Iowa* was let to Ingalls and Avondale in July 1982. Ingalls did not have the capacity to dock the ship and teamed with Avondale to complete the job. The *Iowa* was rushed through reactivation to relieve the *New Jersey* in the Mediterranean, and the *New Jersey* returned for post-shakedown maintenance availability. The *Missouri* was reactivated at Long Beach Naval Shipyard.[44]

Cruisers

The *Ticonderoga* (CG-47) class ships were built at Ingalls and at Bath Iron Works. These are 9,600-ton full-load displacement, 566-foot LOA, 80,000-shaft-horsepower ships. Their hulls and their mechanical and electrical systems are similar to the DD-963 class, with the addition of the Aegis weapon system. On acceptance trials of the *Ticonderoga*, the commander of the Operational Test and Evaluation Force said that the ship outperformed other ships by orders of magnitude. On a second operational evaluation conducted in April 1984, the *Ticonderoga* defeated a "Vandal" sea-skimming target built to simulate anti-ship cruise missiles. In April 1985, the ship defeated multiple low-flying targets. Twenty-seven of this class were planned.

Before this class was authorized, there were several alternate designs considered as the Aegis ship. The guided-missile destroyer (DG) was proposed in May 1973 as a 6000-ton Aegis destroyer. The DG died because Congress decreed that all major combatants would be nuclear propelled. A nuclear-propelled Strike Cruiser design followed, but was opposed by the Department of Defense on the basis of its cost. Congress authorized the destroyer DDG-47 class in 1977. In December of that year a Request for Proposal was issued to Bath, Ingalls, and Quincy. The *Ticonderoga* was delivered 52 months after the contract was awarded. Captain John Bonds was the ship project manager under Rear Admiral Wayne Meyer's Aegis project. Joseph Maurelli was the naval architect for the project. They employed the "design budgeting" process, which allowed the design process to proceed while establishing budgets for the parts that were not complete enough to be included in the contract design.[45]

Destroyers

The *Kidd* (DD-993)-class destroyers were completed during this period. They were begun as Iranian ships with the anti-air warfare modernization capability of the DD-963 class. Some wags called them the "Ayatolla class." These destroyers have improved fragment protection and eight Harpoon cruise missiles in addition to the Standard missiles and a combat system similar to the CGN-38 class.

The DD-963 class have begun an improvement program. Six ships have the Tomahawk cruise missile in armored box launchers. The remainder are scheduled for the vertical launch system for Tomahawk and ASROC, for a towed array sonar, and for Light Airborne Multi-Purpose System (LAMPS III) helicopters with the Recovery Assist and Transfer (RAST) system to secure the helicopters on deck and move them into the hangar. The first ship completed the improvement program in June 1987, the remainder were scheduled to follow closely.

The *Arleigh Burke* (DDG-51) was awarded to Bath Iron Works. This new class is equipped with the Aegis missile system and the SPY-1 radar that first appeared on the new cruisers. It has a new optical fire control system, "Seafire," and a new version of active sonar. While the *Burke* does not have a helicopter hangar, it is capable of controlling the LAMPS III ASW system. The vertical launch system will carry ninety

missiles for Aegis, Tomahawk, and a new anti-submarine ASROC.

Frigates

The *Oliver Hazard Perry* (FFG-7) class continued to be built during this period at Bath, Todd Seattle, and Todd San Pedro. The last of these ships were modified to accommodate LAMPS III and RAST by raking the transom stern aft to increase the LOA without increasing the length between perpendiculars (LBP). They also have increased fragment protection with Kevlar armor in the superstructure. The last of these ships, the *Ingraham*, was added to the program by Congress to keep the San Pedro yard open. She was completed in 1987.

The class was the first of the "design to cost" program—this was changed to "design to Price" in honor of Admiral Frank Price, who dominated the design process. The first project manager in 1971 was Captain Edward Otth. In 1976, he turned the project management over to Captain John Beecher, and when he was promoted, Captain David Stembel became the manager. Captain Bruce Woodruff managed the last of the acquisition.

This project established an enviable record with the twenty-three follow ships built at Bath: the early deliveries totaled to 409 weeks before contract delivery date, and the cost was about 300 million dollars under the target cost.

In addition to the ships built for the U.S. Navy, four were built for the Australian Navy at Seattle and two were built in Australia. The Spanish Navy is building four in Spain.

Amphibious Ships

The LSD 41 class of eight ships was built at Lockheed and at Avondale shipyards. These are diesel-propelled with Pielstick design engines built by Fairbanks Morse. A cargo variant was planned in 1987.

The *Wasp* LHD-1 class is a new design similar to the *Tarawa*-class LHA. This class has a larger well deck that can accommodate three LCAC amphibious air-cushion vehicles. This class is also designed to operate about twenty Harrier VSTOL aircraft and thirty-two CH-46 helicopters or their equivalent. Equivalent probably means the Bell-Boeing tilt-rotor VTOL aircraft that is being designed for the Marine Corps. LHD construction started in 1985 at Ingalls.

The LCAC landing craft was in production at Bell-Halter after a slow start. The first was delivered in December 1984, and the second in March 1985. This program suffered from stretch-out funding throughout the R&D phase that began in 1970. The design was 15 years old before the first production unit was delivered. The surface effect ship and the LCAC were both being developed with two competing designs. There were then four craft being built with funding appropriate for one; the result was very large overhead and very little progress. James Schuler, the R&D manager, observed one day that there was good news and bad news. The good news was that the LCAC was operational; the bad news was that it was Russian.

Mine Warfare Ships

The mine countermeasures (MCM) ship program awarded contracts to Peterson Builders and to Marinette Marine for a class of wooden mine countermeasures ships. Prior to the award of the contract, Vickers and an Italian yard offered licenses for their design methods for reinforced plastic construction. In the 1960s, the United States and the United Kingdom supported a joint R&D program at Dunfirmline, Scotland, to develop a glass-reinforced plastic construction method for minesweeper-size ships. The United States did not continue the development and stayed with wooden construction, despite the growing shortage of suitable timber. The mine countermeasures ship is not a minesweeper of the conventional form, but is equipped to launch and operate a mine neutralization vehicle capable of investigating mine-like targets found by its sonar system. There was some difficulty with the engines for the *Avenger* class. The Navy had a stock of Waukesha engines left over from an earlier program to re-engine the ocean minesweepers (MSOs), and sought to furnish them for the new class. The engines were all of one rotation direction and needed to be reworked to match the required rotation for the *Avengers*. The press had fun with that.

Shortly after the start of the MCM program, the coastal mine hunter (MSH) was proposed and a contract was awarded to Bell Aerospace for the *Cardinal* (MSH-1). This was to be an air-cushion vehicle constructed of reinforced plastic. Experiments conducted in Britain proved that an ACV could survive a mine explosion directly under the vehicle. Earlier, a proposal to design such a vehicle in this country was offered by Norman Jasper, the technical director of the Mine Defense Laboratory at Panama City, Florida. The proposal was turned down by Admiral Kidd, then Chief of Naval Material, as patently impractical. The construction of the MSH-1 was stopped because of the weight growth and a hull section test failure, proving that it is impractical in this country. An Italian-design reinforced plastic minesweeper replaced the MSH class. Congress disapproved a plan to build the ships in Italy, and so they were ordered built in the United States with Italian technology.

Auxiliaries

Most of the auxiliaries built during this period are for Military Sealift Command operation. The T-AGOS 4 class was designed to provide ocean surveillance where there is no bottom-mounted surveillance array coverage. These ships tow the SURTASS array at a low speed and communicate their acoustic data to shore-based command centers. These ships do their job well, but are rough riding in bad weather. A new Small Waterplane Area Twin Hull (SWATH) design has been awarded to McDermott in the expectation that this hull form will allow the crews to perform in bad weather in the high latitudes. The design manager for this class, Philip Covich, has written about the ship and the design process in the May 1987 *Naval Engineers Journal*.[46] The term "SWATH" was invented by Sidney Hersh when he was assigned to the advanced development branch of NavShips.

A class of nine oilers for coastal minesweeper (MSC) operation has been ordered from Avondale and Pennsylvania Shipbuilding. The T-AO 187 class is diesel-powered by Pielstick engines manufactured by Fairbanks-Morse.

Two oceanographic survey ships, T-AGS 39 class, were awarded to Bethlehem Steel, Sparrows Point. They are diesel-powered and are designed to carry an improved bottom mapping sonar.

Four salvage ships of the *Safeguard* (ARS-50) class were built by Peterson Builders. William

Milwee described the design considerations of salvage ships in the March 1984 *Naval Engineers Journal*.[47] These ships are equipped with towing winches, ground tackle for salvage pulling, and diver support systems.

A new class of twenty-two patrol craft, YP-679 class, was built by Peterson and Marinette for instruction and training service at the U.S. Naval Academy. The January 1987 *Naval Engineers Journal*[48] and the ASNE *Patrol Boat Symposium Proceedings* have papers on the design of YPs for the Naval Academy.

Six commercial ships were converted to T-ACS crane ships by the Maritime Administration to support container ships used for wartime sealift. Twelve ships will be converted by 1991. Four Sea-Land SL-7 high-speed container ships were converted to vehicle cargo ships to support Marine battalions. These ships can load and discharge tanks through side doors and ramps, and have cranes for self-unloading of other cargo. Thirteen commercial cargo ships were converted to T-AK types under "build and charter" contracts. This program provided much-needed lift capacity and, at the same time, relieved the glut of shipping that was depressing cargo rates.

The *Mercy* and *Comfort* were converted from supertankers to super hospital ships at National Steel's San Diego yard using modular construction techniques. They each have a twelve-room operating complex and eighty-bed intensive care units.

U.S. COAST GUARD

Medium Endurance Cutters

The Coast Guard is in the process of acquiring a fleet of thirteen 270-foot medium endurance cutters. The first flight of four cutters has been completed by Tacoma Boatbuilding Company, and the cutters have been in service since 1984. The second flight of nine cutters was awarded to Robert E. Derecktor of Rhode Island, a new shipyard located at the former site of the Navy destroyer piers at Newport. Several cutters of the second class have been delivered to the Coast Guard, and the last is expected in 1989.

The 270-foot cutter's armament reflects the close cooperation that exists between the Navy and Coast Guard. In addition to one Mk 75 76-mm dual purpose gun and Mk 92 fire control system, the class has either installed or has provisions to install a towed array sonar, an SLQ-32 electronic countermeasures system, an Mk 36 SRBOC decoy, a Phalanx close-in weapon system, a Harpoon missile system, and a LAMPS-1 helicopter system. This armament is funded by the Navy and would be required by the Coast Guard to perform its wartime responsibilities as part of the Navy.

To reduce the manning requirements of the 270-foot cutters to a minimum, the Coast Guard developed a Command, Display, and Control (COMDAC) System that has the capacity to automate bridge, navigation, and communications functions. Through the use of digitized charts, an optical sight, and radar inputs, navigational functions, including collision avoidance, have been simplified.[49]

Patrol Boats

The Coast Guard has also bought a new class of 110-foot patrol boats, the *Island* class. When Vice President George Bush directed that the level of operations against drug traffic be increased, the Coast Guard decided to request bids for an existing design in the expectation that this would speed up the delivery of the boats. Marine Power and Equipment won the contract, but it was challenged by Bollinger Machine Shop and Shipyard Company because the engine proposed was not identical to that in the parent. Bollinger won the contract after the court directed reevaluation of proposals. The winning design was the Vosper-Thornycroft 110-foot boat powered by two Paxman Valenta 16-cylinder 4,000-horsepower engines derated to 3,000 horsepower to match the torque limitation of the propeller shafts. (The engines had been uprated since being initially specified for the design.) Bollinger is the licensee for United States production of this design, and Vosper engineers assisted in establishing the production. Initial reports stated that the hull plating forward needed additional stiffening for service in the Caribbean, and the second fleet of boats currently under construction have been strengthened to overcome this problem. Although the boat's performance is generally satisfactory, the hull strength problems, coupled with potential logistic support problems of a projected 40-year-old engine, make off-the-shelf procurement of boats for demanding Coast Guard use an open issue. The design of these patrol boats is discussed in a February 1986 article in the Naval Institute *Proceedings*, and two papers were delivered at the ASNE/Coast Guard Patrol Boat Symposium on this subject.[50]

Polar-Class Icebreaker

The Coast Guard has completed the contract design for a replacement polar icebreaker. Although funds have not yet been appropriated for construction, they are expected, particularly since the icebreakers *Northwind* and *Westwind* have recently been decommissioned.

COMMERCIAL SHIPBUILDING

Coal for ship propulsion fuel reappeared in the SS *Energy Independence*, delivered in 1983. The ship is in service transporting coal from Hampton Roads to New England Electric Company utility plants. She was the first coal-burner built in the United States in over 30 years. This coal-burner shifts to oil when entering or leaving port, but trials demonstrated that maneuvering was satisfactory on coal. The predecessor collier for this service sank in a storm on what was planned to be its last voyage.

The one commercial maritime business that has been booming is the cruise business. *Marine Engineering/Log* June 1987 listed the cruise lines operating from American ports. There were 109 cruise ships in service or under construction, ranging from 15 to 2,600 passengers. The total passenger capacity delivered during the 1980s was over 28,000.

The Army Corps of Engineers built a replacement for the dredge *Essayons* at Bath Iron Works on subcontract to Sun Shipbuilding. The ship is a diesel-propelled hopper dredge with extensive automation. Side dragarm suction dredges contain 1,080-kilowatt electric motor-driven dredge pumps. The design for this dredge began on 1 July 1976 and was completed 1 June 1979. The ship was delivered in 1983.

In June 1987 there were four commercial ships under construction in United States shipyards, and no others were on order.[51]

OTHER NAVAL ENGINEERING

The American yacht *Stars and Stripes*, skippered by Dennis Connor, defeated the Australian *Kookaburra III* to return the America's Cup to the United States in 1987. The design teams of the challengers utilized the best research and high technology of this country. Tank testing, numerical hydrodynamics and aerodynamics, CAD/CAM, and even game theory were used in the hull and sail designs. This was revealed at the Chesapeake Sailing Yacht Symposium held at the U.S. Naval Academy in March 1987 and in an article for *Scientific American*.[52]

The British Cunard Line's *Queen Elizabeth II* was re-engined with diesel-electric power. Her nine M.A.N-Burmeister & Wain engines produce 95 megawatts of A.C. electric power. The propellers are constant-speed, controllable reversible pitch, driven by synchronous motors. They had Grim Vane wheels to recover some of the propeller losses, but they were broken during sea trials and were removed. This application of electric drive, while differing from any American application, demonstrates that the concept is economically viable.

The liquid natural gas transport business came to a halt in the United States. The tanker owners were looking for conversion to other service.

The *Sam Rayburn* (SSBN-563), first Poseidon missile submarine, was decommissioned to stay within SALT limitations.

Tennessee-Tombigbee waterway opened, providing access from Mobile Bay to the Tennessee River and the Tennessee Valley Authority rivers and lakes.

A joint French and American expedition discovered the wreck of the SS *Titanic*. The interior was explored by an unmanned tethered vehicle, *Jason Jr.*, controlled from the submersible *Alvin*. The search was led by Robert D. Ballard of the Woods Hole Oceanographic Institution.

The world's first successful guyed tower oil field platform was installed in 1,000 feet of water in the Gulf of Mexico in 1983.

Workers on the Deep Sea Drilling Project, operating from the *Glomar Challenger*, discovered that the accretion of sediment in ocean trenches was much less than expected, casting doubt on some of the theories of tectonic plate movement. They also discovered evidence of mass extinction of sea life that occurred at about the same time as the extinction of dinosaurs.

Admiral Hyman G. Rickover, the Director of Naval Nuclear Propulsion, retired 8 January 1982 and died 8 July 1986.[53]

SUMMARY

This era marked a restoration of some of the power of the U.S. Navy that had been eroded in the previous decade. The Navy acquired ships in large classes that contributed to the economy in first cost and in support costs. The U.S. Navy is well on the way to 600 ships with large classes of submarines, destroyers, and frigates. Were it not for the recent build-up, our Navy would be outclassed.

The Navy built one class of submarines over a period of 20 years, a practice that did great harm to the submarine design experience of the nation. During this decade the Soviet Navy introduced four new classes of attack submarines with startling advances in performance. The Soviet Navy has grown to be a serious challenge to the navies of the free world. Besides their formidable submarine force, they are now building aircraft carriers.

Naval ship propulsion is either nuclear or conventional. The nuclear ships have steam machinery and the new conventional ships are gas turbine or diesel-propelled. There is a single fuel for the conventional ships, and the fuel consumption is less than it would be for steam propulsion. New machinery developments emphasize fuel economy, giving promise of future savings.

American shipbuilding became increasingly for government service; commercial ship orders were nonexistent by 1987. A change in government policy permitted an increasing proportion of ship components to be of foreign manufacture, and foreign sources underbid American sources for auxiliary machinery for some ships. There is cause for concern for the survival of the present marine machinery infrastructure of the nation.

Notes

1 Lehman, John F., "ASNE Day Luncheon Address," *Naval Engineers Journal*, July 1986; *Washington Post*, 18 February 1987.

2 FY 1980, FY 1981 Congressional Hearings, Washington, D.C.: Government Printing Office.

3 Charbonneau, Gary, "The Soviet Navy and Forward Deployment," Naval Institute *Proceedings*, March 1979. Also Hickman, LCDR William F., "Soviet Policy in the Indian Ocean," Naval Institute *Proceedings*, August 1979.

4 Wright, Christopher C., "U.S. Navy Shipbuilding Budgets, 1981," *Warship International*, No. 1, 1982. Also *Ibid.*, "1983," No. 1, 1984.

5 *Soviet Military Power 1986, 1987*, Washington, D.C.: U.S. Government Printing Office, March 1986, 1987; RAdm Butts's testimony reported in Congressional hearings, U.S. Government Printing Office.

6 Naval Submarine League Symposium, Radisson Hotel, Alexandria Virginia, June 1987.

7 *Soviet Military Power 1981, 1982, 1983, 1984, 1985, 1986, 1987*, Washington, D.C.: U.S. Government Printing Office.

8 Hiatt, Fred, "Soviet Sub, Merchant Ship Collide," *Washington Post*, 22 September 1984; "Crippled Sub

Seen Off Japan," *New York Times*, 22 September 1984.

9 "New Developments in the Soviet Navy," *Warship International*, No. 4 1983, No. 2 1984, No. 2 1985.

10 Morison, Samuel L., "The Falklands Campaign: A Chronology," *Warship International*, No. 4, 1983.

11 Walker, CAPT John, "Falkland Lessons," *Naval Engineers Journal*, July 1983.

12 "The Attack on the USS *Stark* FFG-31," *Warship International*, No. 3, 1987.

13 Truver, Scott C., "Mines of August: an International Whodunit," Naval Institute *Proceedings*, May 1985.

14 Tagliabue, John, "Ship Carrying 400 is Siezed," *New York Times*, 8 October 1985; "F-14s Use Latest Electronics in Egypt Air Intercept," *Aviation Week*, 21 October 1985.

15 Ullman, Harland and Paula J. Pettavino, "The Dreary Future of U.S. Maritime Industries," Naval Institute *Proceedings*, May 1985.

16 "U.S. Navy Shipbuilding," *Marine Engineering/Log*, June 1986; "Military Shipbuilding," *Marine Engineering/Log*, March 1987.

17 Auerbach, Stuart, "America, the Diminished Giant," *Washington Post*, 15 April 1987.

18 *Washington Post*, 17 July 1987.

19 Moorhead, Seth B., "The Latest in Ship Weapon Launchers—The Vertical Launching System," *Naval Engineers Journal*, April 1981.

20 Extracts from the unpublished "Official History of the Aegis Program."

21 "All Hands," *Shipmate*, September 1987.

22 Marron, H. D., "Gas Turbine Waste Heat Recovery Propulsion for U.S. Navy Surface Combatants," *Naval Engineers Journal*, October 1981. Also, Donovan, Michael R. and Wayne S. Mattson, "RACER—A Design for Maintainability," *Naval Engineers Journal*, July 1985.

23 Holmes Richard W., II, "Aegis Cruiser Ship Systems Engineering Improvements," *Naval Engineers Journal*, May 1987.

24 McMullen, John J., "The Gas Turbine Installation in Liberty Ship John Seargent," Society of Naval Architects and Marine Engineers *Transactions*, 1955. Also, McLean, H. D., C. C. Tangerini, and W. H. VanCott, "Report on 9000 Hour Operation of Marine Propulsion Gas Turbine in the John Seargent," *Naval Engineers Journal*, November 1960.

25 Bowen, Thomas L. and Daniel A. Groghan, "Advanced-Cycle Gas Turbines for Naval Ship Propulsion," *Naval Engineers Journal*, May 1984. Also, Lewis-Jones, Trevor, "Navy Moving Toward 'Longer Legged' Ships," *Marine Engineering/Log*, March 1987.

26 Robey, H. N., H. O. Stevens, and K. T. Page, "Application of Variable Speed Constant Frequency Generators to Propulsion-Derived Ship Service," *Naval Engineers Journal*, May 1985.

27 Jolliff, Dr. James and Dr. David L. Greene, "Advanced Integrated Electric Propulsion—A Reality of the Eighties," *Naval Engineers Journal*, May 1983.

28 Lavis, David, "Air Cushion Craft," *Naval Engineers Journal*, February 1985.

29 **Marafioti, CDR Ronald J., "Quick Change—Commercial Surface Effect Ship to Coast Guard Patrol Boat," *Naval Engineers Journal*, May 1985.**

30 Butler, Edward A., "The Surface Effect Ship," *Naval Engineers Journal*, February 1985.

31 Gupta, S. K. and T. W. Schmidt, "Developments in SWATH Technology," *Naval Engineers Journal*, May 1986.

32 Covich, Philip, "T-AGOS 19: An Innovative Program for an Innovative Design," *Naval Engineers Journal*, May 1987.

33 Brown, D. K., J. P. Catchpole, and A. M. J. Shand, "Evaluation of Hydrofoil HMS Speedy," *Royal Institute of Naval Architects Transactions*, 1984.

34 Ellsworth, William M., "Twenty Foilborne Years, The U.S. Navy Hydrofoil *High Point* PCH-1," DTNSRDC Contract N00600-81-D-0252.

35 Kehoe, Capt. J. W., and Kenneth S. Brower, "The Israeli *Reshef* Missile Boat," *Naval Engineers Journal*, November 1984.

36 Lehman, John F., "Luncheon Address," *Naval Engineers Journal*, July 1986.

37 Stern, Howard and Robert Metzger, "Automation of Propeller Inspection and Finishing," *Naval Engineers Journal*, May 1985.

38 Adamson, Wayne L. and Ronald W. Schutz, "Application of Titanium in Shipboard Seawater Cooling Systems," *Naval Engineers Journal*, May 1987.

39 Cologer, Christopher P., "Six Year Interaction of Underwater Cleaning with Copper-Based Anti-fouling Paints on Navy Surface Ships," *Naval Engineers Journal*, May 1984.

40 Polmar, Norman, "International Submarine Forces," Naval Institute *Proceedings*, March 1985.

41 Johnson, Robert S., "NFR-90: International Industrial Aspects," *Naval Engineers Journal*, March 1987.

42 Tyler, Patrick, *Running Critical*, New York: Harper and Row, 1986.

43 Wilson, George C., "Departing Hill Specialist Attacks Navy's New Sub," *Washington Post*, January 13, 1988.

44 Sims, Philip J., James R. Edwards, LCDR Robert L. Dickey, and H. S. Schull, "Design for *New Jersey, Iowa*, and *Des Moines* Modernization," *Naval Engineers Journal*, May 1984.

45 Maurelli, Joseph and Robert J. Scott, "Design Budgeting—A New Dimension in Acquisition Strategy," *Naval Engineers Journal*, April 1978.

46 Covich, Philip, "T-AGOS 19 Program and Design," *Naval Engineers Journal*, May 1987.

47 Milwee, William I., "Design Considerations in the Design Architecture of Salvage Ships," *Naval Engineers Journal*, March 1984.

48 Compton, Robert H., Howard A. Chatterton, Gordon Hatchell, and Frank K. McGrath, "The U.S. Naval Academy's New Yard Patrol Craft: From Concept to Delivery," *Naval Engineers Journal*, January 1987.

49 Hall, LCDR Jon W., USCG and LT (JG) Michael D. Anderson, USCG, "The U.S. Coast Guard Multi-Mission Cutter: Command, Display and Control (COMDAC)," *Naval Engineers Journal*, October 1980.

50 Latas, LT Robert M., LT Frank N. McCarthey, Wm. Gary Rook, and CDR William M. Simpson, Jr., "U.S. Coast Guard 110-Ft. Island Class Patrol Boats—Concept to Completion," *Patrol Boats 86, A Technical Symposium*, March 1986.

51 "Cruise Fleets that Sail From U.S. Ports," *Marine Engineering/Log*, June 1987. Also "New Opportunities Must be Found," *Marine Engineering/Log*, June 1987.

52 Letcher, John S., John K. Marshall, James C. Oliver, III, and Nils Salvesen, "Stars and Stripes," *Scientific American*, August 1978.

53 Obituary, *Washington Post*, 9 July 1986.

CHAPTER
TWELVE

Summary

by Randolph King

WHERE WE HAVE BEEN

Early in the 4 years required to prepare this narrative of naval engineering, several prospective authors and others interested in the project discussed how best to proceed. Two general approaches emerged. The first required identification of major naval engineering trends over the hundred years, selecting a manageable number, and covering each chosen topic in a chapter. The alternative method of attacking this formidable task was to divide the century into tractable periods or epochs. An approach by engineering topics was attractive. Subject matter coverage of the book would be readily identified and expertise in a particular field gave promise of being easier to find than an individual willing to take on all aspects of an era. Nevertheless, the chronological approach won out as being more suited to the book's objective as a narrative history.

To assist authors in determining the chapter's scope, a brief list of naval engineering trends was developed and revised as chapter outlines were completed, summaries prepared, and omissions noted. These trends are set forth in Appendix B. Even with this sort of information, the author of each chapter was left with the difficult decisions of determining a manageable scope for the chapter and identifying sources available within the constrained schedule.

As each year, decade, and century changes, pundits review the major topics of the era and prognosticators give us their predictions for the period ahead. There have been efforts to identify the most important events in all of history, or during considerable periods, such as for the Bicentennial of the United States. "What Really Mattered" was the subject of an essay referring to the effort by E. Clifton Daniel to name the most important headlines of the Twentieth century. The piece discusses the choices and omissions and concludes: "Journalism (and history too) is what lives in that all too brief gap between

385

the not yet known and the already forgotten."[1] It was our authors' dilemma to wade into this gap, examine the period to be covered, and make a chronicle of oftentimes poorly recorded implicit naval engineering developments. Some trends have been covered at length in previous works, for example: the shift from sail to steam and then to nuclear energy; the transition from smooth bore broadsides to rifled guns with precise control of firepower; the importance to maritime commerce of container ships and intermodal transportation systems. Somewhat less publicized in maritime applications are such major developments as fiber optics, vertical launch weapons, phased array radars, satellite navigation and communication, improved materials, and fabrication techniques. We expect disagreement with our choices of "what really mattered," and we issue a general challenge to others to choose their topics and either supplement the record or set it straight.

Whatever the consensus on adequacy of coverage of specific topics in this book, we believe we have shown that dedicated, innovative people have contributed to naval engineering and that progress has been much greater than the glacial creep sometimes ascribed to maritime endeavors. We are confident that this multidiscipline field will continue to serve the nation well.

A LOOK TO THE FUTURE

In *The Devil's Dictionary*, Ambrose Bierce defines prophecy as "the art and practice of selling one's credibility for future delivery." With the present far-reaching general economic, Federal budget, and international turbulence, and a United States presidential election in confluence as the 1980s come to an end, it would be foolhardy to attempt long-range predictions. Credibility would most probably end in the trash can. There are certain shorter range indicators, however, that merit attention and have reasonable expectation of importance in the direction of naval engineering.

In remarks that were approximately one quarter ("two bells") into his tenure as Chief of Naval Operations, Admiral Carlisle A. H. Trost speaks of the "complex problem of getting advance technology out of the laboratory and into the fleet while . . . still state of the art." He goes on to say "the challenge during my tenure is to make the decision that will build the Navy with which we enter the 21st century." From the Navy's viewpoint he continues with an excellent summary of the naval engineering challenges:

No one can predict the future. Startling breakthroughs, such as we have seen this year [1987] in things like superconductivity, ceramic turbines, and directed energy weapons, may alter the look of the battle fleets of the 21st century in a completely new way. After more than 2,000 years of naval warfare confined to the surface of the seas, the early 1900s ushered in a true revolution with the advent of the airplane and the submarine. For the first time, the battle area became three dimensional. Will the 21st century see changes just as revolutionary? I'm betting that it will. If we can solve the technical challenges, and if we can maintain our personnel force at the same high quality as we enjoy today, the fleets of the 21st century will have the potential for the total domination of a very large area from the ocean floor to the farthest reaches of space. And that means an even more credible deterrence.

Consider a few possibilities. Nuclear-fusion plants that use sea water as their fuel. Or fossil-fueled engines so efficient that refueling at sea becomes almost unnecessary. Aircraft that travel into space and return. Platforms automatically controlled by other platforms. Equipment that permits one person to do the work of three. Sensors capable of detecting, classifying, and tracking any object on or above the ocean surface. Weapons with inexhaustible ammunition, that shoot particles, beams, and electromagnetic pulses instead of missiles and projectiles. Offensive systems that combine the speed and capacity of artificial intelligence with the imagination, judgment, and moral scruples of the man in the loop. Defensive systems that are nearly impenetrable. These are dazzling prospects, aren't they? As one physicist recently said about superconductors, "the challenge is not to do something that everyone has wanted to do. The challenge is to do something that no one has yet imagined."[2]

Another recently retired senior naval officer summarized informally his views on likely Navy technological emphasis in the near future. These included: cover and deception; smart weapons; activities in space, including the Strategic Defense Initiative, space shuttle flights, extended ability to operate in space stations for extended periods, and sophisticated satellites; and finally, information processing, already of major importance and giving clear indication of further significant impact in robotics, artificial intelligence, and decision-making.

Clearly the Navy's submarine force will continue to stress its trinity of stealth, depth, and speed, using advanced detection and weapon systems of many types. The broad question of extending sensors and secure communications will include additional use of remotely controlled vehicles and perhaps lighter-than-air platforms.

The Navy has conducted research in superconductivity for many years; realization of means to exploit recently reported breakthroughs can lead to significant improvements in electrical and electronic equipment. The ability for both manned and unmanned undersea operations will continue to be important in military operations, commercial endeavors, recreation, and nautical archaeology. Evidence of activity in this area was the report that France launched in 1987 the world's largest civilian submersible.

The Navy's desired composition is well defined into the 1990s by programs already underway, by budget submissions, and by policy statements. Actual budgets, however, are likely to affect adversely the number of ships, aircraft, and personnel. The crunch is summarized in the heading of a 29 August 1985 *Wall Street Journal* article, "Funding the Fleet. Expanding Navy is on a Collision Course with Budget Politics. New Ships and Ports Require More Money to Maintain than Congress Will Allot." The Washington *Post* reported the conclusions of a publicly-funded advisory group to the National Security Council and the Department of Defense (Commission on Integrated Long-Term Strategy). The article included this statement:

> A central message of the report, titled "Discriminate Deterrence," was a call for more selective preparations for military action using 'precision weapons' made possible by dramatic improvements in accuracy brought about by computers and microelectronics.[3]

While this is only one of many public and private examinations of proposals for future directions in national strategy, it is indicative of major issues having impact on the defense establishment.

Severe budget cuts and major internal reorganization beset the Coast Guard and will continue to affect that fine service into the future. The objectives stated by the Commandant in a recent "Long-Range View"[4] cover a wide range of tasks in protection of life, ship safety and security, property damage, protection of the marine environment, cold weather operations, and maintenance of a ready armed force. The Coast Guard has many highly qualified naval engineers, both in uniform and civilian, contributing to the Coast Guard's mission. Undoubtedly, the emphasis on engineering excellence will continue, but it is not clear at what level the effort will be supported nor to what degree the Coast Guard will engage in engineering developments. Design and production of replacement icebreakers is one area, however, that will merit comprehensive and talented effort.

The sorry plight of the U.S. merchant marine continues to be documented, most recently by a high-level commission.[5] The dependence of this country on maritime commerce should be obvious. Moreover, the case has been made frequently that in any extended military emergency or war, the vast quantity of needed material can move only by sea. The deplorable aspect of this situation is that *following a container ship delivery in November 1987 there were no more commercial ships under construction or on order in domestic shipyards.* Engineering research and development relate to the level of ship and other construction; hence, it is reasonable to say that the pace will be slow in the nonmilitary sphere. The related downward trend in shipyard industrial capability and in their suppliers, both major and secondary, will also dampen naval engineering activities. One small bright note is the appearance of several large new cruise ships of non-U.S. construction, and the apparent robust health of that segment of maritime industry. Ocean resource recovery and utilization is another area that may possibly develop and require innovative naval engineering. The mundane-sounding concept of an ocean incinerator ship is a major engineering challenge.

We have devoted but small coverage to recreational boating and its sophisticated relative, ocean racing. Nevertheless, this is a multibillion dollar business in the United States and involves many facets of engineering innovation and excellence. During the America's Cup challenge at Newport in 1983, when research was neglected and the trophy went to Australia, and again in 1987, when it returned to the United States as a result of both research and sailing skill, there was immense worldwide interest. Many reports alluded to winged keels; hydrodynamic development testing; aerodynamic sail design; and mechanical marvels in sail handling, coatings, and myriad other developments. In the latter part of 1987, attention turned to a challenge from New Zealand leading to a race by large boats. Once again, this has captured the attention of a broader spectrum than the yachting community and has even been front-page news. It is almost certain that there will be major design and engineering advances in the boats that meet in this event and that many of these innovations will ultimately find their way to the broader market.

The Annapolis, Maryland, *Capital*, ever-sensitive to yachting, reported on 29 September 1987, "Superyacht pays call," describing the 92-foot *Diablesse*, originally built as a private luxury cruising yacht and purported to be among the largest high-performance modern sailing yachts. *Time* magazine reported on luxury power craft, "High Life Afloat: Superduper Yachts" in its 7 September 1987 issue. In addition to opulence in outfitting, these boats reflect engineering advances that are likely, in time, to find their way to less costly boats. It is probable that Wall Street events of 19 October 1987 will have at least a short term adverse impact on the recreational boating market, but it can still be expected to remain an important segment of the maritime industry. Plans continued for the $1 million purse, winner-take-all "Ultimate Yacht Race" to be held in May 1988 off Corpus Christie, Texas.

Despite the somewhat bleak, or at least cloudy, picture of maritime matters outlined above, competent naval engineers will continue to be needed. A commercial for the BMW automobile speaks to the general theme that "We prefer the judgment of engineers to that of accountants." This may seem self-serving when mentioned in a history of naval engineering. Most certainly operational requirements for military equipment, economic analysis in the commercial world, cost

of the product, and production considerations will affect program decisions at least as much as engineering sophistication and operational adequacy. Nonetheless, the broad implications of the 1916 statement ascribed to Admiral Lord Jellicoe must be remembered: "The prelude to action is the work of the engine room department." The importance of a single, highly innovative technical person was illustrated in mid-1987 by considerable coverage in business reports of the departure of one key designer from a major computer manufacturer following termination of a line of development directly associated with the expertise of that individual. The company's stock promptly fell several points.

Problems and challenges facing the many disciplines within naval engineering are generally similar to those of other areas. Matters of professional ethics, standards of performance, and product liability responsibilities will continue to be important subjects for individual and organization consideration and action. Continuing education will be necessary for all practicing engineers; the myriad courses offered by schools, professional societies, and entrepreneurs include something for everyone but present an increasing problem in cost and selection. Among the serious challenges for naval engineering is that maritime opportunities are generally less known to young people. This calls for appropriate professional societies to remedy the situation by vigorous education and recruiting programs; fortunately some actions are already underway. Whatever the professional issues, it can be predicted that there will be a place for talent and a need for integrity in the many aspects of naval engineering. We must develop and encourage promising individuals to carry on the essential endeavors encompassed within this field. Some will come to be recognized as leaders and professionals of particular merit and may, in the view of future generations, take their place among such past naval engineering giants as Harold G. Bowen, Washington Lee Capps, Edward Lull Cochrane, John Wilkie Collins, John Adolphus Dahlgren, William F. Durand, John Ericksson, Reginald Aubrey Fessenden, Charles H. Haswell, Samuel R. Heller, Jr., William Hovgaard, Benjamin Franklin Isherwood, Albert Kingsbury, Emory Scott Land, John H. MacAlpine, Andrew I.

McKee, George M. Melville, Ben Morell, John Niedermair, William Sterling Parsons, Hyman G. Rickover, Harold E. Saunders, David Watson Taylor, Edward H. Thiele, Nathan P. Towne, and William H. Webb, to name but a few from a century of noteworthy uniformed and civilian naval engineers.

AND FINALLY

Even the most casual reader of this book, whether a neophyte or an expert in naval engineering, will realize that the authors could scratch only the surface of this vast technical area. We trust that the reader from either category will appreciate the sweep of the subject and understand our dilemma. The approach was taken deliberately, with the hope of adding value to the literature on naval engineering, because no other single source was found pointing toward the same objective of narrative breadth and historic span.

Most particularly, we hoped to show major developmental trends in naval engineering and highlight those who made things happen. This last proved most difficult to accomplish. Interesting biographical facts and narratives about naval engineers are in scant supply, with a few notable exceptions. Search was aimed at locating material giving a good picture of individuals and how their interactions took place with important engineering decisions and developments. History's judgment of system success based on equipment performance and operational adequacy shows whether they were wise or in error. We have been less successful than we had hoped in searching out meaningful anecdotes, vignettes, and personal memorabilia. Relatively sterile curricula vitae, official or company biographies, and obituaries are inadequate to bring history to life. The oral histories of the Naval Institute and the U.S. Coast Guard are noted with particular appreciation. We hope that their lead will be followed by both companies and schools to fill significant gaps in the record. Personal accounts are vital to future efforts in achieving historic perspective of the field of naval engineering.

The value of recorded personal insights has been noted by many. In his excellent book *Ultra Goes to War*, Ronald Lewin says, "Goethe's re-

mark is true of military history: 'The most important things are not always to be found in the files.'"[6] Admiral Trost, Chief of Naval Operations, reminded participants in the Current Strategy Forum: ". . . and do keep a record of your thoughts . . . Make that a lifetime habit. . . ."[7]

In his essay in *Time*, Walter Isaacson leads off with: "Pity the poor historian. The wonders of modern technology have combined with the dynamics of government scandals to make his task next to impossible." He then goes on to discuss the adverse impact on searching for the facts of tape recorders, the telephone, Congressional hearings, and "obfuscating memos." He offers an admittedly unlikely solution but with some nostalgia he says:

> Averell Harriman and Robert Lovett, two great statesmen who had been Wall Street partners, talked on the phone regularly when they were apart and then would exchange letters the same afternoon, putting on paper what they had said. 'As I told you over the telephone this morning . . .' they would typically begin. Back then, of course, the post was more efficient: the letter would usually arrive before the next morning's phone conversation.[8]

A fascinating book was noted that makes the following dedication: "This book is dedicated to people who record their lives with good letters, diaries and photographs. And to those who keep and treasure the documents."[9]

Many public and private organizations in the United States are available to "keep and treasure the documents" but apparently many naval engineers do not recognize the importance of doing so. It is hoped that this history, particularly its gaps and inadequate coverage, will raise awareness of this vital matter and reduce the number of sad stories, which are some version of, "I just threw away my [or my spouse's] papers. They were cluttering the house [basement, garage, attic] and I had no idea anyone wanted them." For naval and Coast Guard personnel, uniformed or civilian, there are historians in the Navy, Marine Corps, and Coast Guard organizations who are staffed to discuss personal papers and are equipped to receive and handle pertinent collections. The three Federal sea-oriented academies, Naval, Coast Guard, and Merchant Marine, have capacity and interest for papers from individuals with strong ties to them. Most colleges and universities from which naval engineers receive degrees are pleased to acquire papers and have appropriate facilities to handle them. Other important repositories are maritime museums with significant library facilities and several historical societies, all meriting consideration. No case is made here for particular disposition of private files, but we recommend strongly their consignment to posterity and not to the wastebasket.

Ronald Lewin speaks of the difficulty in writing the history of Ultra, the British World War II code-breaking operation:

> A pioneer work can scarcely be encyclopedic, or always precise, and the Group Captain [Winterbotham] was writing from memory [*The Ultra Secret*], without access to reserved papers, . . . Nevertheless he opened the door and Clio, the muse of history, owes him her gratitude.[10]

We can only hope that this narrative of naval engineering has opened a door.

Notes

1 Friederich, Otto, "What Really Mattered." *Time* Essay, October 12, 1987.

2 Trost, C. A. H., Admiral, U.S. Navy, Chief of Naval Operations, "Two Bells into the Watch." Remarks at the Submarine League Banquet, 9 July 1987.

3 "Report Urges Major Changes in National Security Strategy." The Washington *Post*, January 11, 1988.

4 COMDTINST M16014.1C, "Commandant's Long-Range View." 1 October 1986.

5 Denton, Jeremiah, Chairman, *First Report of the Commission on Merchant Marine and Defense*. 30 September 1987.

6 Lewin, Ronald, *Ultra Goes to War*. New York, N.Y.: McGraw-Hill Book Company, Inc., 1978, p. 19.

7 Trost, C. A. H., Admiral, U.S. Navy, Chief of Naval Operations, "Strategic Options: Bringing Down the Bird of Thought." Speech at the Current Strategy Forum, U.S. Naval War College, 18 June 1987.

8 Isaacson, Walter, *Time* Essay, August 31, 1987.

9 Meier, Peg, *Bring Warm Clothes*. Letters and Photos from Minnesota's Past. Minneapolis, Minnesota: Minneapolis Star and Tribune Company, 1981.

10 Lewin, *Ultra Goes to War*, p. 18.

Even during World War I, women filled many so-called "non-traditional" roles, including the operation of heavy equipment and the performance of highly technical tasks.

Rear Admiral "Amazing Grace" Hopper, Mother of COBOL and originator of the A-O compiler. This brilliant innovator says, "It's easier to beg forgiveness than it is to get permission!"

First-Lady-to-be Betty Ford christens the USS *Dace* (SSN-607) at Ingalls Shipyard 18 August 1962.

Engineering laboratory technician prepares test apparatus for test.

USS *Monongahela* (AO-178) is waterborne after christening at Avondale Shipyards, Inc., in New Orleans, 1979.

USS *Halsey* (DLG-623) and USS *Topeka* (CLG-8) together in dry dock 4 at San Francisco Naval Shipyard, 1963.

There is no need to go into dry dock to change propellers in smaller ships. Here, crew of submarine *Rasher* assists tender personnel as new screw is lowered to waiting divers.

USS *Chicago* (CG-11) at San Francisco Naval Shipyard, 1960.

Controllable pitch propeller for the *Oliver Hazard Perry* class frigates (FFG-7s) on test stand of Bird-Johnson Company.

Deep water basin (top) and turning basin at David Taylor Research Center allow controlled testing of scale hull forms and associated systems.

The largest hydrofoil in the world, *Plainview* (AGEH-1), was one of two experimental hydrofoils assigned to the David Taylor Research Center for developmental tests and evaluation.

Computer-aided design (CAD) allows engineers to alter design parameters and obtain an instant visual representation. Models thus developed may be viewed—and hard copy printed—from any desired perspective.

Rear Admiral John D. Bulkley, in his 20th year as President of the Board of Inspection and Survey, has key role in the Navy's quality assurance program.

Engineering officers and civilian naval architects in shipyards and contractor facilities oversee production to ensure adherence to specifications, maintain quality control, and keep work on schedule.

Gas turbine being prepared for testing in the laboratory.

Civilian engineers and technicians are essential elements in the Navy's engineering program.

The SS *America*, in 1955, represented the latest in engineering advancement for luxury passenger ships.

USCGC *Polar Star* (WAGB-10) is the nation's largest and most powerful icebreaker. She is shown here during 1976 Arctic voyage, off the coast of Alaska.

The container ship was a revolutionary development in maritime commerce, providing a vital link in intermodal transportation. Eight SL/7s were sold to the Navy for conversion to fast supply ships.

The 115,000 ton, 1,005 foot-long tanker *Manhattan* has an icebreaker bow and "ice belt" on her sides. Pictures were taken during month-long ice tests in Viscount Melville Sound.

Led by an Army tank, troops pour forth from an LST (landing ship tank). This versatile ship was produced in less than a year from concept to first launching during World War II.

Model of 1819 history-making steamship *Savannah* went on permanent display in the SS *Savanah*, the world's first nuclear powered merchant ship.

Appendix A

CHRONOLOGY OF NAVAL ENGINEERING

The following chronology of naval engineering is oriented primarily to naval engineering events in the United States, as is the book's narrative. We hope there are sufficient notations for other countries, however, to present a reasonably balanced picture.

This chronology is presented in two columns. The first includes significant events in naval engineering or directly affecting its development in a major way. The second cites pertinent national and international events, legislative, organization, and personnel policy matters. With the exception of a few humorous or miscellaneous entries, events in column two have had significant impact on naval engineering.

In many instances, an arbitrary decision has been made whether to place an entry in column one or two. For example, if a sea battle has strong technological significance it is included in column one. If it is primarily of great strategic importance it is in column two.

Date	Naval Engineering	National & International Events Legislative, Organization & Personnel Policy
?	The Bible records Noah's building the Ark. Some say this may be the oldest ship for which specifications are preserved. (Genesis: 6).	
14th Century B.C.		A trading ship sinks in the Mediterranean in 140 to 170 feet off the coast of Turkey at Ulu Burun. When discovered in 1982 A.D. she will be the oldest known shipwreck. A team from the Institute of Nautical Archaeology (INA) in Texas will spend four years, 1982-1986, excavating and studying the 50-foot long vessel whose hull planks are fastened with mortise-and-tenon joints. Nautical archaeology capabilities advance with naval engineering developments in underwater operations.
2nd or 3rd Century B.C.	Rotary motion obtained directly from steam pressure, is demonstrated by engine invented by Hero of Alexandria.	
311 B.C. circa	First lighthouse, the Pharos of Alexandria, is built at the mouth of the Nile River in Egypt.	
1514	*Henry Grace A Dieu*, nicknamed Great Harry, is built by King Henry VIII of England. Many scholars consider this to be the first ship-of-the-line or capital ship.	
1571		Combined naval forces of Spain and western Italian maritime states, Venice, and Papal States defeat the Turkish navy of Suleyman, thus saving the Mediterranean for European powers. Totals actually in battle are estimated on the Christian side: 203 galleys, 6 galleasses, 13,000 seamen, 43,000 rowers, 29,000 soldiers. Estimates for the Turks are: 208 galleys, 60 galliots and other smaller types, 25,000 troops. A young Spaniard in a Venetian galley, Miguel de Cervantes, loses his left hand in the battle but is able later to write *Don Quioxte* with the other. Among the many factors accounting for the Christian victory is the fact that the bows and sterns of their vessels are covered to form a protection.

Date	Naval Engineering	National & International Events Legislative, Organization & Personnel Policy
1628 August 10	*Wasa* casts off on her maiden voyage, capsizes and sinks in Stockholm harbor. One of the largest naval vessels of the age, inquiry into her loss develops embarassing disclosures of prior knowledge of poor stability shown in a test and ignored by an Admiral.	
1685	The idea of a steamship is presented by French physician Denis Papin. His theories about a steam engine will later be developed by others such as Newcomen, Savery, and James Watt.	
17th Century	Modern version of steam turbine, steam driving a vaned wheel, is conceived by Giovanni Branca of Loretto as a means of operating a grain-milling machine.	
1716 September 14	First lighthouse in America is established at Boston Harbor.	
1775	Fredrik Henrik Chapman publishes his "Treatise on Shipbuilding," which followed his "Architecture Navalis Mercatoria" and turned shipbuilding into a science. The treatise deals in great detail with displacement, location of center of gravity, stability, resistance, shape and dimensions of ships, measurement of tonnage, etc.	
1775 October 13		The Continental Congress passes a resolution creating an American Navy.
1776 September 7	The first submarine attack in the history of warfare reaches its unsuccessful conclusion when *Turtle*, built by David Bushnell of Saybrook, Connecticut, abandons a well-planned attempt to attach a "torpedo" to the hull of HMS *Eagle*, Admiral Howe's flagship anchored off Governor Island in New York Harbor.	
1783 June 15	The small steamboat *Pyroscaphe*, built by the Marquis Claude de Jouffroy, makes her way upstream for 15 minutes on the River Saone near Lyons, France.	
1786	The American inventor John Fitch makes a trip on the Delaware River in his steamboat whose engine works twelve vertical oars.	
1787 December 3	". . . James Rumsey took several ladies and a little girl named Ann on the first (according to Rumsey fans) steamboat ride in history. . . . It was said that 'the crazy man was going to run his canoe with a steam kettle.' . . . General [Horatio] Gates removed his hat and exclaimed, 'My God, she moves.' And she did—for two hours—up and down the river. Jay Hurley of Shepherdstown told me that was because Rumsey hadn't included a stop valve. She ran until the steam died down." Source: Garrett, Wilbur E. "George Washington's Patowmack Canal: Waterway That Led to the Constitution." *National Geographic*. Vol. 171, No. 6, June 1987, pp. 737-738.	
1789		U.S. Congress creates the Lighthouse Service in the Treasury Department. The Service will be under Treasury's Revenue Marine Bureau (1845-1852) and its Lighthouse Board (1852-1903). The latter will pass in 1903 to the Department of Commerce, will be replaced by the Lighthouse Bureau in 1910, which will return in 1939 to Treasury and the Coast Guard.

Date	Naval Engineering	National & International Events Legislative, Organization & Personnel Policy
1790 August 4		The Revenue Marine (subsequently the Revenue Cutter Service and still later the U.S. Coast Guard) is established by bill passed by first Congress and signed by President Washington. Bill responds to request by Alexander Hamilton, first Secretary of the Treasury and father of Coast Guard, for a fleet of armed cutters to ensure collection of tonnage dues and import duties.
1791		Colonel John Stevens has helped bring about U.S. patent laws, and earns one of the initial U.S. patents. He, his sons, and grandsons will apply their inventive genius to many areas including steamboats and naval warfare. He has already been in correspondence with John Rumsey to suggest improvements in the latter's steam engine.
1794 March 27		President Washington signs into law "an act to provide a naval armament," which provides for building six frigates: *Constitution, United States, Constellation, Congress, Chesapeake,* and *President.*
1798 April 30		The Navy Department is established.
1800		President John Adams writes to the first Secretary of the Navy, Benjamin Stoddert, requesting the Secretary "to employ some of his clerks in preparing a catalogue of books for the use of his office. It ought to consist of all the best writings in Dutch, Spanish, French, and especially English, upon the theory and practice of naval architecture, navigation, gunnery, hydraulics, hydrostatics, and all branches of mathematics subservient to the profession of the sea. The lives of all the admirals, English, French, Dutch, or any other nation, who have distinguished themselves by the boldness and success of their navigation, of their gallantry and skill in naval combats." Thus is born the Navy Department Library with emphasis on both operational and technical matters.
1801 February 23		The New York Navy Yard is established and will launch its first ship, the ship-of-the-line *Ohio* (74 guns, 2757 tons, an excellent sailer repeatedly making more than 12 knots) on 30 May 1820. The New York Naval Shipyard will be closed on 30 June 1966.
1801 July 3	Robert Fulton dives his submarine *Nautilus* to a depth of 25 feet and remains there for more than an hour.	
1802 March 16		Congress establishes a Corps of Engineers for the Army, to consist of a "principal engineer," six officers, and ten cadets, to be located at West Point, and to "constitute a military academy" with the Chief Engineer as superintendent.
1804	Colonel John Stevens produces the 20-odd-foot *Little Juliana*, incorporating a multitube boiler and single cylinder driving twin-screw propellers. She is the first successful propeller-driven steamboat in the world.	
1807	Robert Fulton's *Clermont* is the first practical steamship in commission. She will be placed in traffic on the Hudson River between New York and Albany.	
1807		President Thomas Jefferson establishes the Survey of the Coast, forerunner of the present NOAA Corps.

Date	Naval Engineering	National & International Events Legislative, Organization & Personnel Policy
1808	Colonel John Stevens completes *Phoenix*, a paddle-wheel steamboat designed largely by his son, Robert. In June 1809 she will proceed to the Delaware River via the Atlantic Ocean, thereby making the first ocean voyage of any steamboat. She will be a success on the Delaware, operating between Philadelphia and Trenton.	
1811	Colonel John Stevens institutes the first steam ferry service in the world, between Hoboken and New York.	
1812 April 29		An Act provides several important features for effective administrative foundations for academic growth of the U.S. Military Academy. Although it will remain part of the Engineer Corps until further developments in 1815 and 1816, West Point will teach cadets who will serve eventually throughout the service.
1813	Colonel John Stevens proposes a saucer-shaped, ironclad, circular warship for harbor defense. The craft will never be built but is probably the first ironclad ever designed.	
1813ca	Colonel John Stevens and sons, Robert and Edwin, invent forerunner of the armor-piercing projectile. The government orders 5,000 of the shells.	
1815	*Demologos* (also identified as the first *Fulton*), authorized during War of 1812, a catamaran steam frigate and first steam warship in any navy, makes successful trial runs. She is not fitted out for service but is delivered to the Navy in June, 1816, as *Fulton*, placed in ordinary, and used as a receiving ship at Brooklyn Navy Yard.	President Madison sends Sylvanus Thayer to France to observe military schools and practices and to collect books and instruments for the Military Academy.
1817 May		Sylvanus Thayer is named Superintendent of the Military Academy. He will bring about major developments at this first engineering school in the United States. For the first half of the nineteenth century West Point will be one of very few sources in the United States of persons qualified to teach engineering subjects.
1819 May 22	Steamship *Savannah* departs the River Savannah for Liverpool, England, on the first transatlantic voyage by steamship. She is in fact a full-rigged ship with auxiliary single-cylinder engine and collapsible paddle wheel. During the 29.5 day passage her engine operates about 3.5 days and consumes her entire fuel supply of 75 tons of coal and 25 cords of wood. Congress later designates May 22 as National Maritime Day.	
1820		A decked-over small boat is moored at Craney Island in Hampton Roads, Virginia, as the earliest U.S. lightship station. The first outside lightship will be stationed off Sandy Hook, New Jersey in 1824.
1820ca	Robert Stevens makes many improvements to the steam ferryboat: lighter walking beams, placement of boilers outside paddlewheels for safety and more deck space, improved protection for hulls, improved engine control, first use of anthracite coal, first use of pilothouse, yielding piles for ferry slips.	

Date	Naval Engineering	National & International Events Legislative, Organization & Personnel Policy
1824		Rensselaer Institute is established at Troy, New York, and will award the first U.S. formal degrees in civil engineering in 1835. Along with the major changes that will start in 1847 by Benjamin Franklin Greene, the school will become Rensselaer Polytechnic Institute. In 1862 it will be the nation's first civilian school to offer a four-year course in engineering.
1829 June 4	*Fulton (Demologos)* is totally destroyed by a magazine explosion that kills 30 men and wounds many others.	
1830		Robert Livingston Stevens designs, while crossing the Atlantic Ocean, a train rail cross section that will become standard. This is one of many important sea and land inventions of this family.
1832		Federal Administrative reorganization results in newly equipped civilian Survey that produces first navigation charts.
1833 June 4	*Ann McKim* is launched in Baltimore, Maryland, from the shipyard of Kennard and Williamson. She is 143 feet in length, at this time the longest merchant ship in the United States, and is considered by some to be the first clipper ship.	
1833 June 17	*Delaware* is first ship to be placed in a drydock in the United States, at Norfolk Navy Yard.	
1834	SS *John Randolph* is launched in Savannah, Georgia, having been put together with parts made in England by John Laird. She becomes the first successful iron steamship used in U.S. inland commerce.	
1836 February	Charles H. Haswell is directed to prepare working drawings of boilers to be installed in a steam warship then building at Brooklyn Navy Yard.	
1836 September		Charles H. Haswell, is appointed first Chief Engineer to U.S. Navy.
1837		The steamboat *Pulaski* explodes in North Carolina with loss of 100 lives. This provides the catalyst for the Act by Congress the following year initiating commercial vessel inspection.
1838		Congress creates the Steamboat Inspection Service, with the power to license masters and mates and engineers, as well as appoint inspectors of boilers and vessels. Organization proves to be of little help; in fact, boiler explosions aboard ship increase.
1839	Francis Bowes Stevens, son of James Alexander Stevens, and grandson of Colonel John Stevens, designs the "Stevens cutoff" that enables a single person to reverse a steam engine easily.	
1841	First Fresnel lens, invented by Augustin Fresnel in 1822, is imported from France for installation in U.S. lighthouse. Future use of this revolutionary lens will include nearly all U.S. lighthouses as well as aircraft carrier landing systems.	
	Edwin and Robert Stevens resume design of the "Stevens Battery," 410 feet long, beam of 45 feet, and sheathed in 4½ inches of iron. The ship will never be finished but is a major step in development of the warship. The Navy will later accept a scaled-down version, *Naugatuck*, that will see action in the Civil War.	

Date	Naval Engineering	National & International Events Legislative, Organization & Personnel Policy
1842		Congress passes an act establishing a corps of engineers in the Navy, then about twenty in number, under direction of a "skillful and scientific engineer-in-chief."
1842 August 31		Gilbert L. Thompson, a lawyer, is appointed as first Engineer-In-Chief. Act of Congress abolishes the Board of Navy Commissioners and directs the Secretary of the Navy to apportion the Board's functions appropriately among the five Navy Department bureaus authorized by the Act, including Bureau of Ordnance and Hydrography; Bureau of Construction, Equipment and Repairs; and Bureau of Navy Yards and Docks. The latter Bureau administers Navy yards during the nineteenth century.
1843	About the time of its reorganization, the Revenue Marine begins building cutters with iron hulls and auxiliary steam power. They will be ill-starred. *McLane* will run aground while aiding Commodore Perry in carrying out an amphibious assault in the Mexican War at the mouth of the Tabasco River in 1847. She will have her machinery removed and be converted to a lightship in 1848. *Bibb* will leak so badly on her way to Mexico that she will have to be beached. *Polk* will leak on launching and never be used. *Spencer*, found defective, will be used as a lightship at Hampton Roads. *Legare* will be withdrawn from service because of a dangerous boiler and transferred to the Coast Survey. *Walker*, also will be transferred to the Coast Survey, and will be run down and founder off Barnegat.	Under Secretary of the Treasury John Spencer, the Revenue Marine is set up as a bureau within the department with accounting, engineering, personnel, operations, intelligence, and legal branches, and a captain to head the bureau.
1843 July	*Great Britain*, designed by Isambard Kingdom Brunel, makes maiden voyage from Liverpool, England, to New York in 14 days and 21 hours. Built wholly of iron, she is first propeller-driven vessel to cross Atlantic. Brunel originally planned to use paddle wheels but substitutes a six-bladed propeller, 15.5 feet in diameter.	
1843 September 5	Sloop-of-war USS *Princeton*, first propeller-driven steam warship in the world, is launched. Machinery is designed by John Ericsson.	
1844 January		Charles Haswell relieves Gilbert L. Thompson as Engineer-In-Chief of the Navy.
1844 February 28	During the demonstration for notables in Washington, D.C. of the capabilities of *Princeton*, commanded by Capt. Robert F. Stockton, the huge Peacemaker gun on the bow explodes, killing eight people, including Secretary of State Abel P. Upshur; Secretary of the Navy Thomas W. Gilmer; Commodore Beverly Kennon, Chief of the Bureau of Construction, Equipment and Repairs; New York State Senator David Gardiner; Virgil Maxcy, the recent U.S. charge d'affaires at The Hague; two gun crew members; and a personal servant of one of the dignitaries.	

Date	Naval Engineering	National & International Events Legislative, Organization & Personnel Policy
1844 September 29	*Michigan*, first iron warship in the United States, is commissioned, Commander William Inman in command. She was fabricated in parts at Pittsburgh, Pennsylvania, during the last half of 1842, and carried overland and assembled in Erie, Pennsylvania.	
1845	Iron for warships is advocated by Ericsson in report to House Naval Committee.	
1845	British Admiralty conducts tug-of-war between two steam sloops, propeller-driven *Rattler*, and paddle-driven *Alecto*. *Rattler* tows *Alecto* stern first at about 2.5 knots.	
1845 October 10		Commander Franklin Buchanan declares the U.S. Naval Academy to be open, culminating a superb series of steps by Secretary of the Navy George Bancroft designed to establish an academy without arousing Congress by a request for funds. He is able to use the $28,272 for "instruction" included in the Navy Department's budget for 1845; he obtains strong internal Navy support from a board of senior officers that was examining midshipmen completing the course of instruction at the Naval Asylum Philadelphia, in June 1845; and he had arranged to have Fort Severn in Annapolis, Maryland, transferred to the Navy on 15 August 1845 with Buchanan placed in command that day.
1846 December 8	Clipper ship *Sea Witch* is launched in New York. In her short 10-year career, she will break more records than any previous ship her size. Two speed records for Canton, China, to U.S. ports are not equalled under-sail. Dimensions are: LOA 192 feet, Beam 19 feet, Tonnage 19,908.	
1848		The American Association for the Advancement of Science (AAAS) is founded.
1851 August 22	The yacht *America* wins a challenge race, 58 miles around the Isle of Wight at Cowes, England, and a cup. This is the progenitor of one of the most famous of sailing races, for the *America*'s Cup. Races will be held many times off Sandy Hook, New Jersey, during the late 19th and early 20th centuries and will shift to Newport, Rhode Island, in 1930.	
1851 August 31	The clipper *Flying Cloud* arrives in San Francisco after an 89-day passage from New York, a new sailing record. This record will be equalled twice: *Flying Cloud* in 1854 and *Andrew Johnson* in 1859. It will not subsequently be equalled or beaten.	
1852		As a result of seven major steamship disasters, with loss of nearly 700 lives, between December 1851 and July 1852, Congress passes the Steamboat Inspection Act of 1852. This reorganizes the Steamboat Inspection Service, expands responsibilities of the Act of 1838, and corrects major flaw of the earlier law by controlling inspections and licensing. Among short-comings of the new law is that only steamships carrying passengers are subject to its provisions. Steam tugs, freighters, canal boats, etc., are exempt from provisions of the 1852 law, although still remaining subject to those of the 1838 law.

Date	Naval Engineering	National & International Events Legislative, Organization & Personnel Policy
1852	Lighthouse Board is established to administer lighthouses and other aids to navigation.	
1852		A dozen civil engineers in New York City areas form the American Society of Civil Engineers and Architects, to include "Civil, Geological, Mining, and Mechanical Engineers, Architects and other persons who, by profession, are interested in the advancement of science." Attendance will average six the first year, fewer the second, and after 1855 it will be inactive until 1867 when ten civil engineers will meet in New York City and revive ASCE. It will incorporate formally in 1877 and have more than 2,000 members by the end of the century.
1853		The Russian Black Sea Fleet with shell guns annihilates a Turkish squadron that uses round shot. Technologically, the action validates shell against round shot and leads to armored warships. Politically, the event causes France and England to go to war against Russia.
1854	Two records are set by U.S.-built clipper ships: *Sovereign of the Seas*, built in 1853 and designed by Donald McKay, logs fastest speed of 22 knots. *Champion of the Seas*, also designed by McKay, logs 465 nautical miles from noon to noon. The latter ship was one of a group built by McKay for the English Black Ball Line.	
	Reliable compound steam engine is installed in *Brandon* by John Elder of Glasgow. Engine is an instant triumph, burning one-third less coal than single-cylinder engines of comparable vessels.	
1854 May 1	Construction starts on world's largest ship for Eastern Steamship Navigation Company. Originally to be named *Leviathan*, she is named *Great Eastern* when completed in 1858.	
1854 September 16		The Mare Island Shipyard is established and on 3 March 1859 launches its first ship, the USS *Saginaw*, a wooden-hulled, steam driven, side-paddlewheeled gunboat.
1856	Stephen Wilcox designs and patents first water-tube boiler, based on natural circulation of heated fluids. Design is refined with aid of George Babcock and improved model is patented in 1867.	
1857 November	Revenue cutter *Harriet Lane*, built for the Treasury Department by William H. Webb, is launched in New York City. She is first successful steam cutter and a famous ship of Civil War, fighting under both Stars and Stripes and Stars and Bars. As U.S. Navy ship she is credited with firing first naval shot of the war in April 1861.	
1858	Isambard K. Brunel completes *Great Eastern*, which will not be exceeded in size for 40 years. Dimensions are: length 692 feet, hull beam 82.7 feet, beam over paddle boxes 118 feet, draft 30 feet, full load displacement 27,400 tons. Propelled by paddle wheels 56 feet in diameter and a 24-foot propeller, she makes about 15 knots. Six masts can carry about 58,000 square feet of sail. She has passenger accommodations for 4,000 in three classes, crew of 400, and can carry about 6,000 tons of cargo.	

Date	Naval Engineering	National & International Events Legislative, Organization & Personnel Policy
1858 August 10	The U.S. Navy's largest ship, *Niagara*, and the Royal Navy's *Agamemnon*, complete the first transatlantic telegraph cable. It will stop working on 1 September because of manufacturing defects, handling damage, and insulation problems resulting from excess voltage.	
1858 October 27		Birth date of Theodore Roosevelt, considered to be the "Father of the Modern American Navy." His strong support as Assistant Secretary appointed by William McKinley eventually results in establishing Navy Day as October 27 (changed to October 13 in 1972) first celebrated in 1922. In 1948 individual Service dates are combined into Armed Forces Day. Roosevelt is person who orders the term "United States Ship" (USS) to be used with U.S. Navy Ships.
1859		Act of Congress establishes military rank for engineers in the U.S. Navy.
1859 March 2	The paddlewheel gunboat *Saginaw* is launched at Mare Island; it's the first Navy ship to be built on the U.S. West Coast.	
1860	Benjamin Isherwood publishes *Experimental Researches In Steam Engineering* in two volumes, subsequently translated into six foreign languages.	
	In response to the French iron-armored but wooden-hulled frigate *Gloire*, the British lay down HMS *Warrior* built entirely of iron with armor plating amidships. She will be completed in 1861 and her 1,250 H.P. engines will give her a speed of 14½ knots. Her guns will include both breech loaders and muzzle loaders. *Warrior*, the world's first ironclad, will survive and be docked after restoration in the 1980s near *Victory* at Portsmouth, England.	
	Royal Institution of Naval Architects is founded.	
1861 August 4	John La Mountain ascends in a balloon moored to the deck of the Union transport *Fanny* to observe Confederate positions.	
1862		The Morrill Act, or Land Grant College Act, establishes a foundation for military training in public and private universities nationwide.
1862 February 25	USS *Monitor* is commissioned.	
1862 March 9	The first naval battle ever fought between powered ironclads takes place in Hampton Roads, Virginia, between USS *Monitor* and CSS *Virginia* (formerly USS *Merrimack*). Although inconclusive, the engagement revolutionizes naval warfare and ship design.	
1862 April 7		The sidewheel steamer *Red Rover* is seized by the Union gunboat *Mound City* and will be refitted to be the first ship specifically designated by the Navy solely for the care of the sick and wounded.
1862 April 22		American Bureau of Shipping (originally conceived as the American Shipmasters' Association) is incorporated, and is established on a working basis by 23 July 1862.

Date	Naval Engineering	National & International Events Legislative, Organization & Personnel Policy
1862 July 5		Bureau of Steam Engineering is established by act of Congress to be responsible for designing, constructing, maintaining, and repairing steam machinery for naval vessels.
		Name of Bureau of Construction, Equipment, and Repairs is changed to Bureau of Construction and Repair. Function of equipment of naval vessels is transferred to newly created Bureau of Equipment and Recruiting.
		Bureau of Ordnance and Hydrography becomes Bureau of Ordnance when hydrographic functions are transferred to newly formed Bureau of Navigation.
		Title of Bureau of Navy Yards and Docks is changed to Bureau of Yards and Docks.
1863		National Academy of Sciences is founded by Congressional Act of Incorporation.
1863 June	Third Assistant Engineer John Donaldson Ford, who will later serve as president American Society of Naval Engineers and retire as rear admiral, makes port shutters for the guns of the wooden steam sloop of war *Richmond* to protect gunners from the fire of sharpshooters and fits iron to the ship's tops. These are the first port shutters or shields and the first ironclad tops used in the Civil War.	
1864		Theta Xi, professional engineering and science fraternity, is founded.
1864 February 17	A 35-foot cigar-shaped submarine, constructed of iron, CSS *H. L. Hunley*, becomes the first submarine to sink an enemy ship in combat when it rams its spar torpedo into the hull of the steam sloop-of-war USS *Housatonic*.	
1864 July 4	Act of Congress authorizes the Secretary of the Navy to make provision for educating at the U.S. Naval Academy "as naval constructors and steam engineers, such naval cadets and others as may show a peculiar aptitude therefor." (but not established until 1897).	
1864 December 15	The screw frigate, *Wampanoag* (renamed *Florida* on 15 May 1868), is launched at the New York Navy Yard. She contains many design features, with hull design by clipper ship architect B. F. Delano and machinery by Naval Engineer Benjamin F. Isherwood. Debate over design will delay construction, resulting in sea trials starting on 11 February 1868.	
1866	William John Macquorn Rankine, renowned hydrodynamicist, naval architect, and engineer, publishes *Shipbuilding: Theoretical and Practical*.	
1866 April 17	Congress appropriates $5,000 to test the use of "petroleum oil" as fuel for ships' boilers.	
1866 July	*Great Eastern*, designed for transporting 4,000 passengers to the East Indies without recoaling, but used unsuccessfully on North Atlantic routes bankrupting several corporate owners, attains her greatest significance as a cable layer by completing a successful transatlantic cable. A second follows immediately when she is able to recover and splice a cable broken in 1865. A third will be completed in 1869 and a fourth in 1873. By 1926, there will be twenty-four transatlantic telegraph cables. The 1873 cable will operate until 1965 when all will have expired.	

Date	Naval Engineering	National & International Events Legislative, Organization & Personnel Policy
1866 July 20	Modest fleet action between Austrian and Italian navies takes place in battle of Lissa. Limited effect of gunfire confirms age of armored ships. Successful rammings, however, cause continuation of ram bows for several decades longer than their effectiveness warrants as gun range increases.	
1866 July 25		Act of Congress officially establishes the Construction Corps in the United States Navy; establishes military rank for Naval constructors.
1867 March		The system adopted by the American Shipmasters' Association for surveying, rating, and registering vessels takes the form of a list, entitled Record of American and Foreign Shipping, and is published in pamphlet form and continued on a monthly basis.
1868	Siren fog signal is developed in the United States.	
1868 February 11	Screw frigate, *Wampanoag*, begins speed tests in rough water, covering 728 statute miles (633 nautical miles) in 38 hours for an average sustained speed of 16.6 knots, at one point making 17.75 knots. Another naval vessel, American cruiser *Charleston*, will not equal this record for 21 years. Controversy generated by the frigate's unconventional design will reach a peak in 1869 when a naval commission will examine and condemn the vessel, judging the ship unacceptable for active duty in the Navy.	
1868 April 11		The Secretary of the Navy accepts title to 112 acres on East shore of Thames River as gift from State of Connecticut and City of New London, thereby establishing the New London Navy Yard.
1869 June		The Board of Marine Underwriters recognizes the "Record of American and Foreign Shipping," published by the American Shipmasters' Association, as the only approved American publication of the survey and classification of ships.
1869 July 5	Captain Charles R. Raymond, Engineer Officer, enters Yukon territory for 2½ months exploration.	
1869 November 17		The Suez Canal is opened to traffic.
1870		Name of Survey is changed to Coast and Geodetic Survey.
		A legacy from Edwin Augustus Stevens founds the Stevens Institute of Technology.
1870 September 6	HMS *Captain* capsizes with the loss of 412 men from her crew of 489, which event highlights the problems of weight control aboard ship. This loss discredits the turret concept and leads to acceptance of a competing concept, the barbette.	
	Rules for the Surveying and Classing of Wooden Vessels results from a collaborative effort among several organizations, is formally published, and appears as part of the "Record of American and Foreign Shipping."	
1871		Steamboat Inspection Service is reorganized again.
1871 March		Act of Congress reiterates rank for Naval constructors, fixes number of captains in the corps as two and number of commanders as three.

Date	Naval Engineering	National & International Events Legislative, Organization & Personnel Policy
1872	Charles Wyville Thomson of the Royal Society of London commences 3½-year, 68,890-mile voyage aboard a specially equipped 226-foot British naval vessel, *Challenger*. This expedition changes oceanographic knowledge forever.	
1873-79	Albert Abraham Michelson (USNA Class of 1873), instructor at the United States Naval Academy, conducts experiments on the Academy campus leading to measurement of the speed of light. He is later awarded the Nobel prize for his work, the first American scientist to be so recognized.	
1874 June 20		An act to encourage the establishment of public marine schools is enacted by Congress and provides for instruction in ". . . navigation, seamanship, marine engineering and all matters pertaining to the proper construction, equipment and sailing of vessels . . ." Captain (later Rear Admiral) Stephen Bleecker Luce is the guiding force behind the movement for nautical school legislation.
1874 December 10		Operational control of the sloop-of-war *St. Mary's* is transferred from the Navy by Captain Stephen B. Luce to the City of New York's Executive Committee on Nautical Schools, marking the first official start of the New York Nautical School (NYNS), later to become the State University of New York (SUNY) Maritime College.
1875	The U.S. Navy experiments with electric lights as a form of communication.	
1876	British Merchant Shipping Act requires every British vessel in foreign trade to have a load-line mark, culminating years of work of Samuel Plimsoll.	
1876 July 31		An Act of Congress makes mandatory a two-year period of cadet training aboard a school ship prior to qualification for a commission in the Revenue Marine (forerunner of the U.S. Coast Guard). Up to this time, the service has obtained its officers from the enlisted ranks, from the Navy, or from the merchant service. Later this year, nine cadets are appointed by Secretary of the Treasury John Sherman, and thus become the Coast Guard's first Corps of Cadets.
1876 November 27	A ship is completed at the yard of Harlan & Hollingsworth, Wilmington, Delaware, which will bear five names: USS *Ranger* until 30 October 1917, USS *Rockport* until 20 February 1918, USS *Nantucket* until 19 November 1941, then *Bay State*, and finally TV *Emery Rice*, her last name given to her 31 July 1942. Under the latter name she will serve as a training ship for the U.S. Merchant Marine Academy, Kings Point.	
1877	Nathanael G. Herreshoff, MIT Class of 1870, patents catamaran. The American Shipmasters' Association publishes its first *Rules for the Survey and Classing of Iron Vessels*.	

Date	Naval Engineering	National & International Events Legislative, Organization & Personnel Policy
1877 May		The first Corps of Cadets of the Revenue Marine, the nine appointed in 1876, begin training aboard the old tops'l schooner *Dobbin*. Program includes both practical and theoretical instruction.
1878	Operational electric light signal equipment is installed in U.S. Naval vessels.	
1878 January 26	First successful use of self-propelled torpedo occurs in minor engagement when Russian torpedo-boats sink Turkish gunboat *Intibah*, Batum, Black Sea. The torpedo is the invention of Scottish engineer Robert Whitehead, who will perfect a gyroscopically controlled torpedo in 1896.	
1878 Summer		The new bark-rigged clipper *Chase*, especially designed as a cadet school ship, is completed and placed in service, replacing *Dobbin*. She will later be lengthened by 40 feet and will be the permanent home of successive cadet classes for the Revenue Cutter Service for the remainder of the century, except for the period 1890-1894 when the School of Instruction will be closed and the service will depend on the overflow graduates from the Naval Academy. Finally, in 1907, she will be replaced by *Itasca*, a steam-propelled vessel, with auxiliary sail, thus affording the opportunity for much-needed engineering training.
1878 December 7	USS *Ticonderoga* departs on a two-year cruise, and becomes the first Navy steamship to circle the earth. Returns to Hampton Roads, Virginia, 9 November 1880.	
1879	Two cadet engineer graduates of the Naval Academy, later Naval constructors, Richard Gatewood and Francis T. Bowles, are sent to Royal Naval College for course in naval architecture, and to get such a view of the major problems of the profession in Europe as are practicable and permissible by the governments there.	Congress authorizes the Navy to assign a few officers to engineering colleges around the country.
1880	Italian battleship, *Duilio*, is the first major warship built without provision for sails and, at this time, is probably the most powerful warship in the world. She displaces 12,000 tons and mounts four 17.7-inch muzzle-loading rifles in two armored turrets.	
1880	Steamship *Columbia* becomes the first commercial vessel with incandescent electric lighting after three generators are installed under the direction of Thomas A. Edison.	
1880 April 7		The American Society of Mechanical Engineers is officially launched in an organization meeting held in the auditorium of the Administration Building at the Stevens Institute of Technology, Hoboken, New Jersey. Professor Robert H. Thurston is the first president. The first annual meeting will be held in New York City 4-5 November 1880.
1881	HMS *Inflexible* is completed. She carries spars for 18,500 square feet of sail, which prove almost useless for propulsion and serve mainly to get in the way of her big guns.	Secretary of the Navy William M. Hunt appoints a board of officers to study the needs of a new naval construction program and thus takes the first step toward building the New Navy.

Date	Naval Engineering	National & International Events Legislative, Organization & Personnel Policy
1881	Naval officers from the Bureau of Steam Engineering participate in installation of an air conditioning system in the White House during the illness of President Garfield. Filtered air from blowers is passed over ice into the sickroom.	
1881	Inman liner, *City of Rome*, a ship considered by many the most beautiful example of the forced marriage of steam and sail, makes her debut in transatlantic service. She is at this time the largest ship in the world except for I. K. Brunel's *Great Eastern*, which is nearly three times as large, 20 years old and rusting in layup.	Mortimer E. Cooley, a graduate in 1878 of the first four-year engineering officer program at the U.S. Naval Academy (1874-1878), is detailed to serve as Professor of Steam Engineering and Iron Shipbuilding at the University of Michigan.
1881	First large steel-hulled vessel, Cunard liner *Servia*, is launched. She is first liner fitted with electric lighting during construction.	
	First iron-hulled Great Lakes ore carrier, the Steamer *Onoko*, is laid down at Cleveland, Ohio.	
	Edwin Augustus Stevens, Jr. develops the first double-ended propeller-driven ferryboat, *Bergen*.	
1882	First new U.S. oceanographic research ship, *Albatross*, is built. She is first government vessel of any nation to utilize electric power.	
1882 March 23		Office of Naval Intelligence is founded. Until early 1900s, is heavily engaged in overt collection and purchase of information, plans, and equipment from the technologically more advanced European nations.
1883		Congress votes the construction of three protected cruisers and one dispatch boat to be constructed of steel and to be propelled by steam. These are to be the *Atlanta*, *Boston*, *Chicago*, and *Dolphin*. These vessels, the historic White Squadron, mark the beginning of the Modern Navy.
1883 September 18	Ship's log on first day of recommissioning of the wooden-hulled screw steamer USS *Trenton* after installation of electric plant reports merely, "Testing electric lights." She is first American man-of-war to be fitted with incandescent lamps to ascertain practical efficiency of an electric plant on naval vessels. She will be re-wired in 1887, with thirty-nine new lamps added. The plant will continue successful operation until *Trenton* is wrecked by a hurricane in Samoa in March, 1889.	
1884	Charles Parsons tests first practical steam turbine.	
1884 October 6		Navy Department General Order #325 establishes a Naval War College, Newport, Rhode Island, with Commodore Stephen B. Luce as "Superintendent."
1885 December	Dispatch vessel USS *Dolphin* is commissioned, first ship completed for American Steel Navy.	
1886	Teaching of marine engineering, initially as an option in mechanical engineering, begins at the Massachusetts Institute of Technology.	Congress decrees that the Navy use only domestic manufactured material in the construction of naval vessels.

Date	Naval Engineering	National & International Events Legislative, Organization & Personnel Policy
1886	First oceangoing steamer designed and built as a tanker is launched. She is 300-foot, single screw, German-owned *Gluckauf* (means "good luck"). Although nicknamed *Fliegauf* ("blow up"), she ferries oil between U.S. and Europe for seven years. In 1885, 99% of American oil cargoes had been carried to Europe in barrels. Two decades later, 99% will go in bulk.	The honorary scientific Society of the Sigma Xi is founded at Cornell.
1886 July	USS *Atlanta* is commissioned, first major warship in the American Steel Navy, 270-foot, 3,189 tons, equipped for both sailing and steaming.	
1887		War gaming begins at the Naval War College, Newport, Rhode Island, after being introduced into the U.S. about 1886 by the U.S. Army. Its antecedents trace to the 18th century when Prussians began to consider war as a science.
1888	Subjects in Naval Architecture are added to the curriculum at MIT. *Great Eastern* is scrapped. A larger ship will not be built for eleven more years. *City of Paris* is launched. She and her sister, *City of New York*, are first transatlantic steamers to be driven by two propellers. Hulls are steel.	
1888 January 13		The National Geographic Society first meets with thirty-three charter members. Gardiner Greene Hubbard is the first president and the second, in 1898, will be his son-in-law, Alexander Graham Bell.
1888 September 30	The American Society of Naval Engineers is formed.	
1889		The Pennsylvania Maritime academy is founded. It will close in 1947. Bureau of Equipment and Recruiting is redesignated as Bureau of Equipment.
1889 February	The *Journal of the American Society of Naval Engineers* is first published.	
1889 April 2	The State of New York grants a charter to William Henry Webb's Academy to train future designers of ships and marine machinery. The school will be first housed at Fordham Heights in the Bronx. Instruction will start in 1894 with a faculty of three, and the first class of eight men will graduate in 1897. Course length will change from three to four years in 1909 and the name will change to Webb Institute of Naval Architecture in 1920. In 1933, authority will be obtained from the University of the State of New York to award a Bachelor of Science degree. In 1947, the Institute will move to Glen Cove, Long Island.	
1889 November 18	First American battleship, USS *Maine*, 6,682 tons, is launched at New York Navy Yard, Brooklyn, New York.	
1890	*Rules for Building and Classing Steel Vessels* is first published.	Alfred Thayer Mahan completes *The Influence of Seapower Upon History*.
1891	USS *Newark*, last USN cruiser to carry a full set of sails, is launched. American Shipmasters' Association publishes its initial set of *Rules for the Installation of Electric Lighting and Power Apparatus on Shipboard*.	

Date	Naval Engineering	National & International Events Legislative, Organization & Personnel Policy
1891	American Shipmasters' Association publishes *Rules for the Construction, Survey and Classification of Machinery and Boilers for Steam Vessels.*	The Massachusetts Nautical school, forerunner of the Massachusetts Maritime Academy, is founded.
1891 March 3		U.S. Congress enacts the Ocean Mail Act, requiring that mail service vessels "be of the highest rating known to maritime commerce." The U.S. Solicitor General authorizes the American Shipmasters' Association to survey and rate the first vessels built for transatlantic service under the Act.
1892	Rudolph Diesel patents an internal combustion engine.	
1892 December	The American Shipmasters' Association forms its first committee, the Advisory Council of Engineering and Marine Architects, composed of top-level naval architects and marine engineers from industry and the U.S. Navy, and academicians.	
1893	Department of Naval Architecture is established at MIT by Cecil H. Peabody, MIT Class of 1877.	Society of Naval Architects and Marine Engineers is formed.
	First group of "torpedo boat destroyers," later to be called destroyers, is built in England. HMS *Boxer* makes 29.17 knots, highest speed attained thus far by a warship. She is powered by triple expansion steam engines (twin screws) at about 200 psia steam pressure. Dimensions: Length 200 feet, Beam 19 feet, Draft 6 feet (7.8 feet aft), Displacement 250 tons.	
1893 July 31		International Engineer Congress is held in Chicago. The Division of Mechanical and Naval Engineering and Naval Architecture is managed by Engineer-In-Chief George W. Melville, Chief, Bureau of Steam Engineering, Navy Department.
1894	Sir Charles Parsons designs a marine steam turbine and installs it in his 44-ton launch, *Turbinia*. Initial trials are disappointing because of cavitation.	First students are admitted to Webb Institute of Naval Architecture.
1894 July 31		Act of Congress approves creating position of Engineer-in-Chief of the U.S. Revenue Cutter Service (later U.S. Coast Guard).
1894 September 17	Battle of the Yalu confirms identification and development of battleships, armored cruisers, and light cruisers. In fleet action, inferior Japanese force inflicts heavier damage on Chinese fleet by aggressive concentration on alternate Chinese fleet wings. Two Chinese battleships, *Ting Yuen* and *Chen Tuen*, although hit repeatedly, are well protected by armor. The engagement validates small-caliber quick-firing ordnance.	
1895 September 17	Battleship *Maine* is commissioned.	
1896	*Edna G.* is built in Cleveland, Ohio, and named for the daughter of the Duluth and Iron Range Railway president J. L. Greatsinger. She will be the first steam-powered tugboat on the Great Lakes. Except for two years along the Atlantic Coast when taken over by the government in World War I, she will work the Waterfront of Two Harbors, Minnesota, for 85 years. She will be designated a national historic site and become the property of the city of Two Harbors.	
1897	Sir Charles Parsons unveils redesigned *Turbinia* at British naval review at Spithead. She makes 34.5 knots using three shafts, each with three propellers, each driven by a slower-turning turbine than in 1894 tests.	

Date	Naval Engineering	National & International Events Legislative, Organization & Personnel Policy
1897 July 26		Congress creates grade of Captain of Engineers, U.S.R.C.S. John Wilkie Collins, U.S.R.C.S., is appointed to this new position, becoming the first marine engineer in the employ of the U.S. Government to have what is commonly known as positive rank, a desideratum long striven for and subsequently attained by the engineer officers of the Navy.
1897 August 7	*Plunger*, a steam-powered submarine built by John Holland for the Navy, is launched, but will fail to pass acceptance tests.	
1897-99	Engineering curriculum is established at U.S. Naval Academy by Naval constructors Richard P. Hobson and Lawrence Y. Spear.	
1898	Ship Model Basin is built at Washington Navy Yard.	
1898	Marconi conducts first shore-to-ship wireless communication in England, distance: 12 miles.	
1898 February 15	Navy launches its first practical submarine, USS *Holland*.	
1898 March 17		USS *Maine* sinks in Havana Harbor, Cuba, as a result of explosion believed to be caused by Spain's mining of the ship. The event precipitates the Spanish-American war. A future investigation and structural analysis of the wreckage conducted by Captain (later Admiral) Hyman G. Rickover, USN, will conclude that the explosion may have been from within the ship and, therefore, an accident.
1898 March 25		Assistant Secretary of the Navy, Theodore Roosevelt, proposes that the Navy investigate Professor Samuel P. Langley's 'Flying Machines.'
1898 April 9	Captain C. F. Goodrich, USN, is directed to organize the Coast Signal System. This system, consisting of 230 stations on the Atlantic and Gulf Coasts uses signal flags, shapes, torches, and electrical light signal equipment for communication with offshore ships. This system will fall into disuse after the war with Spain but will be considered the predecessor of the U.S. Navy's communication system.	
1898 April 19		United States declares war on Spain.
1898 May 5	First use of communication countermeasures—Commodore George Dewey directs the cutting of the Hong Kong to Manila cable.	
1898 July 3	Mixed U.S. Atlantic squadron of battleships and armored cruisers destroys Spanish Atlantic cruiser squadron at Santiago. Battle further identifies battleships as fleet backbone, with cruisers providing major reconnaissance.	
1898 September 30	First official U.S. Navy radio message transmitted (ashore).	
1898 November 1		The American Shipmasters' Association becomes the American Bureau of Shipping (ABS).
1899	Marconi's wireless communication between USS *New York* and USS *Massachusetts* is first such transmission between U.S. Navy ships.	
1899 February 7		Isaac Rice, lawyer and financier, merges Holland Torpedo Boat Company with the Electric Launch Company to form the Electric Boat Company.

Date	Naval Engineering	National & International Events Legislative, Organization & Personnel Policy
1899 March 3		Naval Personnel Act amalgamates engineering officers with the line. Engineers Corps passes out of existence.
		Number of officers in Construction Corps is fixed at forty by personnel bill, to include five captains and five commanders.
1899 June 7		Columbia University confers its first Honorary Degree of Master of Science on RADM George W. Melville, USN, Engineer-in-Chief of the Navy.
1900 Winter		Revenue Cutter Service training ship *Chase* docks for winter quarters at Arundel Cove, near Baltimore, Maryland. Cadets continue to be quartered aboard ship but classes are held in buildings ashore. Establishment is designated the School of Instruction for the Revenue Cutter Service and is the forerunner of the U.S. Coast Guard Academy.
1900 March 12		General Order No. 544 constitutes Navy General Board.
1900 April 11	U.S. Submarine force begins with acceptance of its first submarine, USS *Holland* (SS-1).	
1900 May		With the issuance fo the 6,807th Commission of Competency, ABS involvement in examining ships' officers comes to an end.
1900 June 7		Congress passes a naval appropriation bill providing for five more boats like *Holland*.
1900 October 12	USS *Holland* (SS-1), Lieutenant H. H. Caldwell, Commanding Officer, is first submarine commissioned in U.S. Navy.	
1901	British coastal passenger ship, the *King Edward*, first turbine-driven merchant steamer, makes 20½ knots on trial trip.	Discovery of Spindletop, Texas oil field, ensures fuel source for U.S. Navy.
	First group of young officers, selected for the Construction Corps, is sent to the Massachusetts Institute of Technology.	U.S. Steel Corporation is formed by merger. Overnight, its fleet of 112 steel freighters is the largest group of American-flagged ships on any waters under one ownership.
1902	Five-masted, full square-rigged ship, *Preussen*, is built in Germany to haul nitrate from Chile to Europe. She is largest sailing ship ever built: 438 feet long, 54 feet in beam, fully loaded displacement of 11,150 tons, and has crew of fifty-eight to handle 60,000 square feet of sail.	
1902	U.S. Navy constructs radio stations in Washington, D.C. and Annapolis, Maryland. First ship testing of wireless of USS *Prairie* and USS *Topeka*.	
1902 July 1		Act of Congress increases number of officers in Construction Corps to forty-six.
1902 November 20		The Navy League of the United States is founded as a result of a meeting of several concerned people at the New York Yacht Club on this date.
1902 November 24	U.S. Navy commissions its first destroyer, USS *Bainbridge*.	

Date	Naval Engineering	National & International Events Legislative, Organization & Personnel Policy
1903	Lydia G. Weld becomes first woman to receive engineering degree from MIT. Degree is in naval architecture.	Congress approves the U.S. Naval Engineering Experiment Station and Testing Laboratory (EES) at Annapolis, Maryland.
	Eight major ships of U.S. Navy fitted with radio. Five North Atlantic Naval shore stations placed in operation.	Letter-and-number symbols begin to be used by the Navy to define its ships. This procedure will be more formally established in 1907 and 1920.
1903		U.S. Coast Guard Academy adds third year to its program.
1903 March 3		Act of Congress increases number of officers in Construction Corps to seventy-five.
1903 December 10		Naval Base is established at Guantanamo Bay, Cuba, as first U.S. military installation on foreign soil.
1903 December 17		Orville-Wright pilots airplane, invented and built with his brother Wilbur, in world's first flight in a power-driven, heavier-than-air machine, at Kitty Hawk, North Carolina.
1904ca	American de Laval Company in Trenton makes a great step forward with construction of new gear cutting machine, achieving extraordinary accuracy.	
1904	Construction starts on sister ships *Mauretania* and *Lusitania*. Special Cunard Line commission decides on turbine power based on *Turbinia's* performance in 1897 at Spithead.	
1904	A major step forward in introducing steam turbines into larger Atlantic passenger ships is made with orders from the Allan Line for *Victorian* and *Virginian*: 11,000 gross tons, power of 8,800 KW (12,000hp) with three shaft arrangement of *King Edward*, 20 knots on trial. *Virginian* will go into operation in 1905, will later be converted to oil-burning, re-engined in 1921-2, and will serve for nearly 50 years.	
1904 June 15		The excursion steamer *General Slocum* burns in New York City's East River with loss of 1,030.
1905		The Navy Collier Service of 1898, consisting of 15 vessels, is reorganized as the Naval Auxiliary Service.
1905 March 3	Congress authorizes two new battleships, to be called *South Carolina* (BB-26) and *Michigan* (BB-27). The chief constructor, Washington L. Capps, will develop the superfiring main battery, which will become the international standard for all big-gun ships. They will launch on 1 July 1908 and 26 May 1908, respectively, after HMS *Dreadnought*.	
1905 May 27	Japanese fleet under Togo decisively defeats Russian fleet of Rohzdesvensky at Tsushima, confirming effectiveness of battleships, heavy long-range naval guns and advanced fire-control. Japanese for first time exploit naval "wireless" to relay intelligence on enemy fleet movement. The Russian Baltic Fleet had conducted a noteworthy feat of seamanship and engineering operation in steaming nearly around the world prior to the battle.	
1905 November 28		September, October, and November have been marked by three great storms on Lake Superior, with loss of 215 lives. On this particular date, two ships are lost and twenty-seven others damaged, resulting in considerable and successful lobbying for lake navigation aids.

Date	Naval Engineering	National & International Events Legislative, Organization & Personnel Policy
1906	SS *Mauretania* is launched. She will be a favorite of transatlantic passengers, will be most successful passenger liner of all, and will hold Atlantic Blue Ribbon for 22 years. Dimensions are: length 790 feet, beam 88 feet, draft 36.2 feet, gross tonnage 37,938 tons. Her 70,000 horsepower turbines drive four propellers and give her a speed of 27.4 knots.	
	Launching of HMS *Dreadnought* commences all big-gun ship era.	
	Radio Direction Finder is installed for test in the collier USS *Lebanon* (AC-2).	
1906 October 28	DeForest applies for U.S. patent on three-element vacuum tube.	
1907	First U.S. Naval steam turbines are installed in destroyers.	
1907	Wilbur and Orville Wright experiment with a hydrofoil catamaran on the Ohio River near Dayton.	U.S. Navy commences radio broadcast of hydrographic bulletin (Notice to Mariners).
1907	U.S. Navy commences tests of radio-telephone in USS *Connecticut* and *Virginia*.	
1907 January 8		President Theodore Roosevelt issues Executive Order 549 specifying that United States Ship or USS shall precede the name of the Navy's ships.
1907 April 13	*Empress*, 1,695 grt, is launched as a cross-English Channel packet. After the outbreak of World War I, she will be purchased by British Admiralty, given a canvas "hangar" aft and will be able to operate three embarked aircraft, served by mainmast derrick. She will be given more substantial conversion in 1915 for aircraft operations and will be returned to owners in 1919.	
1907 November 22		SS *Mauretania* arrives in New York for first time.
1907 December 16	The 'Great White Fleet' leaves Hampton Roads, Virginia, and is first fleet of United States warships to circumnavigate the world.	
1907 October 24		New York Nautical School acquires the barkentine USS *Newport* from the Navy as its training ship. Containing a fully equipped engineroom, the ship will support introduction of courses in marine engines, electricity, and magnetism.
1908	Elmer Sperry patents gyrocompass.	
	Washington Navy Yard model tow-basin is opened.	
1908 March	Construction of Naval Experiment Station is started in Annapolis, first of its kind.	
1908 October 1		Henry Ford introduces the "Model T," a mass-produced automobile designed to be simple and inexpensive. They will be produced until 1927.
1909	Charles A. Parsons makes second major step forward in marine turbines by installing geared-turbine drive in merchant ship *Vespasian*.	
1909 February 22	The 'Great White Fleet' returns to Hampton Roads.	
1909 June	A two-year School of Marine Engineering is established at the Naval Academy for post graduate study. Shorter courses for ordnance specialists and naval constructors will start in November 1912 and February 1913, respectively. These programs will be consolidated in 1913 into the U.S. Naval Postgraduate School at Annapolis.	

Date	Naval Engineering	National & International Events Legislative, Organization & Personnel Policy
1910	The 1st edition of *The Speed and Power of Ships* by RADM D. W. Taylor is published.	Lighthouse Board in the Department of Commerce is replaced by newly organized Lighthouse Bureau.
		The Motorboat Act of 1910 establishes a creditable boating safety program. Advancing technology will require constant updating and major changes in future years, for example, 1940, 1958, 1971.
1910 April 12	*Paulding* (DD-22), built by Bath Iron Works, is first U.S. Navy ship to be launched for operation on fuel oil. USS *Roe* (DD-24), built by Newport News Shipbuilding, will be first oil-burner commissioned, 17 September 1910.	
1910 November 14	Eugene Ely, a civilian pilot, makes first aircraft takeoff from a ship, using wooden platform on USS *Birmingham* (CL-2).	
1910 November 18	The Fuel-Oil Testing Plant is established by the Bureau of Steam Engineering in the Philadelphia Naval Shipyard. Rear Admiral George W. Melville, USN, is credited with this action. Its first mission is principally component problem resolution in finding solutions for the hazards involved when using fuel oil for steam generation in naval vessels. The plant is also tasked with investigation of boiler design, design of instruments and equipment for test and development of boilers, and to provide a nucleus of trained personnel for the Fleet. Its name and mission will be modified in 1932, 1941, 1966, and 1979. (Note: NAVSSES booklet dated September 1986 says organization began in 1910. Paper presented before SNAME Philadelphia Section, 22 April 1947, by Captain Kranzfelder, Director NBTL, says 1909.)	
	In Westinghouse factory, John H. MacAlpine tests large gears, which will be installed in the collier *Neptune* (AC-8), thereby introducing geared machinery to the USA. *Neptune* will be placed in service with a merchant crew at the Norfolk Navy Yard, 20 September 1911.	
1911	Dutch Physicist Heike Kamerlingh Onnes discovers superconductivity, which later in the century will suggest potentially significant developments of many kinds including maritime applications.	
1911 January 18	Eugene Ely, flying a Curtiss pusher aircraft, makes first aircraft landing aboard ship on a specially built platform on USS *Pennsylvania* (ACR-4). Ship is renamed *Pittsburgh* 27 August 1912 to free name *Pennsylvania* for BB-38.	
1911 January 26	Glen Curtiss makes first seaplane takeoff in the United States, at San Diego.	
1911 May 8		Naval aviation is born when Captain W.I. Chambers, Officer in Charge of Aviation, orders Navy's first aircraft, *Triad*, an A-1 amphibian, from Glenn Curtiss.
1911 July 19		Orville Wright delivers the first Navy Wright airplane to Annapolis.

Date	Naval Engineering	National & International Events Legislative, Organization & Personnel Policy
1912	Lieutenant T. O. Ellyson, Naval Aviator #1, works with naval constructor H. C. Richardson in Annapolis to perfect the Chambers compressed-air catapult, continuing work started by Ellyson in Hammondsport, New York, which included experimenting with a wire-launch of the A-1 Triad. Their work will move to the Washington Navy Yard for a successful launch from a barge of Ellyson in a C-1.	
	The U.S. Navy commissions one of designer Simon Lake's submarines, assigning to it the only fractional number ever to encumber a U.S. submarine: the SS 19½.	
	First extensive U.S. Navy test diving conducted from USS *Walke* in Long Island Sound.	
	U.S. Navy officially substitutes word "radio" for "wireless."	
		U.S. Navy commences experiments with radio in aircraft, communicating with USS *Stringham* at 3 miles.
1912 February 14	USS *Skipjack* (SS-24, renamed E-1 17 November 1911 during construction) is commissioned, Lieutenant C. W. Nimitz, U.S. Navy, Commanding Officer. She is first U.S. submarine with diesel power, and will be first U.S. submarine (in 1916) to cross Atlantic under her own power.	
1912 April 14-15		SS *Titanic* strikes iceberg and sinks on maiden voyage. Because she carried mail for the crown, *Titanic* also bore the honorary initials RMS, for Royal Mail Steamer.
1912 December 30		Navy Arlington Radio Station is completed. It is the largest in the world at the time and sets precedent for the Navy's firm role in communications.
1913	Aeronautical engineering course is initiated at MIT by Jerome C. Hunsacker, former Naval Constructor.	Aircraft based ashore at Guantanamo under the command of Lt. John Towers, are used for the first time in fleet maneuvers.
1913 February 1	U.S. Naval Postgraduate School is established at Annapolis, Maryland. The barracks building in which the school is located will be renamed Halligan Hall in honor of the school's first director, Commander John Halligan, Jr. The school will educate an increasing number of students in such fields as mechanical, electrical, and aeronautical engineering and naval construction. USNPGS will close for the duration of World War I and will reopen in June 1919 under the direction of Captain Ernest Joseph King.	
1913 February 6		First seaplane reconnaissance is conducted over Dardanelles by Greek seaplane in First Balkan War.
1913 April 7	USS *Jupiter* (AC-3), first ship equipped with electric drive, is commissioned. She will later be converted to the U.S. Navy's first aircraft carrier.	
1913 November 1		New York Nautical School is transferred to state control and becomes the New York State Nautical School (NYSNS).
1914		Bureau of Equipment is formally abolished.
		School of Instruction for the Revenue Cutter Service is renamed Revenue Cutter Academy.

Date	Naval Engineering	National & International Events Legislative, Organization & Personnel Policy
1914 March 17	USS *K-1* (renamed from *Haddock* SS-32 during construction) is commissioned, Lieutenant (j.g.) E. F. Cutts, Commanding Officer. She is first U.S. submarine equipped with a U.S.-made periscope.	
1914 May 2		Lieutenant (j.g.) P. N. L. Bellinger, USN, flies first mission in direct support of marine ground forces ashore, at Veracruz, Mexico. On 6 May his AH-3, hit by rifle fire, will become the first U.S. Navy aircraft to receive marks of combat.
1914 May 29		*Empress of Ireland*, a British liner, sinks in the St. Lawrence River after colliding with a Norwegian collier. 1,014 are killed.
1914 June 30	Act of Congress authorizes USS *New Mexico* (BB-40), first battleship to employ turbo-electric propulsion.	
1914 August		Panama Canal is first used, extending 50.72 miles from Limon Bay on the Caribbean to Bay of Panama on Pacific. Giant slide in 1915 closes Canal for several months.
1914 September 5		First successful naval employment of a submarine occurs at St. Abb's Head, Scotland, when German submariner Hersing in U-21 sinks the cruiser HMS *Pathfinder*. Impact of submarines on naval warfare is further clearly foreshadowed on 22 September when Weddigen in U-9 sinks HMS *Aboukir, Cressy, Hogue*.
1914 December 10	*Ark Royal* is commissioned, Royal Navy's first purpose-built aircraft carrier. She will serve in various ways in aircraft operations and test until 1941, having been renamed *Pegasus* in December 1934, and in other auxiliary roles until 1946 when she will revert to mercantile status as *Anita I*. She will be broken up in 1950.	
1915	The 1st Edition of *Structural Design of Warships* by William Hovgaard is published by E. & F. N. Spor, Ltd., London.	World's first transatlantic radiotelephone system is set up between U.S. Naval Radio Station-Arlington and Eiffel Tower-Paris. Revenue Cutter Academy is renamed United States Coast Guard Academy.
1915 January 1		Panama Canal is officially opened.
1915 January 24		Battle of Dogger Bank occurs when British battle-cruiser force surprises a surface strike force of German battlecruisers, sinks SMS *Blucher* and heavily damages SMS *Seydlitz*. Germans disengage and escape following hits on British flagship HMS *Lion*. Subsequently, Germans shift to less dangerous gun propellant, but British do not, resulting in heavy losses to British battlecruisers from lighter gunfire at Jutland. There is some dispute about the implications of this battle. Another opinion is that the explosions in gun hoists were due to design of the hoists, and that a change in design made German ships less vulnerable.
1915 January 28		The U.S. Revenue Cutter Service and the Lifesaving Service are merged. The new organization, headed by a captain commandant, is called the U.S. Coast Guard.
1915 March 3	USS *Tennessee* (BB-43), authorized by Act of Congress, with USS *California* (BB-44), become the first battleship class with turbo-electric propulsion.	Office of Naval Operations is formed in the Navy Department.
1915 March 8	First minelayer, USS *Baltimore* (C-3), begins service after her conversion from a cruiser.	

Date	Naval Engineering	National & International Events Legislative, Organization & Personnel Policy
1915 May 7		The Cunard liner, S.S. *Lusitania*, is sunk by Germany off the Irish coast, with a loss of 1,198 lives, including 102 Americans.
1915 June 1		U.S. Navy orders its first non-rigid airship from the Connecticut Aircraft Company.
1915 November 5	Lieutenant P. N. L. Bellinger, USN, makes first catapult launch from a permanent installation on the USS *North Carolina* (ARC-12), with ship underway.	
1915 December		President Woodrow Wilson makes "Preparedness" speech to Congress.
1916		National Research Council is created by the National Academy of Sciences at the request of President Wilson.
1916		By the Naval Reserve Act, Congress establishes the Naval Reserve Force in which men engaged in the seafaring profession are encouraged to join.
1916 February 26		The French cruiser *Provence* sinks in the Mediterranean. 3,100 are killed.
1916 May 31	Battle of Jutland takes place when British Grand Fleet engages German High Seas Fleet in North Sea off Denmark. Despite British command and control failures with repeated loss of contact and initiative, and heavier British combat losses, Germans retire to base and do not again challenge British sea power. U.S. naval assessment of German superiority in gunfire control, damage control, and Zeppelin reconnaissance leads to successful postwar efforts to exploit and utilize these techniques. Jutland discredits the lightly armored, high speed battlecruiser concept, and battleship design will be revised to emphasize protection.	
1916 August 28	USS *Memphis* (ACR-10) (formerly USS *Tennessee*) is totally destroyed by tidal wave while anchored off Santo Domingo City.	
1916 August 29		Act of Congress specifies number of officers in the Construction Corps as percentage of number of officers of line; also numbers in various ranks, including rank of rear admiral, are fixed as percentages of total number of Construction Corps officers.
1916 September 7		Shipping Act, 1916, is approved (39 Stat. 728, Chapter 451).
1916 September 15		Austrian seaplanes sink French submarine *Foucalt* in the Adriatic Sea with bombs in first successful air attack at sea.
1917		Congress converts Coast and Geodetic Survey to a commissioned, uniformed service.
1917 January	American Bureau of Shipping makes agreement with the British Corporation for the Survey and Registry of Shipping, allowing ABS to adopt the British *Rules for the Construction of Steel Ships*, believed to be the best standards and practices at this time.	
1917 March 22		The first Coast Guard Aviation Group graduates from flight training at NAS, Pensacola. Lieutenant Elmer F. Stone, USCG, is designated Coast Guard Aviator #1. Two years later he will copilot the Curtiss NC-4 on its transatlantic flight, for which he will receive the Medal of Honor. Of the six officers shown in the Naval Institute's class picture, one will become a vice admiral and three will attain the rank of rear admiral.

Date	Naval Engineering	National & International Events Legislative, Organization & Personnel Policy
1917 April 6		United States enters World War I. The U.S. Coast Guard passes into the naval establishment and begins operating as part of the Navy.
1917 August 25	RADM David W. Taylor initiates action to develop large flying boats.	
1917 September 27		In first successful use of aircraft mines in war at sea, Russian destroyer *Ochotnik* is sunk in Baltic by a German aircraft-laid mine.
1917 December 6		The French ammunition ship *Mont Blanc* collides with a Belgian steamer in Halifax Harbor. 1,600 are killed.
1918		In less than six weeks, Lieutenant David Sinton Ingalls, U.S. Naval Reserve Force, Naval Aviator #68, shoots down four enemy aircraft and a balloon to become the Navy's first, and only, World War I ace. He had been a member of the First Yale Unit, the first component of the Naval Air Reserve, and went overseas assigned to a British RAF pursuit squadron flying Sopwith Camels. He will become Assistant Secretary of the Navy for Air under President Hoover, serve again in combat in World War II, and retire as a Rear Admiral in the Naval Reserve.
1918 July 19		First carrier strike in warfare is made on Tondern, Schleswig-Holstein, when Sopwith Camels from the first British carrier, HMS *Furious*, destroy naval reconnaissance Zeppelins L54 and L60 at their base.
1918 August 17		General Order 418 establishes use of titles of rank, in address, for all U.S. Navy staff officers.
1918 September	The Royal Navy commissions *Argus*, the first aircraft carrier with an unobstructed, full-length flight deck. She has been converted from partially built Italian merchant ship *Conte Rosso*, construction of which was suspended at outbreak of First World War.	
1918 September 6	U.S. Navy railroad battery equipped with specially converted 14-inch battleship guns commences firing operations against German Army installations in Northern France.	
1919	Hydrofoil boat, HD-4, built by Alexander Graham Bell and Frederick W. (Casey) Baldwin, sets world speed record of 70.85 miles per hour.	The Office of Naval Intelligence defines ship types of the U.S. Navy.
1919 May 16		Lieutenant Commander Albert Cushing Read, USN, with Lieutenants Walter Hinton and James Breese, USN, Lieutenant Elmer Stone, USCG, Lieutenant (j.g.) Braxton Rhoads, USN, and Ensign Herbert C. Rodd, USN, depart Trepassey Bay, Newfoundland, in Read's Curtiss NC-4, to become first flight to cross the Atlantic. They fly for 15 hours and 1,200 miles to Horta, Azores, then via Porta Delgada to Lisbon, Portugal, and, ultimately, to Plymouth, England, for a total distance of 4,514 miles. Sixty-eight destroyers and five battleships have been stationed as "marker buoys" across the ocean.
1919 August 9	Secretary of the Navy authorizes construction of airship ZR-1, the future *Shenandoah*, the Navy's first rigid airship.	
1920 circa	Major shift from coal to oil for marine propulsion is underway.	
1920	Electric propulsion is installed in battleships and aircraft carriers.	

Date	Naval Engineering	National & International Events Legislative, Organization & Personnel Policy
1920 January 17		Coast Guard is given the maritime duty to enforce the Volstead Act implementing the Eighteenth Amendment concerning Prohibition.
1920 June		Dr. Robert H. Goddard receives U.S. Navy contract for rocket-projected depth charge research.
1920 June 4		The Navy's Bureau of Steam Engineering becomes the Bureau of Engineering.
1920 June 5		Merchant Marine Act, 1920 is approved (41 Stat. 988, Chapter 250).
1920 July 6		First test of a radio compass in an airplane. A Navy Curtiss seaplane flies round trip from Norfolk, Virginia, to USS Ohio, 90 miles at sea, guided only by radio.
1920 July 12		Panama Canal is completed by U.S. Army Corps of Engineers and formally dedicated.
1920 July 17		General Order 541 establishes the Navy's system to describe its ships by type classification symbol and hull number as well as by name. The G.O. also provides for annual publication of a "Ship's Data Book," prepared by the Bureau of Construction and Repair and approved by the Secretary of the Navy.
1920 September 1	USS S-5 (SS-110) sinks off Delaware Cape after taking on water through the main air induction system while commencing a dive for a submerged test run. Flooding the torpedo room and blowing the aft ballast and fuel tanks lifts the stern 17 feet above water. The entire crew is rescued through a hole cut by the passing steamer SS Atlanthus, assisted by SS General Goethals. Towline breaks when USS Ohio (BB-12) tries to tow S-5 to more shallow water. She will be struck from the Navy list in 1921.	
1920 December 24 & 30	Edward F. Hennelly, a scientist with General Electric, mentions the magnetron, a key element in early radar, in two letters to Willis R. Whitney, Director of General Electric Research Laboratory. Two patent applications will be docketed on 30 December and 6 January 1921, and will be granted to Hennelly in 1925.	
1921	Pratt School of Naval Architecture and Marine Engineering Building is completed at MIT.	
1921 May 15	The submarine R-14 arrives at Hilo after 5 days under sail. She had run out of fuel southeast of Hawaii during a search for the tug Conestoga, and made sails from blankets and mattresses.	
1921 July 21	Brigadier General Billy Mitchell, USA, participates in U.S. Navy bombing tests off Virginia Coast against old German battleship Ostfriesland (preempts test program to "prove" battleships are sinkable).	
1921 August 10		U.S. Navy's Bureau of Aeronautics is established under Rear Admiral William A. Moffett.
1922	Dr. Harvey C. Hayes, at this time with the Navy's Engineering Experiment Station, develops the first practical deep water sonic depth finder. Later in the year, this equipment in USS Stewart (DD-244) will be used to make a continuous ocean depth track from the United States eastward through the Mediterranean and Indian Ocean to China. Stewart will depart from Newport, Rhode Island, on 20 June for duty with the Asiatic Fleet and will not return to the U.S for 23 years.	

Date	Naval Engineering	National & International Events Legislative, Organization & Personnel Policy
1922 February 6		Washington Disarmament conference results in Washington Naval Treaty, signed on this date by Great Britain, United States, Japan, France, and Italy. Treaty allows agreed naval tonnage to each treaty country, and constrains ship design by class tonnage limitations.
1922 March 20	U.S. Navy's first aircraft carrier, USS *Langley* (CV-1), is commissioned, following conversion from collier *Jupiter*.	
1922 March 24		U.S. Senate ratifies Treaty of Naval Limitations resulting from the Washington Naval Conference.
1922 May 16	*Drottningholm*, renamed from *Virginian* when purchased by The Swedish America Line, completes successful trial after major refit, accomplished by Gotaverken in 11 months. A complete set of new machinery, exchanging the old direct-drive Parsons turbines for a set of geared impulse turbines, was delivered by the Swedish de Laval Company in 9 months from order.	
1922 September 27	Dr. Albert H. Taylor and Leo C. Young of the Naval Aircraft Radio Laboratory at Anacostia, D.C., make the first 'radar observations.'	
1922 October 17		First takeoff from deck of USS *Langley* (CV-1) is made by Lieutenant Virgil C. Griffin in a VE-7-SF.
1922 October 26		First landing on USS *Langley* (CV-1) is made by Lieutenant Commander Godfrey de Courcelles Chevalier in an Aeromarine aircraft.
1922 November 18		Commander Kenneth Whiting, Executive Officer of USS *Langley* (CV-1), is first to catapult from that ship.
1923 April		L. F. Loree (1858-1940) of New York, dean of American railroad presidents, establishes a group now known as "American Newcomen" and interested in Business History.
1923 June		In less than 2 weeks time, fleet aviators and aircraft establish no less than nineteen world records for speed, distance, payload, and duration.
1923 July 1	The Naval Research Laboratory is established. The Naval Radio Laboratory, the Naval Aircraft Radio Laboratory, and the Radio Test Shop of the Washington Navy Yard are combined to form the NRL Radio Division.	
1923 September 8	Nine destroyers of the fourteen in Squadron 11, Destroyer Force, Battle Fleet, run aground at Point Honda, California, with loss of twenty-three men, and total loss of seven ships. This loss points dramatically to the need to put RDF (Radio Direction Finding) equipment in the hands of the ship's navigator, not on shore stations, and starts the process that leads eventually to this outcome.	
1923 November 5	U.S. Navy completes a series of tests to evaluate feasibility of basing aircraft on submarines. A tiny Martin MS-1 seaplane, disassembled and stowed in a hull-mounted container, is assembled and launched at Hampton Roads, Virginia, from the submarine S-1, which submerges to permit the aircraft to become waterborne and take off. A further test will be performed on 28 July 1926.	
1924 February 21		U.S. Army Industrial College is established in Washington, D.C.

Date	Naval Engineering	National & International Events Legislative, Organization & Personnel Policy
1924 August 8	USS *Shenandoah* (ZR-1) makes first shipboard mooring of a dirigible to mooring mast installed aboard USS *Patoka* (AO-9) in Naragansett Bay.	
1924 September 15	Naval Research Laboratory personnel, assisted by personnel from the Bureau of Ordnance and Naval Proving Ground, Dahlgren, Virginia, achieve first successful flight of a radio-controlled pilotless aircraft with takeoff, maneuvering for 40 minutes, and landing.	
1925 September		Commander John Rodgers, Naval Aviator #2, undertakes flight from San Francisco to Hawaii in a PN-9 seaplane. Nearly 26 hours and 1,841 miles after takeoff, plane runs out of fuel and lands at sea. Last 450 miles to Kauai Island is completed in 9 days under sail fashioned from wing fabric.
1925 September 25		USS *S-51* (SS-162) is rammed by SS *City of Rome* and sinks off Block Island, New York. Only three survive of the thirty-six on board. She will be raised on 5 June 1926 under the direction of Captain E. J. King, U.S. Navy, Commanding Officer, Submarine Base, New London, and struck from the Navy list on 27 January 1930.
1925	At sea tests of High Frequency radio during a cruise from San Francisco to Melbourne, Australia, of USS *Seattle* (CA-11), flagship of the Commander-in-Chief of the United States Fleet (CINCUS, an unfortunate acronym contributing in part to a later change in title), prove effectiveness of frequencies to 18 MHz for long range communication.	By the Naval Reserve Act, Congress establishes a Merchant Marine Naval Reserve as a component of the U.S. Navy.
1926 May 9		Richard E. Byrd with his pilot, Chief Machinist Mate Floyd Bennett, complete a 1,360-mile, 15½ hour flight from Spitzbergen Island to the North Pole and back in the ski-equipped Ford trimotor "Josephine Ford."
1926 June 10		Equalization bill establishes Construction Corps promotion in higher ranks, after selection, on basis of percentages of line officers promoted; also limits number of officers in corps with rank of rear admiral to one.
1926 July 28	A further phase of the evaluation previously completed on 5 November 1923 is performed in which the submarine S-1 surfaces, assembles, and launches a small XS-2 seaplane, recovers the aircraft, and resubmerges to complete the cycle.	
1926 Fall		Chester W. Nimitz, a commander at this time, arrives at University of California, Berkeley, to start nation's first NROTC unit.
1927	Active high frequency sonar equipment is first installed in U.S. Navy ships.	
1927 May 20		Charles A. Lindbergh takes off in *Spirit of St. Louis* for solo transatlantic flight, which will end successfully 33 hours later at Paris.
1927 May-July		Lieutenant C. C. Champion, USN, establishes three world altitude records within 11 weeks in seaplane and land-plane configurations of a Wright Apache aircraft.

Date	Naval Engineering	National & International Events Legislative, Organization & Personnel Policy
1927 December 17	USS *S-4* (SS-109) is rammed by USCG *Paulding* and sinks off Provincetown, Massachusetts, with loss of entire crew. She will be raised on 17 March 1928 under the salvage direction of Captain E. J. King, U.S. Navy, decommissioned on 19 March, and recommissioned on 16 October 1928 after repairs at the Boston Navy Yard. This loss of life will expedite development of the McCann rescue chamber.	
1928 January 28	Rigid airship USS *Los Angeles* (ZR-3) makes first dirigible landing on a ship, USS *Saratoga* (CV-3).	
1928 May 22		Merchant Marine Act, 1928, is approved (45 Stat. 689, Chapter 675).
1929	Electronically amplified passive sonar equipment is developed and designated JK.	The California Maritime Academy is founded.
1929 May 10	The "Momsen Lung," intended to improve chances for survival from sunken submarines, is tested by Lieutenant Charles Momsen, U.S. Navy, and Chief Gunner C. L. Tibbals, U.S. Navy, to a depth of over 200 feet.	
1929 July 1		New York State Nautical School becomes New York State Merchant Marine Academy (NYSMMA).
1929 August 20		A Vought UO-1 completes several successful hook-ons to a "trapeze" on a Navy dirigible *Los Angeles*, paving the way for subsequent such "carrier" operations.
1929 December 27		Committee is formed to coordinate Marine Boiler Rules. William McFarland is elected as Chairman and their purpose is to establish Boiler Code Rules.
1930 January 21		Five-Power (England, United States, Japan, France, Italy) naval conference begins in London. Session will lead to the London Naval Treaty.
1930 April 22		London Naval Treaty is formally completed and signed by representatives of the five great naval powers.
1930 July 21		U.S. Senate ratifies London Treaty of Naval Limitations.
1930 September 10		*America*'s Cup Races are held off Newport, Rhode Island, for the first time at this location.
1931	Electric Boat receives submarine contract from the Navy for *Cuttlefish*, a technical milestone because she is partially welded rather than completely riveted. Henceforth, all submarines will be completely welded.	U.S. Coast Guard Academy adds fourth year to its curriculum.
1931 September 23	Lieutenant A. M. Pride, USN, makes the first autogiro landings and takeoffs from USS *Langley* (CV-1). The Navy had ordered an autogiro for evaluation about 2 years after the first U.S. autogiro flight by Harold Pitcairn.	
1931 September 26	Keel is laid for *Ranger* (CV-4), first U.S. aircraft carrier designed from keel up for this purpose.	
1932	The Fuel-Oil Testing Plant at Philadelphia changes its name to the U.S. Naval Boiler Laboratory, recognizing its function of equipment testing as a boiler development plant.	U.S. Coast Guard Academy moves to its present location, just a few miles up the Thames River from Fort Trumbull.

Date	Naval Engineering	National & International Events Legislative, Organization & Personnel Policy
1932 September 25-27		Lieutenants Thomas Greenshow Williams, "Tex" Settle, and Wilfred Bushnell win the Gordon Bennett International Balloon Race, establishing a new world record of 963 miles. Settle receives the Harmon International Trophy, is a naval aviator uniquely qualified in balloons, dirigibles, and heavier-than-air aircraft, and will retire as a vice admiral.
1932 November		The Secretary of the Navy requests Congressional legislation to permit the Naval Academy to grant the Bachelor of Science degree. His plan stresses the desirability of offering a deserved incentive to the increasingly large annual number of graduates for whom no commission vacancies are available, and that such incentives would "raise the efficiency" of the Academy.
1933	The Washington Navy Yard produces twenty sets of quartz-steel echo-ranging equipment, a major sonar development. Lieutenant Robert D. Conrad (CC), USN, receives first graduate scholarship from the Society of Naval Architects and Marine Engineers, the sum of $1,000 for one-year study at Cambridge University, England.	
1933 January		The proposals for legislation to permit the Naval Academy to grant the Bachelor of Science degree are broadened to include the Military Academy and the Coast Guard Academy.
1933 March 3		Intercoastal Shipping Act, 1933, is approved (47 Stat. 1425, Chapter 199).
1933 May 20		A joint bill in Congress is amended to stipulate that Bachelor of Science Degree authority at the Naval Academy, Coast Guard Academy, and Military Academy would be contingent on "the accrediting of said academies by the Association of American Universities."
1933 May 25		President Roosevelt signs into law the bill providing for the Bachelor of Science degree for Naval, Military and Coast Guard Academies. Both West Point and Annapolis have already received accreditation as "approved technological institutions," in 1925 and 1930, respectively. Their authority to grant the BS degree dates from 1933. The Coast Guard Academy will not receive the necessary accreditation until 1941.
1933 October 27	The Portsmouth Navy Yard lays down *Porpoise* (SS-172). She will be the first U.S. submarine equipped with electric reduction gear and high-speed diesel engines.	
1934 June 4		USS *Ranger* (CV-4) is commissioned. She can operate seventy-five aircraft and has complement of 1778.
1934 June 8	USS *Cuttlefish* (SS-171) is commissioned. She is first submarine to have air conditioning installed during construction.	
1934 September	William Beebe and Otis Barton descend 3,028 feet off Bermuda in two-ton steel ball bathysphere, designed by John H. J. Butler.	
1934 September 8		The burning of the *Morro Castle* with a loss of 134 lives will serve as a catalyst for merchant marine legislation concerning ship safety and federally administered maritime training.

Date	Naval Engineering	National & International Events Legislative, Organization & Personnel Policy
1934 December	NRL radar, designed by Dr. R. M. Page and operating at 60 MHz, detects small aircraft at 1 mile. The term "radar" will not be officially accepted until 1940.	
1935 June 5		Aeronautical Engineering Duty (AED) officer specialist community is established in U.S. Navy, with forty-four officers designated AED.
1935 June 5		Naval constructors engaged in aeronautical work are permitted to transfer to line for aeronautical duty only.
1935 August 5		Act of Congress extends selection to lower ranks of Construction Corps; provides for retirement in certain ranks after specified lengths of service and failure of selection.
1936		The Coast Guard is officially tasked to perform icebreaking, but in reality has been performing this mission for decades.
1936 April	NRL radar, operating at 28.6 MHz, detects aircraft at 25 miles, the limit of the display.	
1936 May 6		Congress approves "An Act to authorize the construction of a Model Basin establishment . . . for U.S. vessels including aircraft and the investigation of other problems of ship design . . ."
1936 June 29		Merchant Marine Act, 1936, is approved, (49 Stat. 1985). A primary purpose is to establish a strong merchant marine capable of service as a naval and military auxiliary in time of war or national emergency. The act includes provision for training maritime personnel.
1936 September 18	USS *Mahan* (DD-364) is commissioned under command of Commander J. B. Waller, USN. She has many advanced features and firsts, including: double-reduction, two-pinion locked-train reduction gears, diesel-electric emergency generators for auxiliary light and power in lieu of storage batteries, diesel ship's boats.	
1937	In first successful tests of radar at sea, 200-MHz system in USS *Leary* (DD-158) detects aircraft at range of 18 miles. System uses YAGI antenna attached to 5″ gun barrel for train and elevation. Radar detections on airborne and surface targets at moderate ranges are obtained with the two radars tested. On 19 November 1941 *Leary* will be first American ship to make radar contact with a U-boat.	
1937 January 25	USS *Cheyenne* (BM-10), launched as *Wyoming* on 8 September 1900 and renamed 1 January 1909, is struck from the Navy List. She is the last of the seventy-one monitors ordered for the Navy, of which about fifty actually saw commissioned service. In 1908, *Wyoming* was converted from coal to oil fuel at Mare Island Navy Yard, the first ship to be converted in the U.S. Navy.	
1937 May 6		The hydrogen-filled German dirigible *Hindenburg* explodes, crashes, and burns at Lakehurst, New Jersey, killing thirty-six people, effectively ending this mode of passenger transportation.

Date	Naval Engineering	National & International Events Legislative, Organization & Personnel Policy
1937 Summer	German midshipmen visit USS *New York* (BB-34) assigned to U.S. midshipmen at-sea training, during port call at Kiel, Germany. Germans inquire of Midshipman 1/c F. H. Huron, USN, "Where is your Radio Range Finder?" Midshipman Huron and his shipmates were unaware of radar developments, leading to later reflection concerning knowledge of German intelligence about U.S. activities.	
1937 October 5		Secretary of the Navy directs the new establishment, authorized by Congress on 6 May 1936, to be named the David W. Taylor Model Basin.
1938		By the Naval Reserve Act of 1938 Congress establishes a Merchant Marine Reserve to replace the 1925 Merchant Marine Naval Reserve.
1938 January		The U.S. Naval Academy, having awarded the Bachelor of Science degree to graduates starting with the Class of 1933 as authorized by Congressional Act, now awards this degree retroactively to graduates prior to the Class of 1933.
1938 March 15		The United States Merchant Marine Cadet Corps is established. This is the forerunner of the U.S. Merchant Marine Academy that during the period 1941-1945 will graduate 6,634 officers. 212 midshipmen and graduates will give their lives in service to the country.
1938 May 17		Congress passes Vinson-Trammell Act authorizing "Two Ocean Navy."
1938 May 21		New York State Merchant Marine Academy dedicates its permanent shore base at Fort Schuyler in the Bronx, New York.
1938 November 16	Royal Navy commissions *Ark Royal*, the first large British aircraft carrier designed from scratch. Her World War II career will be brief but noteworthy. She will be torpedoed by *U-81* on 13 November 1941 off Gibralter. Flooding will cause her to capsize and sink.	
1938 December	Model XAF, prototype operational radar installed in USS *New York* (BB-44), is tested very successfully during winter battle practice in the Caribbean.	
1939	*Principles of Naval Architecture* is published by the Society of Naval Architects and Marine Engineers.	Naval Research Laboratory institutes nation's first organized research program in nuclear energy.
		The Lighthouse Bureau is absorbed from the Department of Commerce by the Treasury Department and the U.S. Coast Guard.
		The Navy's Sound School is established in San Diego.
1939 May 23	USS *Squalus* (SS-192) sinks during sea trials with fifty-nine persons on board. She is located by her sister ship, USS *Sculpin* (SS-191). Thirty-three are saved by means of the McCann Rescue Chamber, designed by naval officers Charles Momsen and Allan McCann. *Squalus* is subsequently raised and towed to Portsmouth Navy Yard.	
1939 September 1		World War II starts in Europe with the importance of seapower presaged by the first shot. At 0445 the German battleship *Schleswig Holstein* fires an 11-inch shell that hits an ammunition dump near Danzig and signals the invasion of Poland.
1939 September 8		President Roosevelt declares a "limited national emergency."

Date	Naval Engineering	National & International Events Legislative, Organization & Personnel Policy
1939 September 15	USS *Squalus* (SS-192) is drydocked at Portsmouth Navy Yard after her sinking and salvage. She is rebuilt, renamed *Sailfish* (SS-192), and has a distinguished record in World War II.	
1939 October 14		A German U-boat penetrates Scapa Flow and sinks the battleship HMS *Royal Oak*, first sinking of a capital ship by a submarine.
1939 December 13		First naval engagement in which radar is employed is battle of the river Plate. British cruisers HMS *Achilles, Ajax* and *Exeter*, although badly mauled, force "pocket battleship" *Graf Spee*, engaged in South Atlantic commerce raiding, to seek neutral haven at Montevideo. *Graf Spee* is scuttled to prevent capture in Montevideo.
1939	U.S. Coast Guard Academy becomes first of the service schools to be accredited by the Engineering Council for Professional Development.	
1940	The David W. Taylor Model Basin becomes operational.	
1940	The first Model CXAM air search radar is installed in USS *California* (BB-44). This is an RCA-produced copy of the NRL Model ZAF radar. The CXAM will also be installed in several aircraft carriers, battleships, and cruisers and will be a vital element in the early naval air battles of World War II.	
1940 June		Vannevar Bush persuades President Roosevelt to establish National Defense Research Committee to contract with universities and industry for defense research. Bush becomes NDRC chairman.
		Sir Henry Tizzard's mission reaches the U.S. to deliver its "black box" containing the cavity magnetron, sent by the physicist Sir John Cockroft to increase the power available to U.S. technicians in radar development by a factor of 1000.
1940 June 1		U.S. battleship *Washington* (BB-56) is launched in Philadelphia, Pennsylvania. She is the first American battleship launched since *West Virginia* (BB-48), 19 November 1921.
		The Navy Radio and Sound Laboratory is established in San Diego. During World War II the University of California's Division of War Research will operate as NSRL. On 29 November 1945 the two organizations will be joined into the Navy Electronics Laboratory (NEL). The latter organization will contribute in many ways. For example the QLA scanning sonar, first of its kind, will go into nine submarines that will penetrate the heavily-mined Inland Sea in the closing months of the war.
1940 June 4		The British Admiralty confirms that evacuation from Dunkirk, Operation Dynamo, has been successfully completed. Myriad craft and ships, military and civilian, were the means of crossing the English Channel.
1940 June 12		Civilian Nautical School Act is approved (54 Stat. 346).
1940 June 13	USS *North Carolina* (BB-55) is launched at New York Navy Yard. There has been great rivalry between New York's BB-55 construction and Philadelphia Navy Yard's building *Washington* (BB-56).	

Date	Naval Engineering	National & International Events Legislative, Organization & Personnel Policy
1940 June 20		Navy's Bureau of Ships is established by Act of Congress, taking over functions of the Bureau of Engineering and Bureau of Construction and Repair.
1940 June 25		The Navy's Construction Corps is abolished; officers on the active list of the Corps are transferred to the Line of the Navy as engineering duty officers.
1940 June 30		Maritime Commission replaces Navy as federal agency responsible for providing training ships to the state-operated nautical schools.
1940 July 10		This date is usually given as the start of the Battle of Britain, perhaps the most critical conflict of World War II.
1940 July 19		President Franklin D. Roosevelt signs the Naval Expansion Act, an emergency measure calling for the construction of warships, Naval aircraft, and auxiliary shipping.
1940 August 15		The German Luftwaffe's plan to destroy the British aircraft fighter force on "Eagle Day" ends in a German rout, marking the turning-point in the Battle of Britain.
1940 September		Various British naval vessels report inducing unexplained underwater explosions at a distance.
1940 September 3		President Roosevelt announces "Destroyers for Bases" executive agreement with Great Britain. The U.S. is to give Great Britain fifty destroyers in return for 99-year leases on bases in the Bahamas, Antigua, St. Lucia, Trinidad, Jamaica, and British Guiana.
1940 October		The Battle of Britain is largely over with major favorable impact for the Allies on the course of World War II. Victory for the British results from heroic pilots (900 killed and wounded), British radar, German errors, skillful British strategy and tactics, and intelligence resulting from increasing capability to break Axis codes.
1940 October 1		New York State Merchant Marine Academy initiates a 3-year curriculum, but implementation is delayed by World War II.
1940 October 17		A subpanel of the National Defense Research Committee urges, in a secret meeting, that the radar development program be located at MIT. The resulting MIT Radiation Laboratory radar program becomes America's second largest technical effort of World War II, surpassed only by the Manhattan atomic bomb project.
1940 November 8		SS *City of Rayville* sinks after hitting a mine laid by German raider off Cape Otway, Bass Strait, Australia. She is first U.S. merchant vessel sunk in World War II.
1940 November 11	Obsolete naval aircraft from HMS *Illustrious* torpedo Italian battleships at their base in Taranto, Italy, sinking *Littorio* and *Caio Duilio* and severely damaging *Conte di Cavour*. Feasibility of successful use in harbors of shallow-set torpedoes is confirmed to Japanese for subsequent attack on U.S. fleet at Pearl Harbor.	

Date	Naval Engineering	National & International Events Legislative, Organization & Personnel Policy
1940 November 18	The Chief of Naval Operations directs use of the term "radar," coined by Naval officers E. F. Furth and S. P. Tucker, for the project that is secret at this time.	
1941-44		The Italian Navy, proceeding from essentially the experimental conduct of such attacks in World War II, conducts a series of successful and effective attack with underwater small battle units. Using frogmen, manned torpedoes, and other underwater delivery vehicles, Italian units effect significant damage on British naval and merchant shipping at Gibralter, Malta, and Alexandria. Their greatest exploit is to enter Alexandria harbor early in 1942 and sink HMS *Valiant* and *Queen Elizabeth*.
1941-44		British special forces undertake surprise amphibious raids on selected German coastal targets of opportunity.
1941	Dr. R. M. Page of the Naval Research Laboratory develops the PPI radar indicator. The first radar for submarines becomes operational. LCDR Edward Thiele brings back details of Baltic icebreakers to Coast Guard Headquarters where preliminary designs were started on icebreaker for polar and Great Lakes Service. The U.S. Naval Boiler Laboratory, Philadelphia, becomes the U.S. Naval Boiler and Turbine Laboratory (NBTL). Its expanded role includes initial systems engineering.	
1941 February 1		The U.S. Atlantic Fleet is re-established under Admiral E. J. King, U.S. Navy. This fleet was first constituted on 1 January 1906, but was later discontinued when the U.S. Fleet organization was established.
1941 March 26		The Italian Navy conducts at Suda Bay, Crete, a successful attack with so-called "piloted torpedoes" (British "chariots") with detachable, emplaceable warheads, sinking British cruiser HMS *York* at anchor. This adds new dimension to naval warfare with use of specialized underwater personnel and equipment.
1941 March 28		Admiral Andrew Browne Cunningham, RN, British Commander-in-Chief in the Mediterranean, achieves complete surprise and sinks three cruisers and two destroyers of the Italian Fleet with loss of only one aircraft. Success in this battle of Matapan results, in large measure, from British breaking the Italian code. Henceforth, the Italian Navy's heavy ships will prefer to stay in port.
1941 April 9	Battleship USS *North Carolina* (BB-55) is commissioned at New York.	
1941 May 15		Battleship USS *Washington* (BB-56) is commissioned at Philadelphia, Pennsylvania.
1941 May 21		United States freighter *Robin Moor*, en route to South Africa, is sunk in South Atlantic by German submarine.

Date	Naval Engineering	National & International Events Legislative, Organization & Personnel Policy
1941 May 24		Battle cruiser HMS *Hood* is sunk by German battleship *Bismarck* in Denmark Strait.
1941 May 26	After losing contact by radar, a massive British hunt for the German battleship *Bismarck*, which had broken out from the North Sea, is successful. A Swordfish aircraft from the British carrier *Ark Royal* jams *Bismarck*'s rudder and places her steering gear out of commission. She will be sunk on 27 May by *Rodney*, *King George V*, and *Dorsetshire*. *Bismarck* will be pounded at close range by two battleships, probably receiving more major-caliber hits than any ship in history. She will finally sink when torpedoed by *Dorsetshire*.	
1941 June 2		USS *Long Island* (AVG-1), the first escort carrier, is commissioned at Newport News, Virginia. She was laid down 7 July 1939 at Sun Shipbuilding & Drydock Co. as *Mormacmail* under Maritime Commission contract, launched 11 January 1940, and acquired by the Navy 6 March 1941. She will be redesignated ACV-1 on 20 August 1942, CVE-1 on 15 July 1945, and struck from the Naval Vessels Register on 12 April 1946.
1941 July	The first U.S. Navy Radar school is established at NRL. Many of the officer graduates will return to their ships. Others will be sent to establish new radar schools or to new fleet staff assignments.	
1941 July 24-25		British No. 11 Independent Company (Commandos) undertakes at Merlimont Plage, Le Toquet surprise amphibious raid on selected German coastal targets of opportunity. This action introduces the concept of exploiting superiority at sea with amphibious warfare technology, using Commando Forces.
1941 September 22	USS *Roe* (DD-418) conducts a series of successful tests with the first shipboard installed fire control radar, a model FD mounted on a Mark 37 gun director.	
1941 September 27	Among the first of the installed fire control radars is the model FA (much later to be designated Mark I) in the heavy cruiser USS *Wichita* (CA-45). It was manufactured by Western Electric and operates in the 700-megacycle band.	
	First U.S. Liberty ship, SS *Patrick Henry*, is launched along with thirteen other merchant vessels. Event is commemorated by designating this as Liberty Fleet Day.	
1941 October 31		USS *Reuben James* (DD-245) is sunk while on neutrality patrol and not technically a combatant, with only 44 survivors of 159 men on board. She is first U.S. Navy ship sunk by hostile action in World War II.
1941 November		A German U-boat sinks HMS *Barham* in the Mediterranean, first sinking of a battleship underway.
1941 November 1		Coast Guard is ordered to operate as part of the Navy.
1941 November 4	LST (Landing Ship, Tank) is conceived by John C. Neidermair, the Navy's top ship designer.	
1941 November 19	USS *Leary* (DD-158) becomes first American ship to make radar contact with a U-boat.	

Date	Naval Engineering	National & International Events Legislative, Organization & Personnel Policy
1941 December 2	Contracts are signed between Mare Island Navy Yard and twelve small firms in Denver, Colorado, to pre-fabricate hull structure of what will eventually become thirty-one destroyer escorts and 216 LCT (6) landing craft. This procedure will prove effective in using inland facilities and manpower in shipbuilding. The first DE of this class will be launched 22 August 1942 as HMS *Bentinck* (BDE-13), but will be completed for American use and commissioned as USS *Brennan* (DE-13) 20 January 1943.	U.S. merchant ship *Dunboyne* receives first Naval Armed Guard crew.
1941 December 7		The Japanese bomb Pearl Harbor. U.S. enters World War II.
1941 December 8		HMS *Prince of Wales*, a new battleship, and HMS *Repulse*, a pre-Jutland design battle cruiser, are the first capital ships sunk at sea by torpedo bombers that are shore-based in Saigon.
1941 December 11		Germany and Italy declare war on the United States. U.S. declares war on Germany and Italy.
1941 December 15		USS *Swordfish* (SS-193) is first U.S. submarine to sink a Japanese ship, the SS *Atsutasan Maru*, in World War II.
1941 December 30		U.S. Fleet reorganization is effected with Admiral Ernest J. King as Commander-in-Chief (*COMinCH*) in Washington, D.C.
1942	The first LORAN system is placed in operation.	
1942 January 27	USS *Gudgeon* (SS-211) is first U.S. submarine to sink an enemy submarine, the Japanese IJN *I-173*.	
1942 January 31		Office of Procurement and Material (OP&M) is established in the Office of the Under Secretary of the Navy with Vice Admiral S. M. Robinson as Director.
1942 February 20		U.S. Naval Amphibious Forces are created by order of Admiral Ernest J. King.
1942 February 23		Japanese submarine shells oil refinery at Ellwood, California.
1942 February 25		Coast Guard assumes responsibility for U.S. port security.
1942 March 26		Duties of CNO and COMinCH are combined under Admiral E. J. King.
1942 March 29	USS *South Dakota* (BB-57) is commissioned. She is first Navy ship to have air conditioned hospital spaces.	
1942 April 18		USS *Hornet* (CV-6) launches sixteen U.S. Army Air Corps B-25 medium bombers against targets in Central Japan. This is the first air attack of the war against Japan proper. Lieutenant Colonel (later Lieutenant General) James H. Doolittle leads the raid.
1942 May 3		New York State Merchant Marine Academy becomes the New York State Maritime Academy (NYSMA).
1942 May 4-8		U.S. achieves strategic victory in the Battle of the Coral Sea by halting the heretofore uninterrupted Japanese push southeastward. This is the first battle in modern naval history in which opposing warships do not exchange a shot.
1942 May 13		Navy's Bureau of Navigation is redesignated Bureau of Personnel.

Date	Naval Engineering	National & International Events Legislative, Organization & Personnel Policy
1942 June	*Marine Engineering*, Volume One, is published by the Society of Naval Architects and Marine Engineers. The editor is Herbert Lee Seward, Professor of Mechanical and Marine Engineering, Yale University.	
1942 June 4		Japanese fleet is overwhelmingly defeated at the Battle of Midway by numerically much smaller U.S. fleet in one of the most decisive battles of naval history, ranking with Lepanto, Tsushima, and Trafalgar. It is called a battle won by intelligence. Edward L. Beach says in *The United States Navy*, "To Commander Joe Rochefort must forever go the acclaim for having made more difference, at a more important time, than any other naval officer in history."
1942 July 18		The German Messerchmitt jet-propelled aircraft Me262 is first flown. In 2 years it will be the first jet-propelled aircraft to go into battle.
1942 July 31	*Essex* (CV-9) is launched. Starting with this class of aircraft carriers, mechanical cooling is provided to keep ready rooms at 65 degrees F to permit alerted personnel to stand by in heavy flying clothes. Aircraft carrier ready room temperatures are later raised to 78 degrees Effective Temperature (ET) when combat air patrols and radar give time for donning flying clothes just before takeoff. This is only one of many significant advances incorporated in this class of aircraft carrier.	
1942 August 7		First large scale amphibious assault takes place at Guadalcanal.
1942 August 8-9	A force of four U.S. cruisers (*Astoria* CA-34, *Chicago* CA-29, *Quincy* CA-39, and *Vincennes* CA-44) and the Australian *Canberra* is caught by surprise in the vicinity of Savo Island, off Guadalcanal, by a superior Japanese force. Only *Chicago* survives and more than 1,000 Allied sailors are killed. Battle demonstrates error of keeping crews at high state of readiness for extended periods and need for radar. Surface-search and fire-control radar will soon start flowing to the Pacific in greater numbers. Other U.S. problems include poor tactics and damage control, inadequate training in night operations, and aviation stores and flammables stowed amidships. A near-contemporary account ascribes Japanese success to "sighting us first [and] shooting first."	
1942 August	U.S. Marine Raiders use USS *Argonaut* and *Nautilus* for attack on Makin Atoll by submarine insertion.	
1942 September 1	Naval Construction Battalion personnel (Seabees), the first to serve in an action area, arrive at Guadalcanal, Solomon Islands.	
1942 November 14-15	USS *Washington* (BB-56) leaves Japanese battleship *Kirishima* burning and exploding as a result of radar-directed gunfire in night engagement in fourth battle of Savo Island. This is the first head-to-head confrontation of battleships in the Pacific war. *Kirishima* later is abandoned and scuttled.	
1942 December 2		Enrico Fermi achieves the first real chain nuclear reaction at Chicago. This is the important starting point in the revolution to come in propulsion energy and in ordnance.

Date	Naval Engineering	National & International Events Legislative, Organization & Personnel Policy
1943		The Naval Ordnance Test Station dates from this year when both its Pasadena and China Lake sites begin operation as contract laboratories under Office of Scientific Research and Development (OSRD) administration via the California Institute of Technology. In 1945, the organization will become NOTS, China Lake.
1943 January 5	USS *Helena* (CL-50) fires the first 'VT' proximity-fuse projectile to shoot down an enemy plane.	
1943 February 15		Admiral E. J. King, USN, Chief of Naval Operations, establishes a program for naval development of the unfamiliar aircraft known as the helicopter.
1943 March		First amphibious landing ship, LST-446, arrives in South Pacific operating area.
1943 May 23	USS *New Jersey* (BB-62) is commissioned for the first of four times. Following periods of active service and inactivation, she will be recommissioned on 21 November 1950, 6 April 1968, and 28 December 1982.	
1943 July 24		USS *Tinosa* logs eight point-blank firings of dud torpedoes into Japanese tanker *Tonan Maru #3*.
1943 August 25		German Dornier DO-217E-5 bombers, specially configured to carry, launch, and control the Henschel HS 293 stand-off missile, commence operations against Allied ASW ships.
1943 September	German U-boats commence use of Zaunkoenig ("Wren")-type torpedoes.	
1943 September 9	The Germans sink the modern Italian battleship *Roma* with an air-launched radio-controlled glidebomb, a first. They will put USS *Savannah* (CL-42) out of action for nearly a year with the same weapon on 11 September. 197 men are lost in *Savannah*	
1943 September 30		The U.S. Merchant Marine Academy at Kings Point, New York, is officially dedicated.
1943 October 2		James V. Forrestal, then Under Secretary of the Navy, requests Mr. R. J. Dearborn, President of the Texaco Development Corporation and Chairman of the committee on Patents of the National Association of Manufacturers, to survey policies and procedures of the Navy Department with respect to patents and inventions.
1943-45		U.S. Navy employs frogman teams to covertly survey and clear defended beaches of underwater obstacles, in preparation for amphibious landings.
1944 February 26	CGC *Northland* (CG-96), built by Western Pipe & Steel Co., Los Angeles, California, the first of the seven 269-foot diesel-electric icebreakers of the *Wind* class, is commissioned.	
1944 March 10		R. J. Dearborn submits report and plan, which become the basis for reorganization of Navy Department activities concerned with research, inventions, and related matters.
1944 March		British ASW forces commence employment of FOXER towed noise-maker.
1944 April 28		In a practice drill by 25,000 U.S. troops for the invasion of Normandy, Exercise Tiger, German torpedo boats slip into Lyme Bay on the Southern coast of England and attack the convoy, killing 749 Americans, four times the number who die on Utah Beach.

Date	Naval Engineering	National & International Events Legislative, Organization & Personnel Policy
1944 June	*Marine Engineering*, Volume Two, is published by SNAME.	
1944 June 6		This is D-Day for the American and British landings on the Normandy Coast, Operation OVERLORD. Among many naval operations, a special German U-boat force and a variety of small submersibles deploy in response to the Allied invasion of Europe. "The simultaneous involvement of American forces in the invasion of France and the Marianas [in the Pacific] constituted the most titanic military effort put forth by any nation at any one time in history." (Potter, E. B., *Nimitz.* p. 296.)
1944 June 11	USS *Missouri* (BB-63), last battleship completed by U.S., is commissioned.	
1944 July 25		The Me262 aircraft attacks a Royal Air Force Mosquito bomber, becoming the first jet-propelled aircraft to go into battle.
1944 September 3	First combat employment of a missile guided by radio and television takes place when a Navy PB4-X drone attacks German submarine shelters on Helgoland.	
1944 October 19		Secretary of the Navy issues directive establishing Office of Patents and Inventions. VADM H. G. Bowen organizes and serves as Director of this new office.
1944 November 11		Commander David W. McCampbell, USN, flying his Grumman F6F Hellcat, shoots down his thirty-fourth and last enemy aircraft, the greatest number recorded by any American pilot during a single tour of combat duty.
1944 December 18	The U.S. Third Fleet encounters a typhoon in the Western Pacific, east of the Philippines, resulting in capsizing and loss of USS *Monaghan* (DD-354), *Hull* (DD-350), and *Spence* (DD-512), raising major questions of destroyer stability, particularly in the *Farragut*-class. Major damage is suffered by USS *Monterey* (CVL-26), *Cowpens* (CVL-28), *San Jacinto* (CVL-30), *Cape Esperance* (CVE-88), *Altahama* (CVE-18), *Miami* (CL-89), *Aylwin* (DD-355), *Hickox* (DD-673), and *Dewey* (DD-349). Lesser damage was incurred by nineteen other ships. 146 aircraft were lost or damaged beyond repair. 778 men (some sources say 790) were lost or killed. Ninety-eight officers and men survived loss of the three capsized destroyers. It is the greatest loss taken by the U.S. Navy in the Pacific without compensating return since the First Battle of Savo Island, 8-9 August 1942.	
1944 December 20	CGC *Mackinaw* (CG-121), built by Toledo Shipbuilding Co., Toledo, Ohio, is commissioned. First all-year icebreaker for the Great Lakes.	
1945		U.S. Navy conducts limited strikes against German submarine pens, expending radio-controlled patrol-type aircraft (PB4Ys) loaded with high explosives.

Date	Naval Engineering	National & International Events Legislative, Organization & Personnel Policy
1945 January 8	USS *Norton Sound* (AV-11) is commissioned. She will operate as a seaplane tender until 1948 when she will spend 7 months at the Philadelphia Naval Shipyard undergoing conversion to a mobile missile launching platform. In late fall 1948, she will successfully launch a training missile, thus marking the beginning of the Navy's shipborne family of guided missiles. She will be redesignated AVM-1 on 8 August 1951 and will continue to serve as a test and development ship for guided missiles and ordnance until she is decommissioned on 11 December 1986.	
1945 January 30		A Soviet submarine torpedoes the Nazi transport *Wilhelm Gustloff* in the Baltic Sea; 7,700 are killed. This may be the worst single ship loss in maritime history.
1945 February 13		Commander in Chief, U.S. Pacific Fleet, Fleet Admiral Chester W. Nimitz, USN, issues letter on the subject "Damage in Typhoon, Lessons of," including the admonition not to neglect, "Log, Lead, and Lookout."
1945 March 1		The Naval Research Laboratory's Underwater Sound Reference Division begins operations at Orlando, Florida.
1945 April 13		"Roosevelt, Franklin D., Commander-in-Chief," is first entry on Army-Navy Casualty List transmitted by United Press International this day.
1945 May 5	USS *Haven* (AH-12) is commissioned. Converted from a tanker, *Marine Hawk*, she is first hospital ship to have living quarters as well as hospital spaces mechanically cooled.	
1945 May 6		Victory in Europe (V-E) Day, Germany surrenders.
1945 May 7		General Eisenhower, Supreme Commander of the Allied Forces in Europe, reports to the Combined Chiefs of Staff, "The Mission of this Allied Force was fulfilled at 0241, local time," meaning the end of World War II in Europe.
1945 May 19		Secretary of the Navy issues directive establishing, in his office, Office of Research and Inventions. This action merges Office of Naval Research Laboratory, Special Devices Division of the Bureau of Aeronautics, and Office of Patents and Inventions. VADM Bowen is appointed as Chief of Research and Inventions.
1945 August 6		First atomic bomb is used.
1945 August 9		The second atomic bomb is dropped on Nagasaki, Japan. Captain F. L. Ashworth, USN, is weaponeer in the B-29 aircraft.
1945 August 14	The last Japanese warship sunk in World War II is credited to USS *Torsk* (SS-423), using a new experimental Mark 28 torpedo, followed by a new acoustic Mark 27. Both torpedoes are successful.	
1945 August 16		Victory over Japan (V-J) Day; Japan surrenders.
1945 September 2		Japanese surrender documents are signed onboard USS *Missouri* (BB-63) at anchor in Tokyo Bay, Japan. USS *West Virginia* (BB-48) is only U.S. battleship present at surrender that was also present when Japanese attacked Pearl Harbor on 7 December 1941.

Date	Naval Engineering	National & International Events Legislative, Organization & Personnel Policy
1945 September 29		President Truman issues Executive Order 9653, under authority of the First War Powers Act, to eliminate any doubts about authority of the Secretary of the Navy to make already established organization changes concerning research, inventions, and related matters.
1945 October 10		COMinCH headquarters in Washington are dissolved.
1946		The Association of Senior Engineers (ASE) of the Bureau of Ships is founded under organizing direction of Albert A. Smith, with John C. Nierdermair, Technical Director, Preliminary Design Division, as first president. Organization will later become Association of Scientists and Engineers.
1946 April 1		Army Industrial College is redesignated Industrial College of the Armed Forces (ICAF).
1946 July	Information concerning effects of nuclear weapons on ships is obtained by two major U.S. tests at Bikini Atoll in the Marshall Islands, using devices of about 20-kiloton TNT equivalence. Test Able is an air burst and Test Baker is a burst well below the surface of the lagoon, which is about 200 feet deep.	
1946 July 2	A jet aircraft operates from an aircraft carrier for the first time.	
1946 August 1		National War College opens in Washington with 105 students.
1946 August 1		Public Law 588 of the 79th Congress creates the Office of Naval Research in the Office of the Secretary of the Navy, with Bureau rank to replace existing Office of Research and Inventions. VADM Bowen becomes first Chief of Naval Research, with advice and consent of the Senate.
1946 September 9		New York State Maritime Academy, granted full collegiate status, enrolls first class for an accelerated 3-year course of study leading to the degree of Bachelor of Marine Science.
1946 September 29-October 1		A Navy Lockheed P2V-1 Neptune, "Truculent Turtle," sets record for longest nonstop, unrefueled flight, by flying 11,236 miles from Perth, Australia, to Columbus, Ohio. At end of flight, 160 gallons of gas remain from takeoff load of 8,467 gallons.
1946 December	USS *Irex* (SS-482) is first U.S. submarine equipped with telescopic snorkel.	
1947 February 2		Armed Forces Staff College opens in Norfolk, Virginia, with 150 students.
1947 February 12	First launching of a Loon guided missile from a submarine, USS *Cusk* (SS-348), takes place.	
1947 April 14	The Bureau of Ships' "Longitudinal Strength Committee," chaired by Mr. L. W. Ferris, begins its work that will end 9 October 1950. The group's contribution will be a systematic effort to incorporate, record, and provide continuity to longitudinal strength design criteria over a period of comprehensive postwar naval rebuilding.	
1947 September 6	Captured German V-2 rocket is launched from flight deck of USS *Midway* (CVB-41), the first time in history that a large bombardment rocket has been launched from a ship or a moving platform.	

Date	Naval Engineering	National & International Events Legislative, Organization & Personnel Policy
1947 September 18		National Military Establishment (NME) is established as a unification measure with Army, Navy, and Air Force under Secretary of Defense.
1947 October 8		New York State Maritime Academy awards its first Bachelor of Marine Science degree.
1948 January 20	USS *Cusk* (SS-348) is redesignated SSG-348, becoming the U.S. Navy's first guided missile submarine.	
1948	26,555 dwt *Esso Zurich* is launched, first tanker to be referred to as a "supertanker."	*U.S. Navy Regulations* define classification and status of the Navy's ships and craft.
1948 May		New York State Maritime Academy becomes unit of the State University of New York (SUNY).
1948 September		New York State Maritime Academy initiates a 4-year course of study.
1948 November		A Chinese merchant ship explodes and sinks off southern Manchuria. 6,000 are believed to be killed.
1948 December 3		A refugee ship, *Kiangua*, explodes and sinks near Shanghai with reported loss of 3,920.
1949 April 4		North Atlantic Treaty Organization (NATO) is formed.
1949 April		New York State Maritime Academy becomes the New York State Maritime College (NYSMC).
		Louis Johnson, Secretary of the Defense, orders the cancellation of the construction of the USS *United States* (CV-58), the first-to-be of the "big carriers" and the progenitor of the *Forrestal* class.
1949 May		The third Saturday in May each year is proclaimed as Armed Forces Day for all the military services to replace separate days for the Army, Navy, and Air Force.
1949 August 10		National Military Establishment becomes Department of Defense (DoD).
1949 September		The New York State Maritime College is authorized to award Bachelor of Science and Bachelor of Marine Engineering degrees.
1949 November 26		The Middle States Association of Colleges and Secondary Schools confers accreditation upon the U.S. Merchant Marine Academy as a degree-granting four-year college.
1950	SOFAR (Sound Fixing and Ranging), developed by NEL, becomes operational.	New York State Maritime College becomes the State University of New York Maritime College.
1950 January 31	First round of tactical ship-to-air anti-aircraft missile is delivered for flight test at Naval Ordnance Test Station, China Lake, California, under the Bumblebee Program.	
1950 Mid-February	The first nuclear weapon installation is made on USS *Midway* (CVA-41). This will give the nation an additional arm for such weaponry and will ultimately lead to its deployment on other ship types, most particularly the SSBN.	
1950 June 25		Korean war begins.
1950 November 21	USS *New Jersey* (BB-62) is commissioned for the second time.	

Date	Naval Engineering	National & International Events Legislative, Organization & Personnel Policy
1951 July 31	Preliminary design is finished for the first post-World War II new aircraft carrier, which will be named *Forrestal* (CVA-59). Detail contract plans and specifications will be finished 12 June 1952, in less time than for any prior major warship. There are many innovations, including an armored deck, steam catapults developed by the Royal Navy, and many advances proven in successive modernizations, designated 27A, 27B, 27C, of older U.S. carriers. She will be the last major combatant to retain some riveting, a seam at each shear strake and bilge.	
1952	Hydrofoil craft HC-4, *Lantern*, is developed and built by Dr. Vannevar Bush's company, the Hydrofoil Corporation, Annapolis, Maryland. HC-4 is among first to employ fully submerged foils and be controlled in flying height and pitch by sensor which measures height above water.	By the Armed Forces Reserve Act of 1952, Congress brings together laws relating to Reserve components as an essential step in developing a uniform and unified Reserve program. SUNY Maritime College receives full accreditation from the Commission of Higher Education of the Middle States Association of Colleges and Secondary Schools.
1952 July 3-7	SS *United States* sets transatlantic speed record of 3 days, 10 hours, 40 minutes, breaking record previously held by Britain's *Queen Mary*, and earning the "blue ribbon" and Hales Trophy. She averages 35.59 knots. Her maximum speed is 41.75 knots on full power of 240,000 shaft horsepower.	
1952 September 24		SUNY Maritime College initiates separate deck and engine cadet programs commencing in the fourth class year.
1953 May 8	USS *Tunny* (SS-282) is first U.S. submarine equipped to fire surface-to-surface missiles, the Regulus I.	
1953 July 27		Korean war armistice is effective.
1953 August 1	*Albacore* (AGSS-569), an experimental submarine in advanced hydrodynamic design, is launched at Portsmouth Naval Shipyard. She will have major impact on all future submarine design in U.S. and abroad.	
1953 August	First descent is made by Auguste Piccard's submersible, *Trieste*.	
1953 October 3		Lieutenant Commander James B. Verdin, USN, regains speed record for the United States at 753 miles per hour in a Douglas F4D Skyray.
1954		A funery ship is discovered buried next to the south face of the Cheops pyramid. A claim is made that this 3rd millenium B.C. ship (boat) is the oldest ever discovered.
1954 January 21	Submarine *Nautilus* (SSN-571), world's first nuclear-powered ship, is launched. She is christened by Mrs. Dwight D. Eisenhower, first U.S. President's wife to christen a submarine.	
1954 September 26		The Japanese ferry *Toya Maru* sinks in Japan's Tsugaru Strait with loss of 1,172.
1954 November 11		Congress establishes this as Veterans Day (formerly Armistice Day) to honor all the service men and women who have served the United States.

Date	Naval Engineering	National & International Events Legislative, Organization & Personnel Policy
1955	The 47,450-deadweight-ton *Spyros Niarchos* is launched and is at this time the world's largest tanker.	
	Principles of Guided Missile Design series, edited by Captain Grayson Merrill, U.S. Navy, consolidates knowledge in that subject prior to post-Korea demobilization.	
1955	NEL installs the Long-Range Active Detection (LORAD) system aboard USS *Baya* (AGSS-318) and will test it in following years.	
1955 January 17	USS *Nautilus* (SSN-571) sends message, "Underway on nuclear power."	
1955 February 25	The Royal Navy commissions *Ark Royal*. She has a pair of steam catapults, a 5.5-degree angled deck, a port-side deck-edge elevator, and a mirror landing device. She will be scrapped in 1980.	
1955 May		ONR Committee on Tactical Data Processing established to coordinate the requirements for ships (NTDS), aircraft (ATDS), and Marine Corps (MTDS).
1956	Canadian Hydrofoil, *Massawippi* R-100, employs a three-bladed supercavitating propeller in trials, developed by joint U.S./Canadian effort.	
	Hydrodynamics in Ship Design, Vol. 1, is published by the Society of Naval Architects and Marine Engineers.	
1956	The first transatlantic telephone cable, TAT-1, is laid successfully. It will be retired in 1978.	
1956	A small Advanced Studies Group is set up in the Preliminary Design Branch of the Bureau of Ships. It will prepare many conceptual designs to meet projected needs of the Navy, "The Shape of Ships to Come." The fleet replenishment ship, AOE, carrying oil, ammunition, and stores, will be adopted soon. Other concepts will show merits of the SWATH (Small Waterplane Area Twin-Hulled) ship.	
1956 February 20		Congress amends the Merchant Marine Act of 1936 to establish the permanency of the United States Merchant Marine Academy. The Act provides that cadets at the USMMA may be appointed by the Secretary of the Navy as Reserve Midshipmen in the U.S. Navy and Reserve Ensigns in the Navy upon graduation.
1956 Mid	Development contracts are awarded for the Naval Tactical Data System (NTDS).	
1956 August 21		Commander R. W. "Duke" Windsor, USN, wins the Thompson Trophy by setting a new national speed record of 1,015.4 mph in a Vought F8U-1 Crusader. Aircraft is a production-model carrier fighter equipped with full armament of 20-mm cannon and dummy ammunition, thereby becoming the first operationally equipped jet plane in history to fly faster than 1,000 mph.
1956 October 31		Captain W. H. Hawkes, USN, pilots first airplane to land at the South Pole.
1957	First 'flight' takes place of hydrofoil craft, *Sea Legs*, with fully-submerged canard foils and electronic autopilot stabilization system.	

Date	Naval Engineering	National & International Events Legislative, Organization & Personnel Policy
1957 July 16		Major John H. Glenn, USMC, sets transcontinental speed record of 3 hours, 23 minutes from Los Angeles, California, to Floyd Bennett Field, New York, in an F8U-1P Crusader. This is first upper-atmosphere supersonic flight from West Coast to East Coast.
1957 October 24		USSR launches "Sputnik."
1957 November 7		President Dwight D. Eisenhower gives TV speech that catapults into national focus all of America's scientific and engineering enterprises. He announces appointment of MIT President James Rhyne Killian, Jr. to the newly created post of Special Assistant to the President for Science and Technology, the first White House "science advisor."
1958	WWII Cruiser USS *Boston* (CA-69) is converted to first Navy guided missile cruiser, capable of firing supersonic anti-aircraft guided missiles. Ship is redesignated CAG-1.	
1958	Experimental hydrofoil landing craft, LCVP(H) *Halobates*, completes test program with U.S. Navy's first hydrofoil electronic autopilot and gas turbine power plant.	
1958-1961	NTDS developmental system is tested at shore-based test site at the Naval Electronics Laboratory, San Diego. A mobile van and a "picket ship" are also equipped with data link equipment to test automatic data exchange between mobile platforms.	
1958 February 4	Keel is laid at Newport News for world's first nuclear-powered aircraft carrier, *Enterprise*, designated CVA(N)-65.	
1958 March 7	Last voyage of TV *Emery Rice* begins as she is towed to Baltimore to be broken up by the Boston Metal Company of Baltimore.	
1958 March 8		USS *Wisconsin* (BB-64) is decommissioned, leaving the United States without an active battleship for the first time since 1895.
1958 August 3	USS *Nautilus* (SSN 571) crosses geographic North Pole at 11:15 pm EDT while making first submerged polar transit.	
1958 August 18		Maritime Academy Act of 1958 is approved (Public Law 85-672).
1958 November 7		Navy Electronic Warfare Simulator (NEWS) is commissioned at Naval War College.
1959	*Methane Pioneer*, first LNG tanker, put into operation.	
1959 January 17	USS *Barbel* (SS-580) is commissioned. She is first diesel-powered combatant submarine with *Albacore* hull form.	
1959 March		Navy establishes the Long Range Studies Project at Newport, Rhode Island, under Rear Admiral Edwin B. Hooper. The organization will relocate to Cambridge, Massachusetts, before year's end as the Institute of Naval Studies, with MIT oversight and under a management contract with the Institute for Defense Analysis (IDA).
1959 April 15	USS *Skipjack* (SSN-585) is commissioned. She is first nuclear submarine with *Albacore* hull and single screw, and is first with reduction gears designed to be quiet.	

Date	Naval Engineering	National & International Events Legislative, Organization & Personnel Policy
1959 April 25		The St. Lawrence Seaway, constructed in partnership between the U.S. and Canada, is opened, allowing passage from Lake Superior to the Atlantic Ocean, by way of the St. Lawrence River. It is navigable to 27-foot draft.
1959 July 21	Nuclear ship *Savannah*, world's first nuclear-powered merchant ship, is launched.	
1959 August 27	The first at-sea launch of a Polaris missile, designated UGM-27, is successfully accomplished from USS *Observation Island* (EAG-154) off Port Canaveral, Florida. She will continue to support the FBM (Fleet Ballistic Missile) program for many years, including the first successful at-sea launch of the A-3 Polaris on 17 and 21 June 1963, and hosting President John F. Kennedy as observer on 16 November 1963. She will be redesignated AG-154 on 1 April 1968.	
1959 December 30	USS *George Washington* [SSB(N)-598] is commissioned at Groton, Connecticut. Originally intended to be an attack submarine, *Scorpion* [SS(N)-589], she has been lengthened by insertion of a 130-foot missile section. This innovative and successful modification will advance significantly deployment of the Polaris missile.	
1960		First PhD degree is awarded by the Department of Naval Architecture and Marine Engineering, University of Michigan, to Finn Michelsen.
1960	The American Society of Mechanical Engineers establishes an Ocean Engineering Division.	
1960	NEL enters a development period for the Omega navigation system that will extend until 1968 when the system will become operational.	
1960 January 23	Jacques Piccard and Lieutenant Don Walsh, USN, make man's deepest dive, 35,800 feet, into the Challenger Deep in the Mariana Trench in the bathyscaph *Trieste*.	
1960 May 10	USS *Triton* (SSRN-586) completes first underwater circumnavigation of the earth. Following Ferdinand Magellan's route, she has covered 36,000 miles in 84 days.	
1960 July 20	USS *George Washington* (SSBN-598) successfully fires the first Polaris missile while submerged off Cape Canaveral, Florida. Rear Admiral W. F. Raborn, head of the Polaris project, is on board as an observer.	
1960 November 9	USS *Tullibee* (SSN-597) is commissioned. She has DC electric drive. *Tullibee*, and later *Jack* (SSN-605) and *Narwhal* (SSN-671), are one-of-a-kind efforts to find a substitute for reduction gears.	
1960 November 15	USS *George Washington* (SSBN-598) deploys on her first patrol with a full complement of sixteen Polaris missiles. This is the official operational date for the Polaris system. She will put in at New London, Connecticut, on 21 January 1961, having completed 66 days of submerged running.	
1961		The Newcomen Society in North America, a non-profit membership corporation, is chartered under the Charitable Law of the State of Maine, with headquarters in Pennsylvania.
1961 February 2		Naval Long Range Studies Project becomes Institute of Naval Studies (INS).

Date	Naval Engineering	National & International Events Legislative, Organization & Personnel Policy
1961 April 12		Yuri A. Gagarin, in Soviet spacecraft *Vostok*, is first human being to make earth orbit.
1961 April 24		*Wasa* breaks the surface of Stockholm harbor after 333 years under water. Preservation and restoration work commences.
1961 May 5		Commander Alan B. Shepard, Jr., USN, first American astronaut to go into space, makes 116-mile high, 302-mile-long suborbital flight down the Atlantic Missile Range in Project Mercury "Freedom 7" capsule. Recovery is made by Marine Corps Helicopter Squadron HMR(L)-262, operating from USS *Lake Champlain* (CVS-39).
1961 July	The Fleet Computer Programming Center, Pacific, is commissioned in San Diego, and is the first tactical data system programming facility in the world.	
1961 July 9	USS *Robert E. Lee* (SSBN-601) sets a new underwater patrol record of more than 68 days.	
1961 September	Installation of NTDS service test models is completed in USS *Oriskany* (CVA-34), USS *King* (DLG-10), and USS *Mahan* (DLG-11). Service evaluation will be completed in April 1962.	
1961 September 9	World's first nuclear-power surface warship, USS *Long Beach* (CGN-9), is commissioned in Boston, Massachusetts, CAPT E. P. Wilkinson, USN, in command.	
1961 October 23	USS *Ethan Allen* (SSBN-608) fires the first Polaris A-2 missile while submerged off the Florida coast.	
1961 November 22		Lieutenant Colonel Robert B. Robinson, USMC, establishes new world speed record of 1,606.3 miles per hour in McDonnel-Douglas F-4 Phantom.
1962	*Robert D. Conrad* (AGOR-3), first new construction oceanographic research ship built by the U.S. Navy, is delivered to Lamont Laboratory, Columbia University, for operation. NTDS is installed in USS *Enterprise* (CVAN-65) and USS *Long Beach* (CGN-9) to handle the digital output of SPS-33, a large 3D phased array radar. NEL's Arctic Submarine Laboratory develops the AN/BQS-8 acoustic ice suit.	In response to the need to more closely organize its diffuse studies and analyses resources, the Navy establishes a consortium of the Operation Evaluation Group (NavWag), the Institute of Naval Studies (INS), and the Applied Science Division (ASD) as the Center for Naval Analyses, under a contract with Franklin Institute to manage and direct the conduct of studies.
1962 February	The Surface Missile Systems Project is established in the Navy Department to direct design, development, engineering, construction, test and evaluation, training, and fleet support of the first guided missile fleet armed with Terrier, Tartar, and Talos surface-to-air missiles.	
1962 February 20		John H. Glenn, Jr., in *Friendship 7*, is first U.S. astronaut to make earth orbit.
1962 May 6	USS *Ethan Allen* (SSBN-608) successfully fires a Polaris missile with a nuclear warhead. Nuclear detonation is achieved.	
1962 June 5	Hydrofoil craft, HS *Denison*, is launched at Oyster Bay, Long Island. Craft was developed by cost-sharing program between Maritime Administration and several companies.	
1962 August 2	USS *Skate* (SSN-578) and USS *Seadragon* (SSN-584) rendezvous under the ice and surface at geographic North Pole.	

Date	Naval Engineering	National & International Events Legislative, Organization & Personnel Policy
1962 August 17	Hydrofoil craft PCH-1 is launched and christened *High Point* at J. M. Martinac Shipbuilding Corporation, Tacoma, Washington.	
1962 September	SUNY Maritime College initiates Nuclear Science and the Meteorology and Oceanography curricula.	
1962 November 9	Keel is laid for experimental deep-diving submarine *Dolphin*, AG(SS)-555. She will be launched on 22 May 1968.	
1962 November 12		A combined naval task force, united under auspices of the Organization of American States, sets sail on operational mission in defense of western hemisphere and in support of U.S. naval quarantine of Cuba. Ultimately, task force 137 is comprised of eleven ships volunteered from six American navies, supported by port facilities and material provided by another eight American states.
1963		U.S. Naval Engineering Experiment Station is re-named U.S. Navy Marine Engineering Laboratory.
1963 April 10	USS *Thresher* (SSN-593) sinks during a test dive about 220 miles east of Boston with loss of entire crew. Intensive investigation results in extensive Submarine Safety program, and fosters extensive underwater developments including search, rescue, salvage, and "man in the sea." She will be located in October by the NEL-operated *Trieste*.	
1963 October 26	USS *Andrew Jackson* (SSBN-19) fires the first Polaris A-3 missile while submerged about two miles off Cape Canaveral.	
1963 November 16		President John F. Kennedy, onboard USS *Observation Island* (EAG-154), witnesses firing of a Polaris A2 missile from USS *Andrew Jackson* (SSBN-619).
1964	The first LASH (lighter aboard ship) vessel, a new shipping concept, is put into operation.	
1964 May 8	*Plainview* (AGEH-1) is laid down by the Lockheed Shipbuilding and Construction Company. She will be launched 28 June 1965 and placed in service 3 March 1969, at that time the largest hydrofoil in the world.	
1964 June 5	Following completion by Litton Industries in Minneapolis, Minnesota, the research submersible, *Alvin*, arrives at Woods Hole, Massachusetts, for operation by the Woods Hole Oceanographic Institution. Program is funded by the Navy.	
1964 September 24		DoD institutes the Standards of Conduct for all federal employees.
1964 December 5		The National Academy of Engineering is established by the National Academy of Sciences under the original NAS Act of Incorporation.
1965	An agreement between the Navy and Coast Guard places all icebreakers under Coast Guard Control.	
1965 January 18		President Lyndon Johnson announces plans to develop Poseidon, a more powerful missile than Polaris A-3.
1965 May 11		The Mare Island and San Francisco (Hunters Point) Naval Shipyards are merged forming the world's largest such complex. The merger will end 31 January 1970.

Date	Naval Engineering	National & International Events Legislative, Organization & Personnel Policy
1965 August 28		Astronauts Gordon Cooper and Charles Conrad, orbiting through outer space in Gemini-5, establish communication by radio-telephone with astronaut-turned-aquanaut, Scott Carpenter, who is at that moment conducting a mission in inner space, deep beneath the surface of the Pacific Ocean in Sealab II.
1965 October 14	USS *Abraham Lincoln* (SSBN-602) returns to U.S. for overhaul, having completed eighteen patrols and sailed 140,000 miles, 94% of the time submerged. This date marks retirement of Polaris A-1 from active fleet duty.	
1965	Japanese *Tokyo Maru* is launched. At this time she is largest ship in the world. Dimensions are length 1,005 feet, deadweight 150,000 tons, and displacement 182,500 tons.	Commissioned Survey corps is changed to Environmental Sciences Service Administration (ESSA) Corps.
1966 January	NTDS and Weapons Direction System (WDS) MK 11 are installed in USS *Wainwright* (DLG-28, later to be redesignated CG-28). The coordinated design of these systems achieves a new level of system integration and interface definition for CIC and weapon control systems. This is the first Integrated Combat System.	
1966 February 2	USS *George Washington* (SSBN-598) completes initial overhaul, refitted to carry the 2,500-mile range Polaris A-3 missile.	
1966 March 9		Bureau of Ships is abolished by Defense Reorganization Order.
1966 March 17	The Naval Ship Engineering Center, Philadephia Division, is established, incorporating the U.S. Naval Boiler and Turbine Laboratory, the Submarine Quality Assurance Facility, and the Assurance Engineering Field Facility. The new organization gives increased emphasis to machinery automation. Full scale propulsion system testing is performed for the DD-963 and FFG-7.	
1966 April 7	A USAS H-bomb, lost in the Mediterranean off Palomares, Spain, is located by the manned *Alvin* and recovered by the unmanned Cable-Controlled Underwater Recovery Vehicle (CURV). This vehicle, developed by the Naval Ordnance Test Station, Pasadena, California, validates the utility of ROVs (Remotely Operated Vehicles).	
1966 May		The Coast Guard adopts a new ship designation system.
1966 May 1		The Naval Material Command is established.
		Naval Systems Commands are established. Bureau of Ships is split into Naval Ship Systems Command and Naval Electronic Systems Command. The Bureau of Ordnance becomes the Naval Ordnance Systems Command and Bureau of Aeronautics becomes the Naval Air Systems Command. Of much more importance than name changes is the demise of the bilinear system by which the technical bureaus had formerly reported directly to the Secretary of the Navy. After this date the chain of command will be through the Chief of Naval Operations to the Secretary.

Date	Naval Engineering	National & International Events Legislative, Organization & Personnel Policy
1966 June 20	Proposals to perform contract definition (CD) studies of the Fast Deployment Logistics Ship (FDLS) are submitted to the Naval Ship Systems Command by General Dynamics Corp., Lockheed Shipbuilding and Construction Co., and Litton Systems, Inc. All three are awarded contracts calling for final proposals in January 1967. This is the first use of CD in a Navy shipbuilding program.	
1966 June 25		New York Naval Shipyard is closed.
1966 August 6	USS *Asheville* (PG-84) is commissioned. Her propulsion system includes an LM1500 gas turbine.	
1967	The Israeli destroyer *Filat* is sunk by an Egyptian patrol boat, the first sinking of a warship by an over-the-horizon guided missile attack.	
1967 March 31	USS *Jack* (SSN-605) is commissioned. She has a novel propulsion plant with contra-rotating turbines and propellers.	The Naval Ship Research and Development Center is established with the merger of the Model Basin at Carderock and the Marine Engineering Laboratory at Annapolis.
1967 April 1		The Coast Guard is transferred from the Treasury Department to the new Department of Transportation (DOT).
1967 June 8		The unarmed USS *Liberty* (AGTR-5), at this time the top in U.S. electronic surveillance engineering, is bombed, strafed, and rocketed by Israeli jet fighters and torpedoed by motor torpedo boats. Thirty-four of *Liberty's* crew are killed and 169 are wounded. The American flag is flying prior to both attacks; Israel claims mistaken identity. *Liberty's* commanding officer receives the Medal of Honor for saving the ship and *Liberty* is awarded the Presidential Unit Citation.
1967 July 1		NEL becomes the Naval Command, Control, and Communications Laboratory Center (NCCCLC). NOTS's Pasadena Annex and portions of NEL will join as the Naval Undersea Warfare Center (NUWC). Two weeks later NCCCLC will be the Naval Electronics Laboratory Center (NELC). In 1969, NUWC will become the Naval Undersea Research and Development Center (NURDC), and will become the Naval Undersea Center (NUC) in 1972. NUC and NELC will join in 1977 as the Naval Ocean Systems Center (NOSC).
1967 July 20	Litton Systems, Inc. is named winner of FDLS contract. Congress will drop this program from the authorization bill for FY 1968. It will not be funded subsequently.	
1967 July 29	USS *Forrestal* (CV-59) has serious fire while deployed in Gulf of Tonkin. 134 crew members are killed and there is major damage to the ship. A Board, chaired by Admiral James Russell, USN (Ret), conducts an extensive investigation into causes of shipboard fires and recommends corrective actions. Results are many, including improvements in flight and hangar deck sprinkling systems with flush-deck nozzles, use of Aqueous Film Forming Foam (AFFF), modifications to bomb elevators, and improved Conflagration Station. Changes are made in existing aircraft carriers and in *Nimitz* (CVAN-68), under construction.	
1967 October 4	USS *Will Rogers* (SSBN-659), the forty-first and last of the Polaris/Poseidon FBM (Fleet Ballistic Missile) submarines, deploys on its first deterrent patrol.	

Date	Naval Engineering	National & International Events Legislative, Organization & Personnel Policy
1967 November 6		A Martin SP-5B seaplane of VP-40 makes last operational flight by a U.S. Navy seaplane.
1968		American Bureau of Shipping issues first *Rules for Building and Classing Offshore Mobile Drilling Units.*
1968 February 8		The Congressional Joint Committee on Atomic Energy issues a statement expressing its concern over the "rapidly increasing Soviet submarine threat." This is one of several significant events in development of what is expected to be a single high-speed submarine that eventually becomes the SSN-688 class.
1968 April 6	USS *New Jersey* (BB-62) is commissioned for the third time.	
1968 May	USS *Scorpion* (SSN-589), the sixth ship of that name, is lost in more than 10,000 feet of water, about 400 miles southwest of the Azores, while returning from Mediterranean deployment. She will be declared "presumed lost" on 5 June and struck from the Navy list on 30 June. *Scorpion* will be located in October by USS *Mizar* (AGOR-11) and later viewed by the submarine *Trieste*. Location of the submarine by analysis of acoustic records reflects advances in state of acoustics knowledge and signal processing techniques.	Twenty-seven midshipmen of the Naval Academy Class of 1968 take an Engineer-in-Training examination under auspices of State of Pennsylvania, first time such an exam is given at the Naval Academy.
1968 July 3	From proposals submitted by six shipyards, the Navy awards a contract definition of the DX/DXG program, later to become DD963, each to Bath Iron Works/ Hughes Aircraft, General Dynamics, and Litton Systems, Inc. (Ingalls).	
1968 July 5		Aeronautical Maintenance Duty officer specialist community is established in U.S. Navy, with one hundred officers designated AMD.
1968 August 17	USS *Dolphin* (AGSS-555), capable of operating at depths in excess of any submarine known at this time, is commissioned.	
1968 September	SUNY Maritime College initiates Naval Architecture and Electrical Engineering curricula.	
1969 April 2	Bath/Hughes, General Dynamics, and Litton Systems, each submit a 12-ton proposal for the DX/DXG program.	
1969 June		First designated engineering degrees are granted to qualifying graduates of the Naval Academy Class of 1969. The first dual license (deck and engine) midshipmen graduate from the U.S. Merchant Marine Academy.
1969 July 12	USS *Narwhal* (SSN-671) is commissioned. She has a direct drive turbine and natural circulation reactor. She is reputed to be the quietest submarine in U.S. Naval service at this time.	
1969 July 20		Astronauts Neil Armstrong and Buzz Aldrin exit Lunar Module *Eagle* to begin first human exploration of the Moon's surface "for all mankind."
1970	1970 *Modern Ship Design* by Thomas C. Gillmer is published by the U.S. Naval Institute.	ESSA Corps becomes National Oceanic and Atmospheric Administration (NOAA) Corps.
1970 January 31		The merger of San Francisco (Hunters Point) and Mare Island Naval Shipyards that had occurred on 11 May 1965 is renounced. The shipyards resume their individual identities.

Date	Naval Engineering	National & International Events Legislative, Organization & Personnel Policy
1970 June 23	Litton Systems, Inc., is awarded a multiyear contract for up to thirty destroyers of the *Spruance* (DD-963) class with ceiling price of $2.14 billion. These will be the first U.S. Navy ships to be powered by gas turbines for propulsion and ship's service power. The same platform will be used for two additional DD 963-class, four *Kidd*-class guided missile destroyers, and for the *Ticonderoga* (CG-47)-class guided missile cruisers.	
1970 August 3	USS *James Madison* (SSBN-627) successfully launches a Poseidon C3 missile while cruising submerged off the Florida coast.	
1970 September		SUNY Maritime College introduces graduate level program in Marine Transportation Management.
1971	*Marine Engineering* is published by SNAME.	
1971 March 31	USS *James Madison* (SSBN-627) deploys on patrol with a full complement of Poseiden C3 missiles.	
1972 September	SUNY Maritime College receives accreditation from the Engineers' Council for Professional Development (ECPD) for its Marine Engineering curriculum.	
1972 September 20		USS *John Marshall* (SSBN-611) arrives for refit at Rota, Spain, marking successful completion of the 1,000th Polaris deterrent patrol.
1973	*Globtik London* and *Globtik Tokyo*, sistership tankers, are the largest ships on the water at this time: 1,244-foot length, 93-foot draft, and deadweight of 476,292 tons.	
1973 February 16		The Secretary of the Navy announces selection of Bangor, Washington, as the initial base for Trident submarine operations.
1973 August	Sunken USS *Monitor* is located by a team from Duke University using R/V (Research Vessel) *Eastward*.	
1973 November 15	USS *Johnston* (DD-821), a destroyer, became first ship in history to use coal-derived oil to power its engines.	
1974	The *Glomar Explorer*, specially outfitted for heavy salvage operations at Sun Shipbuilding and Drydock Company by the CIA, recovers a portion of a Soviet submarine that sank in the Pacific in 1968 with loss of the crew.	
1974 February 21		Lieutenant (j.g.) Barbara Allen, USN, becomes first woman naval aviator to win gold wings.
1974 June 28		The San Francisco (Hunters Point) Naval Shipyard is closed.
1974 July 1		Naval Ship Systems Command and Naval Ordnance Systems Command are merged to form Naval Sea Systems Command.
1974 November 9	Hydrofoil ship, USS *Pegasus* (PHM-1), is launched at Lake Washington, Renton, Washington.	
1974 December 21	USS *Glenard P. Lipscomb* (SSN-685) is commissioned. Her propulsion is electric direct-drive.	
1975 July 1		The name David Taylor is added to the title of U.S. Naval Ship Research and Development Center.
1976 January 16		National Defense University (NDU) is formed in Washington, D.C., incorporating Industrial College of the Armed Forces and National War College.

Date	Naval Engineering	National & International Events Legislative, Organization & Personnel Policy
1977 March		The Naval Ocean Systems Center, San Diego, is formed by consolidating the Naval Electronics Laboratory Center and the Naval Undersea Center. NOSC is the principal Navy RDT&E center of command control, communications, ocean surveillance, surface and air launched undersea weapon systems, and supporting technologies.
1977 June 3	The 101,000 cubic meter *Esso Westernport*, at this time the largest LPG carrier in the world, is launched and named at construction shipyard, Chantiers Navals de la Ciotat in La Ciotat, France.	
1977 August 24	Hydromechanics Laboratory at the U.S. Naval Academy is dedicated.	
1978 April 17	A formal continuing (post-license) program begins at the U.S. Merchant Marine Academy with the diesel instruction courses designed to train senior steam marine engineers to serve on diesel ships.	
1978 September	SUNY Maritime College receives ECPD accreditation for its Naval Architecture and Electrical Engineering curricula.	
1978 October 24	A significant double christening takes place when the first heavy-lift cargo ships built to operate under the American flag are named *John Henry* and *Paul Bunyan*. They have been built by Peterson Builders and are owned by American Heavy Lift Shipping Company (AHL).	
1979 April 10	USS *Francis Scott Key* (SSBN-657) successfully launches the first Trident I (C4) missile off the coast of Florida near Cape Canaveral.	
1979 June 20		Lieutenant Donna Spruill, USN, becomes first woman naval aviator to be carrier qualified by completing necessary arrested landings on USS *Independence* (CV-62), flying a C-1A Tracker aircraft.
1979 October 19		The Naval Ship Engineering Center, Philadelphia Division, becomes the Naval Sea Systems Engineering Station (NAVSSES) with the primary function for test and evaluation of ship systems (Hull, Machinery, and Electrical) and provides in-service engineering support for these systems and equipments.
1979 October 20	USS *Francis Scott Key* (SSBN-657) deploys for deterrent patrol carrying sixteen tactical Trident I (C4) missiles.	
1980 April 12		Astronauts John Young and Bob Crippen pilot the orbiter *Columbia* on the inaugural voyage of the Space Transportation System.
1980 November 10	USS *Sam Houston* is redesignated SSN-609 from SSBN. The five ships of this class (SSBN 608-611 and 618) are all redesignated at various times in 1980 and 1981. *Sam Houston* and *John Marshall* (SSN-611) will be converted in 1984-86 to special-mission submarines. The other three will be decommissioned after 2 to 4 years of service as SSN and will then be stricken. Three ships of another five-ship SSBN class, 598-602, will serve for a while as SSN prior to decommissioning and being stricken. Two will decommission directly and then be stricken within 2 years.	

Date	Naval Engineering	National & International Events Legislative, Organization & Personnel Policy
1981	Assistant Secretary of the Navy (Shipbuilding and Logistics) describes as an "unprecedented achievement" the delivery to the U.S. Navy by the Electric Boat Division of seven nuclear submarines (six attack and one Trident) in a single year.	
1981		The Center for Naval Warfare Studies is established at the Naval War College, Newport, Rhode Island, by the Chief of Naval Operations, Admiral Thomas B. Hayward, USN. Its function is broadly based, advanced research on the naval contribution to a national strategy.
1981 May 1		The International Convention for the Safety of Life at Sea (SOLAS) 1978 comes into effect.
1981 June		American Bureau of Shipping and U.S. Coast Guard sign a Memorandum of Understanding to eliminate duplication of plan review and inspection by both parties. This follows an earlier MOU covering acceptance of ABS measurement and tonnage certification of all United States-flag vessels.
1981 June 27		USS *James K. Polk* (SSBN-645) completes the 2,000th FBM deterrent patrol.
1981 July 1		Center for Naval Warfare Studies is established at Naval War College.
1981 November 11	USS *Ohio* (SSBN-726), the first Trident-class FBM submarine, is commissioned.	
1981 December 8		Selection Board is convened to recommend selection to commodore, the first to one-star rank since World War II. Two Engineering Duty and two Aeronautical Engineering Duty officers are selected.
1982 February 22	Secretary of the Navy announces contract for lead production of three landing craft air cushion (LCAC) vehicles.	
1982 April 2-June 15	There are many sea combat and logistics aspects of the British-Argentina Falklands war pertinent to naval engineering. These include success of air-launched Exocet missiles, inability of ships' radars to pick up sea-skimming missiles, failure of anti-missile defenses. HMS *Conqueror*, a nuclear-powered attack submarine, sinks *Belgrano* (formerly a U.S. *Brooklyn*-class cruiser) with a wire-guided torpedo. Loss of various British warships and troop ships points to hazards of aluminum superstructure.	
1982 June	The Accreditation Board for Engineering and Technology (ABET) gives initial accreditation to engineering systems curriculum at the U.S. Merchant Marine Academy.	
1982 June 15	Destroyer tender USS *Dixie* (AD 14), "oldest ship," is decommissioned after more than 42 years of continuous active service.	
1982 September	Ship model towing tank is commissioned at SUNY Maritime College Naval Architecture Laboratory.	
1982 September 25	Battleship *New Jersey* (BB 62) leaves Long Beach Naval Shipyard for first sea trials since beginning activation. First time ship is underway on own power since her third decommissioning 13 years earlier.	
1982 October 1	USS *Ohio* (SSBN-726) departs on first Trident deterrent patrol for this class of FBM submarine.	

Date	Naval Engineering	National & International Events Legislative, Organization & Personnel Policy
1982 December 16	Two Navy divers complete 220-foot open-ocean descent in first operational use of Mark 12 mixed-gas system, which supplies divers with a mix of helium and oxygen.	
1982 December 28	USS *New Jersey* (BB 62) is recommissioned. First of four commissionings was in May 1943.	
1983 January 22	USS *Ticonderoga* (CG-47) is commissioned. She is first of new class of warships equipped with the Aegis weapons system, giving her capability to detect and track hundreds of air targets. She is 563 feet long, with a beam of 55 feet, displaces 9,600 tons, and her propulsion plant is four gas turbine engines driving two controllable-reversible pitch propellers. She will deploy in October only 9 months after commissioning.	
1983 March 23		President Reagan makes speech advocating a Strategic Defense Initiative.
1983 July	Navy divers from USS *Pigeon* (ASR 22) make saturation dive of 850 feet in Pacific Ocean, including walk on ocean floor at that depth, followed by approximately 9 days in decompression chamber. *Pigeon* and USS *Ortolan* (ASR 21), both twin-hulled submarine rescue ships, have saturation diving support capability.	
1983 September 24		U.S. loses America's Cup to Australia in seven races off Newport, Rhode Island.
1983 October		Naval Space Command is established under direction of former astronaut, Commodore Richard Truly.
1983 October 2		The International Convention for the Prevention of Pollution from Ships (MARPOL) 1978 comes into effect.
1983 November 7	The Naval Sea Systems Command officially designates the Naval Ship Systems Engineering Station, Philadelphia, as the Hull, Machinery, and Electrical In-Service Engineering Agent for the Fleet.	
1984 February		Navy space policy is promulgated.
1984 September 29	Final operational shakedown dive is completed for saturation diving facility for hyperbaric biomedical research at the Naval Medical Research Institute, Bethesda. Four divers complete 25 days of hyperbaric exposure, with the deepest depth attained being 1,000 FSW (feet of sea water).	
1984	The first four of twelve jumbo container ships being constructed for United States Lines, Inc. by Daewoo Shipbuilding and Heavy Machinery, Ltd. are christened at the builder's Okpo Shipyard in South Korea. Designed by the New York naval architecture firm, C. R. Cushing & Company, Inc., they are, by far, the largest container ships ever built. First two are delivered to owner in June of this year.	
	The Naval Ocean Systems Center (NOSC) uses a blue-green laser to communicate with a submarine at operational depths.	
1985	There are nine working transatlantic telephone cables, which, together with satellites, move 212 million phone calls, plus telex and telegraph messages.	
1985 June	The Naval Ocean System Center's (NOSC) Advanced Tethered Vehicle dives to 12,100 feet, a record for a tethered vehicle.	

Date	Naval Engineering	National & International Events Legislative, Organization & Personnel Policy
1985 September 1	Hulk of SS *Titanic* is located by a joint U.S.-French expedition under the co-leadership of Dr. Robert D. Ballard and Jean-Louis Michel. *Argo*, an unmanned platform equipped with advanced acoustics and photographic elements, is used to make the discovery. This device is towed by the Navy's research ship *Knorr* (AGR-15), operated by the Woods Hole Oceanographic Institution.	
1985 September 28	The horizontal back-acting compound engine of TV *Emery Rice* (completed 1886, last voyage 1958) is designated a National Historic Engineering Landmark by the American Society of Mechanical Engineers at the U.S. Merchant Marine Academy, Kings Point, Long Island, New York. This is the eighteenth Landmark designated since the program began in 1973.	
1985 December	Karl Alex Muller, a physicist at the IBM Zurich Research Laboratory, and his colleague Johannes Georg Bednorz, use a compound of barium, lanthanum, copper, and oxygen (a ceramic) to obtain indications of superconductivity at 36 degrees Kelvin, by far the highest temperature observed for this phenomenon to this date. This is a further portent of applications in marine propulsion and electrical power generation.	
1986	Ms. Jean Thacher Arnold becomes first female in history of U.S. Merchant Marine to be licensed by U.S. Coast Guard as a Chief Engineer of Unlimited Horsepower Steam Vessels.	USS *Alexander Hamilton* (SSBN-617) returns to New London, Connecticut, after completing her sixty-ninth patrol, the most made to this date by a fleet ballistic missile submarine.
1986 January 28		Seven astronauts are killed when space shuttle *Challenger* explodes shortly after blast-off. Massive sea search retrieves much debris to assist analysis of cause of accident. Submersible *NR-1* proves to be an effective search tool.
1986 May 6	Three nuclear-powered submarines, USS *Ray* (SSN 653), USS *Hawkbill* (SSN 666), and USS *Archerfish* (SSN 678), for the first time rendezvous and surface together at the geographical North Pole.	
1986 May 20	USS *Bunker Hill* (CG 52) becomes first U.S. warship to test fire missiles from a vertical launching system (VLS).	
1986 June 28		Ground breaking ceremony is held at Dahlgren, Virginia, for new Naval Space Command and Control Center.
1986 June 30	U.S. Navy Tomahawk cruise missile with dummy warhead is fired successfully from USS *Long Beach* (CGN-9), first such landing from ship on regular deployment operating outside an established missile range.	
1986 July		British Airline and Record magnate Richard Branson clips 2 hours 9 minutes off transatlantic crossing record of SS *United States* in his 72-foot racing craft, *Virgin Atlantic Challenger II*, powered by two turbocharged 2,000 h.p. diesel engines.
1986 July 4		Renovation of the Statue of Liberty is completed, and centennial celebration takes place.
1986 September 23		The United States Space Command is established in Colorado Springs, Colorado, to consolidate U.S. defense resources affecting activities in space.

Date	Naval Engineering	National & International Events Legislative, Organization & Personnel Policy
1986 October 6		Following an explosion and fire, a Soviet Yankee-I class ballistic missile submarine sinks in the Atlantic Ocean in about 3,000 fathoms about 600 miles east of Bermuda carrying as many as sixteen SS-N-6 missiles. The crew escapes prior to sinking.
1986 December 23		Aircraft *Voyager* completes circumnavigation of earth without refueling.
1987 February		U.S. entry *Stars and Stripes*, skippered by Dennis Conner, regains America's Cup in four straight races off Fremantle, Australia. This is the first time races are televised from cameras aboard racing vessels, and first time televised to world audiences, resulting in convincing most viewers that racing is not akin to watching grass grow.
1987 March 9		Ceremonies mark designation of site of *Monitor* as a National Historic Landmark, the first such designation by the United States of a sunken ship. British Historic Wrecks Act on 1973 gave similar status to Henry VIII's flagship *Mary Rose*, sunk in 1546. Turkish government has had similar policy for decades.
1987 March 30		USS *Seawolf* (SSN-575), at this time the Navy's oldest active nuclear-powered submarine, is decommissioned at the Mare Island Naval Shipyard, 30 years to the day after her commissioning.
1987 April 4		USS *Mariano G. Vallejo* (SSBN-658) is honored in ceremonies and by a message from President Ronald Reagan for completing the 2,500th strategic deterrent patrol by a U.S. fleet ballistic missile submarine. This marks completion of that submarine's fifty-eighth patrol and a combined total of more than 400 cumulative years of deterrence by both Atlantic and Pacific FBMs.
1987 April 14		The Navy approves establishment of a new Special Warfare Command, to be located at the Naval Amphibious Base, Coronado, California, to serve as the Navy component of the newly created unified U.S. Special Operations Command, located at MacDill Air Force Base, Tampa, Florida. Rear Admiral (select) Irve C. Lemoyne, a special warfare officer for 25 years and Seal during the Vietnam War, is first commanding officer.
1987 May 17		USS *Stark* (FFG-31), deployed in the Persian Gulf, is hit by two Exocet missiles fired from an Iraqi F1 Mirage aircraft, resulting in death of thirty-seven men and severe damage to ship.
1987 June 13	*Albany* (SSN-753) is launched on inclined ways at Newport News Shipbuilding and Drydock Company. This will be last such launch at this shipyard, which celebrated in 1986 its first century of operation.	
1987 June 15		Secretary of the Navy James H. Webb, Jr. announces that female civilian employees have the full opportunity to embark in Naval vessels on non-operational, short-term sea trials on the same basis as male civilian employees.

Date	Naval Engineering	National & International Events Legislative, Organization & Personnel Policy
1987 September 9	The high-tech mini-submarine *Nautile* makes its 32nd dive to the wreck of the *Titanic*, reportedly the final dive in a 2-month French-American exploration of the sunken liner. Retrieval of artifacts has caused considerable controversy, but the expedition is a further example of major developments in capability for underwater operations: exploration, archaeology, retrieval, and recovery. Much of this capability results from major developments triggered by loss of the submarine *Thresher*.	
1987 September 10		A Federal Commission decides in favor of New York between Baltimore and New York as host city for the 1992 Columbus quincentennial.
1987 September 12	USS *Avenger* (MCM-1) is commissioned at the yard of her builder, Peterson Builders, Sturgeon Bay, Wisconsin. She has a glass-reinforced, plastic-sheathed wood hull, and degaussing system to give a very low magnetic signature. She is 224 feet long with a 39-foot beam, the Navy's largest wooden ship.	
1987 September 18		The David Taylor Naval Ship Research and Development Center is renamed The David Taylor Research Center.
1987 September 19	*Wasp* (LHD-1), first of a new class of amphibious assault ships, is christened at Ingalls Shipbuilding as the tenth ship of that name, the most popular for a U.S. Navy ship. She is designed to deploy and land elements of a Marine air and ground task force in an assault using helicopters, landing craft, and amphibious vehicles. She is 844 feet long and displaces 40,600 tons.	
1987 September 30		The Commission on Merchant Marine and Defense, chaired by Senator Jeremiah A. Denton, submits to President Reagan its first report. The forwarding letter says, ". . . there is clear and present danger to the national security in the deteriorating condition of America's maritime industries."
1987 October 1		The United States Transportation Command is activated as the nation's newest unified command, responsible for integrating the global air (Military Airlift Command), land (Military Traffic Management Command), and sea (Military Sealift Command) transportation capabilities of the Department of Defense. General Duane H. Cassidy, USAF, is the commander.
1987 November 9	Bay Shipbuilding Company, Sturgeon Bay, Wisconsin, delivers the last of three 700-FEU (Forty Foot Equivalent Units) container ships to Sea-Land Service, Inc. Following this delivery, there will be no more commercial ships under construction or on order in domestic shipyards.	
1987 December 8		U.S. President Ronald Reagan and USSR General Secretary Mikhail Gorbachev sign INF (Intermediate Nuclear Forces) Treaty, eliminating one class of nuclear weapons.
1987 December 10		Delay is announced for eighth test firing at Cape Canaveral of Navy's Trident II missile for Fleet Ballistic Missile submarines. Although no official reason is given, news reports note that this is final day of Summit meeting between President Ronald Reagan and Soviet General Secretary Mikhail Gorbachev. Firing is conducted successfully 11 December. Trident II is scheduled for deployment in December 1989.

Date	Naval Engineering	National & International Events Legislative, Organization & Personnel Policy
1987 December 20		A series of news reports highlights the need for continuing vigilance in connection with safety of life at sea. The passenger ferry *Dona Paz*, en route from Tacloban to Manila, collides with the oil tanker *Victor*. There is an explosion, fire, and both ships sink, resulting in loss of at least 1,500 people. Only 27 survive. The *Binter*, an Indonesian timber carrier, capsizes and sinks in rough weather in the Java Sea. Fifty-five are presumed lost. A helicopter crash on an oil platform with loss of life, and a major fire on another platform are also reported.
1988	The first fiberoptics transatlantic telephone cable, TAT-8, goes into operation with planned service life of 25 years.	Office of the Chief of Naval Operations is reorganized to comply with the Goldwater-Nichols Reorganization Act of 1986. The reorganization transfers to the Secretary of the Navy sole responsibility for acquisition, auditing, comptroller, information management, inspector general, legislative affairs, public affairs, and research and development.
1988 January 19		The DoD administrator for issues involving status of civilians who served in combat zones rules that American merchant seamen who were in active, oceangoing service during the period of U.S. World War II armed conflict, 7 December 1941 to 15 August 1945, are considered veterans for the purpose of all laws administered by the Veterans Administration. The group includes members of the U.S. merchant marine and civil service crew members aboard U.S. Army Transport Service and Naval Transportation Service vessels.
1988 January 21	A Trident II missile for the Navy's fleet ballistic missile submarines is destroyed in early phase of a test launch from Cape Canaveral. This is the first of nine launches that is unsuccessful.	
1988 April 14		Hostile actions in the Persian Gulf continue with underwater explosion damage to USS *Samuel B. Roberts* (FFG-58), presumably from a mine. The engineroom is flooded; ten of the crew are injured.
1988 July 31	USS *Samuel B. Roberts* (FFG-58), damaged by explosion 14 April, arrives at Naval Station Newport, Rhode Island, after 8,027-mile journey from Persian Gulf in the cargo deck of the heavy lift ship *Mighty Servant 2*. She made the last 2 miles from the anchorage in Naragansett Bay to the Navy's Pier 2 in Newport under her own power.	

Appendix B

Naval Engineering Trends

The following list of trends or developments was developed primarily to assist authors of this book. It is included here for reference and with the hope that it may prompt others to further explore and document significant aspects of the history of naval engineering.

Ship Design and Capability

• Longer design time for military ships prior to ship construction contract

• Increased emphasis on risk analysis in determining technical advances to incorporate in ship design

• Relative costs of weight groups of ships; e.g., in 1890 electrical and electronics (a term unknown then) perhaps made up 10% of a warship's cost; today that figure may be 60%

• Improved standards for seaworthiness, seakindliness, stability

• Standards and design specifications for survivability, damage control, fire resistance, and fire fighting

• Improved understanding of loading and response and structural design techniques

• Increased detailed study, during contract design, of access for maintenance, replenishment, and other shipboard routines

• Aircraft/Helo and ship compatibility

• Developments and changes in propulsion systems and propulsors; for example, steam engines, diesel engines, gas turbines, nuclear propulsion, controllable reversible pitch propellers, bow and stern thrusters

• Impact of changes in fuels (coal, bunker oil, diesel, distillate fuel, nuclear) on design, performance, and cost of ships

• Impact of environmental considerations on ship design and cost; e.g., collection and holding systems for sewage and waste

• Improved habitability standards a major factor in increasing ship size

Ship Types

• Development, supremacy, eclipse, and return of the battleship

• Ships and craft for myriad special military operations; for example, mine laying and minesweeping, amphibious, clandestine and "brown water"

• Coast Guard ships and craft for many and varied functions

• Commercial fishing and ocean resource recovery

• Oceanographic ships, long history and development in research and data acquisition

• Special purpose ships and craft for inland waterway and coastal traffic; for example, pusher tugs

• Rise and demise of passenger liners, and their resurrection as cruise ships

• Hydrofoils, SWATH, SES, and other craft formerly loosely grouped as "advanced marine vehicles"

• The burgeoning pleasure craft industry

• Offshore operations and related support craft and facilities

• Capability for underwater and deep ocean manned and unmanned operations including diving equipment and submersibles, both military and commercial

• Icebreakers for both ocean and inland waterway operations

Mission Systems

• Advances in weaponry and combat systems and resulting impact on design and cost of ships

• The advent of digital computers and signal processing causing explosive growth in combat system capabilities

• Improvements in cargo handling resulting in today's Roll-on Roll-off ships, container ships, fast bulk off-loading, etc.

• Major developments to improve speed and accuracy in navigation; ditto for communications and the broad aspects of command and control

Education and Training

• Baccalaureate and advanced degree programs for the various disciplines in the broad field of naval engineering; specialization in the Navy and Coast Guard

- Federal and State maritime schools
- Use for training of shore-based prototype systems and actual operational equipment in training mode
- Development of operational simulators

PERSONNEL

- Design and operational improvements for better utilization of shipboard personnel
- Development of habitability standards for military and commercial ships

FLEET SUPPORT

- Technical developments in logistics: underway replenishment; development of "the train" into multipurpose replenishment ships, many of high speed and large size; strategic sealift; rapid deployment and pre-positioning; forward deployed logistics ships
- Maintenance management in both the military and commercial fleets
- Interaction between port facility design and ship design; e.g., container ships and large bulk carriers

INDUSTRIAL CAPABILITY

- Shipbuilding techniques, processes, and equipment
- Modular construction

- Improvements in hull structure fabrication: riveted, to riveted-welded, to all welded; new types of steels and other materials
- Rise and decline of capability and breadth of major industrial marine suppliers

EFFECTS ON NAVAL ENGINEERING OF MARINE POLICY AND PUBLIC AWARENESS

- Role of professional societies; e.g., Society of Naval Architects and Marine Engineers, American Society of Naval Engineers, organizations such as the U.S. Naval Institute, and special professional groups such as the Association of Scientists and Engineers (formerly the Association of Senior Engineers of the Bureau of Ships)
- Major maritime legislation
- Changes in government organizations; e.g., Maritime Administration, U.S. Coast Guard, Federal Maritime Commission, National Oceanic and Atmospheric Administration
- Rise and fall of National Advisory Committee on Oceans and Atmosphere (NACOA)
- Sporadic recognition of the national importance of maritime matters by formation of groups such as the Maritime Transportation Research Board, Ship Structure Committee, and Marine Board in the National Research Council, and by appointment, from time to time by the President or the Congress, of Commissions to examine various aspects of the maritime industry

Appendix C

SOURCES

Following are representative sources for those seeking information on naval engineering matters. It is hoped that this compilation will help point the way, although it is not intended to be a complete listing. For example, most universities and colleges with programs pertinent to the field of naval engineering are likely to be excellent sources on particular topics. There are many additional museums and other organizations with fine resources.

I MARITIME MUSEUMS

General reference:
Howe, Hartley Edward. *North America's Maritime Museums: An Annotated Guide.*
New York, N.Y.: Facts on File, Inc, 460 Park Avenue S., New York, N.Y. 10016. 1987.

American Merchant Marine Museum
U.S. Merchant Marine Academy
Kings Point, Long Island 11204

American Museum of Naval and Maritime Heritage
Patriot's Point
P.O. Box 986
Mt. Pleasant, South Carolina 29464

Brannock Maritime Museum
P.O. Box 337
Cambridge, Maryland 21613
The Museum Library is primarily concerned with the Chesapeake Bay

Calvert Maritime Museum
P.O. Box 97
Solomons, Maryland 20688

The Chesapeake Bay Maritime Museum
Navy Point
St. Michaels, Maryland 21663

Herreshoff Marine Museum
P.O. Box 450
Bristol, Rhode Island 02809

Intrepid Sea-Air-Space Museum & Foundation
Intrepid Square
New York, New York 10036

Iron Man Museum
401 E. Hendy
Sunnyvale, California 94088

Los Angeles Maritime Museum
Berth 84, Foot of Sixth Street
San Pedro, California 90731

Maine Maritime Museum
963 Washington Street
Bath, Maine 04530
Open seven days a week year round. Has Archives and Library

The Maine State Museum
Augusta, Maine

The Mariners Museum
Museum Drive
Newport News, Virginia 23606

The MIT Museum
Hart Nautical Collection
265 Massachusetts Avenue
Cambridge, Massachusetts 02139

Mystic Seaport Museum
Mystic, Connecticut 06355

U.S. Naval Academy Museum
U.S. Naval Academy
Annapolis, Maryland 21402

Naval Aviation Museum
U.S. Naval Air Station
Pensacola, Florida 32508

Naval Undersea Warfare Museum
Keyport, Washington

Navy-Marine Corps-Coast Guard Museum
Building 1 Treasure Island
San Francisco, California 94130

Navy Memorial Museum
Washington Navy Yard
Washington, D.C. 20374
(Submarine Museum opened here in 1986)

Nautilus Memorial
Submarine Force Library & Museum
Naval Submarine Base, Box 571
New London, Connecticut 06349-5000
Governed jointly by Commanders of the Atlantic and Pacific Submarine Forces. Historical guidance is provided by the Curator of the Navy through the Naval Historical Center. The museum is the official repository of submarine related artifacts and information for the Submarine Force.

New York University
Hall of Fame for Great Americans
New York, N.Y.

North Carolina Maritime Museum
(Hampton Mariners Museum)
315 Front Street
Beaufort, North Carolina 28516

Peabody Museum
East India Square
Salem, Massachusetts 01970

Penobscot Marine Museum
Church Street
Searsport, Maine 04974
The Stephen Phillips Memorial Library is open by appointment throughout the year.

The Philadelphia Maritime Museum
321 Chestnut Street
Philadelphia, Pennsylvania 19106

National Museum of American History
Smithsonian Institution
Washington, D.C. 20560

South Street Seaport Museum
South Street Seaport
New York, New York

Whaling Museum
18 Johnny Cake Hill
New Bedford, Massachusetts 02740

II LIBRARIES WITH SIGNIFICANT MARITIME COLLECTIONS

Library of Congress
1st Street and Independence Avenue, SE
Washington, D.C. 20540

The Maine Maritime Academy
Nutting Memorial Library
Box C-1
Castine, Maine 04420

Stephen B. Luce Library
Maritime College
State University of New York
Ft. Schuyler, New York 10465

U.S. Coast Guard Academy
Waesche Hall
New London, Connecticut 06320

U.S. Merchant Marine Academy
Kings Point, New York 11024

U.S. Naval Academy
Annapolis, Maryland 21402

Navy Department Library
Building 44,
Washington Navy Yard
Washington, D.C. 20374

National Archives
Pennsylvania Avenue at 8th Street, NW
Washington, D.C. 20004
(Much pertinent material can be found in the Archives. For example, official logs for Navy ships in service before June 1945 are stored here.)

Webb Institute of Naval Architecture
Crescent Beach Road
Glen Cove, New York 11542

Library
U.S. Department of Transportation
400 7th Street, SW
Washington, D.C. 20004

III GOVERNMENT AGENCIES

Director of Naval History
Office of the Chief of Naval Operations
Department of the Navy
located at: Naval Historical Center
Washington Navy Yard
Washington, D.C. 20374

Commission on Merchant Marine and Defense
Department of the Navy
4401 Ford Avenue
Alexandria, Virginia 22302

Naval Sea Systems Command
Washington, D.C. 20362-5101

Military Sealift Command
Washington, D.C. 20390

U.S. Coast Guard Headquarters
Department of Transportation
Washington, D.C. 20593

Maritime Administration
U.S. Department of Transportation
400 Seventh Street, S.W.
Washington, D.C. 20590

Federal Maritime Commission
1100 L Street, NW
Washington, D.C. 20005

National Oceanic & Atmospheric Administration
2100 Wisconsin Avenue, NW
Washington, D.C. 20007

The Smithsonian Institution
National Museum of American History
Washington, D.C. 20560

IV THE CONGRESS

The Congressional Maritime Caucus
United States Congress
Washington, D.C.

Merchant Marine and Fisheries Committee
House of Representatives
Washington, D.C. 20515

Energy and Commerce Committee
House of Representatives
Washington, D.C. 20515

House Armed Services Subcommittee on
Seapower and Strategic and Critical Materials
House of Representatives
Washington, D.C. 20515

Senate Merchant Marine Subcommittee
United States Senate
Washington, D.C. 20510

Congressional Research Service
The Library of Congress
Washington, D.C. 20540

Office of Technology Assessment
Congress of the United States
Washington, D.C. 20510

V Clubs and Societies

American Institute of Aeronautics
and Astronautics (AIAA)
1290 Avenue of the Americas
New York, New York 10104

American Society of Civil Engineers (ASCE)
345 East 47th Street
New York, N.Y. 10017

American Society of Mechanical Engineers (ASME)
United Engineering Center
345 East 47th Street
New York, N.Y. 10017

The American Society of Naval Engineers, Inc.
(ASNE)
1452 Duke Street
Alexandria, Virginia 22314

American Society for Testing and Materials (ASTM)
1916 Race Street
Philadelphia, Pennsylvania 19103

Institute of Electrical and Electronics Engineers
(IEEE)
345 East 47th Street
New York, N.Y. 10017

Maine Historical Society
485 Congress Street
Portland, Maine 04101

Marine Technology Society
2000 Florida Avenue, NW
Suite 500
Washington, D.C. 20009

The National Historical Society
P.O. Box 8200
Harrisburg, Pennsylvania 17105-8200

National Maritime Historical Society
132 Maple Street
Croton-on-Hudson, New York 10520

National Space Society
600 Maryland Avenue, S.W., Suite W-203
Washington, D.C. 20024

The Newcomen Society in North America
412 Newcomen Road
Exton, Pennsylvania 19341
(Located here also are The Thomas Newcomen
Memorial Library and Museum in Steam Technology and Industrial History, a reference collection,
including microfilm, open to the public for research.)
The Newcomen Society in North America is affiliated with The Newcomen Society for the Study
of History of Engineering and Technology, with
offices in London. The Society is associated in
union with the Royal Society for the Encouragement of Arts, Manufacturers and Commerce, whose
offices are in London.)

The New York Yacht Club
37 West 44th Street
New York, N.Y. 10036

North American Society for Oceanic History
Mailing Address: c/o Department of History
United States Naval Academy
Annapolis, Maryland 21402
Society's Secretary,
Post Office Box 18108
Washington, D.C. 20036

The Oceanic Society
1536 16th Street, NW
Washington, D.C. 20036

Pan-American Institute of Naval Engineering
Instituto Pan-Americano de Engenharia Naval
IPEN Secretariat
Av. Presidente Vargas, 542-S.2207
20073-Rio de Janeiro, Brasil

SAE
400 Commonwealth Drive
Warrendale, Pennsylvania 15096

San Francisco Maritime Museum Assn., Inc.
680 Beach Street, Room 330
San Francisco, California 94109

The Society of Naval Architects and Marine
Engineers (SNAME)
601 Pavonia Avenue
Jersey City, New Jersey 07306

United States Lighthouse Society
964 Chenery Street
San Francisco, California 94131

The Wisconsin Marine Historical Society
814 West Wisconsin Avenue
Milwaukee, Wisconsin 53233

VI NON-PROFIT ORGANIZATIONS

American Association for the Advancement of
Science
1333 H Street, N.W.
Washington, D.C. 20005

American Military Institute
3309 Chestnut Street, NW
Washington, D.C. 20015

Association of Naval Aviation, Inc.
5205 Leesburg Pike, Suite 200
Falls Church, Virginia 22041

Engineering Foundation
A Department of United Engineering Trustees, Inc.
United Engineering Center
345 E. 47th Street
New York, New York 10017

Institute for Great Lakes Research
Jerome Library
Bowling Green State University
Bowling Green, Ohio 43403

International Commission for Maritime History
National Maritime Museum
Greenwich, London SE10 9NF, England

The Marine Board
National Research Council
National Academy of Sciences and
  National Academy of Engineering
2101 Constitution Avenue, N.W.
Washington, D.C. 20418

National Trust for Historic Preservation
Maritime Department
1785 Massachusetts Avenue, NW
Washington, D.C. 20036

Naval Historical Foundation
Building 57
Washington Navy Yard
Washington, D.C. 20374

Naval Undersea Warfare Museum Foundation
Naval Historical Center
Building 57, Washington Navy Yard
Washington, D.C. 20374

Sea Education Association, Inc.
P.O. Box 6, Church Street
Woods Hole, Massachusetts 02543

Surface Navy Association
P.O. Box 5191
Arlington, Virginia 22205

The Tailhook Association
P.O. Box 40
Bonita, California 92002
(Dedicated to foster, encourage, study, and develop
support for the aircraft carrier, carrier aircraft and
their aircrews of the United States of America, in
their appropriate role in the Nation's defense
system.)

VII OTHER ORGANIZATIONS
(INDUSTRY, UNION, ETC)

American Association of Port Authorities
1010 Duke Street
Alexandria, Virginia 22314

American Bureau of Shipping
and ABS Group of Companies, Inc.
45 Eisenhower Drive
Paramus, New Jersey 07653-0910

American Institute of Merchant Shipping
1000 16th Street, NW — Suite 511
Washington, D.C. 20036-5705

American Maritime Officers Service
Transportation Institute Building
923 15th Street, N.W.
Washington, D.C. 20005

American Petroleum Institute
1220 L Street, NW
Washington, D.C. 20005

American Pilots' Association, Inc.
1055 Thomas Jefferson Street, NW
Suite 404
Washington, D.C. 20007

The American Waterways Operators
1600 Wilson Boulevard
Suite 1000
Arlington, Virginia 22209

Labor Management Maritime Committee, Inc.
100 Indiana Avenue, NW, #301
Washington, D.C. 20001

Marine Engineers Beneficial Association
(MEBA) District 2
Affiliated with the AFL-CIO Maritime Trades
Department
650 Fourth Avenue
Brooklyn, New York 11232

National Association of Passenger Vessel Owners
1511 K Street, NW
Washington, D.C.

National Maritime Council
1748 N Street, NW
Washington, D.C. 20036

National Maritime Union of America
346 West 17th Street,
New York, N.Y. 10011

National Waterways Conference, Inc.
1130 17th Street, NW
Washington, D.C. 20036

The Navy League of the United States
2300 Wilson Boulevard
Arlington, Virginia 22201-3308

The Propeller Club of the United States
1030 15th Street, N.W. — Suite 430
Washington, D.C. 20005

The Shipbuilders Council of America
1110 Vermont Avenue, NW
Washington, D.C. 20005

Transportation Institute
923 15th Street, N.W.
Washington, D.C. 20005

United Shipowners of America (USA)
(Formerly Council of American Flag-Ship
Operators)
1627 K Street, N.W., Suite 1200
Washington, D.C. 20006

Glossary and Abbreviations

Every effort has been made to minimize use of abbreviations and terms that are likely to be unknown to most of our readers. We have attempted, in addition, to include in the narrative the meaning of unusual terms, and particularly to provide the spelled out form of abbreviations. It is probable that our best intentions have gone astray in some degree; the following list is, therefore, provided for ready reference.

NOMENCLATURE AND TERMINOLOGY

Aegis

This word, one of its meanings being shield or protection, is used to identify the major combat system for anti-aircraft and anti-missile fleet defense in the *Ticonderoga*-class cruisers. The word stems from Greek mythology: "A symbol or accoutrement, in Homer ascribed to Zeus." (Webster's New International Dictionary)

Cellulube

Explosion resistant phosphate ester hydraulic fluid.

Electronic Equipment

Where electronic equipment is mentioned in the text, its function is indicated. Joint (Army-Navy "AN") nomenclature is used when known. This alphanumeric system is outlined briefly as follows:

First letter–Installation

A-Airborne
B-Underwater mobile submarine
K-Amphibious
S-Water surface craft
U-General utility

Second letter–Type of Equipment

A-Invisible light, heat radiation
L-Countermeasures
P-Radar
Q-Sonar and underwater sound
R-Radio

Third letter–Purpose

C-Communications
D-Direction finder
G-Gun or searchlight directing
N-Navigation
S-Detecting and/or range and bearing

A number is used to indicate a specific piece of equipment. Those wishing more detailed information on electronic equipment nomenclature are referred to the latest revision of MIL-STD-196 "Military Standard-Joint Electronics Type Designation System."

Hedgehog

Spigot-mortar-array anti-submarine weapon system.

HY (-80, etc)

Category of high yield-strength steels for submarine and other hull use.

Knot

One nautical mile per hour

Level I

Material category, provides for complete information control to origin of fabrication, for nuclear and high pressure steam engineering.

Mile

Statute Mile or Land Mile is 5,280 feet (1,609.35 meters). Nautical mile is an international unit of linear measure equal to one minute of arc of a great circle of the Earth, 6,076.11549 feet (1,852 meters).

Purple K

Powdered potassium compound firefighting material.

Regulus

An early Navy cruise missile.

Schottel Unit

Retractable, bow maneuvering unit.

Styx

A type of Soviet surface-to-surface missile.

Talos

An air defense missile (ramjet), surface-to-air

Tartar

An air defense missile, surface-to-air

Terrier

An air defense missile (solid rocket), surface-to-air

Tonnage

The confusing terminology of modern tonnage measurement has a basis going back to the 13th Century, when merchant ships carried wine in casks called tuns. Volume tonnage is measured in units of 100 cubic feet. Weight measurement is in long tons of 2,240 pounds. The subject has become quite complex, but in simplified terms the various tonnages are: *Displacement tonnage* usually refers to the weight of the ship at its normal full load. *Deadweight tonnage (DWT)* is the number of tons a vessel may carry in cargo, stores, water, fuel, passengers and crew. *Gross tonnage (GT)* is the measure in 100-cubic feet volume units of a ship's closed-in space minus certain exempted areas such as ballast tanks and galleys. *Net tonnage (NT)* is gross tonnage minus space allotted for machinery, engine room, officers' and crew's quarters and similar uses. *Standard displacement tonnage* was defined at the Washington Arms Conference in 1922-1923 as that of a ship complete, fully manned, engined, and equipped ready for sea, including all armament and ammunitions, equipment, outfit,

provisions, and fresh water for crew, miscellaneous stores and implements of every description that would be carried in war, but without fuel or reserve feed water on board. In general, passenger liners are described in terms of gross tonnage, naval ships in displacement tons, freighters and tankers in deadweight tons. (Note: This discussion is obtained primarily from the LIFE Science Library Book, *Ships*. Anyone desiring a more detailed discussion is referred to a text on naval architecture.)

Type XXI
Advanced German World War II diesel submarine with high submerged speed and snorkel.

VERTREP
Vertical replenishment (at sea, by helicopter).

Weapon ABLE (ALPHA)
Rocket launched anti-submarine weapon system.

ABBREVIATIONS

AAAS
American Association for the Advancement of Science

ABET
Accreditation Board for Engineering and Technology (formerly ECPD)

ACC
Automatic Combustion Controls

AEC
Atomic Energy Commission

ANCVE
Advanced Naval Vehicle Concept Evaluation

APL
Applied Physics Laboratory

ASNE
American Society of Naval Engineers

ASSET
Advanced Surface Ship Evaluation Tool

ASW
Anti-submarine Warfare

ATDS
Aircraft Tactical Data System

BAT
Boiler Assistance Team

bhp
brake horsepower

BuShips
Bureau of Ships

CAD
Computer Aided Design

CASDOS
Computer Aided Structural Design Of Ships

CAM
Computer Aided Manufacturing

CC, U.S.N.
Construction Corps, United States Navy

CD
Contract Definition

CF
Concept Formulation

CF/CD
Concept Formulation/Contract Definition

ChNavMat
Chief of Naval Material

CIC
Combat Information Center

CNO
Chief of Naval Operations

CODOG
Combined-diesel-or-gas turbine

CominCh
Commander in Chief

CRP
Controllable Reversible-pitch Propeller

CSS
Confederate States Ship

DARPA
Defense Advanced Research Projects Agency

DCNO
Deputy Chief of Naval Operations

DCP
Development Concept Paper

DIMES
Defense Industrial Management System

DoD
Department of Defense
DSARC
Data Systems Acquisition Review
ECPD
Engineering Council for Professional Development (later changed to ABET)
EDO (ED)
Engineering duty officer (specialist)
EOC
Extended Operating Cycle
EOSS
Engineering Operational Sequencing System
−°F
Temperature in degrees Fahrenheit
FBM
Fleet Ballistic Missile
−in. Hg
Inches of mercury (pressure)
HM&E
Hull, Machinery, and Electrical systems and components. This term has been used for many years to define these three important components of the federation of systems that make up a ship.
HP
Horsepower
HP-IP
High-pressure Intermediate-pressure
Hz
Hertz (cycles per second)
IMA
Intermediate Maintenance Activity
InSurv
Navy Board of Inspection and Survey
IOC
Initial Operational Capability
JP-5
Jet and gas turbine fuel, formula 5
LBES
Land Based Engineering Site
LBTS
Land-Based Test Site
Loran
Dual-base hyperbolic radio location and ranging navigational system (*Long Range Navigation*)
LNG
Liquefied natural gas
LOA
Length overall
MarAd
Maritime Administration
MDCS
Maintenance Data Control System

MHz
Megahertz; one million cycles per second
MSC
Military Sealift Command
MSTS
Military Sea Transport Service
MTDS
Marine Corps Tactical Data System
MTT
Mobile Training Team
NavMat
Naval Material Command
NavSea
Naval Sea Systems Command
NavShips
Naval Ship Systems Command
NBTL
Naval Boiler and Turbine Laboratory
ND
Navy Distillate
NDRC
National Defense Research Committee
NEL
Naval Electronics Laboratory
NIF
Navy Industrial Fund
NME
National Military Establishment
NOR
Navy operational requirement (for equipment)
NRL
Naval Research Laboratory
NSFO
Navy Standard Fuel Oil
NSRDC
Naval Ship Research and Development Center
NTDS
Navy Tactical Data System
OIC
Officer in charge
ONR
Office of Naval Research
OpNav
Office of the Chief of Naval Operations
OTA
Office of Technology Assessment
PEB
Propulsion Examining Board
PERA
Planning and Engineering for Repairs and Alterations
PMS
Planned Maintenance System

PPBS
  Program, planning, and budgeting system of the Department of Defense
PPI
  Plan and Position Indicator (A piece of equipment to present Radar information)
PQS
  Personnel Qualification Standard
psi
  pounds per square inch
RDF
  Radio Direction Finder
RO/RO
  Roll-on, roll-off rapid handling cargo ship
rpm
  revolutions per minute
SAM
  Surface-to-Air Missile
SCB
  CNO's Ship Characteristics Board
SDI
  Strategic Defense Initiative
SecDef
  Secretary of Defense
SEAL
  The Navy's special warfare *Sea*, *Air*, and *Land* teams
SEAMOD
  Modular Ship Research Project
SES
  Surface Effect Ship
SHAPM
  Ship Acquisition Project Manager
shp
  shaft horsepower
SIR
  Submarine Intermediate Reactor
SNAME
  Society of Naval Archhitects and Marine Engineers

SRA
  Selected Restricted Availabilities
STR
  Selected Thermal Reactor
SUNY
  State University of New York
T
  Tons
TCBL
  Tentative Conceptual Base Line
TDP
  Technical Development Plan
TLR
  Top Level Requirement
TLS
  Top Level Specification
TPP
  Total Package Procurement
TRS
  Technical Repair Standards
TS
  Test Site
USCG
  United States Coast Guard
USMMA
  United States Merchant Marine Academy
USMS
  United States Merchant Service
USNA
  United States Naval Academy
USRCS
  United States Revenue Cutter Service
VLS
  Vertical Launching System
WDS
  Weapons Direction System

SHIP TYPE DESIGNATIONS

AC
  Coaling ship, U.S. Navy's designation for a collier
ACR
  U.S. Navy's designation for an armored cruiser
ACV
  Air cushion vehicle (hovercraft)
AE
  Ammunition ship
AF
  Stores ship
AFS
  Combat stores ships

AG
  Miscellaneous (ex-AG, Miscellaneous Auxiliary). This designation is sometimes confusing because, when combined with other designation, AG can mean research; for example, AGOR Oceanographic Research Ship, AGDE Escort Research Ship.
AGC
  Amphibious command ship
AGEH
  Experimental hydrofoil ship
AGSS
  Experimental submarine

AKA
Attack cargo ship

AO
Fleet oiler

AOE
Fast combat support ship

AOR
Fast replenishment oiler

ASR
Submarine rescue vessel

AVC
Auxiliary aircraft carrier (Considered as auxiliary ships until 1943 when they were redesignated CVE and classed as combatant ships.)

AVG
Aircraft escort vessel (Original designation applied to merchant hulls converted to small aircraft carriers; later ACV)

BB
Battleship

CAG
Guided-missile heavy cruiser (term abolished 14 August 1968)

CA
Heavy cruiser

CG
Guided-missile cruiser

CGN
Guided-missile cruiser (nuclear propulsion). The symbol CG(N) was used until 3 October 1967.

CL
Light cruiser

CLC
Task Fleet command ship (Reassigned in 1952 to new command ships category)

CLK
Hunter-killer ship (proposed post-WWII cruiser-sized ASW ships)

CV
Aircraft carrier

CVA
Attack aircraft carrier

CVAN
Attack aircraft carrier (nuclear propulsion). The symbol CVA(N) was used until 3 October 1967.

CVB
Battle aircraft carrier (an early post-war designation)

CVE
Aircraft carrier, escort (ex-ACV; later CVHA, CVHE, CVU, q.v.)

DE
Destroyer escort

DD
Destroyer

DDG
Destroyer (missile)

DL
Destroyer leader

DLG
Missile destroyer leader

DSRV
Deep submergence rescue vessel

EAG
Experimental gunnery ship

ECLC
Experimental communications light cruiser (*Northampton*)

EDD
Experimental destroyer

FDL
Fast deployment logistics (ship)

FFG
Frigate (missile)

GTS
Gas turbine ship

HMS
His/Her Majesty's Ship

JEFF
Type of developmental USS Navy air-cushion vehicle

LASH
Container ship with special handling and stowing gear

LCVP
Landing craft, vehicle and personnel

LHA
Amphibious helicopter carrier

LNG
Liquefied Natural Gas

LPD
Landing transport, dock

LPH
Amphibious assault ship, helicopter

LSD
Landing ship, dock

LST
Landing ship, tank

MS
Motor ship

NR-1
Nuclear-powered research submarine (for deep submergence)

NS
Nuclear ship

PCH
High speed, anti-submarine hydrofoil

PG
Gunboat

PGH
Hydrofoil gun boat

PGM
A fast gunboat

PHM
Missile hydrofoil

RMS
Royal Mail Steamer

RO/RO
Roll-on/Roll-off (cargo) ship

SKMR
An experimental air-cushion vehicle

SS
Steam Ship (commercial); Submarine (Navy)

SSBN
Ballistic missile nuclear submarine

SSG
Early class of cruise missile submarine to carry the Regulus

SSK
Anti-submarine submarine

SSM
Surface-to-surface missile

SSN
Nuclear submarine

TV
Training vessel, e.g. TV *Emery Rice*

ULCC
Ultra Large Crude Carriers

NOTES ON AUTHORS

Commander John D. Alden, USN (Ret)

Commander John Alden was designated as an Engineering Duty Officer in 1950 following service on submarines and an aircraft carrier during and after World War II. He retired in 1965 after serving as Quality Assurance Superintendent at Portsmouth Naval Shipyard. Until 1986, he was employed in professional engineering society activities, including the accreditation of engineering educational programs. Commander Alden has authored many articles on naval and engineering subjects, as well as three books published by the U.S. Naval Institute; he received that organization's Award of Merit in 1973. He is currently working on an analysis of wartime submarine attacks.

Rear Admiral Willis C. Barnes, USN (Ret)

Admiral Willis C. Barnes graduated with distinction from the U.S. Naval Academy in 1944 and served on destroyers and minesweepers before becoming an engineering duty officer with the degree of naval engineer from MIT. His ship design and engineering experience includes ten years in the naval nuclear propulsion program, where he was director of advanced development; command of Mare Island Naval Shipyard; duty as Deputy and Fleet Maintenance Officer, Atlantic; and command of the Naval Ship Engineering Center, from which he retired in 1977. He is a member of several naval engineering societies and the Sigma Xi.

Captain John R. Baylis, USN (Ret)

Captain Baylis graduated from the U.S. Naval Academy with the class of 1946 and served as engineer officer on three destroyers before attending post graduate school at MIT. Following a tour at San Francisco Naval Shipyard, he reported to Portsmouth Naval Shipyard and began his experience in noise reduction in Naval ships. He taught ship design subjects at MIT and then headed the Ship Silencing branch at the Bureau of Ships. Captain Baylis was the Technical Director of the DD-963 Ship Acquisition Project and the Executive Director for Research at NavShips. He is now a Registered Professional Engineer in Virginia.

John Jerome Fee

John Fee is the youngest of the ASNE Centennial History project authors. He first engaged in the Centennial project as a summer intern at the ASNE headquarters. During the summer of 1986, Mr. Fee did most of his research for his chapter and served as an aide to the Centennial project. Mr. Fee is a 1987 graduate of James Madison University. He obtained a Bachelor's degree in History, with his chapter serving as his Honors thesis. John comes from a long line of naval engineering tradition: both his father and grandfather having been engineering duty officers in the United States Navy. John is also a member of the Phi Alpha Theta Historical Honor Society.

Dr. James V. Jolliff

Dr. James V. Jolliff, a 1954 graduate of the U.S. Naval Academy, has received several advanced academic degrees. During 32 years of Naval service, he served in a variety of challenging shipboard and engineering duty officer assignments. Active in ASNE since 1966, he has received numerous special recognitions, including four President's Awards, the Frank G. Law Award, and the "Jimmie" Hamilton Award. He has published over thirty technical papers in the field of naval engineering and is the co-author of the *Naval Engineer's Guide*. He is currently Vice President of Jolliff Enterprises Incorporated, a naval engineering consulting firm based in Annapolis, Maryland.

Rear Admiral Randolph W. King, USN (Ret)

Admiral King graduated from the U.S. Naval Academy in 1943, and, after aviation indoctrination in Florida, joined the USS *Eaton* (DD-510). While serving in that destroyer, he participated in extensive combat operations in the southwest and central Pacific, and qualified in deck, gunnery, engineering, and navigation duties. He then served aboard the USS *Boston* (CA-69) participating in postwar Japanese demilitarization. In 1949, Admiral King was awarded the degree of Naval Engineer for postgraduate studies at MIT. Subsequently, Admiral King's career has been marked by a succession of increasingly significant assignments in naval engineering, research, design, education, construction, and repair. He has worked extensively at technical, managerial, and administrative levels through Engineering Department Head, U.S. Naval Academy; command of the David Taylor Naval Ship Research and Development Center; command of the Norfolk Naval Shipyard; and as Deputy Commander of the Naval Sea Systems Command. Since retirement from Navy duty, Admiral King has served in industry, on the staff of the National Academy of Sciences/National Academy of Engineering/National Research Council, and as President of the American Society of Naval Engineers.

Edward M. MacCutcheon

Mr. MacCutcheon graduated from Webb Institute of Naval Architecture and The George Washington University. He was employed by the New York Shipbuilding Corporation, U.S. Coast Guard, David Taylor Model Basin, Bureau of Ships, and Office of Naval Research. He was Technical Director of the Naval Civil Engineering Laboratory; Chief, Office of Research and Development, Maritime Administration; and Director of Systems Development, National Ocean Survey, National Oceanic and Atmospheric Administration. He is a Council Member, American Society of Naval Engineers; Fellow and Vice President, Society of Naval Architects and Marine Engineers; Fellow, Marine Technology Society; and past President, American Oceanic Organization.

Captain James L. McVoy, USN (Ret)

After graduating from the U.S. Naval Academy in 1949, Captain McVoy served in the USS *Midway* (CVB-41), USS *Marquette*, and USS *W.D. Cobb* (APD-106), and Underwater Demolition Teams, Atlantic. He then completed Submarine School at New London, Connecticut, and served in the USS *Archerfish* (SS-311), USS *Batfish*, USS *Hake* (SS-256), and USS *Tirante* (SS-420). During this time, he earned a B.S. in mechanical engineering at the Naval Postgraduate School, and later, an M.S. in operations research at George Washington University. Captain McVoy was designated an engineering officer in 1961, following which he specialized in design and repair of submarines. Subsequently, he served in numerous material positions concerned with design safety and safety equipment for both submarines and surface ships at the Naval Material Command and the Naval Ships System Command. Captain McVoy served as Inspector General for the Naval Sea Systems Command during the three years before his retirement from active duty in 1980. Since 1980, Captain McVoy has headed the staff of the American Society of Naval Engineers.

Commander Bruce I. Meader, USN (Ret)

Bruce Meader is a 1951 graduate of the U.S. Naval Academy and a career submarine officer. He was Commanding Officer of the U.S.S. *Rasher* in the mid-sixties, and served in three other submarines. Commander Meader has worked extensively in public relations. He holds a master's degree (1982) in that discipline from The American University, where he also serves as adjunct professor teaching "fund raising for non-profit organizations." In 1959, Commander Meader won the National Headliners Club award for cinematography of the U.S.S. *Skate* surfacing at the North Pole, and his documentary film "Operation Sunshine" about the arctic voyage of the *Nautilus* received an Honorable Mention at the Venice Film Festival the following year. He has also won two Freedoms Foundation awards, including the George Washington Medal, for writing. Commander Meader is the director of development for the Navy League of the United States.

Lieutenant Commander Prescott Palmer, USN (Ret)

Lieutenant Commander Palmer graduated from the U.S. Naval Academy in 1943, and, after aviation indoctrination in Florida, joined the USS *North Carolina*. In that battleship, he served in gunnery, deck, and communications duty, participating in combat operations in southwest and central Pacific. Postwar, Lieutenant Commander Palmer served in the aircraft carrier USS *Antietam* until selected in 1949 for postgraduate training at the Naval Intelligence School. At the outbreak of hostilities in Korea in 1950, he was sent to augment naval intelligence at G-2 Division, Commander in Chief Far East (Tokyo) for analysis and planning of the Inchon Landing and other operations. Thereafter, he alternated between line duty at sea as executive officer of the USS *Taylor* (DDE-468); surface operations officer of Carrier Division 2 in the USS *Intrepid*, USS *Roosevelt*, and USS *Independence*; and intelligence staff duty with CinCPacFlt (Pearl Harbor), Office of Naval Intelligence (Washington, D.C.) and NATO Commander Southern Europe (Naples, Italy). On retirement from naval duty, he worked as a technical editor with Control Data Corporation while getting a management M.S. degree at American University. He has since worked at military systems analysis with Analytic Services, Inc.; Potomac Research, Inc.; Delex Systems, Inc.; and other firms in the Washington, D.C. area.

Captain Virgil W. Rinehart, USCG (Ret)

Captain Rinehart is a 1948 graduate of the U.S. Coast Guard Academy, has served in a wide variety of general and engineering assignments afloat and ashore, and received the degree of Naval Engineer from MIT. His last two duty assignments were Chief, Icebreaker Design Branch, and Manager, National Data Buoy Project, both at USCG headquarters. On retirement from Coast Guard duty in 1971, Captain Rinehart served as Chief, Systems Engineering for the National Oceanic and Atmospheric Administration. In 1972, he joined the Maritime Administration R&D staff as program manager for development of the Computer Aided Operations Research Facility. He is currently senior advisor for shipbuilding, and manager of the National Shipbuilding Research Program, which, cooperatively with the U.S. Navy and the private sector, seeks to upgrade technology and methodology.

Dr. Robert L. Scheina

Doctor Scheina received his B.A. from Parsons College, Iowa, in 1964; his M.A. from the University of the Americas, Mexico City, in 1966; his Ph.D. from Catholic University, Washington, D.C., in 1976; and a Senior Analyst certificate from the Defense Intelligence College in Washington, D.C. Doctor Scheina directs the U.S. Coast Guard's historical program, supervising a small staff as well as numerous Reservists and volunteers who supplement the program. Doctor Scheina has authored popular, analytical, technical, and historical works, and over fifty of his articles have appeared in numerous books, magazines, and two encyclopedias. He has authored technical analyses of modern ships' systems, and annually prepares the Latin American navies assessment for the U.S. Naval Institute, and radar, ECM/ESM, and ASW tables for *Jane's Fighting Ships*. He was assistant editor of *Naval Documents of the American Revolution* and co-editor of the *Civil War Naval Chronology*. His works have been translated into four languages. Doctor Scheina has also appeared on numerous television programs as an analyst of Latin American navies.

Captain Keith B. Schumacher, USCG (Ret)

Captain Schumacher is a 1953 graduate of the U.S. Coast Guard Academy, with post-graduate degrees from MIT in Naval Engineering. He has served in both operational and engineering duty billets at sea and ashore. His engineering duties have included regulation of the merchant marine, national and international standards setting, and Icebreaker Design Project for the Polar Class Coast Guard icebreakers. Since retirement from active duty in 1982, he has been active in naval engineering and aviation. He is presently working as a consultant in these fields.

Dr. Michael Vlahos

Doctor Vlahos became the Director, Center for the Study of Foreign Affairs, U.S. Department of State, in 1988. He received his B.A. from Yale College and his M.A. and Ph.D. from the Fletcher School of Law and Diplomacy. From 1977 to 1979, he served as a strategic analyst with the CIA as primary specialist in Soviet doctrine. From 1979 to 1981, he worked on numerous projects for the Defense Nuclear Agency, Lawrence Livermore Laboratory, and the Joint Service Small Arms Program. Thereafter, Doctor Vlahos was with the Johns Hopkins School of Advanced International Studies. In addition to numerous books and articles on foreign and naval affairs, Doctor Vlahos appears on "Good Morning America," "Canada AM," and is a regular commentator for Cable News Network. He is a research Fellow of the Foreign Policy Research Institute, a visiting lecturer at the Army Command and General Staff College, a contributing editor of the *Journal of Defense and Diplomacy*, and a staff consultant to the Johns Hopkins Applied Physics Laboratory.

Captain Joseph F. Yurso, USN (Ret)

In 1952, Captain Yurso received a B.S.ME degree from Pennsylvania State University. He was first employed for two and a half years as a civilian engineer with the Navy's Bureau of Ships in Washington, D.C., before attending Officer Candidate School at Newport, Rhode Island, and being commissioned Ensign in 1955. In 1960, Captain Yurso received a M.S.ME degree from the Naval Postgraduate School, Monterey, California. As a shipbuilding engineer, Captain Yurso's tours of duty involved surface ship and nuclear submarine inspection, planning, construction, overhaul, quality assurance, and logistic support, in both naval and civilian shipyards. Captain Yurso served afloat as damage control assistant, main propulsion assistant, and engineering officer in the USS *Union* (AKA-106). Other assignments included Ship Maintenance Officer for Commander in Chief, U.S. Atlantic Fleet; Production Officer, Norfolk Naval Shipyard; Supervisor of Shipbuilding, Groton, Connecticut; and Shipyard Commander, Norfolk Naval Shipyard. Since retirement from the Navy in 1984, Captain Yurso has worked as a naval engineering consultant and is now employed as chief engineer, ship systems group, QED Systems, Virginia Beach, Virginia.

Naval Engineering Bibliography

This bibliography is intended to be broadly representative of material pertinent to naval engineering. We have aimed for sufficient coverage to suggest avenues for useful search initiation by those wishing to pursue various topics, but without purporting to cover the vast area of naval engineering in great depth.

I MAJOR SOURCES COVERING A BROAD RANGE OF TECHNICAL MATERIAL, TIME OR EVENTS (several eras or epochs)

Journal of the American Society of Naval Engineers, until May 1962. *Naval Engineers Journal*, beginning with the May 1962 issue (Volume 74 No. 2). There are many pertinent historical articles. Several will be listed separately in this bibliography.

Albion, Robert Greenhalgh and Jennie Barnes Pope. *Sea Lanes in Wartime: The American Experience 1775-1945*. 2d. ed. Hamden, Connecticut: Archon, 1968.

Alden, Carroll S., Rear Admiral George R. Clark, U.S. Navy (Ret), Herman R. Kraft, William O. Stevens, *A Short History of the United States Navy*. Philadelphia and London: J.B. Lippincott Company, 1927.

Bauer, K. Jack. *A Maritime History of the United States*: The Role of America's Seas and Waterways. Columbia, South Carolina: University of South Carolina Press, 1988.

Beach, Edward L., *The United States Navy: 200 Years*. Annapolis, Maryland: U.S. Naval Institute, 1986.

Brodie, Bernard, *A Layman's Guide to Naval Strategy*. Princeton, New Jersey: Princeton University Press, 1943.

Brodie, B., *Sea Power in the Machine Age*. Princeton, New Jersey: Princeton University Press, 1941.

Engle, Eloise and Arnold S. Lott. *America's Maritime Heritage*. Annapolis, Maryland: Naval Institute Press, 1975.

Hagan, Kenneth J., USNR (Ret), Editor. *In Peace and War: Interpretations of American Naval History, 1775-1984*, A Second Edition. Westport, Connecticut 06881: Greenwood Press, 88 Post Road West, Box 5007, 1987.

Hovgaard, William. *Modern History of Warships*. London: E. & F.N. Spon, 1920.

Hutchins, John G. B. *The American Maritime Industries and Public Policy, 1789-1914*: An Economic History. New York: Russell & Russell, 1941.

Johnson, Harvey F., Rear Admiral, U.S. Coast Guard, "The United States Coast Guard—Some Adventures," A Newcomen Address. Princeton, New Jersey: Princeton University Press, 1941.

Knox, Dudley W., *A History of the United States Navy*, revised edition. New York: Putnam, 1948. "This is the most ambitious and successful single volume history of the U.S. Navy yet published."—from a review by James Phinney Baxter, President of Williams College.

Mahan, Alfred T. *The Influence of Sea Power Upon History. 1660-1783*. Boston, Massachusetts: Little Brown, 1890. (American Century Reprint, New York: Hill and Wang, 1957.)

Marcus, G. J. *A Naval History of England*. Vol. 1, The Formative Centuries; Vol. 2, The Age of Nelson; Vol. 3, The Empire of the Ocean. Sheffield, England: Applebaum Ltd., 1971.

Office of Naval Intelligence, *General Information Series*. 1888 *et seq.*

Potter, E. B. and Chester W. Nimitz. *Sea Power: A Naval History*. Englewood Cliffs, New Jersey: Prentice-Hall, 1960.

Potter, E. B., *Sea Power*. Annapolis, Maryland: Naval Institute Press, 1981.

Transactions of the Royal Institution of Naval Architects (RINA). RINA was founded in 1860. There is a wealth of information here as in ASNE *Journal* and *Transactions* and other publications of SNAME. RINA Transactions for the Centennial Year 1960, Volume 102, contains for example: "Warships 1860-1960," "Merchant Ships 1860-1960," and "A Marine Engineering Review—Past, Present and Future."

Sprout, Harold and Margaret Sprout, *The Rise of American Naval Power, 1776-1918*. Princeton, New Jersey: Princeton University Press, 1939.

Stevens, William Oliver, Allan Westcott, *A History of Sea Power*. New York: Doubleday, Doran & Company, Inc., 1940.

"The United States Navy." Publication of the Naval History Division, Navy Department, 1969.

II PRIMARY SOURCES

Primary references are cited in specific chapters. A list of representative source organizations is included as Appendix C.

III REFERENCE PUBLICATIONS

Brouwer, Norman J. *International Register of Historic Ships*. Annapolis, Maryland: Naval Institute Press, 1986.

Chapelle, Howard I. *The National Watercraft Collection*. Washington, D.C.: U.S. Government Printing Office, 1960.

Conway's All the World's Fighting Ships. Chesneau, Roger and Eugene M. Kolesnik. *1860-1905*. Published 1979; Gardiner, Robert, ed. *1906-1921*. Published 1985; Gardiner, Robert, ed. dir., Roger Chesneau, ed. *1922-1946*. Published 1980; Gardiner, Robert, ed. *1947-1982*. Published 1983. London, England: Conway Maritime Press. Annapolis, Maryland: Naval Institute Press.

Dictionary of American Naval Fighting Ships. An 8-volume series prepared by the office of the Director of Naval History. Washington, D.C.: U.S. Government Printing Office, 1959-1981.

Fahey, James C., *The Ships and Aircraft of the U.S. Fleet*. Annapolis, Maryland: U.S. Naval Institute (Several editions published since 1946).

"Historic Ship Exhibits in the United States," Publication of the Naval History Division, Navy Department, 1969.

King, J. W., *The Warships and Navies of the World*, 1880. Annapolis, Maryland: Naval Institute Press, 1982, Reprint of 1880 edition.

Landstrom, Bjorn, *The Ship*: An Illustrated History. Garden City, New York: Doubleday & Company, Inc., 1961.

Lewis, Edward V., Robert O'Brien, and the Editors of LIFE. *Ships*. LIFE Science Library. New York: Time Incorporated, 1965.

Rippon, Peter, Commander, RN. *The Evolution of Engineering in the Royal Navy*. Vol. 1 — 1827-1939. Tunbridge Wells, England: Spellmount Ltd, 1988. Volume 2 — 1940-1987 is scheduled to be published in 1989.

Ships, Aircraft and Weapons of the United States Navy. NAVSO P-3564 (Rev. 8/84). Washington, D.C.: Office of Information, Department of the Navy, August 1984.

Silverstone, Paul H. *Directory of the World's Capital Ships*. New York: Hippocrene Books, 1984.

Silverstone, Paul H. *U.S. Warships Since 1945*. Annapolis, Maryland: Naval Institute Press, 1987.

TIME-LIFE multivolume series, *The Seafarer*. The following volumes should be of particular help: *The Great Liners, The Dreadnoughts, The Men-of-War*. Chicago, Illinois 60611: TIME-LIFE Books.

IV SOURCE LISTINGS AND BIBLIOGRAPHIES

Albion, Robert Greenhalgh. *Naval and Maritime History*. An Annotated Bibliography. Mystic, Connecticut: Munson Institute of American Maritime History. The Maritime Historical Association, Inc., 1972 (Fourth Edition).

Allard, Dean C., Martha L. Crawley, Mary W. Edmison, Compilers and Editors. *U.S. Naval History Sources in the United States*. Naval History Division, Department of the Navy. Washington, D.C.: U.S. Government Printing Office, 1979 0-303-704.

Allard, Dean C., Betty Bern, Compilers. *U.S. Naval History Sources in the Washington Area and Suggested Research Subjects*. Third Edition, Revised and Enlarged. U.S. Naval History Division, Department of the Navy. Washington, D.C.: U.S. Government Printing Office, 1970 0-389-167.

United States Naval History, A Bibliography, Sixth Edition. Naval History Division, Department of the Navy. Washington, D.C.: U.S. Government Printing Office, 1972 0-466-781. Stock No. 0846-0067.

Harbeck, Charles T., Compiler. *A Contribution to the Bibliography of the History of the United States Navy*. Cambridge, Massachusetts: The Riverside Press, 1906.

Heimdahl, William C. and Edward J. Marolda, Compilers. *Guide to the United States Naval Administrative Histories of World War II*. Washington, D.C.: Naval History Division, Department of the Navy, 1976.

Higham, Robin, Ed. *A Guide to Sources of United States Military History*. Hamden, Connecticut: Archon Books, 1975.

Smith, Myron J., Jr. *American Naval Bibliography*. Metuchen, New Jersey: The Scarecrow Press, Inc. Volume I, *Navies in the American Revolution*. Published 1973; Volume II, *American Civil War Navies*. Published 1972; Volume III, *The American Navy, 1865-1918*. Published 1974; Volume IV, *The American Navy, 1918-1941*. Published 1974.

Transactions of the Society of Naval Architects and Marine Engineers. Several specific papers will be listed separately. Particular attention is invited to *Historical Transactions 1893-1943*. Published in 1945.

"United States Coast Guard Annotated Bibliography." June, 1982. Washington, D.C.: U.S. Government Printing Office, 1982-0-522-046/8503. (This is an update, expansion, and reformat of CG-230, 1972, compiled by Truman R. Strobridge, at that time the U.S. Coast Guard Historian).

United States Naval Institute *Proceedings* and books.

V Specific Epochs, Eras, Periods, or Status at a Particular Time

War of 1812

Dudley, William S., Ed. *The Naval War of 1812*. A documentary History. 3 Volumes. Washington, D.C.: U.S. Government Printing Office, 1985.

Civil War

Official Records of the Union and Confederate Navies in the War of Rebellion. 31 vols. 10,000 sets of the O.R.N. were authorized by the U.S. Congress and published originally over the period 1894-1927. Hicksville, N.Y.: Republished by The National Historical Society.

Civil War Naval Chronology, 1864-1865. U.S. Naval History Division. Washington, D.C.: U.S. Government Printing Office.

"Civil War Naval Ordnance." Publication of the Naval History Division, Navy Department, 1969.

Jones, Virgil C. *The Civil War at Sea*. New York: Holt, 1960.

Porter, David D. *The Naval History of the Civil War*. New York: The Sherman Publishing Company, 1886.

Scharf, J. Thomas. *History of the Confederate States Navy*. New York: Rogers and Sherwood, 1887. Freeport, New York: Books for Libraries Press, 1969. (c1886)

Spanish—American War

Dorwart, Jeffrey Michael, "A Mongrel Fleet, America Buys a Navy to Fight Spain." *Warship International*, No. 2, 1980.

Long, John D. *The New American Navy*. 2 volumes. New York: Outlook Company, 1903.

Mexican War

Smith, Justin H. *The War With Mexico*. New York: Macmillian, 1919.

World War I

Activities of the Bureau of Yards and Docks Navy Department World War 1917-1918. Washington, D.C.: U.S. Government Printing Office, 1921.

Clephane, L. P. *History of the Naval Overseas Transportation Service in World War I*. Washington, D.C.: U.S. Government Printing Office, 1969.

Daniels, Josephus, *Our Navy at War*. New York: George H. Doran Company, 1922.

Hurley, Edward N. *The Bridge to France*. Philadelphia and London: J.B. Lippincott Company, 1927.

Navy Ordnance Activities. World War 1917-1918. Prepared by the Bureau of Ordnance. Washington, D.C.: U.S. Government Printing Office, 1920.

Sims, William, *The Victory at Sea*. New York: Doubleday, 1920.

Gleaves, Albert. *A History of the Transport Service*. New York: George H. Doran Company, 1921.

World War II

Baker, R., W. J. Holt, J. Lenaghan, A. J. Sims, and A. W. Watson. *Selected Papers on British Warship Design in World War II*. From the Transactions of the Royal Institution of Naval Architects. Annapolis, Maryland: Naval Institute Press. First published by Conway Maritime Press Ltd, London, 1983.

Butowsky, Dr. Harry A., *Warships Associated with World War II in the Pacific*, National Historic Landmark Theme Study. Publication of the History Division of the National Park Service. Washington, D.C.: U.S. Government Printing Office, May, 1985.

Carter, Worrall Reed, Rear Admiral, USN, and Elmer Ellsworth Duvall. *Ships, Salvage, and Sinews of War*. Washington, D.C.: U.S. Government Printing Office (Department of the Navy), 1954.

Charles, R. W. *Troopships of World War II*. Washington, D.C.: Army Transportation Association, 1947.

Connery, Robert H., *The Navy and the Industrial Mobilization in World War II*. Princeton, New Jersey: Princeton University Press.

Furer, Julius Augustus. *Administration of the Navy Department in World War II*. Washington, D.C.: U.S. Government Printing Office, 1959.

Furer, J. A. "Naval Research and Development in World War II." *Journal of the American Society of Naval Engineers*, Vol. 62, 1950, pp 21 53.

Hoyt, Edwin P. *The Lonely Ships*: the life and death of the U.S. Asiatic Fleet. New York: McKay, 1976.

Jones, R. V. *Most Secret War*. London: Hamilton, 1978.

Land, E. S. *Winning the War with Ships: Land, Sea, and Air—Mostly Land*. New York: McBride, 1958.

Lane, Frederic C., et al. *Ships for Victory*. A History of Shipbuilding Under the U.S. Maritime Commission in World War II. Baltimore, Maryland: The Johns Hopkins Press, 1951.

Morison, Samuel E. *History of United States Naval Operations in World War II*. Boston, Massachusetts: Little, Brown, 1947-62. 15 vols.

Morison, Samuel E. *The Two-Ocean War: A Short History of the United States Navy in the Second World War*. Boston, Massachusetts: Little, Brown, 1963.

Roscoe, Theodore, *United States Destroyer Operations in World War II*. Annapolis, Maryland: United States Naval Institute, 1953.

Rowland, Buford and William B. Boyd. *U.S. Navy Bureau of Ordnance in World War II*. Washington, D.C.: U.S. Government Printing Office, 1954.

Schull, Joseph. *The Far Distant Ships: An Official Account of Canadian Naval Operations in the Second World War*. Annapolis, Maryland: Naval Institute Press, Reprint, 1987.

Stillwell, Paul, Ed. *Air Raid: Pearl Harbor!* Recollections of a Day of Infamy. Annapolis, Maryland: Naval Institute Press, 1981.

Young, Brigadier Peter, Ed. *The World Almanac Book of World War II*. Englewood Cliffs, New Jersey: Prentice-Hall, Inc., 1981.

Vietnam

Croizat, Colonel Victor, USMC (Ret). *The Brown Water Navy*. The River and Coastal War in Indo-China and Vietnam, 1948-1972. Poole, Dorset, United Kingdom: Blandford Press, 1984. ISBN 0 7137 1272 4.

Hooper, Edwin Bickford, Dean C. Allard, Oscar P. Fitzgerald. *The United States Navy and the Vietnam Conflict*. Volume I The Setting of the Stage to 1959. Naval History Division, Department of the Navy. Washington, D.C.: U.S. Government Printing Office, 1976.

Marolda, Edward J., Oscar P. Fitzgerald. *The United States Navy and the Vietnam Conflict*. Volume II From Military Assistance to Combat 1959-1965. Naval Historical Center, Department of the Navy. Washington, D.C.: U.S. Government Printing Office, 1986. Stock Number 008-046-00114-6.

Life magazine, "The Fleet Lashes Out—In action with the Navy off Vietnam," cover story August 6, 1965.

Post 1980

Rydén, Inger and Christopher von Schirach-Szmigiel, eds. *Shipping and Ships for the 1990's*. Proceedings of the International Conference, "Supply and Demand of Water Transport," June 18-19, 1979. Stockholm, Sweden: Stockholm School of Economics, 1980.

U.S. Shipping and Shipbuilding Trends and Policy Choices. Washington, D.C.: U.S. Government Printing Office, 1984. Stock Number: 052-070-05949-4.

Villar, Captain Roger. *Merchant Ships at War*. The Falklands Experience. Annapolis, Maryland: Naval Institute Press, 1984.

VI Specific Events

Beach Edward L., Captain, USN (Ret). *The Wreck of the Memphis*. Holt, Rinehart, Winston, 1966.

Calhoun, Captain C. Raymond, USN (Ret). *Typhoon: The Other Enemy*. The Third Fleet and the Pacific Storm of December 1944. Annapolis, Maryland: Naval Institute Press, 1981.

Ellsberg, Edward. *Cruise of the Jeanette*. New York: Dodd, Mead, 1949.

Lockwood, Charles A., Vice Admiral, USN (Ret), and Hans Christian Adamson, Colonel, USAF, (Ret). *Tragedy at Honda*. Foreword by Fleet Admiral Chester W. Nimitz, USN. Fresno, California: Valley Publishers, a Division of Book Publishers, Inc., 8 East Olive Avenue, Fresno, California, 1960. "The greatest peacetime tragedy of the U.S. Navy."

Overshiner, Elwyn E. *Course 095 to Eternity*. Santa Rosa, California: Elwyn E. Overshiner, 92 Buckwood Place, Santa Rosa, California 95404, phone 707-538-0581, 1980.

VII Specific Ship Types and Ship Systems
Aircraft Carriers and Air Capability in Ships

Aviation in the United States Navy. Publication of the Naval History Division, Navy Department, third edition, 1968. Washington, D.C.: U.S. Government Printing Office, 1968.

MacDonald, Scot. "Evolution of Aircraft Carriers," compilation of articles from *Naval Aviation News*, published by the Deputy Chief of Naval Operations (Air), February 1, 1964.

Friedman, Norman, with ship plans by A. D. Baker III. *U.S. Aircraft Carriers: An Illustrated Design History*. Annapolis, Maryland: Naval Institute Press, 1983.

Humble, Richard, *United States Fleet Carriers of World War II*. New York, N.Y. 10016: Sterling Publishing Co., Two Park Avenue, 1986. Photos, illustrations, and index. Offers more than 190 photographs of the U.S. carrier fleet during World War II, including *Lexington, Saratoga, Enterprise, Wasp*, and the late developing "*Essex*" class. Details important sea battles such as Coral Sea, Midway, Eastern Solomons, and Santa Cruz.

Reynolds, Clark G. *The Fast Carriers: The Forging of an Air Navy*. New York: McGraw Hill, 1968.

Wilson, George C. *Supercarrier: An Inside Account of Life Aboard the World's Most Powerful Ship, the U.S.S. John F. Kennedy*. New York: MacMillan Publishing Company, 866 Third Avenue, New York, N.Y. 10022, 1986. 273pp. Photos and index.

United States Naval Aviation 1910-1980. NAVAIR 00-80P-1. Prepared at the direction of the Deputy Chief of Naval Operations (Air Warfare) and the Commander, Naval Air Systems Command, 1981.

Capital Ships (Except Carriers) and Cruisers

Breyer, Siegfried, *Battleships and Battle Cruisers, 1905-1970*. Historical Development of the Capital Ship. Garden City, New York: Doubleday & Company, Inc., 1973.

Ewing, Steve, *American Cruisers of World War II*: A Pictorial Encyclopedia. Missoula, Montana 59801: Pictorial Histories Publishing Company, 713 South Third West, 1984. ISBN 0-933126-51-4.

Friedman, Norman. *U.S. Battleships*: An Illustrated Design History. Ship Plans by Alan Raven and A. D. Baker, III. Annapolis, Maryland: Naval Institute Press, 1984, second printing 1987.

Harris, Brayton, Lieutenant Commander, U.S.N.R. *The Age of the Battleship 1890 1922. The* Watts Histories of the United States Navy. New York, N.Y. 10022: Franklin Watts, Inc., 575 Lexington Avenue, 1965.

Jordan, John. *An Illustrated Guide to Battleships and Battlecruisers*. New York: ARCO Publishing, Inc., 1984.

Parkes, Oscar. *British Battleships*. London: Seely Service & Co., Ltd., 1956.

Sturton, Ian, Ed. *Conway's all the world's battleships, 1906 to the present*. Annapolis, Maryland: Naval Institute Press, 1987.

Whitley, M. J. *German Cruisers of World War II*. Annapolis, Maryland: Naval Institute Press, 1985.

Cargo and Passenger

Flexner, James Thomas. *Steamboats Come True*: American Inventors in Action. Boston and Toronto: Little, Brown and Company, 1944.

Mueller, Edward A., LCDR, USNR (Ret). *St. Johns River Steamboats*. Available from the author, 4734 Empire Avenue, Jacksonville, Florida 32207. 224 pp. Photos, illustrations, maps, charts, and graphs. A collection of original historical accounts of steamboats on Florida's St. Johns River, travel and steamboat excursions.

Ratcliffe, Mike. *Liquid Gold Ships. A History of the Tanker*. London: Lloyds of London Press, 1985.

Sawyer, L. A. and W. H. Mitchell. *The Liberty Ships*. London: Lloyds of London Press, 1970.

Sawyer, L. A. and W. H. Mitchell. *Victory Ships and Tankers*. Devon: David and Charles, 1974.

Young, Robert T., "The Lessons of the Liberties," address given before The Propeller Club of the United States, New York, 8 May 1974. (Concerns World War II experience.)

Communications, Electronics, Navigation, Intelligence

Allison, D. K. *New Eye for the Navy: The Origin of Radar at the Naval Research Laboratory*. Washington, D.C.: Naval Research Laboratory, 1981.

Hezlet, Vice-Admiral Sir Arthur. *Electronics and Sea Power*. New York: Stein and Day, 1975.

Howeth, L. S., Captain, USN (Ret). *History of Communications—Electronics in the United States Navy*. With an introduction by Fleet Admiral Chester W. Nimitz, USN. Washington, D.C.: Prepared under auspices of the Bureau of Ships and Office of Naval History, 1963.

Lewin, Ronald. *Ultra Goes to War*. The First Account of World War II's Greatest Secret Based on Official Documents. New York, N.Y.: McGraw-Hill Book Company, 1978.

Destroyers, Frigates, Escorts

Building Escort and Patrol Ships for the United States Navy. Washington, D.C.: Naval Ship Systems Command, Department of the Navy, 1973.

Building Patrol Frigates for the United States Navy. Washington, D.C.: Naval Sea Systems Command, 1974.

Friedman, Norman: *U.S. Destroyers: An Illustrated Design History*. Annapolis, Maryland: Naval Institute Press, 1982.

Miller, Richards T. "Sixty Years of Destroyers: A Study in Evolution." U.S. Naval Institute *Proceedings*, November, 1962.

Inland Waterways, Great Lakes, Intra-Coastal

Locher, Harry O., Ed. *Waterways of the United States—Rivers—Harbors—Lakes—Canals*. New York, N.Y.: The National Association of River and Harbor Contractors, 15 Park Row, New York 38, N.Y., 2nd ed., 1963.

Mills, James C. *Our Inland Seas: Their Shipping and Commerce for Three Centuries*. Chicago, Illinois: A.C. McClurg & Co., 1910. (Reprinted by Freshwater Press, Inc., Cleveland, Ohio, 1976.)

Iron and Steel

Alden, John D., Commander, USN (Ret), *The American Steel Navy*, Photographic History of the U.S. Navy from the Introduction of the Steel Hull in 1883 to the Cruise of the Great White Fleet, 1907-1909. Annapolis, Maryland: Naval Institute Press, 1972. ISBN 0-87021-681-3.

Baxter, James Phinney III. *The Introduction of the Ironclad Warship*. Cambridge, Massachusetts: Harvard University Press, 1933. Hamden, Connecticut. Archon Books, 1968 (c1933).

"Monitors of the U.S. Navy, 1861-1937." Publication of the Naval History Division, Navy Department, 1969.

Minesweeping, Minelaying, Inshore, Special Operations

All Hands has useful articles on riverine and special operations craft. See, for example: issues of November 1966 and October 1968.

Baldwin, Hanson W. "Spitkits' in Tropic Seas." *Shipmate*, publication of the U.S. Naval Academy Alumni Association, August-September 1966.

Miller, Richards T. "Minesweepers." *Naval Review 1967*. Annapolis, Maryland: U.S. Naval Institute, 1967.

Riverine Warfare: The U.S. Navy's Operations on Inland Waters. rev. 1969. Naval History Division, Navy Department. Washington, D.C.: U.S. Government Printing Office, 1969.

Ordnance, Combat Systems

Lewis, E. R. "American Battleship Main Battery Armament, The Final Generation." *Warship International*, No. 4, 1976.

Padfield, Peter. *Guns at Sea*. London: H. Evelyn, 1973.

Propulsion, Auxiliary Systems

Hewlett, Richard G. and Frances Duncan. *Nuclear Navy 1946-1962*. Chicago, Illinois: The University of Chicago Press, 1974.

Plumb, C. M. *Warship Propulsion Selection*. London: Marine Management (Holdings) Ltd., 76 Mark Lane, London EC3R 7JN for the Institute of Marine Engineers, 1987. ISBN 0-907206-16-6.

Rowland, K. T., *Steam at Sea: A History of Steam Navigation*. New York: Praeger, 1974.

Smith, E. C. *A Short History of Naval and Marine Engineering*. Cambridge, England: University Press, 1938.

Recreation, Yachting

Rousmaniere, John. *The Golden Pastime: A New History of Yachting*. "A richly illustrated account of yachting from the days of King Charles II to 1986. Of special interest. . . are the chapter-length biography of Commodore J.P. Morgan, a two-chapter history of the. . . America's Cup defenses, and a history of cruising."

Research and Oceanographic

Miller, Richards T. "The Navy's Oceanographic Research Ship Designs." Panama City, Florida: U.S. Navy Mine Defense Laboratory, June 1964.

Nelson, Stewart B., *Oceanographic Ships Fore & Aft*. Office of the Oceanographer of the Navy. Washington, D.C.: U.S. Government Printing Office, 1971, Stock Number 0842-0050.

Submarines, Submersibles

Arentzen, E. S. and Philip Mandel. "Naval Architectural Aspects of Submarine Design." *Transactions*, Society of Naval Architects and Marine Engineers, 1960.

Bryan, C. R. and J. R. Wakefield. "The Effect of Weapons on Submarine Design." *Naval Engineers Journal*, February, 1963.

Friedman, Norman. *Submarine Design and Development*. Annapolis, Maryland: Naval Institute Press, 1984.

Jackson, Harry A., *et al.* "ASW: Revolution or Evolution." U.S. Naval Institute *Proceedings*, September, 1986.

McKee, A. I. "Recent Submarine Design Practices and Problems." *Transactions*, Society of Naval Architects and Marine Engineers, 1959.

Soule, Gardner. *Under the Sea*. A Treasury of Great Writing about the Ocean Depths. New York, N.Y.: Meredith Press, 1968.

Tugs, Harbor Craft, Utility, Support

Fry, Eric C. *Lifeboat Design and Development*. London: David and Charles, 1975.

Other

Cooling, B. F. *Gray Steel and Blue Water Navy*. Hamden, Connecticut: Archon Books, 1978.

Ellsworth, Wm. M. *Twenty Foilborne Years:* The U.S. Navy Hydrofoil *High Point* PCH-1. Prepared for the David Taylor Naval Ship Research and Development Center, 1986.

VIII RESEARCH, ENGINEERING DEVELOPMENT
General

Baxter, J. P., *Scientists Against Time*. Cambridge, Massachusetts: M.I.T. Press, 1946.

Breemer, Jan S. *U.S. Naval Developments*. Annapolis, Maryland: The Nautical and Aviation Publishing Co. of America, 1983.

Byer, J. C. and J. C. Tolman, Editors, *New Weapons for Air Warfare*. Boston, Massachusetts: Little Brown and Company, 1947.

Diving and Salvage in the United States Navy. Publication of the Naval Ship Systems Command, Department of the Navy, 1974.

Feld, B. T., Editor, *Impact of New Technologies on the Arms Race.* Cambridge, Massachusetts: M.I.T. Press, 1971.

Innovation in the Maritime Industry. Report of the Maritime Transportation Research Board, National Research Council, 1979. Volume 1 contains findings, conclusions, and recommendations. Volume 2 contains the case studies developed to aid deliberations of the committee.

Jung, Ingvar. *Marine Turbines—A Historical Review by a Swedish Engineer, Volume I Days of Coal and Steam, 1897-1927.* Greenwich, London: National Maritime Museum. (Note: Volumes II and III were expected to be available about June, 1987.)

Morison, Elting E., *Men, Machines, and Modern Times.* Cambridge, Massachusetts: The M.I.T. Press, and London, England, 1966. Two chapters are particularly pertinent: "Gunfire at Sea: A Case Study in Innovation," and "Men and Machinery."

The Ocean Engineering Program of the U.S. Navy. Publication of the Oceanographer of the Navy. Washington, D.C.: U.S. Government Printing Office, March, 1973.

Salkovitz, Edward I., Ed. *Science, Technology, and the Modern Navy.* Thirtieth Anniversary, 1946-1976. ONR-37. Office of Naval Research, Department of the Navy. Washington, D.C.: U.S. Government Printing Office, 1977.

Sapolsky, H. M., *The Polaris Project.* Cambridge, Massachusetts: Harvard University Press, 1972.

Science and the Future Navy A Symposium, October 27 and 28, 1976, In Celebration of the Thirtieth Anniversary of the Office of Naval Research. Washington, D.C.: National Academy of Sciences, 1977.

Pre-1900

American Iron and Steel Association, *History of the Manufacture of Armor Plate for the U.S. Navy.* Philadelphia, Pennsylvania: American Iron & Steel Association, 1899.

Bennett, Frank M. *The Steam Navy of the United States.* Early steam to late 1880. Pittsburgh, Pennsylvania: W.T. Nicholson Press, 1896.

Bruce, Robert V. *The Launching of Modern American Science, 1846-1876.* New York: Alfred A. Knopf, 1987.

Edwards, Emory. *Modern American Marine Engines, Boilers, and Screw Propellers.* Philadelphia, Pennsylvania: 1881.

Tobin, John R. "Report to the Bureau of Steam Engineering on Improvements in Naval Engineering in Great Britain." Washington, D.C.: 1883. This report was forwarded by the Secretary of the Navy to the House of Representatives in response to a resolution from that body.

Post-1980

Abrahamson, James L., *America Arms For A New Century.* New York: The Free Press, 1981.

IX BIOGRAPHY AND AUTOBIOGRAPHY

Biographical Memoirs. National Academy of Sciences of the United States of America. A biography of each deceased NAS member is prepared by another member or members. These are compiled into volumes. Following is a partial listing: Hovgaard, William by William Francis Gibbs, Volume XXXVI, 1962. Taylor, David Watson by William Hovgaard, Volume XXII.

Bowen, Harold G., Vice Admiral USN (Ret). *Ships, Machinery, and Mossbacks.* The Autobiography of a Naval Engineer. Princeton, New Jersey: Princeton University Press, 1954.

Bradford, James C., Editor. *Captains of the Old Steam Navy: Makers of the American Naval Tradition 1840-1880.* Annapolis, Maryland: Naval Institute Press, 1986. (Contains two biographical essays of particular interest concerning naval engineers: "John A. Dahlgren: Innovator in Uniform" by David K. Allison and "Benjamin Franklin Isherwood: Father of the Modern Steam Navy" by Dean C. Allard)

Burnett, Constance Buel. *Captain John Ericsson: Father of the "Monitor."* New York: The Vanguard Press, Inc., 1960.

Coletta, P. E. *Admiral Bradley A. Fiske and the American Navy.* Lawrence, Kansas: Regents Press of Kansas, 1979.

Evans, Holden A. *One Man's Fight for a Better Navy.* New York: Dodd, Mead & Company, 1940.

Gretton, Vice-Admiral Sir Peter, KCB, DSO, OBE, DSC (rtd.) *Former Naval Person:* Winston Churchill and the Royal Navy. London: Cassell & Company, 1968.

Hughes, T. P. *Elmer Sperry: Inventor and Engineer.* Baltimore, Maryland: Johns Hopkins Press, 1971.

Hutcheon, Wallace S., Jr. *Robert Fulton: Pioneer of Undersea Warfare.* Annapolis, Maryland: United States Naval Institute, 1971.

Morison, Elting E. *Admiral Sims and the Modern American Navy.* Boston, Massachusetts: Houghton Mifflin Company, 1942.

Johnson, Robert Erwin. *Guardians of the Sea*: A History of the U.S. Coast Guard, 1915 to the Present. Annapolis, Maryland: U.S. Naval Institute, 1987.

McCollum, Kenneth G., Ed. *Dahlgren*. Dahlgren, Virginia: Naval Surface Weapons Center, June 1977.

McNeil, Jim. *Charleston's Navy Yard*: A Picture History. Naval Civilian Administrators Association, Charleston, South Carolina 29408. Columbia, South Carolina: The R.L. Bryan Co., 1985, ISBN 0-9616176-0-8.

The David Taylor Model Basin, A Brief History. Naval Historical Foundation Publication, Series 11, Number 15, Spring, 1971.

Navy League of the United States, Golden Anniversary, 1902-1952. Prepared for the occasion of the Golden Anniversary Dinner, October 27, 1952, Hotel Astor, New York.

Sinclair, Bruce. *A Centennial History of the American Society of Mechanical Engineers 1880-1980*. Toronto, Canada: University of Toronto Press, 1980.

Tazewell, William L. *Newport News Shipbuilding: The First Century*. Newport News, Virginia: The Mariners' Museum, 1986.

Naval War College Review, Centennial Issue 1884-1984. Sept-Oct 1984.

Cradle of American Shipbuilding: Portsmouth Naval Shipyard, Portsmouth, New Hampshire. Portsmouth, New Hampshire: 1978.

Tidman, Keith R., *The Operations Evaluation Group: a history of naval operations analysis*. Annapolis, Maryland: U.S. Naval Institute Press, 1984.

"U.S. Coast Guard Yard, A History of 'Service to the Fleet'." Publication prepared by the Public Affairs Office, Coast Guard Yard, Baltimore, Maryland 21226, forwarding letter dated 15 July 1985.

XV PERIODICALS

There are myriad maritime periodicals: regional, national, private, industry, official government, and quasi-official. Some cover a wide range of naval engineering related subjects and some are specialized. Only a few are listed here to indicate the types and breadth of the selection.

All Hands Magazine (65th year of publication as of 1988). In addition to pertinent articles in various issues, there have been many special issues over the years, for example: Destroyer Navy, September, 1962. Ships and Yards, October, 1957. Guided Missile Navy, March, 1957. The Carrier Navy, May, 1965, etc.

American Heritage of Invention & Technology. Published three times a year by American Heritage, a division of Forbes Inc. Forbes Building, 60 Fifth Avenue, New York, NY 10011.

Bureau of Construction and Repair *Bulletins*.

Bureau of Ships *Journal*. This publication is an important source. Some issues and articles will be separately cited. An index for the year was usually included in the December issue.

International Defense Review. Published monthly by Interavia S.A., 86 Avenue Louis-Casai, 1216 Cointrin-Geneva, Switzerland.

Jane's *Defence Weekly*. U.S.A.: 4th Floor, 115 5th Avenue, New York, N.Y. 10003. phone: 212-254-9097.

Maine Boats and Harbors. 101 Mechanic Street, Camden, Maine 04843.

Marine Propulsion International. Published 10 times a year by Industrial and Marine Publications Ltd., Queensway House, 2 Queensway, Redhill, Surrey RH1 1QS, England.

Marine Technology. Published quarterly by the Society of Naval Architects and Marine Engineers, 601 Pavonia Avenue, Jersey City, New Jersey 07306.

Life magazine. Over the years there have been many articles on maritime matters, for example: issue of October 28, 1940, devoted almost entirely to the U.S. Navy. "The Fleet's In," November 5, 1945. The Sea, Special Double Issue, December 21, 1962.

National Fisherman. Journal Publications, Inc., 21 Elm Street, Camden, Maine 04843.

Nautical Quarterly. Pratt Street, Essex, Connecticut 06426.

Naval History. Pilot issue in 1987. Regular publication began 1988. Published quarterly by the U.S. Naval Institute, Annapolis, Maryland.

Naval War College Review. Published bi-monthly. Established in 1948.

Proceedings. Published monthly by the U.S. Naval Institute.

Sea Technology. Published monthly by Compass Publications, Inc., 1117 N. 19th Street, Arlington, Virginia 22209.

Seapower. Published monthly by the Navy League of the United States.

Warship International. Roberts, John, Ed. *Warship*, Volume VII, 1983. Gray, Randal, Ed. *Warship*, Volume VIII, 1984. London, England: Conway Maritime Press: dist. Annapolis, Maryland: Naval Institute Press.

XVI HISTORY OF THE AMERICAN SOCIETY OF NAVAL ENGINEERS

Edwards, John R., Rear Admiral, U.S. Navy. "The American Society of Naval Engineers: Its Origin, Scope and Purpose." *Journal of the American Society of Naval Engineers*, August, 1914 (Vol. XXVI, No. 3).

Meader, Bruce. *ASNE: The First 100 Years.* Published 1988 on the occasion of the Centennial of the American Society of Naval Engineers.

Neuhaus, Herbert M. "Fifty Years of Naval Engineering in Retrospect." *Journal of the American Society of Naval Engineers.* Part I 1888-1898, February, 1938 (Vol. L [50], No. 1) Part II 1898-1908, May, 1938 (Vol. L, pp 240-280) Part III 1908-1921, August, 1938 (Vol. L, pp 341-380) Part IV 1921-1938, November, 1938 (Vol. L, pp 527-564).

"The American Society of Naval Engineers." Pre Diamond Anniversary Bulletin, prepared for the Annual Banquet, 4 May 1962.

"Society History—1888 to 1980." Prepared by *ad hoc* ASNE History Committee.

Index

The Illustrations: All photographs are official U.S. Navy photos or otherwise in the public domain. The authors are grateful to the Chief of Information, Navy Department; the Navy Historical Center; Commander, Naval Shipyard, Portsmouth, N.H.; the U.S. Naval Institute; and the National Archives for their contributions. All graphs and charts are from official U.S. Government publications. Line drawings in Chapter 5 are by Bruce Meader; drawings in Chapter 10 are by Joseph Yurso.